HOW ROME FELL

FELL

Death of a Superpower

Adrian Goldsworthy

Yale University Press
NEW HAVEN AND LONDON

First published in the United States in 2009 by Yale University Press.
First published in Great Britain in 2009 by Weidenfeld & Nicholson.

Typeset by Input Data Services Ltd, Bridgwater, Somerset
Printed in the United States of America.

Library of Congress Control Number: 2008933925
ISBN 978-0-300-13719-4 (hardcover : alk. paper)

A catalogue record for this book is available from the British Library.

This paper meets the requirements of ANSI/NISO Z39.48-1992 (Permanence of Paper).

10 9 8 7 6 5 4 3 2 1

Contents

List of Maps   vii
List of Illustrations   ix
Preface   I
Introduction – The Big Question   II

PART ONE – Crisis? The Third Century   27

  1 The Kingdom of Gold   29
  2 The Secret of Empire   53
  3 Imperial Women   70
  4 King of Kings   86
  5 Barbarians   103
  6 The Queen and the 'Necessary' Emperor   123
  7 Crisis   138

PART TWO – Recovery? The Fourth Century   155

  8 The Four – Diocletian and the Tetrarchy   157
  9 The Christian   174
 10 Rivals   194
 11 Enemies   205
 12 The Pagan   223
 13 Goths   245
 14 East and West   264

PART THREE – Fall? The Fifth and Sixth Centuries   283

 15 Barbarians and Romans: Generals and Rebels   285
 16 The Sister and the Eternal City   299
 17 The Hun   314
 18 Sunset on an Outpost of Empire   335
 19 Emperors, Kings and Warlords   353
 20 West and East   370
 21 Rise and Fall   388

Conclusion – A Simple Answer   405
Epilogue – An Even Simpler Moral   416
Chronology   425
Glossary   441
Bibliography   449
Notes   467
Index   511

List of Maps

1. The Roman Empire in the late second century AD   30
2. The Eastern frontier   90
3. The Third Century Crisis   112
4. The fourth century Empire   166
5. Julian's Persian Expedition   231
6. The empire of Valentinian and Valens   239
7. The Gothic War   256
8. Alaric's movements including the sack of Rome   297
9. The initial barbarian invasions in the fifth century   308
10. The Balkan frontier   321
11. The Saxon Shore forts   342
12. The Barbarian kingdoms in Gaul   357
13. Europe and North Africa in the early sixth century   371
14. Justinian's Empire showing the western conquests   395

Charts:
1. Family tree of Septimius Severus   72
2. Simplified family tree of the house of Constantine   190
3. Simplified family tree of the houses of Valentinian and Theodosius   265
4. Civil administration of provinces in the late fourth century   268
5. Central imperial bureaucracy and court   269
6. The command structure of the Roman Army in the *Notitia Dignitatum*   287

List of Illustrations

Bust of Marcus Aurelius (AKG Images/Erich Lessing)
Bust of Septimius Severus (AKG Images/Erich Lessing)
Bust of Caracalla (Ferens Art Gallery, Hull City Museums and Art Galleries/The Bridgeman Art Library)
Statue of the Tetrarchs, Venice (AKG Images/Jean-Paul Dumontier)
Amphitheatre at Dougga in Tunisia (Ancient Art and Architecture Collection)
Regina tombstone (Ancient Art and Architecture Collection)
Relief of Roman soldiers from Trajan's Column (Author's collection)
Relief of Roman emperor kneeling before Shapur (Ancient Art and Architecture Collection)
Collapsed wall at Dura Europos (Dr Simon James)
Wall painting from Dura Europos (Dr Simon James)
Palmyrene gods (AKG Images/Erich Lessing)
Hadrian's Wall (Author's collection)
Fort at Qasr Bashir (Sonia Halliday Photographs)
Roman walls at Porchester castle (Author's collection)
Senate House and Arch of Septimius Severus (Author's collection)
Aurelian walls, Rome (AKG Images)
Constantine coin (Bridgeman Art Library)
Julian the Apostate (AKG Images)
Detail from Arch of Constantine (Author's collection)
Adamklissi Metope: Barbarians on the move (Author's collection)
Roman gateway at Trier (AKG Images/Hilbich)
Mosaic from Piazza Armerina, Sicily (AKG Images/Erich Lessing)
Relief from obelisk base Hippodrome, Constantinople (Chris Hellier/Corbis)
Emperor Honorius (W&N Archive)
Flavius Stilicho (W&N Archive)
Page from the Notitia Dignitatum (Bodleian Library)
Skull from Hunnic grave (AKG Images)
Mausoleum at Ravenna (The Art Archive/Gianni Dagli Orti)

Coin of Justinian (Fitzwilliam Museum, University of Cambridge/
    Bridgeman Art Library)
The walls of Constantinople (Bridgeman Art Library)
Hagia Sophia (AKG Images/Erich Lessing)
Mosaic of Justinian from Ravenna (AKG Images/Erich Lessing)
The aqueduct at Segovia (Author's collection)

Preface

I f people today know anything about the Roman Empire, it is that it fell. This is without doubt the best-known 'fact' about Ancient Rome, just as Julius Caesar is the most famous Roman. Rome's fall is memorable because its empire lasted for so long – more than five hundred years after Caesar's death in Italy and the western provinces, and three times as long in the east, where emperors would rule from Constantinople until the fifteenth century. The Roman Empire was also exceptionally large – no other power has ever controlled all the lands around the Mediterranean – and left traces behind in many countries. Even today its monuments are spectacular – the Colosseum and Pantheon in Rome itself, as well as theatres, aqueducts, villas and roads dotted throughout the provinces. No other state would construct such a massive network of all-weather roads until the nineteenth century, and in many countries such systems would not be built until the twentieth century. The Roman Empire is often seen as very modern and highly sophisticated – glass in windows, central heating, bath houses and the like – especially by visitors to museums and monuments. This makes Rome's fall all the more remark-able, especially since the world that emerged from its ruin appears so primitive by contrast. The Dark Ages remain fixed in the popular mind, even if the term has long since been abandoned by scholars.

Why Rome fell remains one of the great questions of history. In the English-speaking world 'fall' is inevitably coupled with 'decline', for the title of Edward Gibbon's monumental work has become firmly embedded in the wider consciousness. No other eighteenth-century history book has remained so regularly in print in various forms and editions until the present day. There have been plenty of other books written on the subject, and some have been more perceptive in their analysis, even if none has ever challenged *The Decline and Fall of the Roman Empire* as one of the great works of English literature. In later life Gibbon liked to believe that it was his destiny to be an historian and to chronicle the great theme of Rome's fall. He claimed a specific moment of inspiration: 'It was at Rome, on the fifteenth of October, 1764, as I sat musing amidst the ruins of the Capitol, while the barefooted fryars were singing Vespers in the temple of Jupiter, that the idea of writing the decline and fall of the City first started to my mind.'[1]

Gibbon produced several versions of this story, creating the suspicion that he embellished or even invented the memory. On the other hand it is hard for any visitor with imagination not to think similar thoughts, for past and present seem very close beside the centre of Ancient Rome. The 'barefooted fryars' are no longer so obvious, and have been replaced by the ubiquitous hawkers, switching instantly from offering sunglasses to umbrellas whenever the weather changes. Even the crowds of other tourists tramping along the Sacra Via help to give a sense of the bustle and noise of the ancient city, once every bit as busy and active as the modern city that now surrounds it.

Rome is not only a museum, but also a vibrant community, the capital of a modern country and the centre of the worldwide Catholic Church. The reminders of ancient grandeur sit side by side with homes, offices and restaurants. Rome was never abandoned, although it shrank massively in population from the height of the empire in the centuries after its fall. A good number of other modern cities are also built on Roman foundations, something still visible in their grid-shaped street plans. Other Roman cities vanished altogether and those in desert areas produce some of the most romantic ruins visible today. When the Roman Empire fell, life did not simply stop in the lands it had controlled. The context of life certainly changed, sometimes dramatically and quickly, but in other cases much more gradually. As the specialists on the period have long since made clear, the Dark Ages were not wholly dark, although by any reasonable standard they were dark enough in comparison with the Roman period. Many things became more local, such as power and trade, and often the world was a more dangerous place, with raiding and warfare between nearby communities now a real possibility. Quite quickly there was no one with the money or skill to build great monuments such as theatres, aqueducts or roads. In time, it even became difficult to maintain the ones that already existed. Scholars are deeply divided about when, how and why the world changed from the Roman era to the basis of the medieval world that took shape in the following centuries. None doubt that the change occurred.

Gibbon admired the achievements of the Roman Empire at its height, as did all educated Europeans in his day. This in no way reduced his enthusiasm for the modern world, and especially for the constitution of his own country, where the monarch's power was limited and guided by the aristocracy. Gibbon knew that his own country and its neighbours across the Channel all owed their origins to the various barbarian groups that had carved up the Roman Empire. Therefore, in time, good had come from chaos and destruction, and from his perspective the world – or at least the Western world – had in the long run developed along the right lines. This mixed attitude to Rome's fall remains a central part of its fascination. It serves as a warning of mortality. The emperors who built the great arches in the Forum all died like any other human being. Eventually their empire – so rich, so powerful, so sophisticated and so utterly self-confident – also came to an end, its monuments crumbling away into ruin.

The imagery of Ancient Rome has frequently been invoked by more recent states for its associations with the ultimate heights both of power and civilisation. It is never long before talk also turns to Rome's fate. Insiders to the modern great power usually see this as a humbling reminder that everything passes, and perhaps as a warning against complacency and corruption. Outsiders, and especially those resentful of the power of others, tend to prefer the thin comfort of the belief that the current power will eventually fall. Many states have been compared to the Roman Empire. A century ago the most natural comparison would have been with Britain, and then perhaps with France or one of the other great empires of the age. Nowadays, it is inevitably with the United States of America.

The form varies, as does the tone. In recent years the best-selling novelist Robert Harris has written about Roman themes, openly declaring that this was a way of commenting on modern America. The BBC also screened a television series hosted by the former Python Terry Jones called *Barbarians*, with the theme that the reputations of other nations had been blackened by Roman propaganda. It was highly entertaining stuff, even if the message was somewhat strained – the Greeks would certainly have been most surprised to be considered barbarians, since they were the ones who first coined the term for the rest of the world. In interviews at the time, Jones made clear that the series was drawing a direct parallel with the American superpower, and openly criticised the war in Iraq. For many, criticising Rome has become a way of criticising American policy and culture. Inevitably, this affects their view of both.[2]

Milder and less detailed criticism is even more common. At certain sorts of parties, the discovery that I am an ancient historian almost inevitably prompts someone to remark that 'America is the new Rome.' More often than not this is followed by a smug, 'of course, they don't see it.' This at least is utterly false, for Americans have been comparing their country to Rome since its foundation. In shaping the new country, the Founding Fathers consciously hoped to copy the strengths of the Roman Republic and avoid its eventual downfall. These days, it is also fair to say that the different university systems tend to make educated Americans broader in the range of their knowledge than the British. Plenty of engineers or medical doctors in America will at some point have taken a course or two in history or even the classics, something which is unimaginable on this side of the Atlantic. This is one of the reasons why Roman analogies remain exceptionally common in the USA, and are routinely made by politicians themselves as well as journalists, political commentators and the wider public. Usually it begins with the assumption that the USA as the sole superpower left in the world is dominant in a way unmatched by anyone since the height of Roman power.

In the summer of 2001 I took part in a two-day seminar organised by the Center for Strategic and Budgetary Assessments, which was US government-funded by the Office of Net Assessments. Six historians were brought to a nice hotel in Washington DC – as one of the older and more distinguished members of the group put it, 'They obviously don't realise what academics will put up with.' We then gave papers and discussed the grand strategies of various great powers from history. We were just a small part of a wider series of seminars and research sessions aimed at providing insights about future relations between the USA and the emerging power of China. The talks and discussions were enjoyable and fascinating – it is quite rare in academic circles for conferences to cover such a wide range of periods, including First Empire France, Germany in the First and Second World Wars, and British naval policy in the early twentieth century. Yet it was striking that two out of the six of us had been asked to speak about different periods of Roman history.

It is in fact an odd sensation for an historian to talk to an audience that is actually listening to what you are saying. In the university context, most people tend to be thinking more about what they will say in comment on a paper. The subject matter is also literally of no more than 'academic' interest, and however excited and enthusiastic we feel about the topic, this is simply because the hope is always to discover the truth. It is rather humbling to think that at many, many removes, and in the tiniest way, someone may try to shape policy on the basis of your analysis. This naturally focuses the mind in a way no purely academic meeting ever does. It becomes even more important to get at the truth of your subject. At the same time the idea that a government agency is genuinely trying to learn lessons from history is hugely encouraging. Again this is something far more likely to happen in the USA than over here in Britain.

Many people feel that they can see clear similarities between Ancient Rome and the modern world. Comments and questions about this have been overwhelmingly the most frequent during interviews publicising my biography of Julius Caesar. This has been true everywhere, but especially in the USA. Yet the conclusions people draw from these perceived parallels vary immensely and, inevitably, have a lot to do with their own political beliefs. It has always been easy to learn lessons from history, but all too often this is simply the case of using the past to justify modern ideas. Any close look at the Roman Empire will soon reveal massive differences with any modern state, including the United States. None of this means that it is impossible to learn from the past, simply that it must be done with considerable care and a good deal of caution.[3]

This is not a book about modern America and its place in the world, something which others are far better placed to write. It is a book about the collapse of the Roman Empire, which vanished in the west and was eventually left as little more than a rump in the east. The aim is to understand the history on its own terms and in its own context. Historians do not always make the best prophets. The seminar I mentioned earlier was followed just a few months later by the terrorist attacks of 9/11. I would imagine the report produced after the series of conferences is now gathering dust somewhere as immediate priorities have shifted so profoundly. I am pretty sure someone at the seminar made a brief comment about China not posing the only serious threat and about the continued importance of oil and the Persian Gulf, but I may be imagining it. Certainly, none of us gave the impression that we expected that soon America and its allies would be fighting two major conflicts on land. I for one would certainly never have imagined that British Forces would be back in Afghanistan, on the other side of the old North-West Frontier.

This book is about Rome, an empire long vanished and from a world where the technology and culture were so very different from today. Understanding that world is the only way to understand Rome's fall. Filling the pages with constant references to the present day is unlikely to help achieve this. It is more than a little odd to read studies of the Roman period describing the 'shock and awe' of the invasion of Britain in 43. It is even stranger when the discussion of the end of a Roman province provides the opportunity for criticism of Bush and Blair and the war in Iraq.[4]

The Roman Empire did not fall quickly, but as part of a very slow process, and this should warn us against magnifying current events and their likely consequences on the long-term fortune of countries. Britain has been a fairly depressing place in the last decade or so. Ministers caught out in incompetence, corruption or blatant deceitfulness cling on to power like limpets, first denying everything, before finally apologising and expecting this to be enough. Bureaucracy and regulation continue to grow apace, while the basic efficiency of institutions declines, rendering them incapable of even the apparently simple tasks. Yet while the number of civil servants rises, the size of the armed forces shrinks at the very time they are more heavily committed to serious campaigns. It would be easy to draw parallels with the Roman Empire in the fourth century. The self-righteous tone of so much government legislation certainly chimes with Late Roman imperial decrees, as does the apparent failure of so much of this to achieve its aim. Such comparisons are unlikely to assist our analysis of the Roman Empire, and would be no more than the author indulging himself. Understanding the history must come first.

Only at the very end may we reasonably turn to some parallels and even lessons for the present. Some of these will have more to do with human nature than specific policy. I do not claim that any of these ideas are especially profound or original. That does not mean that they are not important and do not apply to any human institution, whether country or company. We should still be thankful that many aspects of the Roman experience are most definitely not mirrored in our own day. Public life is not violent and political rivalries in Western democracies do not explode into civil war.

However, there is perhaps one lesson worth learning from our own times. On an almost nightly basis our television screens carry grim pictures of violence in Iraq and other war zones. Just a few days ago there was the especially sickening incident where initial reports suggested that two young women with Down's Syndrome were employed to carry bombs into a crowd. The explosives were detonated by remote control, murdering their bearers as well as the other victims. Inevitably with attacks where the bombers themselves die it is difficult afterwards to establish the precise facts. However, as usual, these victims were mainly ordinary civilians, not in any way connected with the government or America and its allies. Such dreadful incidents should remind us of the capacity of some human beings to slaughter people who are their neighbours.

Media attention must inevitably focus on such atrocities. They are news, in the way that peaceful daily life is not. What we need to remember is that violence and ordinary life coexist. Frequent targets of suicide bombers or mortar and other attacks are crowded market-places, where people go to buy food and other necessaries. Just a few streets away from an attack, daily routines will be going on much as normal. People go to work and children go to school, people cook and eat, sleep in their beds and do such ordinary things as getting married. Life goes on, because there is really no alternative. Some people will flee, but for many this is not possible. Violence makes all of these things more difficult, and the threat of it spreads fear far beyond the number of direct victims. Yet life will still go on. It is well worth remembering this when we consider the collapse of Roman authority, the end of imperial rule and the barbarian invasions. Perhaps then we will be less impressed when aspects of Roman culture appear to have survived or that occupation by an invader did not result in the flight or extinction of all existing communities.

Looking at the fall of the Roman Empire seemed the logical next project for me after completing the book on Caesar. In some ways it is a departure, for in the past I have mostly studied and written about earlier periods of Roman history. Even after spending the last few years working on this book I still see myself as something of an outsider to the field. I hope that this grants a perspective that is sometimes lost by the period specialist. The work of many others has made it possible for me to write this book. Since it became fashionable a generation or so ago the literature on the later Roman period is now vast and includes some of the most innovative and impressive scholarship seen in any aspect of the study of the ancient world. Newcomers to the field are therefore able to plunder from an array of studies into almost every aspect of the history of these centuries. From the beginning I must acknowledge my debt to these historians and archaeologists, many of whose works are listed in the notes and bibliography. At the same time, the main reason why I wanted to write this book was a dissatisfaction with quite a few of the conclusions and assumptions made in these works. There is no generally accepted explanation for the fall of the Roman Empire in the west in the fifth century. 'Fall' is not a fashionable word with a surprising number of the scholars working on the period, and many talk instead of such things as 'transformation', accepting that there was change, but casting it in a gentler light. A few voices have been raised against this rosy portrait, but any suggestion of decline still seems tantamount to heresy. The empire of the fourth century in particular is regularly depicted as essentially sound, perhaps even stronger and more efficient than the world of Augustus or Hadrian. I simply do not believe this, and hope to show that it makes no sense whatsoever in the light of the evidence, let alone sheer common sense. In addition, the reasons for the collapse of Roman power deserve an explanation, and oddly the most important factor tends to be dismissed.

An academic study would summarise and list the arguments and analysis of all major contributors to the debate on a subject. Such material is meat and drink to historians and an essential tool of their trade. It is also deathly dull to everyone else. Only rarely will any scholar be mentioned by name in the main text of this book. References to their work may then be found in the endnotes. The overwhelming majority of readers will rightly ignore these, but they are there to help anyone wishing to read more or for those wishing to follow the trail that led me to the conclusions presented here. These and the bibliography are not exhaustive and, somewhat unfairly, usually list only those works in English, since many foreign texts will only be readily available to the few readers with access to a good university library.

In the second century AD the Roman Empire was the overwhelmingly dominant power in the known world. It seems reasonable enough to call it the superpower of its time. The term is meant in only the most general sense. I do not intend to define words like 'superpower', 'power', or even 'empire'. Such rigid labelling is common, but in my opinion rarely instructive. At the seminar mentioned above I remember one scholar for whose work I have immense admiration baldly stating that the British Empire was not really an empire. Doubtless what he meant was that it did not share all of its characteristics with other empires, but it is difficult to see what is gained by such strict definition. No such artificial labelling is necessary to show that by the end of the sixth century the power, prosperity and size of the Roman Empire had been massively reduced.

Similarly I have made no real use of the modern terms 'Byzantium' and 'Byzantine', and the emperors who ruled from Constantinople are referred to as Roman even when they no longer controlled Italy and Rome itself. This was how they knew themselves. The accuracy of terms like 'Germanic' and 'tribe' are now hotly debated. I have made use of them because no better alternatives are available. Similarly, the word 'barbarian' is sometimes convenient. None of these terms should be interpreted too rigidly.

This book spans more than four centuries and cannot hope to describe the entire history of the period in equal detail. It would easily be possible to expand each of the chapters into a work of similar length to the entire book. Once again, more detailed studies are cited in the endnotes. I have tried to maintain a coherent narrative, although it is sometimes convenient to concentrate on events in one area before dealing with things happening elsewhere. Some issues, such as religion, law and wider society, are dealt with very briefly for reasons of space. This is not because such issues were unimportant, but simply because they were of minor significance for the slow rotting of Roman power. A very high proportion of our surviving sources are Christian, and it would be very easy for this book to turn into a history of the Church in these centuries. Once again, this would in itself be interesting, but it would be a digression from our real theme. The focus must always be on the factors and events that led to the eventual fall of the empire, and this is the story that this book attempts to tell. It is undoubtedly one of both decline and fall.

Before proceeding it is only right for me to thank the many people who helped me to write this book and listened patiently to my ideas. Some also read various versions of the manuscript and provided very many helpful comments. In particular I would like to thank Geoffrey Greatrex for finding the time amidst his heavy teaching and research load at the University of Ottawa to read all the chapters. Thanks to him I have been pointed to many works that I would not otherwise have found. Both Kevin Powell and Perry Gray were also kind enough to read the text. Each commented in a distinctive way and I can only regret that lack of space made it difficult to include some of their suggestions. Once again Ian Hughes has read and commented on the very first drafts of all the chapters, and has probably been very glad to move into a period more to his taste. Finally, I ought to thank my mother, Averil Goldsworthy, who has proofread almost all of my books in the past and become a little weary of being blanketed with a general thanks to family and friends. All of these have my thanks and have helped to make this a better book than would otherwise have been the case.

I would also like to thank the staff at Orion Publishing, and in particular my editor Keith Lowe, for all their labours in turning a bare text into the finished book. Similar gratitude is owed to Ileene Smith and the people at Yale University Press, both for their past work on *Caesar* and future efforts for this book. Lastly I must thank my agent, Georgina Capel, for once again creating the circumstances in which I could do justice to such a big topic.

Introduction – The Big Question

'The decline of Rome was the natural and inevitable effect of immoderate greatness. Prosperity repined the principle of decay; the causes of destruction multiplied with the extent of conquest; and as soon as time or accident had removed the artificial supports, the stupendous fabric yielded to the pressure of its own weight. The story of its ruin is simple and obvious; and instead of inquiring *why* the Roman empire was destroyed, we should rather be surprised that it lasted so long.' – *Edward Gibbon.*[1]

In 476 the last Roman emperor to rule from Italy was deposed at Ravenna. Romulus Augustulus was in his early teens, the puppet of his father who commanded the imperial army. It was not much of an army, but then they no longer controlled much of an empire. The east was ruled by another emperor at Constantinople and he did not recognise the pretender in Italy. Most of the western provinces – Gaul, Spain and North Africa – had been carved up into kingdoms by warlords of Germanic origin. Now the same fate would befall Italy as an army officer of barbarian origin called Odoacer killed Romulus' father and deposed the emperor. The lad himself was not important enough to be worth killing and was permitted to live out the rest of his life in comfortable retirement. There was a bitter irony that he should be named Romulus after Rome's mythical founder and nicknamed 'little Augustus' after the first emperor Augustus.

It has been common to name 476 as the year when the Roman Empire ended in the west. If so, then five centuries of imperial rule ended with a whimper. The event did not seem to be of massive importance to contemporaries, and probably passed unnoticed by most of the emperor's subjects. Romulus Augustulus was just the last in a succession of puppet emperors manipulated by powerful generals. The empire had split into eastern and western halves each ruled by its own emperor near the end of the fourth century. The east remained strong, but the west had withered, its wealth and power declining under a succession of blows.

By 476 the Western Empire did not have far to fall. In the next century the east Romans would attempt to regain the lost territories, occupying Italy, Africa and part of Spain. They lacked the strength and will to hold on to them in the long run.

The eastern part of the empire – known as the Byzantine Empire to modern scholars, but Roman as far as they were concerned – was a powerful state at the end of the sixth century. Yet it was not a superpower, and its wealth and military might were a pale shadow of the united empire in its heyday, when no enemy or rival had been even remotely Rome's equal. The time when the emperors had governed most of the known world was just a distant memory. By the year 600 the world was a very different place. No new superpower had emerged to take Rome's place and instead there were many smaller kingdoms and peoples. The medieval world had taken shape.

There have been a huge number of theories to explain why the world changed in this way, and very little agreement. Many dispute the importance of 476, even as a landmark. Some argue that the empire had already fallen before this and a few, somewhat bizarrely, that it survived afterwards. Not only are the causes of Rome's fall disputed, but also how long the process took. Some, like Gibbon, see the roots deep in the earlier history of the empire, which produced a slow decline over several centuries. Others suggest a shorter time span, although virtually no one has argued that it took less than a few generations. Debate continues to rage, each age answering the question according to its own obsessions and prejudices. The fall of the Roman Empire remains one of the great mysteries of history.

More recent empires have risen and fallen much more quickly. Hitler's 'thousand-year Reich' and its ally imperial Japan enjoyed spectacular success, both reaching the height of their power in 1942. Three years later they fell in blood and ruin, their power utterly broken. The Second World War also hastened the end of much older empires, whose impact on the wider world was deeper, if often more subtle. Exhausted and impoverished by war, Britain most readily acknowledged the 'wind of change' and gave up its empire in just a few decades. Wars were fought to defeat groups determined to seize power by force, but the inevitability of independence was never seriously doubted. Other countries resisted the change more stubbornly, but all failed to cling on to their colonies in the long run.

The great powers of the eighteenth and nineteenth centuries were a spent force, but they left a deep legacy. Newly independent countries had frontiers based on the decisions of imperial administrators – dramatically so where partition was employed, but more generally and less deliberately throughout Africa and Asia. Much of the world now had English, Spanish or French as a second language, which was very often the language of government and education. Legal and political systems were also derived from European prototypes. Ironically enough Latin law in this way spread to a far wider area than the Roman Empire had ever covered. Control passed almost invariably to an elite drawn from the indigenous population, but who were educated in the European style, and often actually in the country of the colonial power. Rarely is it possible to say more than that the wider population has been no worse off since independence, but all too often the new rulers have proved considerably more corrupt and exploitative than their predecessors. Former colonies now form the bulk of the poorest countries in the world.

Soviet Russia, which had inherited the empire and many of the ambitions of its Tsarist predecessor, survived longer than the west European powers and for forty years was one of two superpowers that dominated the world. Finally, Russia collapsed under its own weight. This happened very suddenly, surprising even its Cold War adversaries. The fate of many regions on Russia's fringes remains to be decided, but has already involved considerable bloodshed in several areas. Soviet Russia's fall left the United States of America as the sole superpower in the world, a situation that at the moment seems only likely to change if the forecasts of China's growth prove accurate. (The idea that the EC may become an equal is clearly fantasy. The periodic suggestions that it could join with Marxist China to form a counterweight to the USA are disturbing, but scarcely realistic.)

Once a colony itself, America became a country through rebellion from Britain. Apart from the expansion westwards, it has never shown much interest in occupying overseas territories, as distinct from maintaining bases around the world. Even so, the Cold War led to fighting open wars in Korea and Vietnam, as well as covert support for combatants in many other countries. Currently, the USA and its allies have substantial forces in Afghanistan and Iraq. In each case this is intended to be a temporary operation, until the supported governments are capable of maintaining themselves without direct military aid. Opponents often dub America an empire, but this is largely rhetoric. However, it is overwhelmingly the strongest country in the world and in this sense its position mirrors that of Rome. Yet the very different experiences of other modern empires should make us cautious about pressing this too far. First we must understand the Roman experience.

There is some irony in the coincidence that the first volume of Edward Gibbon's *The History of the Decline and Fall of the Roman Empire* was released early in 1776, just a few months before the Declaration of Independence. Gibbon was an MP and had been present in the previous autumn, silently approving Parliament's decision to support the government's plan to send more troops against the rebellious colonists. By the time he had completed his mammoth work, Britain had lost the war. It was a serious setback, but proved temporary and the heyday of the empire still lay in the future. The new America was tiny in comparison to today, for the great expansion to the west coast had not yet occurred, and no one would have guessed at its future prominence, although some wild claims were made. America was to have a negligible role in the affairs of the wider world for the next century.[2]

In the nineteenth century it would become more and more common to compare the grandeur of Britain's empire with that of Rome. For Gibbon and contemporaries the parallel was less specific, but there were a number of reasons why he chose to look at Rome rather than any of the other great empires of the ancient world. The first was quite simply the impact of the Romans on the world, and most of all on the Western world. Their empire had been larger and lasted far longer than any of the other great nations of antiquity. As importantly, it had included Gibbon's homeland, as well as most of western Europe. Christianity emerged in the Roman period and eventually became the religion of the empire, hence a Catholic Church and pope in Rome. Gibbon had dabbled with Catholicism in his youth, before being sent away by his father for a properly Protestant re-education in Calvinist Switzerland. Yet the Catholic Church had ensured the survival of Latin – and helped to preserve Greek – as a language and made possible the rediscovery of Greek and Roman literature in the Renaissance. Men like Gibbon were comfortable in both languages, which remained in his day the central pillars of education. The Greek achievement was admired, but Athens' decline was already chronicled by Thucydides and Xenophon. Alexander's empire was vast, but failed to outlive him. The earlier empires of Persia, Assyria, Babylonia and Egypt were known largely through what the Greeks and the Bible said of them. It was still a generation before Champollion would decipher the Rosetta Stone and little was known for certain about the earliest civilisations.[3]

There was also a particular immediacy about Rome for Europe's age of Enlightenment. Only now was there general confidence that learning and culture had once again reached the standards of the classical world, and was even beginning to surpass them. Yet the Roman Empire had collapsed in the west some thirteen hundred years before Gibbon began to write, and even the remnant of the Eastern Empire had disappeared three centuries ago. Looking back, the Middle Ages seemed to present a bleak prospect of ignorance and superstition, in stark contrast to the sophistication and apparent rationality of the Greco-Roman world. This reaction is not uncommon, even today. One recent book examining the transition from ancient to medieval was subtitled 'the Rise of Faith and the Fall of Reason'.[4]

For a long time the human race – particularly that part of it living in western Europe – had regressed rather than progressed, and understanding how and why this had happened was central to understanding the modern world. Yet, for all the reverence for the classics, little attention was paid to the world of the Late Roman Empire, primarily because all of the great Greek and Latin authors were earlier. In some ways Gibbon was treading fresh ground in looking at the fall rather than the rise and heyday of Rome. His concept was grand, original and sophisticated. Not only did he refer to ancient sources, but he also noted and assessed the theories of contemporary authors. Gibbon's breadth of scholarship remains exceptional, and in most respects the *Decline and Fall* can be seen as the first 'modern' history of the ancient world written in English, although in fact academic styles would develop in a different way in the following years. It was also from the beginning recognised as one of the great works of English literature.[5]

The Question

The world has changed since the eighteenth century, as have attitudes to both the past and present. Yet the fascination with the fall of the Roman Empire remains. The link may now be less intimate and obvious, but the influence of Rome upon the modern world – and especially Western culture – remains profound. There is also simple curiosity as to how a state that was so successful and so massive for such a long time nevertheless crumbled – or was shattered – and was replaced by far less sophisticated cultures. Rome's fate seems to act as a warning that strength and success will always prove transitory in the end, and that civilisation will not automatically triumph. It was no coincidence that one of Winston

Churchill's most famous speeches from 1940 foretold that Britain's defeat would result in a 'new Dark Age' – particularly apt since many believed that the Roman Empire had been destroyed by German barbarians in the fifth century.

Each successive generation has returned to the mystery of why Rome fell, and a huge number of different theories have been put forward – not too long ago one German scholar catalogued no fewer than 200. Often parallels have been quite explicitly drawn with problems facing the historian's own country and time, but there is at least one striking contrast between the Roman experience and the demise of the great empires of the twentieth century. Powers like Britain and France were already in decline, exhausted by world wars and their economic consequences, but they also faced huge pressure for independence from their colonies. It is doubtful that either would have had the capacity and will to resist this pressure indefinitely, especially since it was encouraged by the two new superpowers. America had not fought the Second World War to preserve the British Empire and its trade system, while Soviet Russia actively supported Marxist revolutionaries seeking independence.[6]

There is no trace of a comparable desire for freedom from imperial rule in Rome's provinces. The population of the Spanish provinces did not long to become an independent Spanish state, nor were there movements for the liberation of Cappadocia or Greece. Quite simply there were no equivalents in the Roman period of Gandhi or Nehru, Washington or Bolívar, Kenyatta or Mugabe. Even the empire's Jewish population, which had rebelled on several occasions in the first and second centuries, no longer seem to have wanted their own state by the fourth. People wanted to be Roman and associated freedom with belonging to the empire and not independence from it. This is in spite of the fact that the empire's rulers were not elected and enjoyed, effectively, absolute power. In every case power in Rome's former provinces eventually – and sometimes immediately – passed to new foreign invaders. Strikingly, even these usually wanted to become part of the empire and to enjoy its wealth rather than destroy it. The great paradox of the Roman Empire's fall is that it did not end because people inside it – and, indeed, outside it – stopped believing in it or wanting it to exist.

The Romans wanted the empire to exist, and most could not imagine a world without it, but they did realise that it was facing great problems. Most were inclined to see moral decline as the root cause of these: the empire was struggling because people lacked the stern virtue of the earlier generations who had made Rome great. This was a traditional – and particularly Roman – way of thinking. There was also often a religious element. Pagans blamed everything on the Christians for neglecting the old gods who had guided and protected the empire. In turn, Christians blamed pagans for clinging to the old mistaken beliefs, while a few began to link the end of Rome with the end of the world. St Augustine wrote his monumental *City of God* to explain to Christians that in the end all human states, including Rome, the greatest of them all, would pass. Christians were all members of a new and perpetual state that God would create. This was not an encouragement to them to despair of the empire or to try to speed its demise, but to reassure them that a better world lay ahead. Some secular historians – mainly men writing in Greek in the eastern half of the empire long after the west had gone – criticised individual emperors for specific military or political decisions, which were claimed to have had long-reaching consequences. However, none of the surviving works from the ancient world attempted any coherent analysis of why the empire, which spanned the bulk of the known world in 200, was reduced to a small fraction of its power and territory by 500.

Gibbon, primarily a narrative historian, was too subtle to present one single cause for the empire's fall. An Englishman in a country where civil war still cast a long shadow – Culloden was fought just thirty years before the first volume of *Decline and Fall* was released – he drew attention to the frequency of internal strife within the empire and the willingness of Roman armies to fight against each other in support of rival candidates for the throne. With an Anglican's suspicion of the papacy, he saw the adoption of Christianity under Constantine and his successors as a bad thing, which sapped the old Roman virtue and eventually caused too many people to withdraw from public life into unproductive monastic seclusion. His attitude was all the more bitter because he had himself converted to Catholicism during his student days at Oxford. Gibbon's father had withdrawn his son from the university and despatched him for a thorough reprogramming in Calvinist Switzerland. On balance, reflecting both the mood of his sources and the culture of his own day, the sense of moral decline is a constant thread running through Gibbon's account. The Romans failed in the end because they no longer deserved to succeed. At one point, after listing the many problems faced by the empire, Gibbon suggested that we probably ought not to wonder why the empire fell, but marvel that it lasted so long.

In due course many other historians considered this question. Some saw the collapse as internal, the result of failures and decline within the empire. Others preferred to emphasise the attacks on the empire by the Huns, especially the Germanic tribes who forced their way through the frontiers and carved out kingdoms for themselves in the western provinces. In the emotive words of one French scholar, 'The Roman Empire did not die. It was assassinated.' Stressing the role of the Germans had particular appeal in the climate of German nationalism in the nineteenth century. Roman texts contrasting the primitive virtue of German warriors with the decadence of fashionable life at Rome were taken at face value. For some, the empire deserved to die so that power could pass to the tribes that would make the countries of modern Europe. Others saw things in almost as blatantly racial terms and viewed the basic failure of Rome as a consequence of permitting too many barbarian Germans to enter its frontiers. The preoccupations of each age have usually been reflected in their views on Rome's fall. Social problems and class tension have sometimes become fashionable explanations, often in combination with economic factors. For some the world of the later Roman Empire was extremely bleak, with over-taxed peasantry being squeezed to pay for the spiralling costs of maintaining the army. In time the strain was too great and the whole system collapsed. Alternative theories would point to military failures or dwindling population. Others have reflected different modern concerns and suggested that environmental or climate change – perhaps increased by the impact of Roman farming and industry – were the root cause of declining agricultural yields and ultimately economic collapse.[7]

In the last few decades the very nature of the debate has changed within the academic community, and there are several reasons for this. One, common in the West, has been a changed attitude towards empires in general, now that the modern ones have gone. These are no longer assumed by their nature to have been good things. Instead, the pendulum of popular – or at least middle-class and academic – opinion has swung to the other extreme. Instead of being forces for order and progress, bringing peace, education, science, medicine and Christianity to the wilder parts of the world, empires have become nothing more than brutal exploiters of indigenous populations. If empires are automatically a bad thing, then it is comforting also to think of them as inefficient. There has been much emphasis in recent studies of the Roman Empire in the first and second centuries to the lack of central control or planning, its unsophisticated economy, limited technology and simplistic thinking in such matters as geography and military strategy. Instead of the apparently sophisticated, the primitive has been stressed.[8]

Curiously, attitudes towards the later Roman Empire have tended to the opposite extreme. For a long time it was unfashionable for academics to work on the later, rather than earlier periods. The main reason was the lack of good sources – particularly reliable and detailed narrative histories – for the third century, much of the fourth century and all of the fifth century. There is a considerable body of literature surviving from these periods, but it deals little with political or military events, much of it being religious – mostly, but not exclusively, Christian – philosophical or legal. Of little value for studying the great events of these years, it does provide considerable material for various aspects of social, cultural and intellectual history, which have become far more popular with academics in the last generation or so. This encouraged a massive boom in the study of the later empire. Many very important and revealing studies have been produced, and it is fair to say that we now know a good deal more about many different aspects of the period.[9]

Yet something odd has happened as well. In the beginning there was clearly a sense that the historians choosing to work on the later period needed to justify their decision. Many became deeply uncomfortable with the idea of an empire in decline, and emphasised the vibrancy and strength of the fourth- and even fifth-century Roman state. This was especially easy for those dealing with culture and religion. In these fields there was no catastrophic break coinciding with the collapse of the Western Empire. Reassessment of the centuries after Rome's fall has also been an especially fertile field for scholars in recent years, and these two trends have encouraged and fed off each other. Scholars, as opposed to the wider public, had long been unhappy with the term 'Dark Age', and instead the fifth to tenth centuries are now universally referred to as the 'Early Medieval' period. Medieval history is currently flourishing in universities, making this connection both attractive and instructive. At the same time it has been customary to stop talking about the 'Late Roman Empire' or the 'Late Roman period', and instead refer to 'Late Antiquity', stressing the legitimacy, importance and also separateness of study into this period.

Names can be important, shaping the broad mental framework into which specific studies are fitted. In most respects these trends have been positive. Far more imaginative use has been made of the sources we do possess for these periods. Yet there are also inherent problems. Switching the focus to society, culture, religion and even to government and law tends to produce a rather static view, emphasising continuity rather than change. Events such as wars and revolutions, and the behaviour and decisions of specific emperors and ministers, do not necessarily register, but it would be most unwise to see them as unimportant. It seems very hard for many people working on Late Antiquity to consider the possibility that anything was declining. Instead they prefer to see change and transformation. In a gradual – and in no way traumatic – process the world of the Roman Empire morphed into the medieval world. For instance, one scholar who examined government in the Western Empire concluded that: 'It should be clear ... that the Roman Empire did not "fall" in the fifth century, but was transformed into something new.'[10]

The main basis for this conclusion was that some aspects of government, including specific titles and ranks, appear to continue under the Germanic kingdoms. The concept of decline firmly out of fashion, it was probably inevitable that the idea of a fall would also come under pressure. Even when it is admitted that this occurred, it is often portrayed as a matter of little importance. The trend has been for those working on Late Antiquity to be almost relentlessly positive in their assessment of every aspect of it. Institutions such as the army and government are portrayed as very efficient – often more effective than those of the early empire – and any problems seen as inevitable in the conditions of the ancient world and not unique to the later period. Similarly, the slightest trace of continuity is imbued with deep and widespread significance. As an example, the survival of a Roman bureaucratic title in the court of a German king does not necessarily mean that the individual was doing the same job at all, let alone that he was doing it well. Similarly, the find of a stylus pen in a late fifth-century site from Britain cannot be taken to prove widespread literacy in the post-Roman period. Extending the same logic to our own day would mean that the survival of imperial institutions and English as one of the languages of government in India really meant that it was still part of the British Empire. This would doubtless come as a great surprise to the country's inhabitants.

There have been some dissenting voices. Recently two popular books were released in which distinguished specialists on Late Antiquity – curiously enough, both from Oxford – cast doubt on what has become the orthodox view. Brian Ward-Perkins' *The Fall of Rome* (2005) pointed out firstly that the idea of a peaceful transformation between Roman Empire and barbarian kingdom simply goes against the evidence as well as simple logic. Even more importantly, he used the archaeological record to show just how massive a change there was as a result of Rome's fall. Much of this had to do with the everyday life of ordinary people, who, for instance, now lived in houses with thatched rather than tiled roofs, and used simpler, locally produced pottery, rather than a range of finer imported wares. Cultural sophistication declined so sharply that Ward-Perkins felt justified in calling it 'the end of civilisation'. Peter Heather's *The Fall of the Roman Empire* (2005) was more concerned with how the Western Empire fell than its consequences. He employs an essentially narrative structure, feeling that the peaceful transition theory of the empire's end 'has largely established itself ... only because detailed historical narrative has been ignored for half a generation'. Beginning in 376 he charts the century until the deposition of Romulus Augustulus and, like Ward-Perkins, he sees the 'end of the Empire as a major event'. The fourth-century empire is presented as a strong, vibrant state, whose demise was not inevitable. Instead, the new threats posed by peoples from outside, such as the Huns and Goths, presented a challenge that through a mixture of human error and chance was not adequately met.[11]

Each of these books is extremely good in its own way, but both are restricted in what it was possible to cover. Neither makes much effort to link the empire of the fourth century with the earlier empire. Yet this connection needs to be made if we are to understand more fully what the Roman Empire was like and discern why it did eventually fall. Studies of Late Antiquity stress the great strength of the fourth-century empire. They are certainly correct to do so, since Rome in this period was overwhelmingly stronger than any other nation or people in the known world. However, it was not as stable as the empire of the second century, nor was it as powerful. How and why this changed is central to understanding why the later empire was as it was. Put simply, the empire was stronger in the year 200 than it was in 300 – although perhaps it had been even weaker in 250. By 400 the empire was weaker again, and by 500 it had vanished in the west and only the rump was left in the lands around the eastern Mediterranean. A longer perspective is necessary to explain these shifts.

With the concept of decline out of fashion, most historians have tended to stress the pressure from outside the empire. Only recently have some questioned the true scale of the threat posed by the tribal peoples who lived outside the Roman Empire's European frontiers. Even so, many continue to assume that the confederations that appeared by the end of the third century were far more formidable enemies than the barbarian tribes faced by the early empire. It certainly remains an article of faith that the Sassanid Persians who supplanted the Parthian dynasty in the early third century were far more efficient, aggressive and dangerous than their predecessors. This has certainly been repeated so often that no one seems to question its essential truth. The belief that the threats faced by the empire had increased is a convenient one for those wishing to see the massive institutional changes within the empire as sensible reactions to a new situation. Convenience and frequent repetition do not amount to truth, and all of this needs to be questioned.[12]

Civil war was a frequent occurrence from the third century onwards. After 217 there were only a handful of decades without a violent struggle for power within the Roman Empire. Some of these were local rebellions, rapidly suppressed and involving little serious fighting. Others lasted for years and were only decided by one or more major battles or sieges. We have no figures for how many Roman soldiers died or were maimed fighting against other Romans, but the total must have been considerable. It is true that people living in provinces distant from the fighting may not have been directly affected by outbreaks of internal conflict, unless they were related to leading figures on the losing side. This does not mean that such things were of minor importance. Civil war was a fact of life, and everyone who reached adulthood would have lived through one, even if it had no direct impact on them.

Strangely, while most historians note the frequency of internal conflict within the Roman Empire from the third century onwards, they rarely spend much time considering this in any detail. A. H. M. Jones produced a colossal study of the later empire that remains an indispensable reference point even now, more than forty years later. It includes the following curious statement: 'Diocletian maintained internal peace for twenty years, broken only by two revolts.'[13] At this point it is worth noting that one of these revolts lasted for the best part of a decade and both required a major military effort to suppress them. Diocletian had anyway fought and won another civil war to secure himself as emperor in the first place. He was certainly successful by the standards of recent decades, but the stability he gave the empire was limited and brief. His reign was followed by a spate of especially large-scale civil wars. It is significant that Jones devoted only a single paragraph to civil war and internal strife in a long chapter discussing the causes of Rome's fall. His attitude was and is typical, civil wars and usurpations simply being accepted as part of the normal landscape of the later Roman period. One of the reasons for this neglect may simply be that most scholars have worked in countries for whom civil wars were things only of the distant past. It was simply natural for them to assume that foreign threats must always be more serious. In addition, the focus on institutions and culture had little room for civil wars, which rarely if ever involved major changes to such things.

Rarely does anyone pause to consider the consequences of this reality for the attitudes of emperors and their subordinates at all levels.

The aim of this study is to look more closely at both the internal and external problems faced by the Roman Empire. It will begin, as Gibbon did, in the year 180 when the empire still appeared to be in its heyday, before moving on to trace the descent into the chaos of the middle of the third century. Then we will examine the rebuilt empire of Diocletian and Constantine, the move towards division into an eastern and western half in the fourth century and the collapse of the west in the fifth. It will end with the abortive effort of the Eastern Empire to recapture the lost territories in the sixth century. Gibbon went much further, continuing to the fall of Constantinople to the Turks in the fifteenth century. That is a fascinating story in its own right, but is too great a one to be dealt with adequately here. By the end of the sixth century the world was profoundly and permanently different from our starting point. The Eastern Roman Empire was strong, but no longer possessed the overwhelming might and dominance of the united Roman Empire. This book is about how this came about. Central is the story of the individual men and women, the groups, peoples and tribes who lived through and shaped these centuries. In telling the story, we will try to assess the more likely theories about why things happened as they did.

The Sources

We have some important advantages over Gibbon when it comes to considering this theme. Antiquarians had made some effort to collect and catalogue inscriptions from the ancient world, and to describe the visible remains of ancient towns and cities. However, archaeology in any systematic form did not begin until the nineteenth century, and techniques of gathering and understanding data have since become far more refined. New sites are continually being discovered and existing ones better understood, adding to the pool of information about each region and period. Modern methods are very sophisticated and able in the right circumstances to extract a good deal of information. This does mean that the modern trend is to excavate increasingly small areas in greater and greater detail. Given the size of many communities from the Roman period, it is now quite rare for settlements to be excavated in their entirety. Similarly, there are normally only the resources for large-scale work on a small proportion of located sites. This can mean that a general picture of rural or urban life in a province tends to be based on a tiny sample of existing remains, even ignoring what has been lost or the sites not yet located. It is also vital to appreciate the limited amount of unequivocal fact discovered by archaeology. All finds require interpretation, especially if wider conclusions are to be drawn. Any study of the history of the ancient world is incomplete without considering the archaeological record, but impressions derived from the latter are liable to change as new discoveries are made or old ones reinterpreted.

The vast bulk of the literature surviving from the Greco-Roman world was available to Gibbon. There have since been a few discoveries – for instance, the letters of Fronto from the very beginning of our period. Conversely, the poems of Ossian – purportedly heroic poetry surviving in Scotland from the Caledonian tribes who had fought against Rome and mentioned in *The Decline and Fall* – have long since been recognised as an eighteenth-century hoax. However, the genuine finds of texts and fragments from other writers have not fundamentally changed the balance and usefulness of the literary sources. The third century is extremely poorly served. For much of it there are only summaries and epitomes of earlier histories, which are generally brief and often unreliable. There is also the collection of imperial biographies known as the *Historia Augusta*, which purports to be the work of six authors writing in the late third and early fourth centuries. It is now generally considered to have been written by just one man at least a generation after this. An odd mixture of invention and confusion, the author nevertheless seems to include some reliable information. Yet it is an indication of the poverty of our other sources for this period that we are forced to make any use of it at all.[14]

Two notable narrative historians provide detailed – and generally reliable – accounts. Ammianus Marcellinus covers part of the fourth century and Procopius part of the sixth. Both were actual eyewitnesses to some of the events they describe. The same was true to some extent of Cassius Dio and Herodian, who cover the beginning of the period. Apart from these, we rely mainly on snippets of information and brief summaries. As we have seen, the overwhelming bulk of literature from this period is simply not concerned with the great events of politics or war. Some, such as the many panegyric speeches, do address emperors and refer to contemporary concerns and events, but in such a stylised and rhetorical form that it is difficult to glean very much information from them. The belief that these contain coded messages is possible, but easily taken too far. It is vital to remember that we have only the tiniest fragment of the literature that once existed. A large chunk of Ammianus' history is lost, while only the names survive of many other authors and their works. There were doubtless far more who do not even get mentioned in what survives. Most works were preserved in manuscripts kept in church libraries. Inevitably, this meant that the prospects for Christian manuscripts were far better, and also that literary merit rather than historical interest played a part. Chance played an even bigger role.

This is even more true of the other documents – mostly written on papyrus, but sometimes on writing-tablets or pottery sherds, preservation has also largely been a question of luck. These continue to be found where the conditions are right, and sometimes appear in considerable quantities and can include such things as census returns. Such information is highly useful, but never exists in sufficient quantity to generate reliable statistics for population size, age range and the general levels of prosperity on more than a very local and short-term basis. All studies of the ancient world are forced to proceed without the support of statistics. This does mean that it is impossible to prove or disprove some of the theories put forward to explain the fall of the Roman Empire. We simply cannot say whether a serious decline in population played a role in this. Similarly, we cannot measure the state of the economy at any set period or trace the real impact of the staggering devaluation of the currency in the third century. What sources we have may hint at trends, but not everyone will interpret these in the same way.

There is a good deal that we simply cannot now know about the history of the Roman Empire in the third and later centuries. To a greater or lesser extent this is true of most periods of ancient history. Yet we must be careful to ask the questions we want to ask, rather than shifting towards those that the sources make it easiest to answer. In addition, the simple fact that so much Greek and Roman literature has failed to survive does rather suggest that the change from a Roman to medieval world was in many ways drastic. Far more of this literature was simply lost rather than deliberately suppressed or destroyed by churchmen. The medieval world was a far less literate place than the classical world that preceded it, particularly in western Europe. None of this suggests transformation. The fall of the Roman Empire was a major event, even if it occurred over considerable time and cannot be assigned to a specific date. This becomes all the more clear when we consider the empire when it was still at its height.

PART ONE

Crisis?
The Third Century

1

The Kingdom of Gold

'Reflect upon the rapidity with which all that exists and is coming to be is swept past us and disappears from sight. For substance is like a river in perpetual flow ... and ever at our side is the immeasurable span of the past and the yawning gulf of the future, in which all things vanish away. Then how is he not a fool who in the midst of all this is puffed up with pride, or tormented, or bewails his lot as though his troubles would endure for any great while?' – *Emperor Marcus Aurelius.*[1]

Marcus Aurelius died sometime during the night of 17 March 180. Rome's sixteenth emperor was just a few weeks short of his fifty-ninth birthday and had ruled his vast empire for nearly two decades. Later there were rumours of foul play – there nearly always were when any emperor died – of doctors ensuring his death to please his son and heir Commodus. This is very unlikely, and in fact it is in many ways surprising that he had lived as long as he did. Never a robust man, he had driven himself hard during a reign troubled by war and plague. Even so, later generations remembered him as the ideal emperor, and the senator Dio writing in the next century described his reign as a 'kingdom of gold'. Marcus' remarkable *Meditations* – the diary-like collection of his philo-sophical ideas, which was never intended for publication – reveal a man with a profound sense of duty and an earnest desire to rule well. This was not from a desire for reputation – 'It is the king's part to do good and be ill spoken of' – but because it was the right thing to do and the best for everyone. Reputation meant nothing to the dead, and he, like everyone and everything else was destined to die: 'in a short while you will be no one and nowhere, as are Hadrian and Augustus'. Death, and the need to accept it without resentment, is a constant theme, which suggests that he was never quite able to convince himself. His private letters reveal his deep emotion at the loss of friends and family. Yet change was the nature of the world, and even those historians who deny that the Roman empire ever declined or fell describe its transformation. Before looking at this process it is worth examining the world of Marcus Aurelius.[2]

Map 1 The Roman Empire in the late second century AD

BRITANNIA
□ Eburacum
INFERIOR
□
Deva

Isca Silurum □ BRITANNIA
SUPERIOR
□ Londinium

Vetera
2
□ Bonna
⊡ Moguntiacum

BELGICA
Durocortorum •

LUGDUNENSIS

MARCOMANNI

QUADI
Argentorate □ Castra Regina⊡ Aquincur
Lauriacum ⊡
Vindobona
Carnuntum Brigeti
RAETIA NORICUM
1

AQUITANIA
Burdigala • Lugdunum •

3
ALPES
COTTIAE
ALPES
MARITIMAE

4

DALMATIA
Salon

□ Legio
VII Gemina

NARBONENSIS
Narbo

ITALIA
• Roma
□ Albanum

TARRACONENSIS
Tarraco •

SARDINIA
ET
CORSICA

LUSITANIA
Emerita •
Augusta •

Corduba •
BAETICA

Carales •

SICILIA

Tingis •

Caesarea (Iol) •

Carthago •
• Syracuse

MAURETANIA
TINGITANA

AFRICA

MAURETANIA CAESARIENSIS
□ Lambaesis

NUMIDIA

Albis

Rhenus

Danuvius

1 GERMANIA
2 GERMANIA INFERIOR
3 ALPES ATRECTIANAE
  ET POENINAE
4 PANNONIA SUPERIOR
5 PANNONIA INFERIOR

0 ————————— 500 km
0 ————————— 300 miles

Approximate provincial boundaries
• Provincial capital main centre
□ Legionary base
▣ Legionary base and provincial capital
BELGICA Province
PARTHIA Other territories/peoples

ZYGES
□ Potaissa
□ Apulum **ROXOLANI**
DACIA
idunum • Sarmizegetusa
▣▣ Viminacium
Danuvius
OESIA **DOBRUDJA**
UPERIOR □ Durostorum
□ Novae
MOESIA INFERIOR
THRACIA
MACEDONIA
essalonica Perinthus
US
icopolis
ACHAEA
orinthus
Pergamum

BITHYNIA ET PONTUS
Amastris •
□ Satala
• Nicomedia
GALATIA | CAPPADOCIA
ARMENIA
• Ancyra
Melitene □
ASIA
Caesarea
(Mazaca) •
□ Samosata
• Ephesus
□ Resaina
• Myra
CILICIA • Tarsus
• Antiochia
□ Singara
LYCIA ET
PAMPHYLIA CYPRUS
CRETA
ET
YRENE Gortyn
Paphus •
SYRIA COELE
2 legions
□ Raphaneae
SYRIA PHOENICE
Caparcotna □ • Tyrus
Caesarea ▣
• Cyrene
SYRIA PALAESTINA
Aelia Capitolina □
▣ Bostra
PARTHIA
ARABIA
▣
Alexandria/
Nicopolis
AEGYPTUS
Euphrates

Educated people like Marcus knew that the world was round. Greek philosophers had first realised this, but for centuries the Romans had also spoken of the globe or *orb*. There were occasional suggestions to the contrary, but the trend amongst philosophers was to claim that the stars and planets revolved around the Earth rather than the Sun. Knowledge of the night sky was considerable in many cultures of the ancient world, in part because people had a deep-seated belief in astrology. Emperor Hadrian was supposed to have been able to predict even the smallest events in minute detail, including the day and hour of his own death. The world was round, but only three continents were known – Europe, Asia and Africa – and there was no clear idea of the full extent of the last two. Around the land masses was the vast encircling ocean, broken only on its fringes by a few islands like Britain. In the centre of the continents was the Mediterranean, the middle sea. This was the heart of the world, and of the Roman Empire.[3]

In Marcus' day the empire stretched from the Atlantic coast to the Rhine and Danube, and from the line of the rivers Forth and Clyde in northern Britain to the Euphrates in Syria. This was a vast area – by far the greatest part of the known world as far as its inhabitants were concerned. It was all the greater in an age when transport was never faster than a ship could sail across the sea or a horse could gallop overland. It was some 3,000 miles from the easternmost fringes of the empire to its northernmost tip, and yet we know that people made such journeys. In 1878 a tombstone was found near the site of the Roman fort of Arbeia at South Shields overlooking the mouth of the Tyne. It commemorates Regina – Queen or perhaps Queenie – the thirty-year-old 'freedwoman and wife' of 'Barates of the Palmyrene nation'. Palmyra was a wealthy oasis city in Syria and it seems likely that Barates was a merchant, and judging from the size and quality of this monument, a successful one. His wife was more local, a Briton from the Catuvellaunian tribe who lived north of the Thames. Originally she had been his slave, but he had given her freedom and then married her, a not uncommon arrangement. On the tombstone she is shown seated and dressed in the finery of a Roman lady, with a bracelet on her wrist and necklace at her throat, her hair pinned up in one of the ornate styles dictated by fashion. On the husband's part at least there does seem to have been genuine affection. Most of the inscription is in Latin, but the last line is in the curving script of his own native tongue and reads simply, 'Regina, the freedwoman of Barates, alas.'[4]

Neither Barates nor Regina were Roman citizens, but their marriage and presence in northern Britain were all due to the empire. So was the fact that the monument was in Roman style and largely in Latin. The world they lived in was Roman, although never exclusively so. Each proudly identified with peoples that had once been independent. Barates spoke his own Semitic language and Regina is likely to have spoken the Celtic language of her people. Latin was only common in the western provinces and Greek remained the principal means of communication and culture in the east. Throughout the empire many different languages and dialects continued to be spoken locally. There were other differences, too, of religion, customs and culture, and yet the striking thing about the empire was the number of similarities from one province to another. The great public buildings – basilicas, temples, theatres, circuses, amphitheatres and aqueducts – looked much the same in Africa as they did in Gaul, Spain and Syria.

Yet it was more than just a question of architectural style and engineering technique. People dressed in similar and distinctively Roman ways, and particular fashions spread widely. Hadrian was the first emperor to wear a beard, expressing his fondness for this Greek custom, although others said that he just wanted to hide the blemishes on his skin. Many men copied him. Similarly women aped the hairstyles adopted by the emperors' wives and daughters, shown on their portraits throughout the provinces. Virtually identical coiffures can be seen on sculptures from the Rhineland as on funerary portraits from Egypt. These painted portraits decorated coffins containing bodies mummified according to the ancient custom of the region. Becoming Roman rarely, if ever, meant complete abandonment of local traditions.[5]

The Roman Empire was created through conquest, which was often an extremely bloody business. Julius Caesar was said to have killed a million people when he overran Gaul in 58–50 BC, and sold as many more into slavery. This was exceptional, and the numbers are probably exaggerated, but the Romans were ruthlessly determined in their pursuit of victory and the cost could be appalling for the vanquished. The Roman historian Tacitus made one tribal leader proclaim that the Romans 'make a wasteland, and call it peace'. Very few provinces were created without at least some fighting and Caesar himself felt it was natural for the Gauls to fight for their freedom, even if it was entirely proper for him to deprive them of it in the interest of Rome. Yet in Gaul as elsewhere, there were always some communities and leaders who welcomed the legions, seeking protection from hostile neighbours or hoping to gain an advantage over rivals. The Iceni tribe of the famous Queen Boudicca had welcomed the

Roman invaders in 43 and only rebelled in 60 when the royal family was mistreated. The legions were as efficient and brutal in suppressing a rebellion as they were in fighting any other war, and the revolt of the Iceni ended in utter and very costly defeat.[6]

Rebellions often occurred about a generation after the initial conquest, but were extremely rare in most areas after that. By the second century it is very hard to detect any traces of a desire for independence from the overwhelming bulk of the provincial population. Partly this acknowledged the dreadful power of the legions, but the army was not large enough to have held the empire down by force and most regions never saw a soldier, let alone a formed body of troops. More importantly, enough people prospered under Roman rule to want to keep it. The Romans had no wish to occupy a wasteland, wanting provinces that were peaceful and rich. In some periods there was substantial settlement of Roman and Italian colonists in communities in conquered territory, but these were never more than a minority amongst the indigenous population. Provinces would never have been peaceful and paid the required taxes without the efforts of the provincials themselves.

Those to benefit most were the local aristocracies, many of whom kept their land, status and wealth. Local communities were left to run their own affairs for much of the time, since central government had neither the desire nor the capacity to interfere. Some laws were imposed, especially those for incidents involving Roman citizens or to regulate relations with other communities. Usually these communities were cities, which administered the lands around them. Many pre-dated Roman occupation, but where none existed they were usually created. The culture of the empire was primarily urban and local aristocrats were encouraged to become magistrates and city councillors. This gave them prestige, authority and sometimes the chance for an even greater career in imperial service. Many were granted Roman citizenship, but Rome had always been generous with this and it was also extended to many less well-off provincials. In the middle of the first century the Apostle Paul, a Jew from the city of Tarsus in Asia Minor, was a citizen, although there is no evidence that he could speak Latin. His family was able to give him a good education, but do not seem to have been more than moderately wealthy. On a grander scale, entire cities could formally become a Roman town or colony with constitutions modelled on that of Rome itself.

Most of the provinces were artificial creations of the empire, combining different tribes, peoples and cities into divisions that would have had no real meaning before the Romans came. Tribes and cities continued to inspire real emotion. Paul would boast of being a citizen of Tarsus, 'no mean city', as well as a Roman. In the second century cities were at their most prosperous and were fiercely competitive with their neighbours, striving to out-do them in splendour and prestige. Grand public buildings were constructed as physical symbols of a city's importance. Only a fraction survives from what once existed, but such monuments today provide many of the most spectacular reminders of the Roman era. Magistrates were expected to contribute plenty of their own money when presiding over such projects, commemorating this in great inscriptions set up on the completed buildings. Sometimes ambition got out of hand. At the beginning of the second century Pliny the Younger was sent to govern Bithynia and Pontus – modern northern Turkey. He found that Nicomedia had spent over 3 million sesterces on an aqueduct, which had never been completed. Nearby Nicaea had spent 10 million on a theatre that was already collapsing. These were vast sums – a legionary soldier was paid only 1,200 sesterces per year – and give an indication of the huge amounts lavished on improving cities. Most projects were more successful. There were always local peculiarities of custom and ritual, but it is striking just how similar civic life was throughout the empire.[7]

However dreadful initial conquest by Rome may have been, if it created a wasteland, then it was never permanent. The famous *Pax Romana*, or Roman Peace, was a reality, and we should not forget how rare prolonged peace was in the ancient world. Before the Romans arrived warfare and raiding were a common occurrence everywhere, and in some regions endemic. Tribes, peoples, cities, kingdoms or leaders fought each other frequently, and in many cases were wracked by internal violence and civil war. This was as true of so-called barbarian tribes as it was of the Greek world – democratic Athens had proved extremely aggressive in its foreign policy. The Romans, however, stopped all of this. Rome was the most successful imperialist of the ancient world, but it was most certainly not the only expansionist state. It is a mistake to think of conquered peoples as mere victims of Rome rather than aggressive in their own right. The Romans had a unique talent for absorbing others and managed to convince the provinces that remaining loyal to Rome was better than the alternative of resistance. This element of consent was ultimately what made the empire work. By 180 no one could seriously imagine, let alone remember, a world without Rome.

Violence was not completely absent from the provinces. Banditry was a serious problem in some areas at some periods and may at times have had a social or political element to it. Both pirates and bandits figure regularly in Greek and Roman fiction, suggesting that they captured the imagination, which does not necessarily mean that they were common in real life. However, there is frequent mention in a range of sources of other organised or casual violence – of landlords against tenants or any group against the vulnerable. We need to be a little careful, since crimes – especially violent crimes – attract disproportionate attention in today's media, quite simply because no one wishes to report or hear about days when nothing happened. There was no organised police force above a local level and the empire was certainly not without crime, but then this has also been true of other large states. Serious rebellion was very rare. Judaea rebelled under Nero (66–73) and again under Hadrian (132–135), while the Jewish population in Egypt, Cyprus and several other provinces rose against Trajan (115–117). In each case the fighting was bitter and costly, but eventually the Romans brutally suppressed the revolt.[8]

The Jews were unusual in having such a strong sense of nationhood, reinforced by religion, and traditions that emphasised resistance to invaders. There were Jewish communities dotted throughout the cities of the empire, but also many living outside, within the great kingdom of Parthia. The Parthians were the only significant independent power on the empire's borders, ruling a realm that covered much of today's Iraq and Iran. The Romans treated them with a degree of respect unmatched in their diplomacy with other peoples, but never as equals. Parthian cavalry armies were formidable in the right circumstances and had in the past inflicted a number of defeats on Roman armies, although conflicts invariably ended with a treaty favouring Rome. Yet their power should not be exaggerated and was dwarfed by the empire. Trajan had launched a major invasion and had sacked the Parthian capital at Ctesiphon. There was never any prospect of a Parthian army threatening Rome itself. Between Parthia and Rome lay the kingdom of Armenia, which clung on to a precarious independence. Culturally it had more in common with the Parthians, and its throne was frequently occupied by members of their royal family. However, the Romans insisted that only they could grant legitimacy to a new king.

Trajan attempted to annex much of Parthia, but was thwarted by a spate of rebellions in the newly conquered territories and his own failing health. His successor Hadrian withdrew from the new provinces and Parthia gradually recovered some of its strength. Elsewhere along the frontiers Rome faced communities far smaller in scale. The vast majority were tribal peoples, politically disunited and frequently hostile to each other. Occasionally a charismatic leader emerged to unite several tribes for a while, but his power rarely survived to be passed on to a successor. The bulk of the Roman army was deployed on or near the frontiers to face whatever threats emerged. This in itself suggests that serious rebellion was considered unlikely in most of the internal provinces. Writing in the second century, the Greek orator Aelius Aristides compared Roman soldiers to the wall protecting a city.[9]

'More Honourable Men': The Rulers of the Empire

The nine hundredth anniversary of Rome's foundation was formally commemorated in 148 when Marcus Aurelius was in his teens. (It is impossible to know whether or not Romulus existed and actually founded the city in 753 BC, but the traditional date was probably roughly right.) Kings ruled Rome until 509 BC, when the last of these was expelled and the Republic created. In this system elected magistrates provided the state with its senior executive officers, leading it both in peace and in war. They were advised by the Senate, a council that included all former magistrates. The system was supposed to prevent any one individual or group from gaining supreme power. For a long time it worked well, giving Rome an internal stability that was envied by Greek commentators whose own communities were plagued by revolution and internal strife. The Roman Republic expanded to control the Italian Peninsula by the third century BC, and by the middle of the next century dominated the Mediterranean world. Yet eventually Roman politics became increasingly violent. In 88 BC a Roman army marched against Rome itself, beginning the first in a series of civil wars that would tear the Republic apart. Finally, in 31 BC, Julius Caesar's adopted son Octavian defeated his last rival, Mark Antony. Rome became a monarchy once again, although Octavian studiously avoided the word 'king' – Caesar had been murdered because it was claimed that he craved this title.

Octavian claimed to have 'restored the Republic', but during his long reign he created a system that fundamentally altered the balance of power within the state. He and his successors received the name *imperator*, from which we get our word 'emperor'. In Latin it meant 'general', and victorious commanders were traditionally hailed as *imperator* by their armies. It gained a new meaning because Octavian controlled the army. Soldiers swore an oath of allegiance to him, not to their commanders, and were paid and rewarded by him, including a grant of land or money on discharge. He also had permanent control of most of the provinces, oversaw state finances, controlled appointments to most senior posts and could make law. There was no constitutional position of emperor and each power was individually granted to Octavian. Officially he was the *princeps*, the first magistrate and chief servant of the state. Later he was also granted the name Augustus, its dignity helping to replace memories of the bloodstained revolutionary who had clawed his way to power. Both this name and the family name of Caesar became deeply associated with supreme power, and were taken by later emperors who had no connection with the line. The Principate, as it is known to modern scholars, was a veiled monarchy, but few people were fooled. In the Greek-speaking east, Augustus was referred to as *basileus* (king) from the very beginning. Imperial power rested ultimately on armed force. When one senator noted for his skill as an orator was criticised by Hadrian for using a particular word, he meekly submitted, much to the surprise of his friends. Later he cheerfully chided them and asked how could he not 'acknowledge that the man who controls thirty legions is the most learned of all'.[10]

In practice, the emperor was far more than first amongst equals, but the good ones did not parade their power and treated their subjects, and especially the senatorial aristocracy, with respect. The Senate consisted of around 600 members at any one time, but admission to its ranks conferred senatorial status on several subsequent generations so that the class as a whole was a little bigger. A senator had to be freeborn and own property valued at 1 million sesterces. Most senators possessed far more than this, and the bulk of their property took the form of landed estates, sometimes dotted all over the empire, although all were required to own some land in Italy.

The old established families that had dominated the Republic were largely extinct, victims of the civil wars of the first century BC or the purges of nervous emperors. Natural wastage also contributed, for birth rates were low amongst the aristocracy, while infant mortality was exceptionally high. Marcus Aurelius and his wife Faustina were unusual in having as many as fourteen children, but only six of these survived to reach adulthood. Some lines survived through adoption, and others saw their wealth and heritage combine through a daughter's marriage with another family, but many died out altogether. The patricians, Rome's oldest aristocracy, became all but extinct during the rule of Augustus and his family. Later emperors conferred patrician status on other senators as a high honour. Caesar and Augustus had both introduced many Italians into the Senate. Claudius added a large number of men from Gaul and, over the course of time, there were senators from virtually every province in the empire. All were Roman citizens, some the descendants of Roman or Italian colonists, but others were from the provincial aristocracies, men whose ancestors may well have fought against Rome. In time, this was true of the emperors as well. Trajan and Hadrian came from Spain, as did the family of Marcus Aurelius, while Antoninus Pius was from Gaul.

The ancient prestige of the Senate remained, but very few of its members could boast more than a few generations of senators amongst their ancestors. Free elections had ended with the Republic, but the magistracies were still prestigious and important. In addition there were new jobs in imperial service. Most men followed a career that brought them both traditional and imperial posts, and mixed civilian and military responsibilities. The two consuls elected each year had been the senior magistrates of the Republic. Becoming consul was still a great honour, but it was normal for each pair to resign after three months and be replaced, so that there were usually eight in each year, all chosen by the emperor. It was more prestigious to be one of the two consuls who began the year, better again to hold the office twice or even thrice, and best of all to be consul with the emperor as a colleague. A number of provinces were governed by senatorial proconsuls, whose appointment was still the prerogative of the Senate, although it was unlikely that the successful candidate would not also have had imperial favour. Provinces with significant military garrisons were controlled by the emperor's representatives or legates. These men were carefully selected senators and such commands usually represented the pinnacle of their career.

After the senators came the equestrian order, or 'knights' – the name a survival of an earlier age when those wealthy enough to afford a horse had served as cavalry in Rome's militia army. Equestrians were also normally supposed to be freeborn and had to own property worth at least 400,000 sesterces. Once again, many had far more than this. There were substantially more equestrians than senators. Early in the first century the Greek geographer Strabo noted that census returns showed 500 knights in the Spanish city of Gades (modern Cadiz) alone. This was exceptional – even in Italy only the city of Patavium (Padua) could boast as many, although this was perhaps 1 per cent of its population. There may well have been 10,000 equestrians throughout the empire, perhaps substantially more than this. Under the Republic few formal offices had been open to them, but Augustus changed this and created a wide range of administrative and military jobs for them. Smaller provinces were governed by equestrians, as was Egypt, where uniquely the legions were also commanded by knights. Altogether there were around 600 equestrian posts, the vast majority army commissions, compared to just over 100 senatorial jobs.[11]

Equestrians were important men, and some held positions of great responsibility and influence, but they were not a coherent group with common interests. A senator would know every other senator, if only by reputation and family, and at times it was possible to speak of senatorial opinion, but in no meaningful way was there such a thing as equestrian opinion. An even larger and less united group was formed by the curial class, the local aristocrats who held magistracies and formed the ruling councils of the cities dotted around the empire. Their wealth and importance varied with the prominence and size of their home community, but we know that at Comum in northern Italy a man had to own property valued at 100,000 sesterces to be eligible for office – a quarter that required by an equestrian and a tenth of that needed by a senator. Doubtless once again many had more, and it does seem to have been common for equestrians to serve on their local city councils.[12]

The wealthy had grand town houses – the remains at Pompeii and Herculaneum give some idea of their scale and luxury, although it is important to remember that neither of these towns were especially wealthy or important. However, the clearest expression of the elite's wealth came in the grand villas on their country estates. Landowning was the only truly respectable source of wealth and farming for profit offered one of the best – and certainly most consistent – returns on an investment. In addition a country villa provided the perfect environment for periods of leisure, offering peace and quiet unlike the bustling life of cities, as well as opportunities for hunting. Trajan, Hadrian and Marcus Aurelius were all dedicated hunters, as were many senators. Hadrian was badly injured on at least one occasion and set up a monument to one of his favourite horses after the latter had been brought down by a boar. There were also quieter, more intellectual pursuits.

Rome's elite were highly educated and many devoted great efforts to literature and philosophy. All senators would have been at the very least bilingual, for Greek was as essential for an educated man as Latin was for official business. Marcus wrote the meditations in Greek, as a more fitting language for the abstract ideas of philosophy. Skill as an orator was very important for a career in public life, even if most of the speeches made were the formal and predictable panegyrics of emperors. Purity of language, style and expression were judged very strictly and were often more important than content. Literature had a tendency to look back to the distant past and avoid the concerns of contemporary political life. The second sophistic movement – the first sophistic had flourished when democratic Athens was at its height of power in the fifth century BC – was obsessed with the independent past of the Greek cities. The empire became the grand culmination of this glorious antiquity. Much of the literary output of this period is not particularly attractive to the modern reader. Yet the most important thing to notice about it was the standard of learning required to take part in this movement. Only the very wealthy could afford the leisure and acquire the necessary education to be truly men of culture. Their learning confirmed their status at the top of the social ladder.[13]

The emperor needed the wealthier classes to help him run the empire. Senators in particular were the class he lived amongst and their attitude towards him tended to dictate how he would be portrayed in later histories. Literature was mainly written by and for the aristocracy. It was important to treat them with respect and emperors who failed to do this were vilified after their deaths. Hadrian was a clever and able man, but tended to parade his talents too much, delighting in demonstrating his superiority to others. As a result he was unpopular, even though his reign was highly successful, and it was only with great reluctance that the Senate was persuaded to deify him after his death. Yet on the whole Rome had had a series of good emperors in the second century, talented men who took the job seriously and made decisions for the general good. The well-off were certainly content. Roman law had a long tradition of protecting the wealthy and aristocratic from the harsh punishments inflicted on their social inferiors. This continued under the Principate and gradually two distinct groups were acknowledged by law, the 'more honourable men' (*honestiores*) and the 'more humble men' (*humiliores*).[14]

'More Humble Men': The Poor and the Rest

Even adding together senators, equestrians and the curial class, the elite of the empire consisted of a tiny fraction of its total population. There is no reliable figure for this at any period, since the numbers given in the sources are vague, sometimes contradictory and often wildly exaggerated. Usually the estimate of between 50 and 70 million is given for the population in the first century, with many scholars today compromising at 60 million. Ultimately such figures rest on the pioneering work of the nineteenth-century German scholar Beloch, who attempted a systematic study of population densities in the ancient world. Methodical though his work was, it inevitably involved a good deal of conjecture. The same has been true of more recent studies making use of such tools as life tables – charts presenting life expectancy for both genders on the basis of age – from 'comparable' modern societies. Not unreasonably they suggest that birth rates and death rates were both high, as indeed they were in virtually every society before 1800. However, some have opted for an extremely bleak picture of the ancient world, suggesting that life expectancy was as bad as the Neolithic period.

There are no reliable statistics. Ages on tombstones are not necessarily reliable – multiples of five are suspiciously common and there are an improbable number of 100-year-old people from the African provinces. More importantly, only a tiny minority of tombstones have survived and obviously provide no evidence for those unable to afford them in the first place. Census reports from Egypt are again only a minute fraction of the records that once existed and present their own problems. One study found that 35 per cent of all those recorded were under fifteen, but to conclude that the comparatively fewer young adults was the result of high mortality is questionable. People at this age were far more likely to have left their villages, or to have wanted to avoid the census and the taxation that followed in its wake. Without statistics we are left with guessing. It has probably been wise to assume the grimmest possible conditions and, at the very least, it is extremely unlikely that the figure was lower than the range suggested. It may well have been higher, perhaps substantially so. My own suspicion – and it is no more than that – is that the figure will gradually be raised as more and more archaeological evidence accumulates for the number and size of settlements within the provinces.[15]

Whatever the overall size of the population, most people lived in the country, on farms and in villages. Some cities were huge. Rome probably had a population of around a million. Alexandria was half the size, but its population combined with those of Antioch and Carthage probably amounted to another million. A few cities may have had as many as 100,000 inhabitants, although most were far smaller, with populations numbering tens of thousands or even just thousands. Conditions were often crowded, especially in Rome and particularly for the poor. The multi-storey *insulae* (apartment blocks) were often badly constructed and liable to collapse. Fire was an ever-present threat. Even without such hazards living conditions were usually cramped, uncomfortable and expensive. The very poor could not afford to rent such accommodation and lived in shanty towns on waste ground or amongst the cemeteries. Such overcrowding made it very easy for disease to spread.

Some scholars suggest that ancient cities relied on a constant flow of immigrants to maintain their population, since unhealthy living conditions meant that the death rate outstripped the birth rate – or to put it more clinically, that cities were net consumers of people. Public bath houses offered improved hygiene, but the use of the same water by so many people also helped to spread some diseases. Roman cities had public lavatories, as well as drainage and sewage systems – which was considerably more than could be said for most cities before or after the Roman period – and yet these may not always have been adequate. Simply disposing of the dead presented problems in a city as large and as densely populated as Rome. Historians wishing to conjure up a grim image of life there are fond of quoting an incident when Emperor Vespasian was interrupted at dinner by a dog carrying a human hand. We should not forget that this was seen as a dreadful omen, not an everyday occurrence.[16]

Conditions in the cities could be squalid, but they were also places where there was a chance of work. One of the reasons why so many great monuments were constructed was to provide the poor with labouring jobs. At Rome citizens were also entitled to a ration of grain. There were also the great festivals and entertainments. The Circus Maximus could seat between 200,000–250,000 people, and the Colosseum at least 50,000. Even today there are few sporting venues able to accommodate so many. Country areas lacked such attractions, although it is a mistake to think of town and country as completely separate, since most villages were fairly close to a city of some description. The great amphitheatre at Dougga in Tunisia had seats for more people than lived in the city, which suggests that many more would travel to see the games.

Conditions for the poor were different in the rural areas, but may have been similarly grim. We hear of wealthy landlords or their representatives intimidating and robbing their smaller neighbours, when authority was too distant or unwilling to intervene. Obviously, stories of the abuse of power – much like tales of attacks by robbers or pirates – were far more likely to be recorded and so appear in our sources than peaceful and hence mundane coexistence. There is a similar problem with the practice of abandoning unwanted babies on rubbish dumps or dunghills, something that attracted a lot of attention in our ancient sources and has received even more from modern scholars. Such infants were often taken to be raised and sold as slaves, and in Egypt they were sometimes given the unfortunate name of *Kopros* (dung). It is likely that the frequency of such exposures is exaggerated in our sources, which usually have a strongly moral tone and include many Christian manuscripts, and there are cases where *Kopros* became a proud family name, passed on to successive generations after the initial foundling had done well for himself.[17]

Slavery was a fact of life in the Roman Empire, and indeed every other ancient society. There was never any pressure for its abolition, although in the second century several emperors had legislated to relieve some of the more brutal practices, such as the castration of boy slaves to gain a better price as eunuchs. How high a proportion of the overall population were slaves is, once again, unknown. Household slaves were common everywhere – we have already encountered Barates' wife Regina – and the domestic staff of the grander houses could easily measure in the hundreds. Slaves seem to have been rare as the main labour force outside the large estates of Italy, and some of the more dangerous and unpleasant tasks such as mining. Domestic slaves often enjoyed better living conditions than the free poor and stood a fair chance of receiving their freedom. It was also common for a slave to run businesses on his or her owner's behalf and eventually buy his or her freedom for a previously agreed sum from the profits. Yet in the end slaves were still property and suffered from severe legal disadvantages. It was normal for slaves to be interrogated under torture if their master was suspected of a crime, since it was otherwise believed that they would not testify against him.[18]

Scholars today all too often present a very simplistic view of the Roman world. On the one hand are the rich – the senators and equestrians, and at a pinch the curial class as well – and on the other hand are the poor – consisting of everyone else, with slaves as a distinct sub-group. To a great extent this inherits the snobbery of the literary sources, which were almost all written by and for the elite. Viewed from the top, the distinctions between the wider population were unlikely to stand out. A senator might easily own more than ten times the property of a magistrate in a minor city, but this does not mean that the latter was poor. The same logic would dictate that anyone today earning less than the managing director of a multinational company must inevitably live in abject poverty.

It is certainly true that the empire had nothing even vaguely resembling the middle class of Victorian and later Britain. Even the equestrian order did not form a coherent group with interests and attitudes of its own, so this should not surprise us. It is equally obvious from all our sources of evidence as well as simple logic that there were many people in the empire of middling income and property. In every village there were some people wealthier than others, and in towns and cities there was even greater variety of wealth and status. Money was not always enough for respectability – the rich freedman is a familiar and derided figure in literature – but successful freedmen were clearly important figures in many communities. It was common for cities to encourage teachers to set up schools. The elite educated their children at home with personal tutors, and these public schools catered for the more moderately well-off. Literacy was not the preserve of the elite, although few from outside their ranks were able to attain the fluency and purity of Greek and Latin expected of a senator.[19]

Society was a good deal more complex than is often claimed and social mobility was always possible. There were also strong links between individuals at all levels. It was important for senators to have as many clients as possible, individuals and even whole communities obliged to them both for past favours and in confident expectation of new ones. Posts in government and the army were overwhelmingly determined by patronage, and influence mattered in nearly every other aspect of life. The letter of recommendation is the commonest form of writing to survive from the Greco-Roman world and operated at all levels, from senators to anyone able to write and to claim a connection with someone of influence. The following is an extract from a letter written to the equestrian officer commanding the garrison at Vindolanda in northern Britain in the early second century:

> Brigonius has requested me, my lord, to recommend him to you. I therefore ask, my lord, if you would be willing to support him in what he has requested of you. I ask that you think fit to commend him to Annius Equester, centurion in charge of the region, at Luguvalium, . . . you will place me in debt to you both in his name and my own . . .[20]

The emperor was the ultimate source of patronage. Anyone believed to be capable of influencing the emperor would also be courted by people seeking favours. People at all levels had influence, if only because they had a link with someone of greater power. The acceptance of this system as perfectly normal is illustrated in a letter written by Pliny to a provincial governor in the early second century: 'Your command of a large army gives you a plentiful source of benefits to confer, and secondly, your tenure has been long enough for you to have provided for your own friends. Turn to mine – they are not many.'[21]

A man needed to secure plenty of favours if he was to keep his clients content and stop them from seeking preferment from someone else. Inevitably, it is likely that such a system favoured connections over individual talent, but then even modern, supposedly more impartial and scientific systems of selection manage to promote their fair share of incompetents. However, if a man continually recommended clients who were incapable of performing their job adequately, in the long run his appeals were less likely to be successful. Helping an able man gain promotion was also beneficial to the patron, since the former was now in a better position to return the favour. In general the system functioned adequately and seemed as natural to the Romans as it might seem alien to us. In the modern world it is usually considered better to conceal the operation of favour and patronage, even if it is blatant to insiders.

Much the same could be said of the empire's economic system. The academic debate over this has been fierce, all the more so because, once again, it must occur in the absence of any reliable statistics. All agree that it was not exactly the same as a modern market economy, but there is no consensus on just about anything else. It is worth noting that a single system of currency was employed throughout the empire, with just a few exceptions, such as Egypt. Virtually all gold coins in circulation within the empire in the second century had been minted at Rome, as had the majority of silver coins. All carried the head of a Caesar on them. It is also clear that large quantities of goods were able to move over considerable distances. Agricultural products were dominant, and 'factories' – or rather, workshops – producing ceramics, metalwork, textiles and other products seem always to have been fairly small scale. The picture is usually of lots of small workshops, often operating next door to each other, rather than great unified industries. However, we know so little about who owned and drew most profit from such enterprises that it is wise to be cautious about making sweeping conclusions. The Romans did not develop a system of corporate law comparable to that pioneered by the Dutch in the early modern era.[22]

Bulky objects were easier and cheaper to transport by water, on rivers and canals, and most of all by sea. Far more wrecks of merchant vessels have been discovered dating to the first and second centuries than from any other period in the Roman era. There were some extremely large vessels, notably the great ships that carried grain from Egypt to Rome, but the vast majority of vessels seem to have been quite small. Again, the picture is of large numbers of small concerns rather than great centralised enterprises. Some goods are easier to track than others. Barrels were common, particularly in Europe, but are very unlikely to leave much trace archaeologically. In contrast, the ceramic amphorae that were used as containers for wine, oil, fish sauce and many other liquids survive in vast quantities. The famous Monte Testaccio in Rome, an artificial hill consisting of vast quantities of broken amphorae is one of the most spectacular examples, but finds of amphorae, and pottery in general, are extremely common throughout the empire. The wreck of a ship with a cargo of amphorae tends to be particularly visible.

Transporting goods by land was often more difficult, but sometimes the only option. Roman roads are justly famous for their sheer size and obsession with straightness. Originally built for military purposes, they also became valuable all-weather communications routes for civilian traffic. There is a persistent myth that the Romans never developed an effective horse harness, severely restricting the use of wagons for hauling heavy loads. Wheeled transport works best on level or only gently sloping surfaces. Italy is so mountainous that pack animals like mules tended to be preferred and were used in great numbers. Elsewhere in the empire carts and wagons were common, pulled by mules, horses according to availability and, if speed was not a priority, oxen. Camels were important as pack and draught animals in Egypt and some parts of the east. Carts and carriages were well designed for their purpose, and – again contrary to the frequent assertions of historians of technology – in most respects as sophisticated as anything before the modern era.

This was generally true of most types of machinery and engineering. The Romans did not develop windmills, but watermills were common from at least the first century and greatly increased productivity. Water power in general was especially developed in a wide range of activities. There were water-powered saws to cut marble and other stones for building. Mining used water pressure for a range of purposes, shifting earth to uncover deposits, then sifting it to separate out the parts containing ore, which was in turn broken into smaller pieces by hydraulic-powered hammers. Excavation has revealed mine-working on a truly massive scale at sites in Spain and north Wales, outstripping anything seen before the nineteenth century. Some of this occurred in state-run projects, often involving the army, but it is also clear that some private businesses were contracted to exploit the imperial-owned mines. Analysis of core samples taken from the polar icecaps has revealed traces of pollution produced by industrial activity such as smelting. The levels of this for the first century BC through to the second century AD dwarf those of both earlier and later centuries, and indeed of any period before the Industrial Revolution.[23]

Much of the technological sophistication of the ancient world is only now being confirmed by archaeology. The Romans were always willing to copy the innovations of others – the barrel, for instance, appears to have been a north European invention. Most of the innovations in water-powered machinery had been invented in Egypt in the third century BC, but spread widely only after the region's incorporation in the empire. Areas like Gaul were already flourishing before Rome's arrival, with agricultural productivity showing a marked increase and settlements growing in size and sophistication. Contact and trade with the Mediterranean world probably encouraged this indigenous development. There was long-distance trade, widespread mining and such aids as roads in many parts of Europe and in the pre-Roman Iron Age. Roman conquest further encouraged this development, tying all these regions more closely into a wider world and bigger markets. More consumer goods became available to more people, and many were objects that would be familiar in style and function from one end of the empire to another.[24]

It is unlikely that anyone living within the empire could have been unaware of its existence. This was also true of peoples living on the fringes or outside, such as the Garamantes, a tribal people living in the Saharan regions of modern Libya. Excavations at their most important settlement have revealed the presence of pottery, glassware, wine and oil during the Roman period in quantities massively greater than either earlier or later phases. The greater part of these goods had to be carried overland from the Mediterranean coast some 600–700 miles away. The Garamantes also seem to have travelled further, trading over massive distances with peoples further south in Africa, and quite possibly taking slaves as an agricultural labour force. During the creation of the empire Roman and Italian traders had preceded the legions virtually everywhere, although they rarely appear in ancient literature. This continued after the empire stopped expanding. Ireland never attracted the attentions of a Roman army, but there was much trading contact. Other merchants from the empire went to the Baltic to obtain amber.[25]

The most spectacular trade links were with India and China. From the Red Sea ports of Egypt large numbers of merchant ships left in July of each year, catching the monsoon winds that would carry them directly to reach India. Their cargoes included wine, glassware, metals and coin, textiles and frankincense from Arabia. The return journey began in December or January using the north-east monsoon winds to take them back, bringing perfumes, pepper, precious stones, ivory, cotton cloth and silk, which the Indians themselves had obtained from China. Some sailors even went further than this. Chinese records from 166 mention the arrival at the court of the Han emperor of an embassy from the king of Ta-ch'in, whose name was An-tun. Ta-ch'in was the name for Rome, and An-tun was doubtless Marcus Aurelius Antoninus. It was unlikely to have been an official visit and the gifts presented by the merchants – ivory, rhinoceros horn and tortoiseshell – had all been obtained en route.

Both Rome and China were dimly aware of the other's existence, but the distances involved ensured that there was never any direct and meaningful contact. Traders also trekked over vast distances to carry goods overland along the famous Silk Road. Silk was much in demand in the empire and seems to have been available in great quantities. The same was true of pepper. In the first century Pliny the Elder commented on the vast sums spent by Romans on these and other luxuries. It is doubtful that many men travelled the whole route themselves, and the trade was controlled by a succession of middlemen. There were work-shops in Syria that wove silk more finely than anything the Chinese themselves could produce, and this semi-transparent gauze was re-exported back eastwards in considerable quantities. There were persistent rumours in China that the Romans had silkworms of their own pro-ducing this finer material, but in fact it was not until the sixth century that monks smuggled some silkworms to Constantinople and production began in the west. Once again the Romans did not create this long-distance trade, but the conditions of the empire massively increased its scale.[26]

Trade flourished and Pliny was convinced that it was of general benefit: 'now that world wide communications have been established thanks to the authority of the Roman Empire ... living standards have improved by the interchange of goods and by partnership in the joy of peace and by the general availability of things previously concealed'.[27]

The Philosopher Emperor

When Marcus Aurelius became emperor in 161, the empire was at its height. It was prosperous and stable, and the sophisticated culture that mingled Greek and Roman elements with other influences was flour-ishing. It was not a perfect society. Slavery was widespread and the lives of the poorest free citizens were often spent in extremely squalid conditions. Perhaps even more shocking to the modern mind, human beings were regularly slaughtered for entertainment. Yet neither before nor for a long time afterwards was so much of Europe, North Africa and the Near East at peace. More people were better off than had been the case before. For Gibbon, writing in the 1770s, the message was clear:

> If a man were called to fix the period in the history of the world, during which the condition of the human race was most happy and prosperous, he would, without hesitation, name that which elapsed from the death of Domitian to the accession of Commodus [i.e. 96–180]. The vast extent of the Roman empire was governed by absolute power, under the guidance of virtue and wisdom. The armies were restrained by the firm but gentle hand of four successive emperors, whose characters and authority commanded involuntary respect. The forms of the civil administration were carefully preserved by Nerva, Trajan, Hadrian, and the Antonines, who delighted in the image of liberty, and were pleased with considering themselves as the accountable ministers of the laws.[28]

It was not an unreasonable conclusion at the time he was writing, although Gibbon was also appreciative of the advantages of life in Britain and Europe in his own day. The Roman emperors he mentions were probably amongst the most decent and capable men to hold the supreme office. They were all mature men when they came to power, worked hard at the job and eventually died natural deaths.

The reign of Marcus Aurelius was particularly hard. It began with a war in the east, once again sparked by a dispute over Armenia. The Parthians killed a Roman governor and wiped out his army, and launched raids deep into Syria. Marcus had made his brother by adoption co-ruler, giving him the title of Caesar while styling himself Augustus. Caesar Lucius Verus was sent to take command of a grand war effort, although the sources suggest that he was mainly a figurehead and the war was conducted by his subordinates. The Romans repulsed the invaders and then advanced down the Tigris to sack both the Parthian capital Ctesiphon and the nearby Hellenistic city of Seleucia in 165. After this the Parthian king sued for peace. Verus returned to Italy at the end of 166, and the detachments of troops drawn from all over the empire also started to go back to their home bases.

With them came a dreadful epidemic, whose identity cannot now be established, although smallpox and bubonic plague have both been suggested. For the next three decades much of the empire was ravaged by periodic outbreaks of this disease, and in 189 it was said that 2,000 were dying in Rome every day. The overall death toll cannot be estimated – as we have established, there are no reliable figures for how big the population was before the epidemic started. It was certainly seen by contemporaries as an appalling and catastrophic event. The suggestion that some 10 per cent of the total population died, with higher proportions in the crowded cities and army bases, is plausible enough, but is no more than a guess. Census returns from Egypt seem to show a severe drop in the population at this time, with some communities being abandoned altogether. There may be traces of dreadful losses in army recruitment patterns.[29]

While the empire was reeling under this blow – perhaps because of it – a serious problem developed on the Danubian frontier, beginning with a raid on Pannonia by 6,000 Germanic warriors from a number of tribes in 167. This was eventually repulsed, but the perception that Rome was vulnerable encouraged more attacks. A series of bitter campaigns were fought, most of all against the Germanic Marcomanni and Quadi and the nomadic Sarmatian Iazyges. Marcus presided in person over most of these operations. In 170 a raiding band of Germans reached Italy and attacked the city of Aquileia, while another group had penetrated as far as Greece. The sources for these campaigns are poor, but there seem to have been a number of Roman defeats before the tide turned and one by one the tribes were forced to accept peace terms.

Then in 175 Marcus faced an unexpected threat when a false report of his death prompted the Syrian governor Avidius Cassius to declare himself emperor. Marcus' son Commodus was still only thirteen and so could not yet be seen as a viable heir. The revolt collapsed as soon as the truth was known. Cassius and his son were killed, but otherwise there was virtually no bloodshed. However, Marcus was drawn away from the Danube to ensure that the east was secure. Fighting flared up again on the frontier in 177 and the following year the emperor left Rome to resume personal command. He never returned. There was talk of plans to annex two new provinces beyond the Danube. Excavations in the Czech Republic in recent years confirmed that large army bases were established there at this period. A fresh campaign was anticipated when Marcus fell ill and died, perhaps at Vindobona (modern Vienna).[30]

Marcus Aurelius had been a decent, intelligent man who had tried to do his best. His *Meditations* may not be the most original or greatest work of philosophy ever written, but it is striking to read such sentiments from the ruler of most of the known world.

Marcus was to be greatly missed. The senator historian Dio, who grew up under his rule, gloomily wrote that after his death 'our history now descends from a kingdom of gold to one of iron and rust, as affairs did for the Romans of that day'.[31]

2

The Secret of Empire

'for the secret of empire was now revealed, that it was possible to make an emperor elsewhere than Rome' – The senator and historian Tacitus, early second century.[1]

When Marcus Aurelius died there was no doubt about the succession. Commodus was now eighteen and had been ruling as co-emperor with his father since the end of 176. In a sense, Marcus' death meant that the empire had just one emperor instead of two. It was the first time that an emperor was succeeded by a son born during his reign, and Commodus boasted that he was 'born to the imperial purple'. The last four emperors had all been adopted by their predecessors and each had assumed power at a mature age and proved to be capable rulers. This had worked well, but had never been a deliberate plan, since none of the emperors had had a son to succeed him. Nerva, Trajan and Hadrian were childless – Hadrian, and probably also Trajan, showed more passion in their affairs with boys than women – and Antoninus Pius had a daughter, but not a son.

It was only chance that Commodus outlived his father, for several brothers, including his twin, died in infancy. Marcus Aurelius had a healthy, legitimate son, and it would have seemed odd to all concerned had he ignored his son and groomed someone else for the succession. Nor would an adopted heir ever have felt secure while such an obvious rival was alive. Later, with hindsight, many Romans and plenty of modern scholars criticised the failure of the wise philosopher to recognise the inadequacy of his son. This is unfair, and it is doubtful that they would have been generous to a man who had executed his own son to clear the path for an adopted heir.[2]

Fortune dictated that in 180 Marcus had a son old enough to succeed, but still young and inexperienced. The record of young emperors was not good, and only the sixteen-year-old Nero had been younger when he came to power. It was hard for anyone, let alone an inexperienced youth, to resist the temptations of effectively absolute power. In a court where almost everyone was jockeying for position and influence, a ruler was unlikely to be told unpleasant truths or restrained from folly. Hollywood has consistently portrayed Commodus as a monster – most recently in *Gladiator* – and several of our ancient sources agree with this judgement, depicting him as vicious, even in childhood. Dio, who began his senatorial career under Commodus, thought the emperor 'not naturally evil, but simple minded' and easily led astray. He certainly showed little enthusiasm for the work of being emperor. This was less a question of shaping great policy and more about responding to appeals and dealing with problems as they were brought to his attention. An emperor needed to be available, open to requests from individuals and communities, ready to give rulings based on law and precedent. During one of his many journeys Hadrian was pestered by a woman, but brusquely said that he did not have the time to deal with her. Her yelled response – 'Then stop being emperor' – immediately made him stop and listen to her petition. Marcus Aurelius was renowned for the time he devoted to hearing any case brought before him. A conscientious emperor spent long hours in often dull work.[3]

Commodus, however, was not interested. Within a few months he returned to Rome from the Danube and never again left Italy, where he became obsessed with the sports of the circus and arena. Privately, he raced chariots on his estates, but he was less reticent about displaying his other skills in the Colosseum. Days were devoted to watching the emperor slaughter animals with javelin or bow. He also appeared as a gladiator, usually fencing with blunt weapons, but sometimes fighting bouts with sharpened blades, although care was taken to ensure that the emperor came to no harm. While the emperor played, the task of running the empire passed into other hands. A series of court favourites wielded massive influence and power, often becoming rich in the process. None were senators, several were equestrians and others were slaves and freedmen of the imperial household. Some were capable, others utterly corrupt and many somewhere in between, but the empire was not supposed to function this way. It had always been true that anyone with access to the emperor gained importance in relation to their ability to sway his decisions. Yet such power was always precarious, and in turn each of Commodus' favourites lost his trust; others were sacrificed because of their unpopularity. All were executed. Unlike his father, the young emperor had no hesitation in ordering the deaths of his subjects, including many senators and equestrians. From early in the reign there were a succession of real or alleged plots to murder Commodus. Each brought a new wave of arrests and executions.[4]

As the years went by, Commodus' behaviour became increasingly bizarre. Dio recalled one occasion when the emperor decapitated an ostrich in the arena and then moved towards the rows of seats occupied by the Senate:

> holding the head in his left hand and in his right hand raising aloft his bloody sword; and though he spoke not a word, yet he wagged his head with a grin, indicating that he would treat us in the same way. And many indeed would have perished by the sword on the spot, for laughing at him (for it was laughter rather than indignation that overcame us), if I had not chewed some laurel leaves, which I got from my garland, myself, and persuaded others near me to do the same, so that in the steady movement of our jaws we might conceal the fact that we were laughing.[5]

Not everyone may have found Commodus' antics as comic and disturbing as the senators. Some Romans were obsessed with gladiators and perhaps responded to the emperor styling himself the 'Amazon-like, left handed sword-fighter', or dressing and acting as Hercules. The praetorian guard who were the main military force in Rome enjoyed the lax discipline and licence granted to them.[6]

Yet after twelve years many members of the court had wearied of life under such a capricious ruler and a palace conspiracy succeeded where other attempts had failed. The prime movers were the chamberlain Eclectus, Commodus' favourite mistress Marcia and Aemilius Laetus, one of the two prefects in command of the praetorian guard. It was rumoured that Marcia had accidentally discovered an execution order including their three names. Another story claimed that on 1 January 193 Commodus planned to kill both the consuls and then process from the gladiatorial barracks dressed for the arena to become sole consul for the year. Instead, on New Year's Eve Marcia poisoned the emperor's beef. When he vomited and began to show signs of recovery, the conspirators sent in an athlete who strangled him to death. The Caesar born to the purple was thirty-one when he died and had reigned for more than twelve years.[7]

Pertinax: The Freedman's Son

Commodus left no heir, and anyway the conspirators would not have wanted a new emperor likely to avenge his death, so they looked instead for a successor from the Senate. During the night some of the conspirators visited the house of the sixty-six-year-old Publius Helvius Pertinax. Contemporaries believed that he had not been involved in the plot, and most historians accept this. It was an indication of the nervous mood of the times that Pertinax sent a representative to see the corpse before he was willing to accept that the emperor was dead. Reassured, he then went straight to the camp of the praetorian guard. Laetus paraded the soldiers and they were told that Commodus had died of natural causes. Pertinax promised each soldier 12,000 sesterces to recognise him as the new emperor.

Only after securing the praetorians' loyalty in this way, did Pertinax seek approval from his fellow senators. In the early hours of 1 January messengers were sent summoning the Senate to an extraordinary meeting. There was an element of farce when Pertinax and his attendants found the Senate House itself locked, and no one was able to track down the doorman who kept the keys for some time. As a result, Rome's high council met at first in the nearby Temple of Concord. Pertinax made a speech declaring that he did not want to accept imperial rule, pleading age and infirmity. A good emperor was not supposed to want power and there was a long tradition of feigned reluctance. The senators knew how the conventions worked and pressed him to accept the supreme office. Almost all were grateful that Commodus was gone, and in the following days they issued an almost hysterical decree abusing his memory and repeatedly demanded that his corpse be dragged through the streets on a meat hook and degraded. Doubtless many of those who had done well under the previous regime were all the more vocal now in their condemnation. However, Pertinax had already given orders for a proper burial, no doubt eager to avoid upsetting the praetorians.[8]

Pertinax was a distinguished senator, but his career had been highly unorthodox and his background was in marked contrast to the Caesar born to the purple. His father was a freed slave who had done very well in the lumber trade in northern Italy. The young Pertinax had received a good education and spent most of his twenties working as a schoolteacher. Tiring of this, he asked his father's patron to secure him a commission in the army and was eventually made a prefect in command of a cohort of auxiliary infantry. This was an equestrian position and Pertinax must have become a member of the order at this point if he had not already been enrolled in its ranks.

The teacher proved himself a gifted soldier in the arduous wars of Marcus Aurelius' reign, rising through the equestrian ranks. In 175 the emperor made Pertinax a senator in the field – writing to the Senate to notify them – and placed him in command of a legion. He seems to have rewarded other equestrians in the same way. An inscription recounts the career of one Marcus Valerius Maximianus who was commanding a cavalry unit when 'he killed with his own hand Valao, the king of the Naristae' during the campaigns on the Danube. As a reward he was subsequently made a senator and placed in command of a succession of legions. Marcus Aurelius seems to have been eager to promote talent, but it is also probable that the impact of the plague, combined with the losses from campaigns, meant that there was for a while a shortage of senators of the right age and ability to provide enough senior officers for the army.

Pertinax went on to govern a number of provinces and, late in his career, began holding some of the civil posts normal for a senator. Apart from a temporary fall from grace early in Commodus' reign, he continued to flourish and was one of the few intimates of Marcus Aurelius to survive his son's reign. By 193 there seems to have been little objection to his becoming emperor from his fellow senators, including those who had once sneered at him as the son of a freedman. From the beginning the new emperor made a public effort to break with the recent past and return to the style of rule of Marcus Aurelius. A public auction was held, selling off the decadent luxuries from Commodus' palace, including the male and female slaves who had pandered to his sexual needs or his perverse sense of humour. Gossips claimed that Pertinax secretly arranged to rebuy and keep some of these for himself.

Yet some of his attempts to erase the corruption of his predecessor and his ministers upset those who had done well under the old regime. Of more concern was a growing discontent amongst the praetorian guard, who resented the new stricter discipline and feared that even tighter controls might be imposed in due course. Pertinax was an experienced soldier and had something of a reputation as a martinet. Half of the cash donative promised to the guardsmen was paid from the profits of the auction, but the emperor made the mistake of boasting in a public speech that he had paid the soldiers fully, giving them as much as Marcus

Aurelius and Lucius Verus on their accession. This was untrue, for they had given 20,000 sesterces per man. In the first weeks of his reign, elements within the guard twice tried to proclaim an alternative emperor. Order was quickly restored in each case, and Pertinax kept his promise never to put to death a senator by not punishing the men put forward. Yet he did order the execution of a number of the soldiers, which only added to the resentment of their comrades.[9]

On the morning of 28 March between 200 and 300 guardsmen marched from their camp to the palace on the Palatine Hill. They were not part of the normal changeover of sentries, but the palace staff admitted them immediately for many of them still had fond memories of Commodus. Aemilius Laetus covered his head with a hood and made himself scarce rather than confront the mutinous troops. Only the freedman Eclectus stood by the new emperor. Pertinax could have met force with force, summoning the *equites singulares Augusti*, the imperial guard cavalry whose record of loyalty to each emperor was unblemished and who were based nearby, separate from the praetorians. Instead, he decided to confront the mutineers, hoping to shame them back to duty. Dio thought his decision brave, but foolish. For a moment the guardsmen were overawed, until one broke the spell and slashed at the ageing emperor. Eclectus struck down two soldiers before he, too, was hacked to pieces. Pertinax had reigned as emperor for just eighty-seven days.[10]

By this time Laetus had returned to the camp and regained a measure of control over the praetorians – some even accused him of having been behind the murder. He was now approached by Pertinax's father-in-law, who currently held the prestigious administrative post of urban prefect and wanted to be named emperor. The officers of the guard were willing to listen, but were also nervous that a relative might choose to avenge his murdered predecessor. Two of them went down to the Forum and found an alternative candidate, the emperor's consular colleague Didius Julianus. The latter processed up to the praetorian camp accompanied by his attendants, but could not at first gain admission. From outside the gate he gestured up to the men on the ramparts, indicating with his fingers the size of the donative he was willing to pay. Eventually he was admitted, and men shuttled back and forth between the two bidders. Julianus won the contest by promising to give 25,000 sesterces to each guardsman. With all such donatives to secure loyalty, it is important to remember that centurions probably received ten times as much and more senior officers even larger sums. If the guardsmen did well, their commanders, and most of all their two prefects, stood to become very wealthy indeed.[11]

With the praetorian guard behind him, Julianus was duly recognised as emperor by the Senate and granted the imperial powers by formal decree. He was a reasonably distinguished senator, but he could not escape the stigma of having so blatantly bought the empire. On his first appearance he was mobbed by a crowd and there were then protests in the Circus Maximus. Rome itself could be held in check by the armed might of the praetorians, but this was not true of the rest of the empire. As news of the shameful 'auction' spread, the governors of the three provinces with the strongest military garrisons – Britain, Upper Pannonia on the Danube and Syria – refused to recognise Julianus and claimed the throne for themselves. The fate of the empire would be decided by the army for the first time since Nero's death in 68 had led to civil war.[12]

'A wall around the provinces': The Roman Army

The Roman army was the largest and most disciplined fighting force before the modern era, but it was not especially large in comparison to the size of the empire. At its core were the thirty legions, recruited from Roman citizens and each consisting of around 5,000–5,500 men at full strength. A legion was divided into ten cohorts, which were usually 480 strong, apart from the first cohort, which numbered 800. The legions were supported by auxiliaries, recruited mainly from non-citizens. These were not organised at any level higher than the cohort or *ala* – the name given to the similarly sized regiments of cavalry. There may have been somewhat more auxiliaries than legionaries by the end of the second century. In addition there was the navy, which was very active patrolling the sea lanes and protecting merchant trade from piracy. Rome was garrisoned by the praetorians – at nine cohorts of 800 men apiece, equivalent to a strong legion – and the *singulares*, as well as the para-military urban cohorts and the *vigiles*, who acted as firemen and night police. All told, the empire's armed forces numbered some 350,000–375,000 men, a rise of no more than 10–15 per cent from the days of Augustus. This at least was its strength on paper. In reality, like most armies throughout history, many units were more or less under strength for much of the time. Even taking the highest theoretical figure for the number of men in uniform and the very lowest estimate for the empire's population, there were more than 130 civilians for every soldier.

Large parts of the empire rarely saw a soldier, and never an army. The overwhelming bulk of the army was stationed near the frontiers in stone-built bases, each surrounded by its own civilian settlement. In the eastern provinces the pattern was different, with troops in Syria, Judaea and Egypt being stationed in or near the big cities of the region, partly to control their volatile populations. The army was by far the largest source of manpower available to the emperor, so small detachments of soldiers were found dotted throughout the provinces acting as administrators, policemen, traffic regulators and engineers. There were also the *frumentarii*, or 'grain-men', troops responsible for ensuring that the soldiers were supplied with the huge quantities of food needed every day. The complex network of agents required to perform this had expanded its role and come to provide a source of intelligence reports for the emperor, spying on soldiers and civilians alike.[13]

Yet, on the whole, the army lived a separate life away from mainstream civilian society. Citizen legionaries and non-citizen auxiliaries were alike long-service professionals who joined up for twenty-five years. The army preferred volunteers, but conscription was also employed when necessary. Marcus Aurelius enrolled gladiators and other freed slaves during the crisis following the plague, but this was exceptional. However, the levies mentioned in our sources may sometimes have been little more than a press-gang. Legionaries received 1,200 sesterces a year – in contrast, praetorians had an annual salary of 4,000 sesterces and only had to serve for sixteen years.

Pay had remained static since the end of the first century, so that it is probable that its value in real terms had declined. It had never been especially generous and was comparable to the daily rate received by an agricultural labourer, with the distinction that army pay was guaranteed year in, year out. This was set against the hardship and risks of a soldier's life, especially when war broke out. Even units stationed in the most peaceful of provinces were likely to experience a major campaign at least once during the twenty-five years of a man's service. Elsewhere warfare was far more frequent. Even peacetime service was not without its hazards. Surviving unit rosters mention soldiers who drowned, were killed by bandits or ended up sick in hospital for one reason or another. Letters written by convalescent soldiers in Egypt mention being hit by a missile while quelling a riot, as well as a bad bout of food poisoning.[14]

All but the smallest military outposts had a bath house and hospital, probably making a soldier's life healthier than that of poor civilians. This did not all come free – a man's pay was subject to deductions for food, clothing and equipment, not to mention contributions to the cost of festivals and the burial club, which would deal with his remains if he died during service. In addition the soldier was fed a reasonably balanced diet – which included meat, in spite of the persistent myth that legionaries were vegetarian – and for most of his service was accommodated in a stone-built barrack block with a tiled roof, eight men sharing a pair of rooms. Conditions were crowded, but no more so than the *insulae* of the cities – few in the ancient world enjoyed as much private space as we are used to today. If a man survived to be honourably discharged, he was rewarded.

Legionaries received either a plot of farmland or a cash bounty, while auxiliaries were granted citizenship. Yet there were other disadvantages to balance against this. Soldiers were legally barred from marriage and existing marriages were officially annulled on enlistment. Very many ignored this, taking a wife – often a local girl – and raising families. For a long time the unofficial liaisons of auxiliaries had been acknowledged when they were discharged, with any 'wife' or children also receiving citizenship. This had been restricted in the middle of the second century. It was much harder for legionaries to gain legal recognition of their children, and so permit them to inherit. Several emperors legislated to assist this, but the evidence from papyri suggests that retired soldiers and their descendants often had to fight hard to benefit from these decrees in practice.[15]

An educated soldier stood a good chance of promotion, especially if he had influential friends to provide him with a letter of recommendation. A letter survives written by a soldier who joined a legion in Egypt in 107 and, thanks to his connections, was quickly made a clerk. He gleefully told his father that he had only light duties while his fellow recruits were outside breaking rocks. It is hard to know how many recruits to the army were literate, given that we know so little about standards of literacy in the wider population, but they were probably a minority. Discipline in the army was brutal, with floggings and executions being awarded for a range of offences. Leave was a privilege rather than a right, and this and other favours were all too often only available by bribing an officer.

Italians showed little enthusiasm for joining the legions after the first century, preferring the softer and better-paid life of the units stationed in Rome. Some men doubtless joined the ranks of the army for the best of reasons, fulfilling the military theorists' ideal for a recruit. Such high-quality recruits may have been especially common in the *auxilia*, many coming from societies that still greatly admired the warrior virtues. It was also common for sons of soldiers to enlist, often having grown up in and around army bases, and the army welcomed such recruits. Denied legal status, these men had their place of birth listed as 'in the camp' (*in castris*). Yet the majority of recruits, especially to the legions, may well have joined because they had little choice and the army would feed, clothe and pay them regularly. One emperor complained that only vagrants were attracted to the legions. It is also notable that only those guilty of the most serious crimes were barred from military service.[16]

If many soldiers were the failures of civilian life, then this will have reinforced the real sense of the unit as their home. Each legion had a number – the sequence was not logical and there were several First, Second and Third legions – and a name, often supplemented by additional titles and honours. Auxiliary units also had their titles, and all regiments of the army had a strong sense of their own identity. Commanders often encouraged different units to compete with each other and at times the rivalry led to brawling. Unit pride was an important part of military effectiveness, as was the encouragement of individual bravery. Conspicuous courage was rewarded by decorations and status, as well as sometimes promotion and wealth. Like pay, all such medals were nominally awarded by the emperor, whether or not he was physically present. Similarly, recruits joining the army took an oath of loyalty to the emperor and the state. This was regularly renewed. Each regiment also had the *imagines*, images of the emperor and his immediate family, which were kept with the unit's standards in a shrine within the headquarters building.[17]

The emperor controlled the army and took every care to remind the soldiers of their personal loyalty to him. When he did visit a base or lead an army on campaign, he would talk to a unit as 'his' legion or cohort. Yet the army was spread over a wide area and most soldiers would never even see their commander-in-chief, so inevitably others exercised day-to-day control. Senators provided the most senior officers. As part of his career a senator in his late teens or early twenties normally spent one to three years as the senior tribune and second-in-command of a legion. Later, at about thirty, he would become a legion's commander (*legatus legionis*) for a similar period of time. Finally, he would become the legate in charge of a province and its army, a *legatus Augusti*. A privileged handful followed this with a second governorship in charge of one of the three most important military provinces. Each contained three legions and as many auxiliaries. Three years was the average term for a governor in any province, but exceptions were made. Avidius Cassius had been in Syria for much longer than this, but his abortive coup was an indication of the potential threat such long-term commands presented.

Equestrians provided the army with the bulk of its other senior officers. A normal equestrian career involved a man being appointed as prefect in charge of an auxiliary cohort. This would be followed by a spell as one of the five junior equestrian tribunes in each legion and then the command of a cavalry *ala*. Successful men moved on to administrative and financial posts as imperial procurators, and perhaps the governorship of one of the smaller equestrian provinces. *Equites* also commanded the units in Rome, and control of the praetorians was normally shared between two prefects with equal power. Equestrian provinces usually did not include substantial forces because the senatorial legate of a legion could not be made subordinate to an equestrian. Egypt was an exception and in this province the governor and the commanders of the two legions were equestrian prefects. No emperor wanted to trust another senator with control of an area so vital for the grain supply to Rome.[18]

The centurions were the backbone of the army. This was a grade of officer rather than a specific rank. The more junior commanded a century, of which there were six to a cohort, each with a nominal strength of eighty (never 100 in this period). The senior centurion of the six commanded a legionary cohort. Most important of all was the *primus pilus*, the commander of the first cohort, who immediately became an equestrian after this post. All centurions were paid many times the salary of an ordinary soldier and needed a good standard of education. Some reached the post after joining the army in the ranks, but it is a mistake to think of them as akin to modern sergeant-majors. Rather more had been appointed directly to junior administrative or command posts before being commissioned. Others were directly appointed from civilian life without any prior military experience. Pertinax had initially wanted to become a centurion in this way, but his patron had been unable to secure him a commission, which gives a good indication of the status of these posts. It is equally revealing that some equestrians became centurions instead of following the more conventional career. As we have seen there was no single 'middle class' in the Roman world. Yet there were many people of middling income, with a reasonable standard of education even if they fell short of the purity of language expected of the higher levels of the elite. There is a very good chance that the majority of centurions were directly commissioned and came from this social level.[19]

The rank and file were rarely posted from one unit to another, and usually spent their entire service with the same regiment. Many centurions also appear to have remained with the same unit for long periods, although others are known to have served in a succession of different legions, sometimes in widely separated provinces. The more senior ranks moved around far more, and it was rare for a senator to serve more than once in the same province. Pertinax, during his long and unorthodox career as first equestrian and then a senatorial officer, served on all the major frontier zones of the empire apart from North Africa. The Romans did not prize specialists as highly as modern institutions, especially when it came to making appointments to senior posts. As importantly, the emperors were keen to prevent too close a bond developing between commanders and soldiers through long service together. The Republic had been destroyed and Augustus had created the Principate in wars fought between armies more loyal to their generals than the state. On the whole the system he created worked well, and the army remained loyal for the best part of two centuries. It was only when a dynasty ended completely that there was the prospect of legion fighting legion. When it did break down the initiative for rebellion tended to come from the top, and most of all the senatorial governors. A key role was also played by other officers, and especially the centurions.[20]

An Emperor from Africa

The army of Upper Pannonia lay nearest to Italy, and the legate of the province, Lucius Septimius Severus, did not fail to capitalise on the advantage this gave him. He had served under Pertinax earlier in his career and it may be that he was also party to the original conspiracy against Commodus. It was especially convenient that nearby Lower Moesia with its two legions was currently controlled by his brother. Severus marched quickly to Italy; he and his bodyguard – probably the governor's *singulares*, picked cavalrymen chosen from the auxiliary *alae* in his province – are said not even to have taken off their armour in their brief stops to sleep. There was no serious resistance, for Julianus did not have a proper army. A desperate attempt to train elephants taken from the games to carry towers and fighting crewmen in the tradition of classical warfare ended in absurd failure when the creatures refused to carry these unfamiliar burdens. Dio and other senators were highly amused. Julianus grew desperate and had Laetus and Marcia murdered, but soon even the purchased loyalty of the praetorians was withdrawn. Abandoned by everyone, he was killed in the palace by a guardsman. Severus arrived and in a spectacular display of power paraded his army through the city; the Senate duly proclaimed him emperor. Word was sent for the praetorians to arrest the murderers of Pertinax and then to parade without weapons or armour. Severus surrounded them with his own legionaries and then harangued them for their treachery. The murderers were executed, and the remainder dishonourably discharged from service and banned from coming within 100 miles of Rome. New praetorian cohorts were formed from the pick of Severus' own legionaries.[21]

There still remained the two other claimants to the throne. Severus did a deal with the legate of Britain, Decimus Clodius Albinus, giving him the title of Caesar, and making him his junior colleague. The bulk of his forces then went east to fight Gaius Pescennius Niger in Syria. The Severans won a series of battles, culminating in the final victory at Issus in 194 – coincidentally near the site of one of Alexander the Great's victories over the Persians. Niger was killed in the pursuit. Severus had not been present at any of the battles, but did then supervise a brief campaign against the peoples beyond the frontier. Returning from the east in 195 he provocatively named his seven-year-old son Caesar without apparently consulting Albinus. Civil war was renewed, resulting in a climatic battle two years later outside Lugdunum (modern Lyons in France) where the British legate had set up his main base. Dio claims that the armies involved were massive, no fewer than 150,000 men being fielded by each side, which would have added up to the vast majority of the entire army. This is obviously an exaggeration, but it may be that Albinus in particular had raised large numbers of levies since 193. The bulk of the regular army had rallied to Severus. Even so, the fighting was fierce, and at one point Severus himself was unhorsed and narrowly escaped death or capture. There were rumours that his new praetorian prefect deliberately delayed entering the battle in the hope that both leaders would be killed. However, in the end he led the great cavalry charge that won the day. After four years of civil war and turmoil, the empire had a single unchallenged ruler once again. The conflict had been far worse and more prolonged than the 'year of four emperors', which followed the death of Nero.[22]

There was nothing exceptional about Severus' career before 193 – rather like that of Vespasian, who had emerged as victor in 69. They were senators each with a reasonably distinguished career, but it is doubtful that under other circumstances either would have been considered potential emperors. Each man had simply found himself as legate in charge of a large army at a time when there was a power vacuum at the centre, and then had played his hand well – if especially ruthlessly in the case of Severus. In many ways Severus was a typical member of the Senate in this period. He was born in Lepcis Magna (in modern Libya), which had originally been founded by Carthaginians. Carthage itself had been destroyed in 146 BC by a Roman army, the culmination of three massive conflicts with Rome. Even so, Severus grew up with Punic as his first language, and his Latin was always tinged with a provincial accent, which tended to turn an 's' into a 'sh' sound. He may well have pronounced his name Sheptimius Sheverus. Dio says that he desired more education than he actually received, but this should be judged by the exceptionally high standards of the Roman elite. One sixth-century source claims that he was dark skinned, but the only coloured portrait of him to survive shows a fairly Mediterranean complexion. He was from North Africa, just as Trajan and Hadrian were from Spain, but this did not make him any less Roman. His father was not a senator, but the family had been involved in politics for several generations. The African provinces produced a good number of senators in this period, including Clodius Albinus. There is no suggestion that any of these men thought in a distinctively 'African' way.[23]

Severus had won the war, but knew that this did not in itself guarantee his long-term survival. He quickly promoted his two sons to positions of prominence even though they were still infants, marking them down as his heirs to show that his death need not mean a return to civil war. He also looked to the past to give legitimacy to his new dynasty. At first he associated himself closely with Pertinax, for it was useful to appear as his just avenger. However, in an unprecedented step, he declared himself the adopted son of Marcus Aurelius, whose prestige was far greater. One senator caustically congratulated him on 'finding a father'. More disturbingly, this led to an official rehabilitation of Commodus, who had now become the emperor's adopted brother. Senatorial opinion was shocked, but Severus' attitude towards the Senate steadily hardened. His reign began with proclamations that he wanted no senator to be put to death, but before the civil war was over he had ordered many such executions.

There was also resentment and fear of the power wielded by the new praetorian prefect, Plautianus, who was another native of Lepcis Magna. Malicious gossip claimed that he and Severus had been teenage lovers. It is clear that the emperor trusted him and permitted him great patronage and influence, so that in time there were rumours that the prefect was planning to seek the throne himself. In the end Plautianus was executed, after a death-bed condemnation by Severus' brother. So much power was not supposed to be wielded by favourites, especially ones from outside the Senate, and Plautianus' spectacular rise and fall inevitably took others with him. It was a dangerous time to be successful for any senator. Severus spent little time in the Senate – he was away from Italy for most of his reign – and rarely bothered to flatter its members or make them feel secure.[24]

There were other signs that the emperor was worried about maintaining power. He raised three new legions – *I, II* and *III Parthica* – and stationed the *II Parthica* not far from Rome at Alba. It was the first time a legion had been permanently stationed in Italy since the creation of the Principate. Together with the expanded guard units, Severus had an army of some 17,000 men at his immediate disposal. Scholars have often liked to see this as the creation of a strategic reserve, which was supposedly shown to be necessary during the savage wars of Marcus Aurelius' reign. In fact, it had far more to do with the potential threat of a provincial governor rebelling against the emperor. Keeping the army loyal was vital for the emperor. In an effort to secure the soldiers' goodwill, Severus raised their pay and also removed the ban on marriage. Raising the new legions created a lot of new positions for officers – for instance, no fewer than 177 centurions' commissions. Given that many were probably posted in from other units, this meant that a large number of men would owe their initial commission or a step in promotion to Severus. A similar desire to bind the army to him encouraged his foreign wars. From 197–202 Severus campaigned in the east, leading an army down the Euphrates to sack the Parthian capital at Ctesiphon and creating a new province of Mesopotamia. From 208–211 he was in Britain, supervising a series of massive campaigns against the Caledonian tribes of what is now Scotland.[25]

Foreign wars offered military glory free from the taint of winning victories over fellow Romans. The Arch of Severus, which still stands next to the Senate House in the Forum at Rome, commemorates his

Parthian War. It was also no coincidence that Severus chose to operate in the two regions that had provided his rivals in the civil war. There was doubtless some military necessity, since the armies on each frontier as well as the prestige of Rome can only have been weakened when troops were drawn away to fight and die in an internal struggle. It also gave units that had fought on opposite sides in the civil war the chance to campaign side by side under the same leader. Most importantly, Severus had the chance to reward and promote the officers in each area, showing his trust in them, and retiring or posting elsewhere any whose loyalty was suspect. Not everything went well, for there was some tension in the army when it failed to take the city of Hatra, but in general the objectives were achieved. Severus' reorganisation of the east again reveals his concern for his own security. Syria was divided into two provinces, with two and one legions respectively. Mesopotamia was garrisoned by the newly raised *I* and *III Parthica*. The province's governor was an equestrian prefect like the one in Egypt, and both the legions were also commanded by equestrians. This was also true of *II Parthica* at Alba. The process was not quite complete until a year or two after Severus' death, when Britain was also divided, but from then on no province would contain – and hence no governor command – more than two legions.[26]

Septimius Severus was a good emperor, who did his best to rule the empire well, but he was also a man who had won power through military force and feared that someone else might follow his example. This insecurity guided his decisions at all levels. None of this might have mattered too much if he had founded a dynasty that proved solid and enduring. In the last years of his life he made his sons Caracalla and Geta joint heirs. This was a risk, since only in the case of Marcus Aurelius and Lucius Verus had a pair of emperors worked well together. Severus often criticised Marcus for having chosen Commodus as his successor, and so preferring blood to talent, but he was faced with the same problem. As long as Caracalla and Geta were alive, they would inevitably have posed a threat to any alternative emperor. If only one succeeded, then the other would always represent a potential challenge, especially since the pair loathed each other from an early age. Severus is said to have hoped that taking them on campaign would be better for them than remaining in Rome with its many opportunities for vice, and perhaps also teach them to work together. He was disappointed. Stories even circulated that Caracalla tried to murder his father in his eagerness to succeed. Severus' health was anyway failing badly, after years of being plagued by gout. On 4 February 211 the sixty-five-year-old emperor died at Eburacum (modern York) and his two sons jointly inherited the throne. It is claimed that his last advice to them was simple – 'Live in harmony, enrich the soldiers, and despise everyone else.'[27]

3

Imperial Women

'After Alexander's succession to power he possessed the trappings and name of emperor, but control of administration and imperial policy was in the hands of his womenfolk, who tried to bring back a complete return to moderate dignified government.' – *The historian Herodian, middle of the third century* AD.[1]

The two brothers proved utterly incapable of living in harmony. Concluding peace with the Caledonians, they quickly left Britain. On the journey back to Rome they bickered, and then tried to ignore each other altogether. Once there they lived in separate wings of the palace, and had all connecting corridors and doorways bricked up, so that they would never meet by chance. They opposed each other in absolutely everything, even supporting different teams at the chariot races. Rumour said that they actually considered splitting the empire in two, with Caracalla staying in Rome and ruling the west, while Geta controlled the east from either Alexandria or Antioch. The dividing line would be the Bosphorus, and each brother would station legions on their shore to deter the other from aggression.[2]

No one had ever considered dividing the empire in this way, even when Antony and Octavian had carved up the provinces between themselves in the years before Actium. Yet the source for the story wrote his account just a few decades later, long before the empire was actually divided, so this is clearly not an invention from hindsight. The plan was blocked by the emperors' mother, Julia Domna, who demanded to know how they thought that they could divide her. On 26 December mother and both sons met in private in the palace to arrange a reconciliation. Caracalla had other ideas and concealed a party of loyal praetorian centurions near-by. Part way through, these men burst into the room and killed Geta with their swords. Julia Domna was left to cradle the body, and was so covered in his blood that she did not notice a wound to her own hand.[3]

Caracalla left quickly, rushing to the praetorian camp where he declared that he had acted in self-defence, having discovered that his brother was plotting against him. The guardsmen readily accepted his story and pledged their support. He had a harder job convincing the legionaries of *II Parthica* stationed at nearby Alba. They refused him entry and he had to address them from outside the rampart. Even then the soldiers replied that they had sworn an oath to both brothers and not simply one. Persuasion, backed by the promise of a very hefty gift of money, eventually won over the legion. Only after securing the loyalty of the only significant military units in Italy, did Caracalla go to the Senate, telling the same story of his brother's 'plot'. The senators had little choice but to acclaim him, especially since he was accompanied by files of fully armed guardsmen. Geta was formally condemned and his memory ordered erased from the record. Surviving inscriptions from all over the empire show the marks of where the younger brother's name was chiselled away.[4]

Caracalla was twenty-three, older and more experienced than Commodus when he came to power, but still young for an emperor. It is questionable whether Geta would have proved any more capable, although later authors liked to contrast his virtue with his brother's evil nature. Unlike Commodus, Caracalla was neither stupid nor lazy, but he was unpredictable and impatient, and had a vicious temper. He had ordered the execution of several members of the imperial household almost as soon as his father died. The murder of his brother was followed by a far more widespread and even bloodier purge, which included many prominent senators and equestrians. A recently excavated cemetery in York contained a number of skeletons of men who had been chained up and then executed, but yet were still buried with some respect. Pottery fragments dated the find to roughly this period, and it is more than possible that the men concerned were officers and officials killed on Caracalla's orders. There were other victims throughout the remainder of the reign. Pertinax's son, who had been too young and unimportant to be worth killing in 193, died now, because he could not resist making a pun referring to the murder of Geta. Marcus Aurelius' last surviving daughter was also suspected of disloyalty and forced to commit suicide, something that the elderly lady is said to have done with great calmness and dignity. Dio says that in all some 20,000 people perished.[5]

Frequent executions made senators permanently nervous of the emperor's moods, and Carcalla lacked the skill – and possibly also the desire – to win them over. He was not much more successful with the wider population of Rome, even though these were unlikely to feel his anger directly. He gave lavish games, and even took part in a chariot

Chart 1: Family tree of Septimius Severus

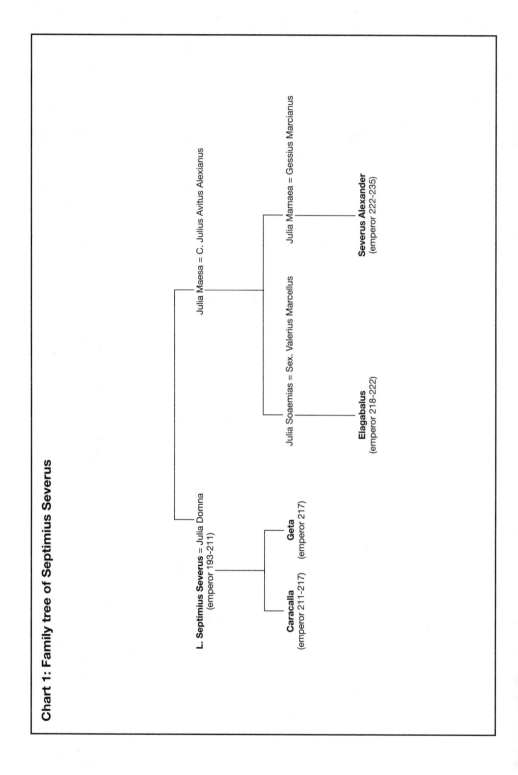

L. Septimius Severus = Julia Domna
(emperor 193-211)

Julia Maesa = C. Julius Avitus Alexianus

Caracalla
(emperor 211-217)

Geta
(emperor 217)

Julia Soaemias = Sex. Valerius Marcellus

Julia Mamaea = Gessius Marcianus

Elagabalus
(emperor 218-222)

Severus Alexander
(emperor 222-235)

race, although he did not emulate Commodus' excessive desire to perform in the arena. Yet he did become unpopular because the crowd saw him as too bloodthirsty when he watched gladiatorial fights. One famous gladiator was made to fight three consecutive bouts, in the last of which he was killed, and this was seen as unfair. Work was begun on a bath complex, the Baths of Caracalla, whose huge ruins are still visible today, providing work for the unemployed as well as the prospect of a future amenity.[6]

After a year Caracalla left Rome and never again returned to Italy. By nature he was restless, and both this and his temper were not improved by his bad health. As he travelled he visited a number of shrines and temples associated with healing deities, following the courses they pre-scribed. Stories circulated that he was troubled by dreams in which Severus silently rebuked him for his brother's murder. Dreams were taken seriously by many in the Roman world and books survive offering detailed interpretations. The emperor was still the emperor wherever he happened to be, and petitioners followed him, seeking an audience and asking for a favour or ruling in a dispute. Surviving records suggest that Caracalla was as prone to rapid and spontaneous replies as our literary sources claim, and confirm that in many cases his judgement was still clear and often sensible. However, he was not always enthusiastic about performing such a dull task. Dio remembered that he and others were frequently summoned to the imperial camp while the emperor was in Syria, having been told that he would see them at dawn. They were then often left to wait – even though there was no chamber to accommodate them – for hours on end, and sometimes sent home at the end of the day because Caracalla had decided not to see them at all.[7]

Small and unhealthy, Caracalla liked to see himself as the rugged, aggressive man of action, and most of all as a soldier. When he spoke to the praetorians after Geta's murder, he had told them to 'Rejoice, com-rades, for now I am in a position to do you favours.' Army pay was raised during his reign, so much so that imperial revenue struggled to cope with the increased burden. On campaign the emperor dressed and acted the part of an ordinary soldier, even going as far as to grind his own ration of wheat into flour to prepare his meal. These theatrics were probably mainly for the benefit of the guardsmen, and it may also have been one of the heavy praetorian standards that he sometimes chose to carry on the march. Most emperors were accompanied by distinguished senators on campaign, but Caracalla preferred the company of army officers – again, probably mainly from the guard. He was also very fond of his cavalry bodyguard, the *singulares Augusti*, many of whom were German. Some of these men were commissioned as centurions and kept in close attendance. The emperor nicknamed them his 'lions'. Dio also remembered seeing him take drinks to the sentries on duty outside his headquarters. Other Roman generals – Julius Caesar prominent amongst them – had played the part of the 'fellow soldier', but here as in so many other things, Caracalla took it to an excess. It was far more than an acknowledgement that his power ultimately rested on control of the army. He also developed an obsession with Alexander the Great, and evidently liked to see himself as resembling the youthful conqueror of so much of the known world.[8]

In 213 he had campaigned on the Rhine and in the following year moved to the Danube. Both frontiers show signs of substantial reorganisation and the construction of new military bases. It may have been during these campaigns that he took to wearing a version of the Gallic hooded cloak (*caracalla*), which gave him his nickname. In 215 he went to the east and remained there for the rest of his life, following in the footsteps of his hero Alexander. He raised – or perhaps reorganised existing legions into – a force modelled on the ancient Macedonian phalanx. That winter he was in Alexandria and summoned the young men of the city to a parade, declaring that he wanted to recruit them as soldiers. Instead, he ordered his troops to kill them – a massacre that has never been satisfactorily explained. He also began a series of campaigns against Parthia, which was split in a civil war between two brothers vying for the throne. Caracalla asked to marry the daughter of one of the claimants, just as Alexander had married Roxanne. His offer was refused and some saw this as no more than a pretext for war.[9]

At the beginning of 217 a large army was concentrated at Edessa in preparation for a fresh invasion. On 8 April Caracalla travelled to visit a shrine near Carrhae – in 53 BC the site of a great defeat at the hands of the Parthians, but now within a province and recently granted the status of a Roman colony. When the emperor stopped to relieve himself by the roadside, he was stabbed to death by one of his own military household, Julius Martialis. The assassin was a former praetorian who had re-enlisted, but was bitter because he had been denied a centurion's commission by Caracalla. Within minutes Martialis was himself cut down by the emperor's 'lions' and died before he could reveal any details of the plot. This was a great relief to its leader, Marcus Opellius Macrinus, one of the two praetorian prefects, who was thereby able to plead complete ignorance. Caracalla was still popular with the guard, and the rest of the army showed no great enthusiasm for his murder. In fact, Macrinus had recently discovered that a message was on its way to the emperor accusing him of disloyalty and decided to strike before he was himself condemned.[10]

There was no heir. Caracalla's marriage had been unhappy and child-less – it was generally believed that illness rendered him impotent in his last years. He had not marked out a successor, mainly because he did not trust anyone, but given his youth this had not seemed important. For two days the empire had no emperor, as Macrinus sounded out the mood of the senior officers. Then he declared himself as the new ruler, assuming all the imperial titles and powers without waiting for the formality of a vote in the Senate. Armies had made emperors in the past – it was only twenty years since Severus had defeated Clodius Albinus – but this was different. Macrinus was not a senator, but an equestrian, who had risen to his position through loyalty and legal skill. Praetorian prefects had always been chosen from amongst the knights precisely because it was believed that they could not aspire to the supreme office. Even Sejanus, who had come close to supplanting Emperor Tiberius in 31, had worked at gradually acquiring offices, including the consulship. At the age of fifty-five, Macrinus leaped straight to supreme power. It was doubtless easier because there were no senators nearby, who might have been considered suitable candidates for the throne. Mesopotamia had from the beginning been an equestrian province, and Caracalla had never been in the habit of taking senior senators with him on campaign. The few that did travel with him were tainted by his favour. The recent division of provinces into smaller units also meant that there was no governor anywhere in the empire who controlled as large a force as that con-centrated at Edessa. The other praetorian prefect pleaded advanced age and stood aside in favour of his colleague.

When the Senate received news of the coup there was relief at the demise of the unpopular and unpredictable Caracalla. Acceptance of the new emperor was more grudging and largely for the want of any obvious alternative. The senators were less bothered by his Mauretanian ancestry and pierced ear – although it is noticeable that all images of the emperor are highly traditional and very Roman in appearance – than his lack of social rank. It did not help that he made no effort to hurry to Rome and win them over. Worse was the appointment of men of similarly undistinguished background to high office, including another equestrian to the post of urban prefect at Rome itself – the city's effective chief magistrate in the emperor's absence. Macrinus tended to appoint men he knew and so inevitably these were mainly from the imperial administration just like himself. Caracalla had given rapid promotion to men he trusted regardless of their social background and had used a lot of equestrians in posts of considerable responsibility, sometimes after a rapid elevation to the Senate. Senators had disliked this, and had no great enthusiasm for a new regime that further promoted many of the same people. Macrinus ruled because he had arranged the death of the last emperor, was able to control the troops on the spot and, for the moment at least, also received the loyalty of the army as a whole.[11]

The Severan Women

Caracalla's mother had accompanied him on most of his travels. Julia Domna had had a prominent public role during Severus' reign, when she received titles such as Augusta and 'The Mother of the camp', and had travelled with him around the empire. Intelligent and capable, she had also worked hard behind the scenes to help her husband with the great task of administering the empire. Augustus' wife, the formidable Livia – called 'Ulysses in a frock' by Caligula – had similarly worked hard to assist him, dealing with correspondence, advising and watching events. In spite of her horror at the murder of Geta, Julia Domna continued to offer the same support to her older son. If anything, her responsibilities increased because Caracalla became so easily bored with mundane tasks. She was in Antioch when he was murdered, tasked amongst other things with opening and reading correspondence to the emperor, so that she could 'sort everything that arrived and prevent a mass of unimportant letters from being sent to him while he was in the enemy's country'.[12] Ironically, the message warning Caracalla about Macrinus was diverted to Antioch in this way, while another went directly to the praetorian prefect himself and prompted him to act. The new emperor treated Julia Domna well until he discovered that she was intriguing against him, after which she was placed under house arrest. In protest she starved herself to death, her end hastened by a long-term illness that may have been breast cancer. She was probably still short of her fiftieth year.[13]

There it might have ended, for both Severus' children were now dead and the dynasty seemed over. Yet Julia Domna had a sister, Julia Maesa, who had usually accompanied her and helped her work, and she in turn had two daughters. All three women were now widows, and the daughters – Soaemias and Mamaea – both had young sons. Maesa returned to her family's home city of Emesa after her sister's death, where it was said that she fretted at no longer living in the imperial household. Emesa (near modern Homs) was in the province of Syria Phoenice, which was garrisoned by a single legion, *III Gallica*, an easy journey to the north at Raphaneae. The origins of the city are obscure, as indeed is the ethnic background of its population. They seem to have been considered Phoenician by some, although there is no evidence for Phoenician settlement there. The bulk of the population spoke Aramaic, but virtually all inscriptions were in Greek, and presumably most official business was conducted in the same language. Trade contributed to Emesa's prosperity, but it was most famous for the great temple of the god Elagabalus ('LHGBL' in Aramaic), whose image was a black, conical stone, said to have fallen from heaven, and who was associated with the Sun.

Soaemias' fourteen-year-old son was the high priest of the cult. His name was Bassianus, but he has gone down in history by the name of his deity, Elagabalus – sometimes in the corrupted and inaccurate later form 'Heliogabalus' used by Gibbon and others. A handsome boy, he cut an especially impressive figure in the regalia of his priesthood. One fourth-century source claims that his grandfather had also been high priest, and it may be that the office ran in the family. The extension of this to assume that Julia Domna and her sister were descendants of the old ruling dynasty of priest-kings is far more questionable than is usually claimed. Their father was a Roman citizen, and they were clearly a well-established and prominent family amongst the local aristocracy. Julia Domna was the wife of a senator – it was said that Severus was attracted because her horoscope predicted that she would be the wife of a king – and Maesa and her daughters had all married equestrians following a public career. They were Romans, and they were also very prominent locally, with influence and family connections in Emesa and throughout the wider region. Already wealthy, the family had grown even richer through close association with the Severan dynasty.[14]

The young Elagabalus was highly visible to the many pilgrims who visited the famous temple. Quite a few men – probably particularly officers – came to the shrine from *III Gallica* and are said to have been especially impressed by the boy. Maesa encouraged a rumour that he was in fact Caracalla's illegitimate son, for he and Soaemias were widely believed to have been lovers before the child's birth. Some claimed that they could spot a physical resemblance. Illegitimate children had few rights in Roman law, and never before had anyone suggested that a bastard son should succeed to the throne, but no one seemed to question this now. Macrinus remained an unknown, and although he grew his beard long to look like Marcus Aurelius and named his son Antoninus, he had no connection with a legitimate dynasty. He had also inherited some major problems from his murdered predecessor. The war with Parthia continued, the enemy only being encouraged when Roman envoys told them that the man who started the war was dead. Macrinus had no experience as a general and may have suffered a defeat before the war was ended by negotiation. The terms were certainly not humiliating for the Romans, but they were far less than the unambiguous military success that his new regime desperately needed. No territory was lost, but the Parthians received a substantial subsidy. The cost of this, added to the expense of paying the army at the rate set by Caracalla, threatened to overburden the emperor's available funds. Macrinus realised that his power to rule relied upon the obedience of the army and knew that reducing the pay scale to the level set by Severus would be hugely unpopular. Instead, he announced that existing soldiers would continue to receive the higher rate, but that all new recruits would be paid the old salary. If the compromise made financial sense, it left the troops suspicious that all pay would be reduced as soon as the emperor felt more secure.[15]

On 16 May 218 the young Elagabalus was taken to the camp of *III Gallica* and proclaimed emperor by the legion. He took the name Antoninus – later Marcus Aurelius Antoninus – to demonstrate his supposed relationship with Caracalla, who in turn had been given the name by his father following his 'adoption' into the family of Marcus Aurelius. Macrinus was at Antioch, but had few troops at his immediate disposal, for the army had dispersed to winter quarters and some detachments may already have started travelling back to their home provinces. He visited *II Parthica*, but failed to win the soldiers over. Soon after he left, the legion declared for the usurper. A scratch force was sent under the command of the praetorian prefect to besiege *III Gallica* at Raphaneae. An initial attack failed, despite the courage shown by some Mauretanian troops who fought well for their countryman. However, when Elagabalus was paraded on the walls of the camp in imperial regalia – and the promise was made that anyone killing a superior officer would assume his rank – the besiegers changed sides. Macrinus was sent the head of his prefect.

With an army that consisted mainly of the units of the guard, he met the advancing enemy not far from Antioch – perhaps near the village of Immae. The praetorians fought well and broke through the enemy line, but the fourteen-year-old boy, his mother and grandmother personally helped to rally the troops and drove the guardsmen back. Macrinus despaired and fled the field – an unforgivable crime for a Roman general. He was hunted down and killed, as was his young son, who had been elevated to imperial rank in an attempt to create a new dynasty. It is doubtful that either army numbered much more than 10,000 men at Immae – far smaller than the armies which had fought between 193 and 197. Almost as importantly, there may have been no senators present at the battle, and certainly none played a significant role. The fate of the empire had been decided in a tiny battle fought far from Rome and with little or no participation by the Senate.[16]

The Boy Emperors

Few mourned Macrinus when news of his death reached Rome, but it was some months before the new emperor arrived. Paintings had been sent ahead, showing him in his full regalia as high priest. Two years younger even than Nero when he had come to power, Elagabalus took his duties to the deity very seriously, and his sense of a special relationship with the god can only have been enhanced by his sudden elevation. Theatrical by nature, he clearly revelled in the very public role of emperor, while showing little taste for the mundane work of administration. In some ways he was little more than a figurehead, while his mother, grandmother and various favourites made decisions behind the scenes. Sometimes their importance was made very public – both women were admitted to at least one meeting of the Senate and may have attended on other occasions. The only woman to have done this before was Nero's mother Agrippina, although even then she had stayed hidden behind a curtain. Senators disliked this breach of tradition, and even more resented the continued promotion of favourites from humble backgrounds to high office. Yet in the main their hatred focused on the emperor himself, whose behaviour became steadily more bizarre.[17]

Elagabalus spent the greater part of his four-year reign in or near Rome and his main concern was to enjoy himself. The stories told of his antics are wild, and doubtless grew in the telling. Yet both Dio and Herodian lived through the reign and we would be rash to ignore their testimony, even though both men hated the emperor. Probably they repeat gossip as well as fact, but it is significant that such stories were circulating – and doubtless being credited. The teenage emperor was married perhaps as many as six times, twice to the same woman. This was the Vestal Virgin Aquilia Severa, whom he divorced his first wife to marry, apparently seeing it as a sacred union appropriate for his status as priest. There was such outrage at his shattering of an ancient taboo, that even the emperor realised his mistake and divorced her. Oddly, after divorcing his third wife, a descendant of Marcus Aurelius, there was no protest when he married Aquilia again, presumably because she was considered to have lost any sacred status. (Curiously his taste for Vestals may have been shared by his alleged father Caracalla, who is supposed to have tried to rape one and was only thwarted by his impotence. The woman was later tried for breaking her vow of chastity and defended herself by saying that the emperor himself could vouch that her virginity was intact in spite of his best efforts. She still suffered the traditional punishment of being entombed alive.)

As well as his marriages, the young emperor made frequent use of prostitutes, although allegedly never the same one twice. He also openly took many male lovers, and like Nero before him, he is said to have been the bride at a wedding ceremony and then lived with his 'husband'. It was even said that he had asked doctors whether they could use surgery to give him a vagina. Roman attitudes to homosexuality were complex, but – in spite of some modern claims – it was always seen as vice. If carried on discreetly it was a minor one, perhaps understandable and easily outweighed by a man's better characteristics. Emperor Trajan was said to have been too fond of boys, but had never let any favourite gain an unhealthy influence over him or persuade him to act wrongly. Elagabalus blatantly paraded and promoted his lovers. It was said that appointments to provincial commands were being allocated to the man with the largest penis. The emperor's behaviour in public was shocking – perhaps deliberately so – and rumours of his antics in private were rife.[18]

The emperor continued to play an active part in the cult of his god, which involved very public dancing and devotees working themselves into a frenzy. The Romans had adopted many foreign deities over the centuries, but usually in a sanitised form. These new rituals shocked them, particularly because the emperor was at the centre of things and expected senators to take part. The senatorial class as a whole hated him for this, even though they took part, the most ambitious of them doing so with great enthusiasm. Daily animal sacrifices on an extravagant scale were carried out, and Dio believed that there were secret ritual killings of children. The teenage emperor changed the cult into something it had never been before, intimately linking it with himself and the empire. The black stone had been brought with the imperial party and installed in the Temple of Jupiter on the Capitol, replacing Jupiter as the most important god of Rome. In 220 the sun god was 'married' to the Roman goddess Minerva, and a very ancient and highly sacred statue physically brought from her temple to join him. Again opinion was outraged, particularly amongst the aristocracy, and a year later the god divorced his wife as too warlike for his nature, and instead 'married' Astarte, whose image was brought from Carthage.[19]

Elagabalus was not a tyrant, but he was an incompetent, probably the least able emperor Rome had ever had. That the empire continued to function was due mainly to the efforts of his grandmother. Never more than a figurehead, he soon became an embarrassment. There were several mutinies in which elements of the army raised rival candidates to the throne, but none had so far gathered enough momentum to mount a serious threat. Even the legion that had first supported him, *III Gallica*, declared for another emperor and seems to have been disbanded, although it was subsequently re-formed. Maesa's skill, money and connections had made Elagabalus emperor. Her other grandson, Alexander, the son of Mamaea, was five years younger than his cousin and had been too young in 218 to be a viable candidate. Now, a little older, he was becoming an alternative, and Elagabalus was made to adopt him in 221. Realising what this meant, the emperor dismissed anyone he felt favoured Alexander, but was aware that the boy was popular with many, including the praetorian guard. On 11 March 222 the thirteen-year-old cousin disappeared from public view and the guardsmen rioted, fearing that he had been murdered. Elagabalus went to the praetorian camp to calm them, but failed and was stopped from leaving. When Maesa and Alexander appeared, the emperor hid. During the night some praetorians found him hiding in a basket or box and beheaded him. His mother was also killed.[20]

The End of a Golden Age

The empire had a new figurehead, but effective control remained with Maesa, passing on her death in 224 to her daughter Mamaea. From the beginning care was taken to avoid the mistakes of the recent past. The black stone was sent back to Emesa by decree of the Senate. Senators were supposed to play a greater role in advising the young emperor and women were formally banned from attending their meetings. There was to be less use of social outsiders in senior posts, more of traditional senatorial governors and commanders. The real changes were superficial and the imperial household, staffed mainly by equestrians, continued to wield massive influence. Alexander reigned for thirteen years, and the decades of turmoil that followed his death made the period seem better than had truly been the case. He never fully escaped the control of his grandmother and then mother. The latter dismissed the wife she had chosen for him when it seemed that she might be able to influence the malleable youth. This became less and less pardonable as Alexander grew older. Throughout his reign sporadic risings occurred amongst the legions as various emperors were proclaimed, although as under Elagabalus none made any headway. The praetorians had grown undisciplined during the latter's weak rule and now were scarcely kept under control. The praetorian prefect and eminent jurist Ulpian was killed by the guardsmen. In 229 Alexander granted Dio the great honour of a second consulship held jointly with him. However, he warned the historian not to come to Rome since he was unable to guarantee his safety as he was known to be unpopular with the praetorians.[21]

Alexander undertook a number of campaigns, but had little success as a general. In 235 he and his mother were murdered by soldiers of the Rhine army who supported a usurper. The new emperor was another equestrian, Maximinus Thrax. He was said to have been from peasant stock and had worked his way up after service as an ordinary soldier. As usual we must allow for the particular perspective of the elite, as well as the propaganda of his enemies. In fact, his parents were probably from the local aristocracy and his career was mainly in the ranks reserved for equestrians, although it is possible that he progressed to this after service as a centurion or junior officer. He certainly took pride in his martial prowess and strength, and sent a painting of himself charging down his enemies for display in the Senate. It was a very different image to Elagabalus, and the senators felt obliged to recognise his rule. Maximinus won power through the support of the troops in one region. In time those elsewhere found other candidates for the throne. He won some victories against these opponents, but was dead within three years, killed by his own men.[22]

The Severan Age is far better documented than the decades that followed, which only adds to a misleading impression of stability. It was a remarkable period, particularly because it saw real power being wielded by four women from the imperial family. Julia Domna herself was probably the ablest of them, and certainly there is evidence that she had a wide intellectual curiosity. She and the others were all clearly ambitious and ruthlessly determined to cling on to power. They also – with the possible exception of Soaemias – seem to have done their best to act in the general good of the empire. Even so, this was not how the Principate was supposed to work, or at least be seen to work. Augustus and his successors were at heart military dictators, but had carefully created a façade of ruling by consent, and especially the consent of the Senate. As a body it was supposed to advise, and as individuals senators filled all the most important posts as magistrates and governors. Bad emperors had not followed these principles or shown the Senate sufficient respect, but there had been more good emperors than bad up to the death of Marcus Aurelius. Individuals – mainly equestrians, but some like Pertinax who had been born to a humbler station – joined the senatorial order without changing its essential nature.

The ever contradictory Caracalla did not respect the Senate, while still writing letters urging senators to diligence and encouraging free debate. Macrinus never visited Rome or the Senate, and probably knew few senators that well. Elagabalus shocked and (privately) disgusted them, and if his cousin tried to treat the Senate with deference, this was weakened because everyone realised that he was a lightweight. Through-out the period a succession of favourites enjoyed spectacular careers. Many were of humble origins, although we should again allow for the exaggeration of senatorial snobbery. Dio was particularly disgusted by the career of Publius Valerius Comazon, who had supported Elagabalus' bid for power as an equestrian – perhaps as the prefect commanding *II Parthica*. He was made a senator, then consul, and held the prestigious post of urban prefect three times. He was said to have been a dancer – and, Dio scathingly implied, a mediocre one, good enough for Gaul, but not for the sophisticated audiences in Rome – although this probably was untrue, even if his father may have owned a theatrical company. Even worse was the growing role of equestrians appointed to commands without the formality of being enrolled in the Senate. As far as senators were concerned, the wrong people were gaining power and influence. Nor were they always convinced of their competence. In the past, members of the imperial women and members of the household had often gained influence, but wise emperors had always ensured that this was kept discreet. Septimius Severus had generally kept to this principle. The rest of his family, just like Commodus, had not managed it.[23]

The twenty years of internal peace from the defeat of Clodius Albinus in 197 to the murder of Caracalla were never to be repeated. Military mutinies and abortive coups occurred sporadically throughout the reigns of Elagabalus and Alexander, but were all unsuccessful until 235. After this, right down to the end of the Western Empire, there were only a handful of decades when there was not a major civil war. The contrast with the first two centuries of the Principate could not be more striking. Then, civil war was rarely more than a remote possibility. For each generation of Romans from now on civil wars and usurpations were normal facts of life. The nature of the conflicts had also changed profoundly, and so had the people bidding for supreme power. Macrinus and Maximinus were both equestrians. Elagabalus was no more than a boy, who claimed to be the illegitimate son of an emperor. All of these men had grown up away from Rome and were seen – at least by the aristocracy – as not fully Roman.

It is hard to imagine that any of them could possibly have become emperor even fifty years earlier. Tacitus had already declared that the secret of empire was that rulers could be made in the provinces. Now it seemed that far more people could aspire to the supreme office, just as long as they could rally troops to their cause. The population as a whole had shown a fondness for dynasties from the beginning of the Principate. For many people in the provinces it mattered little what the emperor got up to in Rome as long as he answered petitions, appointed reasonably honest and capable governors, and did not raise taxes too much. The preference was always to stick with the same family and name. When Severus made himself an Antonine, and Elagabalus and Alexander were declared sons of Caracalla, the political advantage of family connections was weakened.

Men from outside the old senatorial elite were now becoming emperors. The much more numerous equestrian class from throughout the provinces was also filling a growing proportion of the senior jobs in the army and administration. What it meant to be Roman had also changed. In 212 Caracalla issued a decree granting citizenship to virtually the entire free population of the empire. Dio maliciously claimed that this was because he needed to raise funds and so made more people liable to inheritance taxes and other levies to which only citizens were liable. Historians have speculated that Caracalla was once again emulating Alexander the Great's efforts to integrate his subjects of all races. One fragmentary papyrus has survived that seems to be a copy of the decree, but the surviving text consists of general platitudes. The emperor thanked the gods for preserving him – whether from Geta's 'plot' or a dangerous sea voyage is unclear – and wanted the population as a whole to share in his gratitude. In the end we cannot know what motivated the often impetuous emperor. The result did not change most peoples' daily lives to any great degree, although it did make them subject to different laws.

All remained members of their existing communities, whether city or village. Inevitably, with so many more citizens, the value of the franchise was lessened. Roman legal practice had always tended to reserve harsher punishments for the less well off and less well connected. Now laws regularly emphasised the distinction between the 'more honoured' men, and the 'more humble'. There was also increasingly less distinction between Italy and the provinces.[24]

4

King of Kings

'I am the Mazda-worshipping divine Shapur, King of Kings of Aryans [i.e. Iranians], and non-Aryans. ... And when I was first established over the dominion of the nations, the Caesar Gordian from the whole of the Roman Empire and the nations of the Goths and Germans raised an army and marched against Assyria, against the nations of the Aryans and against us. A great battle took place between the two sides on the frontier of Assyria at Meshike. Caesar Gordian was destroyed and the Roman army was annihilated.' – *King Shapur I of Persia, describing his victory over the Romans in 244.*[1]

In March 1920 soldiers from Britain's Indian army were on the banks of the Euphrates in Syria when they stumbled upon a truly remarkable archaeological discovery. Some sepoys digging a position for their machine gun uncovered a temple that had been buried for more than sixteen centuries. Their officer, one Captain Murphy, recognised the building as Roman. All four walls were richly decorated with scenes showing sacrifice. By a strange chance, one of these murals depicted soldiers – Roman soldiers from around the year 238. They were the officers of the Twentieth Palmyrene Cohort, parading beside their standard (*vexillum*) of a square red flag hanging down from a crossbar on top of a long pole. In front of them is their commander, Tribune Julius Terentius – his name is neatly painted in Latin beside him – who offers incense on the altar. Another man, 'Themes son of Mokimos, priest' is named, though this time in Greek. The objects of worship were three figures of gods – or perhaps emperors – and the guardian spirits or Fortunes of two cities, of Palmyra and the place itself, Dura Europos.

Little was known about Dura Europos from literary sources, but this all changed when a programme of large-scale excavation began on the site. By this time Syria had passed under French control and the Franco-American team of archaeologists was aided and protected by soldiers of the Foreign Legion as well as locally raised troops. It was a suitably exotic combination for what had once been a highly cosmopolitan frontier community. Dura was founded around 300 BC as a Macedonian colony and throughout its history Greek probably remained the main language of everyday speech. Yet inscriptions, graffiti and papyri show that a range of other languages, including Aramaic, Palmyrene, Parthian and Latin were also in regular use. The Parthians held the city for two and a half centuries before it fell to Rome in 165 during the campaigns of Lucius Verus. Just over ninety years later Dura fell to enemy attack and was abandoned forever.[2]

Conditions at Dura preserved much that does not normally survive, including wooden shields with ornate painted decoration, shafts of weapons, fabrics and a great quantity of documents written on papyrus. Many of these were associated with the Twentieth Palmyrene Cohort, making it probably the best known unit in the Roman army. Like all bureaucracy, the subjects are generally mundane. There are daily reports listing the number of men fit for duty – the cohort was predominantly infantry, but also had some horsemen and even a few camel riders. Records were kept of men posted away, going on leave or returning to duty. Another records the allocation of horses to the cavalrymen, giving each animal's age and a fairly specific description of its colour.

The Twentieth seem to have been the main part of the permanent garrison. (Interestingly enough, in the past the Parthians had stationed archers supplied by their Palmyrene allies to hold the place.) Other units, including detachments of legionaries, were also often present. The Palmyrenes were auxiliaries, but the real difference in status between these troops and the legions was no longer as important as it had once been. Virtually all of the men in the cohort were Roman citizens. On the nominal role the name 'Marcus Aurelius Antontinus ——————' is most common, revealing that they had gained citizenship following Caracalla's universal grant and taken the emperor's name. Some of them may genuinely have come from Palmyra, but many will have been from other Syrian communities. The Roman army tended to recruit locally whenever this was possible.[3]

Julius Terentius' family owed their name and citizenship to an earlier emperor. As the commander of a cohort he was an equestrian. The painting shows him as tall – although this might be to reflect his status – with a trim beard and a receding hairline. The other officers boast a variety of hairstyles and are almost all bearded. One stands out because his hair is fair. The tribune has a white cloak, in contrast to the darker drab cloaks worn by everyone else. All are unarmoured (although helmets, body armour and shields were employed in battle), wear close-fitting trousers, closed shoes rather than sandals and white tunics with long sleeves. The men's tunics have a red border and Terentius and the front rank of officers have two rings on each sleeve. They do not look too much like the classic image of Roman soldiers, but such a uniform was normal by this period, even emperors conforming to the style.

Officers like Terentius usually served for a few years in a command, before moving on to another post. However, his career was to be cut short. In 239 the Roman outpost came under attack and he was killed in the fighting. Casualties may have been heavy, for the overall strength of the cohort seems to have fallen by 100 men at this time. Terentius' wife Aurelia Arria had accompanied him in this posting and left a poignant memorial to her dead husband. The text, carefully painted in Greek on the wall of a house – perhaps their billet – mourns 'her beloved husband', a man who had been 'brave in campaigns and mighty in wars'.[4]

Persia: The New Enemy

Terentius was not killed by Parthians, but by soldiers of the new Sassanid Persian dynasty. Arsacid Parthia was an essentially feudal state, with the king relying on the great noble families to run the empire and provide him with soldiers. The king needed the nobles, but they were always a potential threat, for if they became too powerful they could overthrow him and place a rival claimant on the throne. Civil wars were frequent. During the second century the monarchy had also been battered by successive defeats in the great wars with Rome, losing more and more territory on the borders. Caracalla's murder in 217 may well have prevented new Roman conquests. Although Artabanus V of Parthia extorted a substantial sum from Macrinus as the price of peace, he was unable to take any more advantage of Rome's weakness because he faced internal problems of his own. One of his brothers was challenging him for the throne, while another rebellion led by a nobleman was also gaining momentum. It was the latter that proved fatal. By 224 Artabanus V had been defeated – the victor's propaganda claimed that he killed the king in personal combat – and the Parthian empire died with him.

The victor was Ardashir I, son of Papak, perhaps grandson of Sassan, although romantic stories later circulated about how the family got its name. He was a Persian rather than a Parthian, but it would be wrong to see his rebellion as a nationalist campaign to overthrow 'foreign' Parthian rulers. Ardashir was simply one of many local aristocrats, if an especially talented and ambitious one. It probably took a decade for him to beat all his local rivals and become undisputed king of his home province of Persis (modern Fars). That he was able to rise in this way gives a good indication of the weakness of central government, which he continued to exploit as he expanded into other provinces. Roman sources make him claim to be the heir of the old Achaemenid Persian kings smashed by Alexander the Great. In Greek his name was Artaxerxes. However, there is no trace of this connection in his internal propaganda and, as far as we can tell, few Persians had much knowledge of this era of their past.

Ardashir won because he was a good soldier and a strong leader. He also followed the traditional Persian religion of Zoroastrianism – a monumental relief set up by his son shows the god Ahura-Mazda crowning the victorious Ardashir. This in itself was a break with tradition, for in the past it had not been considered proper to represent the god in human form. On the monument the earthly king tramples the defeated Artabanus beneath the hooves of his horse, while his heavenly counterpart similarly crushes the evil god Ahriman. From the beginning the new dynasty claimed divine favour and encouraged the construction of the fire-temples central to the cult, but it would be wrong to see them as crusaders. The Parthians had never been hostile to Zoroastrianism and it was only later that it developed into a state church that suppressed other faiths. Ardashir was devout, but tolerant of other beliefs and ideas.[5]

In many ways the new regime closely resembled the old. It was still essentially feudal, although the balance of power had shifted markedly in favour of the king and the administration that developed around the court. At first this had more to do with the strength of Ardashir's character than anything else. As importantly, over time the nobles and lesser kings ruling each region were almost all replaced by members of the Sassanid family. These men and their retinues continued to supply most of the troops for the royal army and the king could not fight a major campaign without them. Ardashir was respected and feared. He was also a usurper who had recently fought his way to power. Few would have guessed that his dynasty would last until the seventh century. If ever he seemed to be weak there was a real danger that another nobleman would depose him. Ardashir needed to keep winning victories to show that he was strong and to reward his followers with plunder. His mind soon turned to the border with Rome.

The rise of the Sassanids had profoundly shifted the balance of power

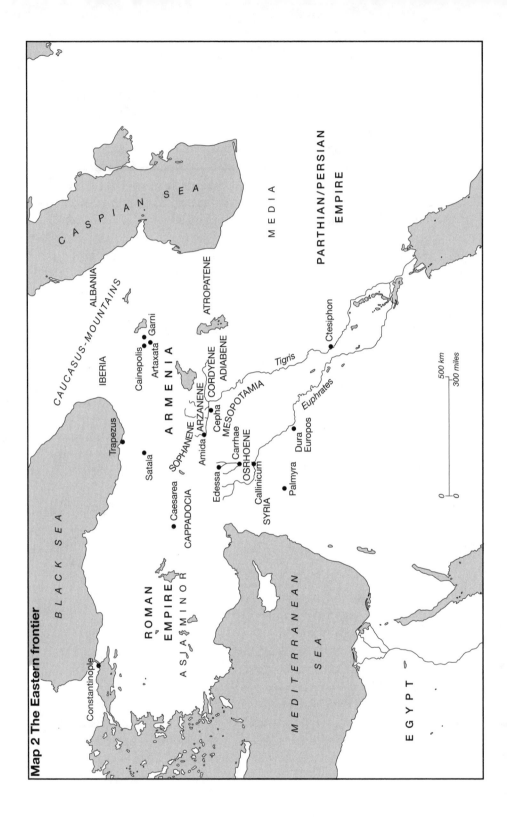

Map 2 The Eastern frontier

on the frontier. Part of the Arsacid family held on to the throne of Armenia and, faced with the threat of invasion, they turned to an ever closer alliance with Rome. Hatra, the desert city that had defied both Trajan and Severus in turn, repulsed a Persian attack in 229, and at some point accepted a Roman garrison. A year later Ardashir attacked the Roman province of Mesopotamia. It was a very tempting target. The twenty-year-old Severus Alexander was seen as weak and under his mother's thumb. Still worse, the Roman troops in this and the neighbouring provinces were not in a high state of readiness. In the last twelve years they had taken part in a civil war and several failed usurpations. Inevitably, discipline had declined, and with it levels of training. Dio mentions that the soldiers in Syria had recently murdered their governor in a mutiny. The Persians easily broke through and raided in Mesopotamia and perhaps beyond.[6]

At first Alexander tried to negotiate, prompting the Persian envoys' boasts about reviving the old Persian Empire as far as the shores of the Mediterranean. Ardashir was not the first to make such claims – in 35 a Parthian king had done the same during a dispute with the emperor Tiberius. Then as now, it was clearly little more than diplomatic bluster to help secure far more modest objectives. When talking failed, Alexander gathered a large expeditionary force from all over the empire and went east. Morale was still a problem and there was at least one mutiny before the campaign began. The details of the operations that followed are hazy, and the Persians had probably already retreated from the Roman province. If not, then they were promptly expelled. Three Roman columns then invaded Persian territory, one being led in person by the emperor. There seem to have been some Roman victories, before Alexander retreated prematurely and allowed the Persians to maul one of the other Roman columns.[7]

The outcome was an uneasy stalemate, neither side mounting any major operations for several years. Alexander left to celebrate a triumph in Rome and then move to the Rhine frontier. The Persian army had dispersed when the Romans withdrew, the feudal element returning home and leaving Ardashir with only his immediate retinue and professional mercenaries. Yet the king was probably content, as raiding will have produced plunder for his nobles and their retainers. There was also glory from winning victories and avoiding any serious defeat. Having strengthened his position on the throne, for the moment he was satisfied.

The Death of an Emperor

In 236 Ardashir launched another attack on Mesopotamia, capturing the cities of Carrhae, Nisibis and Edessa. Again, this may essentially have been a raid aimed at winning glory and gathering plunder. The new emperor Maximinus was too preoccupied with campaigns in the west to respond. He was already facing growing internal opposition. Short of money, his representatives were ordered to be especially rigorous in their collection of taxes, adding to his unpopularity. In March 238 an imperial procurator was lynched in Africa by the tenants of some landowners he had been squeezing for money. They quickly proclaimed the proconsul of the province as emperor. His name was Gordian (fully, Marcus Antonius Gordianus Sempronianus Romanus) and he was senator of good family, but modest talent. He was also extremely old – Herodian says he was eighty. However, his son was with him in the province and was quickly named as co-emperor as they set up court in Carthage. When the news reached Rome the Senate rejoiced and immediately pledged its loyalty, declaring Maximinus a public enemy.[8]

However, they were premature. Africa was not a military province and had no significant garrison. Neighbouring Numidia contained a full legion – *III Augusta* – as well as auxiliaries. Its governor was also a senator, but he had a personal grudge against Gordian and chose to stay loyal to Maximinus. The legion marched on Carthage. The Younger Gordian led a volunteer army against them, but the enthusiasm of peasants was no match for properly equipped and trained soldiers. The army was routed and its commander killed. His father hanged himself when he heard the news.[9]

The rebellion had been crushed after a few weeks, but it was too late for the Senate to change its decision and so a new emperor needed to be found. A board of twenty ex-consuls was given the task of picking out men suitable for the job from amongst the senators' peers. They selected two of their own number, Balbinus and Pupienus, both of whom were probably at least in their sixties. On the day they were proclaimed there was rioting and they were forced to take another colleague, the grandson of Gordian – the child of his daughter and not his recently killed son. Gordian III was just thirteen and the disturbances had almost certainly been orchestrated by senators and senior equestrian officials, who felt that they could gain power through this puppet.[10]

By this time Maximinus had marched on Italy, but became bogged down in the siege of Aquileia. It was there that his officers grew tired of him and killed him. The army then declared its support for the three emperors named by the Senate. It is quite possible that they are the three armoured figures receiving the offering of Terentius and his men on the painting at Dura. However, from the very beginning Balbinus and Pupienus were unpopular with the praetorians and after a couple of months the guardsmen murdered the two men. Once again the empire was ruled by a boy in his early teens – or rather by the people who could control him. The most important of these was Praetorian Prefect Caius Timesitheus, who married his daughter to the young emperor. Although he appears to have been reasonably competent, this was not the way the empire was supposed to work. There were also major problems, not least the same shortage of funds that had caused Maximinus to resort to desperate measures.[11]

Wracked by civil war and once again ruled by a mere boy, the Roman Empire seemed weak and vulnerable to its neighbours. Therefore the Persians pressed their attacks, taking Hatra in 240. By this time Ardashir had died and been succeeded by his son Shapur I, who had shared power with his father in the last few years and already proved himself a formidable soldier. Even so, by 243 the Romans had recaptured Carrhae, Nisibis and Edessa. The army then marched against Ctesiphon – formerly the Parthian capital and still the main seat of government for the new regime. Before it arrived Timesitheus died of natural causes. Early in 244 Shapur met the Roman army in battle near the city and claimed a victory. Roman sources deny that they were defeated, but Gordian certainly did not win and the army soon began to retreat.[12]

At the very least it was a strategic victory for Shapur, reinforced by the death of the nineteen-year-old Gordian. How he died is unclear. The Persians claimed to have killed him, and some of the Roman accounts say that he received a wound that proved mortal. The darker tradition, which says that during the retreat he was murdered in a conspiracy led by the two praetorian prefects, is generally preferred by historians. Certainly the young emperor had presided over a military failure. The two new praetorian prefects had been close associates of Timesitheus and were also brothers – the first time this had ever happened. The younger of the two, Philip (fully Marcus Julius Philippus), was proclaimed emperor by the army. His older brother may simply have been less forceful, but the key factor was probably that Philip had a son, who in due course was made co-emperor. Once again the emperor was an equestrian, and like Macrinus, Philip had risen through the imperial household. By now probably in his forties, he came from an obscure town in southern Syria, which he would later rebuild at massive cost as the grand city of Philippopolis. Later historians dubbed him Philip the Arab, but there is no reason to believe that he was not fully Roman in all important respects.

New emperors were always vulnerable to challengers and Philip wanted to return to the heart of the empire as soon as possible. He made peace with Shapur, giving him 500,000 gold coins and conceding that Armenia lay within Persia's sphere of influence. No Roman territory was ceded, but the Persian king kept Hatra and had won a degree of dominance over the border regions. He also gained a huge amount of glory and was not hesitant in celebrating this. In a victory monument he is depicted on horseback trampling the corpse of Gordian while Philip begs for mercy. The success greatly strengthened his grip on the kingdom.[13]

Philip returned to Europe. Later he would send back his older brother to take charge of the eastern provinces with the title 'commander of the east' (rector orientis), watching the uneasy peace with Persia. In 245–246 Philip himself campaigned on the Danubian frontier, which had come under heavy attack from the tribes beyond. A year later he was in Rome, where he celebrated the one thousandth anniversary of Rome's foundation with a great festival. Most of our sources are hostile to Philip, but as far as we can tell he seems to have done his best to rule well. At this period, however, this was seldom enough. Like all recent emperors he was desperately short of money, not helped by his lavish expenditure. Heavy taxation provoked a rebellion in Syria in 248 and at the end of that year the army in Moesia on the Danube proclaimed a rival emperor. The latter did not last long before his own men turned against him and killed him.[14]

There was soon more trouble on the Danubian frontier, perhaps provoked by the reduction or cancellation of subsidies paid to the tribes to keep the peace. Philip sent an experienced senator named Decius (fully, Caius Messius Quintus Decius) to the region to restore order. In 249 the army there proclaimed Decius emperor and he promptly led a force back to Italy. Philip was defeated and killed in battle near Verona, and his son was murdered immediately afterwards. The fate of Philip's brother is unknown, but he was probably also killed. Decius was soon back on the Danube, fighting against groups of barbarians who had overrun the frontier. From the very beginning he knew that his grip on power was precarious. Probably for this reason one of his first measures was an edict commanding the entire free population of the empire to sacrifice on his behalf. The ritual was to be performed by a set date and had to be witnessed by a local official. Perhaps unintentionally, this decree provoked a crisis for one group within the empire, the Christians.[15]

An Enemy Within?

The first discovery at Dura Europos was a temple and more were found in the subsequent excavations. Like every other community in the polytheistic empire, many different cults seem to have happily coexisted. Decius' decree was quite vague when it commanded people to make an offering to the 'ancestral gods', allowing individuals to address their worship to whatever deities they preferred. More spectacular than the temples at Dura was the uncovering of a synagogue dating to the third century. Its walls were covered in paintings showing scenes from the scriptures, including the Exodus and the arrival in Canaan. This in itself is highly unusual, for normally the Jews of this period were reluctant to represent the human form in art. The style is very similar to the Terentius painting and suggests local taste.[16]

Around the same time that the synagogue was built at Dura, some rooms in a private house were converted into a baptistry by local Christians. Once again, its walls were painted in the same local style, this time with scenes including Adam and Eve, Jesus as the Good Shepherd and with Peter walking on water. In contrast to the later tradition, Jesus is shown as beardless. Another poorly preserved scene seems to have depicted the women going to the empty tomb after the Resurrection. In many ways this discovery was even more surprising than that of the synagogue, for Christianity is almost invisible archaeologically until the fourth century. It did not set up monuments or build distinctively shaped churches, since groups tended to meet in private houses or outside. Without the wall paintings, archaeologists would have been far less confident in identifying the room as a baptistry.[17]

Christians did not sacrifice, something which made them very different from the bulk of the population of the empire. They also denied the existence of any god other than their own, a position which was seen as akin to atheism. The Jews had a similar view, and were seen as perverse by many outsiders, but at least they were a distinct people, whose religion was traditional. For a long time the Christians were seen as just another Jewish sect and it was probably not until the end of the first century that there was a wider perception that the cult stood outside Judaism. Christianity was new, and Christians were drawn from all nations and every level of society. This made many especially suspicious of the religion, since it was hard to be sure how many Christians there were. Critics claimed that converts were usually the vulnerable, poor and ignorant, often slaves or women – groups that educated men felt were by nature illogical. Rumours also spread of terrible secret rituals. The communion service, with its talk of eating flesh and drinking blood, fuelled tales of cannibalism.[18]

Jesus was crucified sometime around 30, during the reign of Tiberius. Although the main charge was one of opposition to Roman power – the claim made that he was king of the Jews – there was no attempt by Roman authorities to suppress his followers. However, in 64 after fire had swept through the heart of Rome, popular opinion turned against Nero and accused him of exploiting the destruction for his own advantage and perhaps even of having arranged it in the first place. In response, the emperor blamed the Christians for starting the blaze, hoping that this unpopular group would make good scapegoats. Many were arrested and executed, some being burned alive as punishment. Both Peter and Paul were said to have been killed during this purge, the former crucified, but the latter beheaded because he was a citizen.[19]

Nero's persecution seems to have focused on the Christians in Rome, but even there it is unclear how long it lasted. The principle was established that being a Christian was a crime against the state, but afterwards the authorities showed little interest in actively suppressing the Church. At the beginning of the second century Pliny the Younger was governor of Bithynia and Pontus, touring from city to city within the province to deal with appeals and dispense justice. At one place people arrested by the city authorities on a charge of being Christians were brought before him. After investigation Pliny concluded that there was no truth in the wild stories of crimes and deviant behaviour, simply of 'excessive superstition'. Those who denied that they were Christians – even if they admitted that they had been in the past – were released. All they had to do was perform a sacrifice and revile the name of Christ. Pliny gave each suspect three chances to escape punishment in this way. If they refused then he had them executed, feeling that they deserved it for their 'stubbornness and rigid obstinacy' as much as anything else.[20]

Emperor Trajan approved Pliny's actions as the correct procedure. The crime was simply being a Christian when questioned by the authorities. Past, and even future, beliefs did not concern the empire, especially if they were kept private. At the end of the second century the Christian author Tertullian, himself a lawyer, claimed that no other crime was treated in the same illogical way. He also emphasised that Christians were model citizens, found in almost every walk of life. The refusal to sacrifice was simply a mark of their integrity, that they could not bring themselves to act out a ritual they knew to be wrong. Yet they were loyal subjects who would obey all other laws, pay their taxes and pray for the emperor and the good of the empire.[21]

After Nero, persecutions of Christians were sporadic and local. They tended to occur at disturbed times or in the wake of natural disasters where people wanted some group to blame. Tertullian claimed that almost any misfortune prompted the cry of 'Christians to the lion!' – lion singular, rather like 'the Hun' in the First World War. Trajan's advice to Pliny was highly revealing, for he stressed that a governor should not hunt out Christians, but merely try those arrested by local authorities. Emperors were not worried by Christianity, but they were concerned to keep individual communities happy. Under Marcus Aurelius there was a large-scale persecution of Christians at Lugdunum (modern Lyons) in Gaul around the year 177. The continuing outbreaks of plague may well have had something to do with creating the nervousness that found this outlet. More immediately, it meant that there was a shortage of suitable criminals to provide victims for the arena.[22]

Even so, there are few signs of a systematic hunt for suspects. The lawyer who came forward to defend those arrested was himself accused of being a Christian during the trial. He confessed and joined the defendants and died in the arena. Later, when a well-known doctor was thought to be encouraging the Christians as they went to their deaths, he too was arrested and sent off for execution. Sometimes arrest and execution were prompted by entirely personal motives. In another account we read of a wife who was converted and subsequently divorced her husband. He in turn publicly accused her and the preacher he blamed for her conversion. On another occasion a recently promoted centurion was reported to the authorities by a colleague who had hoped to gain the same post. Many people seem to have been known to be Christians without this becoming an issue until another dispute arose.[23]

Christian accounts of martyrdoms often emphasise the efforts made to persuade suspects to abandon their faith and go free. Governors are represented taking considerable time and using both threats and reason to convince them. In another case we read of a father begging his Christian daughter, 'have pity on my grey head – have pity on me your father ... think of your child, who will not be able to live once you are gone. Give up your pride!' She refused and was killed in the arena. Not everyone was so determined. On another occasion we read of a man 'who had given himself up and had forced some others to give themselves up voluntarily. With him the governor used many arguments and persuaded him to swear by the gods and offer sacrifice.' Martyrs were revered by the Church, but there was often suspicion of those who volunteered to be punished. Some members of the local church seem to have survived each persecution, and accounts depict them as able to visit and support those held awaiting trial and punishment. The impression is that normally the aim was to arrest some prominent Christians and so deter the others. Governors and even local magistrates seem far more concerned with public displays than private belief.

Sometimes the accounts include moments of grim humour, such as the following exchange between a governor in Spain and a local Christian.

Governor: Are you a bishop? (*Episcopus es?*)
Bishop: I am. (*Sum.*)
Governor: You were. (*Fuisti.*)[24]

The bishop was then burned alive. Public executions for any crime were made especially unpleasant since they were supposed to act as a deterrent. They were also often included in public entertainments. Not all Christians were killed. Men might be sent to labour in the appalling conditions of imperial mines, while women were sometimes sent to work in brothels. On other occasions fines or imprisonment were used, again in the hope of persuading the accused to recant. When the death sentence was imposed, it was often inflicted in extremely savage ways, even by Roman standards. Usually the crowd revelled in the slaughter and only rarely was there any trace of sympathy. On one occasion in Africa around 203 two young women were to be killed by a maddened heifer.

So they were stripped naked, placed in nets and thus brought into the arena. Even the crowd was horrified when they saw that one was a delicate young girl and the other a woman fresh from childbirth with the milk still dripping from her breasts. And so they were brought back again and dressed in unbelted tunics.

The crowd seems to have been quite happy to see clothed women being trampled and gored to death.[25]

Persecutions were spectacular, and appalling for those caught up in them, but they were also rare until the middle of the third century. Most of the time, the majority of people in the Roman world were content for others to follow their own conscience in matters of religion. Many who were not Christians still revered Jesus as a holy man. Julia Mamaea had summoned the famous Christian thinker Origen to Antioch so that she could listen to his ideas. Her son, Alexander Severus, is even supposed to have had a statue of Jesus along with those of other gods and great men he prayed to and kept in his personal chambers. It is easy to forget that the polytheistic mindset made it easy to accept new deities, even if Christians themselves insisted that worshipping Christ must mean a denial of other gods. Philip is said to have been sympathetic to Christians – one later source even claims that he was one himself.[26]

Persecutions were local and occasional and do not seem to have hindered the spread of Christianity. As usual when it comes to statistics, we have no real idea of how many Christians there were at any set period. It appears to have been primarily an urban religion, but then we always know more about life in the cities than the countryside so this assumption may be mistaken. From the beginning Christians produced great quantities of writing, which indicates that a good number were literate and that some were well educated. They probably included many individuals from locally important and prosperous 'middle classes'. Probably Christians were rare amongst the senatorial class, but even this is impossible to prove.

Christianity remained illegal, but only rarely was the law enforced, and most of the time Christians went about their normal lives and even practised their religion in a semi-public way. Decius' edict challenged this and Christians responded in various ways. Some bribed the local officials to purchase the receipt without actually performing the sacrifice. Others complied and made the offering – sometimes one member of the family doing this to protect the others. A few may have abandoned their faith in the face of this government order. Far more resisted, but how they were dealt with depended on the attitude of local magistrates and the provincial governors. Some Christians were executed, even more arrested and punished in other ways, but the sources are too poor for us to know how many suffered. The prominent Alexandrian theologian Origen, who two decades earlier had been summoned by Julia Mamaea, was one of the victims, dying as result of a spell of imprisonment. Decius' edict changed assumptions about the influence of the State over beliefs and also highlighted the ambiguity of the official attitude towards Christians. It was the act of a nervous new ruler, and one worried by foreign invasions, the probability that usurpers would challenge and also the continued impact of outbreaks of plague.[27]

Defeat and Humiliation

Decius' reign lasted less than three years. He had probably already begun to mollify the decree for sacrifices before he was killed in 251 fighting barbarians on the Danubian frontier. The army chose Gallus, the senatorial governor of Moesia, as his successor. We know of at least one attempted usurpation in Syria, before the man Gallus had appointed to replace him in Moesia rebelled in 253. When the rival armies met, they did not fight a battle, but after a conference simply murdered Gallus and his son. The victor, Aemilianus, suffered the same fate within a matter of months. Valerian (fully, Publius Licinius Valerianus) was also a distinguished senator and promptly appointed his son as fellow Augustus. The father soon went to the eastern frontiers where a crisis had developed, leaving his son, Gallienus, to deal with problems in the west.[28]

Shapur had taken advantage of Rome's weakness to intervene in Armenia. At some point he seems to have arranged the assassination of the Armenian king. In 251 he launched a full invasion and drove out that man's successor, who sought sanctuary with the Romans. Shapur chose to take this as a breach of Philip's promise to give him a free hand in Armenia. As importantly, he knew that the Romans were busy fighting amongst themselves. In 252 he marched up the Euphrates and attacked Syria. A Roman army was defeated and Antioch itself captured, along with many smaller cities. However, the Persians never intended to stay. They plundered the cities, took captives and then returned home. Prisoners were an important objective for the Persian king, who settled them in communities deep within his territory where they could labour on large-scale irrigation and building projects. As the Persians pulled back, some minor victories were won by Roman troops and local militias, but really this was just a question of hastening the withdrawal.

The Persians were quiet again by the time Valerian arrived in Antioch in 255. He soon faced other problems from widespread raiding by fleets of Germanic pirates. As resources were shifted to deal with this, the frontier with Persia was once again weakened. Shapur launched a series of small attacks, aimed mainly at capturing border towns. Then in 260 the Persian king led another great invasion, striking first at Mesopotamia. Carrhae and Edessa were attacked. Valerian rushed with a large army to confront the enemy. Concentrating so many troops was dangerous, since it weakened defences elsewhere and, still worse, there had been several recent outbreaks of plague. Again, we do not know quite what happened. There may have been a battle or perhaps simply manoeuvring. What is certain is that Valerian and his senior officers were captured by the Persians, apparently in the middle of a parley. Shapur is shown holding the emperor by the wrist on several victory monuments. He claimed that the defeated Romans numbered 70,000 men, but we should be as sceptical about Persian claims of enemy numbers as we are about those made by the Romans. The Persians raided widely throughout Cappadocia, Syria and even Cilicia. Antioch probably fell for a second time.[29]

Dura Europos was already abandoned by the time Valerian was captured. It seems to have been briefly occupied by the Persians between 252 and 253 before it was retaken by the Romans. The latter were soon working to strengthen the fortifications by building a heavy earth bank behind the main wall, demolishing nearby houses in the process. A few years later the Persians attacked again. With the Euphrates to the east, deep wadis to the north and south, inevitably their main effort was made against the western wall. An initial assault on the main gate failed after heavy fighting which left many arrowheads embedded in the brickwork. The Persians then turned to engineering. Above ground they constructed a ramp that would allow a mobile siege tower or battering ram to be brought against the wall. Underground they dug tunnels to undermine the defences. In response, the Romans laboured to raise the height of the wall in front of the ramp, and also started working on counter-mines. Siege warfare was a battle of ingenuity and engineering skill as much as brute force.

The Persians had some success when one of their mines caused the collapse of a tower that was well placed to shoot at the men working on the ramp. However, soon after this success, the Romans struck back when their tunnels undermined the assault ramp and rendered it too weak to take the weight of a siege engine. Further along the wall Persian miners were already working on another tunnel, this time intended to bring down a tower and the adjacent wall and create a breach in the defences. The Romans guessed what they were up to and dug a mine that eventually broke into the enemy tunnel. Perhaps there was a vicious mêlée fought in the dark claustrophobic confines of the mines. Certainly, almost twenty Roman soldiers died there, along with one Persian, and their remains were found by the excavators. Recently another intriguing reconstruction has been put forward. This suggests that the Persians knew that the Roman raiders were coming and prepared a dreadful surprise, heating sulphur and pitch to give off noxious fumes. The layout of the tunnels meant that the draught carried this quickly into the Roman tunnel, asphyxiating the soldiers. Later, the Romans' bodies seem to have been heaped up into a makeshift barricade, to protect against other attacks, as the Persians prepared to burn the props and collapse the whole mine. Unknown to them, the equally nervous defenders were busy bricking it up at the other end in case the Persians should try to follow it into the city. Later, the Persians collapsed their main mine, but it did not have the intended result. A tower and parts of the wall sunk several feet into the ground, but did not collapse. We do not know how the Persians finally got into Dura Europos. The defenders may have surrendered, despairing of resisting another onslaught, short of food, or because there was no hope of relief. The Persians stayed for a little while, but then abandoned the city to the sands. It was probably too far forward for them to hold in the long term.[30]

5

Barbarians

'. . . wars are decided by courage rather than numbers. We have no mean force. Two thousand of us have gathered in all, and we have this deserted spot as a base from which to damage the enemy by attacking him in small groups and ambushing him. . . . Let our watchword in battle be our children and all that is dearest to us, and to save these let us set out together for the conflict, calling on the gods who watch over and aid us.' – The historian Dexippus' version of his rallying speech to the Athenians after the fall of their city to raiders in 267/8.[1]

In June 251 Emperor Decius attacked a group of barbarians who had crossed the Danube to plunder the Roman provinces. They were led by a chieftain named Cniva, and the emperor had been hunting them and other similar bands for more than a year. At the beginning of his reign he took the name Trajan, in memory of the conqueror of Dacia. Doubtless the idea was to promise new victories on the Danube, but so far there had been few enough. Trajan had been an experienced commander, with a powerful and disciplined army drawn from all over the empire. Both army and empire had been free of civil war for a generation. Decius was less fortunate, a good deal less talented and led forces far weaker than his namesake. Cniva had already beaten him in the previous summer. Afterwards, when Philippopolis in Thrace was besieged, Decius was either unable or unwilling to march to its relief. Abandoned to his fate, the commander of the city betrayed it to the enemy and promptly declared himself emperor. Other usurpers emerged at this time on the Rhine and in Rome itself. All were swiftly killed by loyal officers, but Decius knew that his prestige was at a low ebb. He needed a big victory.

Cniva was on his way home with the spoils of his raid when the emperor caught up with him near Abrittus – an insignificant settlement today near the border between Romania and Bulgaria. Most of the details of what then happened are now lost. There may have been one battle or a series of smaller skirmishes. Initial success turned to disaster when the Romans were ambushed in boggy terrain. Decius was killed, as was his son and co-emperor. One source claims that their horses became stuck in the mud and they were then killed by missiles.

We do not know how many soldiers fell with Decius and his son, although the accounts of the campaign do not suggest that either army was exceptionally big, probably numbering thousands rather than tens of thousands. Roman armies had been beaten by barbarian tribes in the past. Famously, Augustus had lost three legions and their auxiliaries – a force of perhaps 15,000–20,000 men – in an ambush in the Teutoberg Forest in AD 9. The losses were probably lighter at Abrittus, but it was the first time an emperor had been killed by a foreign enemy – and was made worse because his body was never found for proper burial. Ironically enough, the disaster occurred not far from Tropaeum Traiani, where Trajan had built a huge drum-shaped monument to commemorate his Dacian victory, as well as a memorial to honour the war dead.

Cniva's raid was just one of many to burst into the settled provinces of the empire during the middle decades of the third century. Regions that had been peaceful for generations – Gaul, Italy, Spain, Greece, Asia Minor and North Africa – fell prey to marauding bands from beyond the frontiers. Most of the raiders spoke a Germanic language, but the Germans were divided into many separate tribes and some wider groupings. Cniva was from a Gothic tribe, a people who had only fairly recently come into close contact with the Romans. By the end of the third century the Goths, along with other apparently new and powerful peoples like the Franks and Alamanni, posed serious threats to the frontiers on the Rhine and Danube. The balance of power seemed to have shifted profoundly.[2]

The Germans

Julius Caesar claimed that the Rhine marked the boundary between the Germans and Gauls, conveniently providing him with a 'natural' stopping point for his conquests. The restless, aggressive and very numerous Germans were always trying to push westwards into the rich lands of Gaul and beyond. Caesar portrayed the Germanic tribes as semi-nomadic and posing a threat to Rome's allies and even to Italy itself. He dealt with this 'threat' ruthlessly, but it is clear from his own account that the situation was a good deal more complicated than this. Some German tribes were already well established west of the Rhine and were incorporated into the new Roman provinces without difficulty. Caesar also recruited many German mercenaries from east of the Rhine to fight alongside his legions. From the very beginning, the Germans were a valuable source of military manpower as well as a threat.

Augustus tried to annex the lands from the Rhine to the Elbe, but his plan for a great German province died with the legionaries massacred in the Teutoberg Forest. Although Roman armies marched out to punish the tribes for this defeat, the project was never revived and the frontier settled on the Rhine. Neither this nor the Danube was a strict limit to Roman territory, for a strong military presence was maintained on the far banks. Near the end of the first century, the gap between the two rivers was linked by a fortified line, bringing a substantial area of territory, known as the Agri Decumates, under direct Roman rule. A little later, Trajan conquered Dacia, but this was the last major change to the frontier line in Europe for a century and a half. Along it was stationed over half of the entire Roman army – almost two-thirds if the garrison of Britain was included.[3]

To the east were tribal peoples, not all of them Germanic. On the Danube there were the Carpi, relatives of the Dacians who had escaped the conquest of that kingdom, and Sarmatians, originally nomads from the steppes who had moved to the Hungarian Plain. Another tribe, the Bastarnae, may or may not have been Germanic. Yet the overwhelming bulk of peoples who lived next to the frontier were Germans as far as Roman observers were concerned. However, it is doubtful that they saw themselves this way. Some tribes had relations of kinship and shared cults with their neighbours, but there seems to have been no real sense of 'German-ness'. Although their languages had similar roots, it is quite possible that people would have had trouble communicating with anyone from a distant tribe. The important ties were to a tribe, and perhaps even more to smaller groups of clan and family.[4]

Caesar describes the Germans as essentially pastoralists who did not till the soil. Even in his day this was a huge exaggeration. In some areas it does seem to have been common for villages to be simple and short-lived, the people moving on after a few years to a fresh site when they had exhausted the closest fields. Yet the overall picture from the Roman period is one of continuity and stability, and the creation of the static frontier line may well have encouraged this. Several excavated villages were occupied for three or four centuries. Most were small, but some consisted of a dozen or more – in one case thirty – sturdily built rectangular timber houses. The population of such a community most likely numbered a few hundred people. There were no towns comparable to those that had grown up in Gaul and parts of Germany in the Late

Iron Age. Instead the picture is of many villages and isolated farms.[5]

Some tribes had kings, but in the first century it was noted that war leaders were elected from a broader aristocracy. A chieftain's power was measured by the number of warriors he maintained in his personal following – his *comitatus*, to use the Latin word. These men were pledged to fight beside him in battle, and in return he feasted them and rewarded their valour with weapons and gold. Centuries later similar attitudes would be celebrated in poems like *Beowulf*. One powerful fourth-century king had 200 warriors in his band and similar numbers are suggested by spectacular collections of weapons excavated in Scandinavia. These were spoils taken from defeated enemies and then offered to the gods by the victors, who threw them in a sacred lake. At Illerup in Denmark weapons – spear and javelin heads, shield bosses and some swords – sufficient to equip some 300–350 men were dedicated sometime around the year 200. A century later enough weaponry for around 200 warriors was thrown into another Danish lake near Ejsbøl.

Finds like these confirm the impression given by the literary sources about the equipment used by Germanic warriors. Only a few were mounted and armour was rare. The majority of warriors employed a spear, a javelin for throwing and carried a shield for protection. A substantial minority also had swords – by the third century almost invariably Roman-made. More Roman swords have now been found outside the empire than within it and it is striking just how many turned up in the possession of tribal armies in Scandinavia, so far away from the frontier. Some had been captured in raids, but more were probably acquired through trade – much of it illicit – and perhaps in gifts to loyal chieftains.[6]

The semi-professional warriors who made up chieftains' warbands were not especially numerous. At times, larger armies could be formed when they were joined by all those free tribesmen able to equip themselves, but such forces could not stay in the field for long. Most inter-tribal warfare was small scale and mainly consisted of raiding. Occasionally the stakes and scale became higher. At the end of the first century Tacitus wrote gleefully of barbarian tribes wiping each other out without any Roman participation. With just a couple of hundred warriors in his band, a charismatic and successful chieftain could rise to dominate his tribe, and sometimes its neighbours as well, but his power was always precarious. Arminius, the man who had destroyed the legions in the Teutoberg Forest and resisted Roman attacks in the following years, came to lead a confederation including his own Cherusci and a number of other tribes. When the Roman threat receded he was murdered by his own chieftains because they feared he was aiming at permanent rule. Periodically, a chieftain would win great power amongst the tribes, but his status remained personal and tended to die with him. No one managed to establish more permanent authority that could be passed on to an heir.[7]

It was much easier for the Romans to deal with a few kings or chieftains than large numbers of individualistic tribesmen. From the beginning leaders perceived as friendly to Rome were supported with subsidies and even occasionally direct military aid. Many finds of ornate gold and silver vessels from beyond the frontiers are most likely to represent prestigious gifts given to such men. They were not the only ones to benefit from the arrival of the Romans. The new frontiers were very densely populated with crowded army bases and the settlements that inevitably grew up around them, as well as larger towns and cities. Tribesmen farming the lands beyond the frontier found a ready market for any surplus produce.[8]

Trade flourished. Grain and animals from east of the two rivers helped to feed the army and the civilians living on the frontiers. In turn the tribesmen had ready access to many luxury goods only available in quantity from the empire. It was a serious restriction when the Roman authorities barred any group from coming to market in the communities along the frontier and a great privilege to be readily admitted. There was also an impact on barbarian communities further away from the empire. We read of Roman merchants going to the Baltic to buy amber, which was prized as jewellery. Other trades – for instance, in fine furs – seem likely, but are harder to prove. A village discovered on one of the Danish islands shows how a community grew rich through trade, acting as a staging post for markets further afield in Scandinavia. There was also the slave trade, for once the Romans stopped fighting regular wars of expansion there were fewer war captives to be sold. Weapons become more common as grave goods for peoples in eastern and central Europe from around the time the Roman frontier was established. Probably this meant far more frequent predatory warfare, as chieftains raided their neighbours for slaves to sell to Roman merchants in exchange for luxuries.[9]

Chieftains profited most from the slave trade. This was probably also true of agriculture, simply because they were able to amass greater quantities of surplus grain than a single farmer. Already established leaders were also far more likely to attract Roman subsidies. Therefore, although many prospered through the long-term presence of the frontier zone, the impact of Rome also increased divisions within society. In excavated villages all of the houses tend to be of much the same size at the beginning of the Roman period. Later on, it was common for one to be substantially larger and perhaps also fenced off from the rest. Communities prospered through supplying the needs of the densely populated Roman frontier, but it is clear that some individuals benefited far more than others.[10]

Peaceful trade was the most common form of contact between Romans, both civilians and soldiers, living on the frontier and the peoples living beyond. Violent encounters were rarer, but that does not mean that they were less important. Raiding was endemic in most of the societies of Iron Age Europe. It was seen as entirely natural whenever the opportunity occurred and a neighbour seemed vulnerable. For chieftains, successful raids brought glory and the plunder with which to reward their warriors. Caesar noted that German tribes took pride in keeping a wide strip of depopulated land around their territory. This showed that they were a warlike people and so acted as a warning to potential attackers.[11]

The arrival of Rome may well have increased the frequency and perhaps the scale of warfare beyond the frontiers. Certainly, from the middle of the first century BC, weapons appear far more frequently as grave goods in Germanic burials. The new economic conditions meant that previously very rare items such as swords were now available in greater quantities. The slave trade encouraged raiding. Even more importantly, Roman subsidies allowed the chosen chieftains to support larger bands of warriors. This rise in their status and power was often resisted by rivals within the tribes. Competition for power amongst leaders was given a new edge and intensity. Wealth was not enough to guarantee long-term success. Some of the rulers Rome supported were killed by rivals and others fled across the frontier to a life of comfortable exile.[12]

Many tribesmen chose to join the Roman army, presumably viewing it in much the same way as joining the band of a chieftain from another tribe. Some chieftains also took service with Rome, bringing with them the warriors of their household. Raiding the Roman provinces was also a tempting prospect. Although it was more dangerous than attacking another tribe, there was the possibility of far more plunder and glory. Most raids were probably small scale, but if these proved successful then they invited bigger attacks. An inscription from Commodus' reign records the construction of small outpost forts along the Danube to stop 'secret crossings of the river by bandits'.[13] The pattern had been the same on many of Rome's frontiers since the Republic – when the provinces were seen as vulnerable they were liable to be attacked. The size and apparent readiness of the frontier garrison acted as deterrents, but if Roman strength was seen to be an illusion, then it took hard campaigning to restore Rome's position.[14]

It was difficult to catch every band of swift-moving raiders – although easier when they withdrew burdened down with booty – and often the Roman response would be a punitive expedition against those held responsible. Villages were burned, crops destroyed, herds driven off and the people either massacred or enslaved. The aim was short term, to instil fear, but such ruthlessness also sowed the seeds of future hatred. Diplomacy aimed to keep peace more permanently, and tribal leaders were threatened or bribed to refrain from hostilities. The communities closest to the frontiers were generally more inclined to be peaceful, since to them the Romans were a valuable market. As importantly, they were also easily within reach of Roman retribution. Leaders and peoples further afield were harder to control. Maintaining Roman dominance on the frontiers was an on-going task, influenced by the shifting politics of the tribes, as well as events in other parts of the empire.

Frontiers in Crisis

In the middle decades of the third century the frontier defences on the Rhine and Danube proved utterly inadequate as successive bands of raiders broke through into the unprotected provinces beyond. Almost every scholar sees this as a sign that the threat from outside had become greater. Most connect this with the appearance of new confederations of tribes, seen as far more dangerous than the Germanic peoples who had lived next to the frontier in the first century. Opinion has divided between those who saw the confederations as new arrivals and others who believed that they evolved from the already existing tribal groups. These days, archaeologists are far less inclined to resort to migrations to explain cultural change, so that most accept the latter view. Even so, the evidence does suggest that the Goths moved from the Baltic coast to the region of the Black Sea and southern Danube between the first century and the start of the third. They were not a single united people, but a loose grouping of distinct tribes speaking a related language and with many cultural similarities. The same was also true of the Franks, who appear on the Rhineland, and the Alamanni, who emerge to the south of them. Both Franks and Alamanni were certainly important groups by the end of the third century, but it is much harder to say when they first appeared.[15]

The tough wars fought by Marcus Aurelius against the Marcomanni and Quadi are generally portrayed as the first warning signs of this shift in German society. The threat from the barbarians was now greater and it revealed fundamental weaknesses in the defences of the Roman frontiers. The army was dispersed around the perimeter of the empire, so that once an enemy broke through there was no central reserve to cope with it. Furthermore, the difficulties encountered in dealing with barbarian attacks on the Danube so soon after the invasion of Parthia are seen as indications that the Romans had great difficulty fighting two major wars in quick succession.

All of this is dubious. The Marcomanni had been seen as a major threat by Augustus when they and neighbouring tribes had united under a strong king. It may well be that one or more similarly charismatic leaders had appeared amongst them again. A similar pattern is observable with the Dacians, who were perceived as a great threat in Julius Caesar's time, but then disappear until the later first century when another strong king emerged. It is true that during the Marcomannic Wars one raiding army got as far as Italy, but this was never repeated. A rather more important factor in the weakness of Rome's defences at this time was not the slow return of troops from the eastern war, but rather the plague that came with them. The impact of this on the army was not simply a question of the men who died, although sources do suggest that there were very many of these in the crowded barracks. As important were the many who must have fallen sick and the extreme difficulty of carrying on normal training in the midst of an epidemic. Some attacks penetrated the frontiers and, as usual, their success encouraged other chieftains to emulate them. The Roman army was in a poor state and struggled to deal with the problem. Yet in time it did so, although at the cost of a great effort and considerable resources. No territory was lost, and there was even talk of creating new provinces.[16]

There is no record of major fighting along this frontier for well over a generation after the end of these wars. Caracalla spent some time on the Rhine, and Alexander was there when he was murdered. Maximinus spent much of his reign campaigning there and on the Danubian frontier, but also recruited large numbers of German warriors to strengthen his army when he marched on Italy in 238. Soon afterwards Goths and Carpi launched raids across the Danube. For a while the former were bribed to keep the peace, but this payment was stopped either under Gordian or

Philip. Predictably, this provoked a renewed burst of raiding from 243 onwards. Philip had to go in person to the region to restore the situation. In 248 the Quadi and Sarmatian Iazyges – familiar names from Marcus Aurelius' campaigns – attacked Pannonia, and their success encouraged a renewed onslaught from the Goths. Decius was sent to deal with the problem and instead made himself emperor. He soon had to return to the Danube, fighting the campaigns that eventually led to his death at Abrittus.[17]

The new emperor Gallus bought the Goths off, promising them an annual subsidy and allowing them to withdraw, taking their plunder and captives with them. He was far more worried about internal rivals and hastened to Italy. In 253 the man he left as governor of Moesia, Aemilianus, seems to have attacked some Goths and won a victory. The success prompted him to lead off another great chunk of the frontier army in a bid for the throne. Both Gallus and Aemilianus were dead within a matter of months, but the weakness of the frontier defences prompted a new surge of raiding. Cniva's band of Goths were again involved and may have been one of the groups that reached as far as Macedonia.[18]

Around the same time a new threat emerged from the Black Sea. Several groups, including a people called the Borani and several Gothic tribes, began to launch plundering expeditions by sea. At first the targets were local, mainly the few remaining Greco-Roman communities along the northern coast of the Black Sea. By 255 some raiders even harassed the northern coast of Asia Minor. The next year they returned in far greater numbers. The situation was so serious that Valerian had to go to the area, permitting Shapur's Persians to strike at a weakened frontier.[19]

In the meantime there had been more attacks on the European frontiers, on the Danube and southern Rhine. In 254 some Marcomanni reached Ravenna, and in 260 raiders from another tribe again broke into Italy. They were checked by Gallienus near Milan and some of them were defeated on their way home. Recently, an inscription was found at the city of Augusta Vindelicum (modern Augsburg) in Raetia thanking the goddess Victory for this success. It tells of 'the barbarian peoples Semnones or Iuthungi killed or routed on the 24th and 25th April by the troops of the province of Raetia and from Germany and also local militia', and 'the rescue of many thousands of Italian prisoners'. This party of raiders – it is interesting that even the Roman victors seemed uncertain just who they were – had got close to the Rhine before being defeated. A spectacular find of wagons loaded with gold and other valuables

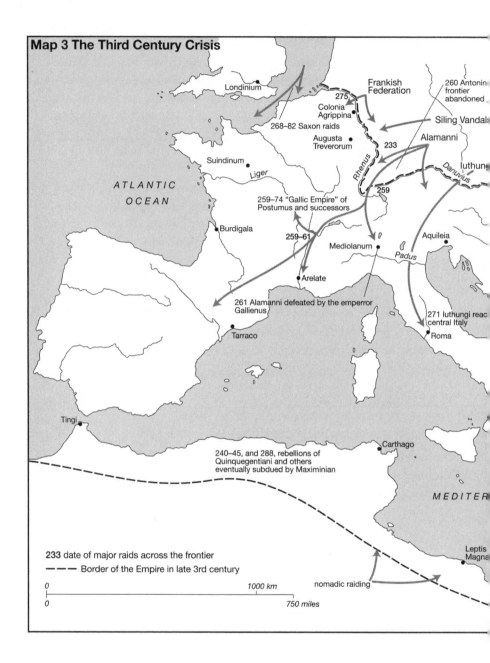

Map 3 The Third Century Crisis

ATLANTIC
OCEAN

Londinium

Frankish
Federation

260 Antonin
frontier
abandoned

275

Colonia
Agrippina

Siling Vandal

268–82 Saxon raids

Augusta
Treverorum

Alamanni

233

Suindinum

Liger

Rhenus

Danuvius

Iuthung

259–74 "Gallic Empire" of
Postumus and successors

259

Burdigala

259–61

Aquileia

Mediolanum

Padus

261 Alamanni defeated by the emperror
Gallienus

Arelate

271 Iuthungi reac
central Italy

Tarraco

Roma

Tingi

240–45, and 288, rebellions of
Quinquegentiani and others
eventually subdued by Maximinian

Carthago

MEDITER

233 date of major raids across the frontier

Leptis
Magna

- - - Border of the Empire in late 3rd century

nomadic raiding

0 ──────────────── 1000 km

0 ──────────────────────── 750 miles

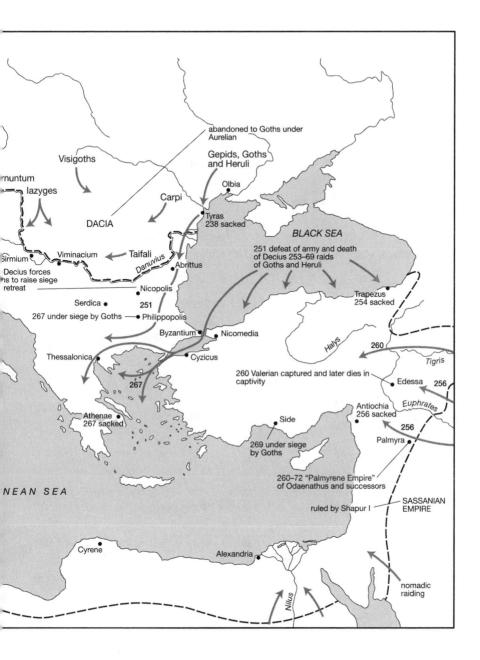

abandoned to Goths under
Aurelian

Visigoths

Gepids, Goths
and Heruli

Olbia

rnuntum

Iazyges

Carpi

Tyras
238 sacked

BLACK SEA

DACIA

251 defeat of army and death
of Decius 253–69 raids
of Goths and Heruli

Sirmium

Viminacium

Taifali

Danuvius

Abrittus

Decius forces
hs to raise siege
retreat

Nicopolis

Trapezus
254 sacked

Serdica

251

267 under siege by Goths

Philippopolis

Halys

260

Byzantium

Nicomedia

Tigris

Thessalonica

Cyzicus

260 Valerian captured and later dies in
captivity

Edessa

256

267

Euphrates

Antiochia
256 sacked

256

Athenae
267 sacked

Side

Palmyra

269 under siege
by Goths

260–72 "Palmyrene Empire"
of Odaenathus and successors

NEAN SEA

SASSANIAN
EMPIRE

ruled by Shapur I

Cyrene

Alexandria

Nilus

nomadic
raiding

dumped in the river itself later in the third century almost certainly represents abandoned plunder.[20]

Some raiding bands were caught and defeated, even if only during their return home, but as many or more were successful. The Roman provinces seemed vulnerable and so inevitably further attacks came. A little later some Germans – in later sources they are said to have been Franks, but this may be an anachronism – marauded through Gaul and into Spain, sacking the city of Tarraco (modern Tarragona). More than a century later a local historian claimed that the scars of this attack were still visible, although no significant trace has been found in archaeology on the site.[21]

In 267 there was a new wave of seaborne attacks from the Black Sea, which spread devastation all along the shores of Greece and Asia Minor. One source claims that the warriors, who included Goths as well as other tribes such as the Heruli, numbered no fewer than 320,000 men sailing in 6,000 boats. The figures are wildly exaggerated, but are an indication of the panic caused by fast-moving attackers who could strike at widely separated targets in a short time. In a later age the Vikings would provoke similar terror. One group attacked Ephesus and burned the great Temple of Artemis, one of the seven wonders of the world. Athens was sacked by a band of Heruli, whose retreat was harassed by Athenians led by a local aristocrat, P. Herennius Dexippus. Sadly the history he wrote of these wars only survives in fragments.[22]

It is difficult to measure the amount of damage done during these raids from the archaeological evidence. Some sites, particularly those along the Rhine frontier, have revealed layers of burning and destruction. Yet it is not always clear whether this was the result of warfare or accident. Dating such a layer can be equally problematic, and often in the past they have been too readily assumed to have resulted from one of the recorded raids. There are also problems in understanding the very large rise in the number of coin hoards buried during the second half of the third century. Some almost certainly were hidden by people afraid of barbarian attack, who were subsequently killed, taken captive or otherwise unable to recover their treasure. Yet there may have been other reasons for hiding money at a time when the quality of coinage was varying hugely, as silver coins in particular contained higher and higher proportions of base metals. Some hoards may simply not have been worth the trouble of recovering.[23]

The impact of a raid can only have been dreadful for those communities and individuals actually attacked. Hardly any cities within the empire possessed modern fortifications. Athens made some effort to repair its ancient walls after the first incursions into Macedonia, but this was clearly not enough to stop the Heruli. Most cities were unwalled and scarcely any had a garrison to man whatever defences they did possess. They were vulnerable, and the news of attacks on other communities can only have increased nervousness. The provinces nearest to the Rhine and Danubian frontiers inevitably suffered the worst. This was especially true of cities and villages along the main communication routes, which were likely to be attacked more often. Northern Gaul suffered a good deal. Many villa farms and small settlements appear to vanish in the second half of the third century, although as usual we are dealing with only a small sample even of the known sites.

By the end of the third century every sizeable city within the empire had acquired a wall. There was no standard pattern, but almost all were very thick and strengthened by towers that projected out from them and so allowed defenders to throw or shoot missiles into the flanks of any attackers. In larger cities these towers were often designed to house artillery. Occasionally the defences looked stronger than they actually were, but the aim was clearly to deter any attack. Almost all of these new walls enclosed an area smaller than the full extent of the city in earlier centuries. Many cities in Gaul shrank dramatically in size, and presumably their populations had fallen as well. Amiens seems to have been attacked several times and in the second half of the third century became much reduced in size. After the sack by the Heruli, the Athenians built a new wall cutting through the old marketplace and excluding a number of great monuments. Much of the stone used was taken from older buildings that had presumably fallen into ruin or were now deliberately demolished. This plundering of old monuments for material to construct new defences was common in many cities.[24]

It was not just urban communities who fortified themselves, for the same inclination is visible in rural areas. The grander villas had often been built with towers, but these were essentially ornamental, increasing the visible presence of a great house and also providing an impressive view. In parts of North Africa during the second century some villas had already taken a more defensive form as a response to the threat from bandits and raiders. Now this became more common in other areas close to exposed frontiers. In Gaul before the arrival of Rome it had been common for settlements to be placed on hilltops. Roman peace brought a move down into the plains as communities grew in size and had no fear of enemy attack. In the later third century the trend was reversed and more and more walled villages appear on high ground as places of refuge during attacks.

The Gallic Empire

The Roman doctrine had always been that the best way of dealing with attacks was to defeat the enemy in open warfare. Ideally, the army presented a façade of overwhelming strength so that potential enemies were deterred from aggression. Every defeat weakened this impression, as did the frequent withdrawal of troops from the frontiers to fight each other in civil wars. Valerian's capture by the Persians was another humiliation at a time when there were already plenty of cracks in the façade. His son Gallienus was later vilified in most of our sources as indolent and far too fond of the luxuries of life in Rome. This was more than a little unfair, as he spent a good deal of time on campaign on the frontiers in Europe. In 268 he was in Greece chasing the bands that had plundered Athens and many of the other famous cities of the classical past. He is said to have won a victory, but the terms extended to the defeated Goths were very generous. Their king was taken into Roman service and given senatorial rank. Gossips also declared that the emperor was infatuated with a Gothic princess whom he took as a mistress.[25]

Soon after his father's defeat, Gallienus lost real control over many of the western provinces as usurpers emerged. In 260 the governor of Germania Inferior, Postumus (fully, Marcus Cassianus Latinius Postumus) declared himself emperor. He had already arranged the murder of Gallienus' infant son and the latter's guardian who had been left in overall charge on the Rhine. Both the German provinces and all of Gaul soon rallied to Postumus, who may well have come from the Gaulish aristocracy. In time they were joined by Britain and much of Spain. Almost uniquely amongst usurpers who lasted for any length of time, Postumus made no effort to march to Italy and defeat Gallienus. Instead, he was content to remain on the defensive, fighting against Roman rivals only when they attacked him. Gallienus' armies were driven back twice. In 269 a challenger emerged in Mainz. Within a few months Postumus had defeated him, but his refusal to let his troops plunder the city led to his murder. The man the army appointed as emperor lasted twelve weeks before he too was killed. His successor Victorinus remained in power for the best part of two years, his murder allegedly being caused by an attempt to seduce one of his officers' wives.

Historians conventionally refer to this regime as the Gallic Empire.

There is no historical basis for this, although one fourth-century historian does talk of Postumus 'assuming power over the Gallic provinces'. As far as he and his successors were concerned they were the legitimate emperors of the whole empire. Consuls for each year were appointed – ignoring the fact that Gallienus continued to appoint them in Rome as well. It is uncertain whether a second Senate was formed. Aristocrats from Gaul filled many of the jobs in the imperial service, but this had more to do with the fact that it was difficult to draw men from further afield and provinces that did not acknowledge these emperors. Culturally, there was nothing particularly Gallic or 'western' about the new regime. The titles and iconography – and also the law – employed by these emperors were entirely conventional. The only unusual thing was their reluctance to seek control of the remaining provinces of the empire.[26]

For much of his reign, Gallienus' rule extended over only Egypt, North Africa, the southernmost parts of Spain, Italy and the provinces behind the Danube. He is counted as the legitimate emperor because he came to power before his various rivals, and ultimately it was the men who succeeded him who would reunite the empire. Rather large claims have been made about his achievements, but these are based on hindsight and tend to ignore the peculiar conditions of his reign. One is a question of strategy. Defeats on all the frontiers are supposed to have shown the need for a central strategic reserve, which could move to confront any enemy who broke through the outer perimeter. Gallienus kept an important part of his army in or near Milan. Coins attest the presence of detachments from at least thirteen different legions – several of them whose parent unit was stationed in provinces no longer loyal to Gallienus. Especially prominent are the cavalry, who seem to have been grouped together under their own distinct commander. Septimius Severus had greatly increased the troops at his immediate disposal by raising *II Parthica* and augmenting the guard. Now, Gallienus had taken this much further by forming a complete army as his reserve and placing a new emphasis on the importance of mounted troops.

None of this makes much sense. We have no real idea of the numbers of troops involved or the proportion of cavalry to give an indication of how revolutionary this force may have been. Cavalry are faster than infantry over short distances, but on longer marches the advantage markedly decreases. Horses are also a lot more difficult to feed and keep in good condition than men. The idea of using a cavalry force as a mobile reserve only makes practical sense if the forces involved were relatively small. Also, northern Italy may at first sight seem like the heart of the empire, but for Gallienus, Milan was actually only just behind the frontier with the 'Gallic Empire'. The circumstances were exceptional, but the deployment of these troops, and as far as we can tell their actual use on campaign, was entirely conventional.[27]

Gallienus' reign was long by the standards of the period, but his ultimate fate was reminiscent of many other usurpers whose power was briefer. In 268 the commander of his cavalry – we do not know the precise title and it may simply have been a senior rank commanding both horse and foot – rebelled against him. Gallienus came back from Greece to attack him, and after a victory in the field began to besiege the usurper in Milan itself. However, he had clearly alienated his other officers and these conspired to murder him. A false alarm was sounded and when the emperor rushed out of his tent to deal with the supposed enemy attack, he was stabbed to death.[28]

Gallienus was about fifty when he was killed. His successor Claudius II (fully, Marcus Aurelius Claudius) was a few years older and was an equestrian from one of the Balkan provinces. It is difficult to know how far he was involved in the conspiracy, but it is clear that a number of officers from this same region formed a powerful group in this period. The usurper in Milan was swiftly dealt with, and then Claudius spent the next two years fighting against barbarian raiders, first in Italy and then in the Balkans. In 269 he won a victory over the Goths and took the names Gothicus and Maximus in celebration. Early in the next year he was one of the victims of an outbreak of plague, achieving the distinction of being the first emperor to die of natural causes since Septimius Severus. His brother Quintillus was proclaimed emperor, but a few months later faced a challenge by one of the senior generals, Aurelian (fully, Lucius Domitius Aurelianus). When the rival armies moved to confront each other, Quintillus' men quickly decided to change sides. He either was killed or committed suicide when he realised what was happening.[29]

Aurelian was another equestrian from Illyria and had been heavily involved in the plot against Gallienus. He was a tough and experienced commander who within five years had reunited the empire. Occupied first on the frontiers and then dealing with the disorder in the eastern provinces, in 274 Aurelian attacked the 'Gallic Empire'. Victorinus' successor Tetricus seems to have had little enthusiasm for the struggle and had serious problems maintaining the loyalty of his own troops. It is even claimed that he betrayed them, sending them out to fight in a hopeless position against Aurelian. Tetricus himself surrendered.

TOP LEFT: The philosopher emperor Marcus Aurelius ruled over the Roman Empire at its height. A serious man who tried to rule well, he was faced by bitter warfare and years of dreadful plague.

TOP RIGHT: Septimius Severus won power by defeating three rivals in four years of civil war. His advice to his sons was pragmatic – 'enrich the soldiers, and despise everyone else.'

ABOVE LEFT: Severus' older son was nicknamed Caracalla after the style of Gallic cloak he regularly wore. A brutal man who disliked the Senate, he was murdered by the commander of his own guard.

ABOVE RIGHT: Diocletian chose to rule with three imperial colleagues and their unity was symbolised by this statue group from Venice. These late third century emperors wear military uniform and have abandoned the philosopher's hairstyle and beard of Marcus Aurelius.

ABOVE: The massive scale of the amphitheatre at Dougga in Tunisia emphasizes the prosperity of many provinces of the Roman Empire. Huge amounts of money were lavished on public entertainments and other leisure activities.

LEFT: This tombstone from near Hadrian's Wall illustrates the mixing of cultures and population under Roman rule. It commemorates Regina, the British wife of a man from Palmyra on the Euphrates. She is shown dressed in the finery of a Roman matron.

RIGHT: Trajan's Column was erected early in the second century to commemorate the emperor's conquest of Dacia, in what is now Romania. A range of different types of soldiers are shown here, including legionaries in the famous segmented armour.

TOP: The Persian King Shapur I celebrated his victories over the Romans on a number of monuments. Here what is supposed to be the Emperor Valerian cowers before Shapur's charger, while the Persian king holds the Emperor Philip by the wrist.

ABOVE: In this wall painting from Dura Europos, the officers of one of the units of the Roman garrison parade to perform a sacrifice. The cohort was commanded by the Tribune Julius Terentius.

TOP: The city of Dura Europos on the Euphrates fell to the Persians after a long siege. This section of its curtain wall was undermined by a Persian tunnel, but failed to collapse completely and create a breach.

ABOVE: Palmyra was an oasis city on one of the major trade routes into the Roman Empire, and for a while under Odaenathus and his wife Zenobia it became a major force. Its wealth was expressed in grand buildings and high quality artwork, such as this statue of the city's three main deities.

Hadrian's Wall is one of the most spectacular Roman frontiers still visible today. Most provincial frontiers lay along rivers, and wall systems were more rare. In all cases the frontiers were not supposed to be boundaries to the Romans, but only to their enemies.

The Roman fort at Porchester near Portsmouth in Britain was built in the third century. Its walls are typical of the period in that they are high and strengthened by projecting towers.

The late third century fort at Qasr Bsheir in modern day Jordan is typical of most Roman bases from this period in that it is small in size, but with a more substantial wall than was common in earlier periods. It contains stabling for sixty-nine mounts and it is likely that many Roman forts housed relatively small units.

TOP: Most of the remains visible today in Rome's Forum were built in Late Antiquity. On the right is the Senate House, constructed by Diocletian. To the left is the Arch of Septimius Severus, commemorating his Parthian campaign rather than his victories over fellow Romans.

ABOVE: Most cities acquired strong defences during the third century and Rome was no exception. Its walls were built by Aurelian on a massive scale: Rome still had huge symbolic importance even if the centres of power had moved elsewhere.

Unusually, he was spared by the victor and even appointed to an administrative post in Italy. Similarly, many men who had held office in the army and administration within the 'Gallic Empire' continued their careers in imperial service afterwards. None of the Gallic emperors had their names formally damned and wiped from the record.[30]

The Barbarian Hordes

It is possible that in the third century some stretches of the empire's frontiers faced an increased threat from the peoples who lived outside. The very existence of the empire, as well as its diplomacy, encouraged the rise of powerful leaders within the tribes. There may have been other factors, too. The archaeological record suggests that the population may have been rising amongst the tribes beyond the Rhine and Danube at this time. It is possible that there were also problems caused by climate change and the exhaustion of soils through farming, although as yet there is not enough evidence to understand this in detail. Sea levels on parts of the North Sea coast do appear to have been rising, so that some parts of the coastline were flooded and in other places the soil became too salty to cultivate.[31]

The scale of the threat to the frontiers had always fluctuated, but the biggest difference between this and earlier periods was the frequency of civil war within the empire. Troops were drawn off from the frontiers time and again to support the ambitions of their commanders. With so many changes in the senior ranks of the army – presumably often followed by considerable alterations at lower levels – it can only have been difficult for the army to train properly. The frontiers were thus weakened. It became easier to mount a successful raid, and each success only encouraged more attacks. It is notable that emperors and usurpers alike invariably saw foreign enemies as less of a threat than internal rivals. Time and again they settled with foreign attackers – including the Persians – or granted them generous peace terms so that they could deal with a challenge for the throne.

There was another side to civil wars. When one Roman army met another in battle it could not count on any superiority in discipline, tactics or equipment. This made numbers crucial, but it was difficult to raise and train new soldiers quickly. Frequent warfare also thinned the ranks of the regular troops and disrupted normal recruitment and training. Hiring the services of a barbarian chieftain and his followers was an attractive option chosen by many Roman leaders. These warriors might lack the discipline of professional Roman troops, but they were certainly more effective than hastily raised conscripts or volunteers. Yet when their Roman paymaster was beaten or murdered, such contingents could not be sure of welcome and employment from the next emperor. It is more than likely that some of the groups to maraud through the provinces had initially been invited into the empire. The desire of Roman leaders to recruit warriors in this way was another factor encouraging the emergence of powerful chieftains. These men were even more dependent on continuous warfare than was normally the case for leaders amongst the tribes. If they were no longer able to find a Roman willing to pay them, then the only other options were fighting against other tribes or attacking the empire. Even usually peaceful farming communities may have found trade disrupted so badly by civil wars that raiding became an attractive alternative. Others no doubt found themselves under attack by emperors keen for quick and clean glory won over foreign enemies and not other Romans.

The victims of a marauding band are unlikely to have been too concerned over the reasons that had prompted the warriors to go on the warpath. The local impact of a raid could be appalling, especially if other raids came in subsequent years. It was probably not much worse to be caught up in a civil war, since even fortifications were not always enough to hold back a Roman army. Civil war and barbarian invasion alike smashed communities and ruined livelihoods, adding to the ranks of the desperate and hopeless. The barbarians who swept across the Black Sea were said to have learned how to make boats and then sail them from the survivors of the cities they had overrun. It is clear that many army deserters and runaway slaves joined the raiding bands, while others set up as bandits on their own. The Marcomannic Wars had been followed by a so-called 'Deserters War' in Gaul, and in the third century there were similar outbreaks of violence.[32]

Some areas – parts of North Africa, southern Italy, Sicily and most of Spain – escaped harm during these disturbed decades and other regions were only lightly touched. Gallia Belgica, the region nearest to the Rhine, suffered badly in spite of the best efforts of the Gallic emperors. Most Roman outposts on the far bank of the river were permanently abandoned and so was the Agri Decumates, the patch of land between the Rhine and Danube. Several forts along the frontier in this area show signs of violent destruction. At the auxiliary fort in Pfünz in Raetia three human jawbones were found inside its south-east tower. The nineteenth-century excavator guessed that these were the remains of sentries. It looked very much as if the soldiers had been taken by surprise, for they did not have their shields – traces of the bindings of these were found outside. If anything, the finds at the fort at Niederbieder in Upper Germany were even more dramatic. The skeleton of a soldier still wearing his hob-nailed army boots was found in the headquarters.

Such finds indicate the difficulty of interpreting some of the archaeological evidence for this period – particularly when it was acquired in early excavations using unsophisticated techniques. These military bases were clearly destroyed by enemy action, but it is harder to identify that enemy. The original excavators assumed that the attackers were Germanic tribesmen. More recently it has been suggested that they were other Roman soldiers, hence the degree of surprise at Pfünz. At Niederbieder a crushed plaque decorated with the head of a youthful emperor was found in the remains of the headquarters building. The young Caesar has been identified as the son of Gallienus who was killed early on in Postumus' rebellion. Hence the garrison may have been attacked because it stayed loyal to the old regime. These interpretations are attractive, but remain conjectural. In the end, we do not know who stormed these bases. It may have been Roman soldiers or barbarian warriors, and if the latter then these could equally have been acting for themselves or as mercenaries and allies hired by one faction in a Roman civil war.

The archaeology does not suggest that the Romans were ejected by a barbarian onslaught from these frontier regions. In time tribes settled in the area, but it does seem to have been a slow and cautious process. After the initial struggles, the Agri Decumates effectively fell in the border region between the territory controlled by Gallienus and the regions loyal to the Gallic emperors. It may have made sense for each side to fall back on the line of the Rhine and Danube, respectively, in case the other attacked. Yet, whatever the cause for abandoning the advanced frontier line and the territory behind it, it is clear that the Romans were either unable or unwilling to reoccupy this region after the Gallic emperors had been defeated and some stability returned to the empire.[33]

On the Danube the situation was similar and there was an even greater loss. Dacia was one of the more recent additions to the empire, but it was rich in mineral resources and for a century and a half had been extremely prosperous. Although it lay beyond the Danube, the natural barrier of the Carpathians protected much of the province from attack. During Marcus Aurelius' wars it had suffered a number of Sarmatian raids, but its major cities had been provided with walls from the beginning and damage was limited to the structures outside. The bulk of the raiding in the third century bypassed the province, yet there are signs of serious problems. From the middle of the century the archaeological record suggests a huge drop in the circulation of coinage. The provincial mint shut down and virtually no new coins seem to have been brought in from outside. Perhaps this was a sign of much of its legionary garrison being posted elsewhere. There is no trace of the auxiliary units moving anywhere else, they just seem to vanish from the record. Government control seems simply to have stopped, perhaps through lack of funds. Aurelian formally abandoned the province, although a new Dacian province was formed west of the Danube. Some of the population from the real Dacia may have moved there or elsewhere within the empire. Others remained behind. There was no rapid inrush of barbarians and for a while a form of Roman lifestyle seems to have continued, perhaps for some time. At the old provincial capital Sarmizegethusa, someone was able to convert the amphitheatre into a defensive redoubt sometime in the fourth century.[34]

6

The Queen and the 'Necessary' Emperor

Zenobia 'was accustomed to hardship, and many even thought her braver than her husband, for she was the noblest of all women of the east and ... the most beautiful.'

'So died Aurelian, an emperor who was necessary rather than good.' – *Anonymous author of the* Historiae Augustae, *fourth century.*[1]

On the monuments commemorating his victory, King Shapur grasps Valerian by the wrist. Envoys were sent to the Roman's senior subordinate, Macrianus, but he refused even to discuss ransoming the captive. Valerian's son and co-ruler Gallienus was far away and never had the ability – and perhaps even the desire – to buy back or rescue his father. Valerian lived out the remainder of his life as a prisoner. Shapur was supposed to have employed him as a mounting block, stepping on the crouching Roman as he climbed on to his horse. One fourth-century source claims that when the emperor died, the Persians flayed his skin, painted it red and then hung it up in a temple as a trophy. The author was a Christian and his book recorded the grisly ends of all those responsible for persecuting the Church – something that Valerian had renewed – so perhaps he let his imagination run away with him. However, he did claim that the trophy was seen by Roman ambassadors in later years.[2]

Shapur had won a great victory. City after city fell and was plundered. In time, the Persian army divided into smaller groups, and some began to make their way home with their spoils and captives. Simultaneously, the Romans started to recover and counter-attacked, winning a few skirmishes. Macrianus exploited these minor successes to declare his two sons joint-emperors – he was lame, so felt himself disqualified from such a public role. Taking his older boy and a large part of the army, he crossed into Europe and marched on Italy. They were destroyed by forces loyal to Gallienus in 261.[3]

The other main leader of the Roman recovery in the east was Septimius Odaenathus, and he stayed loyal to Gallienus. A Palmyrene nobleman – probably the third generation of his family to be Roman citizens – he had come to dominate his home city. He also pursued a career in imperial service, seems to have gained senatorial rank and may well have been governor of one of the Syrian provinces. Perhaps he was still in this office when he led troops against the Persians, although it is equally possible that he acted without formal power and simply as a prominent local man. His loyalties may not always have been clear, and one source claims that he sought friendship with Shapur. Scornfully rejected, Odaenathus won a series of victories over the Persians, hastening their retreat. With the invaders gone, he next suppressed Macrianus' younger son.[4]

Odaenathus was not content merely to expel the Persians from the Roman provinces, and in 262 he led a major offensive that got as far as Ctesiphon. This and a second expedition – probably in 266 – were no more than large-scale raids, but they helped to restore Roman prestige. Shapur remained on the defensive for the rest of his reign – he had already won enough victories to secure his hold on the throne. Gallienus granted Odaenathus a number of honours, and the titles of *dux* (a senior rank and the origin of the medieval 'duke') and 'commander of the entire east' (*corrector totius orientis*), which probably gave him authority over individual provincial governors. Odaenathus had already styled himself 'lord' of his home city of Palmyra. Now he aped the Persian monarch and was named 'king of kings'.[5]

In spite of the grandeur of such titles, Odaenathus never claimed imperial status. He guarded the frontier with Persia and put down any challenge to Gallienus, but, rather like the leaders of the 'Gallic Empire', he made no attempt to expand the territory under his control. For six years he was effectively in control of much of the eastern part of the empire. As far as we can tell he seems to have governed competently – certainly, virtually all of our sources are favourable to him. Even so, he and his eldest son Herodes were murdered in 267 by one of his cousins. It was said that the dispute began with a squabble over precedence during a hunt – Odaenathus, like many other aristocrats, was a very keen hunter. Perhaps there was no more to it than a relative's anger over a public humiliation, but then and later some people have suspected a deeper, more political conspiracy.

Whatever the truth of the matter, its sequel is not in doubt. Power now passed nominally to Odaenathus' younger son Vaballathus, but since he was only a child, effective control lay with his mother, Zenobia. She was Odaenathus' second wife, and the fact that the murdered

Herodes was the product of an earlier marriage added to the rumours of a palace conspiracy. Vaballathus was styled 'king of kings' and 'commander of the entire east'. These were exceptional times and Odaenathus had had an exceptional career, holding power over such a wide area for a long period. His local connections had added to his prestige, but ultimately he had been a Roman official holding rank granted to him by the emperor – even if in truth Gallienus may have had little choice in the matter. This was an appointment, and there was absolutely no precedent within the Roman system for such a rank to be passed on to an heir, or indeed held by any child. For the moment it was tolerated – Gallienus had other, more immediate, priorities, as did his successor Claudius II – and so for the next few years a woman controlled the greater part of the eastern empire.[6]

The Queen of Palmyra

Palmyra – Tadmor in its people's own Aramaic tongue – grew rich through trade, but it existed in the first place because of water. Its springs and wells were rare things in the Syrian desert and its Latin name probably meant the 'place of palm trees'. Early in the first century it was brought under Roman control, but the trade links with Parthia remained strong. Rome's empire demanded luxuries from the east in ever greater quantities and Palmyra became a vital staging point for the great caravans that crossed the deserts. Camels figure prominently in Palmyrene art, reflecting their importance in making the desert crossings. Virtually all the trade came via the Euphrates. Some caravans stopped at Dura Europos, about 130 miles away, where the river was closest, but ultimately most went further down the Euphrates, to the trading ports lower down or even to the Gulf itself. Inscriptions record Palmyrene merchants who sailed from there to India. Others provide more detail about how the caravans were organised and protected, for the high value of the spices and other luxuries they carried were a temptation to attacks from raiders.[7]

In Odaenathus' day, Palmyra was a large and magnificent city, and its romantic desert ruins created something of a sensation when they were discovered by Europeans in the middle of the eighteenth century. Its greatest monument was the first-century Temple of Bel, displaying a mixture of Roman, Greek and local styles in its design. In time the city acquired most of the grand buildings of a Greco-Roman city, with the exception of the quintessentially Roman bath house and amphitheatre, or the equally Greek gymnasium, none of which obviously had much appeal to local tastes. A range of languages was in daily use and a high proportion of monumental inscriptions were bilingual, most often in Greek as well as Palmyrene. Latin seems always to have been fairly rare, even after the city gained the status of a Roman town under Hadrian. As traders, Palmyrenes spread widely. There were many in Rome – and we have already encountered Barates, who left a memorial to his British wife on Hadrian's Wall. Others were at least semi-permanently resident in the communities of the Euphrates Valley, some even becoming officials of the local leaders.[8]

Odaenathus' family was one of several to become massively rich through the caravan routes, but it is hard to say whether Palmyra's aristocracy was created or merely made even more powerful by trade. There is certainly no evidence for Odaenathus coming from a long-established royal family. The city's chief magistrates were called 'generals' (*strategoi*), and although this old Greek title was common in many cities for civil officials, in Palmyra they still had military functions. Strong forces were maintained to protect the caravan routes, in addition to the Palmyrenes who served in the regular Roman army like the cohort at Dura Europos. Palmyra was famous for its archers and its heavy cataphract cavalry, but presumably there were also other lighter horsemen and probably camel riders more suited to escort duty. Odaenathus combined these troops with regiments from the Roman army when he fought the Persians and suppressed the usurper.[9]

Zenobia was probably in her late twenties or early thirties when her husband was killed. Like him, she seems to have come from the Palmyrene aristocracy and was a Roman citizen. Although she educated her children in the language, she is said to have had limited knowledge of Latin herself, but was fluent in Greek and Egyptian, as well as Aramaic. As queen she claimed descent from the Ptolemaic and Seleucid royal houses of the Successor kingdoms established by Alexander the Great's generals. In particular, she seems to have encouraged comparisons between herself and Cleopatra. Several sources emphasise her beauty as well as her intelligence, courage, powers of endurance and fondness for masculine sports like hunting. Unusually for a woman – especially an eastern woman – they do not depict her as sexually voracious, and instead they emphasise her chastity, sometimes to an extreme degree.[10]

For several years after Odaenathus' murder, no emperor in Rome was in a position to do anything to bring the eastern provinces under direct control. Vaballathus was proclaimed with the same titles and authority as his father, but again for several years these stopped short of claiming imperial dignity. An inscription from 271 describes the boy as the 'restorer of the whole east'. Up until the accession of Aurelian the coins minted in the areas controlled by Zenobia and her son followed standard patterns. A few months later they began to produce coins with two 'heads'. A bearded and crowned Aurelian was on one side with his full imperial titles. On the other side was a beardless Vaballathus, styled 'most distinguished man' (i.e., a senator), 'king' of Palmyra, 'victorious general' (*imperator*), and 'leader of the Romans' (*dux romanorum*). It's hard to tell whether or not this actually presented the boy as Aurelian's junior co-emperor.[11]

As Vaballathus' prominence grew, so did the regions under his control. Forces loyal to him had already campaigned to the south, attacking Arabia. An inscription from Bostra records the restoration of a temple to Jupiter Hammon, 'which had been destroyed by Palmyrene enemies'. In 270 an army invaded Egypt, defeating a force led by the provincial governor. The bulk of Zenobia's troops then withdrew, but returned to suppress a rebellion. Oddly, this does not seem to have been seen as a decisive break with the emperor in Rome. Like the forces of Odaenathus, Zenobia's army seems to have been a mixture of Roman regulars and Palmyrene soldiers. Yet its senior commanders, Septimius Zabda and Septimius Zabdai were both Palmyran, and also Roman citizens. Zenobia does seem to have preferred to rely on men from her home city, who may well have been relatives.[12]

The queen now controlled Syria, Egypt, much of Asia Minor – although locally raised forces had repulsed her men in Bithynia – and some of Arabia. The culture of her court certainly had a strong Palmyrene flavour, but was not exclusively so. One of her main advisers was the widely respected philosopher Cassius Longinus from Emesa, who had taught rhetoric at Athens. There is no evidence for an attempt to spread Palmyrene or, indeed, any sort of distinctively 'eastern' culture throughout the areas under Zenobia's control. Instead, government remained essentially Roman, and Roman titles were always paraded alongside specifically Palmyran rank.[13]

In 271 Vaballathus was finally proclaimed emperor. Aurelian's face disappeared from coins produced by the official mints in Antioch and Alexandria, and instead all coins carried the boy's image, sometimes along with that of his mother. He was given the title Augustus, while Zenobia became Augusta. It was an open declaration of rebellion against Aurelian, not against Rome, and Vaballathus was simply presented as the legitimate emperor. Elagabalus and Severus Alexander offered precedents for boy emperors, as they did for emperors from Syria and the behind-the-scenes rule of women. The situation was very similar to the Gallic emperors and, just like them, Zenobia made no effort to expand her territory further and take over the rest of the empire. This does not mean that they made no claim to the other provinces, merely that they did not choose to take them by force at this stage. Perhaps Zenobia hoped to negotiate the acknowledgement of her son as co-ruler with Aurelian, who was childless and so had no obvious heir. If so, then she was disappointed.[14]

The Restorer of the World

In 272 Aurelian led an army into Asia Minor and at first encountered virtually no opposition. When Tyana closed its gates to him, he angrily swore 'not to leave even a dog alive' when he captured the place. In the event the city was quickly betrayed by a man who let Aurelian's soldiers in. The emperor executed the traitor, feeling that a man who would betray his own home could never be trusted, but he refused to let his men sack the town. Instead, he told them to slaughter all the dogs. Having recovered Asia Minor, the army moved south into Syria. The first major clash was near Antioch – probably at Immae where Macrinus had been defeated by Elagabalus more than fifty years before. Worried by the enemy's strong force of cataphract cavalry, Aurelian sent his own lighter horsemen forward to meet them, with orders to give way as soon as the enemy advanced. The Romans did as they were ordered, luring their heavier opponents into a disordered pursuit. Soon they were exhausted from the heat of the sun and the weight of their armour, and were cut to pieces when the Romans rallied and turned on them. Zenobia's army retreated to Emesa – a captive resembling Aurelian was dressed up as the emperor and paraded through Antioch to prevent the people from switching sides before they could escape.[15]

Aurelian pushed on. One hilltop town was stormed when his soldiers advanced up to its walls in the famous testudo or tortoise formation, their overlapping shields held over their heads to protect them from missiles. Soon afterwards he caught up with the enemy army and fought another battle at Emesa. Once again the Roman cavalry were ordered to feign flight and lure the enemy cataphracts into a trap. However, either the Palmyran commanders had learned from their earlier mistakes or the manoeuvre was not carried out so carefully, for this time the cataphracts caught up with the retreating Romans. The battle was won by the Roman infantry, who provided determined support. Aurelian's army included a broad range of troops he had brought with him from Europe, as well as men from the nearer provinces. It is noted that he had a contingent from Palestine – most probably regular units stationed in the region – who carried clubs and maces as well as their normal equipment, and that these proved particularly effective against the armoured enemy. It is more than likely that regular units were still fighting for Zenobia, but obviously it was in the interest of Aurelian to emphasise the foreignness of his enemies. Augustus had done much the same when he fought Antony and Cleopatra.[16]

After this victory Aurelian began to besiege Palmyra itself. Around the same time an army led by one of his commanders retook Egypt. At Palmyra Zenobia despaired, sneaked out of the city with just a few followers and set out over the desert on camels. It was said that she hoped to escape to Persia, but instead she ran into a Roman patrol while crossing the Euphrates and was captured. Abandoned by their queen, the forces in the city soon surrendered and were spared the horrors of a sack. Aurelian was merciful to Zenobia, just as subsequently he would be generous to Tetricus. Instead, the chief blame was placed on her advisers. Cassius Longinus was one of those executed, and was said to have met his fate with great dignity. There is no record of what happened to Vaballathus, which gives some indication of his lack of real importance.[17]

The rebellion was not quite over. When Aurelian withdrew the bulk of his forces, a new emperor was proclaimed by the Palmyrenes in 273. The Roman army returned and stormed the city, and this time its inhabitants paid a heavy price. It was the end of Palmyra's golden age. It shrank in size and became little more than a garrison town – finally getting a bath house to meet the needs of the soldiers. The trade routes shifted away, most probably hastened by the ruin of Dura Europos some years before, and the source of Palmyra's prosperity vanished. Another rebellion in Alexandria was also suppressed, but it is less clear whether or not its leader was seeking imperial rule or had more modest objectives.[18]

Aurelian was back in Rome in 274 and celebrated the grandest triumph seen for many years. Tetricus marched as captive in the parade, as did Zenobia, so laden down with heavy jewellery and golden chains that she struggled to walk. The former emperor of the Gauls then went on to his administrative post, becoming *corrector* of Italy. Accounts differ over Zenobia's fate, but the most convincing – as well as the most appealing – is that she was married to a senator and lived out her life in comfortable peace. Over a century later her descendants were well-established members of the senatorial elite and proud of their famous ancestor.[19]

The treatment of Tetricus and Zenobia emphasises that they were not seen as nationalist leaders who wanted to split away from the empire. The Gallic emperors and Vaballathus and his mother were usurpers, but ones who showed considerable restraint and did not focus their main effort into destroying Roman rivals. Instead, they concentrated on gaining control of parts of the empire that central authority of the 'legitimate' emperor in Rome struggled to govern and protect. For over a decade a greater degree of normality and the rule of Roman law and administration was preserved than the weakened central government could have provided. All of these leaders were ambitious, and doubtless hoped eventually to secure through negotiation or warfare power over the entire empire. Had any of them done so, we would doubtless have talked about the strong man – or woman – whose ambition had been necessary to restore the empire.

Aurelian was praised for this, even in sources emphasising his ruthlessness and cruelty. Defeating Zenobia and Tetricus, and bringing the provinces they ruled back under the control of central government, were the great achievement of his reign. For a short while the empire was reunited under a single emperor. They were not the only wars fought in his reign, and his first two years in power were spent meeting various barbarian incursions. In 270 or 271 raiders again reached Italy and the emperor hastened back from the Danube to deal with them. Aurelian's column was ambushed and badly beaten near Placentia (modern Piacenza) on the Po. This was a rare defeat and he quickly recovered to smash the enemy in two subsequent battles.[20]

Aurelian spent the bulk of his reign away from Rome. He was there in 271, crushing a riot led by workers in the imperial mint, which almost became an open rebellion. It had been provoked by the banning of long-established and highly profitable corruption within the system. Thousands may have died in the fighting before the trouble was crushed. Aurelian was ruthless in quelling this opposition, but seems to have sensed that Rome felt less secure. Therefore, work began on a massive circuit wall, more than $12\frac{1}{2}$ miles in length and almost 20 feet high. Unlike many other cities that shrank in size when they were fortified, Rome's new defences virtually enclosed the entire city. Apart from providing this protection, the emperor also reformed the system for supplying citizens resident in the city with free bread. He regulated the weight of loaves, made the right hereditary, but also extended it to the entire free population of the city. Septimius Severus had also introduced a free distribution of olive oil, much of it from Spain. Aurelian confirmed this and also made salt and pork a regular part of the distribution. Wine was also provided by the state, although this was not free, but simply sold at a fixed and low price.[21]

The emperor boasted of a special relationship with the 'Unconquered Sun' (Sol Invictus) and in 274 dedicated a great temple to the god in Rome. Such claims were not in essence new, and the cult was not unpalatable in the same way as that of Elagabalus. Aurelian's beliefs may have been genuine, and it was certainly no bad thing politically if an emperor's subjects could be persuaded that his rule was divinely supported. No other cults were suppressed. Some later Christian sources claimed that Aurelian was planning a new persecution of the church in the last months of his life. The last empire-wide attack on the Christians had come under Valerian. Unlike Decius, he had specifically targeted the Christians, or rather their leaders. These were to be arrested and executed if they did not publicly abandon their faith. Any who were senators, equestrians or held official office were to be stripped of their status. The Senate seems to have written to Valerian to discover what they were then supposed to do with such men. Christian meeting places may also have been seized.

Perhaps Valerian was not interested in the beliefs of poorer Christians or he may well have hoped that dealing with their leaders would severely reduce overall numbers. We have most evidence for the impact of the persecution in North Africa, where the prominent theologian and writer, Bishop Cyprian, was one of the victims. Gallienus either was less committed to the purge or did not want to alienate any group after his father's capture by the Persians. He issued a new proclamation ending the persecution and granting the Christians freedom of worship. In the eastern provinces Odaenathus and especially Zenobia seem to have had a benevolent attitude and some interest in Christians, Jews and the new faith of the Manichaeans. Christians practised their religion openly, had well-known and public places of worship, while their leaders were often prominent local figures.[22]

After the recapture of Antioch, Aurelian received an appeal from Christians there who were engaged in a dispute with their own bishop, Paul of Samosata. For some time he had preached doctrines considered to be heretical, most importantly denying the divinity of Jesus. After an earlier church council he had publicly renounced this view, but subsequently changed back to his original position. Expelled from his see, he was reinstated by Zenobia, having appealed to her as the closest representative of imperial authority. Now, he refused to leave the building used as the church meeting place and was also accused of living in lavish splendour, attended by followers just as if he were a government official. It was normal for representatives from cults, or indeed any other community or group, to seek a judgement from the emperor when they were unable to resolve disputes to their satisfaction. Even so, it is striking to see the so recently persecuted Christians appealing to an emperor. Aurelian decided against Paul and ordered his expulsion from the church building. The incident gives no hint of a would-be persecutor.[23]

Murder and Civil War

Aurelian was a successful emperor, but most of his closest officers and staff feared him, and some hated him. In 275 he was in Thrace, perhaps on his way eastwards to mount an expedition against the Persians, when he was murdered. None of the conspirators appear to have been especially senior, and stories circulated that they had been duped into fearing for their lives by one of the emperor's secretaries. They had no candidate for the throne and, in any case, would have carried no weight with the army as a whole, since the rank and file remained deeply attached to Aurelian. There was a strange pause while senior army officers chose a successor. Later tradition magnified this into a six-month interregnum, with Senate and army politely inviting the other to name a new emperor. More probably there was at most a matter of weeks before the aged Tacitus (fully, Marcus Claudius Tacitus) was named. One source claims that he was seventy-five, but this may well be an exaggeration. He was another of the successful equestrian officers from the Danubian provinces, who had subsequently received senatorial rank and then retired from active service to live on an estate in Campania.[24]

Taking power at Rome late in 275, Tacitus went on campaign early in the next year, going to Asia Minor, which was again plagued by attacks from seaborne raiders, many of them Goths. Some of the barbarians claimed that they had originally assembled to answer Aurelian's demand for them to serve as auxiliaries in his Persian expedition. Perhaps this was just a pretext, but equally there may have been a genuine misunderstanding. Most of the warriors turned to plundering and Tacitus attacked them, winning a victory – something of great value for a new emperor. Less successful was his choice of his relative Maximinus as governor of Syria, who proved so brutal and corrupt that he was quickly murdered. Fearing punishment, the same army officers then killed Tacitus.[25]

The praetorian prefect Florian (fully, Marcus Annius Florianus) was now named as emperor. Not everyone agreed with his nomination and a senior provincial commander Probus (fully, Marcus Aurelius Probus) was able to rally strong forces from Egypt and Syria to back his own claim. Florian had been made emperor in June. By the end of summer he was dead, killed by his own men when they saw the enemy army approaching them near Tarsus. Yet another equestrian officer from the Danube, Probus was to spend the bulk of his six-year reign on campaign, fighting on the Rhine and Danube, as well as in Asia Minor and Egypt. Not all of the enemies were foreign. There were short-lived usurpations in Syria and more serious ones on the Rhine and in Britain, which were only defeated after some effort.[26]

Gaul was plagued by large bands of robbers. There was also a revolt in Isauria in Asia Minor, led by a bandit leader called Lydius, but this is unlikely to have been a bid for imperial power. The inhabitants of this mountainous region had a reputation as semi-barbarians, but excavations at the city of Cremna suggest that this was greatly exaggerated. Even so, banditry was common in the area and they seem to have taken the opportunity of the disturbed times to raid nearby communities. Probus sent the equestrian governor of Lycia and Pamphylia, one Terentius Marcianus, against the rebels, who were driven back behind Cremna's walls.

What followed demonstrated that the Roman army still maintained much of its skill in siege warfare. The only viable approach to the city was on the western side, and the attackers began by building two long, dry-stone walls to defend against sallies and prevent the defenders from escaping. Heavy catapults were sited on the inner wall and began to bombard the city's fortifications. Then the Roman troops started work on a huge mound little more than 20 yards from the city wall. It was used as a platform for more heavy artillery, but could readily have been converted into an assault ramp at a later stage. Lydius' men responded to the threat by building a much smaller mound of their own behind the wall, for there was a great advantage to having a higher platform. Yet they could not match the regular army's engineering skill or manpower, and even though the city was higher up the slope than the Roman mound, this soon equalled the height of their own platform. Heavy stones – approximately 17–18 inches in diameter and weighing 200–270 lb – from the Roman artillery have been found amongst the debris of the wall nearest to the mound. One tower was smashed, another partially collapsed and had to be hastily repaired. Lydius was shot by a bolt from a ballista aimed by the man who had been in charge of his own artillery, but who had deserted after being flogged. Either his death, or the ominous height of the Roman mound, prompted the city to surrender.[27]

The Roman army was still highly effective when its troops were properly trained, kept supplied, decently led and available in reasonable numbers. Under Probus the Romans won many victories and suffered very few defeats. By the standards of the period he had a long and successful reign, yet it may be that most of the successes were won by his subordinates. He does not seem to have been popular with the army, or at least its officer corps, in part because he employed the troops as a labour force on civil engineering and agricultural projects. There was a long tradition of such work in the Roman army, but it had probably become far less common in recent generations. In 282 Probus was murdered by a group of officers and replaced by his praetorian prefect Carus (fully, Marcus Aurelius Numerius Carus), who ruled jointly with his sons Numerian and Carinus. Carus was another equestrian officer, although unusually for the period his family came from Gaul and not one of the Danubian provinces.[28]

Probus had probably been preparing an expedition against Persia before his death, and in 283 Carus and Numerian advanced into Mesopotamia, which had been more or less under Persian control since 260. The offensive went well and the Romans seem to have won a major battle. Once again a Roman army reached Ctesiphon and this time the city was captured. Carus pushed on, but sometime near the end of the summer died suddenly. Sources claim that he was killed when his tent was struck by lightning, but many historians suspect this was simply a cover story. Perhaps he died of disease, or more likely was murdered. Numerian succeeded him and ruled for most of the next year. The Persian War was abandoned, but as the army withdrew the young emperor fell ill with an eye infection. He was then murdered by the Praetorian Prefect Aper, who managed to conceal the act by pretending that the emperor was simply sick and forced to stay in a covered litter. Eventually the smell exposed the deception, and the army's officers refused to rally behind Aper. Instead, they chose one of their number, Diocletian (fully, Caius Valerius Diocles), as emperor, yet another equestrian officer from the Balkans. He may have had a secret link with Aper, but his first public act after his proclamation on 20 November 284 was to stab the prefect to death, ensuring his silence.[29]

In the meantime, Carus' other son Carinus faced a challenger in Europe when Sabinus Julianus rebelled in Pannonia. In 285 Carinus smashed the enemy in battle near Verona, but by this time Diocletian's forces were also advancing from the east. A few months later the rivals confronted each other close to where the River Margus joins the Danube. The battle was hard-fought and may even have been going Carinus' way, when some of his own officers decided to switch sides and murdered him. One of the motives was said to be the emperor's frequent seduction of other men's wives. For the moment, Diocletian was sole emperor. He would prove to be the most successful ruler the empire had had since Septimius Severus, another man who reached power through civil war.[30]

Carus' invasion had struck a Persia that was itself divided as rival claimants fought for the throne. Shapur I had died in 272. Between them, he and his father had ruled for almost half a century since the defeat of the Parthians in 224. Both were strong leaders and skilful commanders, and together they firmly established their dynasty, but it would be many years before other Persian kings would prove as long-lived and successful. Shapur's son died only a year after becoming king, and his grandson only lasted three. When this man's son, Vahran II, succeeded, the royal family divided, as another branch backed a different candidate and rebelled. It was a sign of the achievement of Ardashir and Shapur that no challengers emerged from outside the Sassanid family. Yet the feudal nature of the kingdom, and its heavy reliance on family members as local kings of each region, always left open the possibility of competition within the royal house for supreme rule.[31]

Modern historians are inclined to see Sassanid Persia as a far more formidable and aggressive opponent than the old Parthian Empire it supplanted. Some talk blithely of a new superpower, posing such a threat to the Romans that they were forced to massively increase their military spending. The cost of this placed a huge strain on the empire's economy and encouraged dramatic political and social changes. Therefore, the radical changes in the State – many of which would occur or be completed under Diocletian – were a necessary if traumatic response to a new situation.[32]

This is a convenient theory, but very difficult to justify. Much of it is based upon the victories won by Shapur I, which were undoubtedly spectacular, but need to be placed in the context of the situation and his own aims. In spite of the boasts of their ambassadors, there is not a shred of evidence for the Persians ever genuinely seeking the reconquest of the old Achaemenid Empire. They did want to restrict Roman power in the areas bordering their lands – Rome had never been a comfortable neighbour and had over time gradually expanded its territory. The Sassanids also needed to eradicate the Arsacid monarchs in Armenia and anyone else likely to challenge their hold on the kingdom. Ardashir and Shapur took advantage of Rome's weakness to dominate the border regions and also to attack the empire itself.

However, this was never a question of permanent conquest. The Persians lacked the strength to achieve this and probably never even considered long-term occupation. Invading armies could and did plunder the Roman provinces over a wide area. Great cities like Antioch fell and were looted, but there was never any question of the Persians holding on to them. Another important objective was the taking of captives in large numbers, and Shapur took many thousands. These were taken deep within his kingdom and settled so far from the borders as to make escape impractical. There they laboured on major engineering projects for the king, building cities, as well as dams and irrigation systems. The results increased agricultural yields on the royal lands, further adding to the king's wealth and power.[33]

The Persian army was effective in the right circumstances – although it is hard to say whether it really differed to any great degree from later Parthian forces since we know so little about these. There is more evidence for some skill in siege craft than had ever been shown by the Parthians, but this should not be exaggerated. Ardashir and Shapur led a very good army, which had carried them into power. Most later kings would not have so many experienced and confident soldiers under their command. It was not a standing army and relied on a part-time feudal element unsuited to garrisoning captured cities. After a big success, many of the contingents would start to disperse and return home with their spoils, leaving the army vulnerable.

As far as we know, after 260 Shapur made no aggressive moves against the Romans. Odaenathus raided as far as Ctesiphon and does not seem to have suffered a serious defeat. The Persian king did not attempt another major attack, even though the Roman empire remained divided. In part this was because Odaenathus and subsequently Zenobia maintained a strong army, although it is doubtful whether this was as powerful as the regular forces in the eastern provinces in more peaceful times. Shapur may have had problems in other parts of his broad realm – it should never be forgotten that he had other borders apart from the one with Rome. More importantly, he had already achieved all that he needed from fighting the Romans – three emperors vanquished and humiliated, armies crushed, long lists of cities taken and plunder and captives in abundance.

The Romans were a powerful and often aggressive neighbour. They posed a threat against which Ardashir and Shapur could unite the subjects of their newly won kingdom. Both men needed victories to secure their hold on power, and a weakened and divided Rome offered an ideal target. Their successes fostered new wars, as the Romans characteristically sought vengeance by invading Persia. Managing to defeat these attacks – or at the very least survive them – brought more glory to the monarch, as well as the reason and opportunity for fresh expeditions against the Roman provinces.

Persia was not the equal of the Roman Empire, and to see Rome and Persia as rival superpowers is deeply misleading. After Rome, Persia was undoubtedly the strongest state in the known world, far greater than any barbarian tribe or even confederation of tribes, but it still had nothing like the wealth, resources and professional army of the Roman Empire. Ardashir and Shapur fought to win and hold on to power. The appearance of such formidable kings and their need for fresh victories coincided with a time of Roman weakness through division and civil war. When Shapur was more secure on the throne he became far less aggressive. Later kings were not so gifted as commanders or were too busy fighting internal rivals to attack Rome. They also faced stronger, more united opposition as civil war became less frequent amongst the Romans themselves. The Persians were unable to repeat the successes of Shapur for many generations.

7

Crisis

'There have never been such earthquakes and plagues, or tyrants and emperors with such unexpected careers, which were rarely if ever recorded before. Some of these men ruled for quite a long time, others held only transient power; some hardly reached the title and fleeting honour before they were deposed. In a period of sixty years the Roman empire was shared by more rulers than the years warranted.' – *Herodian, middle of the third century.*[1]

In the half-century between the murder of Alexander Severus and Diocletian's victory over Carinus, over sixty men claimed imperial power. A precise figure is impossible, since in some cases it is unclear if a rebel leader actually aimed at the throne, or even existed at all. In 2004 a coin was found in Oxfordshire bearing the image and name of the extremely short-lived usurper Domitianus. Briefly mentioned in the literary sources, he was said to have rebelled against Aurelian in 270 or 271. Only a single coin had previously been found with his name, and this had widely been dismissed as a forgery. Now it is clear that he made a bid for imperial power, probably somewhere in the western provinces, and lasted long enough to have coins minted in his name.[2]

Domitianus was one of many would-be emperors who only survived for a matter of weeks. Gallienus lasted longer than anyone else, if his seven years ruling jointly with his father are added to his eight years of sole power. Otherwise, Postumus' nine years represents the longest reign of an emperor without a colleague, albeit over only part of the empire. Both Gallienus and Postumus were murdered by conspiracies involving their own senior officers and staff. This was by far the commonest fate of enduring emperors and short-lived usurpers alike.

The years from 235–285 are often characterised as a time of anarchy and the whole era is dubbed the 'Third Century Crisis'. Certainly, the rapid turnover of emperors was in marked contrast to the first and second centuries – between 31 BC and AD 180 there were only sixteen emperors (seventeen, if Lucius Verus is included as Marcus Aurelius' colleague).

Yet this in turn differs from the fifty-five years following the death of Marcus Aurelius. There were ten emperors (eleven, if Geta is included) from 180 to 235 – and the number could actually be increased if the handful of short-lived usurpers who rose against the later Severans is included. Things were clearly far worse in the middle of the third century, but it was mainly a question of degree. Similarly, although Diocletian ruled with colleagues for two decades, several usurpers emerged during these years, and for a while Britain and parts of Gaul broke away in a repeat of the earlier 'Gallic Empire'. Civil war remained a common event, even if it was never again quite so frequent.

The 'Third Century Crisis' used to be painted in the bleakest terms. It was a time when the Romans suffered defeat after defeat at the hands of new, more powerful foreign enemies. Persian armies took Antioch, fleets of Gothic pirates plundered Greece and Asia Minor, and other barbarians burst across the frontiers into Gaul, Italy and Spain. For years on end much of the east was controlled by the monarchs of Palmyra, and the western provinces broke away under the rule of a succession of their own emperors. There were also outbreaks of plague over wide areas, which may well have rivalled the Antonine epidemic in their virulence and the number of victims. At the same time the economy collapsed, as successive emperors massively devalued the coinage to pay for their wars. Society also changed, some of the poorer citizens in rural areas being reduced to little more than serfs. All of this was accompanied by a crisis of belief, as everywhere people abandoned the old faiths for new religions and wild superstitions.

However, academic fashions change and today few would accept such a grim picture, for the evidence can be understood in other ways. Some would argue that crisis is simply the wrong word, since it is clear that there was never any question about the survival of the empire in some shape or form. Yet no one doubts that this was a period of profound change. Diocletian's empire looked and functioned very differently to the one familiar to Marcus Aurelius. Before moving on to look at the system he created, it is worth pausing to consider some of the wider changes that seem to have occurred.[3]

Render Unto Caesar: Money and the Economy

Emperors were expected to spend lavishly. Almost the first act of any new ruler was to promise a cash gift (or donative) to the army. This was as true for Marcus Aurelius as it was for any usurper seeking power in later years. Even in normal circumstances maintaining the army was the greatest single expense in the imperial budget. Frequent warfare – most especially campaigns that were fought inside the empire and so produced little plunder – greatly added to its overall cost. On the whole, the troops remained loyal to any established imperial family, as long as their rule seemed reasonably effective and they did not suffer too many serious defeats. It was much harder for new emperors to gain this level of loyalty, which only added to their urgent need to treat the soldiers generously. Severus raised army pay for the first time in over a century, and Caracalla increased this again just a few years later. Macrinus struggled to cope with the cost of this and his clumsy handling of the situation prompted his rapid fall.

The emperor was the greatest landowner in the world, the imperial estates including vast areas of farmland, as well as such things as mines, throughout the provinces. Whatever its origins, this quickly ceased to be a personal possession and passed from emperor to emperor regardless of whether there was any family connection. Property confiscated from executed opponents was often added to this, but it was obviously dangerous for any ruler to kill too many rich and influential men. New taxes could be introduced – Dio believed that Caracalla's grant of citizenship was essentially a money-raising venture – or old ones reinterpreted in the government's favour. This, too, was dangerous. The revolt of the Gordians against Maximinus was provoked by resentment at the exactions of the official collecting taxes in Africa. On the whole, the level of taxation throughout the provinces remained remarkably static.[4]

Most of the methods of raising extra revenue quickly were dangerous for any emperor, and especially one who had recently seized power. Yet the need was always there to spend, and it was not just a question of the army. Maintaining even the small-scale administration of the empire cost money and the number of imperial bureaucrats grew steadily during this period. There were also many other things an emperor was expected to pay for. At Rome itself there were the distributions of free and subsidised food, public entertainments, as well as the maintenance of public buildings and the construction of new ones. Emperors were expected to be generous to communities and individuals. If they were perceived as mean and grasping, then that was an invitation for more lavish challengers to emerge. To make matters worse, a good number of third-century emperors could not even call upon the entire imperial resources, since parts of the empire were often under the control of rivals. One of the reasons for Gallienus' survival for so long was that he kept control of the prosperous North African provinces with their substantial imperial estates. Similarly, it was not until after his death that Zenobia took over Egypt, whose grain continued to supply a good part of Rome's needs.

Financial problems appear time and again in the record of the third century. Emperors controlled the minting of gold and silver coinage and there was a constant temptation to make their resources go further by debasing the currency. The change is most striking in the silver coinage. In Trajan's day, a silver denarius contained just over 90 per cent silver (the denarius was the penny of the Authorised Bible, hence the abbreviation before decimalisation of pence as d). Under Marcus Aurelius the percentage of silver as opposed to base metals dropped below 75 per cent at a time when the empire was ravaged by warfare and disease. Septimius Severus increased army pay and let the silver content of his coins drop to 50 per cent. Caracalla introduced a new silver coin, known as the antoninianus and probably worth 2 denarii, although its weight was only equivalent to one and half of these coins. This was abandoned under Elagabalus, but reappeared in the joint reign of Balbinus, Pupienus and Gordian III. By this time the silver content had fallen close to 40 per cent. Around the middle of the century the decline rapidly accelerated and was as little as 3.5–4 per cent silver by the time Aurelian came to power.[5]

The impact of this massive debasement is very hard to judge since, as is usual with the Roman economy, we lack any useful statistics. It is clear that prices by the end of the third century were massively higher than they had been at the end of the second – in some cases by several hundred per cent. There had never been inflation on such a scale in Rome's earlier history. However, the bulk of our evidence for day-to-day rises in costs comes from Egypt, which uniquely had its own system of coinage until Aurelian's reign, when it was brought into line with the rest of the empire.

Prices rose, perhaps suddenly. Farmers, both large- and small-scale, may have been insulated against the consequences of this, since they still had produce to sell or trade. Those who like to see barter as a major part of the rural economy tend to claim that large areas of the empire were unaffected by changes to the currency. Similarly, people involved in manufacture had products to sell, assuming that they, like the farmers, still found a market. Change probably occurred slowly, as the increased number of coins would have only started to circulate gradually, and perhaps people had time to adapt. Yet it was not the only factor. Wars were costly, perhaps especially civil wars, which involved the movements of armies through normally peaceful areas at a time when military discipline tended to slacken. Many suffered; a few probably profited. The population may have been declining – certainly, there must have been substantial local drops in numbers as a result of outbreaks of plague, even if over the long term there was little overall change.[6]

Ultimately, we simply do not know. It is worth bearing in mind that if we had the same amount of evidence for the twentieth century as we have for the third, then we would not have any real idea of the scale of the Great Depression or the impact of two world wars. For instance, Japan's and Germany's growing prosperity would doubtless be seen as inexorable and unbroken in the course of the century. Any talk in literary fragments of the devastation caused by war would doubtless be dismissed as wild exaggeration. It is clear that there were plenty of very wealthy people in the Roman world at the opening of the fourth century. This need not necessarily mean very much – after all, some people remained rich and prosperous throughout the Great Depression. There are no figures to tell us whether the number of wealthy individuals was smaller in the fourth century compared to the second. There were the very poor in both periods, and those at every stage in between, but again we know nothing of numbers or proportions in the overall population.

There are some indications that there was less disposable income around. There is a dramatic drop in the number of surviving inscriptions from the middle of the third century. Since these frequently com-memorated civic benefactions by city magistrates and other leading local figures, this suggests that such things were also becoming far less common. While it is possible that it was simply the inscribed memorials that stopped, the archaeological record does confirm the impression that grand new public buildings were becoming rare. It is worth noting that most cities already had their bath houses, theatres, amphitheatres, basilicas and temples, and so perhaps no longer needed new monuments. Yet the ideology of the local aristocracies in the earlier periods would have seen this as a challenge to build still grander structures, even if this meant risking bankruptcy, like the cities Pliny described from his time as governor in Bithynia early in the second century. The one thing every sizeable city had acquired by 300 was a substantial circuit wall. That so many of these were made from material taken from demolished buildings does not suggest widespread prosperity.[7]

There are also signs that long-distance trade declined. Maritime archaeologists have discovered far more Roman shipwrecks dating from the first century BC through to the second century AD than for any subsequent period. We need to treat this conclusion with a degree of caution – most finds have come from the western Mediterranean because more teams have operated there. Yet it is clear that trade in this area peaked during the early Principate. Perhaps a different pattern will emerge over time as more work is done along other coastlines. Yet excavations on land also suggest that from the third century onwards there was a substantial decrease in the number of objects circulating that had been manufactured outside the province. In part, this was a sign of strong regional development. In Gaul, Britain, Spain and elsewhere there were now locals with the skill to manufacture fineware pottery and glassware, or to lay a mosaic floor. More exotic luxuries such as silks and spices continued to be transported over huge distances – once again, there is no way of knowing whether or not the quantities of such things had changed. However, the trade with India and beyond seems to have declined sharply in the third century, only to revive in the fourth.[8]

In some areas cities shrank in size and population, while villages and farms were abandoned. The fortunes of individual communities had always fluctuated and smaller ones had vanished in the past for various reasons, but in areas such as north-western Gaul such failure and decline undoubtedly became far more common in the second half of the third century. Other areas most directly exposed to frequent warfare also suffered. Dura Europos was abandoned and Palmyra's prosperity dwindled along with its independence. Some regions may already have been in decline before the disturbances of the third century. Italian agriculture was at its peak of productivity in the early Principate, until lucrative markets were lost as the provinces developed. Gauls who made their own wine no longer wanted the produce of Italian vineyards in such great quantities. When trade was booming even the less fertile land tended to be cultivated for profit, but by the second century such fields were no longer worth the effort of farming and we start to hear of deserted land. Spain flourished later than Italy, in part because it came to supply olive oil to Rome and also because of the widespread popularity of the pungent fish sauce, or *garum*, that it produced. In time, its farmers faced competition from other regions, most notably North Africa.

The African provinces were undoubtedly one of the greatest success stories of the third century, although even here there was considerable variation from area to area. On the whole North Africa was rarely disturbed by large-scale warfare – apart from the rebellion of the Gordians, the region was almost untouched by civil war and only parts of it were exposed to barbarian raids – and its economy flourished. Irrigation schemes kept large areas fertile to a degree rarely seen before or since, producing vast surpluses for sale, especially for the markets in Italy and Rome. Its cities show every sign of prosperity, evidenced by the continued construction of grand public buildings. Palestine and other parts of the Syrian provinces also seem to have prospered and show signs of a numerous population, especially in rural areas. Britain was another region that seems to have done well, and it is probably no coincidence that it similarly was generally peaceful. In contrast to Africa, a number of its cities show signs of decline, but this may well have more to do with the local aristocracy remaining at heart more rural than urban. Many villa sites in Britain were at their grandest in the early fourth century.

Fortunes varied from region to region and there were also marked differences within the same provinces. As more archaeological evidence is acquired it will almost certainly suggest an even more complex picture. There is no doubt that some areas suffered badly in these years and went into decline, while others fared much better. A few individuals and whole communities even in the worst affected regions did very well indeed. This is almost always true, even in apparently the bleakest of conditions. It is also probable that there were many tragedies, as those unable to cope with the changes in the economic climate – or subject to any one of many short-term misfortunes – failed and lost everything. Such risks were always there in any commercial enterprise, but became more common in these disturbed times. Those for whom the margins of success and failure were narrow were inevitably most likely to succumb, as indeed they are in any age. In Africa there were plenty of wealthy local men willing to take on civic office and to fund festivals and building work. In other regions there may have been far fewer such men willing or able to keep the cities going.[9]

Roman currency had become hugely debased – the denarius was abandoned and replaced with new silver coins, while bronze coinage vanished altogether for a while – but in many respects it had long been a token coinage. All coins still carried the head of an emperor and throughout the empire were accorded value depending on their denomination and not the actual content of precious metal. (Outside Rome's borders things were different, and there is some evidence for a preference for older, purer coins.) At times there seems to have been concern over whether or not coins bearing the image of defeated emperors would be honoured, but the authorities were generally keen to stress that all properly minted coins were acceptable.[10]

In the year 300 the economy of the Roman Empire was certainly more sophisticated and robust than anything that would be seen in the same regions for well over a thousand years. Without statistics we cannot say how it compared to the conditions of the second century, but it is unlikely to have been stronger and most probably had declined, probably by a large margin. The evidence of traces of pollution in the polar icecaps from the Roman period do suggest a massive boom in the first and second centuries AD, which fell sharply in the third. In most cases, for instance, in the cases of lead and copper, the same levels would not be reached again until the nineteenth century. A number of mine workings in Spain and Britain were abandoned in the late second or early third centuries, even though they still contained extensive deposits. Combined with the loss of the mines in Dacia, it does seem that the empire was producing and refining significantly smaller quantities of minerals. Underlying the problems of the coinage was a real shortage of silver and bronze.[11]

Some of the third-century decline proved temporary and a few regions enjoyed greater prosperity than at any other time, but elsewhere the picture was far less rosy. In the end, the essential fact of the Roman Empire was its sheer size and wealth. Variations between different regions and over time were inevitable. Overall the economy probably did decline, and quite possibly the population had fallen. In spite of this the empire was still massively wealthier and more populous than any other state or people in the known world.[12]

Senators and Knights

Senators remained extremely wealthy – some of them fabulously so – and continued to have influence, but their political role changed profoundly during the third century. Gallienus was said to have banned senators from holding military commands. This was probably an exaggeration, and it is unlikely that there was a specific decree, although he may well have contributed to a well-established trend. Young men from senatorial families stopped serving as the senior tribune of a legion and senators were also no longer given command of a legion as legate. They continued to govern provinces, and in some cases controlled garrisons of troops, but over time ceased to hold command over major armies. The tradition of the chief agents of the state mixing civil and military posts dated back at least to the beginning of the Republic eight centuries before. Now it ended.[13]

Instead, the trend was towards professionals or specialists. Men followed either a career in the army or one in administration and law. All of the senior posts in the army – and indeed the majority of those in the administration – passed to equestrians. To modern eyes professionals ought to be markedly more competent than amateurs. Therefore, on average, equestrians, who spent most of their career with the army, ought to have been better commanders than senators, who interspersed a few years of military experience in a much less specialised career. If so, then the rise of equestrian officers to exclusive control of the senior ranks of the army can be seen as necessary for military efficiency. It is often tied to the emergence of new, allegedly greater threats from Sassanid Persia and the Germanic tribes uniting into confederations under the pressure from new arrivals like the Goths. The Senate's amateur commanders were simply not up to dealing with such tough opponents and so emperors pragmatically turned to experienced equestrian officers instead.[14]

Like many theories, this emphasises the role of external pressures in forcing profound change on the later Roman Empire. Yet we have already seen that the scale of the threat posed by the Persians and Germans in the third century has been greatly exaggerated. Their successes had far more to do with Roman weakness from internal disorder than the inherent failings of the army and frontier systems. It is also very hard to see any noticeable difference in the level of competence displayed by senatorial and equestrian commanders. The evidence is lacking to say much about standards of generalship in the third century, but the 'professional' army commanders in the better recorded fourth century do not seem any more capable than the 'amateur' senators of the Principate. Both led their troops in much the same way.[15]

It is all too easy to impose modern ideas of specialism on the Roman world. Equestrian officers were professional in the sense that their career consisted only of military posts – they did not receive any specialist training. Some rose to higher ranks after service as more junior officers, most notably as centurions, but many were directly commissioned to command a force of 500 or more men (most usually an auxiliary infantry cohort). They had experience of long service, over time in progressively more senior posts, and it was clearly assumed that they would learn as they went along. The same assumption had also been made about senatorial officers, save that they had less time to acquire the skills to command. There is not a shred of evidence that competence was the main criterion for selecting equestrian officers for promotion. In fact, it would be most surprising if patronage did not play the key role in the process. There was also the question of loyalty to the emperor.

Under the Principate, equestrians commanded the praetorian guard and also governed Egypt and led the legions stationed there. No emperor wished the only military force in Rome, or control of the province that supplied the bulk of its grain, to fall to a senator who might easily become a rival. Equestrians could be trusted because they lacked the social status and political connections to make a bid for the throne – at least without first becoming a senator. Septimius Severus rose to power after the murder of two emperors and four years of civil war during which he disposed of three rivals. Unsurprisingly, he greatly increased the troops at his immediate disposal by augmenting the guard units and stationing *II Parthica* near Rome. This and the other two legions he raised were all commanded by equestrians, as was his new province of Mesopotamia. At the same time many existing provinces were split in two. Senatorial legates were left in charge, but none commanded more than two legions. Senators at the head of powerful military forces were potential threats, most of all to emperors who had themselves only recently gained power through armed force. Equestrians were seen as less dangerous, although over time this ceased to be true.[16]

Caracalla disliked the company of senators and preferred to be surrounded by army officers. Hence, after his murder the equestrian Macrinus was able to convince those on the spot to accept him as emperor. As a body the Senate quickly acknowledged his claim. He had an army, and they did not, while the memory of Severus' purges of their class were recent. After this, it was the exception rather than the rule for a new emperor to come from the Senate. Several were infants, but the overwhelming majority were equestrian army officers. As senators ceased to command armies it became even less likely that any of them would be elevated to imperial power.

Only a handful of third-century emperors died a natural death – Septimius Severus and Claudius II are the only two where this was certainly the case. The majority died at the hands of their own subordinates. Assassination and open rebellion by a usurper with an army were frequent occurrences. The men who seized power in these years were obviously ambitious or, in the case of the teenage emperors, had ambitious people behind them. They were also inevitably nervous and insecure. Not one lasted long enough to feel fully safe, still less to found a stable dynasty.

Frightened people will tend to trust only those they know well. Family were preferred and generally proved reliable – one of the main exceptions being the fragile relationship between Elagabalus and Alexander.

Otherwise, men chose former colleagues and subordinates. Therefore, equestrians who had spent their careers with the army tended to choose other army officers to command their armies, govern provinces and fill senior posts in the administration. They did not know many senators intimately, and in any case were wary of those who could boast of senior magistracies, wide connections and great wealth. There was no sudden exclusion of senators from government, it was just that over time all senior appointments, and especially military commands, came to be filled by men from outside the order. Had any emperor lasted several decades in power, then it is possible that he would have felt confident enough to begin trusting more senators with such important posts. This never happened, although our sources claim that some rulers, for instance, Alexander and Tacitus, showed great public faith in the Senate.[17]

The great irony was that in the long run the exclusion of senators from high commands made emperors more, rather than less, vulnerable to challenges. In the first and second centuries only senators were deemed suitable for the throne if there was no acceptable candidate from the imperial family. Furthermore, only the more distinguished members of the order were likely to succeed – at most a few dozen men out of a council of 600. Emperors succeeded by establishing a working relationship with the Senate, tolerable to both sides. Septimius Severus eventually managed to do this, even if his methods were at times brutal.

It was much easier to control the Senate than the larger and more diverse equestrian order. Senators returned to Rome throughout their career, mixed socially and inter-married. An equestrian officer was most unlikely to know men of a similar rank serving with the army in distant provinces. It was now far easier to become emperor, since a man only needed to gain the support of the troops on the spot. Persuading the rest of the empire that his rule was better than any alternative was much harder. The Senate had remained a force for political cohesion long after it lost genuine political independence. Yet its value in this respect was dependent on emperors treating the body with respect and employing senators in the vast majority of senior posts. This was the way Augustus had smoothed the feelings of Rome's elite, helping them to accept the passing of the Republic. For emperors it was a voluntary convention, but it had generally worked well for over two hundred years.

The replacement of senators by equestrians at the head of Rome's armies had nothing to do with military requirements. Still less was it caused by concerted demands from an increasingly prosperous and numerous class for a greater role in public life, for the equestrian order lacked any sense of corporate identity. It had always been possible in the past for the most successful individuals to be enrolled in the Senate. The rise of equestrians to dominate high office in fact led to increasingly stark divisions within the order between those of higher and lower status. The dominance of equestrian officers was a result of the desire of a succession of newly made and normally equestrian emperors to surround themselves with men they felt could be trusted. That this was largely an illusion is shown by the number murdered by such 'trustworthy' subordinates.

As the Senate lost its central role in public life, so Rome itself also diminished in importance, although both were still powerful symbols of the empire's greatness. The Senate continued to meet, debating and passing motions – usually for very formal praise of the emperor. Senators still had influence, and also filled administrative posts in Italy and governed lesser provinces. Rome's population continued to be pampered with free and subsidised food and drink, enjoyed spectacular entertainments in huge venues like the Colosseum and Circus Maximus, and took their pleasures in massive public bath houses. People rarely saw an emperor, and even when one was resident in the city, he was most unlikely to enter the Senate House. Rome remained the largest city in the empire, but it and its Senate had drifted to the margins of political life. Power rested with the emperor and his court, and these rarely came anywhere near Rome.

Surviving the Crisis

Emperors spent little time in Italy, and even less in Rome itself. They frequently went to war, in some cases campaigning every year. Rule of a single emperor became unusual. In some cases this was involuntary, for instance, when rival emperors emerged who were too strong to overcome at the time. More often it was a matter of choice. Emperors with sons tended to elevate these to joint rule almost as soon as they seized power. If they were still infants this marked out a clear successor and so gave the promise of long-term stability. Adult sons could be sent to deal with problems in another region while the father was busy elsewhere.

For many scholars this development shows that it was no longer possible for a single emperor to rule the entire empire. Most also claim that from at least the time of Marcus Aurelius, emperors were expected to preside over major wars in person. They were also expected to win. If there was more than one war at the same time, then there needed to be more than one emperor. Therefore, the trend was towards the division of imperial power, and ultimately this would lead to the split between eastern and western empire at the end of the fourth century. Such analysis not only relies on hindsight, but assumes that this major change was a reasonable, perhaps even inevitable, response to new problems. Once again, this is bound up with the belief that in the third century the empire faced far greater threats from the outside than ever before.[18]

Change was inexorable and stimulated by external pressure. Similar reasoning has often been used to claim that the fall of the Republic and creation of the Principate by Augustus was equally inevitable. If he had not done this, then someone else much like him would have created an essentially similar monarchy. This sort of analysis robs the individuals whose decisions and deeds shaped the process of any independence of action, perhaps even of responsibility. More importantly, a closer examination of the course of events paints a very different picture. Many of the underlying assumptions prove deeply questionable and any sense of inevitability vanishes.

In the second century Trajan spent several years of his reign on campaign, and Hadrian carried out long tours of the provinces. Both also spent a good deal of time in Italy, and Antoninus Pius never left there. The joint rule of Marcus Aurelius and Lucius Verus had nothing to do with any perceived need for two emperors. When Verus died he was not replaced for seven years until Commodus was considered old enough. It had long been normal to mark out a successor by sharing power with him. Commodus ruled alone, as did Septimius Severus until he wished to make clear that his sons would succeed him. Caracalla and Geta inherited jointly because an adult son could not be safely passed over.

Marcus Aurelius took his role as emperor extremely seriously and spent much of the second half of his reign on campaign. This was out of his sense of duty rather than any obligation. Commodus saw things differently and never again went on campaign after he returned to Rome from the Danube. Severus waged war often. At first his opponents were Roman and then subsequently he led major operations in the east and in Britain – the regions that had supported his rivals. There may have been good reasons for these wars, but Severus was also concerned to create a bond with the troops in each area and to win glory – Augustus had been similarly aggressive in the first years of the Principate. Caracalla craved an image as a tough soldier and preferred life on campaign to public life back in Rome. Winning great victories always had valuable propaganda value – hence the taking of triumphal names like Germanicus, Samarticus or Parthicus, and the prominence of symbols of victory on coins.[19]

Military victories were especially attractive to insecure emperors. Success in war showed their competence and, with its implications of divine favour, suggested that their rule was legitimate. Well-established emperors could take credit for wars won by their governors just as Antoninus Pius had done. The less confident needed to preside over the success in person. They were also reluctant to let anyone else gain glory that might rival or surpass their own. The division of the provinces into smaller units anyway ensured that governors had smaller armies at their disposal and these were not always sufficient to deal with a major problem. The third century saw the growth of extraordinary commands – for instance, Philip's brother Priscus over much of the eastern frontier, and the similar rank later granted to Odaenathus. This was necessary because provincial governors now operated on too small a scale to cope in some circumstances. Yet it was inherently dangerous. Time and again a local success by a governor or other commander prompted him to declare himself emperor.[20]

This was the root of the need to share imperial power, far more than an increased threat from outside. Sharing rule with a colleague meant that there was someone else who could – hopefully – be trusted to take command of substantial forces in another part of the empire. Trustworthiness, however, did not ensure competence. Nor did it prevent the colleague from being murdered and a challenger taking over command of his troops. No emperor was ever truly secure in the third century. Long ago, Emperor Tiberius had described ruling the empire as equivalent to 'holding a wolf by the ears'. He had the advantage of succeeding a father by adoption who had ruled for forty-five years, and himself reigned for more than two decades. No ruler lasted that long between Severus and Diocletian.[21]

The Roman army often receives much blame for its role in the disruptions of the third century. Clearly, none of this could have happened without the willingness of Roman soldiers to fight and kill each other. Yet the army did show a clear preference for established dynasties, just as it had done throughout the Principate. Enough of the troops were willing to back Elagabalus, in spite of his extremely dubious claim, because he was seen as a Severan. Similarly, it took major failures on the part of Severus Alexander before a coup succeeded. None of the other emperors could lay much claim to deep loyalty, especially since so many of them had in the first place been involved in killing their predecessor.

The army wanted stability, when it could be sure of being paid and the more ambitious could win promotion. Failing that, soldiers usually wanted to be on the winning side, hence the number of emperors killed when their army was approached by that of a stronger rival.

Soldiers of all ranks certainly took advantage of the chaos of civil war, which inevitably relaxed discipline. There were plenty of opportunities for looting and extortion. It was also possible to rise very quickly to high rank. Elagabalus' leaders promised to promote to the vacant rank any of Macrinus' men who killed a senior officer refusing to defect to them. The best prospects of all were open to officers closest to the emperor. If they joined a conspiracy to arrange for his murder then they could expect rewards from his successor. There were opportunities, but there were also great risks. Backing the wrong side could prove fatal, and certainly risked damaging a career, so that men had to judge very carefully whether to stay loyal or switch allegiance to a challenger. The majority of emperors died at the hands of men who had been close to them. Trust was a precarious thing for the ruler and his subordinates. Fear of execution prompted several assassinations from Commodus and Caracalla onwards.[22]

It was a vicious circle, as each new assassination or rebellion by a usurper – no matter how quickly it collapsed – made a renewal of civil war more likely. A humiliating defeat in a foreign war was likely to provoke an emperor's rapid fall. Others were murdered because of alleged pursuit of their officers' wives. Some died simply because ambitious followers believed that they or an associate could take imperial power for themselves. Emperors were always more worried by Roman rivals than foreign enemies. Even the Persians stood no real chance of seizing large areas of Roman territory. German warriors might raid Italy, Spain or Asia Minor, but they could not stay there.

In the third century the Roman Empire wasted much of its strength fighting itself. Its military system suffered severe dislocation and became less able to deal with foreign threats. Augustus had created a system that veiled the power of the emperor. It was not a clear, constitutional position and so there was no formal arrangement for succession. This was a weakness, but the general stability of the first two centuries make it hard to see this as responsible for the problems of the third century. Chance played more of a role than historians might care to acknowledge. It happened that Marcus Aurelius was survived by a young son who was simply not up to the job of being emperor. Pertinax need not have misplayed his hand and been killed, and Septimius Severus might have lived longer and perhaps taught his sons how to work together and to rule well. Had Commodus, Caracalla, Elagabalus or Alexander been older when they came to power, then they might have proved more capable.

Decisions by successive emperors made the situation worse. The gradual exclusion of senators from military commands and their replacement by equestrians was intended to make emperors safer. In the long run it did the opposite, and emperors came more and more from the ranks of senior equestrian army officers. Similarly, reducing the size, and therefore garrisons, of provinces weakened the capacity of the governors to deal with major operations. Emperors had to go themselves or give sufficient extraordinary power to allow a subordinate the resources to deal with the situation, hoping that it would not also give him the ability to rebel. Not until Diocletian was a measure of imperial control reasserted. Far fewer emperors were assassinated after 285. Civil wars became somewhat less common, although they tended to be much bigger and more costly when they did break out. Things were not as bad as they had been in the half century before he came to power, but we should not exaggerate the change. The stability of the first and second centuries would never be repeated.

PART TWO

Recovery?
The Fourth Century

8

The Four – Diocletian and the Tetrarchy

'... after them the gods gave us Diocletian and Maximian to be our leaders, adding to these great men Galerius and Constantius, of whom the first was born to erase the ignominy of Valerian's capture, and the other to restore the Gallic provinces to the laws of Rome. Four leaders of the world, they were, strong, wise, benign, and ever generous.' – *Anonymous author of the* Historiae Augustae, *fourth century.*[1]

'Capitoline Zeus took pity at last on the human race and gave lordship of all the earth and the sea to godlike king Diocletian. He extinguished the memory of former griefs for any still suffering in grim bonds in a lightless place.' – *Extract from a speech delivered at a festival in Oxyrhynchus in Egypt, probably in 285.*[2]

Diocletian's violent rise to power was typical for the third century, but its sequel was very different. After decades when emperors came and went in rapid succession, he ruled for twenty years. No one had managed anything close to this since the 'golden age' of the Antonines in the second century. Then, while his rule was still strong, he voluntarily resigned and retired to private life – albeit in a grand palace and surrounded by courtiers and guards. No emperor at any time had ever given up power before. Diocletian was different, and so in a number of profound ways was the empire he ruled and the way he governed it.

A striking symbol of his regime is a statue group in St Mark's Square in Venice, most probably brought there in the thirteenth century after the sack of Constantinople in the Fourth Crusade. Carved from porphyry – the purple shade that gave this stone its name was increasingly considered very appropriate for imperial statuary – it shows Diocletian and his three imperial colleagues. He ruled alone for no more than a few months before appointing a junior colleague. Later this man was given equal power, and later still two additional junior emperors were appointed so that imperial rule was shared between four men known as the tetrarchs (which simply means 'the four rulers'). Designed as a corner piece, the four emperors stand in pairs, right hand clasping their colleague's shoulder and left hand holding the hilt of their own sword. Aurelian had been nicknamed 'hand on sword' for his readiness to fight any opponent. The threat of force is here blatant as the tetrarchs stare outwards, searching for any challenger whether Roman or barbarian. Their clothing is military – forage caps, long-sleeved tunics, trousers and boots much like Terentius' men at Dura Europos, and breastplates. In real life they would have seemed less like ordinary soldiers or officers. Their cloaks were of military pattern, but dyed a rich purple reserved solely for emperors. Everything was made from the finest materials, and headgear, tunics and even shoes studded with gems.[3]

It was not just that art styles were different – rougher, heavier carving replacing the smoothness and idealised figures from the art of the early empire – so was the message. Augustus had veiled the military dictatorship he created with a façade of tradition, posing as merely the greatest servant of the state, but still belonging to the senatorial order. The veil had worn very thin over the years, but it was not until Diocletian that it was finally torn down. The tetrarchs were most certainly not 'first amongst equals'. Instead, they existed on a higher level, touched by the divine and far greater than even their most senior subordinate. There was a growing trend in art to depict the emperors as physically bigger than the pygmy figures of courtiers and soldiers surrounding them. Diocletian was addressed as 'lord' or 'master' (*dominus*), sometimes even as 'lord and god' (*dominus et deus*). Surrounded by rigid court ceremony, only a few were ever permitted to approach him. When they did so they had to prostrate themselves in obeisance. A fortunate few were permitted to kneel and kiss the hem of the emperor's robe.[4]

The tetrarchs were far above the people they ruled. They were also always commanders, controlling the vast armies that would be turned against any threat. Their propaganda spoke of the restoration of the empire and the world – for the Romans, the two were effectively synonymous. In one case, the suppression of a usurper was described as 'restoring the light' to a province. Such boasts were not new – Aurelian had made similar claims. Certainly, they gave the empire greater stability than it had enjoyed for generations. For many modern scholars the centralisation of power, massive increase in bureaucracy and the blatantly monarchic public image of the tetrarchs were necessary to deal with the greater problems faced by the empire. A philosopher emperor like Marcus Aurelius simply could not have coped. The time for senatorial amateurism was long past and, instead, tougher rulers were needed, who simply had no time to play out a Republican charade. Leaving aside the point that such arguments have been used to justify dictators throughout the ages, this is very much an analysis based on hindsight. Diocletian's success was not inevitable, nor necessarily was the shape of the fourth-century empire that he did so much to create. The root cause of the ills remained the internal instability producing such frequent civil wars. The tetrarchy proved only a temporary and partial break in this cycle.[5]

The Creation of the Tetrarchy

Diocletian was in his early forties when he was hailed as emperor. He was another equestrian army officer from one of the Danubian provinces. Stories circulated that he was born a slave, which is extremely unlikely, or that he was the son of a freedman, just like Pertinax, which is possible. Very little indeed is known about him or his career up to this point – even the fanciful biographies of the *Historiae Augustae* end with Numerian. Diocletian was married and had a daughter, but no son. Most emperors in the third century quickly nominated a successor, usually by naming a son or other male relative as Caesar. Many of these were infants, incapable of assisting in the task of governing the empire, but it was a promise that the new regime had a future.

Lacking a suitable relative, Diocletian selected an army officer named Maximian (fully, Aurelius Maximianus) and named him Caesar within a few months of defeating Carinus in May 285. Early in the following year Maximian was promoted to Augustus, making him equal – or very nearly equal – to Diocletian. Maximian had an infant son, but Diocletian was seeking a colleague to assist him in the present and immediate future, and was not yet concerned about the long-term succession. He needed a man he could trust, who was capable of dealing with serious problems in one region while he was busy elsewhere. There was no formal division of the empire into two halves, but Diocletian went to the east, while Maximian was sent to Gaul. They styled themselves Iovius (Jupiter-like) and Herculius (Hercules-like) respectively. Diocletian-Jupiter was the senior, father-figure – there is doubt over whether or not he actually adopted Maximian – who cared and planned for the good of the empire. Maximian-Hercules was the heroic son who travelled the world over-coming all enemies and obstacles.[6]

In Gaul his first task was to suppress the Bagaudae (sometimes also spelt 'Bacaudae'), a group of rebels whose main strength seems to have been in the rural areas. The details and cause of this rebellion are obscure, but groups with the same name would appear in the region for several generations. It may simply have been a reflection of the decades of disorder in the area after years of civil war and barbarian raiding. Perhaps there were also wider social and economic problems, but we should be very cautious about accepting official propaganda dismissing them as mere bandits. Coins minted by their leaders claimed full imperial titles.[7]

Maximian seems to have quickly defeated the Bagaudae. In the meantime, he despatched an officer named Carausius to protect the Channel coasts of Gaul and Britain from seaborne raids launched by tribes like the Frisians and Saxons. Again, the Romans quickly achieved success, showing that if properly led and organised, the fleet, like the army, could still prove highly effective. However, doubts were raised about Carausius' methods and motives. It was claimed that he did deals with the raiders or that he waited until they were on the return trip before attacking them, seizing and keeping all of their plunder. The criticism may not have been justified. It was normal Roman practice to mix force with diplomacy, while it was always easier to catch raiders on their way home rather than on the way in.

Whether because he had been planning this all along or was aware that he had come under suspicion, Carausius declared himself emperor in northern Gaul, probably late in 286. The mint at Rouen was soon producing coins bearing his name, and Britain quickly declared for the usurper. Carausius was careful to acknowledge the legitimacy of Diocletian and Maximian, and seems to have hoped for their acceptance as an additional colleague. Any such overtures were rejected. Maximian was occupied for the next two years, campaigning against tribes beyond the Rhine. By 289 major preparations were underway for an expedition to Britain and a panegyric speech relished the prospect of Maximian's inevitable triumph. Similar speeches from the following years are suspiciously silent, suggesting that the campaign was a total failure. It may be that much of the fleet was lost in a storm, or perhaps Carausius was too skilful an opponent. Nevertheless, propaganda continued to dismiss him as no more than a pirate.[8]

Carausius continued to present himself as a colleague of Diocletian and Maximian, and does not seem to have made any aggressive moves against them. If he still had hopes of recognition, these were dashed in the spring of 293 when the tetrarchy was created with the appointment of two junior Caesars. Diocletian took Galerius Maximianus as his subordinate, while Maximian was assisted by Flavius Constantius. Both men were army officers who had probably served with them for some time. Slightly oddly, but perhaps to maintain balance or because of their age and past record, Galerius was named Herculius and Constantius became Iovius. Again, there was no formal division of territory, but in practice Maximian and Constantius ruled the western provinces and Diocletian and Galerius the east. Four colleagues meant four emperors to deal with separate problems, and it was quite rare for even the Augustus and his Caesar to operate together. It was also the clearest possible statement that only Diocletian and Maximian had the right and power to grant imperial status. No one could demand or negotiate for this and hope to succeed.

Constantius moved against Carausius almost immediately. Territory loyal to the usurper in Gaul was the first to be recaptured. Boulogne, long-established main base of the Channel Fleet (the *classis Britannica*), fell after a long siege. Constantius' engineers built a mole to close off the entrance of the harbour. After a few days the structure was swept away by the sea, but it had lasted long enough to isolate the garrison and convince them to surrender. Carausius was murdered around this time by one of his own officials, a man named Allectus. Historians have often connected this plot with the blow to his prestige when Boulogne was lost, but this remains conjectural. Allectus lasted for three years before Constantius invaded Britain and killed him in battle. The actual fighting may have been done by one of his officers, but coins portrayed Constantius' triumphal entry into Londinium (modern London). Between them the two 'British' usurpers had ruled for a decade.[9]

A briefer, though still serious, challenge to the tetrarchs came from Egypt in 297, when a man named Lucius Domitius Domitianus declared himself emperor. Diocletian put down this rebellion, supervising the siege of Alexandria in person. When his men stormed the place, he is said to have commanded them to kill until the blood in the streets came up to the knees of his horse. Fortunately for the Alexandrians, the horse stumbled and fell as it came into the city. The killing was halted and the grateful population subsequently set up a statue of the horse. This romantic story should not conceal the brutality with which any challenge to the tetrarchy was met.[10]

The bond between the four emperors was strengthened by marriage ties, Constantius and Galerius marrying Maximian's and Diocletian's daughters respectively. In addition, each of the Augusti adopted his Caesar. Unity was stressed at every turn. Edicts were issued in the name of all four emperors, whichever was actually the source. In most cases only Diocletian issued rulings or decrees applicable throughout the empire. He was the man who had appointed his colleagues, and his was always the dominant personality. When Galerius suffered a reverse against the Persians, Diocletian is supposed to have made his Caesar run alongside his chariot, still wearing his full regalia.[11]

The Growth of Government

Four emperors meant four men with supreme authority to command and dispense justice in four different regions simultaneously. Ideally, this would prevent regions from feeling neglected and so inclined to support usurpers who promised to deal with local problems and promote local men. Any challenger would have to defeat more than one established emperor at the head of an army. The refusal to negotiate with Carausius demonstrated that no one would be allowed to force their way into power and retain it in the long run. The tetrarchy worked as long as the imperial colleagues remained firm in their alliance with each other and none suffered a cataclysmic defeat. This was not really a product of the system itself, but had far more to do with the competence of the tetrarchs. Even more important was the forceful personality of Diocletian, who imposed solidarity on his colleagues.

Diocletian himself may only have visited Rome once during his reign, when he chose to celebrate the twentieth anniversary of his acclamation in the city. Rome remained a powerful symbol and its population continued to be pampered with festivals, games and free doles. Diocletian ordered the construction of a massive bath complex, larger than any of the earlier public baths. There was also considerable building work in the Forum, repairing and remodelling after a major fire had swept through this part of the City during Carinus' reign. The Curia (Senate House) visited by so many tourists today is essentially a tetrachic building, restored in the twentieth century some thirteen hundred years after it had become the Church of St Hadrian. Politically and strategically, neither the Senate nor Rome were now of more than marginal importance to the empire and its rulers.[12]

When any of the tetrarchs were in Italy they were far more likely to be found in the north at Milan, more conveniently placed to move east into Illyria, or north-west into Gaul. The cities most often chosen for imperial residences give an indication of the tetrarchs' priorities – Trier on the Rhine, Sirmium near the Danube, Antioch in Syria and Nicomedia in Bithynia. All acquired palaces, usually with an adjacent circus, and other grand buildings. Trier's prosperity contrasted with the harder times faced by other communities in the area. It would be wrong to speak of any of these places as permanent capitals as each of the tetrarchs moved frequently. All went to war at various times, and even when they were not actually on campaign they tended to move from city to city. The many decrees and legal rulings of Diocletian preserved in later collections of Roman law were issued from a huge range of different places. The court and, in a real sense, the capital were wherever the emperor happened to be at the time.[13]

Emperors did not travel or live alone. Each of the tetrarchs was protected by thousands of soldiers from guard units. These had grown in number in recent decades so that the praetorians were relegated to a comparatively minor role as little more than the garrison of Rome. Diocletian was the commander of one of these new guard regiments when he was proclaimed emperor. If there was a prospect of actual campaigning – frequently a real possibility when the emperor was in frontier zones – then the guards would be supplemented by more troops. The trend for emperors to keep strong military forces at their immediate disposal had grown since Septimius Severus had increased the numbers of soldiers in and around Rome. One hostile source claimed that under Diocletian the size of the army quadrupled because each of the tetrarchs wanted as many soldiers as their colleagues. This was certainly a huge exaggeration. There were many more units in the army, but each was probably smaller in size than had been the case in earlier periods. Whether or not there was still an overall increase, it is clear that each of the tetrarchs controlled substantial numbers of troops. Superior military force was the ultimate guarantee of imperial power.[14]

Soldiers guarded an emperor, but he could not govern through them. Whatever the size of the army under Diocletian, it is absolutely certain that there had been a massive rise in the number of civil officials. Augustus and his successors for two centuries had run the empire with the tiniest of bureaucracies. Its origins and its basic nature evolved from the household of a Republican senator – the slaves, freedmen and sometimes also friends who helped run his private business and assisted him when he held a public magistracy. The staffs of provincial governors were similar, but smaller, and might be supplemented in military provinces by seconded soldiers. This system did not change in any fundamental way during the first and second centuries. The size of the imperial household grew a little and its organisation became a little more formal. The unpopularity amongst the elite of powerful imperial freedmen led to some reliance on men of higher social background – usually equestrians – in the more senior public roles. A huge amount of day-to-day administration was devolved to local communities, most especially cities, but also villages or tribes where these did not exist. Depending on who is included in the figure, the 'bureaucrats' of the imperial government numbered in hundreds, or at the very most just over a thousand.

By the beginning of the fourth century this total had soared to somewhere between 30,000 and 35,000 – an orator once described the hordes of minor officials as 'more numerous than flies on sheep in springtime'. The growth of bureaucracy was gradual, but it was greatly accelerated under Diocletian. Part of this was simply the natural result of multiplying the number of emperors. Each now had to have a court and administrative departments – for instance, to handle justice, taxation and other forms of revenue, correspondence in both Latin and Greek, controlling provincial governors and maintaining the army. Many offices were simply duplicated. Both Diocletian and Maximian had a praetorian prefect, who had lost virtually all his military responsibilities and was effectively an administrator. The Caesars Constantius and Galerius did not, but did have their own officials and heads for all the other departments.[15]

The Severans had split up the great military provinces to prevent any governor becoming too powerful and so a potential threat. The tendency to divide provinces into smaller regions continued on and off throughout the third century. By the time Diocletian became emperor there were about fifty provinces – roughly a third more than in the days of Marcus Aurelius. Diocletian then 'sliced up the provinces into little pieces' according to one particularly critical source, doubling their number. This was not primarily about protecting himself from usurpers – the great military provinces with garrisons of 30,000–40,000 men had long since gone. Instead, it had far more to do with control and taxation.[16]

There were now many more governors, each in charge of a much smaller area than would have been typical in the first or second century. Italy and a handful of other provinces of no military importance were governed by senators known as *correctores*, but everywhere else the governors were equestrians. By the end of the reign even these had lost virtually all authority over troops. In a radical break from a very old Roman tradition, only emperors still combined civil and military power. Apart from general administration, governors had a particularly important role in overseeing justice and finance in their provinces.[17]

There were more provinces and more governors. Each may well have had a larger staff than was typical in earlier centuries. The result was a huge increase in the number of imperial representatives in each region (even if these would still seem small compared to the bureaucracies of modern states). In one sense this made it harder for the emperors to keep a close eye on what their agents were doing. Provinces were therefore grouped together into larger units known as dioceses. Eventually there were twelve of these – Italy, Spain, the Gauls, Viennensis, Britain, Africa, the Pannonias, the Moesias, the Thraces, Asiana, Pontica and Oriens. Unofficially, Italy was effectively divided into two. In charge of each diocese was a subordinate of the praetorian prefect. These men were called *vicarii* (from which we get the word 'vicar') because they acted in the place of the prefect. It was not a rigid hierarchy. Emperors frequently chose to deal directly with a governor without going through the *vicarius* for that diocese. Similarly, they might deal with a *vicarius* without consulting his praetorian prefect. On occasions, subordinates could also choose to bypass their superiors and appeal to the emperor or prefect directly.[18]

The command structure of the army was entirely separate. The frontier regions and other areas that required a strong military presence were divided up into districts. All the troops stationed in this district were placed under the command of an officer known as a *dux* (duke, pl. *duces*). These military zones did not correspond to provincial boundaries and usually included territory from two or more provinces. Other troops not confined to any fixed garrison were commanded by different officers whose rank was *comes* (count, pl. *comites*). In the past the same term had applied to companions – usually senators – who accompanied the emperor on an expedition. A distinction emerged early in the fourth century between troops likely to serve under the command of an emperor, who became known as the *comitatenses*, and the troops of the *duces*, who became known as the *limitanei*.[19]

Both soldiers and administrators were servants of the emperors. The bureaucrats had ranks and uniforms all clearly derived from the army. They wore military caps, tunics and the belt with its large circular buckle from which a soldier would suspend his sword's scabbard. Time in any government post was described as *militia* (military service), and it became common for members of a department to be nominally enrolled in a legion or other military unit that had long since ceased to exist. Yet in spite of this military façade, the army and civil service were kept utterly distinct. Men pursued a career in one or the other, but did not switch between the two. Over time a huge number of different grades were created within civilian departments, creating a hierarchy even more complicated than the rank structure of the army. Instead of recruiting

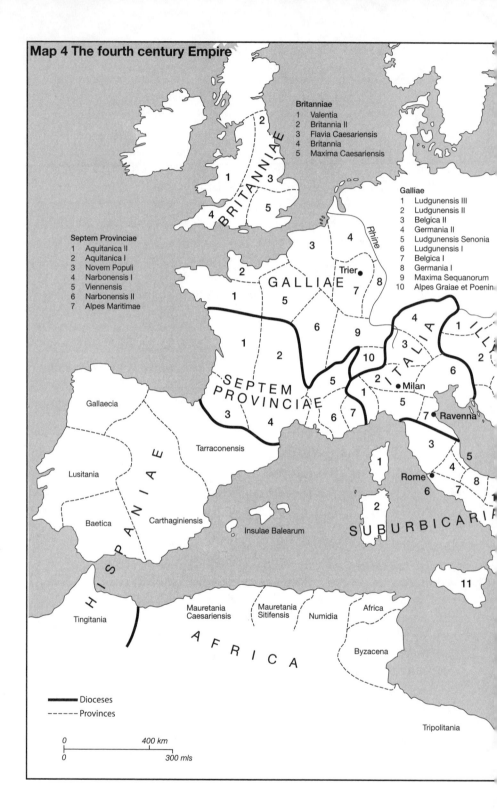

Map 4 The fourth century Empire

Britanniae
1 Valentia
2 Britannia II
3 Flavia Caesariensis
4 Britannia
5 Maxima Caesariensis

Galliae
1 Ludgunensis III
2 Ludgunensis II
3 Belgica II
4 Germania II
5 Ludgunensis Senonia
6 Ludgunensis I
7 Belgica I
8 Germania I
9 Maxima Sequanorum
10 Alpes Graiae et Poenin

Septem Provinciae
1 Aquitanica II
2 Aquitanica I
3 Novem Populi
4 Narbonensis I
5 Viennensis
6 Narbonensis II
7 Alpes Maritimae

BRITANNIAE

GALLIAE

Rhine

Trier

SEPTEM PROVINCIAE

ITALIA

Milan

ILL

Ravenna

Gallaecia

Tarraconensis

Lusitania

HISPANIAE

Baetica

Carthaginiensis

Insulae Balearum

Rome

SUBURBICARI

Tingitania

Mauretania Caesariensis

Mauretania Sitifensis

Numidia

Africa

AFRICA

Byzacena

Tripolitania

— Dioceses
---- Provinces

0   400 km
0   300 mls

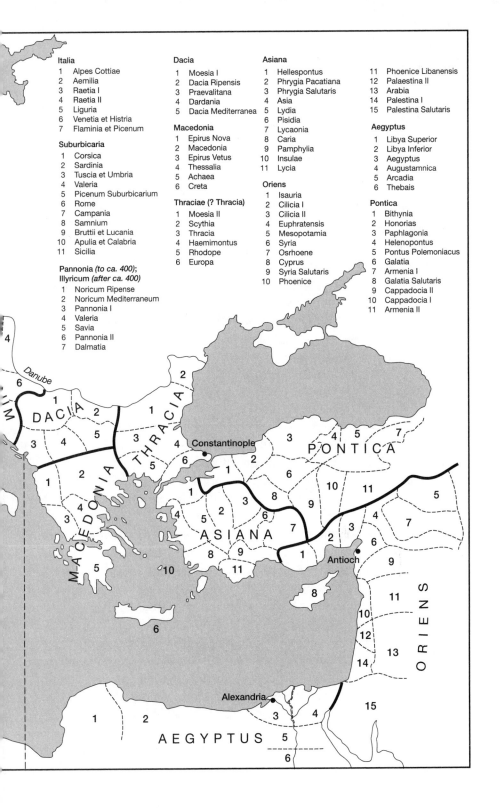

Italia
1 Alpes Cottiae
2 Aemilia
3 Raetia I
4 Raetia II
5 Liguria
6 Venetia et Histria
7 Flaminia et Picenum

Suburbicaria
1 Corsica
2 Sardinia
3 Tuscia et Umbria
4 Valeria
5 Picenum Suburbicarium
6 Rome
7 Campania
8 Samnium
9 Bruttii et Lucania
10 Apulia et Calabria
11 Sicilia

Pannonia (to ca. 400);
Illyricum (after ca. 400)
1 Noricum Ripense
2 Noricum Mediterraneum
3 Pannonia I
4 Valeria
5 Savia
6 Pannonia II
7 Dalmatia

Dacia
1 Moesia I
2 Dacia Ripensis
3 Praevalitana
4 Dardania
5 Dacia Mediterranea

Macedonia
1 Epirus Nova
2 Macedonia
3 Epirus Vetus
4 Thessalia
5 Achaea
6 Creta

Thraciae (? Thracia)
1 Moesia II
2 Scythia
3 Thracia
4 Haemimontus
5 Rhodope
6 Europa

Asiana
1 Hellespontus
2 Phrygia Pacatiana
3 Phrygia Salutaris
4 Asia
5 Lydia
6 Pisidia
7 Lycaonia
8 Caria
9 Pamphylia
10 Insulae
11 Lycia

Oriens
1 Isauria
2 Cilicia I
3 Cilicia II
4 Euphratensis
5 Mesopotamia
6 Syria
7 Osrhoene
8 Cyprus
9 Syria Salutaris
10 Phoenice

11 Phoenice Libanensis
12 Palaestina II
13 Arabia
14 Palestina I
15 Palestina Salutaris

Aegyptus
1 Libya Superior
2 Libya Inferior
3 Aegyptus
4 Augustamnica
5 Arcadia
6 Thebais

Pontica
1 Bithynia
2 Honorias
3 Paphlagonia
4 Helenopontus
5 Pontus Polemoniacus
6 Galatia
7 Armenia I
8 Galatia Salutaris
9 Cappadocia II
10 Cappadocia I
11 Armenia II

Danube

DACIA

THRACIA

Constantinople

PONTICA

MACEDONIA

ASIANA

Antioch

ORIENS

Alexandria

AEGYPTUS

men from specific social groups, status tended to become tied to rank, so that senior posts brought with them promotion to senatorial status. Equestrians enjoyed a virtual monopoly of the higher ranks in the army and civil service, but this led to the creation of several different grades within the order. Again, over time the grade was gained by holding a post and was not a prerequisite for it.[20]

Aspirations and Reality

Government had become a lot bigger. It was certainly more visible and more likely that ordinary citizens would come into greater contact with it during their lives. In theory at least, the development of a much larger bureaucratic machine could have allowed the emperors to run the empire more efficiently. Caracalla's universal grant of citizenship had made most of the population of the empire subject to Roman law, something imperfectly understood in many regions and so only gradually adopted. In the long run this inevitably placed a greater strain on the provincial governors and their small number of subordinates with the power and ability to act as a judge. More governors with enlarged staffs were, in part, intended to deal with this increased business.

Yet the first concern of all emperors was revenue. All knew that they could not stay in power unless they were able to maintain the army and meet the smaller, but still dramatically increased cost of the enlarged bureaucracy. Emperors had significant private funds, for they were the largest landowners in the Roman world. Imperial estates had begun simply as the private property of Augustus and his successors. They were augmented by conquests and the confiscation of property from the condemned. Since the end of one dynasty usually meant that there were no heirs, the imperial estates continued to grow as lines died out and new emperors came to power. A distinct section of the department in charge of revenue administered the income from these lands.

On their own, the imperial estates provided only a fraction of the income needed by emperors. The bulk had always come from taxation, mainly in cash, but always including some paid in goods – usually agricultural produce. Whatever the impact of inflation in the third century on the wider population, it had drastically reduced the real value of taxes. Many of these were levied at fixed rates that had remained static for centuries. Similarly, the salaries paid to those in imperial service – soldiers and civilians alike – did not increase dramatically after the early third century and had fallen in their purchasing power.[21]

Diocletian embarked upon a fundamental reorganisation of the taxation and levy system. Communities were assessed in terms of two basic units, measuring both land and labour force. Land was divided into *iugera*, the size of which varied according to the type of farming possible there and its expected productivity. The second unit was the head count of the adult population available to work the land. From these two units the obligation to the government of a region was established. Setting up the system may have taken a decade or so, as parties of assessors travelled to each province. There were many local variations – for instance, in the age of those counted and whether women were included along with men, as well as the inevitably subjective judgements of land quality. Even so, a uniform taxation system was imposed throughout the entire empire.[22]

In the majority of cases tax was levied in the form of produce, protecting the system from inflation. Much of this was used to supply the army directly, and anything not needed could be sold at the current market rate. In addition, pay for soldiers and civil servants became largely based on rations of food, fodder and other commodities. (This was not true of the donatives issued regularly to commemorate the accession dates of the emperors, which continued to be paid in gold.) What was not needed could be sold or exchanged for what was. Later in the fourth century parts of the system became somewhat artificial as many of the rations were commuted into cash. There is no evidence that this was the case at the beginning, but it is equally unclear how the system functioned in every detail. As an example, how would a clerk in one of the civil departments dispose of unwanted fodder or grain, since there would usually be so many other members of the court trying to sell off their excess at the same time and in the same place? Perhaps there were agents who acted for a group of imperial employees and divided the produce, but it may be that the government did not actually go to the laborious task of delivering each ration to each recipient and instead paid them an equivalent based on an assessment of the going rate.

Diocletian also embarked on a thorough reform of the currency. Gold and silver denominations minted to a reasonably high standard were created. There was also a copper coin with a thin wash of silver known as the *nummus* which was intended for much day-to-day exchange. As part of the multiplication of government more mints were created, producing coins for the immediate use of army and administration in that area. Inflation may have slowed, but did not stop. In 301 Diocletian issued an edict intended to regulate the sale price of goods. Inscriptions bearing parts of the text of this have been found from sites in a number of eastern provinces, but it does not seem to have been circulated or enforced in the western provinces under Maximian.[23]

A great range of items was included. A measure (the Roman unit known as a *modius* = a quarter bushel) of wheat cost 100 denarii, of barley or rye 60 denarii, while the same quantity of oats was worth only 30 denarii. Wine varied from the high quality – for instance, the Falernian wine praised by the poet Horace three centuries earlier – at 30 denarii to the cheapest at a mere 8 denarii. A pound of pork was 12 denarii, while the same weight of high-quality fattened gooseflesh was no less than 200 denarii. Apart from foodstuffs many other goods, from spices to clothing, were listed. Also included were proper rates of pay for many different professions. Teachers were paid per pupil, tailors for each specific job they did and labourers by the day. All values were in denarii, and although it had been a long time since anyone had minted a single denarius coin it still remained the basic unit for currency. A law some months earlier had set the value of a silver coin at 100 denarii and the silver-washed copper *nummus* at 25 and 4 denarii depending on its size.[24]

The only literary source to mention the price edict derides it as an utter failure, ignored by merchants who knew that they could charge more for their goods. Papyri from Egypt do suggest that prices soon rose far beyond the supposed maximums established by the emperor. As far as we can tell it was abandoned fairly quickly, but at least one copy was maintained long enough for a few of the prices to be altered. In his long introduction to the edict, Diocletian reminded his audience of the stability and success his rule had brought, and claimed to be expressly concerned that his brave soldiers were being overcharged. There may also have been a desire to set rates at which the state would pay for goods and services regardless of the market price.[25]

Diocletian's government lacked the machinery to enforce such a rigid pricing system on a day-to-day basis. Perhaps the most striking thing about the edict was its ambition – even if it was economically naive. Combined with the objective of profound change is the highly moral rhetoric. Talk of 'the peaceful state of the world' now that the 'seething ravages of barbarians peoples' have been restrained by great effort, is followed by outrage at a new evil attacking the soldiers. 'There burns a raging greed, which hastens to its own growth and increase without respect for human kind.' A little later the emperor compared this greed to a religion. The tone is typical of the other legislative activity of the tetrarchs and of their recorded rescripts – replies issued to legal questions and appeals sent to the emperor. The sense of outrage was accompanied by savage and often inventively cruel punishments.[26]

Born around 240, Diocletian was far more successful than any of the other emperors in his own lifetime, or indeed for a generation before that. Having lived through decades of disorder and chaos, there was a good deal of truth in the tetrarchs' claims to have brought peace and restoration. Diocletian may genuinely have believed his own propaganda. He certainly felt that the best way to deal with the empire's problems was to impose strong central control. This was not a new idea. Bureaucracy had been growing in the last decades. The turnover of emperors was so rapid that officials, especially those of middle rank who were less likely to be purged when a regime changed, provided the most stable element in government. Diocletian stayed in power longer than his recent predecessors, his strength increasing with each passing year. He was therefore able to take much further the trend towards centralised government.

However, it was still a gradual process. He may have had some long-term plans from early in his reign, even if these ideas were developed or replaced over the years. The creation of new provinces and the growth of government departments were not instant. The tax reforms were probably not completely functioning until near the end of his reign. The new institutions of government helped to strengthen his position, but they were not the cause of his success and longevity. Their effectiveness also depended to a great extent on his own drive, political ability and sense of purpose. Closely supervised and led by carefully chosen and loyal praetorian prefects and governors, the new bureaucracy allowed the emperor to have far more impact on life in the provinces. The scope and tone of his decrees suggest that Diocletian believed that he could and should regulate anything brought to his attention.[27]

The emperors were supreme and ruled through a vast number of officials who had power and status only because they were imperial representatives. The tetrarchs themselves were far above them in dignity and authority. They were distant figures, closely guarded at all times. The slaves who cared for them – now increasingly often eunuchs – became powerful. The senior servants, like the Grand Chamberlain (*praepositus sacri cubiculi*), Superintendent of the Bedchamber (*primicerius sacri cubiculi*), and the Chief Steward (*castrensis sacri palatini*), in due course were ranked higher than the vast bulk of the nobility. When emperors resided in cities they did so in splendour. When they travelled they were surrounded by thousands of troops, bureaucrats and attendants, as well as the hundreds or even thousands more people who had come to the court in the hope of presenting a petition. From Diocletian onwards it was harder to approach emperors, which did at least mean it was also far more difficult to murder them. Some sources and historians have seen this new ceremonial at court as inspired by the authoritarian rule of the Persian kings. This is deeply questionable, and we should remember that there was a very old rhetoric stretching back to Herodotus presenting kings and most especially eastern monarchs like the Persians as the epitome of tyranny. It is far more likely that Diocletian enjoyed ceremony and felt it added to the majesty of his rule. Anything likely to instil obedience in his subjects and deter rebellion was to be welcomed.[28]

The success of Diocletian and his imperial colleagues emphasised the still massive power of the Roman empire. Given a period of relative peace and stability, and most of all a time of continuity in government, the Romans re-established a degree of dominance on their frontiers. Diocletian was able to raise more tax revenue than had been possible for more than a generation, which in turn funded the military activity. New forts were built and old ones repaired. Generally the new bases were smaller, but had higher and thicker walls than earlier forts and fortresses. Victories were won over barbarian tribes, treaties negotiated from a position of strength and, as the reign wore on, fear of Roman might grew once more. Potential raiders became more cautious. There were still attacks, but they were fewer and more often caught and defeated. The situation had improved, but it would have taken far longer to undo all the damage of past defeats.[29]

Sassanid Persia became aggressive again early on in the reign. After a renewed period of civil war – his predecessor only lasted a few months – in 293 or 294 Narses came to the throne. Victor in a civil war, he was both a strong military leader and deeply insecure. A war with Rome offered the prospect of glory and uniting his subjects against a foreign enemy. The Persians attacked, most probably raiding into the Roman provinces in 296. Galerius was sent against them and may well have suffered a reverse – this is the context of the story about Diocletian making his Caesar run alongside his chariot (see page 162). With greater resources, including troops transferred from other regions, Galerius renewed the war and this time won a spectacular victory. Narses' camp was captured, and along with it his harem and much of his household. Ctesiphon was once again taken by a Roman army, probably in 297 or

298. Early in the following year a peace treaty was imposed on the Persian king, who gave up some territory and acknowledged Roman supremacy over a number of independent border kingdoms including Armenia. The frontier between the two powers was set at the Tigris, and the city of Nisibis – now back in Roman hands – was established as the only legal place for merchants to pass between the two empires. This helped each side to control the bulk of contact, as well as to tax the trade passing between the empires. The peace, which was very much to Rome's advantage, lasted for forty years.[30]

Diocletian was one of the most important emperors in Roman history. Just like Augustus, he came to power after a long period of civil war and disorder, and both profoundly changed the state through their reforms. Neither acted in a vacuum, but developed already existing trends in public life almost as much as they innovated. Perhaps more than anyone else, Diocletian established the shape of the fourth-century empire and in doing so removed most of the last traces of the Augustan regime. The military dictatorship was no longer veiled but blatant. The tetrarchy was effective because of the strength and solidarity of its members. Ultimately, its greatest test was the question of succession. In this respect, however, the tetrarchy failed.

9

The Christian

'Constantine, the superior of the Emperors in rank and dignity, was the first to take pity on those subjected to tyranny at Rome; and, calling in prayer upon God who is in heaven, and His Word, even Jesus Christ the Saviour of all, as his ally, he advanced in full force, seeking to secure for the Romans their ancestral liberty.' – *Eusebius, c.325.*[1]

'Now that the whole empire had devolved on Constantine, his arrogance increased and he was carried away with his success.' – *Zosimus, late fifth century.*[2]

On 1 May 305 the tetrarchs simultaneously held two grand parades on opposite sides of the empire. Diocletian and Galerius were just outside Nicomedia, and Maximian and Constantius were at Milan. The cities were the most common residence for the two senior emperors, but in Diocletian's case the spot had a particular significance, for it was there, just over twenty years before, that the army had proclaimed him emperor. Now, aged about sixty and in poor health, he formally resigned his office. Maximian simultaneously did the same at Milan, although subsequent events would make it clear that he acted unwillingly. Galerius stood beside Diocletian and Constantius beside Maximian, and the two Caesars were now each promoted to the status of Augustus. To aid them in their task two new Caesars were appointed. Diocletian unclasped his purple imperial cloak and draped it over the shoulders of Galerius' nephew Maximinus Daia. By the same gesture, Maximian elevated the general Severus to the imperial college.

No senior officer or official can have been surprised by this carefully orchestrated power change, for preparations must have been underway for some time. The promotion of Constantius and Galerius was anticipated, but some sources claim that the choice of Caesars surprised at least the junior ranks in the army. Constantius and Maximian both had adult sons who seemed more obvious candidates. Severus was a close associate of Galerius and it is clear that the latter expected to dominate the new tetrarchy just as Diocletian had controlled his imperial colleagues.[3]

It is impossible to know when and why Diocletian decided to resign. Some scholars see it as a long-held plan, fundamental to his concept of the tetrarchy, but this is surely too schematic. It is more natural to see his regime as developing gradually and not part of some master plan. He had recently recovered from a serious illness and he may simply have lacked the strength or the enthusiasm for the task of ruling the empire. The Christian writer Lactantius, who until a few years before had taught rhetoric in Nicomedia itself, claimed that Galerius pressured the ailing emperor into resigning and then selected the new Caesars himself. We need to be cautious, because Lactantius disliked both men, because they had persecuted the church and his book described the gruesome fates of all who did this. Yet it is undeniable that the new regime was built around Galerius, and in recent years he was the best placed of the tetrarchs to influence Diocletian. Even so, the latter had always proved single-minded in the past and it may be that he believed Galerius was the best choice.[4]

However willingly, Diocletian resigned. For the moment, as in the past, Maximian was unable to resist his more forceful colleague. The empire had four new rulers, one of whom expected to impose his will on the other three and impose solidarity. He failed. It is doubtful that Galerius was as good a politician as Diocletian, but the main difference was the existence of potential rivals with a good enough blood claim to imperial power to rally support. As in the past, one usurpation tended to encourage others. The first came in Britain, just over a year later.

Constantine

Constantius' son Constantine was in his early thirties when he witnessed the acclamation of Galerius and Maximinus Daia at Nicomedia. He had already proved himself a capable officer, fighting on the Danube and against the Persians. For a while he remained with Galerius and stories subsequently circulated of attempts by the latter to engineer his death – ordering him to lead a charge and then withholding reserves, and even commanding him to fight a lion single-handed. Finally, when his father requested that he come to join him in Britain, Constantine is supposed to have slipped away quietly. Using the imperial post with its system of relay stations and fresh mounts, he rode hell for leather to escape, killing the horses he did not need to prevent pursuit. Reaching the bedside of his dying father at York, Constantius had just enough breath left to name him as his successor. Most of this tale is probably romantic invention. In fact, we know that Constantine spent several months in Britain with his father. This was important, for it permitted him to build up a rapport with his senior officers and officials.[5]

Constantius died in York on 25 July 306 and Constantine was immediately proclaimed as his successor by the senior army officers there, backed by their troops. For the moment he claimed only the rank of Caesar and sent envoys with an image of himself in imperial regalia to Galerius, seeking his acknowledgement. This was duly given, in marked contrast to Diocletian's rejection of the claims of Carausius. Galerius also now promoted Severus to the rank of Augustus, completing the tetrarchy once again. However, the appearance of stability did not last.

Maximian had retired to a villa in Italy and his son Maxentius was in Rome in October. Earlier in the year Galerius had issued a decree extending Diocletian's system of taxation to cover Italy as well as the provinces, ending more than four centuries of the region's exemption from direct taxation. Maxentius fed off the unpopularity of this and was proclaimed emperor at Rome by a range of supporters including the praetorian guard – the last time it would make an emperor. Maximian came out of retirement to back his son, once again calling himself Augustus. This time Galerius and Severus were adamant in refusing to accept any more additions to the imperial college.

Severus gathered an army at Milan and marched on Rome in 307, but almost all of his officers and soldiers had been commanded by Maximian before his retirement. They showed no enthusiasm for fighting against their old commander and soon began to desert. Severus fled, but was captured, held prisoner and forced to resign as Augustus. In the autumn Galerius invaded Italy, but he was unable to force the enemy to risk an open battle and was not prepared for such a major undertaking as besieging Rome so late in the year. It is claimed that he was amazed at the sheer size of a city that he had never seen before – a striking reaction from the ruler of the Roman world, but a sign of the city's now marginal importance. Galerius withdrew and did not repeat the attempt. Maxentius responded by having Severus killed, making full reconciliation unlikely.[6]

During this period Constantine campaigned on the Rhine frontier, winning the victories that were expected of an emperor. He did not formally break with Galerius, but nevertheless dealt with Maximian, marrying his daughter Fausta at Trier in 307. (Maximian's older daughter Theodora seems to have died some years before her husband Constantius. She was not the mother of Constantine, for he was the product of an earlier liaison – there is considerable doubt that it was a legal marriage, and Constantine's mother may have been Constantius' mistress rather than his wife.) Maximian proclaimed Constantine as Augustus. He had already squabbled with his own son so remained at the court of Constantine. The Roman world now had five emperors.[7]

In 308 Diocletian came out of retirement to support Galerius. They met with Maximian at Carnuntum on the Danube and appointed as Augustus an officer named Licinius, who was another close associate of Galerius. Maximinus Daia and Constantine were confirmed as Caesars, but permitted to call themselves 'sons of the Augusti'. Maxentius was ignored, but was anyway kept busy by the rebellion of a usurper named Domitius Alexander, who had been proclaimed in Africa and was not suppressed until the following year. After the conference Diocletian went back to cultivate cabbages at his palace in Sirmium – he is supposed to have boasted about their flavour – and Maximian also resumed his retirement.[8]

Diocletian's intervention brought an uneasy truce, but also showed just how far the stability of the tetrarchy depended on the imperial college being dominated by one man. In 310 Maximian once again decided to take back power and rebelled against Constantine. He was swiftly suppressed and executed. Both Constantine and Maximinus Daia soon took back the title Augustus – the latter was said to have been very bitter after seeing first Severus and then Licinius promoted over his head. Galerius died the next year – he was suffering from cancer of the penis and his last days were said by Lactantius to have been particularly unpleasant. Licinius and Maximinus Daia rushed to carve up his territory, eventually accepting a division at the Bosphorus. Diocletian may have died around the same time, but there are a number of traditions about his end, some claiming disease and others suicide.[9]

In 312 Constantine attacked Maxentius. His army was loyal, toughened by campaigns on the frontiers, and he was a very capable general. Marching quickly, he defeated Maxentius' subordinates in northern Italy and then approached Rome itself. The city's walls offered it protection from sudden assaults, but such a long circuit wall was difficult to defend against a properly organised attacker. It would also have damaged

Maxentius' prestige to skulk behind defences against a challenger whom he seems to have substantially outnumbered. He led his army out and crossed the Tiber at the Milvian bridge – the stone bridge had been demolished, so a pontoon bridge had been constructed next to it. In spite of their numbers, neither general nor army was a match for their opponents, and Constantine won an overwhelming victory. Maxentius was killed and many of his panicking soldiers drowned when they streamed across the pontoon bridge and it collapsed under their weight.[10]

Three emperors were left and Constantine and Licinius now allied. In 313 Licinius married Constantine's half-sister Constantia (one of the children of Theodora), before he led his army eastwards against Maximinus Daia. The latter had crossed into Europe and advanced along the main road through the Balkans. They met near the city of Adrianople on 30 April and Daia's army was routed. He escaped, but was hunted down and committed suicide in July. The two emperors left standing now agreed to split the provinces between them, Constantine taking the western and Licinius the eastern provinces.

In 316 Constantine provocatively crossed into Licinius' territory during the course of a campaign against some Sarmatian tribes. If he hoped to provoke a war and not simply assert his seniority, he may have been shocked to find his enemy stronger than expected. There were two battles, the second once again near Adrianople, but although Constantine won both, his victory was not overwhelming. In a negotiated settlement Licinius gave up almost all of his provinces in Europe. In 324 the struggle was renewed. Once again, the road system shaped the campaign and Constantine won his first victory near Adrianople. Licinius retired to Byzantium, but lost a naval battle and then fled to Asia Minor. Constantine pursued and won a final victory at Chrysopolis. Licinius surrendered and was allowed to go into comfortable captivity. Some time later he was charged with conspiracy and executed, along with his infant son. Constantia was spared and lived on as an honoured member of the imperial court.[11]

For the first time in almost forty years the empire was united under a single emperor. It is true that during his reign Constantine named several of his sons as Caesars, but there was never any doubt that he was supreme. Going further than Septimus Severus, who had merely 'found a father', Constantine had long since spuriously declared himself the descendant of the brief, but honoured Claudius II. He made no attempt to revive the tetrarchy and his success rather undermines modern claims that it was now essential to have more than one emperor. Like Diocletian he was a 'strongman' who defeated all his opponents and intimidated any other potential challengers. Unlike Diocletian he chose not to do this through taking and dominating imperial colleagues, but preferred to rule alone. The success of both men had far more to do with personality, political skill and single-minded ruthlessness, than with any of the institutions they employed. Altogether Constantine was an emperor for thirty-two years, although he only controlled the entire empire for thirteen.[12]

The Church

Constantine is famous as the emperor who made the empire Christian. The truth is a good deal more complicated than this, and the preceding narrative has deliberately omitted any mention of his religion. This is not because it was not significant, but because he needs to be understood first as one of the many – though admittedly one of the most successful – usurpers who competed for imperial power in the third and fourth centuries. This was the context of his conversion, and of his religious attitudes and policy. It is misleading to transfer the novelty of his faith to analysis of his political career. Perhaps more than at any other time, there is a great danger of turning a history of Constantine's reign into essentially a history of Christianity – and especially orthodox Catholic Christianity – during these years, simply because this was the concern of the overwhelming majority of the sources.

For a generation after Gallienus called off his father's persecution of the Church, Christian communities across the empire had been free from systematic persecution. This promoted the already pronounced trend for Christianity to become much more visible. Bishops, as Paul of Samosata's controversial career at Antioch had shown, often became well-recognised local dignitaries. Churches were built openly in many towns and cities – there was one next to Diocletian's palace in Nicomedia. There were Christians in many walks of life, including the army and imperial administration, and only occasionally did some of them find that their beliefs became incompatible with their official duties. Tacitly, Christianity seemed to be accepted and no longer seen as a threat to the empire. The wild rumours of cannibalism and incest had largely gone, and many people had a much clearer idea of what the Christians believed. The Neoplatonist philosopher Porphyry based his attacks on the Church on a very detailed knowledge of Jewish and Christian scriptures.[13]

There had been a last burst of persecution under the tetrarchy. Diocletian is supposed to have first become concerned when the priests conducting an unsuccessful augury blamed the failure on Christians in the crowd making the sign of the cross. In 297 all imperial officials and soldiers were required to display their loyalty by performing a sacrifice. Some Christians resigned in response, more probably did just enough to conform, and a few openly refused and were executed. In 303 there was a more concerted move against the Church, prompted in part by a fire in the palace in Nicomedia, which was blamed on Christian arsonists. The focus of the new round of persecution gives a good idea of just how well established and public the Christian movement had become. Churches were targeted – the one next to the palace in Nicomedia was the first to be demolished – and associated assets were confiscated. All Christian scriptures were to be handed over to the authorities and burned. Rather than seeking out every Christian, it was mainly the leaders who were arrested and torture was employed to force them to recant. Those who refused were imprisoned, subjected to more savage coercion and in due course often executed if they continued to resist.

As in the past, Diocletian's main aim was to impose outward conformity and unity throughout the empire. Again, as in earlier persecutions of the Church, much depended on the enthusiasm of governors and other local officials. In some regions it was strongly pressed and extremely brutal, and probably all the more shocking to a Christian community that had been free of such attacks for decades. Diocletian was an enthusiastic persecutor, Maximian and Galerius somewhat less committed, and Constantius decidedly lukewarm. The latter demolished churches, but does not seem to have executed anyone.[14]

The Christians were not the only group to suffer in these years. In 302 Diocletian had also ordered the persecution of the followers of the prophet Mani. Born in Persia in 216, the latter had travelled widely, including a visit to India, and the religion he created showed the influence of Jewish, Christian, Zoroastrian, Buddhist and other ideas. Diocletian seems to have viewed the Manichees as potentially subversive because of their presumed sympathy with the Persians. In his decree he claimed that they 'had sprung forth very recently like novel and unexpected monstrosities from the race of Persians – a nation hostile to us – and have made their way into our empire, where they are committing many outrages, disturbing the tranquillity of the people and even inflicting grave harm on the civic communities'. He feared that in time they would 'infect the modest and tranquil Roman race ... and our whole empire'. It is doubtful that his suspicion was correct, for although Ardashir and Shapur I had treated Mani with respect, their successors had persecuted the cult, executing the prophet himself in 276.[15]

Persecuting the church was scarcely Diocletian's greatest priority in the last years of his reign, although it obviously dominated the accounts of our Christian sources. After his resignation, Galerius and especially Maximinus Daia were enthusiastic persecutors, but again, often had other more important concerns. There is very little evidence that by this time the wider pagan population had much enthusiasm for persecuting Christians. In his last days Galerius issued a decree admitting that persecution had failed to stamp out Christianity. Therefore, Christians would now be permitted freedom of worship and allowed to rebuild their churches, although their confiscated property was not restored. As a result, 'it will be their duty to pray to their god for our safety and for that of the state and themselves, so that from every side the state may be kept unharmed and they may be able to live free of care in their own homes'. Within less than a year Maximinus resumed the persecution, refusing to enforce Galerius' decision. Replying to one petitioner he blamed the Christians' abandonment of the old cults for all the ills of the world, such as war, plagues and earthquakes.[16]

Both Constantine and Maxentius adopted a benevolent attitude towards the Christians when they first seized power, not wanting to alienate any potential supporters. The latter's enthusiasm seems to have cooled once he became more secure. Constantine's father Constantius had not only been very restrained in the years of persecution, but seems to have had a number of Christians in his household. For himself, he remained devoted to the worship of Sol Invictus (the Unconquered Sun) – the popular supreme god whose protection Aurelian had claimed. Throughout the third century there was a tendency amongst many pagans towards a form of monotheism, revering one deity above all others, and perhaps seeing the various gods and goddesses as merely manifestations of a single divine being. Several of the main philosophical schools had taught similar ideas for centuries. Whatever the specific nature of Constantius' beliefs, he certainly did not feel any great hostility towards Christians and may have had a good deal of sympathy, although the 'closet' Christianity claimed for him in later years is unconvincing. Constantine appears to have begun with a similar attitude. Like many people in the ancient world, he believed profoundly in the power of the gods to communicate in dreams. In 310 one panegyrist proudly asserted that he had been granted a vision by the sun god Apollo and this was reflected on his coinage.[17]

Before the Battle of the Milvian Bridge, Constantine ordered his men to paint their shields with a Christian symbol – probably the chi-rho, but possibly a cross with the head turned into a letter 'P'. It was a temporary gesture, probably not repeated in any of his subsequent campaigns. Although the emperor's closest bodyguards seem to have continued to carry shields bearing the chi-rho, the rest of the army kept their traditional insignia, some of it pagan. This was still true at the end of the century and most likely had more to do with unit pride and tradition than particular beliefs. In 312 it was a one-off gesture, intended to inspire his men with the belief that they had divine aid. On a practical level, it also helped to identify the soldiers – always a problem in a civil war fought between armies with identical uniforms and equipment.[18]

The inspiration for Constantine's order was variously explained, and it is likely that the story grew in the telling. The earliest account in Lactantius speaks of the emperor having a dream the night before the battle in which the Christian God instructed him to do this. Later, after Constantine's death, his biographer Eusebius claimed that the emperor himself had spoken of an earlier omen, when he and his army looked up at the noon sun and saw the symbol of a cross against it, with the words in Latin, 'by this conquer' (*hoc signo victor eris*, or 'in this sign you will conquer' in the slightly fuller Latin, although the text gives it in Greek). That night Jesus appeared to him in a dream and explained that using the symbol would bring him victory. In the end, the details do not really matter. Constantine believed that the Christian God had promised and then delivered victory. He was not the first Roman leader to believe that his career was guided by divine help, only his choice of deity was different.[19]

The Christian God had demonstrated His power and this was the basis for Constantine's conversion to Christianity. His army from now on marched under a special flag called the *labarum*, its top decorated with a chi-rho. Allying with Licinius, the two confirmed the Christians' freedom to practise their religion granted by the dying Galerius, but went further, returning confiscated property, including the sites of demolished churches. Eager not to alienate anyone, the two emperors stated that current owners would be compensated. (Traditionally this agreement is known as the Edict of Milan, although – as very many scholars have pointed out – it was neither technically an edict, nor was it issued at Milan.) The subsequent struggle between Licinius and Maximinus Daia was painted in religious terms. The story circulated that Licinius was visited by an angel the night before the critical battle and given a special prayer for his soldiers to repeat. The wording was more generally monotheistic than specifically Christian, but his overwhelming victory seemed proof of its efficacy. Later, when war broke out between Constantine and Licinius, there was an effort to portray this as a new crusade, but there is no convincing evidence that the latter was ever seriously hostile to the church. Perhaps he believed that many prominent Christians were sympathetic to his rival and so mistrusted them, but it is unlikely to have gone further than this. Nevertheless, marching behind the *labarum*, Constantine's forces were victorious.[20]

There were Christians fighting in Constantine's army, but also plenty of pagans, and doubtless more without especially strong formal beliefs. He did not win because he had harnessed a great pool of manpower previously ignored or marginalised by the state. All the evidence suggests that at the beginning of the fourth century Christians were a minority in the overall population. It is also regularly asserted that they were a small minority, but this is by no means clear. As usual, there are no reliable statistics, and, of course, we do not even know how big the empire's population was. One recent study suggested that Christians represented 10 per cent of the total, but this remains purely conjectural.[21]

It is very unlikely that the numbers were smaller than this, and they may as easily have been two or three times higher. We know most about the churches in the eastern provinces, including Egypt, hear quite a bit about those in North Africa, know something about the Church in Rome, but very little indeed about Christian activity in the western provinces. In some areas in the east Christians may locally have been in the majority. Armenia was the first country in the world to become formally Christian when its king converted early in the fourth century. This further increased its closeness to Rome when Constantine fought his way to control of the entire empire. Fairly quickly, Christians living under the Persian kings found themselves under suspicion of sympathising with the Roman enemy.[22]

It is important not to view religious groupings too simplistically. The divide between Christian and pagan was fundamental to the former, but often far less clear to the latter. Pagans were most certainly not one homogenous group, and many would not necessarily have felt any particular sympathy with others who were seen as pagans by Christians. Christianity was far more organised than any substantial pagan cult. It had its own scriptures, supplemented from the very beginning by an ever-expanding literature discussing doctrine, commemorating martyrs and justifying its beliefs to outsiders. Christians sought to convert others to their beliefs in a way that was again highly unusual compared to other established religions. Associated with most Christian communities would have been many people with an interest in and sympathy for the faith, but who had not yet made a firm commitment. Over time some of these would do so, others would drift away and some would simply remain as they were on the fringes. When considering Christian numbers we need to be aware both of this diversity and of a whole range of levels and permanence of commitment.[23]

It is also a mistake to speak too rigidly of a single Church. There were many Christian communities, each distinct in its origins, sometimes its practices and, at times, its doctrine. A division might also be based on language. There was a large Syriac-speaking Christian community in the eastern provinces that seems to have had markedly different traditions to Greek Christianity. Even those churches that would soon come together to form the orthodox Catholic Church were not as uniform as they would become. We should not let hindsight make us assume that its institutions sprang into being instantly, rather than developing over a long period.

The Christian Emperor

Constantine won control of the empire through military force. The support of Christians was an asset, but a relatively minor element in his success. Yet there is no good reason to doubt that the emperor genuinely believed his victory was given to him by God. Virtually every scholar would accept this, although for a long time there was a rather fruitless debate over the question, some preferring to see him as an utterly cynical pragmatist. Apart from oversimplifying human character, this ignored three fundamental points. The first is that individuals respond to religious conversion in different ways. Change in their behaviour and attitudes may be swift or gradual. We should remember that Constantine is unlikely to have had especially detailed knowledge of Christian doctrine before he converted, although it is claimed that he subsequently spent long hours studying the scriptures. Secondly, his faith is often measured against an especially rigorous and rigid ideal, so that he must not only be an enthusiastic supporter of Christianity, but implacably hostile to every other belief system. Constantine was no zealot, but scarcely any Christians at this period seem to have wanted to compel pagans to convert. Finally, Constantine was not just another army officer or private citizen, but the emperor. He spent over half of his reign in a state of rivalry with competitors for power, and often in open war. Like Diocletian before him, his first priority was surviving, and reforms came later and gradually. Simply staying in power and running the empire occupied most of his time and effort.[24]

This last point is all too easily lost in accounts of Constantine's reign, which stay focused almost exclusively on the Church. Christian communities certainly benefited greatly under his rule. Not only was their religion granted formal acceptance by the state, but Constantine was generous in funding the construction of grand church buildings. Some of the first of these were in Rome. The praetorians and other guard units stationed in Rome had supported Maxentius and were disbanded after his defeat, and what is now known as the Church of St John in Lateran was constructed on the foundations of the demolished barracks of the guard cavalry. The Church of St Peter was built on the Vatican Hill where tradition maintained that the Apostle had been buried after his martyrdom under Nero. Given that the site was associated with the grand circus of Nero, it is highly probable that this was in the right place. These and the other churches built by Constantine were not designed like pagan temples, although over the following centuries many of the latter would be taken over and remodelled as churches. Instead, their layout drew more inspiration from the basilica, the traditional Roman meeting place for conducting public business. They were large, with high and often vaulted ceilings allowing large numbers of people to gather.[25]

Constantine built a considerable number of churches, although the scale of his activity in this respect was exaggerated by Christian authors such as Eusebius. There are few traces of new churches in Asia Minor, although this may have been because the local Christian communities did not consider them necessary. Yet, just like the tetrarchs, Constantine was a prolific builder of other monuments, adding another bath complex to Rome. Several of those in the city were completions of projects already begun by Maxentius – most notably the huge basilica whose remains tower over the Forum today. This contained a monumental statue of Constantine himself.[26]

The Arch of Constantine was similarly the reshaping of a monument already begun by his defeated predecessor. Sculptures were plundered from earlier artworks, and the faces of emperors such as Trajan, Hadrian and Marcus Aurelius recarved to show Constantine hunting and offering sacrifice. The text of the inscription is monotheistic but vague, speaking of Constantine defeating his rival 'through the greatness of his mind' and 'with the inspiration of the divinity'. Other slogans were deeply traditional, naming him as 'the Liberator of the City' and 'Founder of Peace'. In contrast, the reliefs showing scenes from his Italian campaign including the Battle of the Milvian Bridge were unprecedented, for no one had depicted the defeat of other Romans in a permanent monument. The Arch of Severus showed only scenes from his Parthian campaign and ignored his victories in civil wars. Attitudes may well have changed, for there is no record of any criticism of this.[27]

Constantine's greatest project was the conversion of the city of Byzantium into the great metropolis of Constantinople. Again, it is important not to assume that he always intended the city to become what it would later be – the capital of the Eastern Empire and the new Rome. It is better to think of it in the context of the tetrarchic practice of developing certain cities such as Nicomedia and Trier. Constantine's concept was probably grander, since he had made himself sole emperor and wished to celebrate his victory. Artwork was brought from all over the empire to ornament Constantinople. Christian claims that there was no trace of pagan cults in the city were exaggerated. There was a large nude statue of Constantine as the sun god on top of what is now known as the Burnt Column, and there were a few temples, mostly on existing foundations. Yet it is fair to say that it was an overtly and overwhelmingly Christian city. Strategically, Constantinople was well placed for an emperor who might wish to move either eastwards or to operate on the Danubian frontier. This in part explains why in time it would outstrip the other tetrarchic capitals.[28]

Constantine did take gold statues and goods from many pagan temples to use in his new projects. A few temples – chiefly ones associated with particularly extreme customs such as ritual prostitution – were shut down altogether. In contrast, other communities sought and received imperial approval to build new temples. Some were associated with the imperial cult, something that had always been more to do with displays of loyalty than piety. Coinage continued to employ well-established pagan imagery for much of the reign, and the emperor himself remained the *pontifex maximus* – the most senior priest of Rome.[29]

Legislation did sometimes reveal the emperor's Christian beliefs.

One law banned owners from tattooing a slave's face, since all men were made in the image of God and it would be wrong to deface that image. There was some restriction on animal sacrifice, but the details of this and how strictly it was imposed at this stage are unclear. Crucifixion was banned, but the death penalty remained and was often imposed in extremely vicious ways. Female slaves who permitted girl children in their charge to be abducted were to be killed by having molten lead poured down their throat. Constantine was particularly keen to punish adultery and other sexual crimes. Yet, while this no doubt chimed with his new beliefs, there was a long tradition of similar legislation stretching back to Augustus. His only break with these earlier laws was to remove the penalties imposed on those who had no children. The tiny minority of Christians who chose a celibate life were not to suffer for this.[30]

Christian bishops and some other priests were granted exemptions from undertaking magistracies and other expensive services for their local community. The same privilege was later extended to Jewish rabbis and synagogue leaders. A few of Constantine's pronouncements are overtly hostile to the Jews as the killers of Jesus, but his actions were not markedly more anti-Semitic than those of many earlier pagan emperors. The Jews were again forbidden to seek converts or to attack those of their own number who converted to Christianity.[31]

Constantine was eager to promote unity amongst Christians and involved himself with two major disputes within the Church. The first was not about doctrine, but was a consequence of the tetrarchic persecution in North Africa. At the time some priests had fled and others came close to collaboration, handing over books they claimed to be scriptures. Others had faced torture and death, while some had the good fortune never to be arrested. When it was all over, a group dubbed the Donatists – their leader was called Donatus – refused to readmit into fellowship those who had fled or collaborated, let alone permit them to resume their priesthood. The dispute came to a head when the Donatists refused to accept the appointment of a certain Caecilian as bishop of Carthage because he was seen as too lenient. There may well also have been a fundamental clash of personalities on both sides. The Donatists appealed to Constantine, just as the congregation in Antioch had once petitioned Aurelian, but with the difference that the emperor was now a Christian. Constantine decided that the issue should be judged by the bishop of Rome. The latter opted to employ the traditional format of Roman justice, but the Donatists' representatives were either unaware or unprepared for this and their case was quickly dismissed. However, they refused to accept this and the result was a schism in the Church in North Africa that persisted for generations.[32]

The other major dispute would also prove an enduring one, but this time the matter was one of doctrine. Fierce debate raged over the precise nature of the Trinity – God the Father, God the Son and God the Holy Spirit. In many ways the arguments show the deep influence of the ways of thinking promoted by the major philosophical schools, with their obsession with specifically categorising things. It was an indication of just how many Christians had received a traditional education, rather weakening the frequently repeated claim that they were invariably of humble status and ignorant. One group known as Arians – it followed the ideas of a presbyter in Antioch named Arius – argued that the Father must have had an earlier, higher existence. Therefore, as the Son, Jesus was, however marginally, not the equal of the Father. In 325 a council was summoned and met under imperial patronage at Nicaea. Constantine was present, but seems to have acted as an interested layman and did not actually take part in the debate. Eventually, it produced a creed in which the Trinity was described as 'of the same substance' (*homoousios* in Greek). Constantine himself was credited with backing and perhaps devising this term. Arius and others who refused to accept this were exiled, although subsequently recalled.[33]

Constantine repeatedly stated that his rule was sanctioned by divine favour. As the reign progressed this became explicitly the support of the supreme, Christian God. He was chosen to govern the empire just as bishops were chosen to shepherd their congregations. Yet it is striking from the beginning how concerned Constantine was to show that bishops were independent and to respect the decisions of church leaders. They acquired the right to dispense justice in church disputes. Christians were also encouraged to enter imperial service and doubtless some people 'converted' in the hope of winning the emperor's favour. Plenty of pagans continued to enjoy very distinguished careers under Constantine, as indeed did Arians and other members of Christian sub-groups. Far more important than issues of beliefs were competence, connections and, most of all, loyalty.[34]

Focusing on Constantine's faith all too easily obscures just how traditional most of his behaviour was. His style of rule was essentially similar to that of recent emperors, and especially Diocletian – so much so that it is often difficult to tell which of the two initiated a reform. The division of the army into frontier-based *limitanei* and the *comitatenses*, in theory kept at the more immediate disposal of the emperor, became more formal. The massive increase in bureaucracy also continued, the various departments of government taking firmer shape. By the end of Constantine's reign there were five praetorian prefects and their role was entirely civil. There were changes in detail to the provincial organisation, and rather more major alterations to the tax system and coinage. Yet, on the whole, the continuity with Diocletian's reign is far more striking than any changes.[35]

The most fundamental difference was Constantine's decision not to renew the tetrarchy itself, or indeed to rule with any colleagues. Unlike Diocletian he did have sons, as well as several half-brothers. In 317 he appointed Crispus, his son from his first marriage, and Constantine II, the oldest son from his second marriage, as Caesars. Simultaneously, Licinius elevated his own son and namesake to the same rank. Crispus was the oldest of the young Caesars, but none of the boys was yet old enough to play an effective role in government. By 324 Crispus was able to fight with some distinction in the civil war, but two years later he was executed by his father. A few months later Constantine killed his second wife, Maximian's daughter Fausta, locking her in an overheated bath house until she was asphyxiated.

Wild stories soon circulated, claiming that Fausta had developed an overwhelming passion for her stepson. When he refused to be seduced, she accused him of attempting to rape her, and his stern father – who had introduced very harsh legislation against such crimes – imposed the death penalty on his son. Afterwards, he is supposed to have learned the truth and so executed his wife. The tale is most likely no more than gossip. Equally false is the malicious claim by some pagan authors, including the Emperor Julian, that Constantine converted to Christianity because only their God would forgive a man guilty of killing his own family. However, he had already been a Christian for more than a decade before these savage events. Whatever the precise details, the desire of Fausta for her own sons to inherit instead of their older step-brother seems the most likely cause.[36]

Palace conspiracies were nothing new, and Constantine's extended family was particularly large and relationships complex. His own half-brothers were not fully trusted and were kept away from power for most of the reign. Their mother, Theodora, was long dead, but his own, Helena, was a prominent figure during the reign, the official line emphasising that she had been Constantius' wife, whatever the actual

Chart 2: Simplified family tree of the house of Constantine

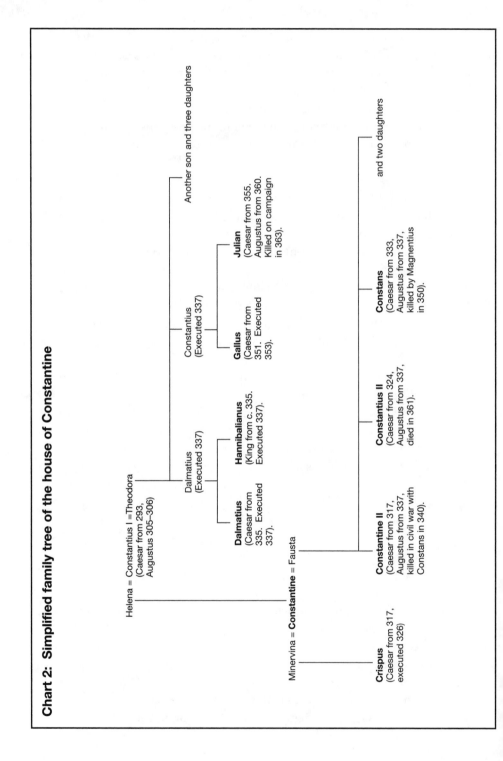

Helena = Constantius I = Theodora
(Caesar from 293,
Augustus 305–306)

Another son and three daughters

Dalmatius
(Executed 337)

Constantius
(Executed 337)

Dalmatius
(Caesar from 335. Executed 337).

Hannibalianus
(King from c. 335. Executed 337).

Gallus
(Caesar from 351. Executed 353).

Julian
(Caesar from 355. Augustus from 360. Killed on campaign in 363).

Minervina = **Constantine** = Fausta

Crispus
(Caesar from 317, executed 326)

Constantine II
(Caesar from 317, Augustus from 337, killed in civil war with Constans in 340).

Constantius II
(Caesar from 324, Augustus from 337, died in 361).

Constans
(Caesar from 333, Augustus from 337, killed by Magnentius in 350).

and two daughters

truth of their relationship. Both she and Fausta were named Augusta. Helena was an especially prominent supporter of the Church and in her last years went on a pilgrimage to Judaea. In 326 she was in Jerusalem and was involved in the construction of the Church of the Holy Sepulchre, raised above what was believed to be the empty tomb of Christ. In later years legends would grow up claiming that she discovered many relics, including fragments of the cross on which Jesus was crucified. Although she died not long afterwards, Helena remained an important figure throughout the Middle Ages.[37]

Constantius II, Fausta's second son, was named as Caesar in 324, and his younger brother Constans was similarly elevated in 333. Two years later Constantine also promoted his nephew Dalmatius, so that there were four Caesars. The empire had five emperors – hence the five praetorian prefects – but only Constantine himself was the Augustus, and there was never any doubt that his power was supreme. This was not a college of equals. In many ways it had more in common with the appointment of relatives as co-rulers by emperors like Gordian, Decius and Philip. It showed to the world that the regime could continue even if the emperor himself died. Nor was it a deliberate revival of the hereditary principle and rejection of deliberate selection of successors. Much like the emperors of the second century before Marcus Aurelius, Diocletian had simply lacked a suitable heir amongst his family and therefore had had little choice but to look elsewhere. Close male relatives could not be readily overlooked. While Constantine was alive they could generally be kept in order, if only by fear, for the fate of Crispus showed that the Augustus would not hesitate to kill even those close to him. Constantine evidently hoped – much like Septimius Severus – that his relatives could be persuaded to live in harmony. Like Diocletian, he was willing to impose harmony, killing his own relatives when he felt this was necessary. In many ways Diocletian and Constantine were alike, both equally determined that one man should wield ultimate power. All of their decisions, including their religious policy, were intended to reinforce this personal supremacy.

Although his greatest victories came in civil wars, Constantine also frequently campaigned against foreign enemies, especially along the Rhine and Danube. Not long after being acclaimed emperor, he had won a victory over a raiding band of Franks. Their captured leaders were fed to the wild beasts in the arena at Trier. In later years he fought against other peoples, including the Sarmatians and Goths. None of our sources mention any significant defeats, and most of the victories claimed by imperial propaganda were probably genuine and substantial. Near the end of his reign Constantine made preparations for a major attack on Persia. The Sassanid king, Shapur II, who had ascended the throne as an infant – legend had it he was actually declared king some months before he was born – was now an adult. Friction developed around the border territories ceded to Rome after Galerius' victory. The Persians resented the loss of these regions and, understandably, were always nervous of future Roman aggression.[38]

The urge to follow in the footsteps of Alexander the Great was often in the minds of Roman generals and emperors who campaigned in the east. More importantly, a victory over Persia offered the prospect of far greater glory than defeating a lesser opponent. In this sense, Constantine's plan was deeply traditional. Yet he added another element, for some years earlier he had written to Shapur, telling him of the power of his God who had 'utterly overthrown' his enemies. He rejoiced at the report that there were many Christians living in Persia, and asked the king to protect and cherish them, 'for by this proof of faith you will secure an immeasurable benefit both to yourself and all the world'. Later, with war imminent, at least one Christian writer looked forward to Constantine's victory uniting all the Christians under one rule.[39]

It was not to be. Constantine died on 22 May 337 at the age of about sixty. He had been baptised just a short time before. It was not uncommon to delay this ritual until very late in life at this period, for it was felt inappropriate to sin after undergoing baptism. The bishop who performed the ceremony was believed to have Arian inclinations, but this is unlikely to have been a concern for the emperor. Instead, as ever Constantine employed people on the basis of his confidence in their reliability and competence.[40]

Constantine was not likeable, but then very few emperors were, especially in the third and fourth centuries. He had been highly successful at a time when civil war remained an ever-present threat. He gave the empire a time of comparative stability, but just like Diocletian, we should not exaggerate the depth of the recovery. Christian authors eulogised Constantine, while pagans condemned him and blamed him for many of the ills that would later befall the empire. In recent centuries, modern historians have all too often had almost as extreme views of him. There is no doubt that his conversion to Christianity was a very significant moment in the history of the world. Yet it is also worth remembering that this religion had already survived repeated attempts to eradicate it. Sweeping claims as to whether it would have survived and spread or faded if Constantine had not converted must be taken with a large pinch of salt.

10

Rivals

'Having troubled the state in all these ways, Constantine died of a disease. His three surviving children succeeded to the *imperium*. ... They managed the affairs of state, giving way to the inclinations of youth rather than to general welfare. For in the first place they distributed the nations amongst themselves.' – *Zosimus, late fifth century.*[1]

'And close kinsmen as we were, how this most humane Emperor [Constantius II] treated us! Six of my cousins and his, and my father who was his own uncle, and also another uncle of both of us on my father's side, and my eldest brother, he put to death without trial.' – *Emperor Julian, 361.*[2]

Christianity made little fundamental difference to the ideology of the Roman empire. Emperors before Constantine had claimed special relationships with particular gods and been declared divine at their death. More recently, Diocletian had styled himself Jupiter-like and was called 'lord and god' in his lifetime. Constantine instead presented his rule as sanctioned by the one supreme Christian God, who had given him victory after victory on the battlefield. Three centuries of tradition was still strong enough at the time of his death for him to be declared divine by the Senate – the last time this was done. The rule of Rome, and especially its emperors, was ordained by God. Constantine was far more concerned that all his subjects acknowledged this than with their actual religious beliefs. It bolstered imperial power, but did not alter the way the army, administration and other organs of the state actually functioned. Nor did it change the Romans' aggressive attitude to other peoples or reduce the savagery of internal rivalries.

Constantine's family members were all raised as Christians. His three surviving sons Constantine II, Constantius II and Constans had all been named as Caesars, as was his nephew Dalmatius. Each of the four men was granted a group of provinces to govern and each had his own praetorian prefect. Constans was still only fourteen, so in his case the day-to-day work was probably carried out by his officials. In 336

Dalmatius' brother Hannibalianus was given the extraordinary title 'king of kings of Bithynia and Pontus'. This was clearly a challenge to the regional dominance of the Persian monarch and part of the pressure put on him in the build-up to Constantine's planned invasion. Therefore five of the Augustus' extended family shared power, and there was much marrying of cousins, both to promote family unity and prevent outsiders from acquiring a claim to the imperial purple.

Constantine died in May, but for four months no new Augustus was appointed and the dead emperor continued nominally to reign. As this peculiar interregnum continued throughout the summer, new laws were issued in his name. In the meantime there was an extremely bloody purge of the male members of the extended family. Both Dalmatius and Hannibalianus were murdered, as were seven other descendants of Constantius' second wife Theodora – posthumous revenge for her displacement of Constantine's mother Helena. By September the three sons of Constantine had disposed of all their rivals. Of their male cousins, only two infants were still alive. It was claimed that the army would accept only the rule of Constantine's sons, although no doubt the brothers had helped the senior officers to reach this decision. All three now took the title of Augustus.[3]

Constantius II played the key role in the purge. He was the first Caesar to arrive at Nicomedia after his father's death, and in due course presided over the funeral at Constantinople. Constantine had prepared a mausoleum for himself, where his body would rest surrounded by memorials to – and in time conveniently discovered relics of – the twelve apostles. The funeral service was Christian and the very public decision not to be buried at Rome was new, and yet in many other respects the rituals were highly traditional. Constantine II and Constans were in Europe during both the ceremonies and the murders, but were probably complicit in the purge and certainly not inclined to hinder the killings. The three brothers met in September near the Danube and shared out the provinces between themselves. Constantius took the eastern provinces as well as Thrace, Constans received the rest of the Balkan regions along with Italy and North Africa, and Constantine continued to control Gaul, Spain and Britain.

All three were Augusti, and the empire was not formally divided, but there was little trace of harmony. Constantine was the eldest and seems to have felt that he was entitled to play a dominant role. This produced friction, particularly with his closest neighbour Constans, and in 340 this erupted into open civil war. The older brother was militarily stronger as well as more experienced, but managed to get himself killed in a preliminary encounter outside Aquileia. Like all Roman civil wars there was no ideology involved and the conflict ended when one of the rivals died. The popularity of Constantine's house was still so great that no outsider had a serious chance of rallying support against the seventeen-year-old Constans, who now found himself in charge of almost two-thirds of the entire empire. Constantius had stayed out of the dispute between his siblings. The Persians, understandably aroused by his father's invasion plans, launched several attacks on the Roman frontier during these years. This gave Constantius good reason – and perhaps a pretext – to remain in his own territory and let the dispute resolve itself.[4]

A decade without a civil war followed – something rare enough to be worth noting. Then, in January 350, an army officer named Magnentius was proclaimed emperor at Autun in Gaul. Precisely how Constans had alienated so many of his senior officers and officials is unclear, but they were now willing to back an emperor from outside the imperial family. Perhaps as the young Augustus – Constans was still only twenty-seven – had grown up, he had proved less willing to be guided by the advisers who had shaped policy in earlier years. Many are also supposed to have been sickened by his blatant homosexuality and the freedom with which he indulged his lovers, handsome youths often selected from amongst the prisoners of war. On the other hand, this may just have been propaganda put out by the victor to blacken his name.

The coup was well managed and Constans failed to rally any support. When one of Magnentius' patrols found him, Constantine's son was attended by just one junior officer. Constans was executed. This provoked a second usurpation, when the army in Illyricum proclaimed as emperor its commander Vetranio. His motives are a little unclear, for within a matter of months he was in negotiations with Constantius. The two met and at a public ceremony Vetranio resigned from power, living out the remainder of his life in comfortable retirement. He may have been working for Constantius all the time, but judged that the best way to control the troops was by letting them proclaim him emperor. This would make them less likely to defect to Magnentius. Equally, Vetranio may not have been playing such a subtle game and simply waited to see how things developed.[5]

If Magnentius hoped for recognition as ruler of the west, then he was disappointed. Constantius had accepted one of his brothers killing the other, but was not about to tolerate an outsider joining in. The ensuing civil war lasted for three years and was fought on a large scale and at considerable cost in lives. Magnentius was also faced with another threat when Nepotianus, a son of one of Constantine's half-sisters, was proclaimed emperor at Rome. Within a month Nepotianus was beheaded and his mother had also been executed. More serious for Magnentius was the defection of one of his senior officers. This man, Silvanus, joined Constantius and may well have taken many of his soldiers with him. This helped Constantius to win a very bloody battle outside Mursa on the Danube in 351. In the next year his forces overran Italy and in 353 they began to reclaim Gaul itself. As defeat followed defeat, Magnentius finally despaired and committed suicide, along with his brother whom he had raised to be Caesar.[6]

Constantius was now master of the entire empire, ruling with just a single junior colleague. This was Gallus, the older of the two nephews of Constantine to survive the bloodletting in 337. He and his half-brother Julian were raised in virtual captivity and were not given any public role or responsibilities to prepare them for high office. The twenty-six-year-old Gallus was appointed Caesar in 351 and left to supervise the eastern provinces, while Constantius went off to deal with Magnentius. At first he seems to have performed this task reasonably competently, but mistrust was surely inevitable between a Caesar and the Augustus who had murdered his father and relatives. It was no coincidence that the friction came to a head just as Constantius was finishing the process of mopping up the rebellion in Gaul. Gallus may have become less restrained in his behaviour, and certainly his relations with many of the senior officials appointed by the Augustus had become tense. He had also made himself unpopular with the wealthy families of Antioch, blaming them for deliberately creating a grain shortage in the city so that they could force prices up. A number of prominent men were arrested, tortured and killed on trumped-up charges. One governor was torn to pieces when Gallus handed him over to an angry mob.

Constantius moved cautiously, fearing that his Caesar would win enough local support to rise against him. Gradually, Gallus was stripped of the military forces at his immediate disposal. Then in 354 he was summoned to join the Augustus in northern Italy, ostensibly for a celebration. On the way, he was arrested and executed. An officer then rode to Milan as fast as the relays of horses from the imperial post service could carry him. There he threw the Caesar's jewel-encrusted imperial shoes down before a delighted Constantius 'as if they were spoils taken from a dead Parthian king'.[7]

The Reluctant Usurper

Our sources for the early decades of the fourth century are poor, and this is especially true of the years following Constantine's death. This situation changes dramatically when the surviving narrative of Ammianus Marcellinus' history begins in 353, providing us with a detailed account of the next twenty-five years. Ammianus was the last great Latin historian, which was ironic given that he came from the eastern Mediterranean – probably from Antioch itself – and so had Greek as his first language. After service as a staff officer in the army, he retired to Rome and subsequently wrote a history covering the period from 96 to 378. Only the last eighteen of the original thirty-one books survive, but it is clear that he covered the events of his own lifetime in greater detail than the earlier periods. This provides us with a detailed account that is not only contemporary, but also sometimes that of an eyewitness. Yet, just like any other source, Ammianus needs to be used with a degree of caution. He was not unbiased, and sometimes his focus on certain events distorts their place in the wider picture. Even so, the detail he provides gives us a very vivid portrait of the fourth-century empire.[8]

Ammianus' surviving narrative begins with the final breakdown in relations between Constantius II and Gallus. The latter is portrayed as an unrestrained tyrant, egged on by his even more ferocious wife, a daughter of Constantine who had earlier been married to the murdered Hannibalianus. Ammianus' account allows us to see the process by which Gallus was gradually stripped of power, isolated and killed. Even more importantly, he tells us of the purges that followed the Caesar's fall and the defeat of Magnentius. Anyone, and especially army officers and civilian officials, connected with them in any way were under suspicion. Senior men were tortured to extract confessions and evidence against others. Many were then executed, a few merely exiled.[9]

In a climate of almost paranoid suspicion, one of the easiest ways for an individual to prove his loyalty was to inform on another. This proof often brought promotion or other favours from a grateful emperor. Additional incentive was provided because such informers were usually rewarded with a share of the condemned man's property. Many wholly innocent men were attacked in this way and the vast majority were executed, for it was extremely difficult to disprove allegations, while evidence was easily fabricated. Ammianus felt that Constantius was too ready to mistrust people, but he was even more sickened by the willingness of officers and officials to turn on their colleagues – or indeed anyone they felt was vulnerable to an accusation. He tells of one frequent informer who was nicknamed 'the count of dreams' because of his skill in twisting innocent stories of dreams told over the dinner table into aspirations for imperial power. Another was called Paul 'the chain' because the evidence he invented would surround innocent men and always proved impossible to escape. Serving in the imperial bureaucracy had become very dangerous and this obviously did not promote efficiency.[10]

Ammianus mentions by name many of the prominent victims of these purges. In 353 he was attached to the staff of the commander of the field forces in the east, the Master of Soldiers Ursicinus. Under suspicion after the fall of Gallus, in part because of the action of his sons, the general was put in charge of courts prosecuting others implicated in the recent disturbances. It was an unusual job for a senior soldier, and his behaviour was clearly monitored to assess his own loyalty to Constantius. Such tribunals condemned many unnamed and less prominent people – the relatives of the more powerful, as well as officers and officials whose careers they had advanced through their patronage. Investigations and arrests were made throughout Britain, Gaul and Spain in the aftermath of Magnentius' revolt. It is only because we have Ammianus' account that we become aware of this ripple effect, as punishments reached out to claim many more individuals than simply the leaders in civil wars and usurpations. This process is normally invisible in the skimpy sources for so many other internal struggles, but needs always to be kept in mind.[11]

Even the briefest of challenges for imperial power caused considerable upheaval, creating a climate of nervousness that filtered a long way down the hierarchies of the army and administration. Men had to choose sides, trying to guess who would win. Even if they remained loyal to the eventual victor, they could not be sure that their innocence would protect them. Ambitious officials grew powerful through accusing others, sometimes out of personal enmity, but also just because they felt that they could get away with it. At the top, the emperor was suspicious that his most powerful subordinates wanted to supplant him – usurpation and civil war remained facts of life. Added to which, the growth in bureaucracy and the grand ceremonies of court life made it harder for him to know what was going on.

The climate of the times is well illustrated by the fate of Silvanus, the officer who had defected from Magnentius during the civil war. When the conflict was over, Constantius rewarded him with the post of commander of the army in Gaul. Silvanus was a Frank, whose father had fought with distinction for Constantine. He was one of many army officers of Germanic descent in the army at this time. A chieftain of the Alamanni had been prominent in Constantine's proclamation as emperor at York in 306. Many of these men adopted Roman names, all had been granted citizenship and social status commensurate with their rank, and were in every important cultural respect Roman. Silvanus was a Christian – something still rare amongst the Franks living outside the empire – and his loyalty was clearly to the empire, even if his earlier defection made it less clear to which specific emperor.[12]

Early on in his command Silvanus gave letters of recommendation to an imperial official operating in the area. It was entirely normal to request such things from those with power in a region, but the man in question had a more sinister motive. He carefully erased the ink carrying the main text of the letters, leaving only the general's signature on each page. Then new letters were written, addressed to a range of senior officers, administrators and other prominent men, hinting at plans for rebellion against Constantius. These were passed on to fellow conspirators, including Praetorian Prefect Lampadius, and several other high-ranking officials. The prefect, whose role gave him access to the emperor outside the restrictions of court ceremony, privately handed these to Constantius.

The emperor immediately ordered the arrest of the men named in the letters. However, some officers – many of them also of Frankish descent and including Malarichus, the commander of one of the guard regiments – staunchly protested Silvanus' innocence. Constantius relented a little, but did not agree to their proposal to send one of their number to bring Silvanus to the court in Milan so that he could explain himself. Instead, he listened to Silvanus' predecessor in the Gallic command, who had no love for his replacement, and selected another emissary. This man went to Gaul, but made no effort to meet or contact Silvanus. Instead he joined up with a local official and started treating anyone vaguely associated with the general as an already convicted rebel. In the meantime the conspirators sent another forged letter, incriminating both Silvanus and Malarichus. It was worded in such a way that the recipient – the man in charge of the arms factory at Cremona in northern Italy – was left baffled, and sent back asking for an explanation.

Malarichus took this to the emperor and loudly proclaimed that a conspiracy was underway. Constantius ordered an investigation that spotted the imprint of the original text and so exposed the letters as forgeries. Lampadius was arrested, but still had enough influential friends to secure his release. One of his fellow conspirators was examined under torture, but he, too, was subsequently released and none of the others were punished at all. The man who had made the forgeries in the first place was soon afterwards promoted to be *corrector* governing one of the regions of Italy.

Although Silvanus had been cleared of any wrongdoing, the slow pace of communications meant that he did not know it. His friends at court had informed him of the accusations and the forged letters, while the behaviour of the emperor's messenger suggested that he had already been condemned without any chance of defending himself. At one point he considered fleeing beyond the frontiers to seek refuge amongst the Franks. Yet another Frankish officer serving in the army persuaded him against this, saying that the tribesmen would either kill him or happily take payment to hand him back to the Romans. The Franks were not a nation, but many loosely connected tribes and clans.

Silvanus had never planned to claim the throne. In the summer of 355 he paid his troops in the name of Constantius, making a speech praising the emperor and urging them to be steadfast in their loyalty. As Ammianus points out, 'if he sought the insignia of imperial power, he would have given out this largesse in his own name'. Yet he felt trapped, found guilty without a hearing. Faced with what seemed inevitable execution, Silvanus decided that his only hope of survival was to make a bid for the throne. Perhaps he could supplant Constantius, or at least negotiate from a position of strength for acceptance as co-ruler. Four days after the pay parade – the date was probably 11 August – he was hailed as emperor by his army at Cologne. It was a hastily organised, makeshift ceremony, with the new emperor wearing a cloak of imperial purple made from small flags taken off several army standards and sewn together.[13]

Constantius was stunned when the news of the usurpation reached Milan. At the court was Ursicinus, still under a degree of suspicion, and it was decided to send him to deal with Silvanus. He did not go with an army, but a few officers and ten of his personal staff, including Ammianus himself. His instructions were to deal with the usurper covertly, but the historian later wrote that they felt like 'beast-fighters thrown down amongst savage animals'. They hastened to Cologne, carrying a friendly letter from Constantius, in which he pretended not to know of Silvanus' elevation. He was to hand over his command to Ursicinus and return with all honours to Milan.[14]

When the party reached Cologne and saw considerable forces gathered with every sign of local support for the usurper, Ursicinus decided instead to present himself as a sympathiser and prostrated himself before Silvanus in the appropriate manner. He was welcomed as a valuable ally, the whole thing made plausible since he, too, had fallen under Constantius' unjustified suspicion. As Silvanus resisted the calls of his men to march on Italy – it was just a few weeks since his proclamation so he may not have been ready, but he may simply have been reluctant to escalate the conflict – the new arrivals secretly went to work. Having discovered that a pair of army units were lukewarm in their support for the usurper, substantial bribes were paid over to persuade them to turn on Silvanus. At dawn a party of these soldiers burst into the palace, cutting down any sentries in their path. Then:

> Silvanus was dragged out of chapel, where he had in terror taken refuge on his way to a Christian service, and was cut to ribbons by their swords. And thus died a general of considerable merit, who had resorted to the most desperate measures to save himself for fear of the calumnies in which he was ensnared during his absence by a faction of enemies.[15]

The usual purge of the dead man's relatives and associates followed, Paul 'the chain' playing a prominent role in 'discovering' information that led to many being executed. Ammianus mentions five victims by name, as well as 'many others.' Even Ursicinus was for a while under suspicion of misappropriating funds.[16]

Silvanus' reign had lasted just twenty-eight days. His murder avoided a civil war, which would inevitably have been far more costly in lives than the executions that did occur in its aftermath. Yet it is important not to measure the costs of usurpations solely in terms of casualties and physical damage. Each emphasised just how precarious a career in the imperial service was. One of the most striking features of this episode is the willingness with which senior Roman officials arranged the disgrace and death of colleagues for their own personal advantage. Another is the difficulty that Constantius had in knowing what was going on in his empire. If anything, the massive increase in bureaucracy kept an emperor less well informed than he had been in the first and second centuries. None of this made for the efficient running of the empire.[17]

Yet good government was not the highest priority for emperors – survival was. Throughout his career, Constantius was always willing to execute, murder or fight a civil war against anyone who challenged his grip on imperial power. The emperors of the Principate had likewise often shown themselves to be utterly ruthless. Ammianus compared the plight of Ursicinus in 354 to that of Corbulo, a distinguished general instructed to commit suicide by Nero. In the first century both Augustus and Vespasian, two men generally treated in our sources as amongst the best emperors, won power in the first place through civil war. Yet the difference was still considerable. Usurpations were not as common in the fourth century as they had been in the third, but they were still frequent. Emperors were harder to murder because of the greater security at court, but the danger of someone winning over a large part of the army remained very real.

No emperor was ever wholly secure. The complex bureaucracy and divided hierarchy, with strict division between military and civil power and complex relations within each one, gave some protection. It was harder for a man to mount a successful challenge. Yet it was not impossible, and if he managed to build up wide support in the different branches of the army and administration then the challenge was likely to be a dangerous one. Emperors were understandably nervous and mistrustful, and their attitude inevitably filtered downwards. Their subordinates knew that they could at any time fall under suspicion. A career could end abruptly in torture and death, or could flourish, quite possibly through the demise of others. Violent competition underlay all levels of government, especially the highest ranks. There was also a degree of ambivalence. For most career soldiers and civil servants, it did not really matter who the emperor was. All that was important was to win his favour and avoid his mistrust. Whoever the emperor was, he would always need his subordinates. Army and bureaucracy survived each usurpation, even if many of the individuals within them became casualties.

Yet, for all the suspicion and paranoia of imperial government, fourth-century emperors lived lives of splendour. Surrounded by ceremony, everything about them was supposed to be blatantly lavish and spectacular. Emperors were special, chosen of God and above the rest of humanity. This was always emphasised, even for men who had just recently proclaimed themselves as rulers. Ursicinus was only behaving as he was expected to do when he prostrated himself before Silvanus. Merely possessing enough purple material to fashion an imperial cloak led some men to their executions.

In reality emperors were always insecure, but in public they were presented as overwhelmingly superior and utterly certain of their rule. This is conveyed well in Ammianus' account of Constantius' entry into Rome in 357. Although not formally holding a triumph, the grand procession of troops suggested just that. Constantius was surrounded by standards and rank on rank of troops, including cataphracts in gleaming armour that even included silvered masks for their faces, so that they seemed 'polished statues and not men'. The emperor

> rode alone in a golden chariot, which shone with the glitter of many precious gems . . . and was surrounded by dragon standards, with woven purple tubes fixed to the golden and bejewelled spear tops, the wind whistling through their open mouths so that they seemed to be hissing in anger, and their tails flicking behind them . . .
>
> And so being acclaimed as Augustus by enthusiastic voices, while the hills and shores echoed the roar, even so he remained utterly still, staying as unmoved as when he was seen in the provinces. And although he leaned a little forward when going under huge gates (even though he was a short man), he stared fixedly ahead, just as if his neck was held in a vice, and glanced neither to the right nor left; he did not even sway when the wheel jolted on a rock, and was never seen to spit, or touch his nose or cheek, or move his hands at all.[18]

11

Enemies

'Shall I now proceed to recall, as though they were something new or previously unheard of, the reconquest, by your valour, of the Gallic province, the subjection of the whole barbarian race, when these triumphs have, in this part of the Roman Empire, been hailed as most deserving of glory by the laudatory voice of popular acclaim, to such an extent as to merit the envy of your cousin the Emperor?' – *Speech of thanks to Emperor Julian by Claudius Mamertinus, delivered 1 January 362.*[1]

For all the magnificent ceremonial of the imperial court, no emperor was ever free from the fear of usurpation. It was a very personal and immediate threat, for challengers obviously did not want to destroy the empire, simply to possess it. Being killed by a rival remained the most frequent cause of death for emperors. Successful usurpers needed the support of a substantial section of the army. Emperors could try to monitor the loyalty of senior officers, giving important commands only to the most loyal. They also continued to make soldiers take an oath of personal allegiance, and to remind them of their loyalty with parades and donatives on significant imperial festivals throughout the year. Yet, inevitably, they remained distant figures to the overwhelming majority of their troops and most of their officers.

The risk that his army might turn against him was something an emperor had to live with. Emperors could not dispense with the army, or even reduce its size substantially and so hope to reduce its power. In the first place, any serious reduction would have created large numbers of unemployed officers as well as demobilised troops. At the least this was likely to increase banditry within the provinces – when Septimius Severus had dismissed the praetorians there was a rapid increase in levels of armed robbery in Italy. More probably it would have created an immediate power base for a usurper who promised to reinstate them.[2]

Yet the main reason the army could not be reduced was simply because it was necessary. None of Rome's foreign enemies threatened its existence. The tribal peoples were disunited – mostly they raided, and at the very worst might nibble away and occupy small areas of land in the frontier zones. The Persians were both more united and more sophisticated militarily, but even they could not hope to do more than win back some of the territory lost to the Romans. Foreign wars were not life and death struggles, at least as far as the Romans were concerned, but they were frequent. Rome had many enemies living alongside its vast frontiers. Just because none of them individually posed an overwhelming threat to the empire did not mean that they posed no threat at all. Violent crime does not threaten the existence of modern democracies, but in turn that does not mean that it can simply be ignored, even if governments and voters seem resigned to its frequency in some areas. For the Romans, raiding across the frontiers needed to be kept at a level the government could accept. Warfare also played a central role in imperial ideology. Winning victories over foreign opponents was the ultimate proof of an emperor's capacity to rule, any success receiving a prominent place in their propaganda. The desire for glory certainly inspired successive emperors to launch frontier campaigns.

A 'New Model' Army

As we have seen, Diocletian and Constantine presided over a major restructuring of the army, alongside their reform of civil administration. Troops were now divided into two distinct grades, the *comitatenses* and *limitanei*. The latter received less pay and had lower physical requirements, but were still full-time professional soldiers. The root of the name was the word for military road (*limes*), although there is some dispute as to the precise significance of this. The *limitanei* were also sometimes called *riparienses*, which came from *ripa* (the banks of a river). They were stationed in provinces, usually in frontier areas, and were commanded by *duces*. Their role was to patrol and police the area around their garrisons and deal with relatively small-scale attacks, such as raiding bands numbering a few dozen or at most a couple of hundred warriors. One study has noted that we never hear of raiding bands of less than 400 men and suggested that smaller groups were routinely stopped by the *limitanei*.[3]

The *comitatenses* had an entirely separate command structure and were more likely to be moved from one region to another. The name was derived from *comitatus* (the imperial household), and the original idea was clearly that they should be at the emperor's disposal. It is possible that under Constantine they were organised as a single army, ready to follow on campaign wherever he went. When his three sons divided up the empire in 337, the *comitatenses* were divided into three separate armies. Over time, more distinct armies stationed in specific regions would be created. In practice, the *comitatenses were* usually commanded by generals with the title 'Master of Soldiers' (*Magister Militum*), such as Silvanus and Ursicinus. Variants of the title included 'Master of Horse' (*Magister Equitum*) and 'Master of Infantry' (*Magister Peditum*), neither of which commanded exclusively infantry or cavalry, but a mixture of both. As subordinates, the Masters of Soldiers had officers with the rank of *comes* (count, pl. *comites*). Again, the word had its root in the personal companions who had traditionally accompanied an emperor on a journey or campaign. In some cases counts were given small-scale independent commands.[4]

The Masters of Soldiers regularly commanded substantial numbers of troops, although it is unlikely that these forces were bigger than the army controlled by a senatorial legate in a major military province in the first or second century. There were only three of them – the number would double by the end of the century, but never increase beyond that – and this made it easier for the emperor to keep a close watch on them. Yet the Silvanus episode had shown that this might not be enough. More important in ensuring the emperor's security were the complex divisions of responsibility and power throughout the provinces. The army was divided into two, with comfortably over half of its units being *limitanei*. However, co-operation between *limitanei* and *comitatenses* does appear to have been common, and senior officers could in practice find themselves with troops of both types under their command during a campaign. A much bigger division was maintained between the army hierarchy and the civil administration.

The army depended on the civilian bureaucracies to supply it with pay, food and clothing. Even weapons and other equipment, which in the early empire had been made in the legions' own massive workshops, were now provided by state-run arms factories under the supervision of the praetorian prefects. A Master of Soldiers planning to challenge the emperor had to secure not just the support of his soldiers, but the co-operation or replacement of large numbers of bureaucrats. It was much harder for one man to know, and win over, everyone who was important. At the same time, there were many people serving in independent hierarchies able to send real or fabricated reports of the disloyal behaviour of others. The system offered some protection to the emperor, at the cost of making it more difficult to get things done. Campaigns could be delayed or hindered by lack of supplies over which the commanders had no control.[5]

The Roman army in the fourth century was large, its manpower still dwarfing that of the swollen bureaucracy. The vast majority of the men paid and under the control of the emperors were soldiers. Yet we do not know how big the army was. Most scholars assume that it was larger than the second-century army, perhaps 50 per cent or even 100 per cent bigger, but the evidence is inadequate and inevitably the calculations involve a good deal of conjecture. We do know that the fourth-century army contained many more units and we have a complete list of those in existence at the very end of the fourth and the beginning of the fifth century. Some units had disappeared since Constantius II's time, others had been created, but this list gives us a fair idea of the overall shape of the army in his day. Unfortunately, we have no certain evidence for the size of each unit so cannot calculate the army's theoretical total size from this.[6]

The *limitanei* included a very broad range of unit types. Some were survivals from the time of Marcus Aurelius and even earlier. There were legions, as well as auxiliary cohorts and cavalry *alae*. Others were new creations. Overall, there was a higher proportion of cavalry units in the *limitanei* than in the *comitatenses*, no doubt because they were useful for patrolling. There were no units including both infantry and cavalry, equivalent to the mixed cohorts of the early empire. Legions were sometimes stationed in several outposts. Several were split amongst five garrisons, while in the early fifth century the *Legio XIII Gemina* provided five garrisons on the Danube, another in Egypt and also had a unit amongst the *comitatenses*. Even so, they were certainly far smaller than the 5,000-man legions of the early empire. It is also more than possible that most units were smaller than the roughly 500-man cohorts and *alae* of the auxiliaries in the second century. Very many of the forts occupied by the *limitanei* were tiny, most a small fraction of the size of earlier auxiliary forts. An Egyptian papryus dating to the start of 300 also suggests some very small units. It mentions a cavalry *ala* with 116 – just over a year later this had risen to 118 – a *vexillatio* of legionary cavalry with 77 men and a unit of mounted archers with 121. A number of units of legionary infantry averaged around the 500 mark, but a camel troop seems to have had just a couple of dozen men.[7]

The situation with the *comitatenses* is no clearer, although there was less variety of unit types. Infantry consisted of legions and a new type of unit known as *auxilia*. All of the latter and some of the former were rated as *palatina,* a title that carried much prestige and some tangible advantages in pay and bonuses, but no difference in function. Cavalry units were all called *vexillationes* and were smaller than the infantry regiments. A common estimate is to give cavalry units a strength of 600 and the infantry somewhere between 1,000 and 1,200. However, the few mentions of regimental strengths in our sources suggest smaller numbers, averaging around 350–400 and 800 respectively. What we do not know is whether such lower figures represent actual campaign strengths, reduced by disease and casualties, or theoretical sizes. A couple of sources mention commanders who kept non-existent men on their unit's role so that they could draw their pay and rations. Infantry units of *comitatenses* were brigaded in pairs, and seem to have permanently operated together. This obviously adds an extra complication since we cannot be sure whether numbers in our sources refer to a single regiment or a pair that the author naturally assumed would be together.[8]

Overall, it is fair to say that the units of the fourth-century army were smaller than their first- and second-century predecessors. Going much further than this quickly becomes conjectural. We cannot even be sure that all units of a particular type had the same theoretical size. Infantry regiments of all types in the field army were probably somewhere between 500 and 1,000 men strong, cavalry units about half the size of infantry. Many units of *limitanei* may have been a good deal smaller, and perhaps we should think in terms of 50 to 200 men, which would make them more like companies than battalions by modern standards. It is possible that on paper the total strength of the army was larger than in Marcus Aurelius' day, but we cannot be sure of this. Its actual strength on a day-to-day basis is even harder to assess.[9]

The evidence is equally poor for the army's recruitment. Some men were volunteers and others conscripts, but the balance between the two is unknown. Sons of soldiers were legally obliged to join the army. Landowners had to supply a set number of recruits as part of the taxation system, but were often able to commute this duty to a money payment or avoid it altogether. There was also a steady supply of drafts for the army from the groups of barbarians settled by treaty within the empire and obliged to provide soldiers for the army. Tribesmen from outside the empire also came as individuals or as groups to enlist in the army.

The old idea that this influx of Germans 'barbarised' the Roman army and over time reduced its efficiency has been discredited. There seems to have been no real difference in reliability and performance between recruits from inside or outside the empire. As we have seen in the last chapter, the senior ranks included many men of barbarian descent who behaved exactly like colleagues of more traditionally Roman stock.

The army took recruits wherever it could get them, and there are clear signs that many people went to drastic lengths to avoid service. In real terms army pay was of less value than it had been in the first and second centuries, while discipline and punishment remained brutal. Repeated laws punished the practice of self-mutilation to avoid being conscripted – potential recruits cut off their thumbs so that they would be unable to hold a sword or shield properly. There was a famous case of an equestrian who had done this to his sons during Augustus' reign, so the practice was not new, but it does seem to have become more common. The frequency of legislation dealing with the problem suggests that the laws were not effective. A letter from a clergyman to a garrison commander in Egypt asked that he exempt a widow's son from conscription or, failing that, at least enlist him in the local *limitanei* so that he could stay near home instead of sending him away to join the *comitatenses*. The fourth-century army did not have massive resources of manpower and this factor played a significant part in shaping its operations.[10]

Whatever the actual size of the fourth-century army, more units certainly meant more officers to command them. Regimental com-manders were usually called tribunes, although other titles such as *praepositus* were also used. Such a post gave a man considerable status – even if, once again, his pay and social importance were somewhat less than those of an equestrian officer in the second century. In comparison to the early Principate, the Late Roman army was top heavy in its command structure. It is more than likely that the desire to reward supporters with high rank – and in some cases their own independent commands – had as much to do with the multiplication of units as any practical concerns. We hear of unattached tribunes, sometimes serving in a staff capacity, and it is more than likely that there were significantly more men with commissions than there were units for them to command. Some tribunes may well have been promoted after service in the ranks. A much more common route was to be commissioned from special units at the imperial court. The *candidati* (candidates) acted as personal bodyguards of the emperor during court ceremony. The *protectores domestici* served as junior staff officers either with the emperor or a Master of Soldiers. Ammianus was one of these. Promotion was officially the emperors' prerogative, but in practice he had to rely on recommendations of senior officers, officials and courtiers. There was no formal system for training these officers or for selecting on the basis of talent. As always in Roman society, patronage played an important role in determining a man's career.[11]

Modern scholars conventionally refer to the *comitatenses* as mobile field armies, and often they go further and dub them elite troops. They are seen as a necessary response to the greater external threats facing the empire. In the past, wars requiring the removal of troops from one frontier zone weakened defences there and left the region vulnerable to attack. In the fourth century the *limitanei* remained permanently in place. They were not as numerous as the forces on the frontiers in the early empire and could not hope to defeat major incursions. Yet their bases were strongly fortified, as were towns and cities, and they were expected to hold out for as long as they could and harass the enemy. A sizeable army of *comitatenses* could then be sent to the region to confront the invader. In essence, they formed the mobile reserves that it is claimed the earlier deployment lacked.[12]

Much of this analysis has been called into question, particularly the sense in which they acted as reserves. Nothing of this sort is ever implied by the ancient sources. No army could ever move faster than an infantryman could march, and more often than not its speed was reduced to that of the plodding draught oxen that pulled its baggage train and carried its food supply. Given the size of the empire, talk of reserves makes little sense, since unless they were fairly close to the theatre of operations then it would take them a very long time to get there. In spite of such criticism, the 'mobile field army' tag has stuck, so that it is worth making a few points about the actual deployment and use of the *comitatenses*.

Unlike the *limitanei*, the *comitatenses* did not occupy permanent garrison posts. When not on campaign they were stationed within the provinces and not on the frontiers. However, they were not kept concentrated as large army corps ready to take the field at a moment's notice, since this would have made it difficult to supply them. Temporary camps, the men living in tents or roughly built shacks, were unhealthy in winter, and in any case it was dangerous politically to keep armies concentrated during the winter months of inactivity in case they rebelled. The army did not build large bases in this period, and even many of the existing legionary fortresses designed to accommodate 5,000 men in the second century were now abandoned or substantially run down. At the beginning of the sixth century the historian Zosimus claimed that Diocletian had kept the empire secure by stationing the whole army along the frontiers in strongly fortified posts. 'Constantine abolished this security by removing the greater part of the soldiery from the frontiers to cities that needed no auxiliary forces.' Once there, he claimed that the soldiers became a burden on the communities and were themselves softened by the pleasures of urban life.[13]

When not on campaign – and even at the most intensive periods of operations these were rarely conducted over winter – the *comitatenses* were dispersed in towns and cities within the provinces. It is doubtful that more than a brigaded pair of units were often stationed in one place. This spread the burden of feeding them and made it harder for the units to join together and back a usurper. In addition, it provided trained soldiers to man the city walls in the case of a sudden threat from a foreign enemy or a rival for imperial power. There was nothing especially new about stationing troops in or near towns. This had been common in the eastern provinces in the first and second centuries, although there was a well-established literary cliché that maintained it had an enervating effect on them.[14]

Yet in the earlier centuries army units had normally lived in their own barracks within or near to cities. This does not seem to have been the case with the *comitatenses* – although admittedly the archaeological evidence for the layout of most towns in the fourth century is extremely limited. Instead, they were billeted in civilian houses, and legal documents talk of officials painting on the door posts the number of men and the unit from which they should come. Throughout history billeting has frequently caused friction between soldiers and civilians. From a military point of view, the dispersal of units in small groups over many separate dwellings was not conducive to good discipline. In their purpose-built barracks the units of the first- and second-century army had been concentrated in one place under the close eye of their officers. They were provided with good sanitation, exercise and bathing facilities, as well as hospitals for their sole use, and had parade grounds and training areas readily available. Facilities in cities and towns were far more limited and not for the exclusive use of the military. Even the largest city might well struggle to find good stabling for the 500–1,000 horses mustered by a couple of cavalry regiments.

Distributing the *comitatenses* in cities was the easiest solution for the government, but was scarcely the best way to keep them in good condition. Military training was and is not a simple thing, permanently instilled once it is learned, but something that must be constantly repeated. As important was physical fitness – essential for the marches required on campaign, let alone actual combat. Both were harder to maintain when the army was split and billeted in civilian settlements. There was also inevitably a delay in concentrating the units before a campaign could be begun. The army may have maintained some pack and baggage animals permanently – and if so these were an extra burden to the communities on top of the cavalry mounts – but still needed to requisition or purchase many more to carry its food and other stores in the field. All this took time and faced the added complication of much of it being controlled by bureaucracies entirely separate from and with different priorities to the army.

It is reasonable enough to call the *comitatenses* field armies. They were more mobile and should usually have been more effective fighting units than the *limitanei*, at least for large-scale operations. Yet, on the whole, there was nothing particularly innovative about them, certainly nothing that would justify calling them elite. The physical requirements were the same as for service in the earlier army, and later in the century even these would be reduced. Over the course of time, some units of *limitanei* were attached permanently to the field forces, receiving the halfway status of *pseudocomitatenses*. This suggests that there was no stark distinction in the military potential of the two grades of troops. In the end, troops were as effective as their training, leadership, tactics and equipment allowed. Only the Persians came close to matching the army tactically, and barbarian armies were markedly inferior. The factory-produced equipment of the fourth-century army has a more functional look than the armour and weapons of the early empire. Both the *pilum* (heavy javelin) and short *gladius* (sword) had fallen out of use. Instead, the standard weapons were a long-bladed *spatha* (sword) – previously only used by cavalrymen – and simpler spears suitable for both thrusting and throwing. As an individual, the Roman soldier was still a well-equipped fighting man. Infantry tactics were probably a little less aggressive, but remained effective. The fourth-century army won the great majority of the battles it fought.[15]

The standards of training and quality of leadership of the fourth-century Roman army inevitably varied – as indeed they had done in earlier periods. On average standards may have been a little lower, but it remained the only professional army in the known world. The demise of the 5,000-man legion removed one command level useful for operating and controlling very large armies in the field. It also meant that it was harder to support large numbers of specialists – engineers, architects, siege specialists, artillerymen etc. – within the army and pass on their experience to successive generations. The *comitatenses* had no permanent bases to act as depots and to maintain records of personnel, their postings, equipment and mounts. Records were still kept, but had to be moved continually if they were to remain useful to the unit. The same was true of soldiers. New recruits, convalescents or detached men returning to normal duty would have to travel to rejoin the parent regiment wherever it happened to be. The frequency with which a unit went on campaign would have steadily worn it down. Some men would be lost to enemy action, many more to sickness or detachment. This meant that large numbers of men may have existed and been rightfully paid by the state, but would not actually be present with their unit when it went on campaign. The probability that most units were heavily under strength most of the time makes it all the harder to estimate their full theoretical complement.[16]

We should not exaggerate the efficiency of the fourth-century Roman army, but neither should we forget just how unique it was in its day. For all the complexity of arranging supplies, the Romans did possess a system for organising these things on a massive scale. The fourth-century army was far from perfect, but still enjoyed marked advantages over all its opponents. We need always to remember that it had been shaped by almost a century spent fighting itself. Diocletian and Constantine did not create an army according to a coldly logical design, changing the military system of the second century because it was obsolete. Instead, they patched together a unified force from the badly dislocated debris left by generations of civil wars. Their first priority was always to protect themselves from challengers, and every other consideration was secondary to this. The immediate threat of civil war never went away and continued to dominate the thoughts of their successors. Given this context, the fourth-century army was highly effective, and it is worth now looking at it in action.

A New Caesar in Gaul

Constantius II was understandably concerned that Gaul had produced a second usurper so soon after the suppression of Magnentius. In the end, he decided that a family connection was the strongest basis for trust and summoned Gallus' half-brother Julian to Milan. On 6 November

355 the twenty-four-year-old was proclaimed as Caesar at a massed parade of the troops. Ammianus notes that the soldiers showed their approval by banging their shields against their knees. If they were displeased, then they lifted the shields off the ground and clashed the shafts of their spears against them. Just like his brother before him, Julian had received no preparation for high office. Unlike his brother, he not only left a considerable body of writings that have survived to this day, but also generally receives much more favourable treatment in our sources, at least for this stage of his life.[17]

The army in Gaul had shown a willingness to rebel against the emperor, but strong forces had to be kept there to protect the provinces from attacks from the tribes across the frontiers. Along the northern stretches of the Rhine were the Franks, and to the south in the lands between the Rhine and Danube were the Alamanni. These were the two main groupings, but other peoples also launched periodic attacks. Neither the Franks nor the Alamanni were unified nations, but a large number of separate groupings of tribes and clans under chieftains whose power rose and fell over the course of time. Some of these smaller groupings would sometimes accept common leadership, but this was never universal. Their attacks on the empire were almost without exception raids aimed at plunder and not occupation. There were no hordes of barbarians hurling themselves time and again against the walls of civilisation. The population of the area occupied by the Alamanni was probably less dense than in the nearest sections of the Roman provinces. Raids on their own would not destroy the empire, but they did make life extremely unpleasant for those caught up in them. We hear of many captives taken back to lives of slavery beyond the frontier. Isolated settlements were destroyed and even some substantial towns overrun and plundered. Having a circuit of walls was not always much protection if they were not maintained or if there was no one organised enough to defend them. Julian later claimed that no fewer than forty-five major towns had been overrun before he arrived in Gaul.[18]

Civil war encouraged barbarian attacks, in the pattern we have already seen in the third century. Internal struggles took Roman troops away to slaughter each other, leaving the frontiers vulnerable. They also tended to dislocate trade with the tribes outside the empire, making some communities desperate enough to resort to warfare. The Alamanni seem to have provided the Romans with timber and building stone in peacetime. Roman leaders were also ever willing to enlist barbarian allies to fight against their rivals. Magnentius hired large numbers of warriors from outside the empire. Constantius doubtless did the same, and also encouraged the Alamannic king Vadomarius to invade the usurpers' territory, granting him the right to settle on the west bank of the Rhine, taking part of the Roman province. Such pragmatic deals were attractive during civil war, but became somewhat embarrassing afterwards. As usual, victors in civil wars were very eager to win some clean glory by defeating Rome's foreign enemies. It was not always easy for tribal leaders to keep up with the dramatic switches of attitude from their Roman allies. Civil wars and raids also created human flotsam – deserters, the dispossessed, runaway slaves and fugitives – and such desperate men joined raiding bands or became bandits in their own right. It must often have been difficult to know the identity of plunderers.[19]

Julian read Julius Caesar's *Commentaries on the Gallic Wars* as he travelled north to take up his new command. The world had changed a lot in the last four hundred years, but the new Caesar soon showed that he could match the famous general's driving ambition. He embraced the military life with enthusiasm. The tradition favourable to him claims that he was hindered by senior officials and subordinates sent by Constantius to keep a close watch on him. This is clearly an exaggeration, and he probably needed a good deal of advice and guidance as he set about his task. Ursicinus initially remained in post as Master of Soldiers to act in this guiding role. However, as a clever man who had spent most of his life alone with his thoughts, Julian was reluctant to accept opinions other than his own.[20]

In 356 Constantius himself led a major operation against some of the Alamanni, which Julian and his troops supported. (A casual reading of Ammianus gives the impression that things were the other way around, with the Caesar playing the dominant role.) Julian led the northern column, while the Augustus commanded a larger army in the south. It was essentially a demonstration of force, intended to show the tribes that the Romans were once more united and ready to deliver a massive attack on anyone who displeased them. The aim was to negotiate new treaties with the tribal leaders from a position of overwhelming Roman dominance. There was little actual fighting, although Julian won a few skirmishes. The initial encounters occurred before he joined the main force – an indication of the time taken to muster a field army – and while he was accompanied only by a unit of cataphracts and another of *ballistarii* (which literally means 'artillerymen', but in this case they were probably equipped as infantry, just possibly with a form of crossbow).

Even with his bodyguard he may not have had many more than a thousand men, but this was easily enough to brush aside the raiding parties he encountered.[21]

The main force was concentrating at Rheims, and en route Julian liberated Autun, Auxerre and Troyes. There were no enemies in any of these towns. Autun had recently been attacked, but the raiders had been repulsed not by the troops in garrison, but by a scratch force of retired soldiers who had banded together to act. At Troyes the gates were barred to him for some time, until he was able to convince those in charge that he was actually a Caesar and the legitimate representative of Roman power. This rather suggests it was sometimes difficult to tell the difference between formed units of the Roman army and a marauding band. Combining with the rest of his army, Julian proceeded to pass through more towns, marching along the Rhine until he reached Cologne. This had fallen to the Franks some time before, but they do not seem to have stayed very long. Again, the campaign was essentially a demonstration of force, showing the government's power to communities who may well have felt abandoned in recent years.[22]

Julian spent the winter in Senon (perhaps modern Sens, but more probably near Verdun) and was blockaded by a band of Alamanni. He did not have many troops with him – as usual, logistic concerns meant the army had dispersed into winter quarters – and so was unable to drive them off. In the end, failing to provoke a surrender, the warriors just sloped off quietly. Julian blamed Ursicinus' successor Marcellus for failing to come to his rescue. Constantius recalled him, refusing to accept his evidently justified explanation that there had never been any serious danger to the Caesar.[23]

In 357 a similar campaign was planned, but Constantius did not take part and left the main force under the command of the new Master of Soldiers Barbatio. The latter had 25,000 men to Julian's 13,000, but the two men failed to co-operate. There may have been a number of reasons for this, including mutual suspicion, but it did not help that Barbatio seems to have had at best modest talent. He suffered a serious reverse and retreated, losing his baggage, leaving Julian to press on alone, launching several raids against tribal settlements. Outside Argentorate (Strasbourg) he encountered a strong army of Alamanni, led by seven kings. Two of these – Chnodomarius and his nephew Serapio – were in command. There were also ten more lesser kings and many noblemen with the army, each with their band of followers, as well as some mercenaries. Ammianus claims that the whole army numbered some 35,000, but this is more than likely an exaggeration. Perhaps the Alamanni outnumbered the Romans. They were certainly confident – some years earlier Chnodomarius had defeated Magnentius' brother. The leaders were willing to fight, but they may have hoped that a display of force would make the Romans negotiate for peace.

Julian did not answer their ambassadors. His army had marched some distance and his initial plan was to fortify a camp, rest his soldiers and fight on the next day. He was persuaded to attack by his senior officials, including his praetorian prefect. They saw this as a great opportunity to defeat so many leaders in one place and claimed that the soldiers would deeply resent being held back. Julius Caesar emphasised that he never gave in to pressure from his men and fought only at times and places of his own choosing, but conditions in the fourth century were different. Julian let himself be persuaded. The Romans advanced and battle developed into a hard slogging match. Julian's cavalry broke and fled – one unit was later made to parade in women's clothes as a punishment. He rallied them, and when a group of warriors led by the chieftains broke through the first line of Roman infantry, they were stopped by reserves. In the end the Romans' discipline and clear command structure prevailed and the Alamanni were routed. Roman losses were 243 men and four tribunes. The Alamanni lost far more, as beaten armies nearly always did in the ancient world, although Ammianus' figure of 6,000 dead is probably another exaggeration.[24]

Strasbourg was a significant victory, but it was also the only pitched battle Julian fought in five years of heavy campaigning in Gaul. More typical was what followed, with a series of savage raids being launched against the tribes. The Roman army won most of the battles it fought during the fourth century, but battles were always risky. A defeat was likely to involve heavy casualties, which it would be hard to replace. Surprise attacks allowed the enemy to be terrified into submission at little risk to Roman lives. Even if a raid was spotted by the barbarians, they were rarely able to gather enough warriors to meet it in time. The worst that was likely to happen was that the raiders would fail to catch anyone. To support the raids a number of abandoned Roman forts were reoccupied, giving the tribes the impression that they were under constant surveillance. This was deeply resented.[25]

The scale of operations is well illustrated by an episode that occurred in the winter of 357–358, when Julian spent a couple of months besieging a band of Franks who had holed up in two abandoned forts. There were only 600 warriors, and he probably kept no more than a couple of thousand soldiers with him to mount the blockade. More would have been unnecessary and very hard to feed in winter. When the Franks finally surrendered they were sent to Constantius as recruits for the army. The episode is striking because the Romans were reluctant to assault such a small force of barbarians. They did not want casualties on either side since the enemy were themselves a useful source of manpower. Even more remarkable is the simple fact that the Caesar himself was willing to devote many weeks to supervising such a small scale operation.[26]

During his time in Gaul, Julian aggressively reasserted Roman dominance along the frontier. In some cases he seems to have turned on communities that had not long past been allied with Rome. Julian wanted and achieved military glory. He needed to be popular with the army and with provincials if he was to avoid the fate of his older brother. He considerably reduced the tax burden on the communities in Gaul in spite of bitter opposition from his praetorian prefect. The scale of the reduction showed the level of graft amongst the officials collecting the levies, but it was a dangerously populist gesture. Constantius had murdered Julian's father and many of his relatives, and more recently executed his brother. It was very hard for either man to trust the other fully.[27]

In 360 Constantius ordered Julian to send four regiments of *auxilia palatina* and 300 men from his other units (whether individual regiments or brigaded pairs is unclear) to reinforce the army in the east. The Persians had launched a major offensive in the previous year so that the need for men was genuine. On the other hand, he had begun the process of removing Gallus by stripping him of his forces. The proposed move was also unpopular with the soldiers in Gaul, many of whom were local or from across the frontiers. Some were supposed to have been promised that they would never serve south of the Alps, let alone further afield. In February 361 Julian was proclaimed Augustus by the troops with him at Lutetia (modern Paris). He feigned reluctance in the traditional way, but soon agreed 'and lifted onto an infantryman's shield, he was raised up, saluted as Augustus, and asked to put on an imperial diadem. When he denied that he had one, they urged him to use a necklace or headband of his wife's.' Julian felt that this would be a bad omen, and similarly disliked the idea of using something from a horse's decorative harness, but finally agreed to wear a neck torque donated by one of the standard bearers.[28]

Ammianus' claim that Julian was genuinely reluctant and pressured by a spontaneous outburst from the soldiers is unconvincing. More probably, the issue of the postings to the east was a convenient moment to implement long-nurtured plans. One *comes* known to be loyal to Constantius had recently been despatched to Britain. On his return he was immediately arrested before he could learn of Julian's elevation. The new Augustus wrote to Constantius, repeating the story of his reluctance and hoping for reconciliation, but he refused to accept the demand that he return to the rank of Caesar. In the summer Julian took his army – presumably including the men who had previously resisted going east – and advanced to confront Constantius. The balance of forces favoured the latter, but in the autumn he fell ill as he crossed Asia Minor on his way back to confront the usurper. Constantius II died on 3 November 361 at the age of forty-four. His only son was an infant and there were no other close male relatives left apart from Julian. Therefore, there was no challenge to the rebel becoming sole emperor.[29]

Julian was especially aggressive during his time in Gaul. He needed glory and the situation was unusually disturbed on the frontier in the aftermath of Magnentius' rebellion. By surprise attacks, which massacred or took prisoner the entire population of some villages, through broader demonstrations of force and the reoccupation of abandoned forts, the idea was to convince the neighbouring peoples of Rome's overwhelming power. Roman methods were often utterly ruthless. The preference was always for one-sided slaughter than the risk of an open battle. In 370 a raiding band of Saxons was overawed by the arrival of strong Roman forces and preferred negotiation to fighting. In return for giving hostages, the raiders were granted the right to return to their homeland. However, the Romans never had any intention of honouring the agreement and instead prepared an ambush. The plan nearly back-fired, when some men emerged from hiding prematurely and were cut up by the Saxons. In the end the barbarians were overwhelmed by weight of numbers and all slaughtered. Ammianus noted that while this might seem 'hateful and treacherous', mature reflection showed that it was only right for the Romans to destroy 'a band of robbers when they had the chance'. Most of these frontier operations were very small-scale. Julian never led his army further than 30 miles east of the River Rhine. The dominance was only intended to be local. It was also likely to be temporary, since the savagery of Roman actions and the unpredictability of their internal politics were bound to instil nervousness and hatred that would burst out in the future.[30]

Alongside the threat and use of military force went active diplomacy. Some tribal aristocrats took service in the Roman army and rose to high rank. Many more were turned into allies and given financial aid. Often their sons were raised as hostages within the empire and given a suitably Roman education. One of the two main Alamannic leaders at Strasbourg was named Serapio because his father had developed a reverence for the god Serapis during his time living within the empire. Chieftains regularly dined with senior Roman garrison commanders in frontier posts, allowing both sides to study the other and guess at future events. On several occasions the Romans exploited this tradition to imprison or murder an important guest.

The tribal peoples were a minor but frequent threat to the empire. At times the Romans were able to gain such a position of dominance in a frontier region that there would be no serious operations for a generation. The Goths along the southern Danube seem to have been fairly quiet for decades after Constantine's campaigns in the region. There was usually friction somewhere along the frontiers with some of the peoples living outside, but most often it was small-scale. Serious incursions in Britain were satisfactorily dealt with by sending a *comes* with just two pairs of *auxilia palatina* regiments from the field army in Gaul. The chief military activity of the barbarian tribes was always raiding. The Romans responded by trying to catch the raiders, usually on their way back, slowed down with their spoils. The Romans relied on fast marching and surprise attacks every bit as much as their enemies. Many of the campaigns described by Ammianus are very small-scale and the details he gives are far more intimate than the sort of thing mentioned in accounts of warfare in earlier periods. We read of raiding bandits overwhelmed when the Romans surprised them while they were bathing and dyeing their hair red in a river. Elsewhere he tells of another group massacred when the Romans deliberately broke the truce during negotiations. At one point during Julian's campaigns, Ammianus notes that: 'Besides these battles, many others less worthy of mention were fought in various parts of Gaul, which it would be superfluous to describe, both because their results led to nothing worthwhile, and because it is not fitting to spin out a history with insignificant details.' This is all the more striking given the small size of most of the skirmishes he does mention. What is so different from earlier periods is the number of times he describes emperors taking personal charge of very small operations. In the first or second centuries such matters would have fallen to a senatorial governor, or often one of his subordinates. It was much harder to get things done in the fourth century.[31]

12

The Pagan

'I call Zeus and all the other gods who protect cities and our race to bear witness as to my behaviour towards Constantius and my loyalty to him, and that I behaved to him as I would have chosen that my own son should behave to me.'

'... does he not rebuke and ridicule me for my folly in having served so faithfully the murderer of my father, my brothers, my cousins; the executioner as it were of my whole family' – *Emperor Julian, 361*.[1]

Julian was just thirty when he became sole ruler of the empire. It was quickly announced that the dying Constantius II had named him as his successor and this may well have been true. In just two generations the male line of Constantine's large family had virtually wiped itself out. No new challenger emerged, and Constantius' generals and officials quickly pledged their loyalty to Julian. This did not prevent a purge when the new Augustus arrived in Constantinople at the end of the year. As usual, only the names of the most prominent victims are recorded. At least four senior bureaucrats were executed – two by being publicly burnt alive – and half a dozen exiled. It was probably not the worst spate of punishments after a civil war, but for the victims and their families it was bad enough. Even Ammianus, who was generally favourable to Julian, felt that at least one of the executed men had done nothing to deserve punishment. Another victim, the notorious Paul 'the chain', was unlamented.[2]

Julian's success was stunning, but did not surprise him for he knew that he was special. Like all of Constantine's family, he was raised as a Christian. His early life was spent in the household of a bishop and he was even ordained as a junior member of the clergy, regularly taking part in services and publicly reading from the Scriptures. He also grew up in virtual captivity, aware that he would always be under suspicion with an emperor who had killed so many of his relations. To all outward appearances Julian grew up to be pious and without ambition. Secretly, he rejected both Constantius and his Christian God. Instead, he became obsessed with the old religion and literature of Greece, something which grew all the more pronounced when he was permitted as a young adult to study in Athens. Julian embraced the teachings of Neoplatonism, the dominant philosophy from the middle of the third century. It had a strong mystical element, embracing revelation as much as logic in the search for understanding. Julian was drawn to an especially extreme form of the school, in the person of Maximus of Ephesus, who was as much magician and showman as he was philosopher. Widely considered to be a charlatan, he put on displays in which he made torches spontaneously catch alight and a statue smile. Julian was thrilled by such 'proof' that the old gods existed and still exercised direct power in the world.[3]

In common with mainstream philosophy and wider attitudes, he believed in one supreme deity who ruled over the other gods and – again, like many others including Aurelian and Constantine's father – identified this supreme god with the Sun. Julian wrote of how 'from my childhood an extraordinary longing for the rays of the god penetrated deep into my soul'. He was a 'follower of King Helios' (one of the many names for the deity), whose 'continuous providence' held together 'this divine and beautiful universe, from the highest vault of heaven to the lowest limit of the earth'. For Julian, it was a very personal and emotional faith. It appealed to his strongly ascetic inclinations and – since it was largely his own creation – satisfied his intellect. Most important of all, it was not the religion of his uncle.[4]

Perhaps Julian's conversion to paganism – known as apostasy, so that he is conventionally known as Julian the Apostate – would have remained no more than a typical piece of student rebellion had he not been made Caesar. Throughout his time in Gaul he concealed his inner beliefs and continued to attend Christian services with every outward sign of enthusiasm. When the civil war began he slowly pulled down the façade, invoking the old gods when he wrote to Athens and other cities to bid for their support. However, it was only after Constantius was dead that he openly rejected Christianity and began publicly to stage animal sacrifices and other rituals. Until this point he had been careful not to alienate any potential Christian supporters. Julian's victory proved to him the power of King Helios in raising him from virtual prisoner to sole emperor in only a few years, just as decades earlier Constantine's continued successes had convinced him to become a Christian.

We know a lot about Julian. Ammianus provides a detailed narrative of his reign and Julian's own writings survive in a quantity unmatched by those of any other emperor. He was the last pagan emperor – at least the last legitimate one, although one short-lived usurper later in the fourth century publicly shared his rejection of Christianity. Modern readers often find much with which they can identify – his intelligence, enthusiasm and years as a student, all of which have particular appeal to academics. For some, his hostility to Christianity also strikes a chord, although usually this is only if they ignore his passion for his own beliefs and addiction to animal sacrifice.

Closer consideration of Julian's career and writings rapidly shatter such apparent connections and any simple image of him as a well-meaning undergraduate. He was ruthless and determined – no emperor could be anything else. There is also very little that might seem especially modern about him. Like anyone else he was a product of his times, and those times were disturbed and his own life particularly traumatic. Being born into the imperial family set anyone apart. Then to survive the massacre of his relatives and endure a youth of captivity and suspicion was scarcely normal, even for his day and age. Julian was an intelligent man, but had spent his formative years in isolation, and that is always likely to promote absolute certainty in a person's own beliefs, making it hard for them to consider alternative ideas. He does not seem to have ever had any close friends as it was inevitably difficult for anyone in the imperial family to relate to others as equals. Added to that was his secret apostasy and development of his own religion. That he was able to hide this from others for many years can only have reinforced his sense of his own cleverness. It may also have encouraged a fondness for play-acting.

Julian did not cut a very impressive figure. He was small, somewhat ungainly and inclined to twitch his head and gabble his words. In Gaul his soldiers nicknamed him 'the little Greek', 'the Asiatic' and 'the chattering mole'. In direct contrast to the imperial styles since the tetrarchy, he grew an unkempt beard – another nickname was 'the goat'. This was quite probably somewhat thin at first, but the coins minted after he had been proclaimed Augustus show him with an abundant and wild growth of facial hair. It was perhaps suitable for a philosopher, but looks far less neat than the well-trimmed beards of the Antonines. Julian idolised Marcus Aurelius as the ideal philosopher emperor. In his satirical work *The Caesars* he imagined a banquet on Mount Olympus where past emperors compete for the approval of the gods. Unsurprisingly, Marcus Aurelius is the ultimate winner. Julian was at home with some of the theatre and ceremony surrounding emperors in the fourth century – his acclamation at Paris was especially well stage-managed. At other times he broke the rules, rushing out of a meeting of the Senate in

Constaninople to greet the arrival of Maximus of Ephesus. Emperors were not supposed to behave so informally and even many of his supporters disapproved. There were similar doubts about his drastic reduction in size of the imperial household inherited from Constantius. Many departments had certainly become swollen under the latter, but even so Julian went too far in his desire to be seen as a simple philosopher who had no need of luxuries or numerous assistants. It was felt that he had diminished the grandeur surrounding imperial rule.[5]

The change in style was short-lived. Julian's peculiarities, and especially his religious ideas and policy, tend to get a lot of attention, but it is important to remember that they had no long-term impact. His reign lasted for little more than two years and ended in disaster and humiliation when he was killed in Persia. The war against the Sassanids and the concessions made by the Romans to buy peace were Julian's greatest legacies to the empire.

War in the East

Julian inherited the struggle with Persia. Constantine had died before launching his grand offensive, but his preparations had only increased tensions in the region, and Constantius II had faced warfare on the eastern frontier for much of his reign. Shapur II was a strong monarch who came to the throne in 309 as an infant and ruled Persia for seventy years. The loss of territory to Rome following the victory of Galerius at the end of the third century had been a deep humiliation for the Persians and the king's principal objective was always to recover these lands. Both sides launched frequent raids into the other's territory, sometimes on a very large scale. As well as their own forces, each also made frequent use of allies, and groups such as the Saracens begin to appear more and more often in our sources.[6]

Control of a region depended upon holding the main cities and other fortified posts. Defensive walls were built on a massive scale by this period, invariably strengthened with projecting towers that were often abundantly equipped with heavy and light artillery. These cities all had their own water supply – indeed, that was their ultimate reason for existence – for they were all situated, usually on higher ground, where the annual rainfall was sufficient to support basic agriculture. Such strongpoints provided bases from which to launch raids or to send out parties to intercept enemy attacks. Any sizeable attacking force had to capture a city or detach troops to mount a blockade if it was not to face a serious threat to its supply lines. The Roman frontier was more heavily and densely fortified than it had been a century before, making it far harder for the Persians to repeat the deep invasions of Shapur I into the provinces.

Fortified cities and towns were vital. This inevitably meant that they were the principal focus for any attack that went beyond a raid. During Constantius' reign the Persians attacked the city of Nisibis three times, but always failed to take it. The intensity of warfare varied. Both Constantius and Shapur II had other concerns, and on several occasions shifted the bulk of their forces to wage war elsewhere. In 357 Shapur was campaigning in what is now Afghanistan and Constantius was busy on frontiers in Europe. Judging that a peace would be welcome to both sides, the praetorian prefect in charge of the eastern provinces sent envoys to the Persians suggesting that they begin negotiations. As it turned out, Shapur had already defeated his opponents, who were turned into subordinate allies. Free to move elsewhere – and also eager to give the newly conquered allies a chance to demonstrate their loyalty by providing contingents for his army – he interpreted the Romans' approach as a clear sign of weakness. He restated the old claims to Persian dominance as far as the Mediterranean and, when these demands were unsurprisingly rejected, prepared a series of major offensives.[7]

In 359 Shapur surprised the Romans by not following the normal invasion route into Mesopotamia. Instead, he attacked further north, avoiding Nisibis and heading instead towards the town of Amida. Ammianus Marcellinus narrowly avoided the Persian patrols to seek refuge in the town and left a vivid account of the siege that followed. Shapur may not have originally intended to stop and besiege the place, instead wanting to keep moving and reach further into the Roman provinces, plundering and taking captives. A renegade Roman official, who had defected to the enemy after he had become overwhelmed with debts, had advised that this would spread more confusion. The same man had provided the information that persuaded the Persians to take the northern route. However, as the Persian army paraded outside the city in a demonstration of strength – the distant hope was that the garrison might be overawed and persuaded to surrender – the son of a client king was killed by the bolt from a Roman ballista. Honour now demanded that Shapur satisfy the bereaved father's yearning for vengeance by taking the town.[8]

In a siege lasting seventy-three days, the Persians tried a mixture of direct assaults with ladders and mobile siege towers; infiltration when a party of archers climbed through a drainage tunnel to seize a tower; and engineering to bring artillery and rams against the defences. Their losses were heavy, especially in the repeated direct assaults. The Roman defenders deployed their plentiful artillery with great skill and beat back every attack. When the Persians brought up a massive artillery tower to suppress the defenders on the wall, the Romans laboured to build a huge mound behind it to regain the advantage of height for their own catapults. Unfortunately for them, the mound collapsed on to the wall itself, providing the Persians with a ready-made assault ramp into the city. Amida was stormed and sacked. Those inhabitants and soldiers who survived the ensuing massacre were led off to lives of captivity in Persia. Ammianus was one of a handful to remain hidden and then escape under cover of darkness.

Shapur had won an important if costly victory – Amida was the first major town to fall to the Persians in Constantius' reign. However, the long duration of the siege meant that the campaigning season was over and so the Persians withdrew with their captives. The collapse of the Roman mound would have made it very difficult to repair the defences, so no garrison was left behind in the ruined town. In 360 Shapur attacked again, this time following the more direct route into Mesopotamia, but still avoiding Nisibis. He stormed the city of Singara, burning it and carrying away its population as captives. On another occasion, Ammianus mentioned seeing the trail of the weak and elderly unable to keep pace with a column of prisoners and so left behind with their hamstrings cut. After this success Shapur moved against the strongly positioned fort at Bezabde and captured it. There was less damage to its walls and, after removing the population, a Persian garrison was installed. With summer almost over the king led his main army back home.[9]

By this time Constantius had arrived. In spite of the news of Julian's acclamation in Gaul, he decided to lead the army in an effort to recapture Bezabde. The Romans brought with them a battering ram left behind by Shapur I after one of his invasions a century before, which was assembled and proved to be still in working order. In spite of this and more modern artillery and siege engines, the Persian garrison bravely repulsed every Roman assault. With winter fast approaching Constantius reluctantly abandoned the siege. In 361 the Persians did not launch a new invasion, supposedly because their priests thought the omens were unfavourable. As importantly, the presence of stronger forces in the region under Constantius himself, and perhaps also the heavy losses in the recent sieges deterred Shapur from further aggression for the moment. Constantius waited near the eastern frontier for some time, before turning back to face Julian, but then fell ill and died.[10]

Julian probably decided to launch a major invasion of Persia almost as soon as he became sole emperor. Although Shapur had only permanently occupied a single stronghold in Mesopotamia, he had destroyed two others. The balance of power had not shifted by much, but Roman prestige was severely dented and needed reassertion. More personally, Julian had won victories on the Rhine and his popularity with the army in Gaul was clear from their willingness to proclaim him Augustus. He was still largely unknown to the army in the east and many of its senior officers. Leading them in a victorious campaign would help to confirm their loyalty. Like any victor in a civil war, Julian was also eager for unambiguous glory against a foreign enemy. The greatest prestige of all would come from defeating Persia. Many emperors had dreamed of eastern conquests, but there was probably more to it than that. Julian had succeeded in everything he had attempted in the last few years. Victory against the odds in a civil war – and a miraculous victory with the convenient death of Constantius – only confirmed his sense of special destiny and divine assistance. It was no coincidence that in *The Caesars* Julian added Alexander the Great to the contest and granted him a distinguished place alongside Trajan, another man who had invaded Parthia. Alexander remained the great hero of the Greek tradition that Julian so cherished. Repeating his exploits would be a spectacular step in returning the world to the classical past of Julian's own imagining.[11]

The preparations for the invasion were extensive. Supplies were stock-piled and a little later some grooms were crushed to death when a towering stack of fodder collapsed in the army's camp beside the Euphrates. Julian moved to Antioch and continued to preside over extravagant animal sacrifices, so that the troops with him were gorged with continual feasts from the victims' meat. The emperor quickly upset most of the great city's population and, in response to their jibes, composed a satire he called the 'beard-hater' (*misopogon*). By the spring of 363 the invasion force was ready. Ammianus, who took part in the expedition, does not tell us how large it was, although he does say that some 20,000 men were engaged in manning the river barges that would carry the bulk of the army's supplies. He also notes that a diversionary force numbered some 30,000 men, and later implied that the main army was only a little larger. A later source claims that Julian's main army alone numbered 65,000. This is possible, and is certainly less than the obviously wildly inflated figures given for other armies in this period by the same author. We still need to be cautious, for it might still be an exaggeration or may include the diversionary force. It does seem safe to say that this was probably the largest Roman army sent to fight a foreign opponent in the fourth century. Julian had absolutely no experience of controlling an army even half the size of this expedition. Nor, for that matter, did any of his officers.[12]

The plan was to surprise Shapur, just as the Persian king had done the unexpected in 359. A diversionary army was formed under the joint command of a relative on Julian's mother's side named Procopius and another officer. Assisted by Armenian allies it was to threaten an advance along the usual routes from Mesopotamia. Shapur took the bait and led his main army to defend against this attack. Julian then advanced down the Euphrates against at first minimal opposition. The Romans passed by the ruins of Dura Europos and the monument to Emperor Gordian with little incident. The region was well watered by a system of irrigation canals and hence highly fertile. However, the Persians broke down dams to flood fields and, where this was not possible, burnt or carried off the crops to prevent them being used by the enemy. Such ruthless scorched earth tactics were common in conflicts between Rome and Persia. The Roman defenders had acted in the same way in 359, devastating the area where they expected – wrongly, as it turned out – that Shapur would advance. Julian's men could gather little food and fodder from the country they passed through, but for the moment their needs were served by the supplies carried on hundreds of river barges.

This did mean that the column had to stick close to the Euphrates and so had little choice but to storm the forts and walled towns along its route. This was done quickly, although at some cost in lives. Julian indulged his taste for dramatic play-acting in one siege when he approached the enemy-held wall with just a few men. His inspiration was an incident in the siege of Carthage in 146 BC. Then, the famous Roman general Scipio Aemilianus, accompanied by the Greek historian Polybius, had led a party of men that cut through an enemy gate. Julian and his men, however, were driven back. Perhaps such risk-taking by their commander inspired the soldiers, although it is doubtful that many had ever heard of Scipio. A good number of officers may have been more familiar with such historical examples and the emperor may well have felt that it was sufficient to impress these men. Yet on the whole, Julian seems to have been more concerned to live up to his own ideal image of the great general and link himself directly with the glories of the past. It was dangerous behaviour for any emperor, and especially for one without an obvious heir. The line between bravery and foolhardiness is often

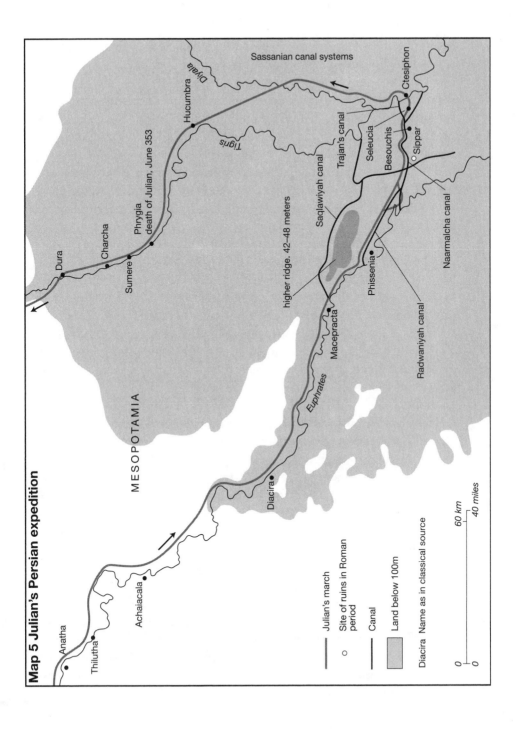

Map 5 Julian's Persian expedition

Sassanian canal systems

MESOPOTAMIA

Anatha

Thilutha

Achaiacala

Diacira

Dura

Charcha

Sumere

Phrygia
death of Julian, June 353

Hucumbra

Diyala

Tigris

Euphrates

Macepracta

higher ridge. 42–48 meters

Saqlawiyah canal

Trajan's canal

Seleucia

Besouchis

Sippar

Ctesiphon

Phissenia

Radwaniyah canal

Naarmalcha canal

Julian's march

Site of ruins in Roman period

Canal

Land below 100m

Diacira   Name as in classical source

0   60 km

0   40 miles

hard to draw, but it is very hard to see any practical gain that could have justified such risks. Julian's sense of his own destiny doubtless convinced him that he would survive any danger.[13]

At another stronghold he led a small party of officers on a personal reconnaissance of the defences and fell into an ambush. Several Persians singled the emperor out because of his conspicuous uniform. He managed to cut down one of them, and the others were swiftly dealt with by his bodyguards, but it was a dangerous moment. When the place was taken Julian took great delight in emulating Alexander and the great Roman general Scipio Africanus (grandfather by adoption of Aemilianus) by treating with great respect some captive aristocratic women. To show that he was unwilling even to feel tempted by their beauty, Julian refused even to look at them. In his case, unlike his famous models, this was little sacrifice, for sex seems to have played very little part in Julian's life. When his wife died – their only child had also not survived – he made no effort to remarry in spite of the advantages of establishing a dynasty.[14]

After just over a month the army reached the Persian capital Ctesiphon. They had made fairly quick progress for a large army, but perhaps not quite quick enough. We cannot be certain about the original objective for the invasion – Julian may not have been that clear on this himself. Ctesiphon was an exceptionally large and strongly fortified city. The Romans lacked a sufficiently large siege train to capture it by a full-scale siege. This would in any case have taken time, creating major problems in keeping the army supplied since it had not captured significant reserves of food from the enemy. To make matters worse, Shapur had by now realised the deception – perhaps the diversionary forces were not aggressive enough – and was approaching with a large part of the main Persian army. A siege would be difficult and dangerous, and Julian quickly decided not to attempt it.

Perhaps capturing Ctesiphon had never been part of the plan, unless it could be taken by stealth or pressured into surrender. On the other hand, the Romans may simply have underestimated the scale of the task, although this would have been a serious failure given that they ought to have had good knowledge of its strength, if only from earlier campaigns. It is worth remembering that Julian's main experience of warfare came from his operations on the Rhine frontier. There, time after time, the Romans would advance quickly into enemy territory, burning villages and crops, seizing cattle and, if they could achieve surprise, killing or capturing the population. Faced with such a dreadful onslaught, the tribal kings would usually treat for peace. If they did not, then the exercise was repeated. In the civil war, a rapid attack into the heart of Constantius' territory had succeeded, albeit mainly because the emperor had so conveniently died. It is hard not to think that Julian saw his Persian expedition in much the same way – a surprise attack deep into enemy territory, capturing towns, devastating the land and defeating any force he encountered. Having shown the Persians that their king could not protect his own realm, Shapur would be forced to sue for peace and accept a treaty on Rome's terms. It is even possible that Julian expected the shock to be great enough to dethrone the king and allow him to be replaced by a royal relative who had long lived as an exile with the Romans.

If this was the plan, then it was seriously misguided. The scale was massively greater than punitive expeditions on the Rhine, both in terms of the number of soldiers involved and especially the distances. Nor was there any reason to believe that the Persians would follow the script and collapse under the pressure of the Roman attack. Shapur was a strong, well-established king with considerable resources for waging war, not some petty tribal leader. It would have taken far more to break his will or turn his subjects against him.

Julian felt unable to take Ctesiphon. He could not advance any further without risk of being cut off altogether, and there was nothing to be gained by staying where he was. Therefore, Julian decided to retreat. Rather than go back the way the army had come through the devastated lands, he decided to follow the line of the Tigris. Stories circulated that he was misled by Persians posing as deserters. Orders were given to burn the supply barges and the vast majority were destroyed before the emperor changed his mind. It would have been difficult to draw these up the Tigris against the current, but even so the gesture was a grim one for the Roman soldiers so deep in enemy country. Foraging did not prove easy on the new route. A large part of Shapur's main army had now arrived and began to harass the Roman column. Julian's men were able to defeat a Persian advance guard, but were unable to bring the main force to a decisive battle. The situation was growing increasingly desperate.[15]

During another attack on the vanguard of the army on 26 June 363, Julian impetuously rushed to the spot without bothering to don his body armour. In the confusion and dust he outstripped his escort and was stabbed with a spear, cutting his own hand as he tried to pull the blade out. The most plausible version is that his attacker was a Saracen fighting as an ally to the Persians, but this did not stop stories circulating that his killer was a Roman – either disgusted by the predicament he had led them into or a Christian who hated his paganism. Taken to his tent, Julian died a few hours later. The emperor is supposed to have been both lucid and calm, conversing with the philosophers on deep questions until the very end. No source claims that he was much concerned with advising his generals what to do next. The stories may be invented – this was the proper way for a philosopher to die – but sound plausible. Whatever else we may think about Julian, he was clearly utterly self-absorbed.[16]

It was later claimed that Julian had nominated Procopius as his heir. However, since he made an ultimately unsuccessful attempt to seize power two years later, this may have been invented. He was not on the spot, and the senior officers and officials with the army knew that they needed to choose someone with the column. It would be far better for an emperor to negotiate directly with the Persians, who would be reluctant to trust any agreement that might quickly be rejected by a new ruler safe back within the empire. The first man chosen refused on the grounds of old age. Then some relatively junior officers proclaimed one of their number as emperor. His name was Jovian and the similarity of this to Julian (in Latin, Jovianus and Julianus) at first produced a rumour that the latter had recovered. Quickly he won enough approval to be accepted by the entire army. Much taller than the diminutive Julian, they were unable to find a purple imperial cloak long enough to reach properly down his legs. This was unsurprising, given that possession of material even vaguely resembling imperial regalia was often enough to lead to arrest and death.[17]

Jovian and the army were in a tight spot. Any emperor, and especially one without any connection to the established imperial house, needed to get back to the heart of the empire quickly if he was to prevent challengers emerging. Fortunately, Shapur was willing to talk. Destroying the Roman army would have taken time and might have involved heavy casualties amongst his best troops. It was far better to negotiate from such a position of strength. He was able to extort massive concessions from the Romans. Some of the territories lost to Galerius were handed back to Persia. With them came the cities of Singara and Nisibis, which the Persians had thrice failed to capture. The populations were to be allowed to leave, but everything else was to be handed over. Finally, Jovian agreed to refrain from intervening in Armenia or supporting its monarch against the Persians. Officers like Ammianus felt that the terms of the peace were humiliating and hated most of all the sight of a Persian banner being raised over

Nisibis. Yet from Jovian's point of view the concessions must have seemed necessary. He had inherited a disaster from Julian and at least he was able to save the army and himself. Most emperors placed their own survival above any other concern.[18]

Faith and Government

The ceding of territory to Persia was Julian's most enduring legacy. At the start of his reign he had declared religious freedom throughout the empire, but it was clear that only some faiths were to be encouraged. The restrictions imposed on sacrifices and other pagan rituals by Constantine and his sons were removed. So were the privileges granted by them to Christian priests, notably exemption from burdensome public duties such as service as a city magistrate. Bishops were also no longer permitted to use the imperial post service when travelling. Men exiled for heresy were permitted to return, although in the case of bishops and other prominent clergy it was not made clear whether they were also restored to their former positions. Julian consciously wanted to foster the enthusiasm of many Christians for bitter internal disputes. Since in the Gospels Jesus foretold the destruction of the great Temple in Jerusalem, which actually occurred in 70, Julian gave orders for it to be rebuilt. The Jewish community was understandably cautious about embracing the ruler of an empire that had so often persecuted them in the past, but some leaders welcomed the decision. The project was quickly abandoned. Even the pagan Ammianus told the story of mysterious fireballs erupting and driving the workmen away.[19]

Julian tried to create an organised pagan church – 'church' is the right word for his was a heavily Christianised vision. Priests were appointed for each region. Their role and behaviour were expected to be very similar to Christian bishops. Julian felt that pagans had been badly shown up by the Christian enthusiasm for charity and his priests were to take care to look after the poor. Some of this structure was put into place. Appointments were made, and cities praised if they embraced the new system, but there is little trace of enthusiasm for Julian's particular brand of paganism. His beliefs remained essentially personal. It was the faith of a clever man, where learning, wisdom and disciplined character were to win favour from the gods. One of the things Julian most disliked about Christianity was the promise of salvation to all. In *The Caesars*, Constantine is rejected by all the gods until he runs to Jesus, who proclaims:

He that is a seducer, he that is a murderer, he that is sacrilegious, and infamous, let him approach without fear! For with this water I will wash him and will straightaway make him clean. And though he should be guilty of those same sins a second time, let him but smite his breast and beat his head and I will make him clean again.[20]

Much of this is doubtless the bitterness of a man whose family had been slaughtered by his avowedly pious Christian uncle. Instead, the gods should reward only the truly virtuous and not evil-doers simply because they repented. It was not a message with wide emotional appeal.

Julian did not formally persecute Christians, or 'Galileans' as he dubbed them. Some Christians were killed in rioting inspired by his decrees, both by pagan mobs and by other Christians in factional disputes. Direct persecution had not worked in the past and there was no indication that it would succeed now that the Church was openly established. Julian's attack was subtler. One measure that provoked especially strong criticism even from sympathetic pagans like Ammianus was the ban on Christians from teaching rhetoric and classical literature in public institutions. The rationale was that no one could adequately teach Homer or any of the other great texts unless they actually believed in the Olympian gods whose deeds they described – not a common view amongst philosophers other than the Neoplatonists. It was widely felt to be unfair to force Christian lecturers who had taught for many years either to recant or give up their posts. Since a traditional classical education was essential for any career in public office the aim was to force ambitious Christian parents to educate their children as pagans.[21]

When Julian died, his newly designed state religion was promptly abandoned. The ban on Christians teaching was repealed and the clergy regained most of their old privileges. There was no such swift end to the doctrinal disputes that had riven the Church from Constantine onwards. In Africa the Donatists still refused to accept the orthodox Catholic Church, and the struggle had taken on a social element and become periodically violent. More widely, there were many who rejected the Nicene Creed with its explicit equality of the Trinity. Constantius II took a much more Arian viewpoint and promoted bishops who favoured this throughout the provinces under his control. Some accepted an alternative creed, where God, Jesus and the Holy Spirit were of like, but not identical substance. There were many variations in just how this was understood and a whole range of sects emerged with distinct views on this and other points.

Some Christians formally rejected the world and chose to live lives of celibacy and frugality. The first monastic communities appeared in Egypt, but the idea quickly spread. Some ascetics achieved great fame for the exceptional simplicity of their lifestyle. Such people were widely revered and frequently written about, but always remained a minute fraction of the overall Christian community. The overwhelming majority of Christians married, raised families and, as opportunity and social status allowed, engaged in commerce or entered public life. It is widely believed that Christianity remained an essentially urban cult and that the population of the countryside clung for generations to the old beliefs. The word 'pagan' comes from *paganus*, or someone who lived in the countryside (*pagus*). Unfortunately, we know so little about the religious life in rural areas that this remains conjectural. *Paganus* was usually derogatory – something like 'yokel' or 'hick' would give the right idea – and may just reflect the common belief of urban dwellers that countrymen were dull and backward.[22]

Jovian was a Christian and quickly abandoned Julian's religious policy. Such concerns were not his main priority, which was to secure his position and minimise the damage to his prestige from the handover of territory to the Persians. Imperial proclamations announced the peace treaty as a great victory for Rome. There were some problems when the news of Jovian's elevation reached Gaul, although this did not develop into an organised challenge to his rule. After spending some time in Antioch, Jovian left for Constantinople but never reached his destination. Early in 364 he was found dead in his room. Fumes from a brazier and poor ventilation were held responsible. Ammianus for one suspected that Jovian had been murdered, but the verdict of accidental death by asphyxiation was publicly announced and accepted. The emperor's son was a baby – he had bawled unceasingly throughout a formal parade at Ancyra some weeks before – and there was no other heir. Without the pressure of an ongoing war, there was more time for court officials and army officers to select a new ruler. In the end, they chose an army officer named Valentinian, who was duly proclaimed as Augustus on 26 February 364.[23]

When the parading soldiers hailed the new emperor, they also demanded that he appoint a co-ruler – the death of two rulers in a year encouraged a desire for more stability. In spite of some blunt public advice from one Master of Soldiers – 'If you love your relatives, best of emperors, choose your brother; if you love the state then pick someone else for the imperial robes' – Valentinian chose his younger brother

Valens and named him as fellow Augustus. The pair divided the empire, the older brother taking the lion's share – geographically some two-thirds of the whole – and the younger being placed in charge of the east. From a family of local importance in Illyria, the brothers continued the tradition of third- and fourth-century emperors coming from the Balkans. Valens does not seem to have had an especially long or distinguished public career before his elevation. The brothers were both Christians. Valentinian supported the Church in his part of the empire and does not seem to have been especially concerned with matters of doctrine. He was tolerant of pagans, and only legislated against a small number of practices and condemned a handful of Christian sects. Valens was enthusiastically Arian, continuing the policies of Constantius II. Arianism was more common in the eastern provinces, although certainly not universal. Practical politics meant that Valens, like any emperor, employed many officials and army officers who were pagans or non-Arian Christians.[24]

The two new emperors were frequently at war. In part this was to win the glory necessary to bolster their rule. They divided up the *comitatenses*, and many individual units were split into two new regiments, named *seniores* and *juniores* respectively. (The terms seem to have already been in use before this date, but most scholars believe that the bulk of units with these titles were created at this time.) For a while, at the very least, such regiments must have been severely under strength until their ranks could be filled with new recruits. The increase in the number of regiments also instantly created more posts for commanding officers, providing a good way of rewarding loyal supporters. Valentinian operated on the Rhine and Danubian frontiers, and sent subordinates to campaign in Britain and North Africa. On and off throughout his reign Valens was occupied with friction on the borders with Persia. Although the treaty of 363 was never formally abandoned, the rival sides each interpreted it in their own way. The Romans continued to involve themselves in Armenian affairs, while the Persians strove to dominate the kingdom and still hoped to regain the remaining territories lost to Galerius. There was a good deal of raiding, and some larger fighting, although the scale of warfare never matched the operations of Constantius' and Julian's reign. Valens was in Syria in 365 when he received news of a serious rebellion. Julian's relative Procopius had been proclaimed emperor outside Constantinople. Within months several provinces acknowledged the usurper.[25]

Procopius' only claim was his connection with Julian, who was himself

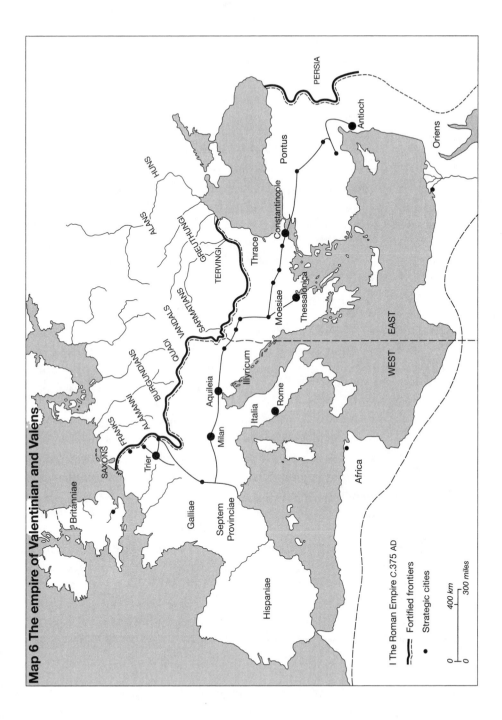

Map 6 The empire of Valentinian and Valens

I The Roman Empire c.375 AD

--- Fortified frontiers
• Strategic cities

0   400 km
0   300 miles

related to Constantine. Having disappeared in the weeks after the latter's death, Procopius emerged from hiding and won over two army units marching past Constantinople on their way to the Danubian frontier. He had grown a beard and was depicted in this way on his coins, but, while he paraded his similarity to Julian, Procopius seems to have remained a Christian. There was clearly no wave of pagan resentment waiting to be tapped by men seeking imperial power. The usurpation began somewhat raggedly – Procopius' imperial robes were a makeshift, almost comic affair. Yet luck was with him and he began to rally more army units to his cause. When Valentinian heard the news of the rising he did not know whether or not his brother was alive or dead. He was engaged in a campaign on the Rhine and decided not to intervene, proclaiming that 'Procopius was merely his own and his brother's enemy, while the Alamanni were the enemies of the entire Roman world'. After eight months, Valens was able to defeat the rebel. Procopius fled, but was handed over by his own officers and beheaded.[26]

Procopius started with very few supporters and gradually pieced together an army from passing units, all of them from Valens' forces. It seems extremely unlikely that he ever mustered an army of 10,000 or more men. In the end, the vast majority of his units deserted back to Valens. Even with such modest resources Procopius had come close to supplanting Valens. It was yet another demonstration of the insecurity of imperial power. Soldiers and officials could often be won over to support a rival. There was a snowball effect, Procopius' initial successes persuading more troops to join him. If a usurper gained local dominance then it was dangerous for officials and soldiers in the area not to join him. It was always better to be on the winning side, and whenever there was internal conflict people had to guess who was likely to win and act accordingly. Like other usurpations, the aftermath of Procopius' revolt brought a round of dismissals and executions, as well as promotions for those who had earned the emperor's favour, often by deserting the rebel at the right moment.[27]

Emperors dressed in a spectacular and ornate clothing that resembled military uniform. Their officials wore more modest versions that nevertheless reflected their delegated power and association with the ruler of the empire. Minor distinctions in colour and decoration – of tunic, headgear, cloak and even shoes – were of great importance in reflecting the hierarchy of office. A larger bureaucracy meant more posts with which to reward supporters. It also meant that many individuals came to represent imperial power wherever they happened to be. Legislation to restrict the demands made on communities by bureaucrats and soldiers suggest that they frequently took more than was necessary for the good of the state. In disturbed times such abuses were likely to be even worse.[28]

During Valens' reign some bandits in Syria disguised themselves as a state treasurer and his escort. Under this guise they entered a town near the end of the day and quite openly seized the house of a prominent aristocrat, announcing that he had been condemned by the emperor. The house was looted and any servants who resisted were killed before the group marched out of town before the following dawn. The success of this brazen raid reveals the general respect for and fear of imperial representatives. This particular gang thrived for some time, living in considerable luxury. In the end, imperial troops found them and massacred them all, even killing their sons in case they grew up to be bandits.[29]

Such thefts of the symbols of imperial authority were exceptionally rare, if spectacular. Keeping a measure of control over legitimate officials, however, was an unending and extremely difficult task. Posts brought privileges with them. The higher ones gave the holder social rank. Almost all provided exemptions from expensive duties to home communities. Salaries were not especially high, at least for the more junior posts, but these were regularly boosted by bribes for favours or fees for services – the slang expression was 'selling smoke'. Patronage and the exchange of favours were deeply embedded in Greco-Roman culture and such arrangements were not considered as corruption unless they went too far, distorting government decisions or resulting in the appointment of candidates staggeringly unsuited to the job. In some cases fees were formally recognised by the authorities. An inscription dating to Julian's reign from the outside wall of the town hall at Timgad in North Africa detailed the charges to both parties in bringing a legal case before the governor's court. Nothing would occur without the specified payment to each of the officials involved at every stage of the process. Charges were all assessed in quantities of grain, although whether they were actually paid in that form or converted into currency is unclear. Costs increased if the officials were required to travel any distance, for instance to serve a writ. Litigation was not cheap – although obviously that has been true in many eras, even if the specific nature of the costs has changed.[30]

No emperor could know all of his officials, still less keep a close eye on all their activities. Rules could be bent or even broken altogether without this ever being brought to the emperor's attention. Therefore, more officials were appointed whose main task was to watch and report on the activities of their colleagues. Chief amongst these were the agents (*agentes in rebus*), and a similar task was often performed by the senior clerks (*notarii*). Neither group was popular either with other officials or the wider public – especially the wealthy and prominent, who were most likely to be investigated. Most emperors liked them, because they seemed to offer them more control over their own administration. Constantius II greatly increased their numbers, particularly expanding the ranks of the agents. Julian publicly dismissed many of them, but the numbers again grew rapidly after his death. Such representatives could investigate specific problems and report directly to the emperor. At best this gave him accurate information about distant problems and permitted him to make an informed decision about them. This assumed that the reports they presented were accurate. Inevitably, there was the chance for human error, as well as deliberate deception.[31]

In the 360s the lands around Septimius Severus' home city of Lepcis were subjected to repeated raids by nomadic tribesmen from beyond the frontier. This followed the execution by the city authorities of one of the tribes' noblemen on a charge of banditry. The city councillors requested help from the local military commander, the *comes* Romanus. The latter gathered some units of *comitatenses* and then demanded 4,000 camels and supplies from the city leaders. It was normal for communities to support the armies with transport animals and food, but the quantities were wildly excessive. It is unlikely that so many animals could have been supplied at short notice, or that Romanus' forces actually needed them. Presumably he was interested in making a profit, either by selling off the bulk of the camels or accepting a bribe to make up for the shortfall in what the city gave him. The leaders of Lepcis refused out of hand, so Romanus waited for a month and then withdrew the army, leaving the city to its fate. Raids continued. As usual, these were evidently small in scale, and agriculture around the city was disrupted rather than destroyed. Yet it was all very galling to the citizens of Lepcis to see that the army was unwilling to protect them. A group of local notables was sent on an embassy to Valentinian, eventually gaining an audience with the emperor at Milan. Romanus sent his own version and this was persuasively presented by his relative, one of the senior officials of the imperial court.

At first nothing was done, but as reports of new and worse raids arrived, Valentinian decided to investigate the matter and gave this task to the clerk Palladius, who was anyway going to Africa to dispense pay to the troops. This last task was urgent and took precedence over the inquiry. Palladius came to private arrangements with the commanders of the regiments in Africa, siphoning off some of the soldiers' pay – perhaps through accepting falsely inflated returns for the number of men in each unit – and sharing the profits. When he finally came to look into the question of the raiding, the clerk quickly established Romanus' culpability. However, the latter had learned of Palladius' financial activities and blackmailed him into falsifying his report. Together they persuaded some locals to contradict the envoys and deny that there had ever been serious raids at all. Therefore, Valentinian was eventually informed that there was no truth in the accusations made against his commander in Africa. Angrily, he turned on the envoys from Lepcis for making 'false' accusations against an imperial official. Some were executed, as was the civilian governor of the province who had backed their story. Other envoys were to have their tongues ripped out.

Only years later did the truth emerge in the aftermath of a tribal rebellion in North Africa, which eventually turned into an attempted usurpation. Romanus was discredited for provoking this episode and placed under arrest. Amongst his papers was a letter from Palladius revealing their secret arrangement. The former clerk had already been dismissed from service. He was arrested, but, being held overnight in a church during a festival, evaded the supervision of his guards and hanged himself. A few of the envoys had been in hiding and so had avoided the savage punishment decreed for them. They now served as witnesses, as those who had backed Romanus' and Palladius' story were sought out and punished.[32]

The whole squalid episode had lasted for over a decade. It revealed starkly the dependence of the emperor on his officials, and the difficulty of establishing what was actually happening in the provinces. The imperial view was limited and the increase in bureaucracy had if anything made it more distant, for all information was filtered and refined by others before it reached the emperor himself. The savagery of the imperial response – both to the envoys and their supporters, and then ultimately to the conspirators when this was exposed – was typical of the fourth century and revealed it to be a very different world from the early empire. In the first and second centuries provincial communities were able to bring unpopular governors to trial after their term of office was over. They might or might not win their case – several of Pliny's predecessors in Bithynia had been found guilty – and the outcome might or might not be just, but the worst that failure would cost them was the waste of money and effort. No one would be executed or mutilated if a prosecution failed.[33]

The Romanus scandal was exceptional. Corruption on such a scale did not pervade the entire administration of the empire and in the end due process caught up with the surviving conspirators. Yet the episode is too readily brushed aside by some modern scholars, eager as always to shed a favourable light on the fourth-century empire. It did reveal what was possible and while it is right to note that behaviour that would seem corrupt to modern eyes would have been perfectly acceptable to the Romans, Romanus and Palladius went far beyond that. Most of all it showed how poorly the government could function. Not only was nothing done about a genuine problem of raiding bands, but the emperor was unable even to find out correctly what had happened.[34]

The governmental system did most of what emperors required of it. It allowed them to harness sufficient resources to support the army. Its complex structure and divided responsibilities also helped to protect them from usurpers. The bureaucracy itself had steadily acquired a life of its own. Departments might bicker for power, but they rarely shrank in size for very long. Officials pursued careers to win themselves wealth, prestige, honours and privileges. The efficient running of the empire was too distant an ambition for individuals and departments within the bureaucracy. Human nature being what it is, such an object was too far removed from their more immediate ambitions. The imperial government more often than not coped with what was required of it in the day-to-day running of the empire. In the last years of Valens' reign, it was to show itself far less capable of dealing with a crisis.

13

Goths

'Now the sun climbed higher ... [and] the Romans were weakened by hunger and thirst, and burdened by the weight of their equipment. In the end the great force of the barbarian onslaught shattered our battle-line ... Some fell without seeing who struck them, or were knocked down by the sheer weight of the attackers, or even killed by comrades.... In amongst the ordinary soldiers the emperor was struck by an arrow, and soon breathed his last – or so it was believed for no one ever claimed to have seen him or been beside him – and his body was never found subsequently.' – *Ammianus' account of the disaster at Adrianople.*[1]

On 17 November 375, Emperor Valentinian was on the Upper Danube, receiving a delegation of chieftains from the Quadi – Marcus Aurelius' old adversaries, who had recently raided into Rome's Pannonian provinces. Valentinian's campaigns were always as much, if not more, about diplomacy than actual use of force. He was known as a quick-tempered man, something that goes beyond the well-entrenched fourth-century stereotype of the irascible and ill-educated Illyrian. When the chieftains claimed that the raids had been launched without their consent by bands of foreigners, and that in fact recent Roman building of new fortifications was provocative, the emperor flew into a rage at such insolence. In the middle of his violent harangue, Valentinian had a stroke and died. He was fifty-four.[2]

Some years before, Valentinian had named his older son Gratian as Augustus. The lad was now sixteen and had been left at Trier by his father. His younger brother Valentinian II was only four, but was immediately also proclaimed as Augustus by troops and bureaucrats on the Danube. Neither Valens nor Gratian had sanctioned this, but they did not feel able to reject the child's elevation. Valentinian, and through him Valens, were both selected as emperor by an influential group of senior bureaucrats and army officers. Throughout their reigns the brothers needed to be careful to keep these men happy. It is notable that a number of the most prominent officials remained in office for many years, far longer than was typical in the past. Julian's reign in particular had been marked by a rapid turnover of men holding senior posts. Distinct cliques of senior officials dominated the administration of the territories controlled by each of the emperors. Such men had no desire for reuniting into a single administration under a sole emperor, unless they could be sure that they alone would monopolise the senior positions. Valentinian and Valens knew that their dynasty was too recent to be fully secure and that they must respect the views of their senior officials. In 375 enough senior men decided that they wanted a separate court and administration under the nominal control of Valentinian II to force the hands of Valens and Gratian.[3]

The empire was once again divided into three. Valens remained in control of the eastern provinces, while Valentinian II was given Italy and North Africa. Illyricum was also technically part of his territory, but in practice this and the remainder of the west was controlled by Gratian. In spite of his age, the latter was active on the frontiers from the beginning of his reign, continuing his father's round of punitive expeditions and forceful diplomacy. For the moment the groups of officials dominating the imperial courts were content with and able to maintain the rule of a youthful and an infant emperor.[4]

Migrants

In 376 a large group of Goths massed on the far bank of the Danube. This was not a raiding party, but an entire people on the move, their women and children riding in wagons. They were called the Tervingi, although they were not all of the people who called themselves by that name. There was another major group of Tervingi, and altogether at least half a dozen distinct groups of Goths are known from our sources – more may well have existed, but are simply not recorded. The Goths, just like the Almanni, Franks and others, remained a deeply divided people, split into tribes and other groups, loyal to many different kings, chieftains and magistrates. In the fifth century kingdoms were carved out from Roman territory by the Ostrogoths and Visigoths. There is no evidence that these groups already existed in Valens' day, under these or any other names. Although they figure in older accounts of the 370s, the Visigoths and Ostrogoths did not come into being for another generation.[5]

The Tervingi sent envoys on ahead seeking permission from Valens to cross into the empire. They asked to be settled on land, preferably in

Thrace, and promised in return to provide soldiers for his army. At the time the emperor was in Antioch, for there was continued friction with the Persians over the control of Armenia, so inevitably there was a delay of a month or more before his reply arrived. His past relations with the Gothic tribes had not always been happy. From the beginning of his reign there was tension. In 365 a contingent of 3,000 Gothic warriors answered the summons of Procopius. They arrived too late to make a difference and excused their action by saying that they felt obliged to honour their old treaty with Constantine by supporting any member of his house, however distant. It is hard to tell whether this was genuine. Roman civil wars must often have been confusing to war leaders from outside the empire. They were also great opportunities to profit and the Goths who rallied to Procopius may simply have felt that a usurper was more likely to be generous if they aided his victory.[6]

Valens was unimpressed by these excuses and spent the next three summers campaigning on the Danube. There was little fighting, for the Goths avoided battle and took refuge in the mountains. Nevertheless, the Romans' display of force was sufficient to prompt negotiation. Valens held a meeting with the Tervingian King Athanaric on a barge moored midway across the River Danube, honouring the latter's solemn oath never to set foot on Roman soil. Both sides paraded their troops on the opposing banks. Valentinian had once similarly conducted talks on a river boat, but in each case the willingness to do so granted a measure of equality to the barbarian leaders involved. Traditionally, representatives of Rome had negotiated in a way that made clear the empire's over-whelming superiority, making the enemy come to them and bow down before a tribunal and the serried ranks of the legions. By the later fourth century it was often more important to gain a quick peace than to insist upon such displays.[7]

Valens needed the Goths to be quiet so that he could deal with the escalating tension with Persia. They agreed to keep the peace and would no longer receive subsidies. At first sight this was clearly a penalty for the Gothic chieftains, but it may well be that in a gift-giving society, receiving anything from an outside power was a clear mark of dependence. They may have seen this as a considerable gain. Similarly, the restriction on any trade across the border except at two nominated posts probably reinforced the power of the Gothic leaders best placed to control access to these points. Athanaric was probably well satisfied by the treaty of 369. Like Valens, he and the Goths were also facing other problems.[8]

The origin of the Huns is shrouded in mystery and discussion of this is best left until later, when looking at their direct attack on the empire (see page 315). In 376 the Romans were only dimly aware of their presence. Wild stories circulated of their savagery and barely human behaviour. They were ugly and misshapen, with shaven heads and beardless faces. Superb horsemen, they could barely walk on their own two feet. Growing no crops they lived on milk and raw meat, which they heated by placing beneath the saddle cloths of their horses.

> They are all without any fixed home, without household gods or laws, or stable way of life, and they always wander from place to place, almost like fugitives, with the wagons in which they live.... Like unthinking animals, they have no concept of right and wrong, are deceitful and evasive in speech, not bothered by religion or belief.

All the old stereotypes of barbarism were revived and repeated, but the spread of such stories gives some idea of the fear inspired by these nomads from the Steppes. Once again, we should not think of the Huns as a single, united people. They were divided into many sub-groups and answered to different leaders. The power of a few kings may have been growing at this time, but the Hunnic attacks in the second half of the fourth century should not be seen as a concerted and organised invasion. Instead, there was an increase in scale and frequency of the raids launched against their neighbours.[9]

The arrival of the Huns added a new factor to the struggles for power within and between the tribes of the region, presenting opportunities as well as a threat. Local chieftains were faced with a choice between opposing Hunnic raiding parties or seeking to ally with Hun leaders to gain the support of their bands. In this way some Gothic chieftains were able to defeat their rivals and expand their own power. Others suffered and were killed, driven from their homes or forced to accept sub-ordination to their enemies. The impact of the appearance of the Huns in the lands around the Black Sea was to make warfare in the region more decisive. The Alans, themselves originally another nomadic people from the Steppes, were the first to feel the brunt and in due course all of their leaders either fled or accepted the overlordship of Hunnic kings. The Goths were next, and the same pattern of resistance and alliance was repeated. At times Huns were hired by both sides in struggles between different Gothic groups. It was not just a case of hopelessly heroic resistance by Gothic kings against the merciless horsemen from the

Steppes. Some Goths quickly came to terms with their new aggressive neighbours and fought with them against other Goths.[10]

Athanaric fought against the Huns and was beaten, retreating into the mountains just as he had done to escape Valens. For the moment at least he was resolute in his refusal to break his oath and seek sanctuary within the empire. It was another group of Tervingi who approached the Danube and asked to be admitted. Two chieftains, Alavivus and Fritigern, are named in our sources, but it is clear that their power was not absolute – they were simply the two strongest and most influential leaders of the warrior bands with the migrants. It is also wrong to imagine a single great caravan rolling towards the empire. For practical reasons of supply as much as anything else, many distinct parties travelled in the same general direction and only massed together when they reached the crossing point on the Danube. They were a loose group, some fugitives from the Huns or enemies within their own people, and others most likely simply eager to enjoy the more comfortable life within the empire. Service in the Roman army was an attractive prospect to many warriors, and the chieftains in particular could look forward to rewarding careers in imperial service.[11]

We do not know how many people there were altogether. One late and unreliable source claims that there were 200,000, but this is likely to be vastly exaggerated. Ammianus simply says that there were too many for the Roman troops on the frontier to count. One modern estimate suggests some 10,000 warriors, along with four or even five times as many women, children and elderly. This is plausible enough, but still no more than conjecture. It remains perfectly possible that the group was larger or smaller than this. Similarly, the ratio of adult males to the rest is very hard to estimate. Clearly, an entire community fleeing from aggression would have contained a higher proportion of non-combatants than bands seeking military service. Soon after the Tervingi approached the frontier, the Romans became aware of another large party of Goths advancing with similar purpose. These were the Greuthungi – although again they were only one section of the people going by this name.[12]

After a round trip of well over 1,000 miles, the Tervingian ambassadors returned from Antioch and their audience with Valens with the news that he had granted their request. Ammianus tells us that his advisers had easily convinced the emperor that the migrants would prove an asset. They would provide a steady supply of recruits for the army. This would mean that the levy of conscripts from other provinces could be commuted into a payment in gold. Thus the empire would have both soldiers and money. There is no support in the ancient sources for the modern suggestion that the ongoing tension with Persia meant that Valens could not have refused the Tervingi entry even if he wanted to do so. Soon afterwards he rejected a similar appeal made by the Greuthungi. Quite why the two groups were treated differently is unknown. Suggestions have ranged from the inability of the authorities to process so many people to a display of strength to emphasise to the Tervingi that the Romans had not been forced to admit them. Just as likely is the possibility that there were differences in the past relationship of their leaders with Rome.[13]

There was nothing new about settling tribesmen from outside the empire within the provinces. Diocletian and Constantine were amongst the many emperors who had chosen to do this. Previously hostile peoples were transplanted to more productive land, so that they ceased to be a threat and in time provided tax revenue and/or soldiers for the army. Precedents for similar behaviour by the Roman authorities went back a long way, to the development of frontiers further and further away under the Republic. In the first century AD a senatorial governor had proudly recorded that 'he brought over more than 100,000 of the people who live across the Danube to pay tribute to Rome, along with their wives and families'. As always the number may be exaggerated, but it was clearly a substantial group of people and was included as one of his greatest achievements.[14]

Yet not all migrants were admitted. Julius Caesar began his Gallic campaigns by refusing to permit a tribe called the Helvetii to move through his province on their way to settle in Gaul. He not only repulsed them when they tried to force their way through, but – claiming that they were plundering Rome's allies – chased after the Helvetii, defeated them in battle and sent them back to their homes. This was an especially robust response from an ambitious general who needed the glory of major victories. Yet it was not that unusual, and there are plenty of other cases where migrating groups were refused entry or driven back by force. The choice was always supposed to lie with the Roman authorities, who would ruthlessly suppress any refusal to accept their decision. In most cases the peoples involved had already been clearly defeated by the Roman army. At other times the submission was more symbolic and a display of Roman might was accompanied by gestures of subservience from the barbarian leaders. In essence, the migrants had first to surrender to Rome. Then they were settled, usually in small groups over a wide area on land that had fallen out of cultivation or was part of an imperial estate. The majority of settlements proved highly successful. The precise legal status of the barbarian colonists varied – descendants of those who had been defeated were one of the few groups not included in Caracalla's grant of citizenship.[15]

The Tervingi had not been defeated, but since they came as suppliants, Valens' decision to grant their request was neither unprecedented nor unreasonable. The details of the treaty elude us, as do the precise terms on which the migrants were to be settled. One of the conditions seems to have been that the Goths convert to Christianity. The Goths certainly did this, adopting the Arian form favoured by Valens himself. A later source also claims that the tribesmen were to be disarmed, although the contemporary Ammianus does not mention this. It is possible that this was part of the agreement, although even if it was, then the gesture of handing over a few weapons may well have been mainly symbolic. In the event, the Tervingi retained a good number of weapons. It took a considerable time to carry the Goths across the Danube – normally there was little need for so many ferry boats. The naval squadron that patrolled the river assisted, but their craft were not especially numerous and certainly not designed to carry large numbers of people or bulky wagons. Many of the Goths crossed in rafts built for the purpose, but a few are said to have tried swimming and drowned in the process.[16]

The Road to Disaster

There were well-established mechanisms for accepting groups of barbarians into the empire and settling them within the provinces. Yet from the very beginning things did not run smoothly for the Tervingi. Possibly there was negligence on the part of Roman officials over the question of disarming the tribe. Certainly there was sloth, incompetence and corruption in almost every other aspect of the affair. Ammianus blamed the two army officers in command on the spot – Lupicinus, the *comes* in charge of the *comitatenses* in Thrace, and the *dux* Maximus, who controlled the *limitanei*. The most basic problem was one of food. The Tervingi may well have used many of their own supplies while they waited for the response from Valens and then during the long process of crossing the river. The Romans were supposed to feed them, but what the Goths were given proved barely adequate. The supplies may simply not have been available. The Tervingi were equivalent in numbers to a very large Roman expeditionary army and it usually took a couple of years to mass the grain and other supplies needed by such a force. The officials on the Danube had had no more than a few months to prepare. Even so, the state received a considerable amount of taxation in the form of agricultural produce and was supposed to store the surplus in granaries within walled cities and army bases ready for use by troops, the court or officials. If the resources were not there to meet the needs of the Tervingi, then the decision to admit them would seem extremely unwise. Perhaps the supplies existed, but had not been moved to the right place. It is hard to believe the suggestion that the emperor ordered his officials to restrict the amounts given to the Goths in order to keep them dependent, since this was bound to be a very risky strategy. The officials on the spot may have decided on such a dangerous course of action. Certainly, they chose to profit from it. Ammianus tells us that once Lupicinus had prised much of the barbarians' wealth from them in exchange for black market food, he began an even more sinister trade. The Goths were desperate enough to sell their children for paltry amounts of dog meat. The going rate was one child for one dog – Lupicinus' men were organised enough to have gathered up stray dogs from a wide area.[17]

Slowly the Tervingi were moved to the city of Marcianopolis where Lupicinus seems to have had his headquarters. They were not admitted to the city or its market, but made to camp some distance outside. To supervise the march most of the Roman troops were drawn away from the frontier leaving it seriously depleted. At some point the Greuthungi, who had been refused entry, crossed into the empire – the concentration of the Roman patrol boats to assist the Tervingi meant that large stretches of the Danube were not being watched. The Roman authorities were rapidly losing control of the situation. Either there were insufficient troops or they were very poorly deployed. The situation at Marcianopolis was already tense when Lupicinus invited the Tervingian leaders to a banquet. Such meetings were a regular feature of Roman frontier diplomacy and also, as we have seen, opportunities for treachery. We do not know whether or not Lupicinus planned to imprison or kill the chieftains. Given the considerable time lag, it is unlikely that he was acting under explicit orders from the emperor.

The trouble began outside the city when an argument between soldiers, townsfolk and the Goths escalated into a small battle. A party of troops was routed. At this point Lupicinus – Ammianus notes that it was late in the evening and he was already more than half drunk – ordered the execution of the chieftains' attendants and the Gothic chieftains were also arrested. When news of this spread outside the city to the Gothic encampments, there was an uproar and more and more warriors arrived to join those who had been involved in the fighting. Fritigern managed to talk his way out, convincing Lupicinus that only he could calm the angry mood of his countrymen. He was released. Nothing more is ever heard of Alavivus.[18]

Lupicinus gathered all of the troops he could and decided to march against the Tervingian camp some 9 miles away from the city. The Goths were waiting and routed the column. Lupicinus himself escaped, allegedly because he was one of the first to gallop for safety. A war had started and quickly began to spread. A group of Goths who had been accepted some time earlier into the empire were waiting at Adrianople to move to the east, presumably to serve with the army. There had already been some friction with a local magistrate, who now raised a force from the city, including the workers from a state arms' factory. These Goths cut this hastily armed militia to pieces, plundering them of their newly made weapons before joining up with Fritigern. Together the combined army tried to besiege Adrianople, but failed dismally. As they withdrew, Fritigern sullenly reminded them that he 'kept peace with walls'.[19]

The Goths lacked skill at siege craft, but far more importantly they lacked the ability to stay in one place for long enough to capture a defended and fortified town. They were now free to plunder the country-side, burning villages and villas, gathering animals for meat and as much grain as they could find. Yet the biggest stores of food were always kept in walled towns and the Goths could not capture such places. So many hungry mouths quickly consumed whatever supplies were available in any stretch of countryside, forcing them to keep moving. The Goths' numbers had grown considerably, as Fritigern's band was joined by the Greuthungi and groups like the one from Adrianople. More came as individuals. Some were Goths recently sold into slavery in exchange for food, or captured years earlier by slave traders or in imperial campaigns. As news spread of the rich plunder for the taking in Thrace, other warbands crossed the Danube to join them. Whatever troops the Romans still had stationed on the frontier were clearly incapable of preventing this. In 377 Fritigern even hired some bands of Huns and Alans with the promise of a generous share of the spoils.[20]

The Goths rapidly became more numerous and powerful, especially since the recent arrivals consisted mainly of eager warriors, not migrants with their families. Many were now equipped with good-quality Roman weaponry and most likely more of them wore mail or other body armour and helmets than was normal for a tribal army. The pressure of the situation, surviving in enemy territory month after month, cemented the authority of their leaders and their ability to work together. None of this altered the basic fact that they were fighting a war they could not win. The main groups of Tervingi and Greuthungi were migrants without homes. Unlike the raiders who had joined them, they could not retire back across the Danube. However much their numbers grew, their military might and resources were dwarfed by those of the empire. The best that they could hope for was to be granted lands by the Roman authorities. The worst outcomes were annihilation, slavery or to make peace with Rome and again suffer mistreatment. Fritigern and the other leaders may have understood this and realised that their best hope was to negotiate from a position of strength. They had no clear military objective. This, combined with the never-ending problem of supply, shaped the apparently purposeless meanderings of the Goths during the next years. They did not remain as one concentrated army, but continually split up into many small parties to forage and plunder. When threatened by Roman forces the different groups would try to re-form as quickly as they could.

In the long run the Romans could not lose this war, but that did not mean that it was easy for them to win it. Lupicinus had lost heavily in his rash and unprepared attack outside Marcianopolis. Other troops were dispersed as garrisons, dotted around the walled cities of the region to defend these against the enemy. At first, all the local forces were capable of doing was holding the vital mountain passes, which kept the Goths bottled up in just one part of the Thracian plain. In 377 a field army was put together from a mixture of units sent by Gratian from the west along with eastern troops. Several successes were scored when isolated groups of Goths were attacked and killed or captured. Rapid movement and surprise attacks were once again the most effective Roman tactics. However, the Goths were sometimes capable of doing the same things, and several Roman units were cut to pieces outside the city of Dibaltum – properly, Deultum – modern Debelt in Bulgaria.[21]

Much of the time the Romans operated in small detachments, harassing the scattered enemy. Only once did they concentrate to attack a substantial number of Goths – we are not sure which particular group this was – who had laagered their wagons in a great circle near the town of Ad Salices. As the Romans gathered, the barbarians also had time to call in many of their dispersed bands of raiders. When the Romans finally launched an attack, there was very heavy fighting around the wagon line. The Roman left wing was broken by a Gothic charge and the situation was only stabilised by the units in reserve. The battle ended in a costly stalemate, but it was the Romans who withdrew some days later. After this they returned to their harassing strategy.

Valens made peace with the Persians in 377 and was back in Constantinople the following year to deal with the problem of the Goths. He had gathered a field force and the plan was to combine with an army brought east by Gratian before confronting the main strength of the enemy. Unfortunately the western army was delayed. An Alamannic soldier from Gratian's guards went on leave and happened to mention the planned move eastwards to his kinsmen. The latter decided to take advantage of the absence of the bulk of the Roman forces by raiding the provinces. Gratian fought a short campaign to punish the tribe involved and only after this was complete was he able to begin the march to join his uncle.[22]

Adrianople and After

It was now late summer and Valens had already decided to advance on his own. At the beginning of August he was at Adrianople, closing with a substantial group of Goths led by Fritigern. His patrols reported that the enemy numbered about 10,000. This proved to be a serious underestimate, but Ammianus fails to tell us how large the Gothic army actually was. At the same time messengers arrived telling him that Gratian was only a few days' march away. Some of his senior officers advised caution, arguing that it was only prudent to wait for Gratian and so make their victory absolutely certain. Others suggested that there was an opportunity for a quick victory over this one section of the enemy. Valens is said to have wanted to win glory for himself, so that he would not be overshadowed by the recent achievements of his nephew and the minor victories won by his own army.

Valens' confidence was boosted when a Christian clergyman acting as Fritigern's envoy arrived. Publicly he asked that the Goths be granted Thrace to settle in, but he also carried a private message in which Fritigern assured the emperor of his goodwill. He asked Valens to mount an impressive display of force so that it would be easier for him to calm his fellow tribesmen and persuade them to accept peace. No answer was given to the envoy, but this seemed a clear sign of the Goths' nervousness. On 9 August 378 Valens marched his army out of Adrianople and moved against the Gothic camp, which once again took the form of a great circle of wagons. The Roman army did not begin to arrive until early afternoon and the men were tired from marching under the hot sun.

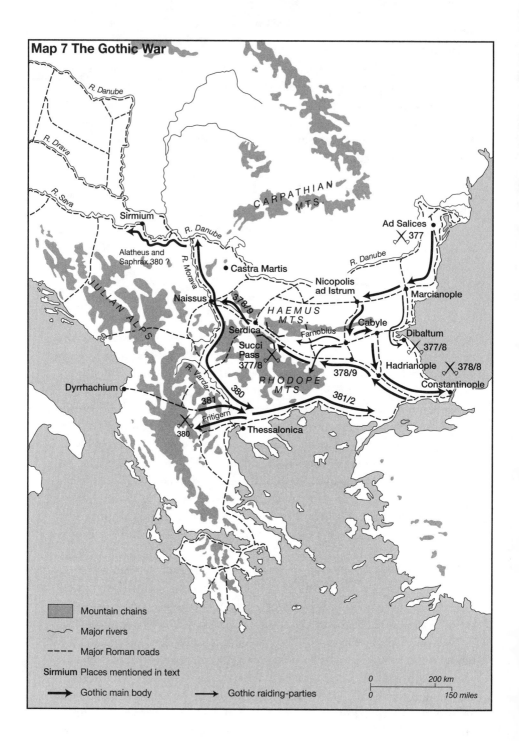

Map 7 The Gothic War

Ad Salices
✗ 377

R. Danube

Sirmium

Alatheus and
Saphrax 380 ?

Castra Martis

Nicopolis
ad Istrum

Marcianople

R. Danube

JULIAN ALPS

Naissus

378/9

HAEMUS
MTS.

Cabyle

Dibaltum
✗ 377/8

Serdica

Farnobius

Succi
Pass
377/8

378/9

Hadrianople ✗ 378/8

Dyrrhachium

R. Varda

380

RHODOPE
MTS.

381/2

Constantinople

381

✗
380

Fritigern

Thessalonica

Mountain chains

Major rivers

Major Roman roads

Sirmium Places mentioned in text

Gothic main body

Gothic raiding-parties

0   200 km

0   150 miles

The column began to deploy by wheeling to the right, so that the units at the head of the column would form the right of the battle line. Ahead of them were bands of Goths in front of the wagon laager, chanting their battle cries. Others lit bush fires, the wind carrying the heat and the smoke into the Roman lines. As well as adding to their discomfort, it reduced visibility. This was important as Fritigern was expecting to be joined by a large group of Greuthungi, including many cavalry.[23]

The Gothic leader may have been playing for time to allow these extra forces to arrive when he once again asked for a parley. Alternatively, he may genuinely have understood that he had absolutely nothing to gain and a huge amount to lose from fighting a battle against the emperor. Valens refused to speak to the first group of envoys because they were too obscure, but the Romans responded to a second approach asking them to send over a senior officer as a hostage. Valens may also have simply been prevaricating, wanting to allow the rest of his army to arrive and form a battle line. On the other hand, he would certainly have been content with a bloodless victory, where the enemy submitted in response to a Roman display of force. Whatever the rival leaders' real intentions, it was not to be.

Fighting began when the two units of Roman cavalry on the far right flank attacked without orders. There was always a danger of such things when two rival armies stood for hours on end facing each other across a short distance. They were quickly driven back, but it seems to have produced a general attack all along the Roman line. On the left flank the units had scarcely arrived and were not properly formed up when they joined the attack. The cavalry units that should have protected the flank of the infantry were not in place, leaving them very exposed. They were completely unprepared to meet the sudden attack of the Greuthungi, along with the Gothic cavalry and a band of Alans. The Roman attack lost momentum, but there was still a long period of savage combat before the battle was over. Some of the infantry were surrounded, the units too confused and densely crowded to form a proper fighting line, but they continued to resist for some time. In the previous year the Romans had been able to deal with the collapse of one flank by sending in reserves. This time the army was not properly formed or under control. A regiment that should have been stationed in reserve could not be found when it was needed, most probably because it had already become drawn into the attack.

Tactically, the Roman army was in a hopeless situation, and in the end the soldiers broke and fled. The Goths pursued with enthusiasm and, as was usual in the battles of this period, the losing side suffered badly. Around two-thirds of the soldiers were killed, along with no fewer than thirty-five tribunes – some commanding regiments and others unattached but with the imperial staff – and two more senior officers. Valens was also among the dead and, just like Decius over a century before, his body was never found. One story circulated that he and his attendants had holed up in a farmhouse. When the Goths were unable to break in, they set fire to the building, killing all save one attendant, who told them how close they had come to capturing an emperor.[24]

We do not know how big Valens' army was at Adrianople and therefore cannot calculate the total loss. Most modern estimates put both the Roman and Gothic armies around the 15,000 mark, so that some 10,000 Roman soldiers are thought to have died. Once again, the figures are plausible but entirely conjectural. We do not know how many of the tribunes who died commanded units – but then, since we do not know how big such regiments were, let alone whether they were present in their entirety or merely as detachments, this would not tell us anything definite. Nor do we know how many tribunes commanding units survived the battle. Clearly, Valens felt confident that his army could deal with a force of 10,000 Goths – presumably all warriors, although Ammianus is not specific. Once again, we are left to guess at whether this would mean having parity or a numerical advantage. Julian was supposed to have beaten an army of Alamanni almost three times larger than his own force at Strasbourg.[25]

Adrianople was a major disaster. Whatever the precise figure, the critical point was that the greater part of the soldiers immediately available to the eastern emperor for active campaigning had been killed. Ammianus compared the defeat to Cannae in 216 BC, where Hannibal had slaughtered some 50,000 Roman soldiers and captured 20,000 more. Adrianople was much smaller in scale, but it was the worst defeat at the hands of a foreign enemy since the third century. Luck played a part, but Valens had been overconfident in closing with the enemy, then indecisive in considering negotiation at the last minute, and had utterly failed to control the attack itself.

The Goths won a great victory, but in the long run it did nothing to improve their situation – they needed to negotiate with an emperor, not to kill one. They followed up by assaulting Adrianople, hoping to capture the supplies there as well as the imperial treasury. Enough troops had been left behind by Valens to repulse every onslaught and an attempt by some turncoats in the army to betray the city was also thwarted. After a while Fritigern and his warriors moved on to threaten Constantinople itself. He had been joined by more warbands, including groups of Alans and Huns. Even so, his army was overawed by the massive size of the city, already bigger than anywhere else save Rome, Antioch and Alexandria. As disturbing were the aggressive sallies of a unit of Saracen cavalry. Ammianus says that one of these riders rode half naked into battle and after killing a Goth by slitting his throat, seemed to drink his blood. Suitably impressed, Fritigern and his men returned to their practice of keeping peace by the use of walls. The Goths had co-operated to fight the battle – although it is more than probable that a number of bands were not present – but remained divided into many separate groups under different chiefs. This and the familiar problems of supply meant that they soon broke up into many fragments, marauding through the region in search of food and plunder.[26]

Fear spread rapidly as the news of the disaster at Adrianople reached the other provinces. In a particularly ruthless series of massacres, groups of Goths throughout the empire were disarmed and slaughtered by the authorities in case they, too, chose to rebel. For a while Gratian was effectively emperor of the entire world, since his younger brother was still too young to assert his own power. Within a few months – probably early in 379 – he acknowledged a recently appointed Master of Soldiers named Theodosius as Augustus of the eastern provinces. Theodosius' father and namesake came from Spain and had enjoyed a distinguished military career under Valentinian, winning victories in Britain and Africa. He was the man who exposed the misdeeds of Romanus. However, in 375 the older Theodosius had been condemned by the emperor and executed. This may have been posthumous revenge from associates of the discredited men or simply the result of the habitual back-biting of the court and paranoia of the emperor. The son was dismissed from service, but may well have been recalled by the time of Adrianople. Soon afterwards he was given a command and won a minor victory on the Danube. He was probably backed by significant figures at the eastern court. Whether or not he was Gratian's choice, the two men did show that they could work together.[27]

Almost the first task was to rebuild an army. Theodosius displayed little of his father's talent as a soldier, but was certainly a great organiser. Men were found from a whole range of sources and a series of strict laws passed against draft dodging, self-mutilation to avoid service and desertion. The army grew in size, but many of the new recruits were not yet properly trained and the confidence of the rest was at a low ebb. The

Romans continued their previous strategy of harassing the individual groups of Goths, blocking their movements and depriving them of food. One attempt at more direct attack ended in failure when a column led by Theodosius himself was badly mauled.[28]

Over the next few years the Goths were gradually worn down by ambushes and surprise attacks. Individual groups surrendered and Gratian settled some in Italy. The details of these campaigns elude us – sadly Ammianus' account stopped a few months after Adrianople and there is no comparable narrative history until the sixth century. In the end all of the Goths who remained within the empire capitulated in 382. Fritigern is not mentioned, and it may well be that he was already dead or killed as part of the settlement. Ultimately, the Goths got much of what they originally asked for – they were settled on land in Thrace or in the adjacent border areas along the Danube. The precise details of the treaty are hotly debated and need not concern us here. It is safe to say that their fierce resistance meant that the conditions under which they were settled were far more generous than was usual. Their own chieftains seem to have retained considerable authority and may, in practice if not in theory, have enjoyed a degree of local autonomy.[29]

There is nothing surprising about the eventual defeat of the Goths, for they simply could not compete against the resources and organisation of the empire. What is startling is that it took six years to force their surrender, and that even then the Roman victory was not as complete as they would normally have expected. This is a serious problem for those who emphasise the strength and efficiency of the empire in the later fourth century. The allegedly enlarged and highly efficient army seems in practice to have struggled to find enough men to deal with the migrating tribes. Yet this was scarcely a new problem or one on a massive scale. Of the major battles of these campaigns the Romans were clearly beaten three times – disastrously, in the case of Adrianople, but badly enough even if on a smaller scale under Lupicinus and Theodosius – and at best managed a hard-fought draw at Ad Salices. This is scarcely an impressive record and again confirms the impression that in this period the army operated best on a small scale, using surprise, speed and ambush rather than direct force. The empire still commanded huge resources, but it does seem to have been difficult to apply these to any problem. There was clearly a shortage of readily available and willing military manpower – the Tervingi were admitted specifically to help meet this need. In these six years of warfare the Roman Empire won not because it was efficient, but simply because it was big. In 386 another group of

Goths attempting to cross the Danube were efficiently blocked by a Roman army. It is more than probable that the best course of action in 376 would have been to refuse entry, since the authorities proved so incapable of effectively processing the migrants. Even if some Goths had broken through by force, they are unlikely to have caused as much damage and disorder.[30]

Just a year after the treaty with the Goths a familiar problem reared its head once more. The local commander Magnus Maximus was proclaimed emperor by the troops in Britain. He was another Spaniard, probably known to – perhaps even a relation of – Theodosius. Gratian refused to recognise the usurper and massed an army to confront him when Maximus crossed into Gaul. There was some skirmishing near Paris, but after several days Gratian's army went over en masse to his opponent. He fled, but was caught at Lugdunum (modern Lyons) and executed. It was clearly a well-orchestrated coup and Maximus had secured the backing of many senior officers and court officials. Some senior members of the court were executed, but the majority switched sides. Less clear is why Gratian had lost their support. His military record was quite good, but he was accused of granting excessive favour to one regiment of Alan cavalry and starting to indulge too much in his pleasures rather than working.[31]

Maximus controlled the European provinces north of the Alps and clearly hoped for recognition as a colleague by Theodosius. He invited the twelve-year-old Valentinian II to move from Milan and join him at his court in Trier, so that they could rule 'as father and son'. Skilfully created delays in the negotiations gave time for troops loyal to the boy emperor to secure the Alpine passes. Maximus still hoped for reconciliation and made no attempt to use force at this stage. For the moment Theodosius recognised the usurper and his name appeared in official documents. He also elevated his son Arcadius – who was no more than five or six years' old – to the rank of Augustus. However, a few years later Maximus launched a sudden attack on Italy, and by 387 he was in Milan and in full control of Valentinian's territories. The latter, along with most of his court, escaped safely to Theodosius.[32]

The extension of Maximus' ambitions signalled a permanent break with the eastern emperor. Valentinian's mother Justina was a formidable woman and had clearly had considerable sway over her son's decisions. Now she is said to have exploited the beauty of the boy's sister to fascinate Theodosius. The two were married soon afterwards and allegedly the bride price was a promise to recover the lost territory from Maximus. Whatever the precise reasons, in the summer of 388 a fast-moving expeditionary force caught the western usurper at Aquileia. Maximus was stripped of the imperial robes and beheaded. There was some more fighting against forces that remained loyal to his family before the west was fully recovered.[33]

Formally the empire now had three Augusti – Theodosius, Valentinian and Arcadius – although it was abundantly clear that real power rested with Theodosius himself. Valentinian remained little more than a cipher. After his mother died actual control rested with some senior officers appointed by Theodosius. The most important of these was Arbogast. Like many senior officers in the army he was of barbarian – in his case Frankish – descent. As time went on, he became more and more contemptuous of the Augustus he was supposed to serve. He assumed the rank of Master of Soldiers without bothering to consult Valentinian. When the emperor dismissed him, Arbogast calmly told him to his face that he did not have the power to do this. The twenty-one-year-old Valentinian II was a pathetic figure and on 15 May 392 he was found dead in his bedroom. It may have been suicide.

Arbogast obviously felt his background barred him from becoming emperor himself, and so named a certain Flavius Eugenius as Augustus. Once a teacher of grammar and rhetoric, his prized literary education had won him a post at Valentinian's court. From the beginning he was obviously a figurehead. At least nominally a Christian – unlike Arbogast who was openly pagan – Eugenius began to cultivate the support of pagans. This probably grew stronger after Theodosius named his younger son Honorius as Augustus at the beginning of 393, making clear that he would not accept the usurper. The civil war that followed was once again decided near Aquileia. In September 394 the two armies met beside the River Frigidus. After very heavy and costly fighting lasting for two days, Theodosius' army was triumphant. Eugenius was captured when his camp was stormed and promptly executed. Arbogast committed suicide before he was taken.[34]

A very sizeable contingent in Theodosius' army was formed by Gothic warriors raised from the peoples settled in 382. On the first day of fighting they bore both the brunt of the fighting and the losses – later some Romans would claim that this made it a double victory for the empire. At Adrianople the Goths had killed Valens, although probably more by accident than design. They never had any prospect of inflicting a permanent defeat on the empire, and Theodosius had been able to wear them down over the next few years. Yet ultimately they represented a valuable resource of military manpower. This was why they had been admitted in the first place, and why the Romans would probably not have chosen to destroy them even if they had been able to do so. Just over a decade later their warriors greatly strengthened Theodosius' army and may even have given him a decisive advantage over Eugenius. Barbarian incursions were a nuisance, but it was always internal enemies who threatened an emperor's rule and very life.[35]

14

East and West

'the law concerning sacrifice was repealed and other traditions handed
down from their forefathers neglected. Thus the Roman empire has
been gradually diminished and become a home for barbarians, or has
been reduced to such a depopulated state that the places where cities
used to be cannot be recognised.' – *Zosimus, late fifth century.*[1]

Theodosius fell ill and died in January 395, just a few months after
the victory of his army at the River Frigidus. The defeats of Eugenius
and Maximus were the two great military achievements of his reign. Like
Constantius before him, Theodosius was better at fighting other Romans
than foreign enemies. After his early campaigns against the Goths, which
resulted in at least one serious defeat, he spent little time with the army,
remaining instead at one of his capitals. This may well have been because
he recognised his limited talents as a soldier and perhaps also wanted to
reduce his direct association with any failures. His sons were still young
in 395 – Arcadius was about eighteen and Honorius just ten – and even
as they grew older they would show no inclination to lead their armies
in person. This would set the pattern for the future. Unlike the third
and fourth centuries, it would be very rare for an emperor to go on
campaign in the fifth century.

That was not the only change. Theodosius is generally acknowledged
by scholars as the last man to rule the entire empire. It is true that he
had colleagues – Gratian, Valentinian II and later his own sons – and
that for substantial periods usurpers controlled the western provinces,
but for much of his reign he was clearly dominant, even if he was not
the sole emperor. More importantly, after 395 the western and eastern
halves of the empire were never again reunited under the same rule and
steadily the division between the two became permanent. Individuals
did not transfer from the army or administration of one half to the other.
A bond remained, but it was loose and more to do with shared history,
ideology and culture than anything else. Both halves of the empire had
the same law and legal system, although over time differences would

Chart 3 - Simplified family tree of houses of Valentinian and Theodosius

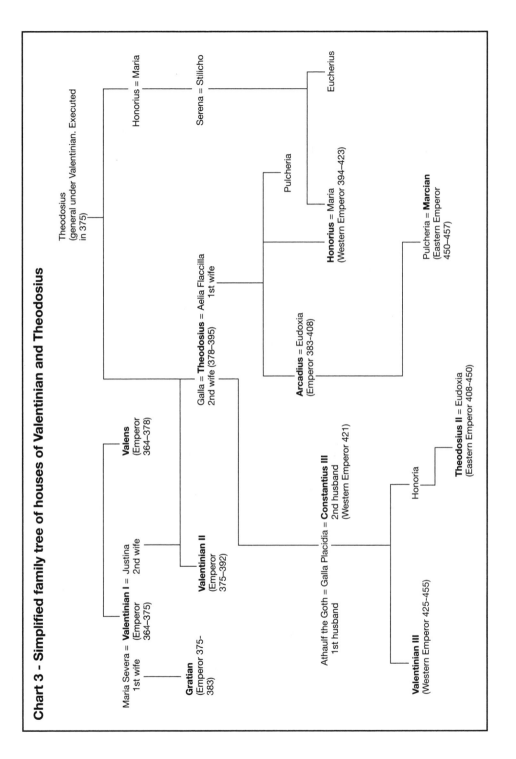

develop. Co-operation between emperors was relatively rare and not always effective. On the other hand, direct conflict only occurred when one supported the claims of a 'legitimate' emperor against a usurper. There was never any attempt to reconquer the entire empire by force. Nor were the two halves of the empire competitors in any way equivalent to modern independent states. They were sometimes rivals, but the rivalry was for limited stakes, for influence rather than control.[2]

The roots of the division went back well into the third century – indeed, the worst that might have happened in the 'great crisis' of that age was that the empire would have fragmented into two or three 'Roman' empires earlier than it actually did. Its survival in some shape or form was never in doubt. Under the tetrarchy the four emperors divided the provinces between them, but generally co-operated under the forceful guidance of Diocletian. Only Constantine was able to repeat this sort of dominance in the later years of his reign when he ruled with his sons. For the rest of the fourth century, there were usually two or more emperors controlling distinct groups of provinces. At times they co-operated and supported each other. More often they appeared indifferent to the fortunes of their imperial colleagues – as when Constantius II watched his brothers fight, or Valentinian decided not to assist Valens against Procopius. Direct conflict was not uncommon.

There was not a conscious decision for a permanent division of the empire in 395. At the time it is doubtful that it was seen as in any way different from arrangements sharing the provinces between imperial colleagues in the past. The divide was in fact the same as that between Valentinian and his brother Valens. It was only subsequent history – most notably a succession of weak and generally young emperors dominated by powerful courtiers – that ensured the split endured. No emperor in the mould of Aurelian, Diocletian or Constantine emerged with the power and will to challenge the situation. In just over eighty years – a very long lifetime, but perhaps better thought of as two or three generations – the line of the western emperors ended altogether.

A permanent split in the empire had become likely from at least the second half of the third century. Precisely when and how it occurred owed more to chance. The ever present fear of assassination and civil war had profoundly changed the way an emperor ruled. None felt secure enough to delegate as much power to their subordinates as had been enjoyed by senatorial legates in the first and second centuries. Provinces were smaller, but much more numerous. The emperors' representatives had also massively multiplied, although individually these tended to have far less power and formed part of a large, complex and often contradictory bureaucracy. Emperors had to do more in person and obviously could not be in two places at once. They needed at least one colleague, and in the long run it was always difficult for two or more emperors to live in harmony, even when they were relatives. More importantly, the slow pace of travel and communication meant that it was impractical for emperors to consult unless they were physically near each other, which rather defeated the object of having more than one in the first place. There was inevitably a tendency for each emperor to go his own way, focusing on immediate problems rather than those affecting distant parts of the empire. The instinct for self-preservation reinforced this tendency. Neglecting local problems was a very good way to encourage usurpation.

The bureaucratic machine created in the late third and fourth centuries was intended to make emperors more secure and give them greater control. It supervised the complex taxation system, which was supposed to channel the resources of the empire into imperial projects. Most importantly of all, it funded, fed, equipped and provided the manpower to serve in the army. Without an effective army emperors could not win the foreign victories that were expected of them, let alone defend themselves against usurpers. The bureaucracy also provided posts with which to reward supporters. Men who entered the civil service gained a salary – modest for many junior posts, but supplemented by semi-official bribery and graft – as well as legal privileges and exemptions from taxation or military service. They were also within a system where their career was ultimately dependent on imperial favour. They were just as much the emperors' men as soldiers in the army.

Civil servants possessed delegated power. Departments and specific offices and posts were also permanent, even if the individuals holding them were not. Those at higher levels enjoyed regular contact with the emperor and could well gain influence over his decisions. At all levels they acted as the main, and sometimes the only, conduit for information passing to the emperors. From the very start of the Principate, anyone with access to the emperor – particularly day-to-day, personal inter-action – was in a privileged position. More than one emperor meant more than one court. The imperial court, like the wider bureaucracy, had also steadily taken on a permanent, institutional form. Together, the courts and the civil service provided a strong measure of continuity, regardless of who the emperors actually were at any one time. They were also highly reluctant to give up their power and influence.

After Constantine's death the empire was only briefly united under

Chart 4
Civil administration of provinces in the late fourth century

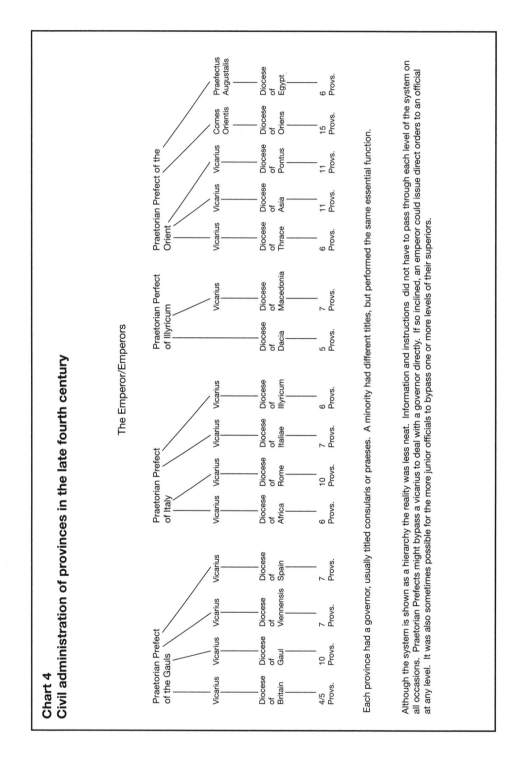

The Emperor/Emperors

Praetorian Prefect of the Gauls

Vicarius	Vicarius	Vicarius	Vicarius
Diocese of Britain	Diocese of Gaul	Diocese of Viennensis	Diocese of Spain
4/5 Provs.	10 Provs.	7 Provs.	7 Provs.

Praetorian Prefect of Italy

Vicarius	Vicarius	Vicarius	Vicarius
Diocese of Africa	Diocese of Rome	Diocese of Italiae	Diocese of Illyricum
6 Provs.	10 Provs.	7 Provs.	6 Provs.

Praetorian Prefect of Illyricum

	Vicarius
Diocese of Dacia	Diocese of Macedonia
5 Provs.	7 Provs.

Praetorian Prefect of the Orient

Vicarius	Vicarius	Vicarius	Comes Orientis	Praefectus Augustalis
Diocese of Thrace	Diocese of Asia	Diocese of Pontus	Diocese of Oriens	Diocese of Egypt
6 Provs.	11 Provs.	11 Provs.	15 Provs.	6 Provs.

Each province had a governor, usually titled consularis or praeses. A minority had different titles, but performed the same essential function.

Although the system is shown as a hierarchy the reality was less neat. Information and instructions did not have to pass through each level of the system on all occasions. Praetorian Prefects might bypass a vicarius to deal with a governor directly. If so inclined, an emperor could issue direct orders to an official at any level. It was also sometimes possible for the more junior officials to bypass one or more levels of their superiors.

Chart 5
Central imperial bureaucracy and court

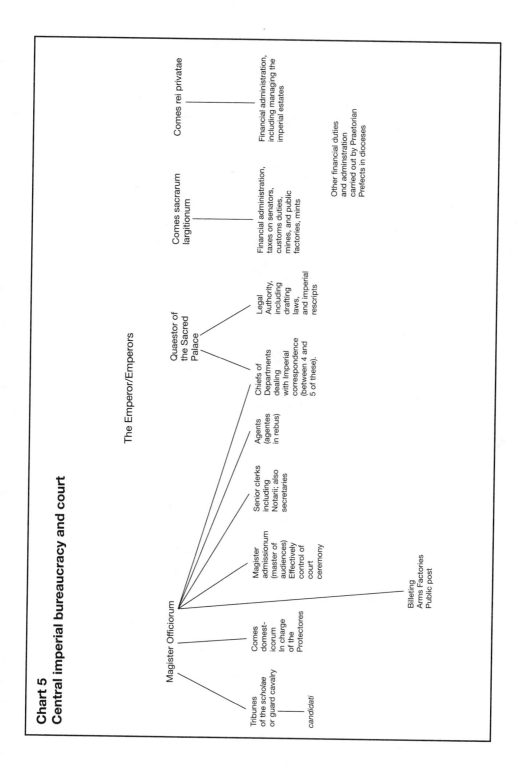

The Emperor/Emperors

Magister Officiorum

Tribunes of the *scholae* or guard cavalry

candidati

Comes domest-icorum In charge of the Protectores

Magister admissionum (master of audiences) Effectively control of court ceremony

Senior clerks including Notarii; also secretaries

Agents (agentes in rebus)

Chiefs of Departments dealing with Imperial correspondence (between 4 and 5 of these).

Billeting Arms Factories Public post

Quaestor of the Sacred Palace

Legal Authority, including drafting laws, and imperial rescripts

Comes sacrarum largitionum

Financial administration, taxes on senators, customs duties, mines, and public factories, mints

Other financial duties and adminstration carried out by Praetorian Prefects in dioceses

Comes rei privatae

Financial administration, including managing the imperial estates the rule of one man – for short spells under Constantius II, just a few years under Julian and Jovian, and finally in the last years of Theodosius. Normally there were two active emperors and therefore two imperial courts and administrations. Most of the time the western and eastern provinces were under different rule. The bureaucracies themselves had become separate and to some extent developed their own agendas. Their main priority was to survive and preserve or even increase their own power. Individually, civil servants hoped to rise to the most important posts and gain as much wealth and influence over others as they could. The senior army officers in each region had similar ambitions. To exist and to hold power, they needed their own emperor. It would have taken a very strong, long-lived and utterly secure emperor to have reversed this trend towards separation. Few enough such men managed to hold power in the third or fourth centuries and none would do so in the fifth. Instead, for so much of the time there were child emperors, utterly dominated by powerful figures at court or – especially in the west – their senior general.

For some time emperors became figureheads. They were less active and stopped travelling. From the tetrarchy onwards a number of capitals had been employed by the emperors, chosen to be near whatever priority they had at the time. Now the court became static, remaining in a single capital almost all the time. In the east this was Constantinople. In the west first Milan, and later Ravenna. In each case the imperial court was located somewhere safe. Emperors did not go to war in the fifth century.

Divided Empire: The World at the End of the Fourth Century

The division of the empire in 395 closely mirrored the division between the Latin-speaking western provinces and the Greek-speaking east. There were many regional differences of language and culture in both areas, but this certainly gave a coherence to the two empires that emerged. In the east, Latin continued to be the language of law and some aspects of government well into the sixth century, and members of the civil service joining the relevant departments were expected to have an extremely good knowledge of it. Over time such skill became less common and eventually this requirement was dropped. Many Latin legal or military terms still survived transliterated into Greek.[3]

United, the empire was massively bigger, more populous and wealthier than any of its neighbours. Divided into two, the difference was less marked compared to Persia, but still huge in relation to anyone else. This remained a world of many tribes and peoples, normally mutually hostile and often riven with internal disputes between rival leaders. Along most of their frontiers, the Romans did not face concerted, organised and large-scale threats but the familiar problems of raiding. In the course of the fourth century large sections of the Rhine and Danube frontiers had been perceived to be weak, encouraging larger and more frequent attacks by bands of plunderers. At times the ferocity and power of the Roman response managed to intimidate the tribes in one area for a short spell. This was never permanent, because the army was unable to maintain a strong and effective enough presence everywhere at all times. Too often the troops were withdrawn to fight elsewhere, whether against foreign or Roman enemies. Equally, it was not uncommon for the defeated tribes to be urged on to attack the provinces again to aid one emperor in his war against another.

Persia had always been different. It was bigger, wealthier and more sophisticated, as well as politically united and able to field large and effective armies. Jovian's peace treaty had ceded strategically important border areas to Shapur II as well as declaring thirty years' peace – treaties stipulating a specific number of years of peace had a long tradition in the Greek world. They had never been that common in Rome's history, in the main because of the Roman tendency to fight on until they had achieved an outright victory. In this case, the treaty was quickly violated. Perhaps from the beginning both sides understood its clauses differently, or maybe attitudes changed later – especially for Valens and Theodosius, who were not in such a precarious position as Jovian had been when the peace was negotiated. The dispute focused particularly on Armenia and neighbouring regions such as Iberia. Shapur II felt that he had been granted sole right to intervene in Armenian affairs. The Romans resisted this and although neither side launched a full-scale invasion of the other's territory, there was still some heavy fighting.

Shapur forcibly removed King Arsaces of Armenia and placed his own man on the throne. The Romans in turn drove this king out and replaced him with Arsaces' son Pap. Shapur ravaged Armenia with his army and then began to make diplomatic overtures to persuade Pap to join him. Learning of this, the Roman commander invited Pap to dinner – the familiar environment for Roman diplomacy and treachery – and murdered him. The intensity of the struggle lessened somewhat when the elderly King Shapur II died in 379 after a reign of some seventy years. Persia had no fewer than three kings in the next decade, as rival family members struggled for power. Equally, the Romans had enough problems of their own and this led to an agreement to partition Armenia in 387 (or possibly 384, as there is some doubt over the date). Persia got the lion's share, with Rome taking around one-fifth of the land. In each case the regions continued to be governed by local satraps and retained considerable local autonomy.[4]

In 421 there was a short-lived conflict between the Eastern Empire and the Persians, when the Romans tried and failed to recapture Nisibis, the great frontier city ceded in Jovian's treaty. Apart from this, there was no major war throughout the fifth century. However, the peace was not quite unblemished. Each side retained well-manned and provisioned fortresses facing each other along the frontier. There was also sporadic raiding by tribes allied to the great powers and sometimes with their tacit backing. Although it took time for this to show itself in imperial pronouncements and propaganda, the Roman attitude towards Persia had shifted significantly. The old dreams of following Alexander to conquer the Persians and absorb them into the empire seem to have died along with Julian. Instead, and at first grudgingly, the Romans began to speak and think of Persia as something like an equal.

It was a realistic assessment. The frontiers between the two were now heavily defended and fortified, making major invasions difficult. Roman power was also weaker than it had once been, and after 395 the eastern half of the empire on its own certainly had nothing like the capacity to drive down and take Ctesiphon in the manner of earlier Roman armies. Conversely, the Persians would find it much harder to raid as deep into the Roman provinces as they had managed in the third century. As importantly, their kings did not have the political need to secure themselves on the throne by leading such spectacular expeditions. Since Galerius' campaigns, Persian ambitions had focused almost exclusively on regaining the lands they had lost, and restoring a frontier that they felt to be both stronger and more proper. In the treaties with Jovian and Theodosius they effectively achieved this aim. For generations to come, both sides were content with the balance of power and realistic enough to understand that they lacked the capacity to change it. Each of them also usually had enough problems to deal with on other fronts.[5]

On other frontiers the ongoing struggle for dominance continued. The Romans relied on the usual mixture of force and diplomacy, which included paying subsidies (or bribes or tribute, depending on how you wish to see these) to tribal leaders to keep the peace. There were now well-established patterns of educating the sons of barbarian kings and chieftains, and then helping to install them in power within their tribes in the expectation that they would prove loyal allies. It did not always work. Some refused to be controlled, while others were expelled by rivals. Such leaders – who may well have brought with them the warriors of their own household – were often then employed as senior officers in the Roman army. King Vadomarius of the Alamanni fought against Constantius II, but eventually made peace and was later used by the emperor to attack Julian in the civil war. Julian captured him – once again the method was to seize him at a banquet organised by a Roman officer – and he was subsequently one of Valens' senior commanders during the fighting with the Persians. His son was also made a king amongst the tribes, but was murdered on the orders of Gratian after his loyalty became suspect.[6]

Life was dangerous for the tribes living next to either Roman Empire. Yet they were never just passive victims of a more powerful neighbour. Raiding continued to be a problem whenever the frontier defences were seen as vulnerable. Mostly it was conducted over fairly short distances and the effects were restricted to certain vulnerable regions. As well as raids there were attempts to migrate and settle within the empire. These seem to have become more frequent at the very end of the fourth century, mainly as the direct or indirect consequences of the growing and aggressive power of the Huns. Raiding and migration were of deep concern to the Roman authorities. Far more common was peaceful interaction. Trade in both directions across the frontiers continued, especially in periods of relative peace and stability. Many of the barbarians who entered the empire did so as individual volunteers for the Roman army which was very eager to enlist their services.

Any consideration of the scale of trade and the economy in general at the end of the fourth century is subject to the usual lack of any meaningful statistics. Some goods certainly continued to be transported over considerable distances. Trade with the far east revived to some extent in the later fourth and fifth centuries. In India the focus moved largely to ports in what is now Sri Lanka. Yet there are signs that there was more competition from Persian and other traders, even if much of the produce eventually made its way into the empire. The port of Aila (modern Aqaba) seems to have been bustling from early in the fourth century, when a detachment of *Legio X Fretensis* was moved there from its old base in Jerusalem. Considerable quantities of incense came through this route. Although later in the fourth century there may have been a brief decline in the demand for incense as pagan rituals were banned, it was not long before the Christians began to adopt it for their own ceremonies.

In 408 or 409 the Roman and Persian authorities acted jointly to regulate cross-border trade, trying to ensure that the states controlled this and that no commerce could occur other than in the appointed places. This suggests that there were plenty of merchants willing to operate independently and that trade between Romans and Persians was common.[7]

It was not only expensive luxury items that were transported over great distances, but also at times products such as grain and wine. The city of Rome had shrunk somewhat in the size of its population – perhaps to between 500,000–750,000 – but still required massive shipments from Africa and Sicily to supply its food. In this case, it remained the duty of emperors to ensure that food was provided – similar provision had also to be made for Constantinople – and was not simply the operation of the market. Yet there is enough evidence for manufacture and farming to show that there was considerable commercial exchange. There was also innovation. A late fourth-century poem mentions water-powered saws for cutting marble in use in the Rhineland. Again, it is always important to remember how different the Roman empire and empires were from the lands outside. The quantity and range of objects available and in wide circulation amongst many levels of the population remained massively greater than all the lands outside – even including Persia, although in this case the difference was less. The division of the empire into two did not do much to restrict trade within the area of the old united empire. The two Roman empires together still represented a massive trading unit and market operating under the same laws and with the same currency, which had stabilised to some extent during the fourth century.[8]

As with the economy, we have no reliable statistics for population of the empire before or after it was divided. Some areas certainly seem to have been booming. There is evidence for a thriving rural population in a number of regions – most notably around the great city of Antioch, but also in parts of North Africa and Greece – for the next few centuries, far larger and more prosperous than in earlier periods. Yet we need to be very cautious about extending this to infer similar conditions throughout the eastern provinces in general, let alone the rest of the Roman world. Archaeological evidence is simply not available in sufficient quantity to permit confident generalisations, and there is always the danger that we will see in it what we expect to see. We know a good deal about some specific sites – and the communities in these variously were founded or abandoned, and grew, declined or remained much the same. Such variety is unsurprising at any period, but should make us reluctant to generalise. The ability of central government to provide land for migrating barbarian groups suggests that some areas were under-populated. However, similar settlements had occurred in earlier periods so this need not in itself be a sign of a new and serious problem.[9]

Considerable regional variation is likely. Areas that were the scene of prolonged warfare can only have paid a price for this in the deaths of people, the destruction of farms and villages, and the loss of crops and animals. Given time and peace, they would recover, but in the short term the impact of conflict could be very great indeed. Whatever the size of the overall population, there is sufficient evidence to show that the authorities struggled to ensure that there were enough people in the right places and doing the right things. The frequency of legislation making it compulsory for sons to follow their fathers' occupations suggests that this was often evaded, and certainly failed to provide sufficient craftsmen and other specialists. The rural labour force was seen as insufficient and again, legislation restricting the movements of peasants and labourers was common. Similarly, it was believed that recruitment to the army was at best barely adequate – so much so that the desire to secure more recruits could influence imperial policy and encourage Valens to admit the Goths. Shortages of manpower were seen as serious problems. That neither agricultural production nor the army collapsed altogether dem-onstrate that neither had reached a critical stage. This does not mean that the authorities' concerns were not real.

The fortunes of cities also varied from region to region, depending on the local situation. Constantinople grew steadily, its population reaching several hundred thousand by the middle of the fourth century. It would grow even more once it became the permanent residence of the eastern emperors instead of one of several capitals. From Constantine onwards the city acquired a growing number of large and magnificent churches, paid for by successive emperors. Churches were built in cities throughout the empire, sometimes with imperial patronage, but more often through the generosity of local aristocrats. Building a church was one of the most common gifts to a community, replacing the older preference for baths and theatres. The number, and in some cases substantial size, of churches built throughout the empire in the later fourth century makes it clear that at least some of the wealthy were still able and willing to make conspicuous donations to cities. Yet there continues to be evidence that in some communities there were not enough local aristocrats who were rich enough or even willing to serve as local magistrates. Some went into the Church, for senior priests and bishops were exempt from civic duties. Others gained similar exemptions by joining the imperial bureaucracy. In each case a proportion wished only for some sinecure, a nominal post sought only because it removed any responsibility to their home community. Successive laws tried to weed out such men and force them to fulfil their obligations, but it is doubtful that the problem was ever properly solved.[10]

The fourth-century empire possessed considerable resources. The essential truth of the Roman Empire remained its sheer size in comparison to all its competitors. No rival had the capacity to destroy it. Yet for all the centralised bureaucracy of this era, there were clearly problems in marshalling and directing its resources of money, manpower and material. It should not have taken six years for the empire's massive superiority in men and wealth to overcome the Goths in Thrace. The division of the empire in 395 did nothing to improve this situation. It had long been the case that the army and administration in one area displayed scant concern for difficulties in distant parts of the empire. Local problems were always their greatest concern. After 395 this only became more marked and, in time, formally acknowledged. Divided empire inevitably meant divided resources. Only rarely would men, money or material from one half be used to assist the other. From the beginning the Eastern Empire was probably wealthier. It faced the major potential threat of Persia, although as it turned out there would be several generations of peace. The Western Empire faced tribal enemies along a much more extensive frontier. None was remotely as powerful as Persia, but they were numerous and there was always a strong chance of conflict somewhere. From the beginning, its resources were more stretched by this very different military problem.

Christian Empire

By the end of the fourth century there was no doubt that the Roman Empire – or empires as it effectively became after 395 – was Christian. Eugenius was the last contender for imperial power to appeal explicitly for pagan support. Bishop Ambrose of Milan was told that the usurper boasted of turning his cathedral into a stable when he returned in victory. We need to be cautious – almost all our sources are Christian and inclined to celebrate the victory of Theodosius as the triumph of the true faith over old superstition. Theodosius' army – like that of all the successors of Constantine apart from Julian – had marched under the *labarum* standard. Whether Eugenius' troops carried symbols of Jupiter is harder to say. Very soon after the battle stories circulated that the victory had been miraculous. An immensely powerful wind – a fairly common phenomenon in the region – had blown into the faces of the usurper's soldiers, robbing their missiles of force while making those of the enemy more powerful.[11]

By the end of the fourth century there were still substantial numbers of pagans, although Christians may already have made up a clear majority of the population. Yet the Christians themselves remained divided into many different groups. In North Africa the Donatists were still strong, maintaining a full church organisation with bishops and other leaders that paralleled that of the state-supported Catholic Church. Theodosius made sure that the official Church would support only the creed and doctrine approved at Constantine's conference in Nicaea. In 380 he declared that:

> We desire that all the peoples who are ruled by the guidance of our clemency should be versed in that religion which it is evident that the divine [divine in the sense of holy or saintly – the same expression was used for the emperors themselves] apostle Peter handed down to the Romans, and which the pope Damasus and Peter, bishop of Alexandria ... adhere to ... We command that those persons who follow this rule shall have the name of catholic Christians. The rest, however, whom we judge to be demented and insane, shall sustain the infamy of heretical dogmas ...[12]

Constantius II and Valens had both been inclined towards forms of Arianism, rejecting the Nicene Creed in favour of one in which Jesus was not absolutely identical to God the Father. Such views were always more popular in the Greek-speaking east. Theodosius was a Spaniard from the Latin west raised to accept the Nicene view of a homoousian trinity – Father, Son and Holy Ghost all being 'of the same substance'. He was also an extremely determined man who felt it was right to impose this view. In 381 bishops who advocated Arian views were sacked throughout the empire. They were no longer to be considered priests, while meeting places of groups other than orthodox Catholics were not even to be counted as churches. Bishops recognised as Catholic were listed for each diocese in the empire. They in turn would grant legitimacy to more junior priests. In addition a number of heretical groups were outlawed.[13]

The structure of the Church mirrored that of the state. There were bishops in all cities. There were also rural bishops, but from very early on these were considered subordinate to their urban counterparts. The diocese of a bishop was defined by administrative divisions of the state. The bishop of the major centre of an administrative diocese – the group of provinces under the charge of one vicar who was in turn under the control of a praetorian prefect – was acknowledged as superior to the bishops of lesser cities. The importance of the bishop of Rome – already sometimes referred to as the pope – was at first a consequence of the real and symbolic importance of that city. Similarly, from the beginning the bishops of Alexandria and Antioch, and in time Carthage, wielded great influence because they were the head of the Church in these massive and prestigious communities. As the fourth century progressed the bishop of Constantinople was eager to join, even to surpass these others. One result was a much more public emphasis by the bishop of Rome on his succession from Peter. The pope remained an important figure, even if emperors rarely visited his city, but for the moment he was still one of a number of senior bishops.[14]

Imperial support for the Church gave its leaders privileged access to the emperor, something that had always brought influence. Cities and provinces would now frequently turn to bishops to make their case for them at the imperial court. Bishops were important men locally. Many came from the ranks of the regional aristocracies and so had a good deal in common with local magistrates and senior men in imperial service. They were also granted the authority to act as magistrates in certain cases. The degree to which any bishop wielded influence at court, or came to dominate his city and the surrounding area, depended much on personality and family connections.

Bishop Ambrose of Milan certainly did not lack a formidable personality. When Justina, the mother of Valentinian II, wanted to provide a meeting place for Arians in the emperor's bodyguard – many may have been Goths – at Milan, Ambrose protested so strongly that she backed down. In 388 a synagogue at Callinicum on the Euphrates was destroyed by a Christian mob, along with a number of pagan shrines. A bishop and his monks were held responsible and Theodosius ordered that the bishop should pay for the synagogue to be rebuilt. In spite of occasional rhetoric, Jewish communities faced little official hostility. Synagogues were respected – many were in prominent places in city centres – and rabbis enjoyed similar legal privileges to Christian priests. Ambrose wrote to Theodosius in immediate protest, and continued to condemn the emperor even after he modified his decision so that the entire community would pay for the costs. In the end he backed down altogether.[15]

More spectacular was their second confrontation. In 390 an army officer was lynched at Thessalonica by a mob outraged at his arrest of a famous charioteer. As punishment Theodosius ordered the garrison to attack the crowd at the circus on a set day. It was not a subtle way of handling the matter and rather suggested that the authorities were not in full control. Whatever the emperor had actually intended, the result was an indiscriminate massacre. Some 7,000 people were alleged to have died, although this is most likely a huge exaggeration. Ambrose wrote to Theodosius telling him that he would boycott the formal ceremony when the emperor was to enter Milan soon afterwards. He demanded that the emperor perform penance before being permitted to receive the sacrament. Theodosius seems already to have regretted his angry order and perhaps wanted to disassociate himself from its dreadful consequences. Therefore, he obeyed Ambrose's demand, and for some time regularly appeared without his imperial robes and regalia, weeping and prostrating himself in penitence in the cathedral at Milan.[16]

The emperor could not fully control the Church, but it would be wrong to see him as controlled by it. Fourth-century emperors were often represented as being persuaded by advisers away from taking especially severe action. Ambrose of Milan was a shrewd politician and may well have judged that the emperor wanted to be convinced. Alternatively, he may have understood Theodosius' emotional character well enough to gauge his moods. Most importantly, we need to remember that this was an exceptional event. Bishops could not tell emperors what to do. They had influence according to their own reputation, personality and importance, but no more than that.[17]

As yet, there was also no single leader to speak with the authority of the entire Church. Of course, there was not really a single Church, for Christians continued to fragment into many different groups. Arianism did not die out immediately just because Theodosius actively supported the Nicene Creed. Even groups he ordered to be prosecuted as heretics proved very hard to eradicate. New disputes continued to occur and led to fresh schisms. One bishop claimed that in Constantinople:

If you ask anyone for change, he will discuss with you whether the Son is begotten or unbegotten. If you ask about the quality of bread, you will receive the answer that 'The Father is greater, the

Son is less.' If you suggest that you require a bath, you will be told that 'There was nothing before the Son was created.'[18]

This was part of a published sermon arguing for a particular view, so should not be taken as evidence that the majority of the population was genuinely preoccupied with doctrinal disputes. Enough people were deeply committed to particular views – and doubtless also to well-liked individual leaders and local traditions – to make possible the splits in the Church that continued to occur. Even so, we need to be aware that such things figure disproportionately strongly in the surviving sources. The ultimate success of orthodox Catholicism also at times makes it difficult to understand accurately the position of its opponents.[19]

The will of the emperor could not make everyone orthodox, nor could it have made everyone Christian in the first place. Early on in his reign Theodosius outlawed Manichaeism, but was otherwise more concerned with suppressing Christian heretics. His mood hardened as his reign went on. More than one law extended the ban on sacrifice. How rigorously this was enforced depended mainly on the local authorities, and animals were still killed to be served up in the banquets celebrating traditional festivals in many communities, something hard to distinguish from formal sacrifice. Yet on the whole, public expressions of clearly pagan ritual became rare. There was little concerted or organised resistance to imperial policy. Rioting did occur between rival mobs, usually when Christian groups – almost always allegedly monks in the service of a local bishop – tried to destroy a pagan shrine. There were spectacular instances of such violence. The great Temple of Serapis at Alexandria was destroyed by such a mob in 391, as was part of the great library in that city, the latter especially disturbing to modern scholars, although how many of the texts lost in this way would have still survived the centuries is impossible to say.

Such conflict was spectacular, but rare. In the main the various religions, and indeed the different branches of Christianity, managed to live side by side in peace, if not necessarily warmth or harmony. There were still many pagans, and indeed Arian Christians, in senior posts in the imperial service. The Senate in Rome still seems to have contained a strongly pagan – or perhaps rather, strongly traditional – element. Constantius II had ordered the removal of the Altar of Victory in the Senate House. For many centuries senators had made offerings of incense on this (or at least a facsimile, as the building itself had burnt down many times over the years) before beginning their debates. Julian allowed the altar to be reinstalled. Gratian took it again and resisted several formal requests from the Senate to restore it. Eugenius reversed this decision, but after his defeat Theodosius once again had it removed and refused all pleas for its return.[20]

Christians trumpeted the failure of pagan deities to protect their own temples and statues from destruction. Valens' death at Adrianople, and especially the story that he might have been burned alive, was similarly seen as punishment for his promotion of Arian doctrine. A common theme in much literature is the greater power of Christian priests and holy men over the followers of false gods or philosophers. Since Constantine, the success of the empire was also due to its worship of the Christian God. Quite quickly the Persians had come to see Christianity as a sign of probable sympathy for Rome.[21]

Others felt the same way. Remarkable accounts survive of Christians living amongst the Goths before they entered the empire. The first were captives from the great raids of the third century, who retained a clear sense of their own distinct identity, as well as their faith. These, like their famous first bishop Ulfilas (literally, 'Little Wolf' – the name is Gothic even if he and his family remained aware of their real origin) were mostly Arians. Ulfilas was sent as an ambassador to Constantius II, presumably under the assumption that the Romans were more likely to pay attention to a fellow Christian. While he was at Constantinople he was ordained as bishop to all the Christians amongst the tribes. Later, the Gothic chieftains evidently decided that Ulfilas and his flock were too closely associated with the Romans for comfort and they were driven by persecution to take refuge within the empire. Ulfilas spent much of the rest of his life translating the Bible into Gothic – something that required the creation of an alphabet, since it was not a written language.

There were also other Christians amongst the tribes who seem to have been converted by missionaries, for they were certainly more orthodox in their beliefs. What is notable is that during periods of tension with their Roman neighbours, Gothic kings instituted several persecutions. We have a detailed account of one of the resulting martyrdoms, that of Saint Saba, who seems to have been especially determined to be killed. It is interesting that on several occasions his fellow villagers tried to protect him, even if in each case he thwarted this by publicly confronting the authorities. On the whole, the picture suggests that the persecution was essentially political. When the Goths were settled within the empire, they willingly became Arian. Their descendants would stick to this doctrine for generations after it had been denounced as heretical by Theodosius and his successors.[22]

*

The united empire in the later years of the fourth century was large and powerful. It is doubtful whether it was quite as large and powerful or prosperous as it had been in 300. Certainly, it was weaker than it had been in the first and second centuries. Divided into two, each of the separate halves was less strong than when they had been joined together. Nor were the two halves equal in power, while the problems they were to face would prove very different. Internal instability had continued to plague the empire throughout the fourth century. Apart from the times of direct conflict, or usurpation and civil war, this could only have a continual wearing effect on the bureaucracy and army. It also steadily reinforced a culture where self-preservation and personal success were the main, almost sole objectives. Both the emperors themselves and their administrations thought less of the wider good of the empire than of their own survival. It was not a recipe for efficiency. What remained to be seen was whether dividing the empire would encourage greater political stability.

One other consequence of the division of the Roman Empire into two is that it inevitably becomes more difficult to follow the story of its demise. Although it would seem simplest to deal with the Eastern and Western Empires separately, this would be misleading. The two empires were neighbours, still closely connected politically, and the problems and decisions of one very often had an impact on the fortunes of the other. Therefore, it is better as far as possible to keep to a chronological approach, even if at times this makes the telling more complex.

PART THREE

Fall?
The Fifth and Sixth Centuries

15

Barbarians and Romans:
Generals and Rebels

'Falling on the barbarians without warning [Stilicho] utterly destroyed their whole force. Scarcely anyone escaped, except a few whom he accepted as auxiliaries.' – *Zosimus, fifth century.*[1]

'All Gaul was filled with the smoke from a single funeral pyre.' – *Orientus, describing the impact of the barbarian invasion in 406.*[2]

A remarkable document from the imperial bureaucracy survives from the end of the fourth century. Its formal title is 'The list of all offices, both civil and military' – in Latin, the *Notitia Dignitatum omnium, tam civilium quam militarium*, although scholars usually just refer to it as the *Notitia Dignitatum* – and it was produced originally for the senior notary or clerk (*primicerius notariorum*) of the emperor Honorius in 395. The recent division of the empire into eastern and western halves is clear throughout the text, the two being throughout shown as utterly distinct. It is highly detailed, setting down each post, saying something about its responsibilities, and in the case of army commanders naming the regiments in their charge. What makes it all the more fascinating is that it is colourfully illustrated. The insignia of each rank is shown, along with symbols of their work – for instance, weapons for those in charge of the factories making equipment for the army or loaves of bread for those responsible for collecting levies of food. Provinces are shown both as personifications and as highly stylised pictures, with miniature walled cities labelled to show the principal communities of the area. Field army regiments have circular images of the devices that were supposed to be painted on their shields.[3]

We do not, of course, have the original document written and illustrated by the staff of the senior notary in 395. Substantial works, whether literary, legal or administrative, survive only because copies were made over the centuries, and the earliest surviving texts are usually medieval. In the case of the *Notitia Dignitatum* we have several sixteenth-century copies of a version made for a Carolingian king in the early middle ages. The illustrations present an odd mixture of Roman and medieval styles. Anything the artist recognised tended to be painted as it looked in his world – hence the little walled towns have a decidedly medieval look. Things he did not understand were more likely to be copied exactly.

Even in the Roman period the *Notitia Dignitatum* seems to have been modified on several occasions. It was clearly used by some parts of the imperial government in the Western Empire, for the sections on the Eastern Empire do not seem to show any changes after 395. The western sections, particularly some of those dealing with military organisation, were altered in the fifth century, perhaps as late as the 420s. The updates were patchy and not always consistently made throughout all of the relevant sections. There are also clearly errors in the pages showing the shield patterns of army units. Quite a few of these are blank, and others look like invented variations on a theme. They are also all shown as neatly circular, when in fact the army used oval shields. Judging from the intricate patterns on the painted shields found at Dura Europos, the miniature versions are also likely to be greatly simplified.[4]

For all its errors and confusions, the *Notitia Dignitatum* is unique in providing an official survey of the imperial bureaucracy and army. It contains a vast amount of information about the structure of the divided empire, including many details not recorded elsewhere. Yet its very uniqueness is also highly frustrating, for if we had one or two comparable documents from earlier or later decades we could trace the developments in the imperial structure far more clearly. There are hints of changes in the text we have, while other sources confirm the existence of much of the administrative and military structure described at other periods. Ammianus, for instance, mentions many of the ranks and posts listed in the *Notitia*, as well as a number of the regiments, and seems to confirm other aspects of organisation. Much of the structure at provincial level, as well as the distribution of *limitanei*, seems unlikely to have changed as a result of the division of the empire in 395.[5]

All this is most encouraging for the wider usefulness of the *Notitia Dignitatum*, but scholars have sometimes been more than a little reckless in its use. Those studying the army have been especially inclined to stretch its lists of units both forward and back for more than a century. It is conventional to assume that a regiment named after an emperor was also formed by him, ignoring the real possibility that already existing units were renamed as a reward or to encourage loyalty. Armies are not always the most logical of structures, especially when it comes to names

Chart 6 The command structure of the Roman Army in the *Notitia Dignitatum*

Units of the Field army are listed under their commander

1. The West

The Western Emperor

The Master of Infantry
The Army in Italy
7 Cavalry regiments
37 Infantry regiments

The Master of Cavalry
The Army in Gaul
12 Cavalry Regiments
46 Infantry Regiments

Comes in Illyricum	Comes in Africa	Comes in Tingitania	Comes in Britain	Comes in Spain
-	19 Cav.	2 Cav.	6 Cav.	-
22 Inf.	12 Inf.	3 Inf.	3 Inf.	16 Inf.

Also
Limitanei grouped into 18 different commands led by 6 *duces* and 12 *comites*.

The Master of Infantry was senior to the Master of Cavalry, and both were senior to the 5 *Comites* in charge of field armies and all of the officers in charge of limitanei. However, once again there was no strict hierarchy and the Emperor might choose to issue orders directly to any commander.

2. The East

The Eastern Emperor

Master of Soldiers at Court I	Master of Soldiers at Court II	Master of Soldiers in the East	Master of Soldiers in Thrace	Master of Soldiers in Illyricum
12 Cav.	12 Cav.	10 Cav.	7 Cav.	2 Cav.
24 Inf.	24 Inf.	21 Inf.	21 Inf.	24 Inf.

Also
Limitanei grouped into 15 commands led by 13 *duces* and 2 *comites*.
The Five Masters of Soldiers were all in theory of equal rank. They were all superior to the commanders of the *limitanei*.

and titles – so that, for instance, in the modern British army a soldier in different infantry regiments may be ranked as rifleman, fusilier, kingsman or guardsman instead of the more prosaic private. It is also unwise to calculate the losses at Adrianople or other disasters on the basis of deducing 'missing' units from the lists in the *Notitia Dignitatum*. As already noted this ignores the probability that some units were lost in other campaigns, while others may simply have been renamed, merged or disbanded for any number of reasons. Field army units at the largest estimate were just a fraction of the size of the old legions and hence more vulnerable to losses and short-term decisions to alter the structure of the army. The frequency of civil war made it all the more likely that the army list would be confused rather than neat and logical.

It is equally important to remember that the objectives of the men who first drew up the *Notitia Dignitatum* were limited. The chief concern of the notaries was in the issuing of commissions for the various military and civil posts listed – a writing desk and a bundle of commissions accompany the insignia of the *primicerius notariorum*. It was the appointments themselves, along with their seniority, that mattered. This was not a work intended primarily to explain how the army and administration functioned. Imperial posts brought their holders power while they were in office and, more permanently, rank, pay and privileges. There were always plenty of men seeking each post and the senior officials with power to bestow or influence appointments expected future favours or immediate bribes to secure success. Inevitably, this encouraged the proliferation of offices, and in some cases these were mere sinecures, for the individual never had any intention of actively performing his supposed duties. As usual, the frequency of imperial legislation intended to curb such abuses suggests that it had only limited success. An archive of letters left by an officer commanding a unit of *limitanei* in Egypt in the fourth century describes how on arrival at the garrison he discovered that several other men had been granted the same commission. Only after considerable difficulty and appeal to higher authority was his own claim acknowledged.[6]

The *Notitia Dignitatum* listed the officially recognised positions – there would be a commander for every army unit even if he is not named specifically – just as its title claimed. There is no mention of the many forces of allies that formed a major part of armies at this period or of the officers who commanded them. Presumably such posts were not the concern of the notaries. Similarly, those who subsequently adapted the text seem to have been interested only in certain sections. Changes in civil posts are rarely noted, and even in the military sphere the priority seems to have been certain units, presumably those of concern to the officer whose staff kept the list.[7]

The overall impression remains of a vast, highly organised and powerful empire, recently divided into two distinct hierarchies in east and west, but still in spirit part of the same entity. Without doubt the *Notitia Dignitatum* has reinforced the views of those scholars who depict the fourth- and to a lesser extent early fifth-century empire as still inherently strong and generally efficient. Its list of army units is the principal basis for the claims that the army was massive, perhaps well over 600,000 strong and so almost twice the size of the forces at the disposal of emperors like Marcus Aurelius. Most will note that such figures would represent 'paper strength' and that the actual number of effectives was likely to be lower, but do not then seem to absorb the full implications of this. The picture still remains of a very large army.[8]

Yet it is very hard to reconcile this with the course of events in the late fourth and fifth centuries. The army – and to some extent the imperial state itself – at times seems invisible, with regions supposed to have been strongly garrisoned apparently undefended. Time and again the question arises of where this supposedly massive army actually was. This raises the fundamental issue of how far the *Notitia Dignitatum* reflected day-to-day reality, especially where the army was concerned. Clearly, the listing of a regiment along with its shield device meant that it actually existed as far as officialdom was concerned. In some cases this may genuinely have meant that the unit had a substantial part of its full complement of soldiers, trained, equipped and ready for service. Alternatively, it could have been massively under strength, although still able to take the field. Another option would be a small cadre, with some key staff and the documentation preserved, all waiting to be turned into a proper unit if ever it was allocated sufficient recruits and other resources. Finally, the regiment may only have existed on paper, its existence reflecting the status of the general in command and perhaps showing what forces he would control in an ideal world. This in itself did not necessarily mean that someone was not enjoying the salary and privileges of being its commander.

All of these options are possible and it is more than likely that there were examples of each of them at various times amongst the regiments listed in the *Notitia*. We have already seen in the conflict with the Goths in 376–382 that the Roman army found it very difficult to deal with a comparatively small number of enemies. At times, when reading descriptions by modern historians of the warfare in this period, it is difficult to avoid the image of Hitler in his last days, planning grand offensives on a map with divisions that had long since ceased to exist. The situation was not so desperate in the years following 395, nor was the enemy so powerful and organised, but the reigns of Honorius and Arcadius were desperate enough.

Stilicho

Even when emperors were strong, their senior officials and commanders routinely and ruthlessly struggled for power, promotion and influence. When emperors were weak or young there was even less restraint in this never-ending contest for dominance. In 395 Theodosius' sons were both young and later events would prove their characters to be extremely weak. Incapable of restraining their subordinates, when old enough they settled for simply playing them off against each other. Anyone able to dominate the emperor effectively gained supreme power. In the east this was first achieved by Arcadius' praetorian prefect Rufinus, who was to be followed by a succession of court officials who virtually ran the Eastern Empire. These men held a range of formal posts and this was in most respects far less important than the hold they were able to develop over the young emperor. This control was never secure, and all eventually fell from power and died violently.

In the Western Empire the real power tended to rest with the man who controlled the bulk of the army, rather than with civilian officials. For the first thirteen years of Honorius' reign this was Stilicho, whose rank – apparently created for and by him – was 'Count and Master of all Soldiers'. This made him formally the supreme military officer in the western armies. There was no equivalent to this post in the east, where several Masters of Soldiers held equal power. In 395 Stilicho had the added advantage that many field army units from the east were still in Italy following the defeat of Eugenius in the previous year. These, combined with western regiments, including many which had previously fought for the usurper, gave Stilicho a military force that none of his potential rivals could match.[9]

Stilicho's father was a Vandal who had commanded a cavalry regiment under Valens, and his 'barbarian' ancestry would be thrown at him by his critics. However, there is no reason to see him as anything other than fully Roman. He had begun his service in the *protectores* and risen rapidly after winning the favour of Theodosius. He married Serena, daughter of the emperor's brother and raised in the imperial family after her father's death. Claiming that the dying Theodosius had entrusted the care and protection of his sons to him, Stilicho swiftly secured control of the ten-year-old Honorius, effectively ruling the Western Empire as regent. He does not ever appear to have sought imperial status for himself, but in due course he would arrange the marriage of his daughter to Honorius.

The new emperors – or perhaps better, the men who controlled them – were faced with problems almost immediately. In 395 predatory bands of Huns raided both Sassanid Persia and Rome's eastern provinces, plundering widely in Armenia, Mesopotamia, Syria and even into Asia Minor. The presence of many eastern army units with Stilicho may well have reduced the capacity of local commanders to deal with this attack. As usual with such raids only a small minority of communities were actually struck, but fear spread much more widely. Away from the borders with Persia, most of this region had been peaceful for over a century and this was clearly a traumatic episode, especially when the Huns returned two or three years later.[10]

Another, closer threat also erupted in 395 when some of the Goths settled within the empire by Theodosius rebelled. They were led by Alaric, an officer commanding troops serving as allies with the Roman army. He was probably from an aristocratic family in one of the tribes, and in due course would be called king, but the source of his authority is not clear. Some of his men may have been bound to him by ties of kinship, others simply by serving under him in the army. He was clearly a man of considerable personality, who would keep his followers loyal for fifteen years. Like the precise root of his power, his long-term objectives are unclear. There had been resentment and some minor outbreaks of rebellion amongst the Gothic communities when they were called upon by Theodosius to provide troops to fight for him against Maximus and Eugenius. However, Alaric and his men had not been part of this and had served with some distinction at the River Frigidus. Perhaps the belief that the Goths had been cynically sacrificed at that battle fuelled resentment. More probably, the succession of two new emperors simply offered an opportunity for profit.

Quite a few of the Goths appear to have resented the settlement imposed on them in 382, even though it was very favourable by Roman standards. We do not know how many men Alaric led, or whether they consisted primarily of warriors who had not settled down in their new lands or also included whole communities. Certainly, they were strong enough to be seen as a dangerous force. From the beginning Alaric sought a senior military appointment from the Romans. Such a commission would have brought with it the right to food supplies for his men from the state. It is possible that all he and his followers hoped for was an improvement in their status and livelihoods well within the Roman system.[11]

The Goths began plundering the provinces in Thrace and Macedonia. Once again, the absence of many regiments in Italy prevented Arcadius and Rufinus from dealing with them. Yet, as usual, they were more concerned with the threat posed by Roman rivals. Stilicho proclaimed that Theodosius had entrusted him with the guardianship of both his sons and led his army eastwards, ostensibly to deal with the rebellious Alaric. However, Arcadius rejected his assistance and instructed him to send the regiments from the eastern army back to Constantinople. There seems to have been friction between the western and eastern troops and it may well be that Stilicho could not control all of his men. In any case, he obeyed the order. He withdrew with all the regiments from the western army and did not engage Alaric.[12]

The eastern regiments were led by an officer named Gainas, who was himself of Gothic extraction. When they arrived outside Constantinople they murdered Rufinus as he rode out to meet them. The latter's influence over the emperor was taken over by his chamberlain, the eunuch Eutropius, who for the moment was more concerned with consolidating his own power at court. For two years Alaric was left to plunder the provinces. In 397 Stilicho returned with an army bolstered by large contingents of barbarian allies. Eutropius and Arcadius proved no more enthusiastic about accepting his aid and thus acknowledging his right to intervene in the east. Alaric was blockaded and forced to retreat into Epirus, but then Stilicho himself withdrew without achieving any permanent victory. Acting on the advice of his favourite, Arcadius had declared Stilicho a public enemy. Around the same time the eastern government began talking to Alaric and eventually agreed to make him Master of Soldiers in Illyricum. The former army officer turned rebel had now become a Roman general. Clearly, Eugenius and Arcadius found this preferable to accepting the dominance of Stilicho.[13]

Late in 397 Gildo, the man left in command of the North African provinces since Theodosius' reign, decided to defect with his province to the Eastern Empire. There was an immediate crisis since Italy and Rome relied so heavily on grain and other food from the region. Stilicho sent Gildo's brother and bitter enemy Mascezel in command of a small expeditionary force, which sailed to Africa from Italy. He was quickly successful. Stilicho was generous with his praise, but shed no tears when Mascezel fell into a river and drowned soon after his return. There were rumours that he had been thrown in by Stilicho's bodyguards.[14]

In the east Eutropius seems to have taken personal command in a successful campaign against the Huns, and this success prompted him to arrange to become consul in 399. It was customary at this time for the eastern and western emperors each to name one of the pair of consuls who took up office on 1 January and gave their names to the year. The post itself was one of prestige rather than real power, but it was ancient – there had been consuls now for nine hundred years – and aristocratic opinion was outraged by the idea of this hallowed office being held by a eunuch. As his unpopularity grew, so other senior men began to see Eutropius as vulnerable. In the same year some Gothic troops operating against bandits in Asia Minor chose instead to rebel, as their commander had a personal score against Eutropius. Gainas led a force against them, but then allied with the rebel troops and urged the emperor to grant their demand to dismiss his favourite. Arcadius' wife Eudoxia joined the chorus of condemnation of the chamberlain and eventually the emperor gave in. Eutropius at first sought sanctuary in a church, but gave himself up when he received the promise that his life would be spared. He went into exile in Cyprus, only to be executed a little later on the false pretext of plotting against the emperor.

For the moment the empress and her favourites dominated the court, but Gainas marched on Constantinople and the implicit threat of this force granted him a short-lived supremacy. He was named as consul for 400. However, his Gothic soldiers were unpopular when they were stationed in Constantinople and eventually he decided to send them to Thrace. However, as the columns formed up to leave, the rearmost parties were attacked by mobs. Large numbers were killed, including many of the soldiers' wives and children. One large group sought sanctuary in a church, but died when the building was set on fire with them still inside. Shortly afterwards Gainas was defeated by an army led by a general called Fravitta, who was also a Goth. Fleeing across the Danube, Gainas eventually died at the hands of a Hunnic king. Fravitta was executed by the Roman authorities just months after his victory on allegations of disloyalty. Generals who were too successful or too popular were seen as dangerous by the powers at court. Eudoxia and her allies had regained control of the court and thus the Eastern Empire.[15]

In 401 Alaric left his haunts of the last few years and headed for Italy. The situation in the east had changed and the new regime was unlikely to be well disposed towards him when it had risen to power by criticising the prominence of 'barbarian' and specifically Gothic generals such as Gainas. Free for the moment from internal disputes, there was a real chance that the imperial government might decide to withdraw his commission and use force against him. For the moment, Alaric judged that he could hope for better terms from Stilicho. We do not know how many men followed him. Those Goths who remained on the land they had been granted in 382 and contentedly farmed inevitably do not get mentioned in our sources. It is probably wrong to think at this stage of a whole people once again on the move, a delayed resumption of the migration that had brought the Goths across the Danube in 376. In the main his followers are likely to have been the young and restless. Perhaps they had failed as farmers or were the children born inside the empire for whom there was not enough land to share. There was also a long tradition in tribal societies of youths seeking glory and wealth as warriors or soldiers, something on which the Roman army had long relied to supply it with recruits. There cannot have been many who had fought at Adrianople more than twenty years before. Some of the warriors were doubtless accompanied by their wives and families, just as camp followers often trailed behind Roman army units. The behaviour of Alaric and his men in subsequent years was not that of a migrating people, but rather of an army.

Alaric's hope was to win negotiated concessions from the Western Empire, most likely including senior military rank and the use of state resources to feed and supply his followers. He was rebuffed. Therefore, while Stilicho was north of the Alps dealing with barbarian raids into Raetia (very roughly equivalent to modern Austria), Alaric invaded Italy in 402, brushing aside one small Roman force to besiege Milan. The city was a frequent imperial residence, but during these disturbed years the court spent more time and eventually settled in Ravenna, which was surrounded by marshland and very hard to attack. It was also more isolated. Stilicho returned to Italy and fought two (perhaps three) battles against the Gothic army. He captured Alaric's wife and children along with other distinguished prisoners, but also suffered losses himself and failed to win a decisive victory. There was a truce, before fighting broke out again and another battle was fought outside Verona, which again left no clear winner. Eventually Alaric withdrew, most probably through lack of food, and moved back into the Balkans for the next few years. There, on the border between the Eastern and Western Empires where neither side could exert much control, he waited, plundering or extorting the supplies he needed from Illyricum. Around 405 Stilicho was willing to negotiate and granted the Gothic leader the rank of Master of Soldiers. The court in Constantinople refused to acknowledge this, especially since it again implied the right of Stilicho to dictate to both east and west.[16]

Stilicho soon faced more immediate problems. Near the end of the year a large force of Goths led by King Radagaisus launched a deep raid and once again reached northern Italy. These warriors were from the tribes beyond the Danube and had no connection with Alaric's men, save that they were all broadly Goths and spoke versions of the same language. Zosimus claims that there were 400,000 of them, but such a figure is clearly absurd for any tribal army, let alone a raiding band. He also tells us that Stilicho concentrated thirty units along with allied contingents in the force that met and utterly defeated the raiders. The *Notitia Dignitatum* lists 181 regiments for the field armies of the Western Empire, forty-six of them in Italy and forty-eight in Gaul. Stilicho seems to have summoned substantial forces from the northern frontiers to form this army. Precise numbers and distribution may well have been different in 405, but this still suggests that it was next to impossible to concentrate more than a small minority of the supposed mobile field army in one place, even assuming that all of Stilicho's units on this occasion were *comitatenses*. Once again, the lack of knowledge about the sizes of units makes it impossible to calculate the size of the army. Nevertheless, it proved sufficient to win a clear victory – the price of slaves is supposed to have fallen sharply when the market was flooded with captive Goths.[17]

During this campaign the first of a series of usurpers was proclaimed emperor by the army in Britain. He was murdered by the soldiers within a matter of weeks and his successor suffered the same fate after just a few months. The third in the line was Constantine, allegedly chosen because of his famous and imperial name, and he proved far more capable as a politician. Distant Britain often seems to have felt neglected by the imperial government and so inclined to make its own emperor, but rarely did these men prove content with just the rule of the island. Like others before him, Constantine crossed the Channel, probably in 407, and soon controlled most of Gaul as well as large parts of Spain. Stilicho sent a Gothic officer named Sarus, a bitter personal enemy of Alaric, to fight against the usurper. He enjoyed some success, but was then in turn forced to retreat.[18]

On New Year's Eve, traditionally in 406, but a good case has been made for 405, raiding bands of two separate Vandal groups, the Silings and Asdings, as well as Suevi and Alans crossed the Rhine near Mainz. Once again, these seem to have been predominantly groups of warriors and not entire tribes migrating in search of new homes. There is no direct evidence for the often repeated story that the river had frozen, although this is certainly possible. Similarly, the claim that this movement was prompted ultimately by pressure from the Huns is unsubstantiated and generally unlikely. It is far more probable that the apparent weakness of the Roman frontier just seemed to offer an opportunity. If the earlier date is correct, then the withdrawal of troops from the Rhine to face Radagaisus could well have created this impression. In this case the usurpations in Britain and Constantine's occupation of Gaul may have been fostered by the failure of Honorius' representatives to stop the invaders. If the attack was only launched at the end of 406, then the warbands themselves may have been taking advantage of the confusion that inevitably followed the outbreak of civil war within the empire. No leader is named for this attack, but the co-operation between several distinct groups suggests the presence of one, or perhaps a few chieftains of considerable charisma. Very quickly the warrior bands overran and plundered the communities near the Rhine, before pushing on into the interior of the provinces. Constantine won some minor victories over them, greatly bolstering his support in Gaul, and seems to have kept them bottled up in the northern regions of Gaul. Yet he did not break them, and for the next few years these bands ranged individually or together through this region, plundering or extorting at will.[19]

In 407 Alaric decided to take advantage of the situation and led his army back towards Italy in the hope of wringing an even better deal from the beleaguered Stilicho. In the next year he demanded 4,000 lb of gold as the price for not launching a new invasion. Stilicho, acting in a way now very familiar for Roman leaders, decided that Constantine was the greater threat and that Alaric could be hired to fight against him. He agreed to pay the gold, and went to the Senate, since such a vast amount was very difficult to secure at short notice and the wealthy senators were one of the most logical sources. In addition, temples and artworks in Rome were stripped to provide the necessary sum, but the senators were bitterly resentful of this bribing of an enemy. One described it as 'not a treaty, but a pact of slavery.'[20]

The priorities of the leading Romans shifted abruptly when news arrived that Arcadius had died on 1 May 408 at the age of just thirty-one. He was succeeded by his seven-year-old son Theodosius II – the infant had been named as Augustus when he was barely a year old.

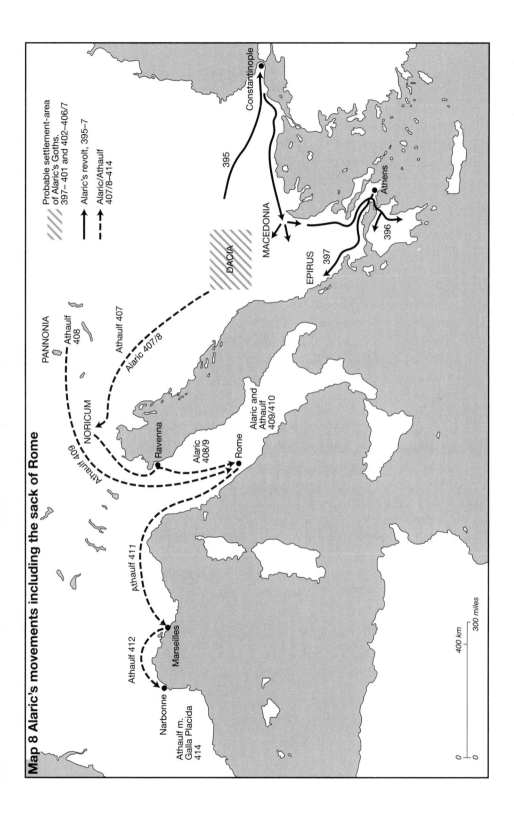

Map 8 Alaric's movements including the sack of Rome

Probable settlement-area of Alaric's Goths. 397–401 and 402–406/7

Alaric's revolt, 395–7

Alaric/Athaulf 407/8–414

395

Constantinople

Athens

396

397

MACEDONIA

EPIRUS

DACIA

PANNONIA

Athaulf 408

Athaulf 407

Alaric 407/8

NORICUM

Athaulf 409

Ravenna

Alaric 408/9

Rome

Alaric and Athaulf 409/410

Athaulf 411

Athaulf 412

Marseilles

Narbonne

Athaulf m. Galla Placida 414

0   400 km

0   300 miles

Stilicho and Honorius both announced their intention to go in person and supervise the accession of the new emperor, in the process no doubt making clear the primacy of the western court. Rivals ambitious to supplant Stilicho had long been encouraging Honorius – who was himself still only twenty-three – to mistrust him. They claimed that the general planned to make his own son emperor, perhaps instead of Theodosius. He certainly was determined to maintain a close link with the imperial family. When Honorius' wife and Stilicho's daughter died, Stilicho promptly replaced her as imperial consort with her sister. The young emperor resented his marginal role in running the empire, just as Valentinian II had before him.

Just who engineered the final confrontation is unclear. The payment to Alaric made Stilicho deeply unpopular and his enemies quickly scented an opportunity to attack him. There was a mutiny of the troops concentrated at Ticinum ready to be sent into Gaul. Several officers and senior civil servants – probably all men appointed by and loyal to Stilicho – were murdered. Honorius was there, but survived the bloodletting. Stilicho was some distance away, attended only by some barbarian troops who were staunch in their loyalty. By the time he reached Ravenna the emperor had ordered his arrest. He refused to fight, in spite of the fact that the soldiers with him were willing. Instead he sought sanctuary in a church, but gave himself up on the promise that his life would be spared. He was promptly executed, once again ordering his men not to protect him. His end was dignified, especially since it was rare for a senior Roman commander to accept death rather than take the chance of fighting a civil war. Perhaps he realised that he had been utterly outmanoeuvred and that his own position was now too weak for him to have any prospect of winning a struggle with Honorius. However, it is hard not to want to believe that he put the good of the empire before his own fate. It may even be true.[21]

16

The Sister and the Eternal City

'In one city the whole world perished.' – *Bishop Jerome reacting to the sack of Rome in 410.*[1]

'At first he ardently desired to eradicate the Roman name and to make all the Roman territory an empire of the Goths in fact as well as in name, and that . . . *Gothia* should be what *Romania* had been.' – *Orosius, fifth century* AD.[2]

The man who profited most from the fall of Stilicho was Olympius, a senior bureaucrat rather than a soldier, who headed one of the main government departments as *Magister Officiorum*. As usual, there was a bloody purge of men associated with the dead leader and the wives and families of the barbarian soldiers who had remained loyal to him were massacred. Most of the men who survived promptly deserted to Alaric. Stilicho's son was hunted down and killed, although the torture of suspects failed to provide any evidence to back the claim that his father had been plotting to make him emperor. Since the deal with Alaric had done so much to discredit Stilicho, Olympius and Honorius refused to honour the agreement and rejected new attempts at negotiation. Yet they also failed to prepare for war and could not prevent Alaric being reinforced by another group led by his brother-in-law Athaulf. Grand claims were made for the victory won over Athaulf by a party of 300 Huns sent by Olympius, but this did not hinder the union of the two Gothic armies.[3]

Alaric invaded Italy once again and was able to advance almost unopposed as far as Rome, which he blockaded in the winter of 408–409. The Gothic army seized Portus, the great harbour town that supplied the city, and so cut off the bulk of its food supplies. Stilicho's widow Serena was now executed under trumped up charges of collusion with the enemy. It is even claimed that the nervous Senate wanted to revive public sacrifice and other pagan rituals in an effort to avert harm from the city. Zosimus claimed that the bishop of Rome – already more and more often known as the pope – grudgingly agreed as long as the rites took place in secret, but since this would have invalidated them nothing was actually done. The story is probably invented, but does give an idea of the fear pervading Rome at this time. Honorius and his ministers in Ravenna did nothing to help. Large numbers of slaves – most of them probably recently captured Goths, many in the war against Radagaisus – deserted to join Alaric's men. The Senate decided to negotiate, paying the Goths to end the blockade and sending a delegation to Ravenna to open talks between the emperor and Alaric. The latter was still hoping for official status within the imperial system and withdrew his army north to Ariminum (modern Rimini) where the discussions would take place.[4]

The talks failed within a matter of months. Olympius refused to grant Alaric a new command, but offered enough concessions to lose face and soon afterwards fled into exile rather than face execution. The new power at the imperial court was Jovius, a sometime associate of Stilicho, now praetorian prefect of Italy and chief negotiator with the Goths. With Olympius out of the way, Jovius became increasingly intransigent in the negotiations, blaming Alaric when these finally broke down. The imperial government similarly spurned further requests from him to be granted Noricum or a similar province even without a formal command. No doubt the emperor and his advisors were happy to see the reduced Gothic demands as a sign of weakness. The Goths marched south and once again blockaded Rome. This time Alaric decided on a new tactic and persuaded a distinguished senator and the current prefect of the city, Priscus Attalus, to allow himself to be proclaimed emperor at the end of 409. Although a pagan he was quickly baptised, for there was unlikely to be much support for an emperor who was not at least nominally Christian. Alaric was named as Master of Soldiers, while Athaulf received a lesser post, as did a number of men who were more obviously Roman – several senior senators were appointed in prominent roles.[5]

Africa, so vital for keeping Rome and Italy supplied with food, remained loyal to Honorius. Attalus showed that he was more than just a puppet by refusing to let Alaric send some of his Gothic warriors – one source claims just 500 of them – to secure the province, instead sending a Roman commander with regular troops. These were seriously defeated, so the new emperor and his Gothic commander led their main army back to Rimini to threaten Honorius more directly. The latter was nervous enough to consider accepting Attalus as an imperial colleague. For his part, the new emperor was determined to depose Honorius and send him into exile, possibly after being mutilated – rendering him unfit for the elaborate ceremonial central to the imperial role. The arrival at Ravenna of some 4,000 soldiers from the eastern army stiffened Honorius' resolve, making him confident that he could defend the city against attack. The talks broke down.[6]

After just a few months Alaric deposed the emperor he had made, although Attalus seems to have remained with him and been treated with some honour. He threatened Ravenna more directly, but any chance of fresh negotiations ended when Sarus, the Gothic officer in service with Honorius, launched a surprise attack on Alaric's men. It was probably no more than a skirmish, motivated as much by a personal vendetta as anything else, but it was enough to shatter any trust. Alaric withdrew and for the third time he marched against Rome itself. There had been little enough reward for his followers in recent years. The grain supply from Africa was most likely still interrupted, while the farmlands around Rome had been plundered twice by his own army when he had threatened the city before. This time he decided to reward the men with Rome itself.[7]

The city had no effective garrison, nor was there any real organisation to defend its high, but very long, circuit of walls. No one wanted to go through another long blockade, nor did Alaric want to keep his army in one place for the months required to achieve this. On the night of 23/24 August 410 the Goths entered Rome through the Salarian Gate. They were probably admitted, for this does not seem to have been a formal assault. For three days they plundered at will. Some houses and monuments were burned in the process, but Alaric had given strict orders to respect churches and the clergy. This restraint by the Arian Goths was widely praised by Christian writers, content for the moment to overlook their heretical doctrine. Churches went unplundered, priests in general were not killed and nuns not raped. Others were not so lucky. The sack of Rome was ordered, but it was still a sack, even if the inhabitants suffered no more than those of any city stormed by a Roman army in the long cycle of civil wars. Rome had shrunk in size and population since the early empire, but it was still vast. Sheer size meant that not everyone was robbed or maltreated, but that was little consolation to those who fell victim.

Alaric had rewarded his soldiers with massive plunder, but sacking Rome destroyed his negotiating power for the immediate future. In this sense it was a sign of failure. Honorius may not have lifted a finger to save the city – there was a story that when the news arrived he misunderstood it and worried that his favourite cockerel named

Rome had died. According to the sixth-century historian Procopius, the emperor cried out and said,

> 'And yet it has just eaten from my hands!' ... and the eunuch comprehending his words said that it was the city of Rome which had perished at the hands of Alaric, and the emperor with a sigh of relief answered quickly: 'But I, my good fellow, thought that my fowl Rome had perished.' So great, they say, was the folly with which this emperor was possessed.[8]

Fool or not, Honorius could never be seen to negotiate with the 'barbarian' who had sacked Rome, especially while there was still a strongly entrenched usurper in the west ready to take advantage if he became unpopular. Alaric headed south, planning to gather ships and take his men across to Africa. This would have provided a largely unplundered and wealthy base, with ample food for his followers and the ability to control the supply so vital to Italy. A bout of storms wrecked both his plans and the vessels he had gathered. Alaric died soon afterwards. Legend claimed that a river was diverted to bury the leader and his vast treasures, then channelled back to cover them. To preserve the secret, the slaves who had undertaken the work were then all killed. Good stories of this sort are worth repeating, but that does not mean that we have to believe them.[9]

Galla Placidia

Athaulf was left as leader of the Gothic army. He and his followers were still very wealthy from the sack of Rome. They also had with them as a prisoner Honorius' sister, Galla Placidia. Now in her early twenties, she had been raised in the household of Stilicho and Serena, but this does not seem to have created any bond of affection. Her first appearance on the political stage was when she aided the Senate in condemning Serena to death. She was unmarried, quite possibly because Stilicho had hoped to arrange a union with his son. Now she was a valued hostage, treated with considerable respect by the Goths.[10]

In 409 Honorius had recognised Constantine as a colleague, since he had been unable to defeat him. The latter had by this time overrun all of Spain and defeated a rebellion raised there by some of Honorius' relatives, who were all executed. Yet even before this was known in Ravenna, relations between the two emperors were strained and broke down completely when Constantine brought troops to Italy to fight against Alaric. Fears of a plot prompted Honorius to execute one of his Masters of Soldiers and there was no significant effort to co-operate with the other army. Constantine withdrew, and the news of the executions in Spain widened the rift. Around this time, the Vandals, Alans and Suevi left northern Gaul and crossed over the supposedly guarded passes of the Pyrenees into Spain. Then they spread out, each moving into a different area to make it easier to survive by plundering and extortion. The Roman army – the *Notitia Dignitatum* lists sixteen field army regiments in Spain – did not hinder them.

Constantine was facing a different threat from Spain, led by the commander he had sent there. This man, a Briton named Gerontius, had heard that he was to be replaced and so had rebelled, declaring his son Maximus as emperor. He may well have drawn allies from the warbands now operating in the peninsula. In 411 he defeated Constantine's son Constans and then besieged the emperor himself at Arelate (modern day Arles). Honorius had also decided to act against the western usurper and sent an army into Gaul. Most of Gerontius' men defected to this force, forcing him to flee. The siege continued until Constantine was forced to capitulate. He was taken prisoner, but then beheaded on the way to Ravenna. The officer who gained most of the credit for the victory was named Constantius. Originally a supporter of Stilicho, he had survived the latter's fall. He would quickly rise to the same sort of prominence once enjoyed by his patron.[11]

Athaulf left Italy in 411, arriving in Gaul soon after a local aristocrat proclaimed himself emperor amidst the wreck of Constantine's regime. The Goths supported him, and in the course of the fighting had the satisfaction of killing Sarus. However, they then changed sides, Athaulf proclaiming that he was fighting on behalf of Honorius against Gerontius. The latter was quickly defeated and shared the same fate as Constantine, being killed during the journey to Ravenna. His defeat was quickly followed by another rebellion in Africa, whose military commander led an invasion of Italy. Athaulf was settled in Aquitania with imperial approval. However, the authorities failed to provide them with supplies of grain, so the Goths refused to release Galla Placidia. Effectively, they had ceased to be under Honorius' control. Athaulf and his men raided widely, captured the cities of Narbo and Tolosa (modern Narbonne and Toulouse respectively), and even attacked Massilia (modern Marseilles). Constantius blockaded the coast.

In response, Athaulf took the truly remarkable step of marrying Galla

Placidia. Never before had an emperor's sister become the wife of a barbarian leader, let alone one who was fighting against forces loyal to her brother. The ceremony took place on 1 January 414 at Narbo, with the groom dressed as a Roman general and the wedding song sung by Priscus Attalus. The former emperor was once again named as Augustus. The marriage produced a son, who was given the blatantly imperial name of Theodosius, especially significant because Honorius was childless. Nevertheless pressure on the Goths was growing as a result of the blockade and they moved again, crossing into Spain and occupying Barcelona and the surrounding area. The infant Theodosius died at this point, then in 415 Athaulf was stabbed while inspecting his horses in a stable and died of his wounds. The man then proclaimed king was Sarus' brother. He publicly humiliated Galla Placidia, making her walk ahead of his horse, but he was then himself murdered within a week and a new leader called Wallia emerged.[12]

Wallia and Constantius soon afterwards agreed terms. The widowed Galla Placidia was sent back to Ravenna – Constantius was probably already hoping to marry her himself, despite her loathing for him. Attalus was also handed over and was led in triumph when Honorius visited Rome. Two fingers were cut off his hand to symbolise the two occasions when he had usurped imperial status, but he was not executed and instead sent into exile to the island of Lipari. Without the backing of the Goths, he was simply not important enough to be dangerous. Wallia and his men were now enlisted to fight against the other barbarians still in Spain. The state provided them with food. They attacked and shattered the power of the Siling Vandals and Alans. This may have been enough of a demonstration for the other groups to accept peace on terms more favourable to the imperial authorities. In 418 Constantius recalled the Goths from Spain to Gaul and settled them in the province of Aquitania Secunda. The details are obscure, but it is more probable that they were given land rather than simply a share of tax revenues. Wallia died in this year, but his successor Theodoric I continued to rule as king, running the Goths' internal affairs, but with the obligation to aid the Western Empire as allies.[13]

Constantius married Galla Placidia in 417 and she bore him a son in 419, who was named Valentinian. There was no trace of the genuine affection she seems to have felt for Athaulf and she was still attended by loyal Gothic retainers. An ungainly man, with a long neck, bulbous eyes and large head, Constantius was in public inclined to slump in the saddle and shoot shifty glances in all directions. Privately he was far more effusive, at banquets matching the professional comedians and clowns. Whatever his character, he had successfully suppressed the usurpers and rebellious groups within the empire and brought some degree of control to the frontiers. Already holding Stilicho's old rank of Master of all Soldiers, and the title of patrician, he was made consul three times.

Constantius effectively ruled the Western Empire and in 421 he was formally named as Augustus and colleague by Honorius. Galla Placidia was named as Augusta, but her husband died of natural causes before the year was out. The court at Constantinople throughout failed to recognise either of the new imperial titles. A struggle to replace Constantius swiftly erupted, with some open fighting. Galla Placidia fled with her son to Constantinople. Her brother, still childless, died in 423. A usurper promptly was proclaimed with the backing of senior members of the court at Ravenna. It took a hard-fought campaign by strong elements of the eastern army and navy, as well as a fair dose of betrayal, to defeat this man. Finally, in October 425 the six-year-old Valentinian III was proclaimed Augustus at Rome.[14]

Theodosius II had only been a year older than this when his father died and he succeeded to sole rule of the Eastern Empire in 408. In spite of their youth, both would go on to have unusually long reigns – technically Theodosius, who was made Augustus when he was an infant, ruled for longer than any other emperor. Inevitably, their power could only be nominal until they reached at least their late teens, and neither would ever truly break free of the rule of others. Galla Placidia accompanied her son to Rome. Formally she was the Augusta, and although there was no legal title of regent, this was in practice her role. There was a conscious effort to strengthen the bonds between the two halves of the empire and her son was betrothed to the daughter of Theodosius II, herself a mere child of three. The support of the Eastern Empire came at a price, and Illyricum was ceded to the government in Constantinople in return for supporting Valentinian III in the civil war.

Imperial women played a prominent and at times very public role in the politics of the fifth century, and not simply as a convenient means of cementing alliances by marriage. In 414 Theodosius II's older sister Pulcheria was only about fifteen or sixteen, and yet she suddenly emerged as a major influence at court, being named as Augusta. A deeply religious woman, she pledged herself to a life of chastity and convinced her sisters to make the same gesture. Piety – whether in the traditional pagan rituals or since Constantine in a distinctly Christian form – had always been admired in emperors and their relatives. Politically, their refusal to marry prevented potential rivals to their brother gaining a connection to the imperial house. She took personal charge of her brother's education, dismissing his tutor. During these years the life of the court was described as more like the cloistered life of a monastic community than the heart of an empire. Theodosius was raised to study the scriptures, and to pray and fast. Yet for all the alleged simplicity of court life the pomp and elaborate ceremonies surrounding the person of the emperor as well as his senior officials continued unabated.

Neither Galla Placidia nor Pulcheria went unchallenged. Officials and army officers continued to jockey for power and influence. Both women tried to build up and maintain support amongst such men, but not all could simultaneously be kept happy with promotions and other rewards. Some loyal men also proved inept and were discredited. Inevitably, there were also disappointed men who could only advance through the fall of others. The sources may be inclined to exaggerate the role played by these women. The Roman tradition remained deeply uncomfortable with the idea of women wielding genuine political power. They were not the sole powers behind the young emperors, but they were certainly amongst the most important. In the eastern court another woman emerged as a competitor to Pulcheria. This was Eudoxia, the wife Theodosius had married in 421, who was also granted the title of Augusta two years later. Daughter of a noted – and pagan – philosopher, she had become a Christian, probably before the marriage. Although she retained an interest in traditional literature and scholarship, there was never any indication that her conversion was not sincere.[15]

Galla Placidia, Pulcheria and Eudoxia were all intelligent and in many ways capable individuals, but their power was in the end dependent entirely on their influence over the two emperors. This was equally true of all the court officials, members of the household and army officers who gained prominence during these years. Whatever the merits of the decisions they persuaded the emperor to take, or made on his behalf, their positions remained uncertain. At any time someone else could supplant them. In both halves of the empire power remained concentrated in the hands of the emperor. Neither Valentinian III nor Theodosius II proved able to take permanent control even when they grew older, but remained indecisive and readily susceptible to the influence of others. Weakness and instability at the very heart of government made it harder for either empire to maintain consistent policy, let alone direct its efforts and resources effectively.

Warbands and Armies

Thirty years after the death of Theodosius, his grandchildren reigned as eastern and western emperors. During these decades civil war had been frequent, especially in the west, which had always produced more usurpers than the east. Even more striking was the escalation of the now endemic rivalry between senior army officers and bureaucrats into open violence. Young and weak emperors created a power vacuum at the top of the imperial hierarchy that others struggled to fill. The rise of Constantius from officer to army commander, to brother-in-law of the emperor and finally to imperial rule himself, showed what was possible. Others did not quite climb so high, but a succession of men in both the eastern and western courts came to possess effective rule in these years. Constantius was almost unique in dying of natural causes, and virtually all the others were executed. In most cases their fall was accompanied by the deaths of many of their supporters.

This constant competition within the imperial hierarchy, along with the climate of suspicion, fear of violence and ruthless personal ambition that it created, provides the context for history of this period. Alaric rebelled in the hope of exploiting a time of imperial weakness to gain position and status. He and Athaulf survived because the imperial governments were never strong enough to destroy them. Stilicho's propaganda claimed that he had the Goths at his mercy on three occasions, but was always forced to pull back. This is unconvincing. Yet it is probably also true to say that the Gothic army was too useful to be destroyed, even if this had been possible. Certainly, Alaric was given appointments as Master of Soldiers by both the eastern and later the western emperors, even if each rank was subsequently withdrawn. During his career he alternated between rebel and Roman general. Constantius preferred to send the Goths against the Vandals and Alans in Spain than try to complete their defeat. In civil wars emperors routinely hired the same barbarians who had recently been ravaging the provinces to fight against their Roman opponents. Almost always, Roman rivals were seen as the most dangerous foes.

We do not know how large the Gothic army was at any stage. It is said to have mustered 40,000 men outside Rome. The figure is not impossible, especially if it included camp followers as well as the fighting men, but we have no idea whether or not it is accurate. The demand for 7,000 silk garments as part of the price for breaking the first siege of Rome has been used to infer that there were that number of properly

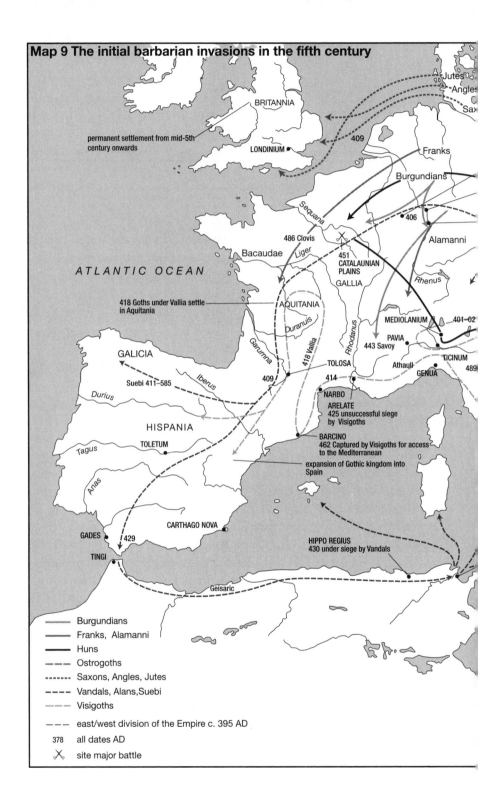

Map 9 The initial barbarian invasions in the fifth century

BRITANNIA

Jutes
Angles
Sax

permanent settlement from mid-5th
century onwards

LONDINIUM

409

Franks

Burgundians

ATLANTIC OCEAN

Sequana

406

Alamanni

486 Clovis

Bacaudae

Liger

451
CATALAUNIAN
PLAINS

GALLIA

Rhenus

418 Goths under Vallia settle
in Aquitania

AQUITANIA

Duranuis

MEDIOLANIUM

401–02

PAVIA
443 Savoy

GALICIA

Garumna

Rhodanus

418 Vallia

TOLOSA

TICINUM

Athaull

GENUA

489

Suebi 411–585

Iberus

409

414

Durius

NARBO

ARELATE
425 unsuccessful siege
by Visigoths

HISPANIA

TOLETUM

BARCINO
462 Captured by Visigoths for access
to the Mediterranean

Tagus

Anas

expansion of Gothic kingdom into
Spain

CARTHAGO NOVA

GADES

429

HIPPO REGIUS
430 under siege by Vandals

TINGI

Geisaric

Burgundians

Franks, Alamanni

Huns

Ostrogoths

Saxons, Angles, Jutes

Vandals, Alans,Suebi

Visigoths

east/west division of the Empire c. 395 AD

378   all dates AD

✕   site major battle

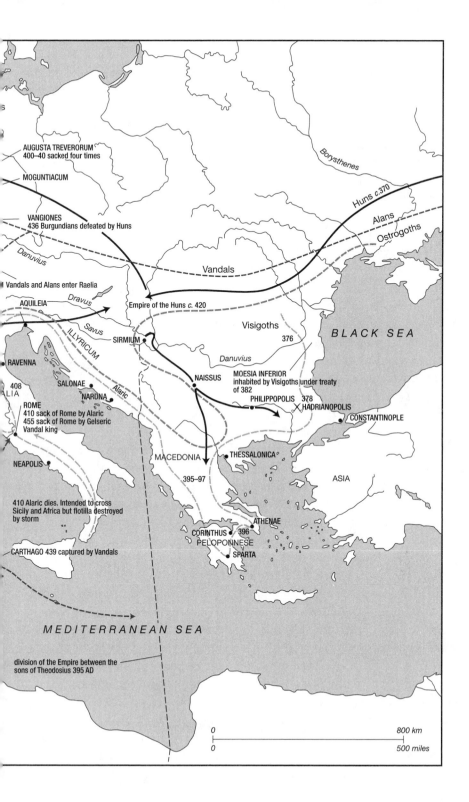

AUGUSTA TREVERORUM
400–40 sacked four times

MOGUNTIACUM

VANGIONES
436 Burgundians defeated by Huns

Danuvius

Vandals and Alans enter Raetia

AQUILEIA

Dravus

ILLYRICUM

Savus

SIRMIUM

RAVENNA

408
...LIA

SALONAE

NARONA

Alaric

ROME
410 sack of Rome by Alaric
455 sack of Rome by Gelseric
Vandal king

NEAPOLIS

410 Alaric dies. Intended to cross
Sicily and Africa but flotilla destroyed
by storm

CARTHAGO 439 captured by Vandals

Borysthenes

Huns *c.*370

Alans

Ostrogoths

Vandals

Empire of the Huns *c.* 420

Visigoths

376

BLACK SEA

Danuvius

NAISSUS

MOESIA INFERIOR
inhabited by Visigoths under treaty
of 382

PHILIPPOPOLIS   378
HADRIANOPOLIS

CONSTANTINOPLE

MACEDONIA

THESSALONICA

ASIA

395–97

ATHENAE

CORINTHUS   396
PELOPONNESE

SPARTA

MEDITERRANEAN SEA

division of the Empire between the
sons of Theodosius 395 AD

0   800 km

0   500 miles

equipped, genuine warriors. Again, this is perfectly possible. The Goths never attempted a formal siege or assault on Rome. Whatever the size of their army they were vastly outnumbered by the inhabitants of the city, but these were not organised or equipped. The Goths needed only to be numerous enough to prevent substantial supplies of food from reaching the city. In these circumstances even a few thousand confidently led warriors could make life extremely hard inside Rome. Similarly, the various barbarian groups that crossed the Rhine seem unlikely to have been especially numerous – bands of a few thousand warriors from each group seeming more likely than armies of tens of thousands or more. Their behaviour, much like the ability of the Goths to move about, crossing mountain passes when necessary, surviving for years on plunder and foraging within the provinces, does not suggest big forces. Wherever such groups struck, the local impact was doubtless terrible, but their numbers meant that only small areas would be affected at any time. The Goths were probably the largest force, supplied at times from imperial resources and by this time largely equipped with the products of state-run arms factories. In appearance, they probably looked little different to regular Roman troops.[16]

There is equally little impression of especially large and unambiguously Roman armies in these years. Stilicho's thirty units with allies may well have been one of the largest forces to take the field. It is also worth noting that the 4,000 soldiers sent from the east to Ravenna profoundly affected the balance of forces in the campaign. In 409 it was said that 6,000 soldiers were sent to defend Rome itself, although they were ambushed and only a handful got through. If the figure is accurate then evidently such a number was considered adequate to protect the city. The *Notitia Dignitatum* does show signs of losses and desperate improvisation in the make-up of the western field armies. Many units were newly created – or at least renamed – after 395 and a significant proportion composed of units of *pseudocomitatenses*, regiments transferred permanently to the field army from the *limitanei*. It is doubtful that such units were replaced amongst the frontier troops. Yet, in considering the strength of the army, we come back to the basic problem that we do not know what size regiments were in practice or, indeed, how many existed at all other than on paper. The ease with which the mixed group of raiders crossed the Rhine, then survived in Gaul and finally went into Spain raises the question of just where the Roman army was. This problem is only increased if, as seems very likely, the number of barbarians was relatively small. Many Roman units may well have been drawn away to Italy by

Stilicho or, as time went on, become caught up in the civil wars. Yet in the end it is hard to avoid the conclusion that many simply did not exist.[17]

What is certain is that none of the leaders during the operations in these decades was willing to risk heavy casualties. This was as true of men like Alaric, as well as whoever led the tribal bands of Vandals, Alans and others, as it was of the Romans. Major battles were extremely rare and none of them decisive. Stilicho and Constantius both seem to have had a fondness for blockading the enemy into submission rather than direct confrontation. In Stilicho's case, his military experience and talent may well have been modest, and perhaps he was aware of this limitation. Constantius may have been more gifted, but both men were primarily political soldiers. Heavy losses could not easily be replaced and might well involve a loss of face that could precipitate rapid dismissal and execution.

Similarly, Alaric depended for his significance on maintaining a formidable force of warriors under his command. The same was true of the other barbarian leaders. Warbands or armies isolated deep within the provinces had no ready source of substantial reinforcements. It is more than likely that successful groups would attract new recruits from warriors who had crossed into the empire individually or in small bands. The empire's frontier defences were in no state to prevent this. There were also army deserters and runaway slaves. Yet these would only join a leader they believed to be successful. Even minor defeats, especially several in a row, would discourage such men, as well as perhaps prompting desertions from amongst the existing warriors. Major battles were simply too risky unless a leader had an overwhelming advantage, in which case the enemy were unlikely to fight in the first place. Therefore, campaigns were generally tentative, each side aiming to gain an advantage to be used in negotiation. For the imperial governments, the enemy all too often offered the prospect of effective soldiers for their own uses. These were wars of skirmishes and raids, and doubtless the Roman army continued its fondness for ambush and surprise attacks. Campaigns would be decided by many small actions rather than major set-piece battles. For the men involved this difference was doubtless academic, and a small skirmish could be as vicious and dangerous as a famous battle.

Alaric and his successors hoped to win rank, position and as much security as possible within the Roman system. They could not overthrow the empire for there were simply not enough of them. There were stories that the Goths had taken oaths to overthrow the empire even before they crossed the Danube and Athaulf is supposed to have spoken of his plans to replace a Roman with a Gothic empire. He changed his mind when he decided that Roman laws were necessary to run a peaceful state. Yet the simple fact that they were exploiting periods of instability within both the empires also made their object harder to obtain. The rapid rise and fall of successive powers behind the emperors produced radical shifts in Roman policy. On several occasions this robbed both Gothic leaders of the chance of successful negotiation.[18]

Within a few short years of the sack of Rome, Emperor Honorius celebrated a triumph in the city – and a triumph over a Roman rival, something that would have been unimaginable in the first or second century. Life in the city continued. The Senate met and, when not interrupted by civil war, the people continued to enjoy entertainments and state-supplied doles of food. Politically, the Gothic blockades and actual plundering of Rome had made no impact on the life of the empire, the centre of which had long since transferred to wherever the imperial court happened to be. Psychologically, the news of the sack shocked the Roman world, including the eastern provinces, which now had their own emperor and capital at Constantinople. Pagans blamed the disaster on the abandonment of the old gods. Christians struggled to refute these claims, with ideas we shall consider later (see page 353). Today scholars are inclined to play down its significance in the long term. In practical terms they may well be right, for the Western Empire continued to run after 410 much as it had done before. Yet this is to miss the fundamental point that the imperial government had been incapable of preventing the sack happening in the first place.

In the end, it is the impotence of the imperial government that most stands out during this period. Riven with in-fighting, nominally led by weak emperors and in practice by favourites or dominant officers whose position was always precarious, it proved even less capable of dealing with problems than the regimes of the fourth century. The military challenges it faced were not markedly greater than those faced in earlier periods. The Goths were somewhat different, in that they were an enemy that came from within the provinces, largely as a consequence of the earlier failure to defeat them fully in 382. Even so, they do not seem to have been overwhelmingly numerous. Yet there were never enough imperial troops to defeat them or, indeed, any of the other enemies that emerged, with the exception of Radagaisus' raiding party. The weakness of the empire certainly encouraged more attacks, just as it had always done, but again, there was nothing new about this. No one was ever able to marshal the still considerable resources possessed by either the Eastern or Western Empire effectively enough to meet these challenges. In the end, the Western Empire was content to accept the existence of allied, but at least semi-independent, tribal groups within the provinces. The power of the emperor in Ravenna was gradually seeping away.

17

The Hun

'The barbarian nation of the Huns ... became so great that more than a hundred cities were captured and Constantinople almost came into danger ... and there were so many murders and so much bloodshed that the dead could not be counted. They even captured the churches and monasteries and slaughtered great numbers of monks and nuns.' – *Callinicus, describing the Hunnic invasion in the 440s.*[1]

Attila the Hun remains to this day a byword for savagery and destruction. His is one of the few names from antiquity that still prompts instant recognition, putting him alongside the likes of Alexander, Caesar, Cleopatra and Nero. Of these, only Nero has a reputation so wholly negative, for Attila has become *the* barbarian of the ancient world. All too often his life merges with that of a later – and far more successful – conqueror, Ghengis Khan. The images are of thousands of narrow-eyed men on ponies, pouring out of the Steppes beneath wolf-tail standards to spread blood and ruin, of burning towns and mounds of skulls. At the close of the nineteenth century, first the French, and then more often the British, would dub the Germans as Huns. They did not choose Goth or Vandal, or any of the other names of peoples who could plausibly be seen as ancestors to the modern Germans. In 1914 it was the Hun who 'raped' neutral Belgium. It helped that the name was short and catchy, which was highly convenient for slogan writers as well as poets like Kipling. More importantly, it conveyed an image of an enemy utterly opposed to all that was civilised and good.[2]

Within this stereotype is at least a shadow of the real fear inspired by the Huns in the late fourth and fifth centuries. Some of this was based on race. Huns looked different, even to other barbarians already in contact with Rome. They were short and stocky, with small eyes and faces that seemed almost featureless to Roman observers. Many accounts emphasise their ugliness, although curiously none mention the elongated skulls that a minority of Hunnic men and women sported – a deformity deliberately created by tightly binding a child's head to distort the cranium. No one knows why this was done, although similar practices have been fairly common in other cultures. For once, we are probably right to assume a ritual motive for something we do not understand.[3]

The Huns appeared alien to Roman and Goth alike. They also seemed terrifyingly ferocious and deadly warriors. Yet they were not invincible. Attila's empire was large, if not quite as extensive as his boasts – and some historians – would have us believe. His armies travelled deep into the Roman provinces spreading destruction, but they could not stay there. Some frontier regions were ceded to him, and more were devastated, but overall his territorial gains from Rome were modest. Attila's empire was also very short-lived, tearing itself apart in the years after his death as his sons squabbled for power and subject peoples rebelled. The Huns themselves are unlikely ever to have been especially numerous, and Attila's great armies seem always to have included a majority of allied warriors, including Goths, Alans and other peoples. Nor were the Huns only ever enemies of Rome. Both the Eastern and Western Empires frequently enlisted bands of Huns who fought very effectively on their behalf.

Attila the man is a good deal more interesting than the myth. He was not the same as Ghengis Khan, nor were the Huns identical in every way to the Mongols of the Middle Ages. Nomadic peoples do not all conform to a single, unchanging culture. The Huns have been blamed for provoking the barbarian invasions that eventually broke up the Western Empire. They have also been credited with preserving that empire for several decades, postponing its collapse by holding the Germanic tribes in check. There is an element of truth in both claims, but neither is the whole story. Nevertheless, it is fair to say that for a generation the Huns and their kings were the single most powerful force confronting the Romans in Europe.[4]

From the Steppes to the Danube

For the Romans, the Huns had simply appeared in the fourth century and, in spite of various attempts to link them to groups 'known' from classical tradition, they had no real idea of their origin. Nothing has survived from the Huns' own oral culture to tell of their own beliefs in this matter. In the eighteenth century it was suggested that the Huns were the same people as the Hsuing-Nu – Xiongnu is the modern spelling – known from Chinese sources. This powerful confederation of nomadic tribes had posed a serious threat to the borders of China from the end of the third century BC until they were broken up in the late first century AD. Driven away by a resurgent Chinese empire, the survivors were then supposed to have drifted further and further west until they reached the fringes of the Roman world several centuries later. While this remains a possibility, the case is not at all strong. Certainly, the Huns seem to have originated somewhere on the great steppe, but that area of grassland is so vast and contained many different nomadic groups, so that this in itself does not tell us very much.[5]

We simply do not know why the Huns drifted westwards. Classical sources repeat the myth of their first contact with the Goths being accidental, a party of Huns chasing a straying animal further than ever before until they stumbled over a people previously unknown to them. Such stories are common in ancient literature, but rarely credible. Nomadic groups like the Huns include some highly skilled craftsmen, including metal workers, and more especially the men who made the wagons they travelled in and the bows with which they hunted and fought. However, they have tended always to be short of luxury items and were dependent on settled communities for such things. In the end, it was probably the wealth of Rome, and indeed Persia, as well as of the peoples living on their borders, which drew the Huns towards them. In the second half of the fourth century they reached the Black Sea. By its end some had come as far west as what is now the plain of Hungary.[6]

As with the Goths or Alamanni and other peoples, it is a mistake to think of the Huns as a single unified nation. On the Steppes, nomadic groups often spend much of the year in small parties consisting of a few families, moving from place to place to find seasonal grazing for the sheep and goats that provide them with so many of the necessities of life. There may well already have been kings and chieftains amongst them, even if their power was loose, as well as something vaguely resembling clans or tribes. Contact and conflict with peoples like the Goths and Alans, and eventually the Romans, encouraged the importance of such groupings and the power of individual leaders to grow. Large-scale raiding required leaders to control the bands of warriors and direct their attacks. Successful raids brought plunder and glory, adding to the prestige and power of the man in charge. The warfare that caused such large groups of Goths to seek refuge across the Danube in 376 will have fostered the growth in power of successful Hunnic war-leaders. Some groups fled from the onslaught of the Huns. Far more remained, joining them as more or less subordinate allies. Hunnic leaders came to have chieftains and kings from other races loyal to them as subordinate allies. Over the next half-century the trend was clearly towards a smaller and smaller number of Hunnic war leaders acquiring more and more power. This would culminate in Attila, although even then some groups of Huns do not seem to have acknowledged his rule. After his death they fragmented into many separate bands.

The military success of the Huns against the tribal peoples they encountered needs some explanation, although not perhaps as much as is often thought. We do not know enough about these initial conflicts to assess the role played by numbers, leadership and the strategic or tactical situation. In warfare success can feed off itself, making the victors more and more confident, while at the same time demoralising their enemies until they expect to lose. This is especially true when the victors look and act differently to their opponents, making it easier to believe that these strange enemies are invincible. In the earliest encounters the Huns had an advantage in that while they could strike at the enemy's farms and villages, it was hard for these opponents to respond and attack anything that was vital to the nomads. The Huns were mobile, and the wagons with their vital resources of families and food could withdraw to places beyond the range of most enemy attacks. As importantly, the Huns, all of whom were mounted and used to travelling great distances on horseback, could strike deep and move fast in their raids. Even in defeat they could often escape with only minimal losses.

The Huns were horse archers. Their horses were smaller than Roman mounts, but tough and with great stamina, which allowed them to survive the harsh winters on the Steppes. A sixth-century east Roman manual recommended attacking the Huns at the end of the winter when their horses were at their weakest. Most warriors would have owned more than one mount. On campaign, and especially during a raid, men would have regularly changed to a fresh horse, allowing the band to keep moving at a fast pace. This should not be exaggerated. There is not a shred of evidence for the claim that each Hun needed a string of ten horses. A few of the wealthier men may have had as many – although they would not necessarily have taken them all on campaign. Most ordinary warriors may have aspired to owning two or three mounts, but even as many as this required considerable amounts of fodder. The Huns used a wooden-frame saddle different in design to the four-horned type used by the Romans, but better suited to mounted archery. They did not use the stirrup, which was as yet still unknown in Europe.[7]

The Hunnic bow was a complex piece of craftsmanship. It was a composite bow, which combined wood with animal sinew, horn and bone. Sinew has great tensile strength, while horn has compressive strength. In combination they massively increase the power of a bow in relation to its size. When strung such a composite bow curves back elegantly from the hand grip. Its length is increased by bone or horn 'ears' or laths. These are flexible and effectively make the string longer and so again add power. When the bow is unstrung, it will bend back in the opposite direction, hence these are commonly known as recurved bows. Composite bows were widely known in the ancient world. The Persians used them, as did nomadic and semi-nomadic peoples like the Sarmatians and Alans. Composite bows had been standard in the Roman army for centuries and laths are relatively common finds from military sites. Hunnic bows were unusually large – especially for use on horseback – and thus more powerful. The ear laths added to this. They were also asymmetric, so that the arm of the bow above the hand grip was longer than that below. This did not increase power, but made it easier to handle for a mounted archer. Hunnic bows were of extremely high quality. It probably took years to make a bow and required great specialist knowledge and experience, which was passed on from bowyer to bowyer. A good bow lasted for a long time and it is interesting that the traces of those found in burials seem to have been from broken weapons. A bow was too valuable to bury unless it was already damaged.[8]

Technology explains some of the deadliness of Hun warriors. Each of them used an exceptionally powerful and sophisticated bow. He also had a saddle that provided a secure seat, even when riding at speed and controlling the horse with his knees because both arms were needed to shoot. A bow is not like a firearm or crossbow, where the energy to propel the missile comes from the weapon itself. It is much easier to train men to use such weapons. Becoming a good archer takes far more practice and individual skill. A bow draws most of its energy from the person who shoots it. The composite design increases this power, but does not in itself create it. Archers need to be physically strong, especially in the chest and arms. Skill comes only with constant training. This is doubly true for horse archers, where the warrior must be an expert rider as well as proficient with a bow. Hunting provided practice for war, and to survive on the Steppes every Hun needed to be both an expert horseman and archer. Later, when the Huns had moved to lands closer to the Roman Empire and their lifestyle was modified, these skills were evidently still valued and practised.[9]

The initial encounters between the Huns and Goths tend to be painted in simple terms of warriors on foot, most of them without armour and protected only by a shield, almost helpless in the face of swift-moving archers on horseback. The comparison is often made to the hunt, where a group of riders systematically breaks up the herd and coldly kills individuals and small groups. However brave the foot soldiers, they simply could not catch their mobile opponents, who would only close with them when they had an overwhelming advantage. At that point the Huns would turn to their secondary weapons of slashing swords and lassoes. There may have been encounters like that, although we should note that the Alans were traditionally famous for their own cavalry and mounted archers and yet were also quickly overcome by the Huns. After their initial successes, Hunnic armies tended to include substantial contingents of allies fighting in their own traditional style. Many were infantry armed with javelins, spears or swords and not bows.[10]

The Hunnic bow was deadly in skilled hands, but it was not a wonder weapon and there were limits to what Hun armies could achieve. Horse archers were only truly effective in open country, such as the Steppes or the Hungarian plain. Another disadvantage was that the long training and constant practice required for proficiency tended to limit their numbers, even when the nomads became a little more settled and their population may have increased. There may never have been that many Hun warriors and certainly heavy casualties were very hard to replace quickly. The expansion of the power of Hun leaders to control allies and subjects provided far greater resources of manpower, but ensured that armies were of a more mixed composition.

The Romans had fought very successfully against horse archers and nomadic peoples in the past – Sarmatians and Alans were two prime examples. In another age it is doubtful that the Huns would have enjoyed such spectacular success. Yet, as we have seen, the early fifth century was characterised by very tentative warfare. Roman generals like Stilicho and Constantius – and also war leaders like Alaric – could not afford to suffer serious casualties or risk the loss of prestige resulting from a defeat. It was not an era of frequent and decisive battles. Nor was the Roman army willing to embark on concerted aggressive campaigning, at least in Europe. There were always too many other problems with which to deal, not least the threat posed by Roman rivals. In this era Attila was able to field armies that were large and formidable by the standards of the day, and to maintain them on campaign for considerable periods. Only rarely were they faced by strong opposition. The success of the Huns was to a great extent a product of Roman weakness.[11]

A New Threat on the Danube

The Eastern Empire was most exposed to Hunnic raiding. This seems to have escalated gradually from the start of the fifth century, so that in the usual way successful raids encouraged larger and more frequent attacks. Powerful Hunnic leaders emerged, such as Rua, the uncle of Attila. In 422 the government in Constantinople agreed to pay him 350 lb of gold every year as the price for his keeping the peace. In 434 he demanded that this be increased, and when the Romans refused, he launched an attack on the Balkan provinces. However, Rua died soon afterwards and was succeeded by Attila and his brother Bleda. They appear to have split their uncle's kingdom between them rather than ruling jointly. For a while the pressure on the Roman frontier was reduced, but by 440 the brothers were able to extort an annual payment of 700 lb of gold from the Eastern Empire. Theodosius II's ministers faced other military problems and this sum may have seemed a small price to pay for peace.[12]

Blackmailers inevitably interpret compliance as a sign of weakness and increase their demands. Peace proved illusory and within a year the Huns began raiding Illyricum and Thrace once again. One of the pretexts for the renewal of war was the alleged activity of the bishop of the city of Margus, who was supposed to have crossed the Danube to plunder gold from the graves of some Hun kings. Margus itself was soon targeted and the bishop began to worry that its citizens would prefer to hand him over to the enemy rather than all perish in his defence. Therefore he deserted to the Huns and promptly betrayed the city to them, arranging for some of his associates to open the gate and let in the enemy during the night.[13]

Other walled cities fell to direct attack. Fragments of a contemporary history mention the Huns employing battering rams, scaling ladders and mobile towers to mount formal assaults. They may have copied such technology from the Romans or, alternatively, now included many contingents that had once served with the Roman army. As important as such comparatively simple machines were the numbers of troops they deployed, the capacity to keep them in one place long enough to mount

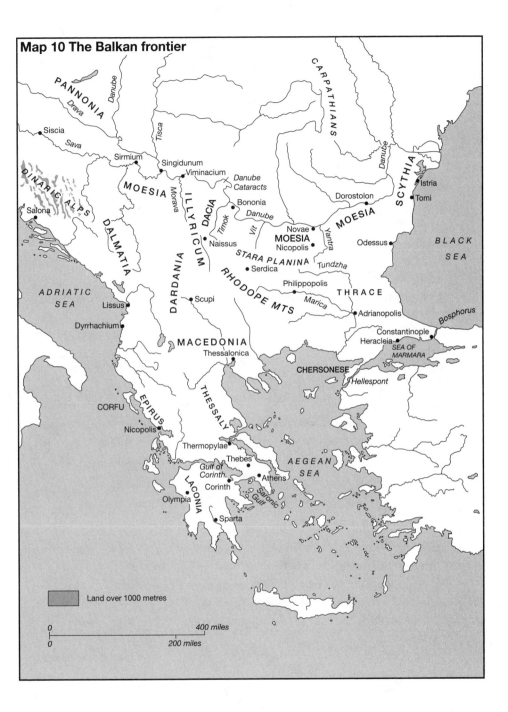

Map 10 The Balkan frontier

PANNONIA

Drava
Danube
Sava
Tisca
CARPATHIANS

Siscia
Sirmium
Singidunum
Viminacium

MOESIA
Morava
ILLYRICUM
DACIA
Timok
Danube Cataracts
Bononia
Danube
Vit
Novae
MOESIA
Nicopolis
Yantra
MOESIA

DINARIC ALPS
Salona
DALMATIA

DARDANIA
Naissus
STARA PLANINA
Serdica
Tundzha

RHODOPE MTS
Philippopolis
Marica
THRACE

Scythia
Danube
Istria
Tomi
Dorostolon
Odessus

BLACK SEA

ADRIATIC SEA
Lissus
Dyrrhachium
Scupi

MACEDONIA
Thessalonica

Adrianopolis
Bosphorus
Constantinople
Heracleia
SEA OF MARMARA

CHERSONESE
Hellespont

CORFU
EPIRUS
Nicopolis
THESSALY

Thermopylae
Thebes
Gulf of Corinth.
Corinth
Athens
Saronic Gulf
AEGEAN SEA

Olympia
LACONIA
Sparta

Land over 1000 metres

0   400 miles
0   200 miles

a siege and the willingness to take casualties in an assault. The Hunnic ability to take fortified places set them apart from other tribal armies. Singidunum (modern Belgrade) and the major city of Sirmium were amongst their victims and were left in ruins. In 443 Naissus, another major city and the birthplace of Constantine, was also burned to the ground. Several years later some travellers noted that a few people lived a basic existence in the remaining buildings. More ominously, they had to camp in the open away from the nearby river, because 'all the ground adjacent to the bank was full of the bones of men slain in war'. Even more people were carried off to lives of slavery. Of these, some would subsequently be ransomed, while a lucky few were able to win their freedom and even gain honours and status amongst their masters. Yet, for the overwhelming majority, slavery under the Huns was as brutal and unpleasant as in any other society.[14]

The Romans strengthened the army in the region by bringing troops from elsewhere and were eventually able to drive the raiders back. Payment of the subsidy ceased for some years. In 445 Attila killed his brother and became sole ruler of an enormous Hunnic empire. No other rival emerged during his lifetime. Much of central Europe seems to have been under his control, although we must be sceptical about claims that his rule stretched as far as the North Sea. Under Attila some other Huns enjoyed considerable power, as did a number of kings from other tribes. He took a larger number of wives, not only for pleasure but also no doubt to cement political alliances. We also know that at least one of Bleda's wives survived and was treated with considerable honour. Loyal followers were rewarded and prospered under Attila's rule. Gothic burials from within his empire are often accompanied by spectacular gold objects and in some cases reveal emulation of Hunnic customs, such as deliberately deformed skulls. Disloyalty was ruthlessly punished. A constant feature of treaties with the Romans was Attila's demand that anyone – and given that they were named he clearly meant prominent individuals – who fled from his rule into the empire must be returned to him. We know of two princes who were impaled as soon as they were handed over to Attila's men.[15]

After two years of poor harvests and outbreaks of plague, a succession of earthquakes spread devastation throughout the Eastern Empire in 447. Constantinople was badly affected, with substantial parts of its great walls collapsing. Attila scented an opportunity and launched a major attack. A Roman general – as so often in these years, he was a man of German extraction – chose to risk a battle and was badly beaten. Once again, cities fell to the invader and were sacked. At Constantinople, the Praetorian Prefect Flavius Constantinus enlisted the services of the two factions into which the enthusiastic circus-going population of the city was divided. The Blues and Greens were normally bitter rivals, but under his leadership they agreed to work together and in some sixty days had cleared up much of the damage in the city. Its walls were repaired long before the Huns were able to take advantage of its vulnerability. Elsewhere they spread devastation. One group even reached as far as Thermopylae in Greece, the famous pass where in 480 BC an army of Greeks led by the Spartans had made a sacrificial stand to delay Persian invaders.[16]

Once again, the Eastern Empire felt forced to buy peace from the Huns. Attila was now to be sent no less than 2,100 lb of gold each year, and in addition received an immediate payment of 6,000 more, which he calculated were the arrears due since the Romans had stopped paying the earlier subsidy. For the first time he was also granted land south of the Danube – a stretch of territory some 300 miles long, from Singidunum to Novae in Pannonia, and five days' journey in width, which could have meant anything from about 20 to 100 miles. This included all of the province of Dacia Ripensis – one of those named to conceal the abandonment of Dacia proper in the third century – and parts of three other provinces. Much of the area had suffered badly in the recent raids and it is unclear to what extent Attila actually occupied it. He may simply have wanted a depopulated strip of land to advertise his power and his ability to force concessions from the Romans. His main aim in his relationship with Rome was to profit from plunder during warfare and extortion in peacetime. Both reinforced his prestige and gave him the wealth to be generous to supporters.[17]

The sums paid to Attila were considerable, although not wholly out of proportion to the amounts paid to other foreign leaders in the past. In the long run the Eastern Empire could well afford the expense. In the short term it meant an increase in taxation, including levies on the senatorial class, something that this group always resented. Yet Attila was never a comfortable neighbour, and the fear remained that he would choose to renew his attacks if ever he decided that the Eastern Empire was vulnerable. He was constantly sending embassies to Constantinople. One reason was the Roman convention of plying the ambassadors with lavish gifts to demonstrate the friendliness of the Roman authorities and in the hope of winning the envoys' goodwill. Attila exploited this by routinely choosing different men to go to Constantinople. In this way he rewarded his nobles at the expense of the Romans. The frequent embassies and their insistence on negotiation over often trivial matters also helped to keep the emperor and his senior advisers off balance, reminding them that peace could not be taken for granted.[18]

A remarkable account survives written by Priscus, a member of a Roman delegation sent from Constantinople to visit Attila on his home ground in 448. It was tasked with returning some deserters or refugees from Attila's empire – although only five out of the seventeen individuals named by the Huns were taken back. After a lengthy journey, escorted much of the way by a group of Huns returning from an embassy to Constantinople, they finally reached Attila's camp. It was late and they attempted to pitch their tents on a hillock, but were promptly warned off by some riders: no one was permitted to camp on higher ground than the king. It was sometime before they managed to secure an audience. Messages were sent alternately telling them to leave, since they had failed to bring all the deserters and had nothing new to offer for negotiation, and then holding out the possibility of talks. On a more intimate scale, it was very similar to Attila's use of diplomacy in his relations with the Romans, keeping them off balance and threatening force, in the hope of winning concessions when the actual bargaining began. The Roman party went to a succession of important individuals, plying them with gifts and flattery to persuade them to use their influence to secure a hearing with Attila himself.[19]

They encountered a number of remarkable characters. One was the widow of Bleda, who was clearly still a woman of wealth and local authority. She rescued the Roman party after a storm had knocked down their tent, providing them with food, warmth and several attractive young women – a gesture of hospitality amongst the Huns. Priscus primly reports that they allowed the women to share their meal, but did not otherwise take advantage of the situation. They also tried to approach Onegesius, Attila's most important deputy, but, when they could not reach him, instead went to his brother Scottas. Another person to receive the Romans was one of Attila's wives, held in considerable honour because she had given him his first son. All the while the ambassadors trailed behind Attila, as he toured his lands, stopping at one village to take an additional wife. Eventually they came to one of his more permanent residences, where he lived in a grand wooden hall surrounded by an impressive ornamental palisade. Onegesius had a smaller compound, which also included a Roman-style stone bath house. This had been built by Roman captives taken in the attacks on the

Balkan provinces. There was no local source of stone in the Hungarian plain, so all of the materials had had to be carried hundreds of miles to the spot. The engineer who designed it had hoped to win his freedom by doing a good job, but instead found himself kept on permanently as the attendant.

He was not the only Roman to be found there. Priscus was surprised when a 'Hun' greeted him in Greek. The man proved to have been a merchant taken prisoner when a city on the Danube had been sacked. Over time, he had won the trust of his master, a Hunnic nobleman, fighting as one of his warriors against both the Romans and other peoples. He won his freedom, took a Hunnic wife and told Priscus that his new life was preferable to the old, complaining of the empire's heavy taxes, corrupt government and the unfairness and cost of the legal system. Priscus claims to have convinced the man of the superiority of the emperor's rule, but it is hard to be sure whether he really meant this or sympathised with the criticism he attributes to the man in his account. There was also a long tradition in classical literature of contrasting the primitive honesty of barbarians with the corruption of civilised societies. Apart from such survivors, there was also an embassy from the Western Empire. It was there to placate Attila over an issue of some gold treasure from Sirmium in Pannonia. The bishop there had handed this over to one of Attila's secretaries, a Roman named Constantius, supplied to him by the Western Empire. This man promised to ransom the clergyman if he was taken captive or, if the bishop died, to use the treasure to pay for the freedom of his flock. In the event, Constantius kept the gold for himself and later pawned it on a visit to Rome on Attila's behalf. However, he later lost royal trust and was executed, and Attila was now demanding not simply the gold but the banker with whom Constantius had made the deal. The Roman ambassadors were hoping to persuade him to accept just the equivalent sum in gold.[20]

It was a while before Priscus and his party got to see Attila and at first it was only from a distance. They saw the grand processions organised around him, and witnessed his courtesy to one of his hosts when he stopped in a village, remaining on horseback to take food and drink from them. Finally, they were invited to a feast in his hall. It was a ceremonial occasion, with guests seated according to their precedence. The Romans were placed on his left rather than his right – the latter was more honourable – and even there precedence was given to an important nobleman. There was a long succession of toasts, first by Attila, who saluted each of his guests from the most senior down. Then:

A luxurious meal, served on silver plate, had been made ready for us and the barbarian guests, but Attila ate nothing but meat on a wooden platter. In everything else too, he showed himself temperate; his cup was of wood, while his guests were given goblets of gold and silver. His dress too was simple, affecting only to be clean. The sword he carried at his side, the straps of his Hunnic shoes, and the bridle of his horse were not adorned, like those of the other Huns, with gold or anything else costly.[21]

The ceremony was perhaps not quite as elaborate as that of the imperial courts, but it was far more directly imbued with the spirit of Attila himself. He confirmed his favour to his leading men, as well as demonstrating his power by treating the Roman representatives with less honour. Much of the time he appeared indifferent to what was going on, but punctuated this with outbursts of rage and only showed clear affection to one of his sons. He ignored the performance of the dwarf jester Zerco, who had been a favourite of Bleda. (The presence of this man, who was originally from North Africa and spoke a bizarre mixture of Latin, Gothic and Hunnic, is doubtless the source of the persistent myth that Attila himself was of diminutive stature.)

Attila treated the Romans to a few displays of anger, with more conciliatory signals coming via others. This seems to have been his normal method, although in this case he had more than usual grounds for displeasure. Priscus was assistant to the head of the embassy, a man named Maximinus. The latter had already tried and failed to persuade Onegesius to defect to the Romans. They were themselves unaware that the authorities in Constantinople had an ulterior motive in sending the embassy in the first place. Accompanying them was another official named Vigilas (in older books this is often rendered Bigilas), who had the rare distinction of being able to speak the Hunnic language. When the Hunnic embassy was in Constantinople, this man had secretly negotiated with its leader Edeco. Vigilas persuaded him to assassinate Attila for the price of 50 lb of gold and promise of sanctuary within the empire. It is hard to know whether Edeco ever considered fulfilling his part of the deal, for on his return home he quickly informed the king of the plot. With Attila's blessing, he then continued to play along with Vigilas. In the end, they caught him red-handed bringing the gold to pay the assassin. He and his son were taken prisoner and more money was extorted from the Roman authorities before they were released.[22]

Assassination plots were obviously not conducive to successful dip-lomacy, and Maximinus and Priscus unsurprisingly achieved very little. Yet Attila was moderate in his response, using his discovery of the plot to give him the advantage over the Romans in subsequent negotiations. Even at its highest, the subsidy and other sums paid to him were comfortably affordable to the Constantinople government. Yet they were still an indication of its impotence in dealing with the Huns militarily. At best, when there were no other major military commitments else-where, they could hope to hold them in check. There was no prospect of attacking and permanently defeating Attila, hence the willingness to try assassination instead. Attila was too feared by those closest to him for this to be viable. For the moment the Eastern Empire had no choice but to live with him and continue to pay the subsidies. Fortunately for it, Attila was beginning to look further afield, transferring his attentions to the Western Empire.[23]

The Last Roman

Flavius Aetius was born into one of those military families from the Balkan provinces that had filled the higher ranks of the army and provided a good number of the emperors in the third and fourth centuries. Like many of those emperors, he spent his career almost permanently at war, regularly leading troops on campaign against foreign and Roman opponents. For some twenty years he was by far the most powerful man in the Western Empire. Consul three times and Master of All Soldiers, he was named patrician in 435 and yet never made any attempt to become emperor himself. The civil wars he fought were struggles over who would dominate the imperial court. There were other ways in which his life showed just how different conditions were in the fifth century. Twice during his youth he was sent as a hostage to foreign leaders, first to Alaric and subsequently to a Hunnic leader. In earlier centuries the Romans had often taken hostages, who were given a properly Roman education in the hope that this would also create sympathy. The Romans did not themselves give hostages to others. By the fifth century the balance of power had shifted profoundly.

Aetius received a thoroughly Roman education, supplemented by the experience of living amongst foreign peoples. He became a highly proficient horseman and archer following his years with the Huns. Even more importantly, he gained an understanding of them and formed associations that would be of great use to him during his life. Following the death of Honorius, he was one of the most prominent supporters of the usurper John and went to raise a force of Huns as auxiliaries – perhaps better, as mercenaries – from the leaders he knew. Aetius and these warriors arrived in Italy too late to take part in the campaign and found John executed and Valentinian III established as emperor by an eastern army. His Huns remained loyal and, in return for not reigniting the war and instead pledging himself to the new emperor, Aetius was promoted to Master of Soldiers in Gaul. At least some of the Huns seem to have remained with him and fought in his subsequent campaigns against the Franks west of the Rhine and the Goths established within Gaul itself.[24]

There were two other commanders vying for supremacy in the Western Empire during these years. Galla Placidia tried to play them off against each other, hoping to prevent any of the three from becoming too powerful and so impossible to control. Eventually in 427 Felix, the senior Master of Soldiers in command of the imperial army in Italy, sent troops to attack his colleague Boniface, who commanded in Africa. This force was defeated and by 430 Aetius had supplanted Felix in his post and engineered his execution. Two years later Boniface led his army into Italy to fight for supremacy. He won the ensuing battle, but suffered a mortal wound in the process. Aetius fled, eventually going to the Huns and raising a new force of these warriors. In 433 he returned and once again assumed the supreme military command – Boniface's successor had fled to Constantinople without fighting. Galla Placidia's hopes were dashed; until his death some two decades later, Aetius would not face a serious rival.[25]

As usual, the Roman preoccupation with in-fighting had seriously compromised the empire's ability to deal with other military problems. The Goths settled in Aquitania – now increasingly identified as the Visigoths or 'West Goths', to distinguish them from the 'East Goths' who still lived on the Danube – and on several occasions launched attacks on neighbouring parts of the Roman provinces. This seems to have been largely opportunism, although it is possible that some of the friction was provoked by the Roman authorities. Other tribal groups, such as the Franks and Burgundians, expanded the territory they controlled nearer to the frontiers. Raids from outside the empire also increased. In Spain the Suevi became more aggressive, taking the provincial capital at Merida and attacking Seville. From 429 onwards they were the single most powerful group in the Iberian Peninsula, for in that year the Vandals and surviving Alans migrated to North Africa. A later source claims that their leader, King Geiseric, was followed by some 80,000 people – women, children and the elderly, as well as warriors. The figure is not impossible, although as always we should note that we have no idea whether or not it is accurate. It may well be inflated. Yet even transporting a group far smaller than this would have required a high degree of organisation. Probably the migrants were ferried across the Straits of Gibraltar over the course of several weeks.[26]

At first the Vandals do not seem to have met serious opposition. There were units of *comitatenses* in Africa, as well as *limitanei*, but they had to protect a huge area. It is more than probable that, like most other Roman armies by this time, some of the units existed only on paper or were pale shadows of their theoretical strength and efficiency. Add in the preoccupation with the struggle between Boniface and the other army commanders and it is less difficult to explain the repeated successes of the Vandals. The rumours of collusion and claims that Boniface invited the Vandals to cross may be no more than propaganda to blacken his reputation. Although the use of barbarian groups as allies was common, the Vandals did not in the event ever aid him. Over the next years Geiseric and his men moved gradually eastwards. The major city of Hippo Regius was captured and sacked in 431 – its famous bishop St Augustine had died more than a year before, but his last letters reflect the fear caused by the invaders. By this time the Vandals were Christian, but like the Goths they followed a distinctly Arian interpretation of the faith, making them heretics in the eyes of the Church.[27]

Whether or not Boniface ever colluded with the Vandals, in the end he fought against them and was badly beaten. He retreated and soon decided to take his army across to Italy and instead try his fortune there. By 435 Aetius was left unchallenged by any rival commanders, but was too preoccupied with problems in Gaul to use force against Geiseric. The Vandals were granted a substantial part of Numidia by a formal treaty, but the peace proved brief. In 439 Geiseric took Carthage, one of the greatest cities in the world. Shiploads of Vandal raiders soon became a menace to merchantmen and coastal communities. In 440 Geiseric led a major attack on Sicily. North Africa remained one of the wealthiest regions of the Western Empire, supplying a substantial part of the food consumed in Italy, as well as tax revenue and perhaps also some manpower for the army. Its loss was probably the single most serious blow suffered by the government of Valentinian III.

In 441 a major expeditionary force of soldiers was concentrated in Sicily in preparation for an invasion of North Africa. Theodosius II sent substantial numbers of troops from the eastern army as well as warships to support his western colleague. Yet the invasion was never launched. Negotiations began and there was soon pressure for the eastern forces to return and bolster the Balkan frontier against the attacks of the Huns. In 442 a treaty granted the Vandals control of most of the more prosperous regions of North Africa. Around this time Valentinian's daughter Eudocia was betrothed to Geiseric's son Huneric. The latter was already married to a daughter of the Visigothic king. Geiseric swiftly terminated this by accusing the young woman of attempting to murder him. She was mutilated – her ears and nose cut off – and sent back to her father. The Visigoths were too far away for their enmity to matter and the prospect of the alliance with the imperial family was far more tempting to the Vandal king. Eudocia was still a child and for the moment remained in Italy.[28]

Aetius dominated the Western Empire for two decades. He went on campaign in virtually all of these years, fighting against, amongst others, the Visigoths, Alamanni, Franks, Burgundians and Seuvi, as well as the rebels known as Bagaudae who had appeared in north-western Gaul. Just like Stilicho and Constantius before him, court poets celebrated his bravery, skill and sweeping victories in the grandest of styles. His cuirass was 'not so much protective armour as his everyday clothes'. Almost always actively campaigning, Aetius used even the rare breaks from fighting to prepare for future wars. Yet the very frequency of operations reveals that his successes were limited and almost never decisive. He was also careful to prevent any potential rival from controlling troops and winning victories. There was effectively only one army and it was under the direct command of Aetius. If he did not deal with a problem, then it was unlikely that it would be dealt with at all.

The loss of much of Africa, as well as the continued occupation of parts of Gaul by the Visigoths and Spain by the Seuvi, produced a massive drop in the revenue and resources available to Valentinian's government. Inevitably, Aetius had substantially fewer troops at his disposal than Stilicho or Constantius. Some of this may also have been deliberate, as the emperor and senior figures at court tried to impose some limit on their general by restricting the resources available to him. A great deal of Aetius' success was due to his Hunnic allies, and it was largely through their efforts that the Burgundian kingdom was shattered in 436–437. The Burgundians' disastrous defeat later became the basis for the epic tale of the *Nibelungen*, more familiar to us today through Wagner's operatic cycle, although obviously this is far removed from the real events. It was the most decisive victory of Aetius' career and due almost entirely to his allies. The Huns also operated with success against the Bagaudae and the Visigoths, until they were badly beaten outside Arelate (modern Arles) in 439.[29]

It is unclear how well Aetius and Attila knew each other. There seems to have been frequent diplomatic contact between the Western Empire and the Huns, and we know that Aetius supplied Attila with men to serve as his secretaries when writing in Latin. This need not suggest anything more than the desire to placate a powerful leader. By 450 Attila seems already to have been considering an attack on the Western Empire. Territorial expansion was never his primary aim in warfare and the Balkan provinces had already been thoroughly plundered during previous Hun attacks. Attila's power rested ultimately on his ability to reward his supporters lavishly. For this he needed to fight successful wars, to both gain plunder and maintain the fear that prompted payments of tribute. He was good at finding pretexts for attacks in small disputes and at first, he talked of fighting the Visigoths on behalf of Valentinian III. There were also rumours of a connection with Geiseric. In the end, he found an excuse from an extremely unlikely source.

Honoria was the sister of Valentinian III and daughter of Galla Placidia. As yet unmarried – no doubt to prevent any possible rival gaining a connection with the imperial family – she had an affair with her estate manager and became pregnant. The lover was executed and Honoria married off to a senator who was politically trustworthy, probably elderly and certainly dull. Determined to escape from this condition, she somehow managed to send a letter and her ring to Attila, pleading for his aid. The Hunnic king happily accepted this as an offer of marriage and laid claim to half of the Western Empire. Although this story sounds like a romantic invention, it appears quite early in our sources and may well be true. Honoria's mother had married the Goth Athaulf, admittedly while she was a captive and so may not have had much freedom to refuse. More recently, Honoria's niece, the emperor's daughter Eudocia, was promised as bride to a Vandal. Marriage to the powerful king of the Huns was not quite so unimaginable as it would have been in the past, even if it was still not up to the women of the imperial family to choose their own husbands.[30]

The appeal from Honoria provided Attila with a convenient pretext and useful negotiating tool, but there is no good indication that his war was planned as anything other than a massive plundering raid. In 451 he led his army across the Rhine near modern Coblenz – after a considerable journey if scholars are correct to assume that it set out from Pannonia earlier in the same year – and quickly overran most of the neighbouring cities. Trier, so often used as an imperial capital in the late third and fourth centuries, was one of the cities sacked. The Hunnic army – in reality, a large majority of the troops were allies, including a strong contingent of Goths – pushed on, but seems to have lost momentum when it failed to capture Orleans. By this time Aetius had mustered an army to meet it. This also consisted mainly of allied troops fighting under their own leaders. There were Franks, Burgundians, Alans and Saxons, as well as a strong force of Goths from Aquitania led by their King Theodoric. A major battle – something rare for this period – was fought somewhere in the region known as the Catalaunian Plains (Campus Mauriacus). Attila certainly failed to win this encounter, and may have suffered a clear reverse. King Theodoric was amongst the fallen and a later Visigothic source claims that Attila was reduced to despair after the battle. He is supposed to have prepared a funeral pyre for himself, using the saddles of his men, and only at the last minute decided against suicide. However, Aetius' army swiftly broke up as the allied contingents went home. This was probably as much to do with the problems of supplying the concentrated force, although our sources allege that he deliberately persuaded his allies to leave since he did not want them to destroy the Huns. The threat of Attila was the best way of keeping the Visigoths and others docile.[31]

The Huns had been checked, but Attila had not suffered catastrophic losses to his army. In 452 he attacked again, surprising Aetius by striking not at Gaul but at northern Italy. Aquileia, the old city on the border with Illyricum, was besieged and captured. Other cities, including Milan, were plundered, although the imperial capital at Ravenna was once again protected by its surrounding marshes. For a while Attila headed south, before retreating and returning to his own lands. Legends quickly grew up attributing this withdrawal to a meeting with the pope. Rather more probably it was due to supply shortages and a disturbing outbreak of plague within his army. Attila and his men had already acquired considerable quantities of plunder and many of the warriors were probably keen to carry this back to their homes before the winter.

The western Romans had not defeated Attila, but neither had he forced them to offer him tribute and other concessions. Even a failure to win an outright victory could be damaging to a war leader whose power rested on continuous success. While he was away the Eastern Empire had become more hostile. Theodosius II had died in 450 without an heir and been replaced by a fifty-eight-year-old army officer named Marcian. Pulcheria, herself well into middle age, renounced her vow of chastity and married the new emperor to make him legitimately a member of the Theodosian family. Marcian was fortunate that Attila was already committed to a western campaign and was unable to retaliate when he stopped paying tribute to the Huns. Troops were also sent to aid Aetius in 452. At the same time the eastern army was launching minor offensive operations against Attila's kingdom, exploiting the fact that his main forces and attention were elsewhere. It provided another reason for the Huns to withdraw from Italy.[32]

Attila would doubtless have resumed the war in the next year. However, early in 453 he took yet another wife and celebrated the occasion by prodigious drinking, something that was common at his court. The next morning he was found dead next to his hysterical bride. He had passed out and then choked to death from internal bleeding. Much later romantic stories would be invented of his wife murdering him to exact revenge for wrongs done to her family. Attila had not marked out a successor and his numerous sons soon began to fight each other for power. At the same time, many of the allied and subject peoples made bids for power. In just a few years the Hunnic Empire collapsed.[33]

Valentinian III's mother Galla Placidia had died in 450. His sister Honoria may not have survived their mother by very long and never again appears in our sources. The emperor was only in his early thirties, but never became his own man. Influence at court shifted and there were new opportunities for ambitious men. At the same time, Aetius' position had become weaker. In recent years, even before the attack of Attila, he had been less able to recruit Huns to fight for him. While Attila was alive, Valentinian clearly needed his most powerful general to oppose the enemy invasions. Now that the Hun was dead, Aetius seemed less necessary. The general understood his new vulnerability and hoped to secure his position by arranging a marriage between his son and Valentinian's daughter Placidia. The emperor continued to resent Aetius and was encouraged to act by a wily senator named Petronius Maximus. In September 454 the general came to the palace at Ravenna for a meeting. During the discussion Valentinian and his eunuch chamberlain suddenly attacked Aetius with swords and hacked him to death. One of the emperor's advisers told him that he had cut off his right hand with his left. Yet the instigator Petronius was disappointed with the scale of his emperor's gratitude.

Recruiting two members of Aetius' bodyguard, he arranged for them to murder Valentinian III on 16 March 455. Petronius Maximus then immediately declared himself emperor.[34]

18

Sunset on an Outpost of Empire

'The barbarians over the Rhine ... reduced the inhabitants of Britain and some of the Gallic peoples to such straits that they revolted from the Roman empire, no longer submitted to Roman law, and reverted to their native customs. The Britons, therefore, armed themselves and ran many risks to ensure their own safety and free their cities from the attacking barbarians.' – *Zosimus, late fifth century.*[1]

'However, the Romans never succeeded in recovering Britain, but it remained from that time on under tyrants.' – *Procopius, mid late sixth century.*[2]

Sometime after 446 Aetius was said to have received an appeal for aid from the Britons who were under attack from the Picts, Scots and other barbarians. They complained that 'the barbarians push us back into the sea, the sea pushes us back into the barbarians; between these two kinds of death we are either drowned or slaughtered'. There had not been Roman governors in Britain for a generation, but the island was still clearly considered part of the empire in a general sense. Leading Britons obviously felt the same way, hence their appeal to the military commander of the west. In the event, Aetius had other priorities and sent no aid. Left to their own devices the British 'councillors' agreed with a local warlord or king – literally a 'proud tyrant' – to hire Saxon mercenaries. These beat back the northern barbarians, but then turned against their employers, sacking towns and forcing many to flee across the sea. Eventually, a nobleman named Ambrosius Aurelianus, described as the 'last of the Roman race', emerged as leader of the survivors. The Britons won some victories, culminating in a great triumph at Badon Hill.[3]

The story is first told by the British cleric Gildas sometime in the sixth century. He provides no dates, although the impression is that this account covered a considerable period – decades at the very least. He does mention that the initial appeal was to a man who was three times consul, and this was only true of Aetius from 446–454. Actually,

Gildas calls him Agitio, but a later version of the story was surely right to correct this to Aetius. Yet the mistake does raise the question of just how much Gildas actually knew of events a century or more before his lifetime. He was also not writing a history and this passage comes from the introduction to a bitter attack on the 'tyrants' and priests of his own day. Literary sources for fifth-century Britain are very sparse and were almost all written long after the events they describe. Some facts may be accurate, others confused and perhaps merged with myth, or deliberately distorted by later propaganda. Separating these strands is certainly not easy, and a few scholars would say that it was altogether impossible.[4]

Yet there is nothing inherently implausible about Gildas' account. The Saxons – a term that was used at the time to embrace a range of different groups including the Angles, Jutes and Frisians – did end up dominating much of what would become England by the late sixth century. Other sources suggest that there was serious conflict with them in the middle years of the fifth century. That some Saxons were hired to fight against other 'barbarians' and later came into conflict with their employers was a familiar enough tale in the Roman world at this period. We also know that significant numbers of Britons fled to north-western Gaul, so that in time Armorica became known as Brittany.[5]

Dates are rare in the sources, and often both they and some of the accompanying details must be suspect. There is archaeological evidence for the period, but even by normal standards this presents considerable problems of interpretation. As a result, radically different accounts of life and politics in fifth-century Britain continue to be produced. On the fringes of this there is the constant flow of material about Arthur, much of it aimed at the more popular end of the market and extending into fiction and film. This varies from quite serious history to highly fanciful studies. Gildas never mentions Arthur and it is a later source that associates him with the victory at Badon Hill. It is better to begin trying to understand the Britain of this era before any attempt to describe an 'historical' Arthur. Recently, there has been much more emphasis by academics on placing events in Britain within the wider context of the history of the Western Empire. This has proved fruitful, although if anything has added to the variety of interpretations of the same evidence. Here the emphasis will be the other way around, looking at what the experience in Britain tells us about the last years of the Western Empire.[6]

Britannia

Britain was one of the last major additions to the Roman Empire. Julius Caesar had landed in the south-east in 55 BC and returned with a larger force in the following year. There was no permanent occupation. The expeditions were huge propaganda successes, but achieved little in practical terms and did not result in the creation of a province. Trade with Britain increased massively in the following decades and there was some diplomatic contact. A string of royal refugees fleeing the power struggles within and between the tribes of south-eastern Britain arrived at the imperial court seeking support. Augustus decided against intervening, feeling that the cost of occupation would be greater than any likely profit.

In 43, the emperor Claudius was desperate for military glory to cement his tenuous hold on power. Therefore he ordered a massive expedition to invade Britain and even travelled to the island himself. The tribes of the south-east were quickly overcome or surrendered. Progress elsewhere was slower, and it is not at all clear just how much of Britain the Romans planned to conquer. In 60 they came close to losing the territory they did control. Queen Boudica of the Iceni rebelled and was joined by many other previously pro-Roman tribes. The three largest cities of the province – Londinium (London), Camulodunum (Colchester) and Verulamium (St Albans) – were all sacked. Finally a decisive battle, followed by ruthless punitive action, broke the back of the rebellion and it was never repeated. Over the next decades more conquests were made in the west and north. What would become Wales and the north of England were occupied only after heavy fighting. In 84 a Roman army won a victory somewhere in Scotland, while elements of the fleet circumnavigated Britain and proved that it was an island.[7]

Claudius sent four legions and a strong force of auxiliaries to invade Britain. A generation later the garrison was reduced to three legions, although the number of auxiliaries seems to have increased. One estimate of the garrison of Britain in the middle of the second century places this as high as 50,000 men, although this rather assumes that all units attested in the province were there simultaneously. Even if the actual garrison was smaller, it was certainly a substantial part of the entire Roman army – somewhere between one-tenth and one-eighth. Some troops were stationed in the west, especially in Wales, but the bulk of the provincial garrison was deployed to the north. It was also in the north that a series of frontier defences were created, before the main line settled permanently on Hadrian's Wall. All of this was immensely costly. It was also dangerous for such a large army to be given to a single governor, and it was no coincidence that one of the challengers for the throne in 193 was the legate of Britain. Septimius Severus' campaigns against the Caledonians may have permitted a substantial reduction in troop numbers. Barrack blocks built in the forts of Hadrian's Wall in the following years all appear to have been about half the size of those in earlier periods. It is quite likely that centuries in these units were halved in size from eighty to forty men, although they still remained under the command of a centurion. If this occurred more generally, then the size of the army in Britain may have been reduced by as much as 50 per cent. The provincial command was also divided.[8]

Even if the garrison in the third century was substantially smaller than in earlier periods, it was still large and costly. Britain's mineral resources were exploited from very soon after the conquest. The island also produced a substantial surplus of grain, and a large part of this was either from imperial estates or taken by the state as tax, so that British wheat helped to feed the troops stationed in the Rhineland. Even so, it is doubtful that the profits of occupying Britain ever covered the expense of maintaining government and garrison there. Over time just under thirty cities were created. Most were local capitals and administrative centres for groups based around the old tribes. Some of the cities, notably London, Cirencester, Silchester and St Albans (Verulamium) were large and in due course gained basilicas, theatres, amphitheatres and bath houses. No circus with chariot racing was known in Britain, until one was discovered in 2004 at St Albans. In the fourth century all major cities almost certainly did build large churches – a basilica-type building that may well be a cathedral has been identified in London. Other capitals were more modest and it is fair to say that none acquired the splendour of so many cities in other provinces, especially those nearer the Mediterranean. In many areas there were no cities and only what are known as 'small towns' by archaeologists. Usually lying on the main roads, these communities acted as market towns and housed various local industries.[9]

Many British aristocrats sided with the Romans from the beginning and did very well out of the conquest. The grand villa or palace complex at Fishbourne was built in the first century, most probably as a residence for the client ruler Tiberius Claudius Togidubnus, who was described as a 'great king'. It was normal Roman practice to win over the leaders of conquered peoples, and prominent British families soon gained citizenship and a Latin education. However, it does seem to have taken the

British nobility a very long time to break into the higher levels of imperial service. Many built villas and grand town houses, but the ethos of civic life so typical of other provinces was less developed in Britain and it seems to have been rarer for them to spend money on major endowments for their communities. Britain has produced markedly fewer inscriptions than most other sizeable provinces, and a large part of those that do survive are military. In many areas the focus of life remained essentially rural. Much of the population continued to live on farmsteads and in small villages. Some changed to more Roman styles of buildings, but others continued to live in the traditional – and highly functional – roundhouses familiar from the Iron Age.[10]

Geographically, Britain was on the very margins of the empire – indeed, of the world as far as Greeks and Romans were concerned. There was contact with Ireland, but the Roman official line was that it would not be worth the expense of conquest and occupation. Britain required a large garrison and never quite developed as much or in the same way as some of the provinces nearer the heart of the empire. It might therefore be tempting to see its conquest as a failure, a costly burden imposed on the empire by the vanity and urgent need for glory of Claudius. This would be a mistake. Not all provinces developed identically, and Britain remained under Roman rule for three and a half centuries during which time life there changed profoundly. If there was a significant drop in troop numbers in the third century, then this may have brought the province closer to making a profit for the empire. If it was not the wealthiest province in the empire, there was still considerable prosperity for a wide section of the population. The recent claim that 'for every winner under Roman rule, there were a hundred losers' is very hard to substantiate, and the same author himself notes that 'it does not follow that life would have been any better without Rome.' It does seem true that the gap between richest and poorest widened. Then as now the fact that some of the population became substantially wealthier does not automatically mean that the lifestyle of the remainder declined or that they became poorer in real terms. The sheer quantity of finds on virtually every British site from the Roman period compared to Iron Age or post-Roman occupation makes it clear that many objects were far more readily available to the general population.[11]

Willingly or not, the population of Roman Britain accepted Roman rule. There was some armed resistance, particularly in northern Britain, but nothing to unite the communities elsewhere in opposition to imperial government. Britain seems to have been spared the worst of the disruptions of the third century, if only because it was physically harder for large armies to cross the seas to reach it. Even if numbers were less than at their height in the second century, there were still significant forces stationed on the island. This, and the tendency for emperors to see Britain's problems as distant and rarely urgent, made it a fertile ground for usurpers. Constantine the Great was by far the most successful, but all of the others also had ambitions beyond simply controlling Britain itself and all took troops across the Channel. This weakened the provincial garrison, but did mean that, with the exception of the suppression of Allectus, all of the campaigns in the resulting civil wars were fought outside Britain.

The End

By the end of the fourth century Britain formed a diocese under a *vicarius* based in London and responsible to the praetorian prefect. The diocese was subdivided into either four or five provinces – the existence of a fifth is uncertain. Valentinian I formed a province named Valentia after himself, but it is unclear whether this involved the creation of a new province or the renaming of an existing one. The *Notitia Dignitatum* lists three military commands in Britain. The *Comes Britanniae* commanded a force of *comitatenses* consisting of three infantry and six cavalry units. The proportion of foot to mounted regiments is unusual, even if the former were normally larger than the latter. It suggests a force tailored to chase small bands of raiders rather than fight massed battles. This small field force is usually seen as a late creation, perhaps by Stilicho, given recorded cases of despatching field army units from Gaul to deal with problems in Britain during the fourth century. The *Dux Britanniarum* commanded units of the *limitanei*, mostly stationed in the north and including the garrisons of some named forts on Hadrian's Wall. Finally, there was the 'Count of the Saxon Shore' (*Comes Litoris Saxonici per Britannias*) controlling *limitanei* based around the east and south coasts from Brancaster, near the Wash, to Portchester, not far from modern Portsmouth. One survey estimated the maximum total strength of these troops as 20,000, but guessed that it was actually lower at nearer 12,000. As always, the real number of effectives at any one time is likely to have been substantially less than the army's paper strength.[12]

The garrison of Britain created three usurpers in 406–407. There were clearly still enough troops for the last of these, Constantine III, to cross into Gaul and gain control of a large part of the Western Empire. He must have taken some, perhaps most, of the British army with him and it is unlikely that any of these troops returned. This can only have weakened the defences of Britain, just like previous, ultimately unsuccessful usurpations. The garrison was weaker, but opinion is divided over precisely what threats it faced. No one would dispute that there were enemies to the north. The Picts – the name was most likely derived from 'picti' or 'painted men' because it was believed that they commonly wore tattoos – seem to have emerged when the old Caledonian tribes became a little more united. To their west were the Scotti, who are likely to have migrated from Ireland and would eventually give their name to Scotland. Both peoples had launched serious raids into the British provinces during the fourth century. Many of the attacks came by sea along the coast, and there seems also to have been some forays made by the tribes still living in Ireland. The sixteen-year-old St Patrick was taken as a slave by just such a group of raiders, although it is unclear whether this took place before or after the end of direct Roman rule.[13]

The name 'Saxon Shore' is only attested in the *Notitia Dignitatum*. Ammianus mentions the Saxons launching raids against Britain in 367, as part of a simultaneous onslaught by the Picts, Scots and also the Franks. Otherwise there is little explicit evidence for Saxon raiding on the coast of Britain, unlike frequent mention of their attacks on the northern coast of Gaul. This may simply be because the sources are much better for Gaul and extremely sparse for Britain. A literal reading of the accounts of Carausius' operations against pirates in the English Channel would suggest only attacks on Gaul, although raids on the British coast are usually assumed. If the Saxon Shore was named after the enemy it was supposed to defend against, then this would make it unique in Roman history. On the other hand, the suggestion that it was named because large numbers of allied Saxon troops were stationed or settled there is even less convincing and unsupported by any evidence.[14]

Some have questioned the ability of raiders from what is now northern Germany and Denmark to reach Britain. Far less is known about the sea-going vessels of the tribes in this period than the ships of the Viking age. The few to survive archaeologically may only have been intended for inland waterways. None have sails and it has been claimed that their keels were too small to have supported a strong enough mast to mount one. It would have been possible for a group of warriors to row to Britain and return with any spoils, but it would certainly have been difficult. More probably, we have simply not yet discovered an example of a sailing ship intended for longer voyages. A carving of a boat with a sail has been

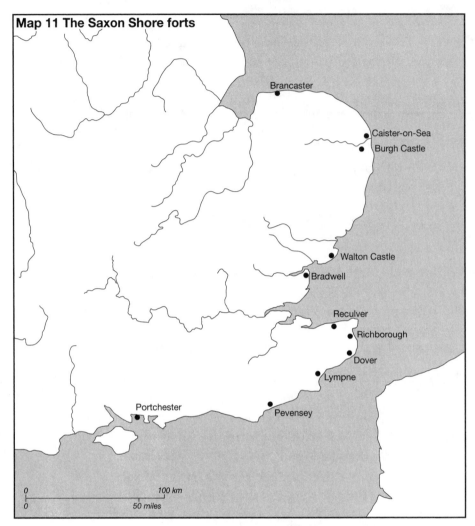

Map 11 The Saxon Shore forts

Brancaster

Caister-on-Sea
Burgh Castle

Walton Castle
Bradwell

Reculver
Richborough
Dover
Lympne

Portchester
Pevensey

0   100 km

0   50 miles

found in Denmark and it does seem inherently unlikely that the peoples of the area never adopted this technology. It is harder to say how well a shallow-keeled boat would perform under sail, but it is important to remember that fighting at sea was always rare. These vessels were only ever meant to deliver and carry off a group of warriors.[15]

It is doubtful that any such vessel was especially large, and later – admittedly somewhat questionable – sources tend to talk of between one and four boats in any force. A raiding group numbering hundreds of warriors was probably exceptionally large and most parties would have been smaller. Normally they would only strike at targets near the coast or reached along an easily navigable river. Other than in their means of transport these attacks were essentially the same as other barbarian raids. The late fourth-century military writer Vegetius mentioned that the English Channel was patrolled by small warships, whose sails, rigging and even the sailors' uniforms were coloured to blend in with the sea. Although this may well have made them harder to see at a distance, it can rarely have been possible to intercept the raiders on their way in. They were more likely to be caught before or after they landed, and most of all as they retreated. Again, the pattern was much like raiding on land and, in just the same way, successful expeditions would encourage more attacks. Maritime raiding does seem to have been fairly common throughout the Roman period. It may well have occurred before this period and would certainly persist for many centuries after the Western Empire had gone, most famously in the Viking Age.[16]

The Saxon Shore forts varied in design. They were probably built over a long period and not as a single planned system. Other third-century forts, such as the one on the Taff at Cardiff, which were not included in the later command, seem to share many common features. All were strongly fortified and situated on a navigable river, usually at its mouth. Little is known of their internal arrangements. The purpose of the Saxon Shore forts has been as hotly disputed as their name. One suggestion has been to see their role as primarily logistic. This assumes that grain from imperial estates or gathered as tax was transported along the rivers to be massed in a supply dump within the Saxon Shore fort. It could then be transported by the Roman navy to the Rhineland or wherever else it was required. There is no evidence at all to support this, and it has largely been based on the mistaken assumption that there was no significant Saxon raiding.[17]

The Saxon Shore forts could not have prevented every attack, but did restrict access to the major rivers. This made it harder for raiders to reach deep into the countryside. We do not know whether by the start of the fifth century the Romans still maintained naval squadrons in Britain as they had done in earlier years. None are mentioned in the *Notitia Dignitatum*. Seaborne patrols would have been useful in making raiders more wary and might on occasions have caught them on shore or returning home. It is impossible to know when Vegetius' camouflaged patrol boats ceased to operate. As a general rule naval forces were and are more expensive to operate than troops on land and so are especially vulnerable to shortages of funds. The garrisons of the forts would have been capable of patrolling the land around their bases. Like anywhere else, there were not enough troops to keep the entire frontier perfectly secure. The best the Romans could hope for was to make it dangerous for raiders to operate, intercepting enough groups to prevent the coast of Britain becoming seen as an easy target. Their presence may have done a little to make the local population feel that they were protected, and the larger forts such as Porchester may also have served as places of refuge.

All of Britain's cities were strongly walled by the fourth century. Opinion is divided whether they were in decline by this period. There are cases of public buildings such as basilicas and theatres falling into ruin. Significant numbers of large town houses were also abandoned. Only a minority of communities seem to have had a working public bath house by 400. Yet cities were clearly not abandoned. There was still some building, although more often in timber than stone, and several former public buildings were turned into workshops or factories. More problematic is what is known by archaeologists as 'dark earth', a thick layer of dark grey soil often containing plant remains, animal bones and charcoal, which is found on top of earlier Roman buildings on many urban sites. Although some have seen this as traces of less well-constructed timber structures, more probably it represents the abandonment of these parts of a city for building. It may have been cultivated or perhaps no more than a convenient dumping ground. Perhaps the population of many cities and of the small towns declined. Certainly, they were less grand than they had once been, but this in itself does not mean that they ceased to function altogether.[18]

The fourth century saw the construction of many of the largest and most luxurious villas ever built in Roman Britain. It is possible that some aristocratic families chose in these years to spend more time on their estates than in their town houses, but equally, completely different factors may have caused this phenomenon. By the end of the century very few new villas were being built on such a scale and some existing ones fell into disuse. As with the decay of major buildings in the towns, this did not in itself mean that the lands were abandoned. The estate may have continued to function as a unit based around a rather humbler dwelling and we really cannot say very much at all about the state of the rural economy. There is also little direct archaeological evidence for Christianity in Roman Britain. Pagan temples did continue in use especially in the rural areas, but suggestions of a pagan revival in the countryside are unconvincing. A better case can be made for the majority of the urban and rural population being at least nominally Christian by the start of the fifth century.[19]

Whatever the gradual changes in the fortunes of towns, villages and country estates, the end of formal Roman rule in Britain was both abrupt and unexpected. Constantine III flourished for four years before finally suffering defeat. Many of the prominent men in Britain had already lost enthusiasm for his rule. As far as we can tell he had shown no real interest in Britain or its problems once he crossed to the Continent. His resources were stretched very thin and the success he enjoyed was really just a reflection of the weakness of central government. Around 407–408 some British leaders rebelled and expelled Constantine's officials. Zosimus tells us that in about 410 the rebels appealed to Emperor Honorius, who replied from Ravenna 'urging them to fend for themselves'. Doubt has been raised about this passage and some have suggested that a copyist's error has changed Bruttium in Italy to Britain. This is not especially convincing and raises problems of its own. In the end, it probably does not matter whether or not Honorius actually did instruct the leaders in Britain in this way. Direct Roman rule certainly ended at about this time. The government at Ravenna was simply incapable of reasserting rule in such a distant province. Even when Constantine was finally defeated there were too many other problems to deal with and its resources were inadequate.[20]

After the End

Roman rule in Britain was ended by a rebellion against Constantine III. As far as we can tell it was not a revolt against Rome or the empire itself. For at least the next century the educated inhabitants of the island still seem to have referred to themselves freely as Romans or Britons. In a way it was unusual that the rebels did not proclaim a new emperor. By this time the army left in Britain must have been small, probably no more than skeleton units of *limitanei* dotted around the frontier outposts. They were neither numerous nor united enough to impose a single ruler, whether as emperor or representative of Honorius' government. No one had the power or money to hold the diocese or even the individual provinces together. New coinage stopped reaching Britain in significant quantities after 402. None of the communities or leaders to emerge in the fifth century minted their own currency. This lack of new coinage makes it much harder to date sites from this period. It does not mean that the economy entirely ceased to be monetary, and money may still have been used for some exchanges for a considerable time. It is an indication, however, that there were no more professional, salaried soldiers. The imperial taxation system also ceased, and gold or grain or other levies no longer had to be gathered and transported on such a vast scale.[21]

Britain broke up into many separate communities. It was not simply a reversion to the old tribes pre-dating Roman rule. Too much time had passed for these to have great meaning and, instead, the administrative states created by the Romans had more significance. Even so, the powers that would emerge did not follow these boundaries very precisely. Instead, new states or kingdoms were created. Most, if not all, were ruled by kings – or tyrants, as Gildas and other sources tend to dub them. They may not have been the only authorities, and some civic leaders seem to have continued to exist, but such warlords were undoubtedly stronger than any other powers to emerge. Central imperial power had gone and in its place anyone capable of controlling enough force, influence and wealth was able to carve out a kingdom.[22]

A source written in Gaul in the middle of the fifth century talks of Britain being 'devastated by a Saxon invasion' in 410. There is no archaeological evidence for this attack, but then the same is true of most barbarian raids on Britain and other parts of the empire. Certainly, settlement by Saxons or other north German peoples in early fifth-century Britain seems to have been limited to a few small communities in the south-east. These may as easily have been mercenaries brought in by British leaders – or before that by the imperial authorities – as settlers who seized territory by force. The example of Alaric's Goths shows that the same group could easily appear in both guises over the course of just a few years. The attacks in 410 were most likely heavy raids and need not have involved huge numbers of warriors or any attempt at permanent occupation. Some might prefer to date the attacks earlier and associate them with the ones that are supposed to have provoked the rebellion against Constantine. Alternatively, Saxon attacks may have become heavier to exploit the weakness in Britain following the expulsion of the imperial authorities.[23]

Saxon raids posed a problem, especially to those communities in vulnerable areas. The same was true of plundering bands of Picts, Scots and Irish. All were likely to have been quite small-scale, especially when the attackers came by sea. Roman rule in Britain was not ended by outside attacks, nor were the British powers that emerged rapidly overrun by these foreign enemies. There is some sign of the Britons organising to combat their foes, especially on Hadrian's Wall where several forts were reoccupied in the fifth century. Sometimes the evidence of activity is slight, but at Birdoswald a large timber hall was built on the foundations of the Roman granary. Someone also repaired the defences at Housesteads, although in earth rather than stone. At the very least this suggests local war leaders with warbands were based in partially restored former army bases. One scholar would even see this as the sign that a leader emerged able to revive something of the old military command of the *Dux Britanniarum*, albeit doubtless on a more modest scale.[24]

Britain's kings and warlords most likely fought each other as often as foreign enemies – the Romans had no monopoly on civil war – and the fragmentation of the provinces into many small kingdoms does not suggest harmony. Like the emperors, it would be surprising if they did not employ barbarians as allies or mercenaries to fight against their neighbours and rivals. For at least a few decades it was British leaders who remained in control throughout the old Roman diocese. No light was switched off, immediately extinguishing all aspects of culture and life from the Roman period. Most cities and towns continued to be occupied, as did many villas. Some substantial buildings were built within the old walls of towns, even if they were invariably of timber construction. Systems to supply water remained in use for most of the fifth century, in at least one case being repaired. Some baths continued to function, but in general these were one of the first things to decay and be abandoned both in cities and at villas. Very soon no one had the skill or wealth to maintain such sophisticated pieces of engineering, let alone build new ones. There were also more mundane changes. It quickly became rare to use pottery that was not made locally, and before long the potters ceased producing wheel-turned pottery.[25]

Some things survived, but that is not to say that the changes were not major and fairly rapid – certainly within a generation – even if they were not instant. Life in Britain became less sophisticated, with few signs of prosperity comparable to the Roman period. The wealthiest were cushioned to some extent, and it was easier for them to leave and settle in Brittany, but their comforts were fewer both there and in Britain itself. Western Britain, notably Wales, Cornwall and Cumbria, had been amongst the least developed parts of the Roman province. Paradoxically, this may have changed in the century or so after Roman rule, with these areas becoming a little more 'Roman' and almost certainly more thoroughly Christian. There is no good evidence for a substantial pagan community in Britain in the fifth and sixth centuries before the creation of the Saxon kingdoms.[26]

Britain was not cut off from all contact with the Roman empires after 410. Trade declined massively, and it was no longer part of the imperial bureaucratic and fiscal systems, but as far as both Romans and Britons were concerned it remained part of the Roman world. The church played a key role in maintaining this connection. Bishop Germanus of Auxerre in Gaul was later canonised and his biographer recorded two visits to Britain, the first in 429 and the second sometime in the next fifteen years. Travel to Britain was evidently still possible and not excessively dangerous. Nevertheless, it is hard to judge how much the biographer really knew of life on the island. Germanus seems to have visited St Albans (Verulamium) and went to the shrine of its famous martyr. In one city he healed the blind daughter of a local dignitary, called a tribune, but whether this was the correct title is questionable. He also rallied the locals to defeat a band of Saxons and Picts – in itself a fairly unlikely combination – teaching his men to raise a shout of 'Alleluia!' This is said to have been enough to rout the enemy.[27]

Yet the main reason for both visits was to combat heretical Christians rather than foreign plunderers. Germanus held debates with priests adhering to a doctrine named Pelagianism after its founder. Pelagius was originally from Britain, although his preaching mainly attracted attention after he moved to Italy in 380. His particular brand of asceticism was moderate by the standard of the day, but his emphasis on the ability of individuals to become virtuous through effort and make themselves acceptable to God was far more controversial. Over time he attracted many prominent critics, including St Augustine, who accused him of effectively denying that salvation depended on grace alone. Pelagius was finally condemned as a heretic in 418. Germanus' biographer claims that the bishop easily confounded the British Pelagians in debate. He also characterises them as boastful and ostentatiously dressed, but this may just be conventional criticism. It is hard to say whether it can be used to show that there were substantial numbers of wealthy aristocrats and priests in the British towns.[28]

Invaders

Older books tend to depict the arrival of the Saxons, Angles, Jutes and other tribes as a massive invasion, which killed or drove off all of the British inhabitants of the south-east. Later these peoples would continue to expand, creating kingdoms and in time merging into the Anglo-Saxons, speaking their own Germanic language and with their own customs and laws uninfluenced by Roman or British ideas. The descendants of the population of Roman Britain were dubbed the 'Welsh' or foreigners and forced into enclaves in Cornwall, Wales and the north-west. Thus was England created.[29]

More recently, ideas about this and other ancient migrations have changed profoundly. Scholars have doubted the scale of any movements, suggesting that the invaders were far outnumbered by the indigenous population. At the same time, the violence of their arrival has often been played down, particularly by emphasising the idea that many arrived as mercenaries. The discovery of graveyards that appear to show Saxon and Briton being buried on the same site has been interpreted as demonstrating that the two groups could and did peacefully coexist. Others would see the spread of Saxon styles – again, largely through grave finds and mainly of metalwork such as brooches and belt buckles – no longer as an indication of the advance of these people. Instead, it has been suggested that the Britons deliberately aped these styles, willingly associating themselves with the Germanic peoples for political reasons.[30]

As usual in such cases, the pendulum has swung too far and it is important to look again at the evidence. Saxon finds become markedly more common around the middle decades of the fifth century. Most are in eastern England, and the greatest single group are from burials. Initially, these take the form of cremations, but gradually inhumation becomes normal, with the body usually accompanied by grave goods. In roughly the same period, literary sources speak of a great war beginning when Saxon mercenaries rebelled against their British employers. In one tradition, the king responsible for enlisting the Saxons' services is called Vortigern. The names of the warriors' leaders, the two brothers Hengist and Horsa, mean literally 'stallion' and 'horse' and may well be later inventions.[31]

The details and precise dates of this conflict are impossible now to reconstruct, but there does seem to have been an increase in the area dominated by Saxon groups at this time. Events elsewhere in the empire have shown that barbarian warbands did not need to be especially large to cause a fundamental shift in the local balance of power. The imperial government rarely had enough soldiers to defeat these groups. Usually this was only possible when they hired another set of barbarians to fight on their behalf. Such leaders as emerged in Britain can only have been massively weaker and so even less capable of dealing with barbarian groups. Given that there was no central authority as powerful as the empire at the start of the fifth century, even very small bands of warriors would have presented a major problem. On the other hand, it does seem that many settlements in northern Germany and Denmark were abandoned in the fifth century. In some areas sea levels rose and previously fertile fields were flooded or turned into salt marshes. A significant migration to better land in Britain is perfectly possible.[32]

Mixed cemeteries apparently containing both Saxon and British burials are not straightforward to interpret. In the first place, considerable caution needs to be used before assuming that a particular object automatically denotes someone of a particular race. Brooches were both functional and valuable. They would not be discarded or remade simply because the design was not traditional to the owner's culture. In the end, brooches and belt buckles were there to hold up clothes more than to express identity. Any such item could as easily have been acquired through violent acquisition as peaceful trade. It is not impossible that the mixed cemeteries do indicate peaceful coexistence of two races within the same community. This does not mean that both sides lived willingly in this way. Many repressive regimes would not necessarily reveal themselves in the burial record. Britons apparently able to bury their dead according to their own customs and in the same general area as Saxons does not necessarily mean that they were not a more or less subject race.

There were significant numbers of Saxon war leaders in eastern and southern Britain by the second half of the fifth century, and they were strong and powerful. This was simply a reality that no one could afford to ignore, least of all the British leaders and communities closest to them. It is certainly quite plausible that some decided their best advantage lay in joining the new arrivals, hoping to benefit from their power. Plenty of British nobles had done much the same when Claudius invaded in 43. Some Britons may have tried to 'become' Saxons, just as some of their ancestors had once been keen to 'become' Romans. In neither case was this spontaneous, but simply a response to the arrival of a new power, which it seemed unwise or impossible to oppose.

One great difference was that the Saxons were no more united than the Britons. Apart from the term embracing groups from a range of different peoples, the Saxons themselves appear as disunited as other tribal groupings. It was not simply a question of allying with *the* Saxons, but finding a way to placate or defend against each of their war leaders within striking distance. Raiding is likely to have continued to be a normal part of life for the invaders. There is no particular reason to believe that rivalry and fighting between Briton and Briton or Saxon and Saxon ceased. There were also still other enemies, such as the Picts and Scots. Parts of western Britain seem to have been permanently occupied and settled by war leaders from Ireland. Nor was the conflict all in one direction. St Patrick wrote to the British King Coroticus condemning him for allowing his warriors to raid and take slaves from amongst Christian converts in Ireland. We also hear in 469 of a British war leader named Riothamus who had taken his band of warriors over to Gaul and become a local power. We do not know whether he had been forced to leave or simply scented better opportunities for profit and employment on the Continent.[33]

Given the thinness and questionable reliability of our sources, we cannot chart the wars of the fifth and sixth century in any detail. Yet the overall pattern was one of gradual expansion by the Germanic tribes. The Britons who migrated to Brittany or the western parts of Britain itself must have been fleeing from something. Doubtless conflict was not unceasing and there were periods of general peace as well as longer and more sustained local lulls. Perhaps the Britons did win some great victories as Gildas and others claimed, but in the sixth century Saxon power waxed stronger and began to shape Anglo-Saxon England. Not all Britons will have fled or died, but the survivors were absorbed by their conquerors. Celtic language was replaced by Saxon in a large part of the island and Latin for the moment was virtually or wholly abandoned. Until St Augustine of Canterbury's mission in 597, the Saxon kingdoms were all pagan, although it is impossible to know whether pockets of Christian belief remained within them. By this time the Western Empire was only a distant memory, but the Catholic Church preserved some of its international connections.[34]

Roman Britain had not fallen to outside pressure. The leaders who threw out Constantine III's governors quickly started to squabble amongst themselves. They were Romans as much as Britons and the rebellion was still essentially a civil war. Its result was to create many tyrants or kings instead of one imperial usurper. Constantine himself was too busy fighting for his own survival to try to regain control of Britain. Honorius and his successors lacked the power to do so. There were foreign enemies, and gradually some of these overran much of the island, but it is worth remembering how long this took. Everything, including power, trade and warfare, became far more local than had been true under the Romans. Some things survived, especially in the areas longest controlled by the Britons themselves. Christianity was one of the most important and mainly responsible for at least some continuation of literacy, both in Latin and eventually also in the Celtic languages. Debate continues to rage over how much, if any, continuity there was between Roman Britain and Anglo-Saxon England. Some towns were important to both, although whether occupation was unbroken is less easy to say. The evidence in favour of this is not good, but even the continuities that can be traced should never obscure the massive scale of the change. It would be five hundred years before even the greater part of the old Roman diocese would again be united under a single authority. The better part of seven centuries would pass before Norman cathedrals would match in scale the basilicas of Roman cities or the headquarters buildings of legionary fortresses.[35]

There is no firm evidence that Arthur actually existed and the mentions of him are all comparatively late. On the other hand, there is no reason that he could not have existed, and it is hard for anyone – perhaps especially anyone British – not to wish that he did. The fifth and sixth centuries were clearly years of frequent conflict, a time that produced many warriors and warlords. That one of them was especially successful and charismatic is plausible enough, although equally the later stories may be an amalgam of the deeds of many men generously fleshed out with myth. There is much more besides the reality or otherwise of Arthur about the history and society of Britain after the end of the Roman province that we simply do not know. In the long run there were probably fewer traces of the Roman presence left in Britain than almost any of the western provinces. Yet on the whole its experience may well have had more things in common with the wider experience, at least in the fifth century. It is now time to look at the final years of the Western Empire.[36]

19

Emperors, Kings and Warlords

'Since the Roman state is now either dead or at the very least dying in those areas where it still seems alive.' – *Salvian, middle of the fifth century.*[1]

S alvian's view was deeply pessimistic and part of a work condemning the wickedness, greed and corruption of Roman society. This sinfulness was all the worse because the Romans were now Christians and ought to have known better. Many churchmen expressed much the same idea. Expectation of Jesus' Second Coming had always been strong amongst Christians. To many the disasters suffered especially by the Western Empire in the fifth century seemed clear signs of the coming Apocalypse. There was a long tradition in classical literature of understanding events in moral terms. For Christians this was even stronger. Salvian claimed that the barbarian invaders were being used by God to punish the sinful Romans. Inevitably, such beliefs encouraged him to paint a very bleak picture of life in the empire. We need to be very cautious in using such sources, but also should note that his attitude was shaped by real experiences. In 418 Salvian had witnessed the Frankish sack of Trier. For some three decades up to his death he was presbyter at Massilia (Marseilles), not far away from the Gothic kingdom established in Aquitania. Just a few years after Salvian's death the last emperor to rule in Italy would be deposed.

The house of Theodosius the Great had already failed in both empires around the middle of the fifth century. Theodosius II died in 450, and his cousin Valentinian III was murdered just five years later. Neither left a son to succeed him or, indeed, had made any clear effort to mark out a successor. Some link with the imperial family was provided in the east when Marcian married the emperor's sister Pulcheria. Yet she was now well into middle age and even if she renounced her long-held vow of chastity in more than just name, there was never any prospect of the couple producing children. It would in fact be some time before an emperor was succeeded by his son. Instead, the choice of new emperors –

and indeed the disposal of the current incumbent – usually had more to do with the decisions of powerful generals and other figures at court.

The Western Empire very quickly relapsed into the familiar pattern of usurpation and civil war. Petronius Maximus had encouraged the killing of Aetius and then arranged the murder of Valentinian III. Others were also eager for imperial power, but he was the most determined and best organised in the immediate aftermath of the assassination and was able to proclaim himself emperor. He married Valentinian's daughter Eudocia – the same girl betrothed some years before to the son of King Geiseric of the Vandals. It is not clear whether this was the provocation that sparked the subsequent Vandal attack on Italy. Some eastern sources alleged that the girl's mother Eudoxia actually appealed to Geiseric for assistance. On the other hand, a naval expedition on such a large scale needed considerable preparation, making it more than likely that the Vandal king was already contemplating some form of attack before this occurred. With Aetius dead, the armies of the Western Empire had yet to find another strong leader. Italy was easy for the Vandals to reach and highly vulnerable, at least in the immediate future.[2]

The Vandals arrived outside Rome itself in May 455. Petronius Maximus was there, but had neither the forces loyal to him nor the spirit to mount a defence. He fled, along with many others, and was killed during the confusion. One story says that he was knocked from his horse by a stone flung by one of his own soldiers and then finished off by a mob. His reign lasted less than three months. Shortly afterwards the Vandal army was admitted to the city – no one made any effort to defend its walls – and for two weeks it thoroughly plundered Rome. Like Alaric's Goths the Vandals were Arian Christians and they responded to the appeal of the pope to treat the churches with respect. Yet their plundering of Rome lasted far longer and gives every impression of having been more systematic than the sack of 410. Geiseric and his men had considerable experience of piracy and looting since they had established themselves in Africa and taken to the seas as raiders. It made practical sense to maintain a level of order and control during the pillaging, rather than simply killing, destroying and stealing at the will of each individual. Such activities were likely to waste much of the spoils and reduce the profits for all. The inhabitants of the city were less likely to resist if they could see this, in the hope that the enemy would refrain from more random and concerted brutality. For them it was simply a question of surviving as best they could. Amongst the treasures carried off were the remnants of the plunder taken by Titus from the Temple in Jerusalem when it was destroyed in 70. Apart from gold, the Vandals also took with them Valentinian's widow Eudoxia and her two daughters. They were not the only captives, and the prospect of those taken simply as slaves was not pleasant. The bishop of Carthage sold church plate to buy the freedom of many of these prisoners. Others may have been less fortunate.[3]

Petronius Maximus had not been recognised by Constantinople and, indeed, his rule was only in the process of being acknowledged throughout the Western Empire when he was killed. Representatives had been sent to key figures throughout the provinces to ensure their support. Petronius had chosen a senior ally by the name of Avitus to go to the Gothic kingdom in Aquitania, currently ruled by Theodoric II. The Goths had helped Aetius repulse the Huns just a few years ago. The Gothic kings were more often than not loyal allies of the empire. There were periods of friction, but they were certainly far less consistently hostile than the Vandals. Nevertheless, their goodwill and support could not be taken for granted by any emperor. As the most powerful of all the tribal kingdoms established within the provinces, they were a major factor in determining the balance of power and hence the success or failure of a regime.

While Avitus was still at Toulouse the news arrived of the death of Petronius. The ambassador promptly persuaded the Goths to proclaim him emperor. Only later did Avitus receive backing from a more unambiguously 'Roman' source, when a gathering of leading men from the Gallic provinces acknowledged his rule at Arelate (modern Arles) in July. There was no matching support from the army and civilian leaders in Italy. For more than a generation the posts in both Gaul and Italy had tended to be filled almost exclusively by local men. The aristocracies in each area were becoming more regional and so reluctant to accept rule by 'outsiders'. The troops in Italy – mainly mercenary and allied contingents, although it is possible some regular units survived if only in name – were commanded by Ricimer and Majorian. These men adamantly refused to accept the new emperor. Constantinople also refrained from giving its seal of approval to Avitus.[4]

In 456 Avitus led an army into Italy, but was defeated in the Po Valley outside Placentia (modern Piacenza). Giving up power, he retired to become a bishop, but died within a matter of months. There were rumours of foul play. After concerted negotiation with the eastern court, Majorian was made Augustus of the Western Empire at the very end of 457 with the full backing of his colleague in Constantinople. Marcian had died in January and a relatively obscure army officer called Leo was made emperor in his place. Leo's acclamation was elaborate and protracted even by the standards of imperial ceremony, and suggests a conscious effort to establish the legitimacy of his rule. For the moment the eastern imperial court remained dominated by the senior commander Aspar and his family. Leo was his choice, and it would be some time before the new emperor was able to break free from the influence of his senior general. In the east the contest was mainly over who could control the emperor. In the west competition for power was less focused and more often openly violent.[5]

Power Lost and Found

The Gothic kingdom was the single greatest power block within the Western Empire, simply because it was able to field the strongest army. No other group – including the remnants of the Roman army – was on its own capable of matching the force wielded by the Gothic king. There were other powers, such as the Burgundian kingdom settled in eastern Gaul by Aetius, and the Franks, now firmly established west of the Rhine. In Spain the Suevi had never fully been under Roman control, while North Africa had long since been lost to the Vandals. In some ways these different groups held each other in check and the Romans continued to employ one barbarian group against another. Avitus sent the Goths, as well as contingents of Franks and Burgundians, to attack the Suevi. Majorian continued to employ the Goths to fight in Spain, in spite of a brief conflict with them in Gaul. They were too valuable as allies and too dangerous as enemies to risk prolonged confrontation. It was simply far more attractive to employ their aggressive tendencies against other threats. In a relatively short time, the Suevi were confined permanently to the extreme north-west of the Iberian Peninsula. Their kingdom would survive in that region for centuries, but never again became more than a limited local threat. It is doubtful whether the Goths' successes ever genuinely brought territory back under direct imperial control. This was blatantly true after 466, when Theodoric II was murdered and replaced by his younger brother Euric. The new king openly expanded his own realm in Gaul and Spain.[6]

Unlike the Suevi, the Vandals were harder to reach and could not be dealt with simply by persuading another barbarian group to attack them. Reaching Africa required a fleet large enough to carry a sizeable army over to North Africa as well as the supplies needed to keep it there. Even

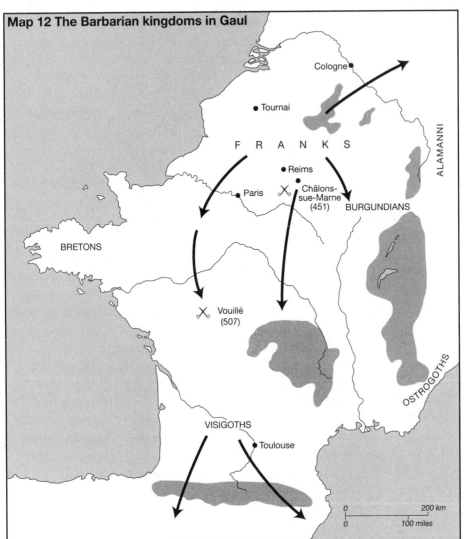

Map 12 The Barbarian kingdoms in Gaul

Cologne

Tournai

F R A N K S

ALAMANNI

Reims

Paris

Châlons-sue-Marne
(451)

BURGUNDIANS

BRETONS

Vouillé
(507)

OSTROGOTHS

VISIGOTHS

Toulouse

0   200 km
0   100 miles

with substantial resources, such an operation was inevitably complex and risky. In 460 Majorian prepared to invade from bases in Spain, but before the invasion could be launched he lost the bulk of his fleet to a sudden attack by Geiseric. The project had to be abandoned since no replacement ships were available in the foreseeable future. Roman prestige in Spain, such as it was, suffered a serious blow. Even worse was the damage to Majorian's own reputation. When he returned to Italy in 461 Ricimer had him deposed and executed. The general – like most senior officers a man of barbarian, in his case Suevic, ancestry – may have disliked having an emperor who was clearly determined to act on his own initiative. The failure of the North African expedition offered a good opportunity for disposing of him. A few months later Ricimer had the much weaker Libius Severus proclaimed emperor. This time there was no recognition from Constantinople.[7]

For some time the rule of the new emperor was scarcely acknowledged outside Italy itself. In Gaul the commander of the troops in the region was in rebellion against Ricimer, but was too busy trying to control the Goths to mount a serious offensive. Another general broke away in Dalmatia, declaring loyalty to the eastern emperor Leo, but refusing to accept the rule of Libius Severus in Ravenna. This was an extreme although not unprecedented situation. The Western Empire had been steadily losing more and more of its territory and revenue throughout the fifth century. Each settlement of a barbarian group, whether it was made under the authority of the emperor and his representatives or independently through blatant force, further reduced the imperial resources. Each region occupied in this way ceased to pay tax into the imperial coffers.

In 395 the Western Empire was the less prosperous of the two halves into which Theodosius' empire was divided. Since then it had suffered successive blows as Britain, Spain, North Africa and much of Gaul ceased to be under its direct control and to yield revenue. Stilicho, Constantius and Aetius had enjoyed prolonged periods of dominance, but had always lacked the resources of money, food and men to do much more than juggle the various threats and problems. They were able to keep them from becoming fatal, without ever winning more permanent victories. The settlement of groups of barbarians within the provinces was often attractive in the short term. Yet it inevitably meant another area removed from the imperial taxation system. The income of the Western Empire continued to shrink. Those regions not permanently lost were not necessarily fully under control, and many areas had suffered from raiding and civil wars. All of the barbarian groups established within the provinces at times chose to attack or try to conquer the neighbouring communities. Thus threats increased and were established within the heartland of the empire at the same time as the resources to deal with them dwindled away.[8]

The greatest single blow to the fortunes of the Western Empire was the loss of Africa to the Vandals. Italy had long relied on African grain to supply its needs and, more generally, it was one of the most productive areas of the entire Roman world when it came to tax and resources.

Majorian's attempt to recapture North Africa made considerable sense. In 468 there was another effort, this time with the massive participation of the Eastern Empire, which sent troops and a fleet of more than a thousand vessels – many of them doubtless small transport ships. Relations between the eastern and western courts had improved following the death by natural causes of Libius Severus in 465. It took almost two years of negotiation before Ricimer agreed to accept a new emperor nominated by Leo. During this time there was no emperor in the west, although it is doubtful if this made much difference to life there. The new emperor was called Anthemius and Ricimer married his daughter to seal their alliance. For all the massive preparation and pooling of resources – substantial numbers of troops supplied by the western government were also involved – the second expedition also ended in disaster. This time the great fleet reached the African coast, but its commander then hesitated, halted operations and began to negotiate. A few days later, Geiseric seized the opportunity offered by a favourable wind to break up the invasion fleet with fire-ships and then attacked the scattered and already panicking remnants.[9]

After this second humiliating failure the Vandals were not attacked again until the sixth century. It took the Eastern Empire many years to recover from the massive and wasted cost of Leo's expedition in 468. The Western Empire continued to do without the revenues from North Africa, and in the following years the aggressive example of King Euric was followed by other leaders established within and alongside the remaining provinces. The already small resources at the disposal of the Western Empire continued to decline. In parts of Gaul there were risings by groups dubbed Bagaudae, first encountered in the late third century (see page 159). Dismissed as little better than bandits in our sources, the reality was probably much more complicated. At this and other times there are signs that some of their leaders were educated and had at least started life as members of the local aristocracy.[10]

In many regions powerful landowners maintained considerable bands of followers on their estates. Some of these men were effectively mercenaries and, like the bulk of the troops who fought for the western emperors, they were usually of barbarian origin. Scholars these days tend to refer to such local forces as 'self-help groups', implying a broadly benevolent and defensive role. They are seen as an indication that local communities had to look to their own devices to protect themselves in an increasingly dangerous world. This may have been the case in some instances, but other interpretations are equally possible. The local landowner with his gang of hired thugs may genuinely have been willing to use this force to protect his tenants and neighbours from bandits and raiding barbarians. Possession of such a force may equally have allowed a man to dominate the lands around, using threats or force itself to bully his neighbours. As in any period the lines between an informal police force, a group of vigilantes and a paramilitary/criminal gang controlling and 'protecting' its own patch are narrow and often unclear.[11]

The trend in the fifth-century west was for power to become more local. An extreme example was Britain after the end of formal government. Northern parts of Gaul similarly seem to have fragmented into many separate units at a quite early stage. In contrast, by the end of Euric's reign the Goths controlled an area larger than several Roman provinces, although his realm did not neatly follow the old administrative boundaries. Other barbarian leaders controlled less territory than the Goths at this stage. Then there were the smaller, much more local powers, whether city leaders, major landlords or smaller chieftains able to dominate a small area and take by force or extort what they needed to support their followers.

The degree of independence enjoyed by all of these figures from kings to landowners and bandit leaders varied. Some may have acknowledged the principle of imperial control, even if they ignored the emperors with impunity on a day-to-day basis. By no stretch of the imagination were they part of a clear hierarchy of imperial administration. No emperor could simply replace, or even bring to trial, one of the tribal kings. Stopping even minor infractions could only be done by the threat, and usually the actual use of force. Yet the imperial power no longer possessed a clear and decisive dominance when it came to the use of force. The rise of numerous regional powers was the key development in the west during the fifth century. The most powerful were all direct results of barbarian settlement. Each marked another stage in the decay of the Western Empire, which in the end would lead to the disappearance of emperors ruling from Italy. Yet they were from the start consequences of imperial weakness. They were not its root cause. Successive governments had more or less willingly agreed to, or at least accepted, the creation of kingdoms within the provinces. That this was felt unavoidable, or at best the most attractive of available options, demonstrates just how weak the empire was in the first place.

There were other signs of the steady seepage of power away from the emperors. We have already observed that even in the fourth century it was often extremely difficult for the emperor to control imperial officials and army commanders. In the fifth century powerful generals and senior court figures more often dominated emperors than the other way round. The general Aspar was exceptionally powerful in the Eastern Empire for decades, relying in part on the promotion of his relatives to key posts and the continued loyalty of mainly Gothic troops within the army. Emperor Leo recruited very heavily from the Isaurian highlanders of Asia Minor to provide himself with a force to counter this power block. These men came from within the empire, but the region had a long history of banditry and rebellion and they were seen as effectively barbarians and bandits. In the end, he felt able to have Aspar murdered in 471. It is notable, as with Aetius, that an emperor preferred informal killing to dismissal or trial. That these were not safe options was promptly demonstrated by the rebellion of Aspar's supporters. Peace was only achieved after granting considerable concessions.[12]

Another sign of the decay of central authority was the growing prominence of bishops as leaders in local affairs. To some extent this was a result of the type of wealthy, well-educated and connected men attracted to the Church. It is probably mistaken to lament that such men did not instead seek imperial service. The imperial administration was not any more notably efficient before this trend became pronounced. In addition, those who went into the Church often displayed as much enthusiasm for intrigue and fierce competition as those who took posts in the imperial bureaucracy. On several occasions the election of a bishop, including the pope, was contested by mobs willing to fight for their favoured candidate. There were also disputes over the supremacy of the major metropolitan sees, Alexandria in particular proving itself unwilling to submit to the authority of the much newer church at Constantinople, even though the latter was the imperial capital and centre of secular government. Politics and the individual ambition often coloured the theological disputes that continued to divide the Church. The nature of the Trinity was no longer controversial and, instead, disputes concerned the precise definition of Christ's nature during his incarnation, and whether or not distinct human and divine natures had existed simultaneously.[13]

Early in the fifth century the potential abuse of a bishop's power and position was well illustrated by the career of Cyril, bishop of Alexandria from 412. It was significant that his predecessor was his own uncle, which shows that his family was already prominent. Cyril made frequent use of bands of monks to intimidate not only other bishops, but also the provincial governor. In successive attacks on pagans, Jews and Christian heretics he went far beyond imperial legislation and in the process flexed his muscles. At the same time he was careful to send regular 'gifts' to powerful figures at court. In 415 his followers murdered in spectacularly brutal fashion the famous Neoplatonist philosopher Hypatia, who was the rarest of things in classical history – a woman holding a post at one of the most famous universities in the world. Although pagan, we know that she included prominent Christians amongst her circle of friends, including priests and the governor Orestes. The latter had already come into conflict and even been attacked by Cyril's monks. The bishop even tried to portray the governor as a secret pagan. In many ways Hypatia was killed simply so that Cyril's men could demonstrate their power. Afterwards they were only briefly dispersed and in due course the bishop would call on similar support in his other projects. Willing to make free use of intimidation and violence, Cyril was also a skilful operator in Church politics. He was willing to appeal to the pope in Rome when in dispute with the bishop in Constantinople. For all his use of violence, he remained highly respected as a theologian and played a key role in several church councils. During these he also demonstrated his skill as a politician, making concessions when necessary to preserve his prominence.[14]

Cyril was not an attractive figure and it would be easy to see the rise of men like him as a direct consequence of the abasement of Theodosius before Bishop Ambrose of Milan. It is impossible to imagine Constantine permitting such licence in a bishop. Yet this was not simply a case of the Church as an organisation independent of the imperial hierarchy steadily increasing its power at the expense of the state. Instead, it expanded into a vacuum already created by the decay of central authority. It would have required major and united effort on the part of the provincial and imperial authorities to control a man like Cyril. The imperial bureaucracy had long since ceased to be united in purpose and Cyril was a shrewd enough politician to win or buy favour from enough influential senior officials to protect himself. Time after time the authorities decided that it was not worth the effort of controlling him. Ambitious bishops of this sort – rather like the barbarian kings in the western provinces – knew that they could not simply act as they wanted. There were limits, but they also understood that the power of the central authorities was weaker than it once had been. They could get away with a great deal, especially if they waited for a suitable opportunity when the authorities were preoccupied with other problems. Cyril's talent for politics, high reputation as a theologian and the current weakness of imperial authority allowed him to succeed. Other bishops, including his successors, were not always so fortunate and sometimes suffered deposition or exile when they incurred imperial displeasure.

The Changing World

Bishops appear in a less negative light as leaders rallying the local population to defend themselves against attack. St Germanus was credited by his biographer with leading a scratch force of Britons to defeat a raiding army. A less spectacular and ultimately unsuccessful role was performed by Sidonius Apollinaris, the bishop of Clermont, in opposing the aggression of Euric's Goths. A member of the Gallic provincial aristocracy, Sidonius had entered the Church comparatively late in life. By both education and inclination deeply traditional, his writings tell us a good deal about how the leading provincials adapted to the new reality of barbarian kings living beside and amongst them. Sidonius left a very detailed and generally flattering portrait of the Gothic king, Theodoric II:

> His figure is well proportioned, he is shorter than the very tall, taller and more commanding than the average man. The top of his hair is round, and on it his curled hair retreats gently from his even forehead.... His chin, throat, and neck support not fat, but fullness; the skin is milk white.[15]

Describing the king's routine, including before dawn attending an Arian service where 'he worships with great earnestness, though between ourselves one can see that this devotion is a matter of routine rather than conviction'. Afterwards he devoted himself to administration, receiving deputations, before breaking for a visit to his treasury or stables.[16]

The description is far from the well-established stereotype of a barbarian. Even the claim that petitioners were more likely to be successful if they let Theodoric win at board or dice games only in part approaches such cliché. In many respects Sidonius could as easily have been describing the daily routine of an early third-century emperor. He and other Gallic aristocrats felt able to deal with such a man, without themselves becoming in any way less Roman.[17]

Living the sophisticated, leisurely and highly literate life of a Roman aristocrat was important to Sidonius and his contemporaries. One of his letters describes in great and, after the fashion of the day, hugely overblown terms the bath house at a friend's villa in Gaul. Another describes a much more primitive bathing experience, because he claims the hosts had yet to complete the construction of their bath. Instead, their servants hastily dug a trench 'close to a spring or river'. A pile of heated stones was poured into the flooded trench and 'while the ditch was heating it was roofed over with a dome constructed of pliant hazel twigs turned into a hemispherical shape'. The guests got in and 'here we while away the hours with no lack of witty and humorous conversation'. Men like Sidonius were determined to be 'Roman' regardless of the limited facilities at the disposal even of aristocrats in fifth-century Gaul.[18]

Sidonius was one of those who felt that Romans could not accept the aggression that became characteristic of the Goths in Euric's day. Other members of the provincial aristocracy were more favourably inclined towards the Gothic leader or perhaps simply pragmatic. As bishop, Sidonius defended his city against a concerted Gothic siege. The fighting seems to have been very small scale – we read of a party of fewer than twenty horsemen who were able to fight their way through the enemy blockade. Yet there was little real help from outside and eventually the emperor in Ravenna decided to give Clermont and other border towns to the Goths as the price of peace and to secure more important cities, including Arelate (modern Arles) and Massilia (modern Marseilles). Euric was fairly moderate in victory and Sidonius was only imprisoned for a few months. During his captivity he was able to study and write, but complained about two elderly and inebriated Gothic women who kept him awake by talking throughout the night outside his room.[19]

Sidonius had witnessed the acclamation of Avitus, who was his father-in-law, and came into contact with several other emperors and their courts, seeking favour and office. His writings never give the impression that any of the emperors or their representatives were especially powerful in Gaul itself. There is no trace of the regular army that had once existed. Sidonius' father had been praetorian prefect of the Gallic diocese around the middle of the century, but it is hard to say just how much control such a senior official actually had in this area by that period. All of Sidonius' writings demonstrate the need for tact when speaking of Gothic and other barbarian leaders.

Even less sense of central government is given by *The Life of St Severinus*, a biography of a holy man – he does not seem actually to have been a priest – active in Noricum (modern Austria) on the Danube from just after the middle of the fifth century. A few small units of *limitanei* appear. One tribune – interestingly, the man later became a bishop – pleaded his inability to confront a group of barbarian raiders, because his soldiers were very few in number and virtually unarmed. Encouraged by Severinus, he and his men chased the raiders, surprising and routing them. A few prisoners were taken, but allowed to go free after Severinus had warned them not to return.[20]

More generally we are told that:

At the time when the Roman Empire was still in existence, the soldiers of many towns were supported by public money for their watch on the wall. When this arrangement ceased, the military formations were dissolved and, at the same time, the wall was allowed to break down. The garrison at Batavis, however, held out. Some of these had gone to Italy to fetch for their comrades the last payment, but on their way had been routed by the barbarians.[21]

The bodies of the dead men eventually floated back down the river and were discovered. The impression is of the last remnants of the frontier army simply vanishing when the pay, supplies and other support stopped arriving. At least one community hired a group of barbarians to protect them, but the garrison thus introduced to the walled town was soon seen as a burden. In the confusion caused by an earthquake the barbarians were driven from the town, some even killing each other in the confusion.[22]

Life was dangerous in Noricum during these years, but there was no single enemy. A range of tribal groups appear, including the Rugi, Heruli, Goths and Alamanni, as do a number of chieftains or kings. All of these raided into the province, usually on a fairly small scale. The aim was to take plunder and captives. Occasionally, whole communities were destroyed, usually after ignoring Severinus' warnings. Some chieftains, notably King Feva of the Rugi, seem to have established themselves permanently within the province and subjected some of the provincial population to their rule. Severinus was able at times to moderate the actions of some of these leaders. However, even his successes were always temporary. The general trend was to the destruction or abandonment of community after community and a withdrawal of the population away from the Danube. Eventually, a large part of the surviving population abandoned the province altogether, taking with them the remains of St Severinus who had died in 482.[23]

The world of *The Life of St Severinus* is more obviously gloomy and dangerous than that conjured up in Sidonius Apollinaris' letters. Noricum appears as a considerably bleaker place than Gaul, the only encouraging notes coming from the faith and power of Severinus. Each reveals life at a time when the Western Empire was weaker than it had been even a generation before. The professional army had disappeared, as had the allied and mercenary forces with which Constantius and Aetius had held things together for a while. Central government lacked the capacity to intervene in local affairs as a matter of course. In contrast, there were various leaders of barbarian origin, either established within the provinces or able to attack them. These were not invariably hostile, nor were they irredeemably and implacably savage, but they were foreign. They were also facts of life. There was no force capable of destroying them – even defeats over the smaller groups were generally limited and short term. Circumstances varied from area to area and individual to individual, but there was little choice but to come to terms with these new powers.

The Last Emperor

In the Western Empire relations between Anthemius and Ricimer soured over time, and in 472 open war broke out between the emperor and his general. Anthemius employed the services of an army of Goths from the Danube – part of the wider group now conveniently known as Ostrogoths or 'East Goths', as distinct from the Visigoths or 'West Goths' established in Gaul. (The terms themselves did not appear until the sixth century and at this stage the Ostrogoths remained divided into a number of distinct groups.) This Gothic aid proved insufficient and the emperor was defeated and executed in July. Ricimer replaced him with one of the few men left with even the vaguest connection to the house of Theodosius. This was a Roman aristocrat named Olybrius, who was married to Valentinian III's younger daughter Placidia. Diplomacy had secured the couple's return from captivity amongst the Vandals some years before. The new regime was short-lived. Ricimer and Olybrius both died of disease within a few weeks of each other in the autumn of 472.[24]

Command of the army in Italy now passed to Ricimer's nephew Gundobad. In 473 he created a new emperor, choosing a court official named Glycerius. Emperor Leo refused to acknowledge this appointment. Gundobad was a Burgundian prince as well as a Roman officer, and at some point he seems to have decided that his best prospects for power and success lay amongst his own people. He left Italy to pursue other ambitions and never returned. In 474 the Eastern Empire backed an invasion of Italy led by the general Julius Nepos. Glycerius was deposed, but his life was spared and he retired to become a bishop. Julius Nepos was proclaimed emperor. Like that of his immediate predecessors, his rule was scarcely acknowledged outside Italy, even though he was accepted by Constantinople. It was one of his decisions that surrendered Clermont to the Visigoths, much to the disgust of Sidonius Apollinaris.

Nepos' power was not unchallenged, even in Italy itself. The troops there – all apparently contingents from the Germanic tribes, including significant numbers of Rugi and Heruli from the Danubian frontier – were commanded by Orestes. Even more than Gundobad, this man illustrated the confused loyalties and career patterns of the fifth century. Decades before, he had served Attila the Hun as a secretary and ambassador. In 475 he rebelled against Nepos, who fled from Italy and returned to his old base in Dalmatia. Constantinople protested, but did nothing tangible to assist him. Leo had died in 474. He was succeeded jointly by his son-in-law Zeno and the latter's son and his grandson, the seven-year-old Leo II. The boy died within a year, leaving his father as sole ruler. Zeno – his original name was Tarasicodissa – was an Isaurian nobleman promoted to senior rank and married to the emperor's daughter. His rise was one of the more spectacular consequences of Leo's favouring of the Isaurians to create a military force loyal to him over senior generals like Aspar. In 475 the new emperor faced a serious challenge from the usurper Basiliscus. Zeno fled from Constantinople, which until late in the next year remained under the control of his rival. In the end Zeno prevailed, and he would go on to survive further challenges to his rule, but the struggle within the Eastern Empire ensured that there was no prospect of major intervention in the west during these years.[25]

Orestes named his young son as emperor in 475. The boy was called Romulus, but swiftly acquired the nickname Augustulus or 'the Little Augustus'. He was the most obvious puppet ruler in a succession of weak emperors created by the commanders of the forces in Italy. The importance of these generals depended on the loyalty of their troops. In 476 Orestes lost this to another officer named Odoacer. There was discontent amongst the soldiers because the new government had refused their demands for land – or perhaps the tax revenue derived from it. Orestes was killed, his son merely deposed and allowed to live out his life in comfortable seclusion. He was not worth the trouble of killing. Nor did Odoacer feel that it was worth creating a new emperor to replace him. Instead, the imperial regalia was formally sent to Constantinople. Officially the empire was united again, with Zeno and his successors ruling as sole emperors from Constantinople. In practice, the lands of the former Western Empire would go their own way, as a number of separate kingdoms.[26]

Odoacer was a Scirian, and evidently did not consider it possible or wise to seek imperial rule himself. Perhaps under pressure from his followers, he proclaimed himself as king and ruled Italy in this rank rather than simply as the head of the army there. As far as possible he preserved the existing regional and local administrative structures. The Senate still met and there continued to be city prefects and other magistrates at Rome. Major repairs were conducted on the Colosseum in 484. The absence of an emperor in the west may not have been immediately obvious to many living in Italy, let alone the other provinces. Imperial power had long since become so weak as to make the western emperors almost irrelevant. With hindsight, many in the Eastern Empire saw the year 476 as significant. Nepos lived on in exile in the Eastern Empire until his death in 480, but no effort was made to restore him to power. Odoacer minted coins with Nepos' name on them in spite of his refusal to acknowledge his rule.[27]

Yet few can have ignored the simple fact that ultimate power rested now with an essentially foreign army simply because it possessed superior military might. Odoacer was in his turn supplanted by a stronger war leader, King Theodoric of the Ostrogoths who invaded Italy in 489. The struggle between the two kings took several years, during which time Odoacer was able to hold out in Ravenna for a considerable period. In the end the two leaders negotiated a peace settlement by which they would share power. Shortly afterwards Theodoric had Odoacer murdered and ruled alone.[28]

The people of Italy had no say in these events. This was as true of the fabulously wealthy senator as much as the slave or peasant. Continuity of culture and institutions should not hide the basic truth that the creation of the kingdoms in the west was a consequence of the blatant military power of the leaders involved. The tribal leaders did not batter down and invade a still formidable Roman Empire. They certainly used force to achieve their ends, and the settlement was at times an extremely violent and brutal process, but it was made possible by the decay of central power. The only people capable of defeating the major barbarian armies – and, indeed, many of the small warbands – were other tribal leaders. The story of the fifth century was one of the exploitation of imperial weakness. Thus the Western Empire died. Each of the new kingdoms was another serious blow to already diminishing power and resources. They were important stages in a gradual process already long underway.

20

West and East

'Theodoric ... secured the supremacy over both Goths and Italians. And although he did not claim the right to assume either the garb or the name of emperor of the Romans, but was called "*rex*" to the end of his life ... still, in governing his own subjects, he invested himself with all the qualities which belong to one who is by birth an emperor. For he was exceedingly careful to observe justice...' – *Procopius, an eastern Roman historian, c.551.*[1]

'Our kingship is an imitation of yours ... a copy of the only empire.' – *Cassiodorus, an Italian aristocrat who had a career in service to the Ostrogothic kings, c.537.*[2]

By the end of the fifth century the territory once controlled by the Western Empire was now split into a number of separate kingdoms. The Visigoths controlled much of Gaul and almost all of the Iberian Peninsula. Only in the north-west did the rump of the Suevic kingdom survive. Similarly, the Vascones – from whom the modern Basques claim descent – were effectively independent in their lands along the north-east coast. The Visigoths, however, were not the sole power in Gaul. There was a substantial Frankish kingdom in the north, and smaller Burgundian and Alamannic states in the east. In the far north some areas had been settled by Saxons. Brittany was controlled by a combination of its old provincial population and the descendants of the refugees who had fled there from Britain. Across the Channel, Britain was divided into many separate groupings, and the east was now overwhelmingly dominated by rulers who were Saxon or from other north Germanic tribes. The Vandals remained in control of North Africa, although to the south they were under pressure from the Moors. Finally, Italy itself was in the hands of King Theodoric and the Ostrogoths.

It would be misleading to give an impression of stability or permanence at this stage. Conflict was frequent between and within the emerging kingdoms. Leaders murdered and killed rivals from within their own families, as well as chieftains from other lines. One branch of the

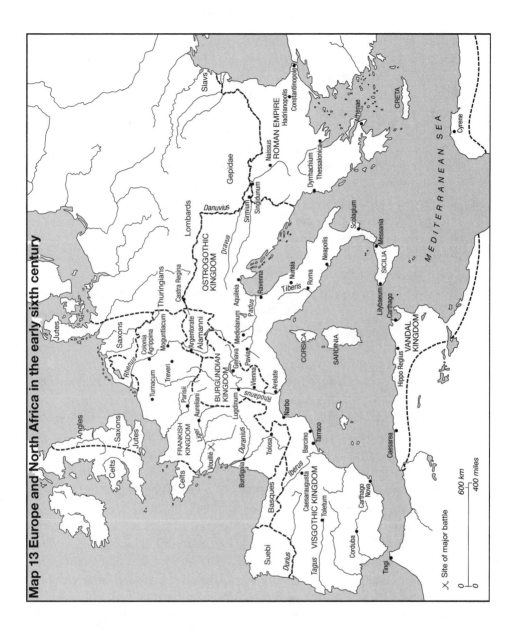

Map 13 Europe and North Africa in the early sixth century

Merovingian family had come to dominate the other Frankish groups and would continue to do so for several generations. This was achieved through the ruthless eradication of anyone who threatened their power. They were similarly aggressive in their relations with the other forces in Gaul. Early in the sixth century King Clovis of the Merovingian Franks attacked the Visigoths and eventually forced them permanently south of the Pyrenees. He also fought with great success against the Alamanni and Burgundians. The boundaries of early medieval Europe were not inevitable, but the product of long and often grim conflict. Individual leaders and their followers competed for power and eventually the overall winners were able to create fairly permanent kingdoms.

It has long been fashionable for academics to speak of the transformation of the Roman – or, more usually, Late Antique – world into the kingdoms of the early Middle Ages. Certainly, change did occur, and some things changed gradually and so might reasonably be described as having been transformed over time. Yet on the whole this characterisation is deeply misleading. Transformation tends to suggest a voluntary and relatively gentle process, but the changes to occur in the Roman west were anything but voluntary as far as the wider population was concerned. The barbarian leaders who emerged in the late fourth and fifth centuries mattered because of the number of fighting men who obeyed them. The chieftains and kings employed by the imperial authorities were only useful in the first place because they wielded significant military force. Controlling armed force made such leaders significant. This persuaded successive emperors to permit them to settle within the empire. It also allowed them to take lands they were not given. Whatever the origins of settlement, no group remained content with the territory on which it first settled and all subsequently tried to expand by force.[3]

The new kingdoms came into being and took shape through the military strength of their leaders. The scale was smaller, and there were many separate powers instead of one large one, but such men were as much imperialists as the generals who had once carved out Rome's empire. Force created the new kingdoms and maintained them as distinct units. This was a profound difference to the Roman period. The empire had been plagued by civil war since the third century. Roman armies had fought each other time after time to place a rival claimant on the throne. These campaigns had invariably occurred within the provinces, so that it was Roman cities and villages that were sacked and the produce of Roman farmers that was consumed by the rival armies. Linked with the constant in-fighting was a weakness on many frontiers. Large parts of some provinces had been exposed to raiding bands from outside the empire for generations. In both these respects the Roman Peace had been far less than perfect for a very long time. It is hard to say whether or not life became more or less dangerous when the empire vanished and the kingdoms were created. As always, so much depended on where an individual lived, as well as the vagaries of chance. Yet in one respect the change was profound and clearly for the worse. In the past one province of the empire did not arm itself to raid or conquer a neighbouring province. Civil wars had always occurred at a higher level. Now warfare was more local in focus and the probability is that as a result it also became more frequent and less decisive. Warlike competition was common between the new kingdoms.[4]

This is not to revive the old stereotype of relentlessly savage and violent barbarians. Force lay behind the creation of the new kingdoms, but all of the most successful barbarian leaders realised that threats were often more powerful than violence itself, and that conciliation offered even greater possibilities. In winning power, and defeating foreign enemies and rivals from amongst their own kin, such leaders were utterly ruthless. Warfare in the ancient world tended to be a savage business in all circumstances. Clearly, at times there was dreadful brutality, massacre and rape. Yet these were not mere thugs intent only on destruction. The successful leaders were all shrewd and highly ambitious as well as ruthless men, who did not want to destroy the empire, but to gain control of part of it and enjoy the comforts and wealth of civilisation. The aim was to create permanent kingdoms, not simply plunder and destroy. As the emperor Tiberius had once put it, the aim was to 'shear' the provincials and 'not flay them alive'.[5]

More than just pragmatism restricted their behaviour. As usual, we have no reliable statistics for population sizes in this period. However, even the most generous estimate of the largest barbarian groups would tend to number them no bigger than 100,000 people, including men, women and children. If such a population was even reasonably balanced, it would be hard pressed to field more than 30,000 warriors and nearer 20,000–25,000 would be more likely. In reality, the barbarian groups that settled within the empire were probably substantially smaller, their warriors counted in thousands rather than tens of thousands. No one would assess the provincial population of Spain, North Africa, Gaul or Italy as less than several millions each. There was no question of the eradication of the existing population and its replacement with new settlers. Perhaps one of the few exceptions to this was in eastern Britain as the fifth century progressed, although as we have seen the evidence for this can be interpreted in more than one way. Normally, the followers of the war leaders who created the new kingdoms had no choice but to live alongside the existing population. Similarly, the latter had no real choice about accepting new masters. This was still true even if, in some cases, they rarely saw a Goth or Frank. Both the occupying army and the occupied provincials simply had to accept and make the best of the new situation.[6]

The New Kingdoms

Compulsion and occupation underlay the barbarian settlement in the western provinces. The survival of institutions and a good deal of the existing culture should never blind us to this. In each of the new kingdoms an elite formed by the leading warriors of the new regime was imposed on all existing structures. Many wealthy families from the existing aristocracy survived with their riches and lands more or less intact. Persuading such men to accept the new regime helped to prevent them becoming leaders of wider resistance. Some embraced life in the royal court with enthusiasm. Sidonius Apollinaris joked with a friend who had become so fluent in the Burgundian language that he claimed the Burgundians themselves deferred to his knowledge of their own tongue. On another occasion, Sidonius mocked the supposed Burgundian habit of using rancid butter to grease their hair. Private disdain did not prevent Romans from showing respect in public, especially to barbarian leaders. A few fashions were copied from the tribes, although since these had themselves aped Roman styles in recent generations, and the Romans in turn had long since adopted 'Germanic' long tunics and trousers, the result was already something of a hybrid. We hear of provincials who served at the Vandal court, because anyone wearing Vandal dress – which evidently included many of these men – was barred from attending services in a Catholic rather than an Arian church.[7]

Debate continues to rage over precisely how land was allocated to the barbarian groups in the new kingdoms. For some, estates were confiscated from their existing owners and physically transferred to individual barbarians who then ran them as their own. The main alternative argues that it was not the land itself that was taken and transferred, but the tax revenue due from it. Effectively, the two-thirds of taxation that had once gone to the imperial administration – and in theory at least was mainly then spent on the costs of the army –

ABOVE: Famous for his open support for Christianity, the Emperor Constantine's greatest victories came in civil wars. Afterwards he gave the Empire just over a decade of internal peace and strong rule. His death was soon followed by fresh civil conflict.

RIGHT: Constantine's nephew Julian grew up as a virtual prisoner until he was made Caesar in Gaul in 355. He mounted a successful bid for supreme rule, but later died during a disastrous invasion of Persia. He was most remembered for his unsuccessful attempt to replace Christianity with an organised pagan church.

BELOW: Traditionally victors in civil wars did not openly commemorate or depict the defeat of Roman enemies. However, the Arch of Constantine blatantly celebrated his defeat of his Roman rival Maxentius at the Battle of the Milvian Bridge.

This early second century AD monument from the Danubian frontier depicts a barbarian and his family on the move. The Romans had long experience of controlling such movements, which makes their failure to deal with the Goths in 376 all the more striking.

The Porta Nigra (Black Gate) at Trier is one of the most impressive examples of Late Roman fortification. Trier was frequently used as a capital by western emperors and was consequently developed on a grand scale.

This scene from a mosaic in the lavish villa at Piazza Armerina in Sicily depicts Roman soldiers engaged in an animal hunt. They are not armoured, but otherwise are dressed in the standard army uniforms of the late Empire.

ABOVE: This base for an obelisk was set up in the hippodrome at Constantinople by the Emperor Theodosius I in 389. Despite his defeat of the usurper Magnus Maximus, only barbarian leaders are shown begging for imperial clemency.

FAR LEFT: The Emperor Honorius inherited the rule of the Western Empire at the age of just ten, and was never as impressive a figure as this image suggests. In 410 he failed to prevent the sack of Rome by the Goths.

LEFT: Flavius Stilicho, a Roman with barbarian ancestry, dominated the early years of Honorius' reign and controlled, but did not defeat, Alaric the Goth. Stilicho was subsequently executed on the orders of Honorius.

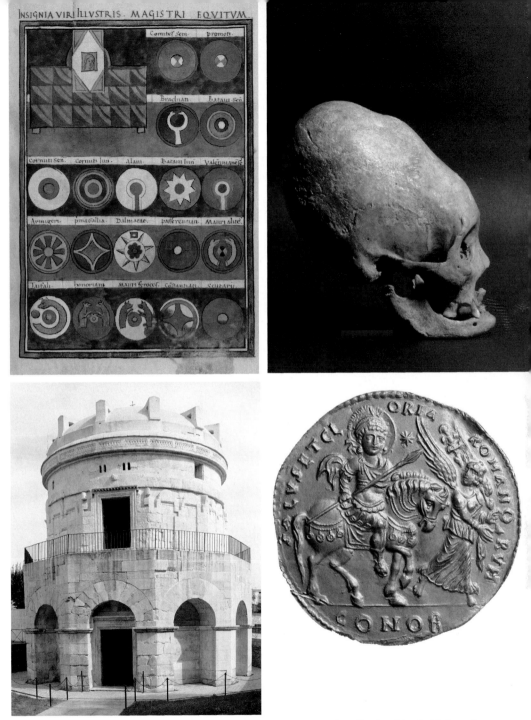

TOP LEFT: The *Notitia Dignitatum* is a remarkable document listing the officials of the divided empire around the turn of the fourth and fifth centuries. It lists army units and has pictures of the insignia painted on their shields. TOP RIGHT: Some Hunnic children had their skulls deliberately distorted to create the elongated shape shown here. It is not clear precisely why this was done, but seems to have been a mark of distinction. ABOVE LEFT: Theodoric the Goth established himself as king in Italy at the end of the fifth century. Many aspects of Roman life, law, and administration continued under his rule, and the style of his mausoleum at Ravenna is Classical in many respects. ABOVE RIGHT: The Emperor Justinian devoted considerable effort and resources during his long reign to retaking parts of the collapsed Western Empire. However, in the long term it proved impossible to hold on to much of this territory.

TOP: The massive defensive walls of Constantinople were completed in 413 during the reign of Theodosius II. The walls were not overcome by an enemy until the Fourth Crusade in 1204.

ABOVE: On this mosaic from the Church of St. Vitale in Ravenna, the Emperor Justinian is shown surrounded by courtiers and soldiers. Beside him is Maximianus, the bishop of the city. The soldiers' shields carry the chi-rho symbol of the *labarum*, adopted as his standard by Constantine.

The spectacular dome of the Hagia Sophia cathedral demonstrates the engineering skill and wealth still available to the Eastern Roman emperors like Justinian in the sixth century. The first dome collapsed in an earthquake, but was subsequently repaired.

Although Roman power collapsed, legacies of the empire remained in many of the former provinces. Some were cultural, and others more physical, such as the great aqueduct at Segovia in Spain. This late first century structure was still supplying the city with water at the beginning of the twentieth century.

now went to individual barbarians. In Italy Theodoric and his successors stressed that the roles of the Romans and Goths were complementary: 'While the army of the Goths makes war, the Roman may live in peace.' Therefore the taxation formerly devoted to funding the Roman military machine now supported Gothic soldiers directly. This transferral of revenue rather than the land itself is seen as likely to have been much less traumatic, hence the lack of substantial evidence for friction between the landowners and Goths. On the other hand, the suggestion that the warriors allocated the revenue probably collected in person creates a less amicable picture, and suggests considerable room for abuse and extortion.[8]

In the end, the evidence is insufficient to know precisely how the barbarians were supported from the land. We are probably wrong to expect this always to have been done in the same way in different areas and also not to have evolved over time. In due course it is clear that noblemen of barbarian descent came into direct possession of substantial estates. How they did so is uncertain, and purchase, theft or confiscation, royal gift and marriage into the existing aristocracy are all possibilities. The law codes set down by the rulers of the various kingdoms all maintain a clear distinction between the wider provincial population and the barbarian settlers and their descendants. Some of the former clearly had privileged status, but this was always lower than the equivalent members of the barbarian group. Nor was it simply the same as the distinction in Roman law between soldier and civilian. The Goths in Italy, and other groups elsewhere, were not simply soldiers, but the soldiers of an occupying power.[9]

Assimilation of the newcomers was never fast. In a real sense the continued authority of the new king and his troops relied upon their remaining distinct, as the controllers of all military force within the kingdom. There is a fierce and ongoing debate over the extent to which the Ostrogoths, Visigoths, Vandals, Franks or any others were truly a homogeneous ethnic group. There is good evidence that all at one time or another incorporated individuals and whole groups from other peoples. Yet whatever the precise ethnic composition, each group did remain distinct from the wider population it controlled. Any merging between the two was gradual and took several generations. Vandal Africa and Ostrogothic Italy both fell before the process was anywhere near complete. Elsewhere, in the long run the culture and language of the provincial population tended to prove most enduring. The Franks and the Visigoths would eventually become Latin speakers, so that today both the French and Spanish languages have clear Latin roots. Britain was an exception, the Anglo-Saxons continuing to speak a Germanic language, although Latin remained in use for literature and administrative writing.

One of the main obstacles was religion. By the period of settlement, virtually all of the barbarian groups had become Christian. The Franks were one of the last in mainland Europe to convert; the Saxons in Britain seem to have been the only ones to persist longer than this. Unusually, the Franks became Catholic. Almost every other Germanic group consisted of Arian Christians and this served as a constant reminder that they were different, distinct from the wider population. The Vandals were the most militant in their attacks on Catholicism, making use of the same imperial laws elsewhere applied to heretics. The peculiar conditions of North Africa, where since the Donatist schism there effectively existed two church organisations side by side with each other, ensured that hostility to Catholicism did not automatically alienate the entire population. Catholic bishops and priests were exiled from their sees and suffered other restrictions. Arians and others were favoured, although by the sixth century the attitude of Vandal kings became more moderate and some Catholic bishops were restored.

Elsewhere direct attacks on the Catholic Church were very rare. The Gothic kings in Italy and Spain built and endowed Arian churches, but there does not seem to have been any significant effort to turn Catholics into Arians. Indeed, there was usually official respect for Catholic churches and bishops, if only because this made sound political sense. Arianism was just another distinction of the occupying power, along with its physical appearance and style of dress. In the form followed by the rulers of the western kingdoms it may have had little in common with the ideas of Arius and his immediate followers. It is hard to discern any signs of major religious friction within these kingdoms. On the other hand, there is no evidence to suggest that the conversion to Catholicism of the Frankish King Clovis and his successors created more enthusiasm for their rule. In the long run, all of the kingdoms to survive eventually became Catholic.[10]

Even in the initial phases of settlement most leaders – and also probably many of their followers – had already had considerable exposure to Roman culture. Clovis' father Childeric was buried near Tournai in a grave first discovered in the seventeenth century. The grave goods suggest a fusion of Roman and traditional styles. These included a ring with the

Latin inscription 'of King Childeric' (*Childerici Regis*) for use as a seal. Theodoric, the ruler of the Ostrogoths who took Italy from Odoacer, readily illustrates the changing allegiances and experiences of his age. He was born within the Hunnic Empire probably a little before Attila's death. Later, from the ages of eight to eighteen, he was a hostage educated at the court of the eastern emperor in Constantinople. Afterwards he returned to his people and led a group of the Ostrogoths, proving himself a highly successful war leader. During these years he fought variously against different barbarian groups, most notably other Ostrogoths such as those loyal to the powerful Theodoric Strabo, or 'Squinty'. He fought both for and against the Romans, although it may ultimately have been with imperial approval that he moved to Italy. A story later circulated that Theodoric himself was only semi-literate. It was claimed that he had a stencil with the word *legi* ('I have read') so that he could write this on any document to show his approval. There is good reason to doubt the tale. More importantly, whatever his personal education, the kingdom he founded was fully literate in its administration and government.[11]

Men like Theodoric knew something of the ritual and symbolism surrounding the Roman emperors. This makes it all the more striking that they did not copy it, but presented themselves as lesser powers. For all the ceremony at the courts of the new kingdoms, the rituals and honours were always far less than those of the imperial court. Kings behaved more like Roman magistrates or provincial governors than emperors. Sidonius Apollinaris' detailed description of the routine of the Visigothic King Theodoric mentions that he held court sitting in a chair like a magistrate, not an imperial throne. In the early years all this may have helped preserve the fiction that each kingdom remained in a meaningful way part of the empire. Roman law was preserved throughout the provinces of mainland Europe. The kings did not usurp the imperial prerogative by issuing new legislation. Instead, they modified the existing laws and in several cases issued new codes that collected existing legislation and also laid down the relationship between barbarians and Romans. The former were always granted the right to trial by their own countrymen. The legal principles of the new codes seem to have owed more to Roman ideas than any 'Germanic' tradition. The key point was that they institutionalised the superior status of one section of the community. The barbarian kingdoms upheld the rule of law, but they simply made it favourable to the occupying power.[12]

There is little evidence for an immediate and abrupt decline in the standard of living for the provincial population within the new kingdoms. In some regions it is in fact hard to see any obvious distinction at all between the Roman and post-Roman periods. Some of the barbarian monarchs continued to stage games – usually beast fights – and many circuses and amphitheatres remained in use for some time. Water supplies were maintained to many cities. There was some building, usually of churches and since these were most often Arian, such things tended not to be given much mention in the essentially Catholic sources. In general, these were smaller than the churches constructed under imperial patronage. More work was done to repair and maintain existing structures. The Visigoths rebuilt the middle spans of the great arched bridge that still stands today at Merida (then, Augusta Emerita) in Spain. There was little or no construction of grand new monuments, but then that had been true of many cities in the later empire after the heyday of the second century. Technical skill seems to have been lost fairly gradually. In time, lack of knowledge as well as funds prevented all of the more sophisticated pieces of engineering so common under the Roman Empire. Even more basic techniques faded from regular use. In much of Europe thatch replaced tiles as roofing, and timber or wattle and daub became far more common than construction in stone or brick.[13]

On the whole, those areas with best access to the sea, and especially those on or near the Mediterranean, tended to fare better. Long-distance trade remained more frequent in these areas, if only of the light, luxury items that yielded the greatest profits. The Eastern Empire continued to bring in silks, spices and other exotic goods from India and beyond, and some of these items found their way into the west. Further from the Mediterranean, trade seems to have become much more local – in some cases this had already happened under Roman rule. The vast majority of the population came to use cruder pottery than had been common in the past. The new kingdoms do not seem ever to have improved the economic life of an area or the levels of comfort for those living there. The best that can be said was that they did not invariably have an immediate and detrimental impact on these. Yet the trend was certainly towards a less sophisticated and prosperous lifestyle. The luxuries of the empire – glass in windows, central heating, bath houses and the sheer quantity of consumer goods – had never been evenly distributed, but they had been fairly common. In due course they would cease altogether to be features of life in early medieval western Europe.

This change was not deliberate and in most instances it occurred very gradually over several generations. The sheer size of the old empire, with its single political authority, universal law and currency, and complex system of taxation had all stimulated the economy. Conditions were simply different by the late fifth and sixth centuries. Not only was trade massively reduced in scale, but life in general was simpler and its focus more local. Even ideas were exchanged less freely. For at least a few generations the surviving provincial aristocracies in the old western provinces seem to have maintained a fairly traditional education. Most were literate, some highly so. Very few, if any, were bilingual in Greek and Latin in the way that had once been common and the mark of the truly educated.[14]

The Church helped to preserve the use of Latin. It also maintained contacts between regions regardless of political boundaries. Yet we need to be careful. The institution of the medieval Catholic Church did not spring instantly into life, but developed very gradually. Over time the pope in Rome assumed something of the old role of the western emperors, even adopting some of their titles and ceremonial. Yet the pope's power was extremely limited and at times contested. Although various Church institutions had acquired wealth and lands, there was as yet little central marshalling of this. The kings of the west – and especially the Ostrogoths in Italy – generally respected the bishops and most of all the bishop of Rome. They did not do this because they had to, but because it made sound political sense. Respecting the Church helped to keep their new subjects content with their rule.

The survival of aspects of language, culture and institutions is important, but should never blind us to the degree of change. The kingdoms in the former Western Empire were fully independent. They had diplomatic contact with the emperors in Constantinople, but were not in any meaningful way subject to them. The kingdoms sometimes fought and also traded with each other, and their inhabitants had much in common with the peoples of other kingdoms. However, they were still utterly separate – far more so than the same regions had been as provinces. In the modern world many former colonies show the deep legacy of long-term occupation by an imperial power. Common survivals are in language, law and the shape of their political institutions. Many follow boundaries once created by imperial administrators and as a result often incorporate several ethnic or cultural groups. The imprint of the imperial power is clear. In spite of this, it would rightly come as a great surprise to their inhabitants to be told that they were anything less than fully independent.

The Empire That Did Not Fall

Emperor Zeno was hard pressed for money throughout his reign, in part as a legacy of the huge cost of the failed expedition to Africa in 468. He also faced a succession of serious internal threats and in many ways it is remarkable that he was able to survive in power for seventeen years. It took almost two years to suppress the rebellion of Basiliscus, Emperor Leo's brother-in-law, and during some of that time Zeno was forced to flee to his home territory in Isauria. Basiliscus made some serious mistakes, and when one of his main military supporters was wooed back by Zeno the rebellion began to collapse. Zeno reoccupied Constantinople in 476. Basiliscus was executed, along with his son whom he had named as co-ruler. Another victim in the months that followed was the commander whose defection from the usurper had made Zeno's victory possible. The restored emperor was taking no chances.

The next usurper was Leo's son-in-law Marcian. He was proclaimed emperor in 479 and attempted to seize control of Constantinople, but was narrowly defeated. This time there was greater clemency and the usurper was ordained as a priest and sent into exile. Both the challengers to Zeno had been supported by the Goth Theodoric Strabo. For a while he allied with the other Theodoric and their combined forces ravaged the Thracian provinces and even came close to taking Constantinople itself. Attempts to break Strabo's power by force had all ended in failure, but in 481 he died accidentally. Zeno gave the other Theodoric the rank of Master of Soldiers – a post also held by Strabo at various times when he was in favour with the Constantinople regime – and employed him to defeat Strabo's son. Many of his surviving warriors joined Theodoric's own forces, greatly increasing his power.[15]

Zeno was the most successful of the Isaurian noblemen promoted to senior ranks by Leo. Yet there were clear signs that the rise of the Isaurians was resented by other officers, and their wider unpopularity was suggested when they became targets of the mob during rioting in Constantinople. The mere fact that the emperor was himself an Isaurian did not guarantee the loyalty of all the officers drawn from the same region. Disappointment, and quite probably also long-established personal enmity, led to rebellion by two such men in Isauria itself in 484. The rebel leaders had approached the Persians for aid, but the only practical support came from some of the Armenian satraps. Zeno managed to muster an army consisting of strong contingents of Goths and Rugians, as well as regular troops. The rebels were quickly defeated in battle, although it took four years of blockade before their last stronghold fell and the revolt was finally over. By this time Theodoric and his men had left the Danubian frontier for Italy. Whether or not Zeno had enlisted them to fight against Odoacer, he was certainly glad to see this powerful and uncertain ally removed from the Eastern Empire.[16]

Zeno died of disease in 491. He left no heir, and after considerable discussion at court it was decided to let his widow Ariadne, who was the daughter of Leo, decide the succession. She chose a man already in his sixties, the palace official Anastasius, and promptly married him. His elevation prompted a new round of unrest in Isauria, initially on behalf of Zeno's brother Longinus, who had most pointedly not been selected as emperor by the court. Anastasius quickly exiled Longinus and met the rebellion with armed force. He was equally brutal in his response to unrest in Antioch and Constantinople itself, which seems to have been motivated by a wider unpopularity of his rule. In spite of this rocky start, as well as his age and comparative obscurity, Anastasius proved himself to be a gifted politician and a highly successful emperor, who reigned until his death twenty-seven years later. Under his rule the finances of the empire improved considerably, allowing him to leave a substantial surplus in the treasury.[17]

The Eastern Empire he ruled was recognisably the same as the one created in 395. Although he reformed the currency, and took considerable effort to make the bureaucracy as efficient as possible, the structures of the civil service, its offices and departments remained virtually unchanged. Latin continued to be used in law and much official documentation, even if very few of the bureaucrats were native speakers. Anastasius reformed army pay, turning the bulk of this back into coin rather than allowances of clothing, equipment and food. He seems to have made military service considerably more attractive so that volunteering was enough to satisfy the army's needs. A little less use would be made in future of mercenary bands and allied contingents.[18]

In 395 there had been little fundamental difference between the civilian bureaucracy and the military structure in the two halves of the empire. In less than a century the army had vanished in the west, as had administration above the level of the individual provinces. Even more obviously there had ceased to be emperors in the west. The survival of the apparently identical eastern half of the empire after the collapse of imperial power in the west is often used to argue that the external threats in the west were greater than internal problems. If the east survived, so this logic runs, then the basic structures of the late fourth- and fifth- century empire cannot have been terminally flawed.[19]

The most obvious difference between the east and west was the barbarian settlement. The Eastern Empire faced serious attacks along the length of the Danubian frontier – Attila's great empire had targeted this region repeatedly, inflicting considerable damage. He only turned against the west in the final years of his career. Hunnic power collapsed rapidly after his death, but his sons led several major raids into Roman territory. Some of the powers to emerge from the wreck of Attila's empire, notably several groups of Ostrogoths on the Pannonian and Thracian frontiers, proved equally hostile. Later in the fifth and sixth centuries new groups such as the Bulgars, Slavs and Avars would be drawn into contact with the Roman frontier and would prove equally warlike and aggressive. Some barbarian groups had been permitted to settle in imperial territory from 382 onwards. Of these a portion had subsequently migrated again, invariably moving into the lands of the Western Empire. Inevitably, we hear much less about any group that remained peaceful. Unlike their western colleagues, the eastern emperors were not forced to accept the permanent occupation by barbarian groups of substantial parts of their provinces.

Geography played a role in this. The Bosphorus provided a permanent obstacle making it very difficult for any hostile group to cross into Asia. Persia was a major power, its wealth and military capacity only a little inferior to the Eastern Empire. Yet it was easier to deal with a single neighbouring king than a large number of competing chieftains and war leaders. This was especially true in the fifth century when the Persian monarchs were often weak and rarely inclined towards major aggression against their Roman neighbour. They also faced a serious problem on their northern frontier from the growing aggression of the 'White Huns'. The problems on the eastern and southern frontiers of the empire were profoundly different in nature to those in Europe. There was not pressure from many different leaders eager to stake a permanent claim to parts of the empire. The eastern emperors did not successively lose provinces and their revenue to barbarian settlement. Their resources remained essentially undiminished throughout the fifth century. The support for expeditions to recover Africa from the Vandals proved costly to the Eastern Empire, but for all their concern over this the losses they endured were temporary.[20]

At the end of the fifth century the Eastern Empire remained essentially intact and in possession of all its resources. The archaeology suggests that many of the eastern provinces were thriving, with high populations and good agricultural productivity. Again, the general freedom from raiding over the course of the century was in marked contrast to the western provinces and doubtless contributed to this prosperity. Thrace and Pannonia suffered far more from enemy attack, and territory closest to the border was permanently abandoned and occupied by barbarian peoples. Revenue from elsewhere funded a degree of defence for these regions. It also made possible the construction of major defensive works, most notably the Theodosian Walls, which kept Constantinople secure from foreign attack until the thirteenth century, when the city was stormed during the Fourth Crusade. The region was never fully secure throughout the fifth century and successive emperors had to balance fighting, conciliating and bribing the war leaders operating in this area. Many of these received Roman subsidies or tribute to keep the peace, and others were appointed to army commands. Disturbed as this frontier so often was, the essential geography kept the problems confined to a limited area and encouraged successive enemies to move westwards.[21]

The Eastern Empire remained prosperous enough to support a large regular army and the imperial bureaucracy. Neither was any more perfect than the equivalent institutions in the west at the end of the fourth century, but they were not forced into terminal decline through lack of funds. As always it is worth reminding ourselves that the simple possession of such institutions, however imperfect, set the Romans apart from all their neighbours with the exception of the Persians. None of the barbarian kingdoms created in the Western Empire were able to maintain especially large or notably efficient professional armies. The Eastern Empire could do this and after Anastasius' reforms was less dependent on mercenary and allied contingents or unwilling conscripts. The Eastern Empire was a large, wealthy and powerful state. In most circumstances it did not need to be especially efficient.

At the end of the fourth and beginning of the fifth centuries both Western and Eastern Empires underwent decades of rule by emperors who came to power as children, and always remained weak and easily influenced. During this period emperors withdrew from active participation in campaigning, and indeed from much of public life beyond the complex ceremonies of the court. This trend was only partially reversed when men like Marjorian presided over campaigns in Gaul and the unsuccessful African expedition. The competition to dominate this succession of weak emperors was often fierce. In the Western Empire a series of generals became rulers in all but name. Their power was not formal, and was always subject to challenge by rivals, but was no less real for all that. Ricimer demonstrated how easy it was to make and break emperors, especially once the line of Theodosius had ended.

The western provinces had always produced a disproportionately high number of usurpers. All usurpers needed military support and large numbers of troops were stationed there, so there may be no more to it than this. However, more probably the constant threat of raiding and invasion encouraged these regions to feel neglected by central government. There was also the simple fact that each civil war tended to encourage further outbreaks. A successful usurpation showed what was possible. A defeat inevitably left some discontented survivors, who had little to hope for from the current regime and were therefore inclined to replace it. This pattern repeated itself again and again in the Western Empire during the fifth century, whether the conflict was actually to create a new emperor or simply to dominate the existing one. The majority of fifth-century western emperors died violently, as did many of their leading generals. Stilicho and Aetius were both killed, and Boniface died of his wounds. In contrast, Constantius and Ricimer survived long enough to die of natural causes.

The Eastern Empire was not altogether free of civil war, most especially in Leo's reign. Yet these were still markedly less frequent than in the west. Competition within the court remained fierce, but was only occasionally violent and even less often led to all-out warfare. Although several very powerful generals emerged in the Eastern Empire, and some had considerable power, they never quite achieved the dominance of men like Aetius in the Western Empire. In most cases there were other powers within the court, so that no single influence was overwhelming. Zeno was probably the most successful of these generals, rising through the army to marry the emperor's daughter and ultimately succeed him. With the exception of Zeno's short-lived son, all the men who became emperor after the death of Theodosius II did so at a mature age. None was a mere puppet, even if each had to struggle to free himself from powerful figures in the army and at court. Their success was not inevitable, but that they were able to overcome such challenges shows that the balance of power was very different to that in the west. The same was true of the failure of all the usurpers who appeared in the east. Success as usual fed off itself. Marcian, Leo, Zeno and Anastasius all had comparatively long reigns and died of natural causes at ages that were advanced for those days. Had any of them been supplanted then this would doubtless have fostered further instability.

Once again, the greater and more stable wealth of the Eastern Empire played a part. Shortage of funds contributed a good deal to weakening Zeno's power and making his reign so turbulent. In the west emperors and their commanders struggled to control ever diminishing resources, knowing that a serious failure could readily prove fatal. In the east there was usually money and sufficient troops to deal with any problem. It was just a question of controlling these and directing them reasonably efficiently. Another force for stability was the existence of Constantinople itself as the imperial capital. It was a large city, if not quite so big as Rome had been in its heyday. Housed there was a senatorial aristocracy consisting of the wealthiest individuals from the provinces, most of them former officials. There were also the key officials and departments of the imperial administration, all possessive of their responsibilities, and with their seniority marked and jealously guarded by the intricate details of uniform and insignia. The bishop of the city was one of the most important figures in the Church, in spite of rival claims from Alexandria, and the continued acknowledgement of the ultimate authority of the pope in Rome. Finally, there was the wider population itself, which, like the inhabitants of most ancient cities, was often unruly and willing to express its opinion.[22]

Constantinople was a genuine capital, the centre of life for the court and administration. It contained many individuals and groups with more or less political influence and importance. The contrast with Ravenna – or even the earlier capital of Milan – could not be more marked. There the western emperors were isolated. The Senate's power had long since become symbolic, but it still consisted of rich and influential men. Both they, and other important figures including the pope, were in Rome, some distance away from ready access. A constant stream of petitioners and people seeking favours from the emperor still flowed to Ravenna, or wherever the court happened to be, but in no other respect was it an especially important city. Constantinople was genuinely the heart of the Eastern Empire. Controlling it did not guarantee the success of an emperor, as the ultimate failure of Basiliscus had shown, but it was a major asset.[23]

The eastern emperors intervened on several occasions in disputes over the succession in the west. Zeno was too weak to provide meaningful support for Julius Nepos following his expulsion in 475. The latter lived on in Dalmatia until his death in 480, an emperor solely in name. The government in Constantinople never again tried to revive the Western Empire. It was content instead to deal with the individual kings, who were wooed in various ways. The Frank Clovis was even given the honour of a consulship, although he obviously did not travel to take this up in person. The break-up of the Western Empire did not pose a serious threat to the Eastern Empire. If anything, it made it more secure, since there was no longer a court in Italy that might seek to interfere in the politics of the east, backing a rival to the throne with either diplomacy or direct force. There was now no one in the west with the prestige even of the last few western emperors. No Gothic or Frankish king could claim the right to intervene in the east.[24]

It is fair to say that the threats faced by the Western and Eastern Empires in the fifth century were different. No independent kingdoms were created in the Eastern Empire and throughout the century its territory remained essentially intact. This does not mean that the structures of both empires were essentially sound and that the Western Empire only succumbed because the threats it faced were overwhelming. It is true that each new settlement robbed the state of precious resources, weakening its capacity to function in the future. It became harder and harder to deal with any problem, but this does not alter the fact that even before the first major settlement of the Goths in Gaul, the Western Empire consistently failed to deal with the threats it faced. It won no permanent victories and the only way it could break up one of the new kingdoms was by using another barbarian group. All too often, this simply meant replacing one group with another, not restoring a region to imperial control. At times, the western authorities seem consciously to have aimed at limiting the victories won by barbarian leaders fighting on their behalf. A leader fighting as an ally one year could easily become an enemy the next.

The survival of the Eastern Empire had less to do with the efficiency of its institutions than its sheer size. As in the past, the essential reality of its size and strength meant that it did not have to be especially efficient. Even the Western Empire did not fall quickly, in spite of the successive losses of major provinces and their revenue. The enemies it faced were disunited. They fought for dominance of their own people and were equally aggressive in their relations with other barbarian groups. For decades the western emperors survived by playing off one barbarian group against another.

The failure of the two Roman expeditions to Africa was not inevitable, with luck and human error playing a part. If the Vandals had been defeated and these lucrative provinces recovered, then this would have meant a substantial increase in the resources of the Western Empire. This assumes that the Romans would have been able to hold on to Africa in the long run. It is always possible that another barbarian group would have tried to seize this rich area, just as Alaric and others seem to have planned to do before the Vandals succeeded. Access was relatively easy from Spain, which the Romans no longer controlled. Even with the resources of Africa it is hard to imagine that the Western Empire would have been capable of destroying any of the barbarian kingdoms in the other provinces. Yet it could easily have survived, perhaps for generations. On the other hand, it is hard to believe that it would have remained free from civil war and usurpation, conditions that always created opportunities for ambitious barbarian war leaders.

The Eastern Empire was large, populous and wealthy. Throughout the fifth century it was simply bigger and more powerful than any of its neighbours and potential or real enemies. The advantage over Persia was slight, and the two now treated each other much more as equals. The comparative weakness and lack of aggression of the Persian monarchs in the course of the fifth century had clearly fostered the prosperity of the Eastern Empire. This attitude would change early in the sixth century, beginning a prolonged period of conflict between Rome and Persia. This test would give a clearer idea of the real strength of the Eastern Empire.

21

Rise and Fall

'God has granted us to make peace with the Persians, to make the Vandals, Alans and Moors our subjects, and gain possession of all Africa and Sicily besides, and we have good hopes that he will consent to our establishing our empire over the rest of those whom the Romans of old ruled from the boundaries of one ocean to the other and then lost by their negligence.' – *Emperor Justinian, April 536.*[1]

Emperor Anastasius was in his late eighties when he died on 9 July 518. He had no son and had failed to mark out a successor. After a good deal of manoeuvring within the imperial court, Justin, the commander of the emperor's close bodyguard (*excubitores*) bribed his way to power. There were rumours that he used money given to him by the chamberlain, who as a eunuch could not aspire to the throne himself. Allegedly, Justin had agreed to buy support for another candidate, but then changed his mind and used the cash on his own behalf. Now in his mid sixties, he came originally from a rural part of the Latin-speaking Balkan provinces. Justin was not a member of the established aristocracy, but as usual we should be careful about accepting the snobbery of our sources and labelling him a peasant. The malicious claim that he was illiterate is extremely unlikely for someone so senior in rank. Nevertheless, his rise was certainly spectacular and demonstrated once again the influence of the senior officers and officials at court.[2]

One of Justin's nephews was a junior officer in another of the imperial guard units, the *candidati*. This man, Petrus Sabbatius, was rapidly promoted and then adopted, taking the name Justinian. Before the emperor died in 527, Justin made Justinian his imperial colleague, so that this time the succession was smooth. Justinian would rule as sole emperor until his own death in 565. Some saw him as the real power behind Justin, and even if this was an exaggeration, it is fair to say that he was at the centre of power for well over forty years. This was an exceptionally long period of continuity, even in an era of long-lived emperors. During these years Justinian took a direct interest in many things, from theology to law, and through his generals – he never went on campaign in person – fought a long series of wars. The provinces in North Africa were retaken and the Vandal kingdom destroyed. After a much longer struggle, Ostrogothic Italy also fell to Justinian's armies, as did Sicily, Sardinia, Corsica and part of Spain. Only a few of these conquests proved lasting and much of the regained territory was lost within a few years of Justinian's death. His successors were inclined to blame Justinian for over-stretching the empire's limited resources and creating the massive problems they faced. It was a convenient excuse and there was at least a measure of truth in it.[3]

Justinian's actions and their consequences were always deeply controversial. Like his uncle, he came from one of the few Latin-speaking regions of the Eastern Empire. There is no doubt that he was well educated and fluent in Greek as well as Latin, but he did not come from the ranks of the aristocracy and was always resented by them. Many of the sources – especially those written or released after his death – are deeply hostile to him. He was a stickler for court protocol, and anyone presented to him had to prostrate themselves on the floor and, if they were so favoured, kiss the hem of the imperial robe. Other emperors had permitted the more distinguished senators and officials merely to bow. Justinian and his wife Theodora seem to have revelled in expensive displays of imperial grandeur and dignity.[4]

In many ways the empress was even more remarkable than her husband. Theodora was born into a family of entertainers who worked in the great circus adjacent to the palace in Constantinople. As a girl she became maid to one of the mime actresses who performed in the intervals between chariot races. Later she became an actress and dancer herself. A career of this sort tended to be brief and Theodora, like many of these women, chose to exploit her celebrity and looks by becoming a courtesan. The more lurid stories about her allegedly rampant sexual appetites were doubtless mere gossip repeated by sources who loathed Theodora. Yet even accounts favourable to her did not hide the fact that she had been a prostitute. She gave birth to an illegitimate daughter and there may have been other children. After a while she was hired as mistress by the governor of Egypt, only to be abandoned by him in Alexandria. There, she seems to have had a profound religious experience. When Justinian met her she was back in Constantinople working as a seamstress. She became his mistress, but they could not legally marry since a man of his status was forbidden from marrying a woman who had once been a prostitute. It took some time for them to persuade Justin to introduce a special law permitting the wedding. As far as we can tell, Theodora was always faithful to Justinian, although the couple never had a child.[5]

Theodora was undoubtedly a very strong-willed woman. Justinian had a deep affection for her and respected her opinions, and emperor and empress often appeared as equals at ceremonial events. Theodora was known to influence his policy and decisions over the appointment, promotion and dismissal of officials and army officers. Emperors believed to be dominated by their wives or other female relations were invariably criticised in later sources, and Justinian was no exception. Yet domination certainly seems too strong a word. Justinian relied on his wife, but his was not a weak character and after her death no one individual in any way controlled him. Theodora's humble and rather discreditable background provided plenty of ammunition for the couple's detractors. Three of her old friends from the circus days were brought to live as her companions in the palace and were found wealthy husbands. Theodora also gave over another palace building as a refuge for girls rescued from prostitution. Some Christian groups later remembered her as extremely devout. Yet there was no doubt that she could also be devious and vindictive, engineering the fall of a number of prominent men.[6]

The Old Enemy

In the fifth century relations between the Eastern Empire and Sassanid Persia had generally been peaceful, in marked contrast to earlier centuries. It became normal for the Roman emperor and Persian king to refer to each other as 'brother' in their diplomatic exchanges. Persia was effectively acknowledged as the empire's equal and Roman dreams of her conquest had long since faded. The long peace was encouraged by the other problems faced by both sides. The Persians were confronted with the growing threat of nomadic groups – the Sabir Huns in the north and the Hephthalite or 'White Huns' to the north-east. To what extent either of these groups were related to the Huns of Attila is questionable, and the name 'Hun' may simply have been given to any nomadic group felt to fight in a similar way. Their raids were frequent and several expeditions sent to punish them ended in disaster. One Persian king was even killed in battle, something that the Romans had never managed in all their long wars with Persia. Several bouts of civil war further weakened Sassanid power and made them reluctant to provoke serious fighting with their Roman neighbours.[7]

Things began to change with the accession of the Persian King Kavadh in 488. Eight years later he was expelled in a civil war and took refuge amongst the Hephthalite Huns. With their support he defeated his rival in 499 and then reigned until his death in 531. His son Khusro I succeeded him and ruled until 579. For some eighty years Persia was ruled by just two kings, providing a level of stability that more than matched the longevity of contemporary emperors in Constantinople. Yet it took some time after his return from exile before Kavadh could feel secure and he was desperately short of money. Hephthalite assistance had come at a high price. He also needed wealth to pay soldiers, reward loyal followers and prevent the nobility from supporting rival claimants to the throne. The irrigation systems that made agriculture possible in large parts of his kingdom were expensive to maintain and even more costly to expand.[8]

Kavadh needed funds and sent ambassadors to Constantinople requesting money from Anastasius. The ostensible justification for this was the cost of maintaining garrisons to deny the Sabir Huns access to the passes in the Caucasian mountains, most notably the pass known as the Caspian Gates. The Persians argued that this was a service to the Romans as well as themselves, since Hunnic raiding parties could other-wise easily reach into the Roman provinces, as they had done in the past. The Romans had paid subsidies to the Persians on several occasions during the fifth century. However, it is uncertain whether there was ever a formal arrangement to help fund the defence of the Caucasian passes. Such a deal would have smacked of paying tribute to a superior foreign power and have been deeply damaging to any emperor. Whatever the background, Anastasius refused to pay. Therefore, in 502 Kavadh launched an attack on the Roman provinces, determined to take by force the wealth he needed. He took and plundered several important towns, including Amida, which fell only after a siege lasting more than three months. The Roman response was sluggish, but by 505 their counter attacks were strong enough to persuade Kavadh to accept a truce. He had already acquired considerable plunder and large numbers of captives to settle on royal lands. The Romans probably paid him a considerable sum to secure the peace. All in all Kavadh was most likely content, and anyway faced a new burst of aggression from the Sabir Huns.[9]

The peace lasted for two decades, by which time Kavadh was well into his seventies and becoming concerned about the succession. Choosing Khusro over an older son, the Persian king asked his 'brother' the Roman emperor to ensure that his choice was respected. Kavadh actually asked

Justin to adopt Khusro as his son. Although the emperor was enthusiastic, his advisors eventually persuaded him that this would be dangerous, as it would also give the youth a direct claim to the imperial throne. That the proposal was made and seriously considered and even the reason for its rejection emphasise how far Roman attitudes towards Persia had changed. In the end, Justin offered a lesser form of adoption, which was often used with barbarian leaders, but eventually the talks broke down.[10]

Disappointed, Kavadh returned to his familiar demands for money from the Romans. Skirmishes escalated along the frontiers and in 530 the Persians launched a major invasion. Their first target was Dara, a fortress city built not far from Nisibis. Anastasius had begun its development into a major stronghold and Justinian had added to the work. Led by a general named Belisarius, a sizeable Roman army met the larger Persian force outside Dara and inflicted a sharp defeat on them. In 531 Belisarius was in turn routed by another invading Persian army at the Battle of Callinicum. Fortunes were mixed in the following months, but the Persians were gaining little and by the end of the year were eager for peace. This mood was only reinforced when Kavadh died and Khusro became king in his place. In 532 the Romans and Persians agreed what they called the 'eternal peace'. Justinian agreed to pay the Persian king 11,000 lb of gold – a figure almost twice as large as the biggest payment to Attila, but still comfortably affordable for the Eastern Empire.[11]

In 540 Khusro broke the treaty and attacked. It was simple opportunism. He knew that Justinian's armies were heavily committed elsewhere and that therefore Roman defences in the east were weak. Like his father, he was also very short of funds, and like most earlier Persian campaigns, the invasion was essentially a large-scale raid. It did reach further into Syria than any Sassanid attack since the third-century triumphs of Shapur I, and in this respect was exceptional. Antioch was captured and sacked, and Khusro bathed in the waters of the Mediterranean. Then the king retired, taking his plunder and tens of thousands of prisoners with him. There was never any prospect of permanently occupying the captured cities.[12]

The fall of Antioch was a major humiliation for Justinian, but a year later a far more serious blow was struck by a dreadful plague. It began in Egypt and swiftly spread throughout the provinces. The fatalities in Constantinople were said to have been massive and it has been common to compare this epidemic with the Black Death of the fourteenth century. The disease was probably a form of bubonic plague, although it is perfectly possible that other infections spread simultaneously and claimed many victims. Like the medieval plague it returned a number of times during the next decades, but as usual we have no reliable statistics to assess its full cost in lives and its wider economic and social consequences. In spite of the impact of the plague, Justinian recalled Belisarius from the west and sent him against the Persians. The Romans attacked Persian territory in Assyria, although the offensive, much like enemy operations, amounted to little more than a grand raid. There were no more spectacular successes for either side in the following years.[13]

By 545 Justinian and Khusro made peace in Mesopotamia, although hostilities continued in the far north, near the Caucasus. Both Rome and Persia had long struggled to dominate the kingdoms of this area, such as Lazica and Iberia. Religion played a role in the contest, for both areas became Christian, providing the Romans with a pretext for supporting them. Over-enthusiastic Persian efforts to promote Zoroastrianism provoked several defections to Rome. In turn, the maladministration and corruption of Roman officials at other times convinced peoples to break their link with the empire. The balance of power swayed back and forth between the two powers and much of the actual fighting was done by allies. This was also true in the south, where the two main Arab groups – the Ghassanids allied to the Romans and the Lakhmids who were backed by the Persians – were enthusiastic raiders. The two powers encouraged these allies to harass the other's territory. This was often a way of putting pressure on the rival power and was rarely considered by either side to constitute a real war.[14]

In 561/2 a more complete peace treaty was agreed – this time supposedly to last a modest fifty years instead of being eternal. The Romans were to pay the Persians an annual subsidy of 500 lb of gold. Justinian could see little advantage to further fighting against Persia, especially since he had continued military commitments elsewhere. It is striking just how limited the operations in this conflict had been. Most campaigns were essentially raids. Fortified towns remained of critical importance, providing protection from enemy attacks and bases from which raids could be launched. As such they were often the targets of major offensives. Both sides scored successes, but sieges could be costly and were not invariably successful. The Persians repeatedly failed to capture Edessa, just as the Romans were always unsuccessful in their attempts to regain Nisibis. The Persians had resented the strengthening of Dara so close to their own border and in 532 had persuaded the Romans to withdraw the bulk of the troops stationed there.[15]

Into the West

The wars against Persia were the largest conflicts fought by the Romans in the sixth century. On several occasions they mustered armies of 30,000, and perhaps even 40,000 men. These were large by the standards of any period of Roman history and were matched by Persian armies, which were as big or even bigger. The cost of maintaining the many fortresses on the eastern frontier was also huge. On several occasions these were found to have decayed, something that the spate of earthquakes to hit the area in this period is unlikely to have helped, but they were always rebuilt. Justinian also spent heavily on defending the Balkan frontier against the various tribal peoples who threatened the region. Yet even though this was closer to Constantinople itself, it is clear that the Persians were always seen as the most dangerous and important enemy. Resources would be taken from any other theatre to bolster the defences of the east. This makes it all the more striking that the most spectacular successes of Justinian's reign were won in the western Mediterranean.[16]

In 533 Justinian despatched Belisarius to invade the Vandal kingdom in North Africa. The previous year's eternal peace with Persia had made the eastern front secure, but this was still a risky venture. Senior advisers reminded the emperor of the costly disaster in 468 and urged him to abandon the plan. Yet Justinian scented an opportunity. The Vandals had recently become embroiled in a dynastic squabble and also faced rebellions, both in Africa and some of the islands they controlled. In addition, the Ostrogoths agreed to let the Romans use their ports in Sicily as staging posts for the invasion fleet. Justinian decided to take the gamble. Belisarius was given a large support fleet and an army of at least 15,000 men – there is some doubt about the total as it is unclear whether this figure included his own strong regiment of cavalry. The real total for the army may have been up to a few thousand higher. This was a considerable force by the standards of the day. However, the army and fleet were certainly not larger than those involved in the disastrous fifth-century expeditions. There was absolutely no guarantee of success and a failure would have seriously damaged Justinian.[17]

The result was a spectacularly rapid and overwhelming success. The main Vandal forces were elsewhere when the Romans landed. King Gelimer was in the south of the country dealing with rebels, while many of his best troops were far away in Sardinia dealing with another uprising. Wrong footed from the start, the Vandals concentrated what troops they could and rushed to confront the invaders. Belisarius smashed them in

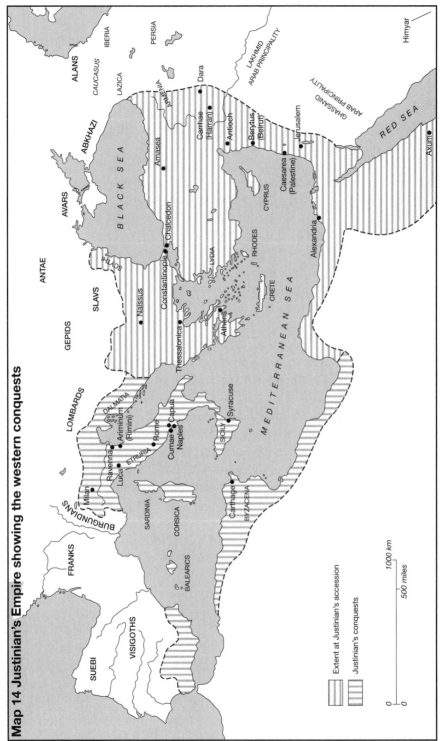

Map 14 Justinian's Empire showing the western conquests

ALANS

IBERIA

PERSIA

CAUCASUS

LAZICA

ARMENIA

ABKHAZI

Dara

Amasea

Carrhae
(Harran)

Antioch

LAKHMID
ARAB PRINCIPALITY

Berytus
(Beirut)

Jerusalem

GHASSANID
ARAB PRINCIPALITY

Himyar

RED SEA

Caesarea
(Palestine)

Axum

Alexandria

CYPRUS

RHODES

CRETE

AVARS

B L A C K   S E A

ANTAE

ILLYRI

Chalcedon

Constantinople

LYDIA

SLAVS

Naissus

GEPIDS

Thessalonica

Athens

M E D I T E R R A N E A N   S E A

LOMBARDS

DALMATIA

Ariminum
(Rimini)

Ravenna

Luca

ETRURIA

Rome

Cumae
Naples

Capua

Syracuse

SICILY

BURGUNDIANS

Milan

SARDINIA

CORSICA

BALEARICS

Carthage

BYZACENA

FRANKS

SUEBI

VISIGOTHS

Extent at Justinian's accession

Justinian's conquests

0   500 miles

0   1000 km

two battles, both fought almost entirely by his cavalry. Gelimer fled to a mountain refuge, but eventually surrendered a few months later and was taken back to Constantinople. Justinian allowed Belisarius the honour of a triumphal procession, although the victorious general walked through the streets rather than riding in a chariot in the ancient fashion. Gelimer was led in the procession and kept repeating a verse from the Old Testament Book of Ecclesiastes: 'Vanity of vanities, all is vanity'. The culmination of the ceremony came when Belisarius and Gelimer both came before a seated Justinian and Theodora. Both the general and his captive prostrated themselves before the emperor. For all the honour done to Belisarius, the ceremony made it abundantly clear that the true glory belonged to Justinian.[18]

The stunning success against the Vandals encouraged the emperor to consider further adventures in the west. Italy now seemed vulnerable as a group of Ostrogothic nobles turned against Theodoric's grandson, who was seen to be both too 'Roman' and far too much under the control of his mother. When the young king died, she tried to replace him with his cousin, but she was soon imprisoned and eventually killed. In 535 Belisarius was sent with just 7,500 men to take Sicily. Once again, his success was speedy, encouraging Justinian to order the invasion of Italy itself. From the beginning this conflict was to be fought with very limited resources compared to the African campaign. Italy, with its many walled cities, also presented a far larger and more difficult theatre of operations. At the same time the Goths proved less willing than the Vandals to seek immediate confrontation. The result was a far longer and bitterly fought series of campaigns over the following decades, during which many of the communities of Italy suffered badly. Belisarius occupied Rome at the end of 535 at the head of just 5,000 men and was besieged there for over a year before finally repulsing the Ostrogothic army.[19]

In Africa the Roman army had generally been welcomed by the wider population. Belisarius took care to keep his men on a tight rein when they entered Carthage, preventing looting or other misbehaviour. The situation in Italy was more complicated. Naples held out against the Romans and was sacked when they finally managed to force their way in. Elsewhere the Romans were welcomed, but each community to defect to Belisarius was another place he needed to protect from Ostrogothic reprisals. Even though the number of Roman troops in Italy gradually increased, many of these had to be dispersed in small garrisons. In 539 another of Justinian's most trusted generals, the eunuch Narses, was sent to Italy with reinforcements. He and Belisarius did not get on well and failed to co-operate. Milan was occupied by the Romans, but then quickly retaken and brutally sacked by the Ostrogoths. Friction and bickering between Roman commanders became a common theme for most of the Italian campaigns. Individual commanders went their own way, content with controlling their own small forces and dominating one patch of territory. Many proved themselves spectacularly corrupt, extorting as much money as possible from the local inhabitants. There were several cases of individuals and whole communities regretting their allegiance to the Eastern Empire and defecting back to the Goths.[20]

The record of the Roman army during Justinian's wars was extremely mixed. It won most of the major battles in the west and a fair few of those fought against the Persians. In some of these it fought with exemplary discipline and skill. On the other hand, battles were comparatively rare and much of the fighting was on a far smaller scale. More importantly, there were far more cases of generals unable to control their own soldiers. On more than one occasion, including the defeat at Callinicum, Belisarius was pressured into joining battle against his better judgement because he felt unable to resist the enthusiasm of his men. After the victory in Africa one soldier got drunk and accidentally shot and killed his own commander with an arrow. Looting and other misbehaviour could not always be prevented, even when it weakened the Romans' cause by alienating the locals. It did not help that the soldiers' pay was often heavily in arrears and this provoked a number of mutinies. Before the Italian campaign, Belisarius had to be recalled to Africa to deal with a serious outbreak amongst the troops he had left there. A major contributing factor in this outbreak was the fact that many of the soldiers had married the former wives of the Vandals and were eager to retain their property.[21]

Justinian's wars in the west were fought with limited numbers of troops, who were sometimes poorly disciplined and even mutinous. The senior officers rarely co-operated well – a problem not helped by a reluctance at times to appoint a clear supreme commander. Many Roman officers and officials were more interested in personal profit and succeeded only in alienating the people they had supposedly come to liberate and restore to the empire. The resurgence of war with Persia in 540 also shifted the conflict in Italy to a lower priority. Narses had already been recalled, and Belisarius was sent to fight in the east in 541. The impact of the plague can only have reduced the manpower and funds at the emperor's immediate disposal. Belisarius returned to Italy in 544 and found himself desperately short of all resources. He retook Rome, which had fallen to the Goths, but was able to achieve very little before being recalled again in 549. Narses returned to take charge of the forces in Italy and, as relations with Persia improved, was able to demand and receive more troops. In 552 he defeated and killed the last Ostrogothic king, Totila, in battles where the Romans significantly outnumbered the Goths. This was in spite of the fact that some troops were despatched to intervene in a civil war in Visigothic Spain. Justinian seems to have believed that this offered another opportunity to exploit the weakness of one of the kingdoms.[22]

From the beginning, there was a strong element of opportunism in Justinian's wars in the western Mediterranean. Periods of temporary internal weakness in Vandal Africa, then Ostrogothic Italy and finally Visigothic Spain were exploited. If the forces deployed by the Romans to fight these campaigns were modest in comparison with those fielded in the struggle with Persia, it is also worth noting how comparatively weak the western kingdoms proved. Luck played a major part in the swift collapse of the Vandals, but the slow progress of the war in Italy had more to do with the Roman failure to commit sufficient resources than Ostrogothic strength. The intervention in Spain was on a limited scale and had very limited results. A Roman-controlled coastal enclave was created around Cartagena. In Italy Narses defeated a Frankish invasion in 554. There was further trouble in Africa, with a succession of difficult campaigns against the Moorish tribes to the south of the provinces. For both Italy and Africa new praetorian prefectures were created to oversee their administration. Justinian had no intention of reviving the Western Empire, instead the recovered territories were simply treated as additional provinces of the east.[23]

Africa was the biggest long-term success in the reconquered west and by the end of the sixth century was a relatively peaceful and prosperous part of the Eastern Empire. Most of the gains in Italy were lost within a decade of Justinian's death. In 568 Italy was invaded by the Lombards, yet another tribal group that in the past had as often appeared as allies as they had as enemies of the empire. The Roman forces stationed in Italy were weak and poorly co-ordinated. The bulk of the Italian Peninsula was overrun and carved up into separate territories ruled by Lombard chieftains called *duces* by the Romans. The empire managed to hang on to just a few areas on the coast and around cities such as Ravenna and Rome. Sicily and the other major islands were also preserved, but even the most generous assessment of Justinian's aggressive policy in the western Mediterranean would have to see it as extremely limited in its success. It had also been highly expensive and produced a need for permanent garrisons to protect territories that in most cases yielded little revenue to central government. Ironically, the fall of the Ostrogothic kingdom in a long and costly conflict, followed not long after by the Lombard invasion, probably destroyed many aspects of Roman culture and society that had survived the collapse of the Western Empire.[24]

A New World: The Age of Justinian and After

Justinian's empire suffered from prolonged conflict with Persia, other wars on many other fronts, as well as natural disasters of which by far the most catastrophic was the great plague. Some of the wars were of his own making, and in all cases any profits or gains were more than balanced by the expenses and losses. The empire was not markedly stronger by the end of Justinian's reign and its resources were certainly stretched very thin. The events of these years clearly exposed the limited power of the sixth-century empire. It did not have the capacity to take back the lost Roman territories in the west and recreate the grandeur of the old, united empire. There was considerable sympathy for the arrival of the eastern Romans amongst the wider population of the western regions. In spite of this it was usually some time before the provincials were convinced that the presence would be permanent and so safe to support.

The corruption and venality of eastern commanders and officials in several cases quickly destroyed this goodwill. The emperor could not fully control his representatives, in much the same way that his generals often struggled to control their troops. The military successes of Justinian's reign owed something to the talents of a handful of gifted generals – most notably Belisarius and Narses – and far more to the still considerable resources of the empire. At times the Romans were able to commit troops and funds to a campaign on a scale that no one apart from the Persians could match. If the Constantinople government was determined enough and willing to commit the resources, then none of the western kingdoms was likely to be able to resist in the long run.[25]

For all the problems of his reign, Justinian was spared an outbreak of full-scale civil war. In 532 riots broke out in Constantinople led by the factions supporting the two main chariot-racing teams in the circus. Traditionally these two groups were bitterly hostile, but when they joined together the trouble escalated rapidly into something far more serious. Some powerful individuals seem to have seen this as an opportunity to replace the existing regime and they may have helped to foster the violence in the first place. One of the surviving nephews of Anastasius was proclaimed as emperor and initial attempts to suppress the rebels by force failed. One story claimed that Justinian was ready to flee and only Theodora's resolution dissuaded him, quoting the old tag, 'Monarchy is a good burial shroud'. Since the actual saying was 'Tyranny is a good burial shroud' it is more than likely that this was a malicious story aimed at the imperial couple. For whatever reason, Justinian resolved to fight. Belisarius and Narses led their soldiers against the rioters and massacred them. The recently proclaimed emperor was executed, even though he had probably been an unwilling pawn.[26]

This was the closest Justinian came to being overthrown by a rival, but like all emperors he was always suspicious of any possible threats. For the moment Belisarius had proved his loyalty by slaughtering the rioters – in much the same way that Napoleon was promoted by the Directory after his famous 'whiff of grapeshot'. Later, Belisarius came under suspicion when the Ostrogoths offered to proclaim him western emperor. Similarly, there were rumours that he and others had plotted to control the succession when it was expected that Justinian might succumb to the plague. More than once Belisarius was removed from his command and sent into retirement when the emperor lost confidence in his loyalty. This in spite of the fact that he was certainly one of the most competent and probably also one of the most loyal of Justinian's commanders. As always, an emperor tended to make his own security his first priority, sacrificing the wider needs of foreign wars. Theodora also arranged the dismissal and disgrace of one of her husband's most trusted senior officials, the praetorian prefect John the Cappadocian. Inventing a conspiracy, her agents – including Belisarius' wife Antonina – managed to convince John to incriminate himself.[27]

Suspicion of colleagues was as deeply entrenched in the imperial bureaucracy as corruption. Justinian made some attempts to combat this, in particular trying to prevent the now normal practice of selling appointments and governorships. Despite the emperor's best efforts his success was extremely limited. Men entering a career in the imperial service expected to make substantial profits through informal gifts given to secure their favours. This was simply the way things worked, and had been for as long as anyone could remember.[28]

Justinian's codification of Roman law proved a far more lasting legacy. In 529 his team of legal experts produced the *Codex Justinianus*, which collected all imperial legislation and confirmed its validity. Legislation excluded from the collection was automatically repealed. In this way it superseded all earlier collections of law, including that carried out under Theodosius II almost a century before. In 533 this was supplemented by the *Digest*, which summarised the rulings and ideas of all notable Roman jurists from the imperial period. Another major work was the *Institutes*, which was intended to guide those studying law. In the following year a new edition of the *Codex* was released. All of these works were in Latin and eventually they would have a profound influence on the development of law in Europe. Justinian also continued to issue new laws or legal rulings – known as *novellae* – many of which were in Greek.[29]

Throughout Justinian's legal work it was always made clear that these were the laws of a Christian emperor. He seems to have taken far more seriously the concept that as emperor he was God's representative on earth. Certainly, while many previous emperors had tried to promote unity within the Church, Justinian took a much more direct role in defining what was orthodox theology. The main point of contention continued to be the question of whether Jesus during his life on earth had possessed a single combined nature, or distinct human and divine parts. A version of the latter defined by the Council of Chalcedon as long ago as 451 was the orthodox position that Justinian attempted to impose. There was considerable resistance and Theodora was widely known to be sympathetic to opponents of this doctrine. Both Justinian's direct interventions and the periodic inconsistencies in his attitude caused suspicion in many churchmen. This certainly contributed to periods of friction with successive popes, although the continued reluctance to admit equality with the see in Constantinople also formed part of this. However, the emperor's power was unquestioned. Justinian felt free to dismiss any bishop, including the pope and the senior bishop or patriarch of Constantinople.[30]

By Justinian's day it was clear that the basic culture of the empire had changed and its ideas owed more to Christianity than to the classical tradition. There were still some notable pagans, but the long-established types of literature, including secular history and many forms of poetry, were disappearing. The philosophical schools in Athens were closed – at one point a group of philosophers fled to Persia to be freer to continue their studies. In time they became disillusioned and were permitted to return to the empire as part of the treaty between Justinian and Khusro in 532. Books of all types became less common. Purity of language – mostly Greek, for most of the inhabitants of the Eastern Empire had never esteemed Latin that highly – ceased to be quite so important as the mark of true refinement and education, as did knowledge of Homer and the other great works of pagan literature.[31]

At the same time the physical shape of cities and their central importance to society also changed. The central open space for public business, ceremonies and commerce had been the Forum, or *Agora*. By the sixth century these functions were more likely to be performed on a single straight road, the *cardo*, which was lined with stalls. Over time such roads tended to become crowded with more or less permanent structures, looking much like the Souk in later Middle Eastern cities. Churches rather than other public buildings were most likely to be the main focal points for the community. Theatres were no longer very important and public bath houses were in decline. The complex rituals and luxury of Roman bathing ceased to be one of the main elements of civilised life.[32]

In the Renaissance the term 'Byzantine' was coined for the Eastern Empire, in part because this made it easier for people in western Europe to claim to be the real heirs of Roman civilisation. The population of the Eastern Empire never stopped referring to themselves as Romans and their empire as Romania. (Sometimes they would also call themselves Christians, seeing this as synonymous with being Roman.) Justinian's empire was the clear descendant of the empire of Augustus and his successors, but in terms of power it was a lesser descendant. It remained powerful, but its strength was matched by Sassanid Persia. The superpower that had once so utterly dominated such a large part of the world – almost all of the known world – was a distant memory. The events of the century after Justinian's death would only ram home this truth.[33]

He was succeeded by his nephew Justin II, after allegedly naming the latter as his heir during his final hours. In 572 Justin started a new war with the Persians. It was the only time in the sixth century when the Romans initiated a major conflict against their eastern neighbour, which is in marked contrast to their aggression towards Parthia and Persia in earlier periods. In the event the war went very badly and the ageing Khusro I captured the fortress of Dara. The shock seems to have plunged Justin into complete mental collapse from which he never recovered and so an imperial colleague was created. A senior and loyal court official named Tiberius was chosen and under him the Romans started to enjoy more success in the struggle with Persia. During these campaigns a general called Maurice made a name for himself, and his popularity with his soldiers encouraged key figures at court to make him emperor when

Tiberius died in 582. The war continued to go well for the Romans, aided by a Persian civil war in 590.[34]

Fortunes continued to sway one way and then the other, often aided by periods of internal chaos affecting either the Romans or Persia. In 602 a usurper named Phocas rebelled against Maurice, who fled from Constantinople and was killed. Another usurper emerged to challenge Phocas within the year. The Persians were not slow to exploit this weakness and launched a series of major offensives. Large parts of Mesopotamia and Roman Armenia were systematically conquered. Another Roman civil war erupted in 608. A few years later the Persians overran Syria, capturing Antioch once again. Palestine also fell, with the Persians entering Jerusalem in 614. It took almost a decade for the Romans to recover and then there were more years of heavy fighting before they retook most of the lost provinces.[35]

In the meantime, something unexpected by either Rome or Persia had occurred to the south. A merchant named Muhammad from the Arab trading town of Mecca preached a new religion and united the Arab tribes. He taught that there was only one God – not a Trinity of complex definition as the Christians had claimed and argued over. Jesus was revered as a prophet, one in a succession that culminated in Muhammad, the greatest of them all. Muhammad died in 632, but his followers swept on to success after success. Both Persia and Rome had exhausted their strength in their long conflicts with each other. Sassanid Persia was the first to fall, collapsing in just a few years. Then in 636 the Arabs won an overwhelming victory over the Romans near the River Yarmuk. They soon took Palestine, Syria and, not long afterwards, Egypt itself. Later their armies would sweep across North Africa and overwhelm the Roman provinces there.[36]

How the Arabs united and achieved such incredible conquests is a fascinating story, but it is too long a tale to tell here. By the end of the seventh century the Eastern Empire survived, as it would do until the fifteenth century, but it was a tiny rump even of the territories ruled by Justinian. The superpower had died centuries before his day. By the time of the Arab conquests the shape of medieval Europe was still developing. Society there lacked the comforts common in the centuries of Roman rule. It was also less sophisticated, with low levels of literacy and patterns of trade far reduced in distance and quantity from the height of the empire. By comparison the Muslim world preserved far more aspects of Greco-Roman civilisation, to which the Arabs would add ideas and refinements of their own. In part this was because their heartland lay in regions that had known civilisation long before the arrival of the Greeks and Romans. Both the Islamic world, and in time the 'barbarians' of the west, would develop further, rediscovering old ideas or inventing new ones. Marcus Aurelius understood that the world was always changing, but by the seventh century it is doubtful that he would have seen much that was familiar in the lands that had once been his empire.

Conclusion: A Simple Answer

'It will be enough for me, however, if these words of mine are judged useful by those who want to understand clearly the events which happened in the past and which will (human nature being what it is), at some time or other and in much the same ways, be repeated in the future.' – *Thucydides, writing at the very end of the fifth century BC.*

The Western Roman Empire ceased to exist in the fifth century. Even those scholars who talk of transformation admit this simple fact. The Eastern Roman Empire lasted for another thousand years until it was overrun by the Turks. Even at its height it could never hope to dominate the world. It was a power, rather than a superpower. The sixth century demonstrated that it lacked the capacity to recapture the lost western provinces. In the seventh century the Arab conquests stripped it of even more territory. It continued to exist as just one amongst many powers in the known world, and some of these were geographically larger and both militarily and financially stronger. Even so, none could be said to have replaced the Roman Empire or matched its former size and power.

None of this happened quickly, but viewed in the long term it cannot be seen as anything other than decline and – in the case of the Western Empire – fall. It was a long process and no single event, lost war or decision can be said to have caused it. The basic question remains of why this occurred, and whether the most important cause was internal problems or external threats. Throughout their history the Romans had always fought a lot of wars against very varied opponents. They had suffered some serious defeats, but had always recovered. There was never any question that such defeats could cause the collapse of the empire. Yet this did happen in the west in the fifth century and therefore we must ask whether the threats faced by the Late Roman Empire were greater than those of earlier periods. This in turn raises two basic possibilities. Either one or more individual enemy was more formidable, or there were simply so many simultaneous threats that the empire could not cope.

It is usually asserted that the Sassanid Persians were far more formidable than the Parthians, or indeed any enemy the Romans had faced
for centuries. They certainly won more victories over the Romans than
the Parthians. On the other hand, the levels of Persian aggression varied
enormously and there were long periods of peace. Some Persian kings
needed the wealth and glory offered by a successful war with Rome.
Usually this was necessary to secure their own hold on power. The largest
Roman armies of the period were those sent east to face the Persians and
massive resources were expended on frontier fortifications. Having said
that, only border territory was ever actually lost to Persia and even this
was on a fairly modest scale. The idea that from its first appearance in
the third century Persia was an especially deadly opponent – even a rival
superpower – remains firmly entrenched in the minds of scholars. It is a
belief that is very hard to reconcile with the evidence, but this does not
mean that it will not continue to be asserted.

Groups from the tribal peoples of Europe eventually took control of
the Western Empire. However, it is extremely difficult to see major
change in the military efficiency of the tribal peoples of Europe from
Julius Caesar's day to that of Stilicho's or Aetius'. To some degree larger
tribal confederations appeared, but we should never exaggerate the degree
of unity. It is convenient to talk of *the* Franks or *the* Goths, in spite of
the fact that these remained divided into many separate and sometimes
mutually hostile tribes. At no stage before the creation of the barbarian
kingdoms inside the provinces was there a single king of all the Franks
or any other people. Attila united both his own people and allied and
subject races to a remarkable degree. Yet, once again, he was unable to
take much territory from the Romans and was essentially a raider and
extortionist on a grand scale. Other powerful barbarian leaders had
emerged in the past and, like Attila, they had proved unable to pass on
their power to a successor. The Huns were a frightening enemy, but it is
worth remembering that their power had been broken before the final
collapse of the Western Empire and that they had anyway devoted most
of their attentions to the Eastern Empire.

There is no good case for claiming that the enemies of the Late Roman
Empire were simply more formidable than those of earlier periods. This
also makes it harder to argue that the Roman Empire had to adapt in
the third century to face new and more dangerous threats, most of all
the Sassanid 'superpower'. Does this mean that it was the sheer quantity
rather than the scale of individual threats that was the problem? There
certainly do seem to have been more major wars in the third and

subsequent centuries than in the early Principate. In particular, raiding by barbarian groups in Europe is much more prominent in our sources. Such predatory attacks, often on a small scale, were not new. In the past they had always increased in scale and frequency whenever the frontier defences were perceived to be weak. An impression of vulnerability encouraged attacks and this makes it hard to judge whether an increase in raids and invasions was the consequence of a rise in barbarian numbers and strength or a result of Roman weakness. It is clear that all of Rome's enemies, including the Persians, exploited the empire's frequent internal disputes and civil wars.

There may be other reasons for Roman weakness and we need to consider these. Unfortunately, for so many of the theories about long-term problems we lack the basic information either to confirm or deny them. There are no good figures for the population of the empire at any period and, therefore, we cannot say with any certainty that this was in long-term decline. Similarly, we must study the economy without any adequate statistics. It seems more than probable that levels of trade and prosperity fell from the end of the second century onwards and never again achieved the levels of the early Principate. However, sources at best hint at such trends, and some scholars will interpret these glimpses of the past in radically different ways. The same is true of the traditional picture of a Late Roman world where the burden of tax was oppressive and fell disproportionately heavily on the poor, who were already oppressed by their rich landlords. Land fell out of cultivation and the rural population was reduced to the level of serfs. None of this is implausible, but that is also true of other models and it is impossible to prove any of them. Far more data – the bulk of which must come from archaeology if it can ever be found – is needed before we can speak with some confidence on these topics. The same is true of claims about climate change and other wider problems.

The type of evidence we have, as well as the interests of scholars, has meant that a good deal of the work on Late Antiquity has focused on economy and society, law and government, intellectual life, culture and religion. Studies tend to concentrate on broad themes and inevitably this emphasises continuity rather than change. By comparison, narrative history has all too often been neglected and certainly has made only a minor contribution to most scholars' mental picture of the period. There are exceptions and study of the frontier relations and foreign wars has often been more traditional in style, since a narrative or chronological element is obviously essential. At the same time civil wars and internal conflict have not received such detailed and coherent treatment. This is odd, for these are the one aspect of the empire's internal problems for which we have considerable evidence.

It is worth once again emphasising that from 217 down to the collapse of the Western Empire there were only a handful of periods as long as ten years when a civil war did not break out. Some of these conflicts were very brief and some were confined to a small region – the usurpers who were proclaimed and then suppressed, or rejected and murdered by their own men after a reign lasting just a few weeks. Challenges for imperial power were sometimes resolved without serious fighting. On the other hand, some conflicts were fought on a very large scale and lasted for years. It is easy to remember Constantine as the great emperor who united the entire empire under his control, but we should not forget that he was a usurper who fought or prepared for civil wars for the first half of his reign.

Civil war and challenges to the imperial throne were common occurrences. Every adult emperor from Septimius Severus onwards experienced at least one such conflict during their lifetime. Usurpers never wanted to destroy or change the empire. These were not conflicts about ideology, but purely for political power. A small minority of the losers in these wars were allowed to keep their lives, although only a tiny handful were permitted to continue in a public career. In the vast majority of cases such conflicts only ended with the death of one of the rivals. Usurpers were the most direct and personal threat faced by any emperor and tended to be treated accordingly. It was normal for an emperor to abandon a war against a foreign enemy to deal with a Roman rival.

Usurpers did not act alone. They needed supporters and the most important of these expected rewards including promotion and riches if the rebellion was successful. If a usurper was suppressed, then many of his backers were likely to suffer with him. Punishment was often extended to their families, especially those holding any office or whose wealth made them appealing targets for informers. In this way even a localised rebellion could mean life, death, imprisonment or ruin to people in distant provinces who had not been involved in it in any direct way. This was a world of patronage, where the powerful exerted themselves to secure benefits for relatives and friends. Such webs of favour and gratitude could become very dangerous for all concerned at times of internal conflict.

All usurpers needed military backing to succeed. Emperors from Augustus onwards tried to keep their soldiers loyal through solemn oaths and regular donatives. On the whole, the army tended to stay loyal to an established dynasty unless the emperor seriously alienated them. Few usurpers could count on similar loyalty. Losses were considerable in some civil wars, as the army wasted its strength fighting against itself. Soldiers fighting an internal struggle could not simultaneously operate on one of the frontiers. Time and again substantial parts of the army were drawn away and Roman military dominance across its borders reduced or utterly shattered. Successive civil wars dislocated the army's administrative and logistical structures, its training patterns, recruitment and also its discipline, which suffered whenever licence was given in an effort to win loyalty. Ordinary soldiers could usually expect to change sides to join the victors after a failed rebellion. This was not so easy for more senior officers.

Each civil war cost the empire. Anything gained by the winning side inevitably had to be taken from other Romans and a prolonged campaign was likely to involve widespread destruction within the provinces where fighting occurred. Almost as important as the physical price of civil war was its impact on attitudes and behaviour from the emperor down. Personal survival became the first objective of every emperor and shaped all of their decisions and the very structure of the empire. In the quest to protect themselves successive emperors gradually reshaped the empire itself and, ironically enough, often made themselves more rather than less vulnerable.

The biggest change was the marginalisation of the senatorial class in the third century and, along with them, the city of Rome as a real rather than merely spiritual capital of the empire. Senators – and most of all a handful of distinguished men and those trusted with senior provincial commands – were for a long time the only possible rivals for imperial power. At first the major military provinces were divided up so that no one man commanded too large an army. By the end of the third century senators had virtually ceased to hold military rank of any kind. They had also all but ceased to become emperor.

Emperors could now come from a far wider section of the empire's population. Any connection with the imperial family – even spurious claims to be the illegitimate son of an emperor – was sufficient to make a claim. In the past Rome's emperors had had to be wary of only a small number of senators, men who were known to them personally and whose careers meant that they spent many years in and around Rome. Now a rival could be almost anyone. They did not need political connections or family reputation, simply the ability to persuade some troops to back them. Many emperors were equestrians, and almost all were army officers or imperial officials.

The trend towards smaller provinces continued. In addition, military and civil power were made separate. This helped to protect an emperor against challengers, but made it far harder to get things done. In particular, it was very difficult to raise and supply a large enough army to deal with a serious problem on the frontiers. From the emperor's point of view this was comforting, since the same army could easily have been turned against him by a rival. At times extraordinary commands were created so that one commander could deal with a problem, but emperors had to be wary of offering such power to a potential usurper. More often emperors chose to go themselves and take personal command of a campaign. From the middle of the third century onwards Roman emperors spent much of their time performing tasks that would once have been dealt with by an imperial legate. Again, it is worth emphasising that it was not the scale of the problems that had increased, but the ability of the empire to employ its resources to deal with them.

An emperor could not be everywhere at once. If he was unwilling to trust anyone else with sufficient power to deal with a distant problem, then it would simply not be dealt with at all. Time and again this sense of neglect by central government prompted a region to rebel and proclaim its own emperor. One solution was to have more than one emperor. The tetrarchic system is often praised, but its success was always limited and no one was able to repeat the dominance of Diocletian for any great length of time. In a way, the acceptance that more than one emperor would exist offered usurpers the prospect of advancing to supreme power in stages. It also tended to encourage regionalism as separate military and civil hierarchies developed in different parts of the empire. Each group was naturally inclined to give priority to its own aims and problems, and often proved reluctant to assist other parts of the empire.

Emperors had always travelled in some state, surrounded by members of their household, bureaucrats and guards. This increased massively in scale during the third century. All wanted to have sizeable military forces under their direct control. If the field armies were intended to perform a strategic role, then this was first and foremost to guard against Roman rivals. Emperors surrounded themselves with more and more attendants and personal bodyguards, and made court ceremonial increasingly elaborate. In part this was to dignify and secure the rule of men who had often seized power in brutal fashion comparatively recently. It was also intended to protect the emperor's person. Assassination was less common in the fourth century than the third. At the same time all of this tended to isolate the emperor. It made it harder for him to know personally even his more senior officials and commanders, let alone the vastly inflated number of bureaucrats who now worked in the imperial administration. Control over the activities of the men who represented imperial authority throughout the provinces was extremely limited.

All emperors lived with the fear of usurpation. It shaped their behaviour and also that of all of the officials and officers who served under them. A career in the imperial service offered the prospect of legal privileges and wealth, gathered both through pay and, even more, from bribes and payments for services. The most successful achieved very high rank with all the patronage and influence this brought. A small minority were even able to reach imperial rank. However, alongside the advantages came serious risks. Any suspicion that an individual was plotting against the emperor was likely to be punished severely. The same was true of anybody associated with a failed usurper or their supporters. In a system where careers were routinely advanced by personal recommendation, such networks of patronage inevitably put many individuals in danger. Personal survival and personal success and profit were the foremost aims of most officials.

The imperial bureaucracy in the Late Roman Empire was certainly far larger than in the first and second centuries. The army may or may not have been bigger, but certainly consisted of far more small, independent units. Size on its own does not mean that either of these institutions was more efficient. There were far more administrators than could readily be supervised, especially since they formed part of a bureaucracy that was both divided and confused in its structure. The imperial administration raised funds and resources to support both itself and the army. Such short-term expedients as debasing the coinage suggest that at times this supply proved inadequate. However, on the whole the system seems to have functioned in the third and fourth centuries, at the very least to a minimal necessary level. It still left plenty of room for inefficiency and corruption, and such wastage may well have been on a massive scale. Most individual members of the bureaucracy did their job well enough to keep the system functioning and prevent their peculation becoming too blatant. Some may genuinely have been both honest and competent.[1]

Civil wars were most common in the third century, but remained frequent afterwards. The state developed in ways intended to protect emperors from internal rivals, but singularly failed to do so. Personal survival had always been an important concern for all emperors since the creation of the Principate. Augustus had fought his way to power through a series of civil wars. Assassination plots and open rebellion were threats faced by each of Rome's rulers from the very beginning. Augustus was a monarch, but created a system in which his power was carefully veiled. Since he was not formally a king, there was no clear institution to arrange the succession. Some have seen this as a fatal flaw in the system of the Principate – effectively, an accident waiting to happen. Others would go further and see the Augustan system as a 'millstone', revered by tradition that prevented proper reform of the empire in the third and fourth centuries.[2]

This cannot explain the quite staggering difference between the Principate and the Late Roman Empire. There was civil war for a year after the death of Nero in 68 and another longer conflict after Pertinax was murdered in 193. Claudius, Domitian and Marcus Aurelius each faced a challenge from a rebellious governor, although all of these revolts swiftly collapsed. Assassination plots and attempted coups at Rome were a little more common, although some of these may have been imagined by nervous emperors or invented by their ruthless subordinates. The early Principate was not wholly free from the reality or threat of internal conflict, but for more than two hundred years it still suffered only rarely from these. This is also in marked contrast to the last half-century of the Republic. If the system created by Augustus was so seriously flawed, then only remarkable luck could explain this. With Gibbon, we might stop 'inquiring *why* the Roman empire was destroyed', and instead 'be surprised that it lasted so long'.

It stretches credibility to see two centuries of largely unbroken internal peace as a mere fluke, especially when they were followed by a longer period when civil war was so very frequent. It is true that each fresh bout of internal conflict weakened imperial authority and the institutions of the state and therefore made future usurpations and rebellions more likely. Yet, once again, it cannot have been solely chance that such a cycle did not develop earlier. In the third century the empire largely lost the Republican façade so carefully constructed by Augustus. He and his successors ruled through the Senate. As a body this had no real political independence, but sensible emperors took care to respect its dignity. More importantly, they employed senators in virtually all important posts, effectively ruling the empire through them.

It may seem odd in this day and age to praise a system based on an aristocratic elite, consisting of men who were amateurs in the modern sense. Yet the system had many advantages in the Roman context. It provided a manageable group of senior soldiers and administrators – an emperor could know all of these men and their families. Only a minority were potential rivals and these could be closely observed. Public life remained focused on the fixed location of Rome itself, making it easier to sense the mood of the aristocracy. Emperors in the first and second centuries were able to trust selected senators to control substantial armies and large provinces. Only rarely – usually during times of major conflict with Parthia – was it necessary to appoint a commander to control more than one province and this did not automatically lead to an attempt at usurpation. In the first and second centuries emperors were able to delegate and did not feel obliged to direct campaigns in person. Rome was the centre of the empire in more than just a spiritual sense. We do not need to idealise the senatorial legates of the early period. Some were incompetent, a few untrustworthy and probably quite a lot were more or less corrupt. In all these respects they seem at the very least no worse than the senior officials of the Late Roman Empire. Politically, the small senatorial class was simply easier for an emperor to control. Reliance on the Senate was a Republican tradition, but actually made sound sense.

The governments of ancient states had limited ambitions and did not concern themselves with major programmes of health, education or the detailed day to day regulation of markets, industry and agriculture. For all its size and sophistication, the Roman Empire was not fundamentally different in this respect. It raised revenue and other resources and made use of these in a range of ways. The army was the biggest single cost, but there was also the maintenance of many buildings, some ports and a vast road network, as well as the subsidised or free doles of food to the population of Rome and later Constantinople. None of these duties of the empire ground to a halt in the third or fourth century. However, this does not mean that they were functioning well.

The Roman Empire did not fall quickly, but to use this as proof that its institutions were essentially sound is deeply misguided. The empire was huge and faced no serious competitors. Persia was the strongest neighbour, but there was never a prospect of a Persian army reaching the Tiber. Rome was massive, heavily populated and rich. This remained true even if the population and economy were in decline. It had a transport system of all-weather roads and busy commercial routes by river, canal and sea on a scale unmatched again in Europe until recent centuries. Although we may note the difficulties emperors had in making their will felt in distant provinces, their capacity to do this at all was still far greater than the leaders of any other people. The Roman army was a large, sophisticated, permanent and professional force backed by an extensive logistical system. Like the empire itself, it was different from anything else in existence in the known world. The Romans possessed many great advantages over all of their competitors. None of these rivals had the power to push the empire over in the third or fourth centuries. The empire was huge and did not need to operate at the highest levels of efficiency to succeed. It possessed massively greater resources, technological and other advantages. There was also the probability that somewhere along the line some officers and officials would do their job at least moderately well. This meant that the Romans were likely to prevail in the long run. None of its enemies were capable of inflicting more than a limited defeat on the Romans.

None of this meant that the cost of repeated civil war was not felt. It is not difficult to make the case that the majority of emperors in the first and second centuries had the wider good of the empire as their main ambition. All were concerned with personal survival, but this had not become the overwhelming priority it would be for their successors in later eras. That is not to say that the later emperors were more selfish, but simply that they could never be as secure. Many may have had the best of intentions to rule well, but the government of the empire became first and foremost about keeping the emperor in power – and at lower levels, about the individual advantage of bureaucrats and officers.

The Late Roman Empire was not designed to be an efficient government, but to keep the emperor in power and to benefit the members of the administration. Many of these could enjoy highly successful careers by the standards of the day without ever being effective in the role that they were theoretically supposed to perform. Sheer size prevented rapid collapse or catastrophe. Its weakness was not obvious, but this only meant that collapse could come in sudden, dramatic stages, such as the loss of the African provinces to the Vandals. Gradually, the empire's institutions rotted and became less and less capable of dealing with any crisis, but still did not face serious competition. Lost wars were damaging, but the damage was not fatal to the empire itself. As an example, from 376–382 the Romans could not lose the war against the Goths, but they still struggled to win it. Even defeats at the hands of the Persians did not deprive the empire of major or essential resources.

The Roman Empire continued for a very long time. Successive blows knocked away sections of it, as attackers uncovered its weaknesses. Yet at times the empire could still be formidable and did not simply collapse. Perhaps we should imagine the Late Roman Empire as a retired athlete, whose body has declined from neglect and an unhealthy lifestyle. At times the muscles will still function well and with the memory of former skill and training. Yet, as the neglect continues, the body becomes less and less capable of resisting disease or recovering from injury. Over the years the person would grow weaker and weaker, and in the end could easily succumb to disease. Long decline was the fate of the Roman Empire. In the end, it may well have been 'murdered' by barbarian invaders, but these struck at a body made vulnerable by prolonged decay.

Epilogue: An Even Simpler Moral

In the Victorian era the British were fond of comparing their empire to the Roman, confident that their own territories were significantly larger. Nowadays, comparisons tend to be made to America. Countries like China and India have their own very ancient and civilised past to draw upon and are far less likely to concern themselves with the more Western idea of Rome as *the* great empire of history. The United States in the early twenty-first century is not the same as Queen Victoria's empire, and neither of these are identical to Rome. The world has changed enormously. Looking at the globe today – or indeed at a photograph taken from space – the former territories of the Roman Empire at its greatest extent do not look quite so big. The Roman world had only three continents, and the size of both Africa and Asia was massively underestimated. Technology was primitive and the pace of invention and change seems to us incredibly slow. It was a world that accepted slavery as normal, killed animals and people for entertainment, and celebrated military glory as one of the highest human achievements. Today we live on a planet whose population dwarfs that of the Victorian era, let alone the ancient world. At the same time travel is far faster and communication from one side of the planet to the other can be virtually instant.

The closer you look at Rome, then the more obvious it is just how very different it was to any modern state, let alone the United States. We should be very glad indeed of these differences, for there was much about the Roman Empire that was brutal and unpleasant, even if it was no worse and in most respects better than its neighbours. At the time of writing the Republican and Democratic Parties in America are selecting their presidential candidates. Before this book is released this process will be complete and someone will have been elected and installed in the White House as president. We do not yet know who this will be, but we can at least be sure that the defeated candidate will not try to rally part of the United States Armed Forces and plunge the country into civil war.

Apart from cultural and institutional differences, it is easy to list many profound contrasts in the situation of Rome and modern America. Rome was effectively a superpower, but it existed in a world that did not include a serious challenger. Parthia and then Persia were strong sophisticated kingdoms, but it was only after the division of the Roman Empire – and really then only after the collapse of the west – that it could be seen as Rome's equal. The United States is the sole superpower in the modern world, but there are many other powers amongst just under 200 recognised countries. None of these other powers are yet America's equal, but they cannot be ignored. The economic and military strength of some Asian countries is clearly growing and states like India will in time gain more and more influence in world affairs. China may become a true superpower. A growing number of countries now possess nuclear weapons, capable of devastation on a scale far beyond the worst conflict of the ancient world. The United States faces challenges to its dominance unlike anything experienced by the Roman Empire. At the same time there is no equivalent for America of the tribal peoples who lived beyond Rome's borders. Illegal migrants are a very different proposition to bands of raiders or groups intending to seize and occupy land by force.

Recently, Cullen Murphy's *Are We Rome? The Fall of an Empire and the Fate of America* (2007) drew some broad similarities between the Roman and American experience. Interestingly, he focused in particular on the Late Roman Empire and the reasons for its eventual collapse. Without ever pushing the analogies too far, he noted broad similarities in attitudes in both government circles and the wider population. Even more serious was the extension of government functions to many private or semi-private agencies, all much harder to control and inevitably with priorities and aims of their own. As part of this he also highlighted the huge reliance of America and its allies on private companies to provide the manpower to support its war efforts. Only in part is this the result of a shortfall in recruiting for the regular army. Private companies do not need to be paid when not being used, nor does the government directly pay pensions and other benefits to their employees. Superficially, this can make them seem far cheaper (especially since at government level the payment may well come from a different part of the budget), and in the very short term this might even be true. In the long term it is likely to make the regular forces lose some of their capability. What was once a choice then becomes an unavoidable necessity and alongside this goes a loss of control.[1]

In the Late Roman Empire, government became primarily about survival. Senior men wanted power – that was why there was never a shortage of men ambitious to become emperor. At all levels in the civil

417

service and army, promotion brought rewards and privileges. With these came considerable risk, which increased as a man rose in rank. Everyone in imperial service, including senior army officers, was far more likely to be killed or tortured and imprisoned on the orders of other Romans than to suffer at the hands of foreign enemies. Although only a minority – and logic would dictate overall a very small minority – would actually suffer such punishment, these risks were very real. There was little incentive for genuine talent. Officials and officers understood that ability would not matter if they came under suspicion of disloyalty. It was not a recipe for efficiency.

At a basic level the emperors and government officials of the Late Roman Empire had forgotten what the empire was for. The wider interests of the state – the *Res Publica*, or 'public thing', from which we get our word 'Republic' – were secondary to their own personal success and survival. This was not at root a moral failing. There had been plenty of selfish and corrupt individuals in earlier periods of Roman history, just as there have been in all other societies. The difference was that by the late empire it was difficult for them to behave in any other way. Emperors lived lives of fear, fully aware that they stood a good chance of meeting a sudden and violent death. Officials were equally nervous and suspicious of colleagues, as well as their imperial master.

It is only human nature to lose sight of the wider issues and focus on immediate concerns and personal aims. In the Late Roman Empire this was so often all about personal survival and advancement – the latter bringing wealth and influence, which helped to increase security in some ways, but also rendered the individual more prominent and thus a greater target to others. Some officials enjoyed highly successful careers through engineering the destruction of colleagues. Performing a job well was only ever a secondary concern. Even emperors were more likely to reward loyalty over talent. Officials and commanders needed only to avoid making a spectacular mess of their job – and even then enough influence could conceal the facts or pass the blame onto someone else. None of this was entirely new, but it became endemic. When 'everyone' acted in the same way there was no real encouragement to honesty or even competence. The game was about personal success and this often had little connection to the wider needs of the empire.

It was not a phenomenon unique to the Late Roman Empire, nor are its implications only of significance to the United States or indeed any other country. All human institutions, from countries to businesses, risk creating a similarly short-sighted and selfish culture. It is easier to avoid in the early stages of expansion and growth. Then the sense of purpose is likely to be clearer, and the difficulties or competition involved have a more direct and obvious impact. Success produces growth and, in time, creates institutions so large that they are cushioned from mistakes and inefficiency. The united Roman Empire never faced a competitor capable of destroying it. These days, countries and government departments do not easily collapse – and Western states do not face enemies likely to overthrow them by military force. In the business world the very largest corporations almost never face competitors that are truly their equal. Competition within the commercial market at any level is obviously rarely carried out on entirely equal terms.

In most cases it takes a long time for serious problems or errors to be exposed. It is usually even harder to judge accurately the real competence of individuals and, in particular, their contribution to the overall purpose. Those in charge of overseeing a country's economy generally reap the praise or criticism for decisions made by their predecessors in office. Often both they and their predecessors will be inclined to act for immediate political reasons. For the vast majority of people, their work is less open to the public gaze, but is similar in that the real consequences of what they do are not obvious. Comparatively few people these days actually make or even sell something, or work in a profession where at least some of the goals are obvious. A doctor or nurse knows if their patient recovers. A hospital manager operates at a completely different level, dealing with numbers and budgets and not individual patients. Such distance is inevitable and in many walks of life the wider goals are even less clear.

By their nature bureaucracies tend to grow. This was true in the Roman Empire, let alone with the massively larger government agencies of modern countries. Individuals within a department obviously have to focus on their particular task. It is only natural to believe that with more people they could deal with this more effectively. The larger they grow, then the more distant most members will be from the reality of the overall function of the department, and they will become even more removed in their way of thought to anyone outside. This is not inevitably a bad thing, but does mean that they will continue to expand unless restrained, since their problem or concern is the only one they will see. In Britain, and to some extent in the USA, the number of people employed directly or indirectly by the government is now staggeringly large. For much of history states have usually employed more soldiers than civilian officials. Successive governments in Britain have drastically reduced the size of the Armed Forces. Perhaps this might have been justified if they had not subsequently committed them to several major overseas operations.

Given that it is difficult to deal with a major and distant task, it is normal to break this up into many separate and much smaller tasks. Certain individuals are given limited objectives that can more easily be measured. Once again this is reasonable, but can easily be taken too far. The limited goal can too easily become the end in itself. The culture of targets has been especially prevalent in the United Kingdom for some time. In part it is a result of the desire to spread the efficiency of business management into many more walks of life. Sadly, what has been introduced is not the skill of the genuinely gifted business manager – something that would obviously be difficult to duplicate – but a far more rigid facsimile of supposedly general rules for running a business. Talent is hard to teach and the methods employed tend to reinforce the distancing of the individual from the real function for which they are employed. Management is simply turned into a taught skill, which with minor modification brings success in any environment.

This is especially dangerous in large institutions, where the individual's real contribution is so hard to measure. Targets themselves will over time tend to distort this sense of the wider goals even further. The temptation, most especially in government, is to make them readily achievable so that success can be declared. As often, the targets are chosen because they are something that can be measured. How can you really judge how good a school or a hospital is, especially if you are an administrator only able to see evidence in written form? The targets become ends within themselves, robbing individuals within the system of any initiative. Improvements in communications make it easier for those at senior levels to intervene and send instructions to those lower down and this has a similar tendency to destroy initiative. Even more damage has been done to this as a side-effect of the widespread reliance on computers, where the system makes most of the decisions on an automatic basis.[2]

At no point does anyone in authority appear to have wondered whether the business model is actually appropriate for all situations. An army, for instance, is by its very nature not a profit-making enterprise. Targets and other government initiatives have to succeed, since no government can admit repeated failures. Such things quickly develop a life of their own, almost wholly independent of reality. Everything is supposed to be improving and yet institutions prove incapable of the simplest tasks. Thus in Britain we have a National Health Service in which the number of administrators has increased as the number of beds for patients has fallen. Seemingly incapable of such basic tasks as keeping wards clean, as an institution its attitude at times seems ambivalent to the fate of patients, concerned only with numbers passing through the system.

It is very easy for a large institution to lose sight of its real function. This is especially true if the task is large, complex and unending. Government can all too easily become a question of trying to stay in power under any circumstances. It would be tempting to see democracies as especially susceptible to this were it not for the fact that all types of regime readily fall prey to the same thing. Individuals within the institutions tend to start thinking along similar lines, putting personal ambition and advantage above everything else. Real success or failure is hard to measure, especially in the short term. Targets and personal gains are attractive alternatives.

In public life a scandal of some sort – whether someone is revealed as corrupt, deceitful or simply incompetent – no longer prompts resignation if there is any chance at all that brazen denial and/or an apology will suffice. 'I take full responsibility' must now stand alongside such things as 'This is totally unacceptable' as ministerial statements that mean the exact opposite of what they actually say. In other instances, the guilty parties demand that a code of conduct be created for them to understand how they should behave. Apparently, simple honesty and common sense are inadequate. In government or business it is quite possible to be very successful and richly rewarded without ever having been efficient. Meeting short-term targets or making short-term savings or profits, all of which may be done in ways that in the long run actually weaken the institution, can be sufficient.

The generally slow pace of real events helps to make this possible, and this is something the Roman example illustrates well. For all the inefficiency and corruption of the Late Roman Empire, its sheer size and in-built strength meant that it was a very long time before its weaknesses became more obvious and serious in their consequences. Today the media regularly employs terms like 'meltdown' or 'crisis' about businesses and government departments alike. Rarely does this lead to the predicted catastrophes. Like the Romans, the bodies involved are usually just too big to come to immediate and final collapse. Life continues, and so does the institution or company. In-built strength helps to carry them through. In bodies like the National Health Service or Armed Forces, there are usually still enough talented and dedicated individuals at lower levels to permit them to function in spite of woeful management and inadequate resources. Yet the warning from the Roman experience is that major catastrophic failures often arrive both suddenly and unanticipated.

Time plays another role. One lesson of Rome's fall is that it happened very slowly. This means that we should not be too ready to predict rapid shifts in the balance of power in our own world. When Gibbon released the first volume of the *Decline and Fall* in 1776, he and others could be reasonably optimistic that Britain would win the war in America. The second and third volumes appeared early in 1781, when the picture was less rosy. By the end of the year Cornwallis had surrendered his army to the American and French forces at Yorktown. The final volume came out in 1788, when the American colonies were irrevocably lost to Britain and a new country had emerged. Gibbon's tone became noticeably more pessimistic as the book progressed. The subject matter was partly responsible for this. There is something very depressing about the collapse of Roman power (which may in part explain the tone of this epilogue). Yet, as we noted in the Introduction, the loss of America did not prevent the British Empire becoming even stronger and more successful in the next century.

In spite of its propaganda, no empire – or, for that matter, superpower – is guaranteed its supremacy. This is as true of modern America as it was of Rome. Such dominance requires not simply strength, resources and the willingness to use them, but also the ability to direct them efficiently. This depends to a great degree on culture. From the third century onwards Roman emperors lost a sense of their wider role and instead concentrated on survival. The rot began at the top, and in time a similar attitude pervaded the entire government and army high command. Sheer size meant that for a very long time the Romans either kept winning or, at the very least, did not suffer defeats that were catastrophic. The empire was in decline, but it was able to continue for many lifetimes.

Modern America is not perfectly efficient – no country has ever or will ever achieve this. Some of its weaknesses and problems may seem echoed in the Roman experience, but none are anywhere near as pronounced. Nothing suggests that the United States must inevitably decline and cease to be a superpower in the near future. We ought to be glad of this, since none of the likely alternatives to this situation are very appealing. This certainly does not mean that America can afford to be complacent.

The Roman experience suggests that imperial decline is likely to start at the top. In their case the fatal decline of the empire came from internal problems. If governments or agencies forget what they are really for, then decline will occur, however slowly. It is no easy thing to keep or to recapture this sense of perspective and purpose. Bureaucracies are stubborn, they tend to expand on their own and develop their own agendas. This is not inevitable, but it is always likely. If the trend is to be reversed, then this process needs to start at the very top. So perhaps we should expect more from our political leaders. If they do not set an example by placing the wider good before personal or party interest then it is most unlikely that anyone else will behave any better. A greater willingness to take genuine responsibility would be a good start, but seems unlikely to occur.

Decline is not inevitable, but the risk is always there. It is much easier to proclaim such remedies than for anyone to implement them. Rome's fall was to a great extent self-inflicted. It is hard to say when the process became irrevocable, but it began with the four-year civil war that followed the successive murders of Commodus and Pertinax. Emperors tried to make themselves safer and in doing so weakened the capacity of the empire to act. They also failed to prevent the regular appearance of internal challengers. Like Gibbon, it is difficult not to become somewhat pessimistic in tracing this story. My last words come from a comment made by an American student at a seminar during my days as graduate student at Oxford. After a paper discussing schisms within the Church in the fifth and sixth centuries, this rather urbane individual affected a rural accent to sum the debate up: 'You know', he said, 'people are kinda stoopid.'

Chronology

Legitimate emperors' reigns are shown in capitals. Usurpers and their reigns are shown in italics. The distinction between the two was often blurred. Many legitimate emperors, like Constantine, began their careers as usurpers.

161–180	REIGN OF MARCUS AURELIUS.
162–165	War with Parthians. The Romans capture Ctesiphon.
166	First major outbreaks of plague.
167	Barbarian raiders cross the Danube and one group reaches Aquileia in northern Italy.
168–175	Marcus Aurelius oversees a series of campaigns along the Danubian frontier.
175	Usurpation by *Avidius Cassius* in Syria after false rumour that Marcus Aurelius had died. The rebellion quickly collapses without serious fighting.
178–180	Marcus Aurelius campaigns on the Danube.
180–192	REIGN OF COMMODUS.
192	Commodus murdered on 31 December. Pertinax proclaimed emperor.
193	Pertinax murdered. Julianus proclaimed emperor. Septimius Severus proclaimed emperor in Pannonia, Pescennius Niger proclaimed emperor in Syria and Clodius Albinus proclaimed emperor in Britain. Severus and Albinus ally and the latter is named as Caesar. Severus occupies Rome and Julianus is killed.
193–211	REIGN OF SEPTIMIUS SEVERUS.
194	Severus defeats and kills Pescennius Niger.
195	Break between Severus and Albinus, who is declared Augustus.
197	Severus defeats and kills Albinus at Lugdunum (modern Lyons).
197–202	Severus campaigns in the east.
208–211	Severus campaigns in Britain.

211	Severus dies in Britain and is succeeded by his sons Caracalla and Geta. Geta murdered by Caracalla.
211–217	REIGN OF CARACALLA.
212	Caracalla pronounces the *Constitutio Antoniniana*, granting Roman citizenship to almost every free inhabitant of the empire.
214–217	Caracalla campaigns in the east.
217	Caracalla murdered outside Carrhae. The praetorian prefect Macrinus proclaimed emperor. He is the first equestrian to become emperor.
217–218	REIGN OF MACRINUS.
218	Elagabalus proclaimed emperor in a rebellion engineered by his mother, Soaemias. His supporters defeat Macrinus in battle. Macrinus flees and is killed.
218–222	REIGN OF ELAGABALUS.
218–222	Precise dating is uncertain, but there were unsuccessful usurpations in Syria by *Seleucus*, *Uranius*, *Gellius Maximus* and *Verus*.
221	Elagabalus adopts his cousin Severus Alexander.
222	Elagabalus and Soaemias are murdered.
222–235	REIGN OF SEVERUS ALEXANDER.
222–235	Date is uncertain, but at some point during the reign there was an unsuccessful usurpation by *Taurinus*, probably in Syria.
224	Parthian King Artabanus V defeated and killed by the rebel Ardashir, king of Persia. Creation of the Sassanid dynasty, which will rule the Persian Empire until the seventh century.
230	Ardashir invades the Roman province of Mesopotamia.
232	Severus campaigns against the Persians, but fails to achieve anything.
234	Maximinus Thrax proclaimed emperor by troops in Pannonia.
235	Severus Alexander murdered by mutinous soldiers on the Rhine.
235–238	REIGN OF MAXIMINUS THRAX.
235-238	Persians occupy much of Mesopotamia, capturing Nisibis and Carrhae.
235–238	Dates uncertain, but there were unsuccessful usurpations by *Magnus* and *Quartinus* in the Rhineland.

235–237	Maximinus campaigns on the Rhine and Danube frontiers.
238	Gordian I and his son Gordian II rebel in North Africa. The rebellion is quickly crushed by the legate of Numidia. Both Gordians perish. In the meantime the Senate has declared in support and so is forced to find replacement emperors. It chooses Pupienus and Balbinus and the infant grandson of Gordian I, known as Gordian III. Pupienus and Balbinus are subsequently murdered by the praetorian guard. Maximinus invades Italy, but fails to capture Aquileia and is murdered by his own men.
238–244	REIGN OF GORDIAN III.
240	Rebellion of *Sabianus* at Carthage is quickly defeated.
241	Ardashir dies and is succeeded by his son Shapur I.
242	Prophet Mani begins to preach his new religion
242–244	Gordian III campaigns against the Persians. There are some successes, but the war ends in failure. Gordian III dies or is killed. The praetorian prefect Philip is proclaimed emperor.
244–249	REIGN OF PHILIP THE ARAB.
244–249	Dates and details uncertain, but there were unsuccessful usurpations by *Marcus* in Syria, *Silbannacus* in Germany and *Sponsianus*, probably in Pannonia.
248	Philip holds ceremony at Rome to commemorate one thousand years since the city's foundation. Decius campaigns successfully on the Danube.
249	Decius proclaimed emperor and defeats and kills Philip in northern Italy. Unsuccessful usurpation by *Jotapian* in Syria.
249–251	REIGN OF DECIUS.
249–250	Decius issues a decree to sacrifice, leading to persecution of the Christians.
250 (or 251)	Unsuccessful usurpation by *Julius Priscus* in the east and *Valens* at Rome.
251	Decius defeated and killed by barbarians (probably Goths) led by Cniva. *Hostilianus* and *Trebonianus Gallus* proclaimed emperors. The former dies shortly afterwards.
251–253	REIGN OF GALLUS.

252	Shapur I deposes the king of Armenia and once again invades Mesopotamia.
253	*Aemilianus* rebels on the Danube. He defeats and kills Gallus, but is himself killed just a few months later by his own troops. Valerian proclaimed emperor on the Rhine and appoints his son Gallienus as Augustus. Goths launch seaborne raids from the Black Sea. Shapur I launches heavy raid and captures Antioch. Usurpation by *Uranius Antoninus,* who campaigns successfully against the Persians.
253–260	REIGN OF VALERIAN AND GALLIENUS.
253–259	Date and details uncertain, but unsuccessful usurpation by *Mareades* in Syria.
254	Heavy raiding across the Rhine and Danube. *Uranius Antoninus* defeated by Valerian. Persians capture Nisibis again.
255	Second major outbreak of Gothic raiding by sea. The north coast of Asia Minor is heavily attacked.
257–260	Valerian's persecution of the Christians.
258	Usurper *Ingenuus* rebels on the Danube, but is quickly defeated by Gallienus.
259	Barbarian raiders (possibly Alamanni) raid widely in Gaul. A group of Iuthungi penetrate into Italy.
260	Valerian campaigns against the Persians, but is captured and held prisoner for the rest of his life. This prompts a spate of usurpations, including *Regalianus* in Illyricum, *Valens* in Macedonia, *Postumus* in Gaul, *Regalianus* on the Danube, *Macrianus* and *Quietus,* and *Ballista* in the east, and others in Egypt, Italy and possibly Africa.
260–268	RULE OF GALLIENUS WITHOUT A COLLEAGUE.
260–269	*REIGN OF POSTUMUS OVER WESTERN PROVINCES.*
261	*Macrianus* defeated and killed by Gallienus' army, *Quietus* killed by Odaenathus, who is named as *dux* and 'commander of the east'. *Valens* rebels in Macedonia, but is later killed by his own troops. Unsuccessful usurpation by *Mussius Aemilianus,* governor of Egypt.
262	Odaenathus campaigns successfully against the Persians and reaches Ctesiphon.

265	Gallienus attacks *Postumus,* but is repulsed.
266	Odaenathus again raids Ctesiphon. Goths raid Asia Minor again.
266/267	Odaenathus killed. Power passes to his wife Zenobia in the name of their son Vaballathus.
267	Gallienus' general *Aureolus* rebels against him. Goths raid widely in the Balkans and Greece. Athens sacked.
268	Gallienus murdered. *Aureolus* defeated and killed. Claudius II proclaimed emperor. He defeats the Alamanni in Italy.
268–270	REIGN OF CLAUDIUS II GOTHICUS.
269	Claudius defeats Goths. *Postumus* assassinated. *Marius* is proclaimed emperor in Gaul, but quickly killed. He is in turn succeeded by *Victorinus.* Zenobia begins to extend her control of the eastern provinces.
270	Claudius II dies of plague and is succeeded by his brother Quintillus. He is overthrown by Aurelian. Zenobia occupies Egypt, Syria and Asia Minor.
270–275	REIGN OF AURELIAN.
271	*Vaballathus* declared emperor. Aurelian defeats *Victorinus,* who is murdered and replaced by *Tetricus.* Dacian provinces abandoned. Aurelian orders construction of massive defensive wall around Rome.
272	Aurelian defeats Zenobia and recaptures eastern provinces. Death of Shapur I.
273	Aurelian suppresses new revolt in Palmyra.
274	Aurelian attacks *Tetricus* who surrenders.
275	Aurelian murdered. Tacitus declared emperor with approval of Senate.
275–276	REIGN OF TACITUS.
276	Tacitus murdered. He is succeeded by the praetorian prefect Florianus. *Probus* rebels and is declared emperor by the eastern legions. He defeats the Goths. Florianus is murdered by his own men who defect to his rival.
276–282	REIGN OF PROBUS.
279	Rebellion in Isauria and siege of Cremna.
280	Unsuccessful usurpations by *Bonosus* and *Proculus.*
281	Unsuccessful usurpation by *Saturninus.*
282	Probus murdered and replaced by Carus, who then campaigns against barbarians on the Danube.

282–283	REIGN OF CARUS.
283	Carus attacks Persia, but dies near Ctesiphon. He is succeeded by Carinus, who rules in the west and Numerian, who rules in the east.
283–284	REIGN OF CARINUS AND NUMERIAN.
284	Numerian murdered by plot led by Praetorian Prefect Aper. Diocletian proclaimed emperor and immediately kills Aper.
284–305	REIGN OF DIOCLETIAN.
285	Diocletian defeats Carinus at the Battle of Margus. Maximinian campaigns in Gaul and on the Rhine. Diocletian campaigns on the Danube.
286	Maximian named as Augustus. *Carausius* rebels in Britain.
286–293	*REIGN OF CARAUSIUS IN BRITAIN AND NORTHEN GAUL.*
289	Diocletian campaigns on the Danube. Maximian attacks *Carausius*, but is defeated.
290	Diocletian campaigns in the east.
293	Constantius and Galerius named as Caesars to create the tetrarchy. Disputed succession in Persia – Narses eventually becomes king (possibly 294). Constantius captures Boulogne. *Carausius* murdered and replaced by *Allectus.*
296	Constantius defeats *Allectus* and recovers Britain. Persians invade Armenia.
297	Galerius defeated by Persians near Carrhae. *Domitius Domitianus* rebels in Egypt, proclaiming himself emperor.
298	Galerius wins major victory over Persians and captures Ctesiphon. Diocletian personally suppressed *Domitianus* in Egypt.
299	Peace treaty negotiated with Persia. The terms are very favourable to Rome.
301	Diocletian reforms currency and issues edict on prices.
302	Diocletian orders persecution of Manichaeans.
303	Diocletian initiates major persecution of Christians.
305	Diocletian and Maximian abdicate. Constantius and Galerius are each named as Augustus with Severus and Maximinus Daia as their Caesars.

306	Constantius dies at York. His soldiers proclaim *Constantine* as emperor. *Maxentius* proclaimed emperor in Italy with support of his father Maximian.
306–337	REIGN OF CONSTANTINE. HE ONLY CONTROLS ENTIRE EMPIRE FROM 324.
307	Galerius and Severus invade Italy, but eventually withdraw. Severus captured by *Maxentius* and subsequently executed.
308	Maximian retires again under pressure from Diocletian. Licinius named as Augustus. In North Africa *Domitius Alexander* rebels against *Maxentius*.
309	*Domitius Alexander* defeated and killed.
310	Maximian declares himself emperor once again, but is defeated and killed. Maximinus Daia proclaimed as Augustus.
311	Death of Galerius. Before he dies he issues an edict of tolerance granting rights of worship to groups including the Christians. This is to some extent ignored by Maximinus Daia. Diocletian also dies at this point (or possibly in 312).
312	Constantine invades Italy and defeats *Maxentius* at the Milvian Bridge.
313	Constantine and Licinius ally. Licinius defeats *Maximinus Daia*. The allies issue an edict confirming freedom of religious belief, the so-called 'Edict of Milan'.
314	Constantine campaigns on the Rhine.
316	War breaks out between Constantine and Licinius. Constantine wins victory at Cibalae. Licinius cedes virtually all of his European provinces as the price of peace.
317	Constantine declares his sons Crispus and Constantine II Caesars.
324	Renewal of war between Constantine and Licinius, who is defeated and sent into retirement, but subsequently executed. Constantine's son Constantius II declared Caesar. Constantine orders work begun on Constantinople.
326	Constantine executes his son Crispus, and his wife Fausta. Constantine's mother Helena visits Jerusalem and is supposed to have located many sites and relics.
327	Death of Helena.

330	Constantinople formally dedicated.
332	Constantine campaigns on the Danube against the Goths.
333	Constantine's son Constans declared Caesar.
334	Constantine campaigns on the Danube.
335	Constantine's nephew Dalmatius declared Caesar.
337	Death of Constantine. Constans, Constantine II, and Constantius II proclaimed emperors after killing off Dalmatius and several other male relatives.
337–340	REIGN OF CONSTANTINE II.
337–350	REIGN OF CONSTANS.
337–361	REIGN OF CONSTANTIUS II.
340	Civil War between Constantine II and Constans. Constantine is killed in a skirmish.
343/4	Battle of Singara between Romans and Persians.
346	Persians attack and fail to take Nisibis.
350	*Magnentius* proclaimed emperor in Gaul. Constans defeated and killed. Persians repulsed at Nisibis again.
351	Constantius II appoints Gallus as Caesar.
353	*Magnentius* defeated and commits suicide.
354	Gallus executed for alleged conspiracy.
355	Brief usurpation by *Silvanus* in Gaul. Franks sack Cologne.
355	Julian proclaimed as Caesar and sent to Gaul.
355–359	Julian campaigns on the Rhine.
357	Julian wins victory over the Alamanni at Strasbourg.
359	Amida captured by Persians.
360	*Julian* proclaimed as Augustus by his soldiers in Gaul.
361	Civil war between *Julian* and Constantius II ends with the latter's death by natural causes.
361–363	REIGN OF JULIAN.
363	Julian launches major invasion of Persia. However, he is stalled at Ctesiphon and begins to retreat, but is killed in a skirmish. The army proclaims Jovian as emperor.
363–364	REIGN OF JOVIAN.
364	Jovian agrees peace treaty heavily favouring the Persians. He cedes territory to them, including the crucial border fortress of Nisibis. Jovian dies – perhaps accidentally – near Ancyra. Valentinian proclaimed emperor and appoints his brother Valens as Augustus. They divide the empire, Valentinian taking the west and Valens the east.

364–375	REIGN OF VALENTINIAN.
364–378	REIGN OF VALENS.
365	Rebellion of the usurper *Procopius* outside Constantinople.
366	*Procopius* defeated.
367	Valentinian campaigns on the Danube.
369	Valentinian campaigns on the Danube.
372	*Firmus* proclaims himself Augustus in North Africa.
373	*Firmus'* revolt suppressed by the elder Theodosius.
375	Valentinian campaigns on the Rhine, but suffers a stroke and dies. His sons Gratian and Valentinian II succeed him in the west. Elder Theodosius executed.
375–383	REIGN OF GRATIAN.
376	The Tervingi, a Gothic people, are allowed to cross the Danube into Roman territory. However, their reception is mishandled and they rebel. Another Gothic group, known as the Greuthungi, force their way across the Danube.
377	Indecisive battle with the Goths at Ad Salices.
378	Valens defeated and killed by the Goths at Adrianople.
379	Theodosius proclaimed as emperor in the east.
379–395	REIGN OF THEODOSIUS.
382	Gothic War finally concluded, with the Goths being settled in Roman territory. Altar of Victory removed from the Senate House in Rome.
383	*Magnus Maximus* rebels in Britain and invades Gaul. He defeats and kills Gratian. For the moment he is recognised as emperor by Theodosius.
383–388	*REIGN OF MAGNUS MAXIMUS OVER MUCH OF THE WESTERN EMPIRE.*
387	*Magnus Maximus* overruns Italy, but fails to capture Valentinian II. The latter is taken by his mother to Constantinople. Theodosius marries Valentinian II's sister and is persuaded to fight *Magnus Maximus*.
388	*Magnus Maximus* defeated and killed.
390	Massacre of rioters in Thessalonica for which Theodosius will later do penance.
391	Destruction by monks of the Serapaeum, an ancient shrine to Serapis in Alexandria. Theodosius introduces legislation to restrict pagan practices.

392	Valentinian II is found dead and may have committed suicide. His senior general Arbogast proclaims the senator *Eugenius* as emperor. The latter makes some attempt to rally support from pagans.
394	Theodosius defeats Arbogast and *Eugenius* at a great battle fought at the River Frigidus.
395	Theodosius dies at Milan. He is succeeded by his sons Honorius in the west and Arcadius in the east. Both are young and real power lies elsewhere. The Western Empire is dominated by the general Stilicho. Bands of Huns raid Persia and the Eastern Empire. Alaric leads a rebellion of Goths in the Balkans. Eastern troops return to Constantinople led by Gainas. He engineers the murder of Rufinus and achieves a short-lived dominance of the eastern court.
395–408	REIGN OF ARCADIUS IN EASTERN EMPIRE.
395–423	REIGN OF HONORIUS IN WESTERN EMPIRE.
396	Alaric plunders widely in Greece.
397	Stilicho campaigns against Alaric, but the eastern emperor Arcadius and his court refuse to accept his dominance. Stilicho withdraws without achieving anything. Alaric given rank of Master of Soldiers by Arcadius. In Africa the governor Gildo rebels. He does not declare himself emperor, but wishes to defect to Arcadius.
398	Gildo defeated by his brother Mascezel on behalf of Stilicho. Mascezel dies or is killed soon after returning to Italy.
399	Gainas and others pressure Arcadius into executing his chamberlain Eutropius.
400	Gainas flees from Constantinople. Massacre of Goths as they leave the city. Gainas defeated by another Gothic officer named Fravitta, who is also executed some months later.
401	Alaric moves into the territory of the Western Empire.
402	Alaric invades Italy, but Stilicho fights several engagements with him and the Goths eventually withdraw.
405	Alaric named as Master of Soldiers by the Western Empire.
406 (or 405)	Vandals, Alans and Suevi cross the Rhine on New Year's

Eve and raid widely in Gaul.

406 Radagaisus leads a large raiding force of Goths across the Danube, but is defeated by Stilicho. Three usurpers in succession declare themselves emperor in Britain. The last is *Constantine III* who crosses to Gaul and soon controls much of the Western Empire.

406–411 *REIGN OF CONSTANTINE III.*

407 Alaric once again invades Italy.

408 Arcadius dies and is succeeded by his seven-year-old son Theodosius II. Stilicho agrees to pay Alaric to avoid another attack on Italy, but the deal damages his prestige. Honorius turns against him and after a army mutiny Stilicho is arrested and executed. Alaric invades Italy.

408–450 REIGN OF THEODOSIUS II IN EASTERN EMPIRE.

408–409 Alaric blockades Rome.

409 *Priscus Attalus* is proclaimed emperor by Alaric, but quietly deposed some months later. Honorius recognises *Constantine III* as his colleague.

410 Alaric sacks Rome, but dies soon afterwards and is succeeded by Athaulf. Britain rebels against *Constantine III.*

411 Gerontius rebels against *Constantine III* in Spain and declares his own son *Maximus* as emperor. He besieges *Constantine III*, but is killed after his army defects to Honorius' general Constantius. Constantius completes the destruction of *Constantine III.* Another usurper, *Jovinus*, appears in Gaul. He is first supported and then destroyed by Athaulf's Goths.

413 *Heraclius*, the governor of Africa, rebels and invades Italy, but is defeated and killed.

414 Athaulf raids widely in southern Gaul, and marries Galla Placidia. *Attalus Priscus* is again proclaimed emperor.

415 Athaulf murdered and leadership of Goths eventually falls to Wallia. He hands over *Priscus Attalus* who is sent into exile by Honorius. Wallia and his warriors fight in Spain on the emperor's behalf.

418 The Goths are settled in Aquitania. Wallia dies and is succeeded by Theodoric I.

421 The general Constantius named as Augustus, but dies soon afterwards.

422	Eastern Empire agrees to pay King Rua of the Huns so that he will not raid them.
423	Death of Honorius. *John* is proclaimed emperor at Rome.
424	Theodosius II refuses to acknowledge John and assembles an army to enforce the claim of Valentinian III, the son of Constantius and Galla Placidia.
425	*John* defeated and killed. Aetius arrives too late to play a part in the campaign with the force of Huns he has recruited. He is given an appointment by the new regime.
425–455	REIGN OF VALENTINIAN III.
427	Civil war fought between senior generals in the west over who was to dominate the weak emperor. Felix defeated by Boniface.
429	Vandals cross from Spain to North Africa.
430	Felix supplanted and killed by Aetius.
431	Vandals sack Hippo Regius.
432	Boniface takes troops to Italy and defeats Aetius, who flees. However, Boniface dies of his wounds.
433	Aetius returns and becomes the supreme commander in the Western Empire.
434	Rua demands an increase in the subsidy paid him by the Eastern Empire in return for not raiding.
435	Aetius given title of patrician. Rebellion of Bagaudae in north-west Gaul.
436–437	Defeat of Burgundians by Aetius and his Hun allies. Goths from Aquitania attack city of Narbo.
438	Theodosius II issues the collection of laws known as the Theodosian Code.
439	Vandals take Carthage.
440	Vandals attack Sicily. Rua's nephews Bleda and Attila force the Eastern Empire to a further increase in the subsidy paid to the Huns.
441	Western and Eastern Empires combine to prepare a major expedition against the Vandals, but this is never launched. In Spain the Suevi extend their control.
441–442	The Huns raid widely in Illyricum and Thrace.
442	Treaty with Vandals acknowledges their control of much of North Africa.
445	Bleda murdered and Attila becomes sole ruler of the Huns.

447	Attila launches very heavy raids on Eastern Empire, devastating Thrace and even threatening Constantinople. Theodosius II grants him a stretch of territory close to the Danube as well as a greatly increased payment in gold.
448	Embassy to Attila described by Priscus.
450	Death of Theodosius II. He is succeeded by Marcian.
450–457	REIGN OF MARCIAN IN EASTERN EMPIRE.
451	Attila attacks Western Empire, but is checked by Aetius at the Catalaunian Plains.
452	Attila attacks Italy, sacking several cities, but eventually withdraws.
453	Death of Attila.
454	Aetius murdered by Valentinian III.
455	Valentinian III murdered and *Petronius Maximus* declares himself emperor. He is killed when the Vandals attack and plunder Rome. In Gaul *Avitus* is proclaimed emperor with the support of the Goths.
456	*Avitus* invades Italy, but is eventually defeated.
457	*Avitus* abdicates and becomes a bishop, but soon dies. Majorian named as western emperor with the support of the Eastern Empire. Marcian dies late in the year. Leo is named eastern emperor with the backing of the Master of Soldiers Aspar.
457–474	REIGN OF LEO IN EASTERN EMPIRE.
457–461	REIGN OF MAJORIAN IN WESTERN EMPIRE.
460	Majorian prepares to invade Africa from Spain.
461	Majorian's expedition to Africa suffers catastrophic defeat off the coast of Spain. He is subsequently deposed and executed by Ricimer, the commander of the army in Italy. Ricimer names Libius Severus as emperor.
461–465	REIGN OF LIBIUS SEVERUS IN WESTERN EMPIRE.
463	Rebellion by *Aegidius* at the head of Roman army in Gaul.
465	Assassination of *Aegidius*. Libius Severus dies and is not replaced as western emperor for nearly two years.
467	Leo backs one of his generals, Anthemius, to become western emperor. Ricimer accepts his rule.

467–472	REIGN OF ANTHEMIUS IN WESTERN EMPIRE.
468	Second expedition against the Vandals in Africa ends in disaster.
471	Aspar murdered on orders of Leo.
472	Civil war between Anthemius and Ricimer. The emperor is defeated and executed. Ricimer proclaims *Olybrius* as emperor. Ricimer dies soon afterwards, and is shortly followed by *Olybrius*.
473	Ricimer's command is inherited by Gundobad the Burgundian. He names *Glycerius* as western emperor.
473–474	*REIGN OF GLYCERIUS IN WESTERN EMPIRE.*
474	Death of Leo. Zeno becomes eastern emperor. Gundobad abandons *Glycerius* and instead plunges into Burgundian politics. Julius Nepos leads an army from Dalmatia to depose *Glycerius* and make himself emperor.
474–491	REIGN OF ZENO IN EASTERN EMPIRE.
475	The army of Italy led by Orestes rebels and drives out Nepos who takes refuge in the Eastern Empire. Orestes proclaims his son Romulus Augustulus as western emperor. *Basiliscus* rebels against Zeno and captures Constantinople.
475–476	REIGN OF ROMULUS AUGUSTULUS.
476	Odoacer leads a rebellion of a large part of the troops in Italy, killing Orestes and deposing Romulus Augustulus. He sends the imperial regalia to Constantinople. Zeno defeats and executes *Basiliscus*.
479	Usurper *Marcian* rebels against Zeno, but is defeated and becomes a priest and exiled.
480	Death of exiled Julius Nepos.
481	Death of Gothic leader Theodoric Strabo.
484–488	Rebellion against Zeno in Isauria eventually defeated.
489	Theodoric and his Ostrogoths invade Italy.
491	Death of Zeno. He is succeeded as eastern emperor by Anastasius.
491–518	REIGN OF ANASTASIUS IN EASTERN EMPIRE.
493	Odoacer surrenders to Theodoric at Ravenna. After a brief period of joint rule Odoacer is killed.
502	Persians launch major offensive against Eastern Empire.

505	Romans force Persia to accept a truce.
518	Death of Anastasius. He is succeeded by Justin I as eastern emperor.
518–527	REIGN OF JUSTIN I IN EASTERN EMPIRE.
527	Justin dies, but has already made his nephew Justinian his co-emperor. Justinian succeeds him.
527–565	REIGN OF JUSTINIAN IN EASTERN EMPIRE.
528	Justinian releases the first version of his Law Code.
530	Belisarius defeats Persians at Dara.
531	Belisarius defeated at Callinicum.
532	Serious rioting by circus factions in Constantinople nearly supplants Justinian. The trouble is brutally suppressed. Treaty of 'eternal peace' signed with Persia.
533	Justinian releases the *Digest*. Belisarius invades North Africa and rapidly defeats the Vandals.
534	Belisarius celebrates triumph for African victory.
535	Belisarius invades Sicily.
536	Belisarius invades Italy and occupies Rome.
537	Belisarius besieged in Rome
539	Ostrogoths sack Milan.
540	Persian King Khusro attacks Eastern Empire and sacks Antioch.
541	Belisarius recalled from Italy. He is soon sent against the Persians.
542	First major outbreak of plague in Eastern Empire.
544–549	Belisarius campaigns in Italy.
545	Justinian and Khusro agree peace in Mesopotamia, but fighting continues on other fronts.
548	Death of Empress Theodora.
550	Offensive launched against Visigoths in Spain.
552	Narses defeats Ostrogoths in Italy at Taginae.
553	Narses defeats Ostrogoths at Vesuvius.
554	An army of Franks invades Italy and is defeated at Casilinus.
561–562	'Fifty year' peace agreed between Eastern Empire and Persia.
565	Death of Justinian, who is succeeded by his nephew Justin II.
565–578	REIGN OF JUSTIN II IN EASTERN EMPIRE.

568	Lombards invade Italy.
572	Justin II attacks Persia.
573	Persians capture Dara. Justinian suffers permanent mental collapse. From this point on his rule is nominal.
574	Tiberius appointed as Caesar and effectively becomes sole emperor.
574–582	REIGN OF TIBERIUS IN EASTERN EMPIRE.
578	Death of Justin II.
582	Death of Tiberius who is succeeded by the general Maurice.
582–602	REIGN OF MAURICE IN EASTERN EMPIRE.
602	Usurper *Phocas* rebels. Maurice is deposed and killed.
608–610	Civil War. Several rebellions against Phocas, of which the most serious is led by Heraclius, the commander in Africa. Phocas is defeated.
610–641	REIGN OF HERACLIUS IN EASTERN EMPIRE.
632	Death of prophet Muhammed.
636	Romans suffer heavy defeat at the hands of a Muslim Arab army at the Battle of Yarmuk.
638	Arabs capture Jerusalem.
640	Arabs conquer Egypt.

Glossary

Agentes in rebus: From the fourth century, the 'agents in matters' were representatives of the emperor whose official task was to carry despatches. Since this involved travel and contact with many individuals, they also reported on the activities of other members of the imperial system. They were especially concerned to root out the disloyal. Their reports were one of the few ways that an emperor had of finding out what was going on in a distant province. Since their accusations so frequently led to the disgrace or death of officials and officers, they were as widely disliked as they were feared.

Arianism: This version of Christianity was declared heretical by the Council of Nicaea in 325. However, it continued to be widespread, especially in the eastern provinces throughout the fourth century. Its originator was Arius, a priest who taught at both Antioch and Alexandria. He asserted that Jesus was neither identical nor quite equal to God the Father. Precisely how this difference was defined varied amongst Arians. One of the commonest definitions was to say that God the Father and God the Son were 'of like substance' (in Greek *homoios*). A version of Arianism remained common amongst groups like the Goths and Vandals into the sixth century.

Bucellarii: Soldiers paid and supported by a particular commander and forming part of his household. These men were still part of the regular army and supposed to be loyal to the emperor. The name derives from the ration hard-tack biscuit (*bucellatum*) and emphasised the commander's obligation to feed his soldiers. Such troops were common in the fifth and sixth centuries.

Candidati: Forty *candidati* were selected from the *scholae* regiments of the imperial bodyguard. They acted as personal bodyguards to the emperor. Their name was derived from their white uniforms. (Under the Republic, men standing for political office had also worn specially whitened togas, hence our word candidate.)

Cataphract: Heavily armoured cavalryman often riding an armoured horse. The Romans first encountered such warriors in eastern armies, but later made use of them themselves.

Clarissimus: Literally meaning 'most distinguished', under the Principate the term was reserved for senators. By the fourth century it is instead associated with many imperial posts, both in the civil service and army.

Clibanarius: Heavily armoured cavalryman, whose horse may also have worn armour. It is unclear whether or not the term was synonymous with cataphract. The name came from a nickname meaning 'bread-oven'.

Cohort (cohors): Under the Principate both legionaries and auxiliary infantry were divided into cohorts. This was the basic tactical unit of the army. Most cohorts were 480 strong, but the first cohort of a legion and some selected auxiliary units numbered 800. By the fourth century only some units of *limitanei* were still organised into cohorts. These seem to have been much smaller than the earlier cohorts.

Cohortales: The staff and functionaries of provincial governors. From Constantine onwards this role was hereditary.

Colonus (pl. coloni): The *coloni* were tenant farmers. Diocletian tied such individuals to the land they worked in an effort to ensure regular tax revenue. Their descendants inherited the same obligations.

Comes (Count): Officers of the later Roman army, ranking below the Masters of Soldiers. A few of these officers were placed in charge of specific regions. Others were given command of parts of the *comitatenses*. *Comes* literally meant 'companion' of the emperor and the title was also employed for a range of different posts.

Comes Domesticorum (Count of the Domestic Staff): From the middle of the fourth century this officer commanded the imperial bodyguard known as the *protectores*.

Comitatenses: The units of the 'field armies' in the fourth, fifth and sixth centuries. In theory they were kept at the immediate disposal of the emperors or their commanders. They received better pay and privileges than the *limitanei*.

Consul: The year's two consuls were the senior elected magistrates of the Roman Republic and the year was named after them. The post of consul remained prestigious long after its real power had diminished. Emperors often held the consulship themselves. By the fifth century it was customary for the eastern and western emperors to appoint one consul each.

Cuneus: Title given to some cavalry units in the Late Roman army.

Curia: Town council composed of wealthier male members of the community. Its members were expected to spend considerable sums of their own money on local projects. In the Late Roman Empire it became difficult in many regions to find enough local men willing and able to serve on the councils.

Denarius: The basic silver coin under the Principate. It was the 'penny' of the Authorised Bible, hence the pre-decimalisation abbreviation of *d* for pence. Denarii ceased to be minted in the third century, but many sums were still calculated in this unit.

Diocese: Having reduced the size of individual provinces, Diocletian created fourteen larger groupings known as dioceses for civilian administration. Each was the responsibility of a *vicarius*, who was himself junior to the praetorian prefects.

Dominate: Augustus and his successors had been known as *princeps*, or first citizen/magistrate. From Diocletian onwards, emperors preferred to be called *dominus*, which meant 'lord' or 'master'. Therefore, it is conventional for scholars to refer to the Late Roman Empire as the Dominate.

Donatists: This schismatic group took its name from its first leader Donatus. This split in the North African Church was not initially about questions of doctrine. Donatists objected to the readmission and continued service as priests or bishops of men who had fled or otherwise been discredited during the persecution of the Christians. Eventually, wholly parallel and distinct church organisations existed in many North African communities.

Dux (pl. duces): Senior officer in the Late Roman army, commanding a region and its garrison of *limitanei*.

Equestrian Order (Equites): The social class immediately below the senatorial order, the *equites* were named from their traditional role as the cavalrymen in the army of the Republic. Equestrians greatly increased their share of military and civil posts during the third century. Eventually, equestrian status was automatically bestowed by the holding of specific imperial posts, and the class itself was divided into several sub-groups of varying seniority.

Equites singulares Augusti: The emperor's own horse guards for the first three centuries of the Principate, these provided an elite cavalry force to support the praetorian guard. They seem to have been abolished when Constantine abolished the praetorian guard.

Foederati: Allied barbarians, obliged to provide military service to the emperor, who usually served in their own units and sometimes under their own commanders who usually held Roman rank.

Homoousios: This doctrine described Jesus as 'of the same substance' as God the Father. It was adopted as the orthodox position by the bishops at the Council of Nicaea. In spite of some fierce resistance, it would eventually be confirmed as the doctrine of the orthodox Catholic Church.

Honoratus: retired imperial official, usually ranked as *clarissimus*. Such men enjoyed considerable prvileges.

Legatus: The senatorial representatives or deputies of the emperor. Under the Principate two types of imperial legates were most important: (1) The *legatus Augusti pro praetore* who held command in all imperial provinces (apart from Egypt) containing a legionary garrison; (2) The *legatus legionis* who commanded a legion.

Legion (Legio): Under the Principate the legion was a large formation of *c.*5,000 men. Legions continued to exist in both the *comitatenses* and *limitanei* in the fourth and fifth centuries, but it is clear that they were much smaller in size. Legions of *comitatenses* are unlikely to have been much larger than 1,000 men and may well have been considerably smaller.

Limitanei: The grade of troops commanded by the *duces limitis*, the military commanders of the various regions, usually on the frontier, into which the provinces of the later empire were divided. They were paid less than the *comitatenses*.

Magister Officiorum (Master of Offices): The *Magister Officiorum* is first attested in the fourth century. The power of this rank gradually increased, until it became one of the most senior in the entire imperial bureaucracy and court. In addition to civil responsibilities, the *Magister Officiorum* controlled state arms factories and had some degree of control over the *scholae*.

Magistrates: The Roman Republic had employed elected magistrates as its senior executive officers. The most senior of these were the two consuls. Most of the posts continued to exist under the empire, but lost any political independence and were often appointments made by the emperors.

Manichaeism: This religion was founded by the prophet Mani in the third century. He had travelled widely, including a visit to India, and his ideas showed the influence of a wide range of different faiths, including Judaism, Christianity and Zoroastrianism. Mani spoke of a struggle between Light, or good, and Darkness, or evil. The world was a creation of Darkness that trapped elements of the Light within it. His most ardent followers lived rigorously ascetic lives in an effort to win redemption. Initially welcomed in Persia, he was eventually executed by King Bahram I in 276. Diocletian persecuted the followers of this religion, as did later Christian emperors.

Master of Soldiers (*Magister Militum*): These were the most senior military commanders below the emperors themselves from the fourth century onwards. There were several variations of this title. These included the Master of Horse (*Magister Equitum*) and Master of Infantry (*Magister Peditum*). In some cases the title also defined the region or sphere or responsibility. Not all Masters of Soldiers were of equal seniority, but the details of the rank structure varied over time.

Montanists: A Judaising Christian sect that appeared in the late second century and subsequently flourished, especially in Asia Minor. The Montanists initially were inspired by two women prophets who predicted the rapid approach of the Second Coming. The sect also emphasised the achievement of ritual purity through fasting, penances and retreat from ordinary life. The Montanist Church persisted with its own distinct hierarchy until the eighth century.

Neoplatonism: This descendant of Platonism developed in the third century from the teachings of the philosopher Plotinus, but incorporated ideas from other philosophical schools and fresh concepts. Neoplatonism became the dominant philosophical school of the Late Roman world. It included strong mystical elements.

Nicene Creed: *See* Homoousios.

Numerus (pl. numeri): Name given to units of irregular auxiliary soldiers under the Principate. Later the title was adopted by some cavalry units.

Palatini: Units of higher status and prestige than the *comitatenses*, the *palatini* also formed part of the field armies of Late Antiquity (4th–6th Century AD).

Patrician (Patricius): Although once an inner elite within the ranks of the Senate, in the fifth century this was used as a title by powerful generals, most notably Stilicho and Aetius.

Pilum (pl. pila): The heavy javelin that was the standard equipment of the Roman legionary for much of Rome's history, but seems to have fallen out of use during the third century.

Praepositus: Unit commander in the Late Roman army. It seems to have been virtually synonymous with tribune or prefect.

Praepositus sacri cubiculi: The senior eunuch official of the emperor's household. At times these men gained considerable influence. Theodoric, the Ostrogothic king of Italy, had one of these officials in his own court.

Praetorian Guard: The military bodyguard of the emperors of the Principate commanded by tribunes and the whole corps commanded by two praetorian prefects. Its position as the strongest armed body in Rome gave it considerable power. It was disbanded by Constantine in 312 after supporting his rival Maxentius.

Praetorian Prefect: Originally the commanders of the praetorian guard, as the third century developed the praetorian prefects developed into something more like senior bureaucrats or grand viziers. By the fourth century they had lost all real military responsibilities and did not command troops. Their number also increased and the post tended to oversee a specific region of the empire. The vicars were their subordinates.

Primicerius notariorum (Head of the Notaries): The senior notary had particular charge of issuing appointments and commissions. The *Notitia Dignitatum* was originally prepared by his department.

Primicerius sacri cubiculi: This was the second most senior eunuch of the imperial chamber. Once again, close access to the emperor himself often meant that these acquired considerable influence.

Principate: Augustus claimed to be merely the *princeps*, the most senior magistrate/citizen in the state. Therefore the regime he created is conventionally referred to as the Principate. It lasted from the late first century BC until its collapse during the third century.

Protectores domestici: This was the close imperial bodyguard. It seems to have existed from at least the time of Diocletian. In some respects it served as an officer cadet unit, since its members were frequently given command of units in the wider army.

Rescript: Formal reply issued by an emperor in response to a petition. These rulings were legally binding.

Schola: Guard cavalry regiment in the later Roman army. In the *Notitia Dignitatum* five *scholae* are listed for the Western Empire and seven for the Eastern Empire.

Senate: This body of some 600 members that met in Rome enjoyed considerable prestige even after it had ceased to wield real political power. Later, Constantinople acquired a Senate of its own.

Senatorial Order: In the Principate membership of the senatorial order required the possession of considerable property, including at least some land in Italy. The status was kept for two generations after an individual had actually been a member of the Senate. Later, senatorial status came as a result of holding high imperial office.

Solidus: This gold coin was introduced in the fourth century, in part because the taxation system and other imperial finances needed to be based on more stable gold values. There were seventy-two coins to a pound of gold.

Spatha: The name conventionally used to describe the longer swords used by Roman cavalrymen and, in Late Antiquity, also many infantrymen.

Stoicism: One of the main philosophical schools popular in the Principate, stoicism was founded by the philosopher Zeno in the late fourth century BC. Marcus Aurelius was one of its most prominent adherents.

Tetrarchy: The Rule of Four Emperors was introduced by Diocletian. There were two senior colleagues, each with a title of Augustus, and each of these had a junior assistant, who was titled Caesar. Pronouncements and laws were all issued in the four names. The system did not last in this form.

Trecenarius: Junior officer in the Late Roman army.

Vicar (Vicarius): The vicar was the civil administrator in charge of a diocese.

Zoroastrianism: The religion of ancient Persia, which may well have originated around 1000 BC. It was revived and became far more prominent with the establishment of the Sassanid dynasty by Ardashir in the third century. Its worship was marked by specially designed temples, which housed the sacred fire.

Bibliography

Three volumes of the *Cambridge Ancient History* are frequently cited in the Notes, abbreviated as *CAH²*. These are:

Bowman, A., Garnsey, P. & Cameron, A. (eds.), *The Cambridge Ancient History*, Vol. XII: *The Crisis of Empire, A.D. 193–337* (2nd edn, 2005).

Cameron, A. & Garnsey, P. (eds.), *The Cambridge Ancient History*, Vol. XIII: *The Late Empire, A.D. 337–425* (1998).

Cameron, A., Ward-Perkins, B. & Whitby, M. (eds.), *The Cambridge Ancient History*, Vol. XIV: *Late Antiquity: Empire and Successors, A.D. 425–600* (2000).

Adams, J., 'The Poets of Bu Njem: Language, Culture and the Centurionate', *Journal of Roman Studies*, 89 (1999), pp. 109–134.

Alfödy, G., *Noricum* (trans. Birley, A.) (1974).

——'The Crisis of the Third Century As Seen By Contemporaries', in *Greek, Roman and Byzantine Studies*, 15 (1974), pp. 89–111.

Alston, R., *Soldier and Society in Roman Egypt* (1995).

Amory, P., *People and Identity in Ostrogothic Italy, 489–554* (1997).

Austin, N., *Ammianus on Warfare: An Investigation into Ammianus' Military Knowledge (Collection Latomus 165)* (1979).

Austin, N., & Rankov, B., *Exploratio: Military and Political Intelligence in the Roman World from the Second Punic War to the Battle of Adrianople* (1995).

Baatz, D., 'Cuiculus – Zur Technik der Unterminierung antiker Wehrbauten', in Schallmayer, E., *Niederbieder, Postumus und der Limesfall* (1996), pp. 84–89.

Bagnall, R., & Frier, B., *The Demography of Roman Egypt* (1994)

Balty, J., & Van Rengen, W., *Apamea in Syria: The Winter Quarters of Legio II Parthica* (1993).

Banaji, J., *Agrarian Change in Late Antiquity: Gold, Labour, and Aristocratic Dominance* (2001).

Bar, D., 'Was there a 3rd-C. economic crisis in Palestine?', in Humphrey, J. (ed.), *The Roman and Byzantine Near East*, Vol. 3, Journal of Roman Archaeology Supplementary Series, 49 (2002), pp. 43–54.

Barbero, A., *The Day of the Barbarians: The First Battle in the Fall of the Roman Empire* (trans. Cullen, J.) (2007).

Barnes, T., 'Legislation against the Early Christians', *Journal of Roman Studies*, 58 (1968), pp. 32–50.

——*Constantine and Eusebius* (1981).

——*The New Empire of Diocletian* (1982).

——'Constantine and the Christians of Persia,' *Journal of Roman Studies*, 75 (1985), pp. 126–136.

——*Athanasius and Constantius: Theology and Politics in the Constantinian Empire* (1993).

——*Ammianus and the Representation of Historical Reality* (1998).

Barnwell, P., *Emperors, Prefects and Kings: The Roman West, 395–565* (1992).

Bell, H., Martin, V., Turner, E. & van Berchem, D. (eds.), *The Abinnaeus Archive: Papers of a Roman Officer in the Reign of Constantius II* (1964).

Bellinger, A., Brown, F., Perkins, A., & Wells, C. (eds.), *The Excavations at Dura-Europos: Final Report*, VIII, Part 1, *The Synagogue* (1956).

Beloch, K., *Die Bevölkerung de Griechisch-römischen Welt* (1886).

Berchman, R., *Porphyry Against the Christians* (2005).

Birley, A., 'The Economic Effects of Roman Frontier Policy', in King, A. & Henig, M. (eds.), *The Roman West in the Third Century*, BAR International Series, 109 (1981), p. 40.

——*Marcus Aurelius* (rev. edn 1987)

——*Septimius Severus: The African Emperor* (1988).

——*The Roman Government of Britain* (2005).

Birley, E., *The Roman Army* (1988).

Bishop, M. & Coulston, J., *Roman Military Equipment from the Punic Wars to the Fall of Rome* (2nd edn, 2006).

Blockley, R., *East Roman Foreign Policy: Formation and Conduct from Diocletian to Anastasius* (1992).

Boak, A., *Manpower Shortage and the Fall of the Roman Empire in the West* (1955).

Bowersock, G., *Julian the Apostate* (1978).

Bowman, A. & Thomas, J. (eds.), *The Vindolanda Writing Tablets* (*Tabulae Vindolandenses II*) (1994), 250.

Bradford Welles, C., *The Excavations at Dura-Europos: Final Report*, VIII, Part 2, *The Christian Building* (1967).

Brandon, P., *The Decline and Fall of the British Empire* (2007).

Breeze, D. & Dobson, B., *Roman Officers and Frontiers* (1993).

Bremmer, J., 'The Vision of Constantine' in Lardinois, A. et al. (eds.),

Land of Dreams: Greek & Latin Studies in Honour of A.H.M. Kessels (2006), pp. 57–79.

Brown, P., *The World of Late Antiquity: From Marcus Aurelius to Muhammad* (1971).

——'The Rise and Function of the Holy Man in Late Antiquity', *Journal of Roman Studies*, 61 (1971), pp. 801–101.

Bruun, C., 'The Antonine Plague and the Third Century Crisis', in Hekster, O., Kleijn, G., & Slootjes, D. (eds.) *Crises and the Roman Empire* (2007), pp. 201–217.

Burgess, R., 'The Dark Ages Return to Fifth Century Britain: The Restored Gallic Chronicle Exploded', *Britannia*, 21 (1990), pp. 185–195.

——'The Summer of Blood: The "Great Massacre" of 337 and the Promotion of the Sons of Constantine', *Dumbarton Oaks Papers*, 62 (forthcoming, 2008).

Burns, T., 'The Battle of Adrianople: A Reconsideration', *Historia*, 22 (1973), pp. 336–345.

——*Barbarians Within the Gates of Rome: A Study of Roman Military Policy and the Barbarians, ca. 375–425 A.D.* (1994).

——*Rome and the Barbarians, 100 B.C.–A.D. 400* (2003).

Bury, J., *History of the Later Roman Empire from the death of Theodosius I to the death of Justinian*, 2 Vols. (1958).

Campbell, D., 'What happened at Hatra? The Problems of the Severan Siege Operations', in Freeman, P. & Kennedy, D. (eds.), *The Defence of the Roman and Byzantine East*, BAR International Series, 297 (1986), pp. 51–58.

Campbell, J., 'The Marriage of Soldiers Under the Empire', *Journal of Roman Studies*, 68 (1978), pp. 153–166.

——*The Emperor and the Roman Army* (1984).

Casey, P., *Carausius and Allectus: The British Usurpers* (1994).

Casey, P., 'The Legions in the Later Roman Empire', in Brewer, R. (ed.), *The Second Augustan Legion and the Roman Military Machine* (2002), pp. 165–176.

Chadwick, H., *The Church in Ancient Society: From Galilee to Gregory the Great* (2001).

Chambers, M. (ed.), *The Fall of Rome: Can it be Explained?* (1963).

Chrishman, R., *Arts of Mankind: Iran: Parthians and Sassanians* (trans. Gilbert, S. & Lemmons, J.) (1962).

Claridge, A., *Rome: Oxford Archaeological Guides* (1998).

Coello, T., *Unit Sizes in the Late Roman Army*, BAR International Series, 645 (1996).

Corcoran, S., *The Empire of the Tetrarchs: Imperial Pronouncements and Government, AD 284–324* (1996).

——'Before Constantine', in Lenski, N. (ed.), *The Cambridge Companion to the Age of Constantine* (2006), pp. 35–58.

Coterill, J., 'Saxon Raiding and the Role of the Late Roman Coastal Forts of Britain', *Britannia*, 24 (1993), pp. 227–239.

Coulston, J., 'Roman Archery Equipment', in Bishop, M. (ed.), *The Production and Distribution of Roman Military Equipment: Proceedings of the Second Roman Military Equipment Research Seminar*, BAR International Series, 275 (1985), pp. 230–348.

Cunliffe, B., *Greeks, Romans and Barbarians: Spheres of Inter-action* (1988).

Danzinger, D. & Purcell, N., *Hadrian's Empire* (2005).

Dark, K., 'A Sub-Roman Re-Defence of Hadrian's Wall?', *Britannia*, 23 (1992), pp. 111–120.

——*Britain and the End of the Roman Empire* (2000).

Davies, R., *Service in the Roman Army* (1989).

de Blois, L., *The Policy of the Emperor Gallienus* (1976).

——'The Crisis of the Third Century A.D. in the Roman Empire: A Modern Myth?', in de Blois, L. & Rich, J. (eds.), *The Transformation of Economic Life under the Roman Empire* (2002), pp. 204–217.

——'Monetary Politics, the Soldiers' Pay, and the Onset of Crisis in the First Half of the Third Century AD', in Erdkamp, P. (ed.), *The Roman Army and the Economy* (2002), pp. 90–107.

Delbruck, H., *The Barbarian Invasions* (trans. Renfroe, J.) (1980).

Dermandt, A., *Der Falls Roms: Die Auflösung der Römischen Reiches im Urteil der Nachwelt* (1984).

Devijver, H., *The Equestrian Officers of the Roman Army*, 2 Vols. (1989 & 1992).

Diaconescu, A., 'The towns of Roman Dacia: An Overview of Recent Archaeological Research', in Hanson, W. & Haynes, I., *Roman Dacia: The Making of A Provincial Society*, Journal of Roman Archaeology Supplementary Series, 56 (2004), pp. 87–142.

Dignas, B. & Winter, E., *Rome and Persia in Late Antiquity: Neighbours and Rivals* (2007).

Dixon, K. & Southern, P., *The Late Roman Army* (1996).

Dodds, E., *Pagan and Christian in an Age of Anxiety* (1965).

Dodgeon, M. & Lieu, S., *The Roman Eastern Frontier and the Persian Wars, AD 226–363* (1991).

Drake, H., 'The Impact of Constantine on Christianity', in Lenski, N. (ed.), *The Cambridge Companion to the Age of Constantine* (2006), pp. 111–136.

Drijvers, J., *Helena Augusta: The Mother of Constantine the Great and the Legend of the Finding of the True Cross* (1992).

Drijvers, J. & Hunt, D. (eds.), *The Late Roman World and its Historian* (1999).

Drinkwater, J., *The Gallic Empire: Separation and Continuity in the North-Western Provinces of the Roman Empire AD 260–274, Historia Einzelschriften*, 52 (1987), pp. 1–270.

——'The Bacaudae of Fifth Century Gaul', in Drinkwater, J. & Elton, H. (eds.), *Fifth Century Gaul* (1992), pp. 208–217.

——'The Germanic Threat on the Rhine Frontier: A Romano-Gallic Artefact', in Mathisen, R. & Sivan, H. (eds.), *Shifting Frontiers in Late Antiquity* (1996), pp. 20–30.

——*The Alamanni and Rome 213–496: Caracalla to Clovis* (2007).

Duncan-Jones, R., 'Pay and Numbers in Diocletian's Army', *Chiron*, 8 (1978), pp. 541–560.

——*Money and Government in the Roman Empire* (1994).

——'The Impact of the Antonine Plague', *Journal of Roman Archaeology*, 9 (1996), pp. 108–136.

Dyson, S., 'Native Revolt Patterns in the Roman Empire', *Aufstieg und Niedergang der römischen Welt*, II. 3 (1975), pp. 38–175.

——*The Creation of the Roman Frontier* (1985).

Edwards, C. & Woolf, G. (eds.), *Rome the Cosmopolis* (2003).

Edwards, M., 'The Beginnings of Christianization', in Lenski, N. (ed.), *The Cambridge Companion to the Age of Constantine* (2006), pp. 137–158.

Elton, H., *Warfare in Roman Europe: AD 350–425* (1996).

——'Military Forces', in Sabin, P., Van Wees, H. & Whitby, M. (eds.), *The Cambridge History of Greek and Roman Warfare*, Volume II: *Rome from the Late Republic to the Late Empire* (2007), pp. 270–309.

Errington, R., *Roman Imperial Policy from Julian to Theodosius* (2006).

Esmonde Cleary, A., *The Ending of Roman Britain* (1989).

Evans, J., *The Age of Justinian: The Circumstances of Imperial Power* (1996).

——*The Empress Theodora: Partner of Justinian* (2002).

Fabech, C., 'Booty Sacrifices in Southern Scandinavia – A History of Warfare and Ideology', in Björklund, E., *Roman Reflections in Scandinavia* (1996), pp. 135–138.

Faulkner, N., *The Decline and Fall of Roman Britain* (2nd edn, 2004).

Ferguson, J., 'China and Rome', *Aufstieg und Niedergang der Römischen Welt*, II. 9. 2, pp. 581–603.

Fields, N., *The Hun: Scourge of God AD 375–565* (Osprey Warrior Series 111, 2006).

Fink, R., *Roman Military Records on Papyrus* (1971).

Foss, C., 'Syria in Transition, AD 550–750: An Archaeological Approach, *Dumbarton Oaks Papers*, 51 (1997), pp. 189–269.

Frakes, R., 'The Dynasty of Constantine Down to 363', in Lenski, N. (ed.), *The Cambridge Companion to the Age of Constantine* (2006), pp. 91–107.

Freeman, C., *The Closing of the Western Mind: The Rise of Faith and the Fall of Reason* (2002).

Frend, W., *Martyrdom and Persecution in the Early Church* (1965).

Frere, S., *Britannia* (3rd edn, 1987).

Frier, B., 'Roman Demography', in Potter, D. & Mattingly, D. (eds.), *Life, Death and Entertainment in the Roman Empire* (1999), pp. 95–109.

Garnsey, P., *Social Status and Legal Privilege in the Roman Empire* (1970)

Garnsey, P. & Humfress, C., *The Evolution of the Late Antique World* (2001).

Gibbon, E., *The History of the Decline and Fall of the Roman Empire*, 3 Vols. (1776–1781).

Gilliam, J., 'The Plague under Marcus Aurelius', *American Journal of Philology*, 82 (1961), pp. 225–251.

Goffart, W., *Barbarians and Romans: The Techniques of Accommodation Revisited* (1980).

——*Barbarian Tides: The Migration Age and the Later Roman Empire* (2006).

Goldsworthy, A., *The Roman Army at War, 100 BC–AD 200* (1996).

——*The Complete Roman Army* (2003).

——*In the Name of Rome* (2003).

——*Caesar: The Life of a Colossus* (2006).

——'War: The late Republic and Principate', in Sabin, P., Van Wees, H. & Whitby, M. (eds.) *The Cambridge History of Greek and Roman Warfare*, Vol. 2 (2007), pp. 76–121.

Goodburn, R. & Bartholomew, P. (eds.), *Aspects of the Notitia Dignitatum*, BAR Supplementary Series, 15 (1976).

Goodman, M. (with the assistance of Sherwood, J.), *The Roman World 44 BC–AD 180* (1997).

Grainge, G., *The Roman Invasions of Britain* (2005).

Grant, C., *The Emperor Constantine* (1993).

Gray, P., 'The Legacy of Chalcedon: Christological Problems and Their Significance', in Maas, M. (ed.), *The Cambridge Companion to the Age of Justinian* (2005), pp. 215–238.

Greatrex, G., 'The *Nika* Riot: A Reappraisal', *Journal of Hellenic Studies*, 117 (1997), pp. 60–86.

——*Rome and Persia at War, 502–532* (1998).

——'The Gothic Arians after Theodosius (to Justinian)', *Studia Patristica*, 34 (2001), pp. 73–81.

——'Byzantium and the East in the Sixth Century', in Maas, M. (ed.), *The Cambridge Companion to the Age of Justinian* (2005), pp. 477–509.

——'The Early Years of Justin in the Sources', *Electrum*, 12 (2007), pp. 99–115.

Greatrex, G. & Lieu, N. (eds.), *The Roman Eastern Frontier and the Persian Wars: Part II AD 363–630* (2002).

Greene, K., *The Archaeology of the Roman Economy* (1986).

Greene, K., 'Technology and Innovation in Context: The Roman Background to Medieval and Later Developments', *Journal of Roman Archaeology*, 7 (1994), pp. 22–33.

Grigg, R., 'Inconsistency and Lassitude: The Shield Emblems of the *Notitia Dignitatum*', *Journal of Roman Studies*, 73 (1983), pp. 132–142.

Gutman, J. (ed.), *The Dura Europos Synagogue: A Re-evaluation (1932-1972)* (1973).

Haarer, F., *Anastasius I: Politics and Empire in the Late Roman World* (2006).

Haldon, J., *The Byzantine Wars* (2001).

Halsall, G., *Warfare and Society in the Barbarian West, 450–900* (2003).

——*Barbarian Migrations and the Roman West, 376–568* (2007).

Harries, J., *Sidonius Apollinaris and the Fall of Rome, AD 407–485* (1994).

Haywood, J., *Dark Age Naval Power: A Re-assessment of Frankish and Anglo-Saxon Seafaring Activity* (1991).

Heather, P., *Goths and Romans, 332–489* (1991).

——*The Goths* (1996).

——*The Fall of the Roman Empire: A New History* (2005).

——'The Fall of the Roman Empire' in *Oxford Historian*, 4 (May 2006), pp. 17-20.

Hedeager, L., 'The Evolution of German Society 1–400 AD', in Jones, R., Bloemers, J., Dyson, S. & Biddle, M. (eds.), *First Millennium*

Papers: Western Europe in the 1st Millennium, BAR International Series, 401 (1988), pp. 129–401.

Hekster, O., *Commodus: An Emperor at the Crossroads* (2002).

Herzteld, E., *Archaeological History of Iran* (1934).

Hodgson, N. & Bidwell, P., 'Auxiliary Barracks in a New Light: Recent Discoveries on Hadrian's Wall', *Britannia,* 35 (2004), pp. 121–157.

Holden, P. & Purcell, N., *The Corrupting Sea: A Study of Mediterranean History* (2000).

Holden, P., 'Mediterranean Plague in the Age of Justinian', in Maas, M. (ed.), *The Cambridge Companion to the Age of Justinian* (2005), pp. 134–160.

Holum, K., 'The Classical City in the Sixth Century: Survival and Transformation', in Maas, M. (ed.), *The Cambridge Companion to the Age of Justinian* (2005), pp. 87–112.

Hopkins, C., *The Discovery of Dura Europos* (1979).

Hopkins, K., 'Taxes and Trade in the Roman Empire (200 BC–AD 400)', *Journal of Roman Studies,* 70 (1980), pp. 101–125.

——'Early Christian Number and its Implications', *Journal of Early Christian Studies,* 6 (1998), pp. 184–226.

Howard-Johnston, J., 'The Two Great Powers in Late Antiquity: A Comparison', in Cameron, A. (ed.), *The Byzantine and Early Islamic Near East III: States Resources and Armies* (1995), pp. 157–226, (reprinted in Howard-Johnston, A., *Early Rome, Sassanian Persia and the End of Antiquity* (2006)).

Howe, L., *The Praetorian Prefect from Commodus to Diocletian, AD 180–305* (1942).

Howgego, C., 'Coin Circulation and the Integration of the Roman Economy', *Journal of Roman Archaeology,* 7 (1994), pp. 5–21.

Humfress, C., 'Law and Legal Practice in the Age of Justinian', in Maas, M. (ed.), *The Cambridge Companion to the Age of Justinian* (2005), pp. 161–184.

Hunt, D., 'The Outsider Inside: Ammianus on the Rebellion of Silvanus', in Drijvers, J. & Hunt, D. (eds.), *The Late Roman World and its Historian* (1999), pp. 51–63.

Ilkjærm, J. 'The Weapons' Sacrifice at Illerup Ådal, Denmark', in Randsbourg, K., *The Birth of Europe* (1989), pp. 54–61.

Isaac, B., 'The Meaning of the Terms Limes and Limitanei', *Journal of Roman Studies,* 78 (1988), pp. 125–147.

——*The Limits of Empire* (2nd edn, 1992).

James, S., 'Britain and the Late Roman Army', in Blagg, T. & King, A.,

Military and Civilian in Roman Britain: Cultural Relationships in a frontier province, BAR International Series, 136 (1984), pp. 161–186.

——*Excavations at Dura-Europos 1928–1937: Final Report*, VII: *The Arms and Armour and Other Military Equipment* (2004).

——'The Deposition of Military Equipment During the Final Siege at Dura-Europos, with Particular Regard to the Tower 19 Countermine', *Carnuntum Jahrbuch 2005, Archäologie der Schlachtfelder – Militaria aus Zerstörungshorizonten: Akten der 14. Internationalen Roman Military Equipment Conference (ROMEC), Wien, 27–31 August 2003* (2005), pp. 189–206.

Jeffreys, E., Jeffreys, M., Scott, R. et al., *The Chronicle of John Malalas: A Translation* (1986)

Johnson, M., 'Architecture of Empire', in Lenski, N. (ed.), *The Cambridge Companion to the Age of Constantine* (2006), pp. 278–297.

Johnson, S., *The Roman Forts of the Saxon Shore* (1976).

——*Later Roman Britain* (1980).

——*Late Roman Fortifications* (1983).

Jones, A., *The Later Roman Empire, 284–602*, 2 Vols. (1964).

Jones, M. & Casey, J. 'The Gallic Chronicle Exploded?', *Britannia*, 22 (1991), pp. 212–215.

Jones, T. & Ereira, A., *Terry Jones' Barbarians* (2006).

Jongman, W., 'Gibbon Was Right: The Decline and Fall of the Roman Economy', in Hekster, O., Kleijn, G. & Slootjes, D. (eds.) *Crises in the Roman Empire* (2007), pp. 183–199.

Kassai, L., *Horseback Archery* (2002).

Kelly, C., *Ruling the Later Roman Empire* (2004).

——'Bureaucracy and Government', in Lenski, N. (ed.), *The Cambridge Companion to the Age of Constantine* (2006), pp. 183–204.

Kennedy, D., 'European soldiers and the Severan Siege of Hatra', in Freeman, P. & Kennedy, D. (eds.), *The Defence of the Roman and Byzantine East*, BAR International Series, 297 (1986), pp. 397–409.

Kulikowski, M., 'Barbarians in Gaul, Usurpers in Britain', *Britannia*, 31 (2000), pp. 325–345.

——'The *Notitia Dignitatum* as a Historical Source', *Historia*, 99 (2002), pp. 358–377.

——*Later Roman Spain and its Cities* (2004).

——*Rome's Gothic Wars* (2007).

Lander, J., *Roman Stone Fortifications: Variation and Change from the First Century to the Fourth Century AD*, BAR International Series, 206 (1984).

Lane Fox, R., *Pagans and Christians* (1986).

Lang, J., 'Two Sides of a Coin: Aurelian, Vaballathus, and Eastern Frontiers in the Early 270s', in Mathisen, R. & Sivan, H. (eds.), *Shifting Frontiers in Late Antiquity* (1996), pp. 59–71.

Le Bohec, Y., *The Imperial Roman Army* (1994).

——*L'Armée Romaine Sous le Bas-Empire* (2006).

Leadbetter, B., 'The Illegitimacy of Constantine and the Birth of the Tetrarchy', in Lieu, S. & Montserrat, D. (eds.), *Constantine: History, Historiography and Legend* (1998), pp. 74–85.

Lee, A., 'Traditional Religions' in Lenski, N. (ed.), *The Cambridge Companion to the Age of Constantine* (2006), pp. 159–179.

——*War in Late Antiquity: A Social History* (2007).

Lendon, J., *Soldiers and Ghosts: A History of Battle in Classical Antiquity* (2005).

Lenski, N., '*Initium mali Romano imperio*: Contemporary reactions to the battle of Adrianople', *Transactions of the American Philological Association*, 127 (1997), pp. 129-168.

——*The Failure of Empire: Valens and the Roman State in the Fourth Century AD* (2002).

——'The Reign of Constantine', in Lenski, N. (ed.), *The Cambridge Companion to the Age of Constantine* (2006), pp. 59–90.

Leveau, P., 'The Barbegal Water Mill and its Environment: Archaeology and the Economic and Social History of Antiquity', *Journal of Roman Archaeology*, 9 (1996), pp. 137–153.

Levick, B., *Julia Domna: Syrian Empress* (2007).

Lewit, T., *Agricultural Production in the Roman Economy*, BAR International Series, 568 (1991)

Liebeschuetz, W., *Barbarians and Bishops: Army, Church, and State in the Age of Arcadius and Chrysostom* (1990).

——*The Decline and Fall of the Classical City* (2001).

——'Cities, Taxes, and the Accommodation of the Barbarians: The Theories of Durliat and Goffart', in Noble, T. (ed.), *From Roman Provinces to Medieval Kingdoms* (2006), pp. 309–323.

——'Was there a Crisis of the Third Century?', in Hekster, O., Kleijn, G. & Slootjes, D. (eds.), *Crises and the Roman Empire* (2007), pp. 11–20.

Lieu, S., 'Captives, Refugees and Exiles: A Study of Cross-Frontier Civilian Movements and Contacts between Rome and Persia from Valerian to Jovian', in Freeman, P. & Kennedy, D. (eds.), *The Defence of the Roman and Byzantine East*, BAR International Series, 297 (1986), pp. 475–505.

Lillington-Martin, C., 'Archaeological and Ancient Literary Evidence for a Battle Near Dara Gap, Turkey, AD 530: Topography, Texts, Trenches', in Lewin, A. & Pellegrini, P. (eds.), *The Late Roman Army in the Near East from Diocletian to the Arab Conquest* (Oxford, 2007), pp. 299–311.

Lindner, R., 'Nomadism, Huns and Horses', *Past and Present*, 92 (1981), pp. 1–19.

Liverani, M., 'The Garamantes: A Fresh Approach', *Libyan Studies*, 31 (2000), pp. 17+.

Luttwak, E., *The Grand Strategy of the Roman Empire from the First Century AD to the Third* (1976).

Maas, M., 'Roman Questions, Byzantine Answers: Contours of the Age of Justinian', in Maas, M. (ed.), *The Cambridge Companion to the Age of Justinian* (2005), pp. 3–27.

Mackensen, M., 'Late Roman Fortifications and Building Programmes in the Province of Raetia: The Evidence of Recent Excavations and Some New Reflections', in Creighton, J. & Wilson, R. (eds.), *Roman Germany: Studies in Cultural Interaction*, Journal of Roman Archaeology Supplementary Series, 32 (1999), pp. 199–244.

MacMullen, R., *Soldier and Civilian in the Later Roman Empire* (1963).

——*Enemies of the Roman Order* (1967).

——*Roman Social Relations* (1974)

——*Roman Government's Response to Crisis, AD 235–337* (1976).

——'How Big was the Roman Imperial Army?', *Klio*, 62 (1980), pp. 451–460.

——'The Epigraphic Habit in the Roman Empire', *American Journal of Philology*, 103 (1982), pp. 233–246.

——*Christianizing the Roman Empire, A.D. 100–400* (1984).

——'The Legion as Society', *Historia*, 33 (1984), pp. 440–456.

——*Corruption and the Decline of Rome* (1988).

Maenchen-Helfen, O., *The World of the Huns: Studies in Their History and Culture* (1973).

Man, J., *Attila: The Barbarian King who Challenged Rome* (2005).

Mango, C., *Byzantium: The Empire of the New Rome* (1980).

Manley, J., *AD 43: The Roman Invasion of Britain: A Reassessment* (2002).

Mann, J., 'What was the *Notitia Dignitatum* for?' in Goodburn, R. & Bartholomew, P. (eds.), *Aspects of the Notitia Dignitatum*, BAR Supplementary Series, 15 (1976), pp. 1–9.

Matthews, J., *Western Aristocracies and Imperial Court: AD 364–425* (1975).

——'Mauretania in Ammianus and the Notitia', in Goodburn, R. & Bartholomew, P. (eds.), *Aspects of the Notitia Dignitatum*, BAR Supplementary Series, 15 (1976), pp. 157–186.

——*The Roman Empire of Ammianus* (1989).

Mattingly, D. 'Impact Beyond Empire: Rome and the Garamantes of the Sahara', in de Blois, L. & Rich, J. (eds.), *The Transformation of Economic Life Under the Roman Empire: Proceedings of the Second Workshop of the International Network Impact of Empire* (Roman Empire, *c.*200 BC–AD 476) (2002), pp. 184–203.

——*An Imperial Possession: Britain in the Roman Empire, 54 BC–AD 409* (2006).

McGeorge, P., *Late Roman Warlords* (2003).

McLeod, 'W., The Range of the Ancient Bow', *Phoenix*, 19 (1965), pp. 1–14.

McLynn, N., *Ambrose of Milan: Church and Court in a Christian Capital* (1994).

Meeks, W., *The First Urban Christians* (1983).

Millar, F., 'P. Herennius Dexippus: The Greek World and the Third-Century Invasions, *Journal of Roman Studies*, 59 (1969), pp. 12–29.

——'Paul of Samosata, Zenobia and Aurelian: The Church, Local Culture and Political Allegiance in Third-Century Syria', *Journal of Roman Studies*, 61 (1971), pp. 1–17.

——*The Emperor in the Roman World, 31 BC–AD 337* (1977)

——*The Roman Empire and its Neighbours* (1981).

——'Emperors, Frontiers and Foreign Relations', *Britannia*, 8 (1982), pp. 1–23.

——*The Roman Near East, 31 BC–AD 337* (1993).

Millett, M., *Roman Britain* (1995).

Mitchell, S., 'Maximinus and the Christians in AD 312: A New Inscription', *Journal of Roman Studies*, 78 (1988), pp. 105–124.

——*Cremna in Pisidia: An Ancient City in Peace and War* (1995).

——'The Cities of Asia Minor in Constantine's Time', in Lieu, S. & Montserrat, D. (eds.), *Constantine: History, Historiography and Legend* (1998), pp. 52–73.

——*A History of the Later Roman Empire AD 284–641* (2007).

Moorhead, J., *Theodoric in Italy* (1992).

——*Justinian* (1994).

——*The Roman Empire Divided 400–700* (2001).

Morgan, M. & Lieu, S. (eds.). *The Emperor Julian: Panegyric and Polemic* (2nd edn, 1989).

Morris, J., *The Age of Arthur: A History of the British Isles from 350 to 650* (1973).

Murdoch, A., *The Last Pagan: Julian the Apostate and the Death of the Ancient World* (2003).

Murphy, C., *Are We Rome? The Fall of an Empire and the Fate of America* (2007).

Murray, J. (ed.), *The Autobiographies of Edward Gibbon* (1896).

Musurillo, H., *Acts of the Christian Martyrs* (1972).

Nicasie, M., *Twilight of Empire: The Roman Army from the Reign of Diocletian until the Battle of Adrianople* (1998).

Noble, T. (ed.), *From Roman Provinces to Medieval Kingdoms* (2006).

Nylam, E., 'Early *Gladius* Swords in Scandinavia', *Acta Archaeologia*, 34 (1963), p. 185.

O'Flynn, J., *Generalissimos of the Western Roman Empire* (1983).

Odahl, C., *Constantine and the Christian Empire* (2004).

Okamura, L., 'Roman Withdrawals from Three Transfluvial Frontiers', in Mathisen, R. & Sivan, H. (eds.), *Shifting Frontiers in Late Antiquity* (1996), pp. 11–30.

Oost, S., *Galla Placidia Augusta: A Biographical Essay* (1968).

Parker, A., *Ancient shipwrecks of the Mediterranean and the Roman Provinces*, BAR International Series, 580 (1992).

Parker, H., *The Roman Legions* (1928).

Parkin, T., *Demography and Roman Society* (1992)

Pearson, A., *The Roman Shore Forts* (2002).

——'Piracy in Late Roman Britain: A Perspective from the Viking Age', *Britannia*, 37 (2006), pp. 337–353.

Perkins, A. (ed.), *The Excavations at Dura-Europos: Final Report*, V, Part 1, *Papyri* (1959).

——*The Art of Dura Europos* (1971).

Piganiol, A., *L'Empire Chrétien (325–395)* (1947).

Pohl, W., 'Justinian and the Barbarian Kingdoms', in Maas, M. (ed.), *The Cambridge Companion to the Age of Justinian* (2005), pp. 448–476.

Pomeroy, S., 'Coprynyms and the Exposure of Infants in Egypt', in Cameron, A. & Kuhrt, A. (eds.), *Images of Women in Antiquity* (1983), pp. 207–222

Porter, R., *Gibbon* (1988).

Potter, D., *Prophecy and History in the Crisis of the Roman Empire: A*

Historical Commentary on the Thirteenth Sibylline Oracle (1990).

——*The Roman Empire at Bay, AD 180–395* (2004)

Rathbone, D., 'Villages, Land and Population in Graeco-Roman Egypt', *Proceedings of the Cambridge Philological Society*, 36 (1990), pp. 103–142.

Ratjár, J., '*Die Legionen Mark Aurels im Vormarsch*', in Oexle, J. (ed.) *Aus der Luft – Bilder unserer Geschichte* (1997), pp. 59–68.

Reece, R., The Third Century: Crisis or Change?', in King, A. & Henig, M. (eds.), *The Roman West in the Third Century: Contributions from Archaeology and History*, BAR International Series, 109(i) (1981), pp. 27–38.

Rees, R., *Diocletian and the Tetrarchy* (2004).

Richardson, J., *The Romans in Spain* (1996).

Rives, J., 'The Decree of Decius and the Religion of Empire', *Journal of Roman Studies*, 89 (1999), pp. 135–154.

Rodwell, T. & Rowley, T. (eds.), *Small Towns of Roman Britain*, BAR, 15 (1975).

Rostovtzeff, M. (ed.), *The Excavation at Dura-Europos: Preliminary Report of the Fifth Season of Work, October 1931–March 1932* (1934).

Rostovtzeff, M., Bellinger, A., Hopkins, C. & Wells, C. (eds.), *The Excavations at Dura-Europos: Preliminary Report of the Sixth Season of Work, October 1932–March 1933* (1936).

Saller, R., 'Promotion and Patronage in Equestrian Careers', *Journal of Roman Studies*, 70 (1980), pp. 44–63.

——*Personal Patronage under the Early Empire* (1982).

Salway, P., *Roman Britain* (1998).

Scheidel, W., *Measuring Sex, Age and Death in the Roman Empire: Explorations in Ancient Demography*, Journal of Roman Archaeology Supplementary Series, 21 (1996).

Schonberger, H., 'The Roman Frontier in Germany: An Archaeological Survey', *Journal of Roman Studies*, 59 (1969), pp. 144–197.

Seeck, O. (ed.), *Notitia Dignitatum* (1876).

Sherwin-White, A., *The Letters of Pliny: A Historical and Social Commentary* (1966).

——*The Roman Citizenship* (1973).

Snyder, C., *An Age of Tyrants: Britain and the Britons AD 400–600* (1998).

Sotinel, C., 'Emperors and Popes in the Sixth Century: The Western View', in Maas, M. (ed.), *The Cambridge Companion to the Age of Justinian* (2005), pp. 267–290.

Speidel, M., *Riding for Caesar: The Roman Emperors' Horse Guard* (1994).

Stephenson, I., *Romano-Byzantine Infantry Equipment* (2006).

Stephenson, I. & Dixon, K., *Roman Cavalry Equipment* (2003).

Stoneman, R., *Palmyra and its Empire: Zenobia's Revolt Against Rome* (1992).

Stuart Hay, J., *The Amazing Emperor Heliogabalus* (1911).

Swift, E., *The End of the Western Roman Empire: An Archaeological Investigation* (2000).

Syme, R., *The Roman Revolution* (1939).

——*Emperors and Biography: Studies in the Historia Augusta* (1971).

Tchalenko, G., *Villages Antiques de la Syrie du Nord* (1953–1958).

Termin, P., 'A Market Economy in the Early Roman Empire', *Journal of Roman Studies*, 91 (2001), pp. 169–181.

Thomas, C., 'Saint Patrick and Fifth-Century Britain: An Historical Model Explored', in Casey, P. (ed.), *The End of Roman Britain: Papers from a Conference, Durham 1978*, BAR British Series, 71 (1979), pp. 81–101.

Thompson, E. (revised & ed. Heather, P.), *The Huns* (1996).

Todd, M., *Roman Britain* (3rd edn, 1999).

——*The Early Germans* (2nd edn, 2004).

Tomlin, R., '*Notitia Dignitatum omnium, tam civilium quam militarium*', in Goodburn, R. & Bartholomew, P. (eds.), *Aspects of the Notitia Dignitatum*, BAR Supplementary Series, 15 (1976), pp. 189–209.

——'Christianity and the Roman Army', in Lieu, S. & Montserrat, D. (eds.), *Constantine: History, Historiography and Legend* (1998).

Tougher, S., *Julian the Apostate* (2007).

Treadgold, W., *Byzantium and its Army, 284–1081* (1995).

Turton, G., *The Syrian Princesses: The Women Who Ruled the Roman World* (1974).

Vervaet, F., 'The Reappearance of the Supra-Provincial Commands in the Late Second and Early Third Centuries CE: Constitutional and Historical Considerations', in Hekster, O., Kleijn, G., & Slootjes, D. (eds.), *Crises and the Roman Empire* (2007).

Veyne, P., *Bread and Circuses* (1990).

von Petrikovits, H., 'Fortifications in the North-western Roman Empire from the Third to Fifth Centuries AD', *Journal of Roman Studies*, 61 (1971), pp. 178–218.

Wacher, J., *The Towns of Roman Britain* (2nd edn, 1995).

Walker, S. & Bierbrier, M., *Ancient Faces: Mummy Portraits from Roman Egypt* (1997).

Ward-Perkins, B., *The Fall of Rome and the End of Civilization* (2005).

Watson, A., *Aurelian and the Third Century* (1999).

Watson, G., *The Roman Soldier* (1969).

Webster, G., *The Roman Imperial Army* (1985: reprint with updated bibliography, 1998).

Weiss, P., 'The Vision of Constantine', *Journal of Roman Archaeology*, 16 (2003), pp. 237–259.

Wells, C., *The German Policy of Augustus* (1972).

Wells, P., *The Barbarians Speak: How the Conquered Peoples Shaped Roman Europe* (1999).

Wheeler, E., 'The Laxity of the Syrian Legions', in Kennedy, D. (ed.), *The Roman Army in the East*, Journal of Roman Archaeology Supplementary Series, 18 (1996), pp. 229–276.

Whittaker, C., *Frontiers of the Roman Empire: A Social and Economic Study* (1994).

Whittaker, M., *Jews and Christians, Greco-Roman Views* (1984).

Wiesehofer, J., *Ancient Persia: From 550 BC to 650 AD* (1996).

Wightman, E., *Gallia Belgica* (1985).

Wildberg, C., 'Philosophy on the Age of Justinian', in Maas, M. (ed.), *The Cambridge Companion to the Age of Justinian* (2005), pp. 316–340.

Wilken, R., *The Christians as the Romans Saw Them* (1984).

Willems, W., *Romans and Barbarians: A Regional Study in the Dutch Eastern River Area* (1986).

Williams, S., *Diocletian and the Roman Recovery* (1985).

Williams, S. & Friell, G., *Theodosius: The Empire at Bay* (1994).

Williams, W., 'Caracalla and Rhetoricians: A Note of the *Cognitio de Gohairienis*', *Latomus*, 33 (1974), pp. 663–667.

Wilson, A., 'Machines, Power and the Ancient Economy', *Journal of Roman Studies*, 92 (2002), pp. 1–32.

Wilson, R., *Roman Forts: An Illustrated Introduction to the Garrison Posts of Roman Britain* (1980).

Witschel, C., 'Re-evaluating the Roman West in the 3rd c. A.D.', *Journal of Roman Archaeology*, 17 (2004), pp. 251–281.

Wolfram, H., *The Roman Empire and its Germanic Peoples* (trans. Dunlap, T.) (1997).

Wood, I., 'The End of Roman Britain: Continental Evidence and Parallels', in Lapidge, M. & Dumville, D. (eds.), *Gildas: New Approaches* (1984), pp. 1–25.

——'The Fall of the Western Empire and the End of Roman Britain', *Britannia*, 18 (1987), pp. 251–262.

Woolf, G., 'Roman peace', in Rich, J. & Shipley, G., *War and Society in the Roman World* (1993), pp. 171–194.

Yarshater, E. (ed.), *The Cambridge History of Iran*, Vol. 3 (1): *The Seleucid, Parthian, and Sassanian Periods* (1983).

Young, G., *Rome's Eastern Trade: International Commerce and Imperial Policy, 31 BC–AD 305* (2001).

Zahran, Y., *Philip the Arab: A Study in Prejudice* (2001).

Zwalve, W., 'Callistus' Case: Some Legal Aspects of Roman Business Activities', in de Blois, L. & Rich, J. (eds.), *The Transformation of Economic Life under the Roman Empire: Proceedings of the Second Workshop of the International Network Impact of Empire*, (Roman Empire, *c.* 200 BC–AD 476) (2002), pp. 116–127.

Notes

Preface

1. J. Murray (ed.), *The Autobiographies of Edward Gibbon* (1896), p. 302.
2. The same case is also made in the book that accompanies the series, T. Jones & A. Ereira, *Terry Jones' Barbarians* (2006); for an example of Robert Harris comparing Ancient Rome to modern America, see his article on the Pirate War of 68 BC, published in various papers, and online at http://www.nytimes.com/2006/09/30/opinion/30harris.html.
3. A marvellous example of the best approach to doing this sort of analysis is C. Murphy, *Are We Rome? The Fall of an Empire and the Fate of America* (2007). It is a very witty book – I am still rather taken with idea of Tacitus writing for *The Economist* – and also a very perceptive and thought-provoking study by someone who has done his research well.
4. For 'shock and awe', *see* D. Mattingly, *An Imperial Possession: Britain in the Roman Empire, 54 BC–AD 409* (2006), p. 123. Septimius Severus' campaign in Caledonia in the early third century AD is dubbed the 'war on terror' on p. 124. More direct linking of Roman imperialism with the current war in Iraq may be found in N. Faulkner, *The Decline and Fall of Roman Britain* (2nd edn, 2004), pp. 15– 16. I have not yet seen the same author's *Rome: The Empire of Eagles, 753 BC–AD 476* (2008), but this seems to expand on similar themes to those explored in his study of Roman Britain.

Introduction – The Big Question

1. E. Gibbon, *The History of the Decline and Fall of the Roman Empire*, Vol. 3, (1781), ch. 38. The quotation appears on p. 509 of Vol. 2 of the Penguin Classics edition (1995). There have been many different editions of Gibbon and the page numbering varies greatly.
2. *See* R. Porter, *Gibbon* (1988), pp. 101, 161.
3. In general, *see* P. Brandon, *The Decline and Fall of the British Empire* (2007).
4. C. Freeman, *The Closing of the Western Mind: The Rise of Faith and the Fall of Reason* (2002).
5. For more detailed discussion, *see* Porter (1988), pp. 67–93.
6. A. Dermandt, *Der Falls Roms: Die Auflösung der Römischen Reiches im Urteil der Nachwelt* (1984).
7. A. Piganiol, *L'Empire chrétien (325–395)* (1947), p. 222; for good general discussions of the various theories about Rome's fall, *see* B. Ward-Perkins, *The*

Fall of Rome and the End of Civilization (2005), pp. 1–10, 169–183, and P. Heather, *The Fall of the Roman Empire: A New History* (2005), pp. *xi–xvi*, 431–459.

8. E.g., F. Millar, *The Emperor in the Roman World* (2nd edn, 1992) or B. Isaac, *The Limits of Empire* (2nd edn, 1992).

9. The single most influential work in this field was clearly P. Brown, *The Making of Late Antiquity* (1978).

10. P. Barnwell, *Emperor, Prefects and Kings: The Roman West, 395–565* (1992), p. 174.

11. P. Heather, 'The Fall of the Roman Empire', in *Oxford Historian*, 4 (May 2006), pp. 17–20, quotes from pp. 18 & 19.

12. For a discussion of the real threat posed by the tribal peoples of Europe to the Roman Empire, *see* G. Halsall, *Barbarian Migrations and the Roman West 376–568* (2007).

13. A. H. M. Jones, *The Later Roman Empire 284– 602*, Vol. 2 (1964), p. 1033.

14. E. Gibbon, *The History of the Decline and Fall of the Roman Empire.* Vol 1 (1776), ch. 6, fn. 13–14.

1–The Kingdom of Gold

1. Marcus Aurelius, *Meditations* 5. 23, taken from the Wordsworth Classics of World Literature Series, trans. R. Hard (1997), p. 41.

2. A. Birley, *Marcus Aurelius* (rev. edn. 1987) is the most recent and thorough biography; quotations from *Meditations* 7. 36, 8. 5; on loss of children, *see* Fronto, *Epistulae ad Marcum Caesarem* 4. 11, 5. 19 (34), 5. 45 (60), Marcus Aurelius, *Meditations* 1. 8, 8. 49, 9. 40, 10. 34, 11. 34, and Birley (1987), pp. 106–108.

3. SHA, *Hadrian* 16. 7; for an innovative analysis of Mediterranean history touching on many of the issues discussed in this chapter, *see* P. Holden & N. Purcell, *The Corrupting Sea: A Study of Mediterranean History* (2000).

4. *RIB* 1065, cf. *RIB* 1171.

5. A well-illustrated collection of mummy portraits can be found in the British Museum exhibition catalogue, S. Walker & M. Bierbrier, *Ancient Faces: Mummy Portraits from Roman Egypt* (1997).

6. Tacitus, *Agricola* 30; Plutarch, *Caesar* 15, with discussion in A. Goldsworthy, *Caesar* (2006), p. 335; for a discussion of rebellions, *see* S. Dyson, 'Native Revolt Patterns in the Roman Empire', *Aufstieg und Niedergang der römischen Welt*, II. 3, pp. 38–175.

7. Acts 21: 39; Pliny, *Epistulae* 10.37 & 39; for a discussion of civic life and aristocratic patronage, *see* P. Veyne, *Bread and Circuses* (1990).

8. For some general discussion, *see* G. Woolf, 'Roman Peace', in J. Rich & G. Shipley, *War and Society in the Roman World* (1993), pp. 171–194.

9. Aelius Aristides, *Roman Oration* 79–84.

10. SHA, *Hadrian* 15. 13; for a detailed survey of the creation of the Principate, *see* R. Syme, *The Roman Revolution* (1939).

11. Strabo, *Geog.* 3. 5. 3 (C 169), and R. MacMullen, *Roman Social Relations* (1974), pp. 89, 183 n. 1.

12. *See* MacMullen (1974), pp. 90–91.

13. Hadrian and hunting, *see* SHA, *Hadrian* 26. 3.

14. SHA, *Hadrian* 15. 11–13; for a readily accessible and broad-ranging picture of Hadrian and this period, *see* D. Danzinger & N. Purcell, *Hadrian's Empire* (2005); for a discussion of the law and social status, *see* P. Garnsey, *Social Status and Legal Privilege in the Roman Empire* (1970), esp. pp. 221–223 on the terms *honestiores, humiliores* and their synonyms.

15. A good introduction to the question of demography is B. Frier, 'Roman Demography', in D. Potter & D. Mattingly (eds.), *Life, Death and Entertainment in the Roman Empire* (1999), pp. 95–109.; *see also* K. Beloch, *Die Bevölkerung de Griechisch-römischen Welt* (1886), R. Bagnall & B. Frier, *The Demography of Roman Egypt* (1994), T. Parkin, *Demography and Roman Society* (1992), W. Scheidel, *Measuring Sex, Age, and Death in the Roman Empire: Explorations in Ancient Demography* (1996), and D. Rathbone, 'Villages, Land and Population in Graeco-Roman Egypt', *Proceedings of the Cambridge Philological Society*, 36 (1990), pp. 103–142.

16. *See* C. Edwards & G . Woolf (eds.), *Rome the Cosmopolis* (2003), esp. W. Scheidel, 'Germs for Rome', pp. 158–176 for a very bleak picture of living conditions; Suetonius, *Vespasian* 5.

17. S. Pomeroy, 'Coprynyms and the Exposure of Infants in Egypt', in A. Cameron & A. Kuhrt (eds.), *Images of Women in Antiquity* (1983), pp. 207–222, and also Parkin (1992), pp. 91–133.

18. On the role of slaves and freedmen in business, *see* W. Zwalve, 'Callistus' Case: Some legal aspects of Roman Business Activities', in L. de Blois & J. Rich (eds.), *The Transformation of Economic Life under the Roman Empire* (2002), pp. 116–127.

19. *See*, for example, the discussion of the language in poetry written by centurions in J. Adams, 'The poets of Bu Njem: Language, Culture and the Centurionate', *JRS*, 89 (1999), pp. 109–134, esp. 125–134; *see also* Horace, *Sat.* 1. 6. 72–74, and Suetonius, *Gramm.* 24. 1.

20. A. Bowman & J. Thomas (eds.), *The Vindolanda Tablets (Tabulae Vindolandenses II)* (1994), 250.

21. Pliny, *Epistulae* 2. 13. 1–3 (Penguin translation); for patronage in general, *see* P. Saller, *Personal Patronage under the Early Empire* (1982).

22. *See* K. Greene, *The Archaeology of the Roman Economy* (1986), and 'Technology and Innovation in Context', *Journal of Roman Archaeology*, 7 (1994), pp. 22–33, and T. Lewit, *Agricultural Production in the Roman Economy* (1991); *see also* de Blois & Rich (2002), *passim*, and esp. W. Jongman, 'The Roman Economy: From Cities to Empire', pp. 28–47, and J. Drinkwater, 'Prologue and Epilogue: The Socio-Economic Effect of Rome's Arrival In and Departure From Gaul', pp. 128–140, and P. Termin, 'A Market Economy in the Early Roman Empire', *JRS*, 91 (2001), pp. 169–181; on currency, *see* C. Howgego,

'Coin Circulation and the Integration of the Roman Economy', *Journal of Roman Archaeology*, 7 (1994), pp. 5–21.

23. On mills, *see* Greene (1986), Holden & Purcell (2000), pp. 255–257, A. Wilson, 'Machines, Power and the Ancient Economy', *JRS*, 92 (2002), pp. 1–32, and P. Leveau, 'The Barbegal Water Mill and its Environment', *Journal of Roman Archaeology*, 9 (1996), pp. 137–153.

24. *See* A. Wilson, 'Machines, Power and the Ancient Economy', in *JRS*, 92 (2002), pp. 1–32, esp. 17–29.

25. D. Mattingly, 'Impact Beyond Empire: Rome and the Garamantes of the Sahara', in Blois & Rich (2002), pp. 184–203, and M. Liverani, 'The Garamantes: A Fresh Approach', *Libyan Studies*, 31 (2000), pp. 17+.

26. Reweaving silk, Pliny, *NH* 6. 20 (54); for discussion, *see* J. Ferguson, 'China and Rome', *Aufstieg und Niedergang der Römischen Welt*, II. 9. 2, pp. 581–603, and G. Young, *Rome's Eastern Trade* (2001), esp. pp. 27–89, 187–200.

27. Pliny, *NH* 14. 2 (Penguin translation, J. Healy).

28. E. Gibbon, *The Decline and Fall of the Roman Empire*, Vol. 1 (1776) (Penguin Classics edn, 1995), p. 103; this passage seems to have been inspired by very similar comments made by William Robertson some years before, *see* R. Porter, *Gibbon* (1988), pp. 135–136.

29. *See* Birley (1987), pp. 121–131, 140–152, and J. Gilliam, 'The Plague Under Marcus Aurelius', *American Journal of Philology*, 82 (1961), pp. 225–251, Rathbone (1990), pp. 114–119, R. Duncan-Jones, 'The Impact of the Antonine Plague', *Journal of Roman Archaeology*, 9 (1996), pp. 108–136, Bagnall & Frier (1994), pp. 173–178.

30. For a discussion of the difficulty in reconstructing the course of these campaigns, see Birley (1987), pp. 249–255; for some of the archaeological evidence, *see* J. Ratjár, '*Die Legionen Mark Aurels im Vormarsch*' in J. Oexle (ed.), *Aus der Luft – Bilder unserer Geschichte* (1997), pp. 59–68.

31. Dio 72. 36. 4 (Loeb translation).

2–The Secret of Empire

1. Tacitus, *Histories* 1. 4.

2. Commodus' boast that he was 'born to the imperial purple', Herodian 1. 5. 5–6; Trajan's fondness for boys, Dio 68. 7. 4, who notes that this harmed no one; Hadrian's famous affair with Antinous, Dio 69. 11. 3–4, SHA, *Hadrian* 14. 5–8.

3. Apart from *Gladiator* (2000), the most notable screen depiction of Commodus was in the *Fall of the Roman Empire* (1964); on the role of the emperor, *see* F. Millar, *The Emperor in the Roman World, 31 BC–AD 337* (1977); Hadrian and the petitioner, Dio 69. 6. 3; Marcus Aurelius and justice, Dio 72. 6. 1–2, SHA, *Marcus Antoninus* 24. 1–3

4. For summaries and discussions of Commodus' reign, *see* A. Birley, *Septimius Severus: the African Emperor* (1988), pp. 57–62, 78–88, and D. Potter, *The Roman Empire at Bay, AD 180–395* (2004), pp. 85–93.

5. Dio 73 21. 1–2 (Loeb translation).

6. For the argument that some of Commodus' propaganda was effective, *see* O. Hekster, *Commodus: An emperor at the crossroads* (2002).

7. Dio 73. 22. 1–6, Herodian 1. 16. 1–17. 12, SHA, *Commodus* 17. 1–2.

8. Dio 74. 1. 1–5, Herodian 2. 1. 1–3. 11, SHA, *Commodus* 18. 1–20. 5, *Pertinax* 4. 5–5. 6, and discussion in Birley (1988), pp. 88–90, who argues that Pertinax was involved in the conspiracy.

9. Dio 74. 3. 1–2. 6, 5. 1–9. 1, Herodian 2. 4. 1–5. 1, SHA, *Pertinax* 1. 1–4. 4, 5. 7–13. 8, Birley (1988), pp. 63–67, 91–94; for the career of Valerius Maximianus, *see L'Année épigraphique* (1956), 124.

10. Dio 74. 9. 2–10. 3, Herodian 2. 5. 1–5. 9, SHA, *Pertinax* 10. 8–11. 13.

11. Dio 74. 11. 1–6, Herodian 6. 1–14, SHA, *Didius Julianus* 2. 4–7, with Birley (1988), pp. 95–96, Potter (2004), pp.96–98, *CAH²* XII, p. 2; by the late third century donatives may have been the same for all ranks, *see* R. Duncan-Jones, 'Pay and Numbers in Diocletian's Army', *Chiron*, 8 (1978), pp. 541–560, but this is unlikely to have been true in earlier periods.

12. Dio 74. 12. 1–14. 2, SHA, *Didius Julianus* 3. 1–4. 9.

13. For good overviews of the Roman army, *see* G. Webster, *The Roman Imperial Army* (1985: reprint with updated bibliography, 1998), Y. Le Bohec, *The Imperial Roman Army* (1994), H. Parker, *The Roman Legions* (1928), and A. Goldsworthy, *The Complete Roman Army* (2003); on the *frumentarii*, *see* N. Austin & B. Rankov, *Exploratio: Military and Political Intelligence in the Roman World from the Second Punic War to the Battle of Adrianople* (1995), esp. 136–137, 150–154; the classic study of the army and politics is J. Campbell, *The Emperor and the Roman Army* (1984).

14. On conditions in the army, *see* R. Davies, *Service in the Roman Army* (1989), G. Watson, *The Roman Soldier* (1969), and R. Alston, *Soldier and Society in Roman Egypt* (1995); *see* Davies (1989), pp. 229–230 for the letters from soldiers in hospital, *Tabulae Vindolandenses II* 154, for a cohort strength report listing men sick in hospital, and R. Fink, *Roman Military Records on Papyrus* (1971) No. 63, for a return listing men killed by bandits and drowned.

15. On the question of marriage, *see* J. Campbell, 'The Marriage of Soldiers Under the Empire', *JRS*, 68 (1978), pp. 153–166, and Alston (1995), pp. 54–59.

16. Low quality of recruits, Tacitus, *Annals* 4. 4, for a discussion, *see* A. Goldsworthy, *The Roman Army at War, 100 BC–AD 200* (1996), pp. 28–30, and Davies (1989), pp. 3–30.

17. Unit pride, *see* R. MacMullen, 'The Legion as Society', *Historia*, 33 (1984), pp. 440–456, and Goldsworthy (1996), pp. 252–257.

18. For the career patterns of Roman officers, *see* many of the articles in E. Birley, *The Roman Army* (1988), H. Devijver, *The Equestrian Officers of the Roman Army*, 2 vols. (1989 & 1992), D. Breeze & B. Dobson, *Roman Officers and Frontiers* (1993), and R. P. Saller, 'Promotion and Patronage in Equestrian Careers', *JRS*, 70 (1980), pp. 44–63.

19. Goldsworthy (1996), pp. 13–15, 30–32.

20. Campbell (1984), esp. pp. 106–109, argues that the influence of the centurions was not in itself enough to control the soldiers.

21. Dio 74. 14. 3–17. 6, 75. 1. 1–2. 1, Herodian 2. 11. 7–14. 4, SHA, *Didius Julianus* 6. 1–8. 10, *Severus* 5. 1–6.9, with Birley (1988), pp. 97–105, and Potter (2004), pp. 101–103.

22. Dio 76. 6. 1 for the claim that there were 150,000 men on each side at Lugdunum; for narrative and analysis of the civil war, *see* Birley (1988), pp. 108–128.

23. Birley (1988), pp. 8–56; the sixth-century source claiming he was dark-skinned is John Malalas, *Chronicle* 12. 18 (291). This is available in translation by E. Jeffreys, M. Jeffreys, R. Scott et al, *The Chronicle of John Malalas: A Translation* (1986), *see* Birley (1988), p. 36.

24. Dio 76. 7. 1–8. 4; finding a father, Dio 77. 9. 4; on Plautianus, *see* Birley (1988), pp. 137, 161–164.

25. On the horse guard that was doubled in size, *see* M. Speidel, *Riding for Caesar: The Roman Emperors' Horse Guard* (1994), pp. 56–64.

26. Problems at Hatra, Dio 76. 11. 1–12. 5; the campaigns in Mesopotamia, *see* Birley (1988), pp. 129–135, with D. Kennedy, 'European soldiers and the Severan siege of Hatra', in P. Freeman & D. Kennedy (eds.), *The Defence of the Roman and Byzantine East* (1986), pp. 397–409, and D. Campbell, 'What Happened at Hatra? The problems of the Severan Siege Operations', in Freeman & Kennedy (1986), pp. 51–58; on Britain, *see* Birley (1988), pp. 177–187, M. Todd, *Roman Britain* (3rd edn, 1999), pp. 144–155.

27. Dio 77. 15. 2–4, 17. 4, Herodian 3. 14. 1–3, 15. 1–3, SHA, *Severus* 19. 14.

3–Imperial Women

1. Herodian, *History of the Empire* 6. 1. 1 (Whittaker's translation, Loeb edition).
2. Dio 78. 1. 1–6, Herodian 4. 1. 1–5, 3. 1–9.
3. Dio 78. 2. 1–6, Herodian 4. 4. 1–3.
4. Dio 78. 3. 1–3, Herodian 4. 4. 4–5. 7, SHA, *Caracalla* 2. 5–11, *Geta* 6. 1–2.
5. Dio 78. 3. 4, 1a–5, Herodian 4. 6. 1–5, SHA, *Caracalla* 3. 2–5. 3, *Geta* 6. 3–7. 6.
6. Dio 78. 6. 1a– 2, 10. 1–11. 7, Herodian 4. 7. 1, SHA, *Caracalla* 4. 9–10, 9. 4–11; gladiator forced to fight three bouts, Dio 78. 6. 2.
7. Dio 78. 15. 2–7; important visitors kept waiting, Dio 78. 17. 3–4; for a discussion of Caracalla's style of rule, *see* D. Potter, *The Roman Empire at Bay* (2004), pp. 140–146, including mention of his visiting shrines, and *see also* G. Fowden, in *CAH²* XII (2005), pp. 545–547; for an example of Caracalla's method of hearing a petition, *see* SEG XVII. 759 with discussion in W. Williams, 'Caracalla and Rhetoricians: A Note of the *Cognitio de Gohairienis*', *Latomus*, 33 (1974), pp. 663–667.
8. Dio 78. 7. 1–9. 1, 13. 1–2, Herodian 4. 7. 4–7; 'Rejoice, fellow soldiers . . .', Dio 78. 3. 1; Herodian 4. 7. 7 says that he carried legionary standards and speaks of their great weight, but it is interesting that Suetonius emphasised the

heaviness of praetorian standards, Suetonius, *Gaius* 43; the lions, Dio 79. 5. 5–6. 2; for the emperor as fellow soldier, *see* J. Campbell, *The Emperor and the Roman Army, 31 BC–AD 235* (1984), pp. 32–59, esp. 51–55, and for discussion of changing styles of command in general, *see* A. Goldsworthy, *In the Name of Rome* (2003).

9. On his campaigns, see *Dio* 78. 13. 3–15. 2, 18. 1–23. 2, 79. 1. 1–3. 5, Herodian 4. 7. 3–7, 8. 6–11. 9, SHA, *Caracalla* 6. 1–6; for discussion, see Potter (2004), pp. 141–144, F. Millar, *The Roman Near East, 31 BC–AD 337* (1993), pp. 142–146, B. Campbell, in *CAH²* XII (2005), pp. 18–19.

10. Dio 79. 4. 1–6. 5, Herodian 4. 12. 1–13. 8, SHA, *Caracalla* 6. 5–7. 1.

11. Dio 79. 11. 1–21. 5, Herodian 4. 14. 1–15. 9, 5. 1. 1–2.6, SHA, *Macrinus* 2. 1–4, with Potter (2004), pp. 145–147.

12. Dio 79. 4. 3 (Cary's translation, Loeb edition).

13. Dio 78. 18. 2–3, 79. 4. 2–3, 23. 1–24. 3, Herodian 4. 13. 8; 'Ulysses in a dress' (*Ulixes stolatus*), Suetonius, *Gaius* 23; quote from Dio 79. 4. 3 (Cary's translation, Loeb edition); for Julia Domna, *see* the excellent B. Levick, *Julia Domna: Syrian Empress* (2007), and *also* A. Birley, *Septimius Severus* (1988/1999), *passim*, esp. 191–192, and in general, G. Turton, *The Syrian Princesses: The Women Who Ruled the Roman World* (1974); much later sources contain the fictional story of an incestuous relationship between Domna and Caracalla, SHA, *Caracalla* 10. 1–4, Aurelius Victor, *De Caesaribus* 21.

14. Dio 79. 30. 2–4, Herodian 3. 2–5; for discussion, *see* Millar (1993), pp. 119–120, 145, 300–309, Potter (2004), pp. 148–150.

15. Dio 79. 28. 2–29. 2, Herodian 5. 3. 6–11, Aurelius Victor, *De Caesaribus* 23; for discussion of army pay, *see* G. Watson, *The Roman Soldier* (1969), pp. 90–91.

16. Dio 31. 4–41. 4, Herodian 5. 3. 12–5. 1, SHA, *Macrinus* 15. 1–2; Millar (1993), pp. 144–147, Potter (2004), pp. 148–152.

17. Dio 80. 17. 2, SHA, *Elagabalus* 4. 1–2, 15. 6, 18. 3.; Agrippina in the Senate, *see* Tacitus, *Annals*, 13. 5; for a discussion, *see* R. Talbert, *The Senate of Imperial Rome* (1984), p. 162.

18. On Elagabalus' sexual exploits, *see* Dio 80. 13. 1–14. 1, 14. 3–17. 1, Herodian 5. 5. 6, 6. 1–2, SHA, *Elagabalus* 5. 1–5, 6. 5–7, 10. 4–7, 25. 4–6, 26. 3–5, 31. 1–8; Caracalla and the Vestal, *see* Dio 78. 16. 1–3.

19. Dio 80. 11. 1–12. 2, Herodian 5. 6. 3–10, 7. 2, SHA, *Elagabalus* 3. 4–5, 6. 78. 3; Potter (2004), pp. 153–157.

20. Dio 80. 17. 2–21. 3, Herodian 5. 7. 1–8. 10, SHA, *Elagabalus* 13. 1–17. 3; on attempted rebellions during the reign, *see* Dio 80. 7. 1–4; one of the very few biographies of Elagabalus is fairly sympathetic, J. Stuart Hay, *The Amazing Emperor Heliogabalus* (1911); disbanding of *III Gallica*, *see* ILS 2657.

21. Herodian 6. 1. 4–10; Dio 80 (81). 4. 2 on military mutinies; for the praetorians, *see* Dio 80 (81). 2. 2–3, 4. 2–5. 2; for a discussion of the reign, *see* R. Syme, *Emperors and Biography: Studies in the Historia Augusta* (1971), pp. 146–162, Potter (2004), pp. 158–166, and B. Campbell, in *CAH²* XII (2005), pp. 22–27.

22. For Maximinus in general, *see* the discussion in Syme (1971), pp. 179–193; Herodian 6. 8. 1–8, SHA, *Maximinus* 2. 1–5. 1 on Maximinus and 'humble origins'; Herodian 6. 9. 1–8 on the murder of Alexander, SHA, *Maximinus* 7. 1–6; for his images, *see* Campbell (1984), pp. 68–69.

23. Dio 80. 4. 1–2, 21. 2–3, *see also* R. Syme (1971), p. 142.

24. On the edict of Caracalla, *see* Dio 78. 9. 5, and SHA, *Caracalla* 5. 8 on his surviving a shipwreck; for discussion, *see* A. Sherwin-White, *The Roman Citizenship* (1973), pp. 275–287, 380–394, and Potter (2004), pp. 138–139.

4–King of Kings

1. *Res Gestae Divi Saporis* 1–2, 6–8. This translation from M. Dodgeon & S. Lieu, *The Roman Eastern Frontier and the Persian Wars, AD 226–363* (paperback edn 1991), pp. 34, 35–36. The full text is edited and translated by A. Maricq, *Syria*, 35 (1958), pp. 245–260.

2. For Dura and its discovery, *see* C. Hopkins, *The Discovery of Dura Europos* (1979), S. James, *Excavations at Dura-Europos 1928–1937: Final Report*, VII, *The Arms and Armour and Other Military Equipment* (2004), pp. xxiii, 39, A. Perkins, *The Art of Dura Europos* (1971), and F. Millar, *The Roman Near East, 31 BC–AD 337* (1993), pp. 445–452, 467–471.

3. *See* A. Perkins (ed.), *The Excavations at Dura Europos: Final Report*, V, Part 1, *Papyri* (1959), R. Fink, *Roman Military Records on Papyrus* (1971), pp. 18–86, 90–105, 125–136, etc., and the selection of texts in Dodgeon & Lieu (1991), pp. 328–335.

4. Epitaph, *AE* 1948, 124, and quoted in Dodgeon & Lieu (1991), p. 32, along with a piece of graffito recording the attack; extracts from the Dura strength reports are on pp. 328–331, esp. p. 331, n. 4 for the possible link between a drop in numbers and the Persian attack.

5. On the rise of Ardashir and the Sassanian state, *see* in general E. Yarshater (ed.), *The Cambridge History of Iran*, Vol. 3 (1) (1983), esp. pp. 116–180, R. Frye, in *CAH²* XII (2005), pp. 461–480, E. Herzteld, *Archaeological History of Iran* (1934), J. Wiesehofer, *Ancient Persia: From 550 BC to 650 AD* (1996), B. Dignas & E. Winter, *Rome and Persia in Late Antiquity: Neighbours and Rivals* (2007), pp. 18–32, and the sources in Dodgeon & Lieu (1991), pp. 9–33; R. Chrishman, *Arts of Mankind: Iran: Parthians and Sassanians* (1962) has good photographs of the triumphal monuments of Ardashir and Shapur I.

6. Dio 80. 3. 1–4. 2, Herodian 6. 2. 1–2; presence of Roman troops in Hatra, *AE* 1958, 239–240, translated in Dodgeon & Lieu (1991), p. 33; E. Wheeler, 'The Laxity of the Syrian Legions', in D. Kennedy (ed.), *The Roman Army in the East* (1996), pp. 229–276 shows that the poor quality of the armies in the east was a literary cliché. However, this does not mean that at some periods and in some circumstances legions stationed in the east might not actually be of low quality.

7. Herodian 6. 2. 3–7, 3. 1–6. 3, SHA, *Alexander Severus* 55. 1–3; mutiny in the army, 6. 4.; on the question of Persia's ambitions, *see* B. Isaac, *The Limits of Empire* (1992), pp. 20–33, 50–53.

8. Herodian 7. 5. 2 says that Gordian was eighty years old; for a full discussion, *see* R. Syme, *Emperors and Biography: Studies in the Historia Augusta* (1971), pp. 163–178.

9. For the fullest account, *see* Herodian, 7. 4. 1–6. 9, 9. 1–10. 1, SHA, *The Three Gordians* 7. 2–10. 8, 15. 1–16. 4.

10. Herodian 7. 10. 1–9.

11. Herodian 8. 6. 1–8. 8, with D. Potter, *The Roman Empire at Bay, AD 180–395* (2004), pp. 169–171, and J. Drinkwater, in *CAH²* XII (2005), pp. 31–33.

12. Sources in Dodgeon & Lieu (1991), pp. 34–45; see also the summaries and discussion in Potter (2004), pp. 217–236, and Drinkwater, in *CAH²* XII (2005), pp. 35–36.

13. See Potter (2004), pp. 236–241, Drinkwater, in *CAH²* XII (2005), pp. 36–38; the most recent biography of Philip in English is Y. Zahran, *Philip the Arab: A Study in Prejudice* (2001); the Greek of Shapur's inscription says denarii, which were silver, but it is generally accepted that the payment was in gold, *see* Potter (2004), p. 237 (p. 634, n. 94).

14. See Dodgeon & Lieu (1991), pp. 45–48 for Philip's activity in the east and the appointment of his brother Pirscus as *rector orientis*.

15. On Decius, *see* Syme (1971), pp. 194–203, Drinkwater, in *CAH²* XII (2005), pp. 38–39, Potter (2004), 241–246, and J. Rives, 'The Decree of Decius and the Religion of Empire', *JRS*, 89 (1999), pp. 135–154, including discussion of the edict on sacrifices.

16. On the synagogue, *see* Perkins (1971), pp. 55–65, M. Rostovtzeff, A. Bellinger, C. Hopkins & C. Wells (eds.), *The Excavations at Dura-Europos: Preliminary Report of the Sixth Season of Work, October 1932–March 1933* (1936), pp. 309–396, A. Bellinger, F. Brown, A. Perkins & C. Wells (eds.), *The Excavations at Dura-Europos: Final Report*, VIII, Part 1: *The Synagogue* (1956), and J. Gutman (ed.), *The Dura Europos Synagogue: A Re-Evaluation (1932–1972)* (1973).

17. On the baptistery, *see* Perkins (1971), pp. 52–55, and M. Rostovtzeff (ed.), *The Excavations at Dura-Europos: Preliminary Report of the Fifth Season of Work, October 1931–March 1932* (1934), pp. 259–289, and C. Bradford Welles, *The Excavations at Dura-Europos: Final Report*, VIII, Part 2: *The Christian Building* (1967).

18. The literature on the early Church is truly vast, but good starting places are W. Meeks, *The First Urban Christians* (1983), R. Wilken, *The Christians as the Romans Saw Them* (1984), M. Whittaker, *Jews and Christians, Greco-Roman Views* (1984), E. Dodds, *Pagan and Christian in an Age of Anxiety* (1965), and R. Lane Fox, *Pagans and Christians* (1986), esp. pp. 419–492.

19. Tacitus, *Annals* 15. 44.

20. Pliny, *Letters* 10. 96–97, with A. Sherwin-White, *The Letters of Pliny: A Historical and Social Commentary* (1966), pp. 691–712.

21. *See* in general W. Frend, *Martyrdom and persecution in the Early Church* (1965), and T. Barnes, 'Legislation Against the Early Christians', *JRS*, 58 (1968), pp. 32–50; Tertullian, *Apology* 1. 4–2. 20, 8. 1–20, 10. 1–11, 30. 1–32. 337. 4–8.

22. *Christianos ad leonem!*, *see* Tertullian, *Apology* 40. 1–2; Lyons, *see* Eusebius,

Ecclesiastical History 5. 1–63, and H. Musurillo, *Acts of the Christian Martyrs* (1972), pp. 62–85.

23. Musurillo (1972), 'The Martyrs of Lyons', 1–10, 49–53, 'The Martyrdom of Saints Ptolemaeus and Lucius', 1–10, 'The Martyrdom of Saint Marinus', 1–2.

24. Musurillo (1972), 'The Martyrdom of Saints Perpetua and Felicitas', 5. 2–4, 'The Martyrdom of Polycarp', 4.

25. Musurillo (1972), 'The Martyrdom of Bishop Fructuosus and His Deacons, Augurius and Eulogius', 2. 8–9. In Latin the exchange is even more laconic – *Aemilianus praeses Fructuosum dixit: Episcopus es? Fructuosus dixit: Sum. Aemilianus dixit: Fuisti, et issuit eos vivos ardere;* the two women in Africa, Musurillo (1972), 'The Martyrdom of Saints Perpetua and Felicitas', 20. 1–4.

26. Origen, *see* Eusebius, *Ecclesiastical History* 6. 21. 3–4; 6. 36. 3 for his writing letters to the Emperor Philip; Philip described as a Christian, 6. 34. 1; Alexander Severus, SHA, *Alexander* 29. 2.

27. G. Clarke, in *CAH²* XII (2005), pp. 625–637; Origen's death following imprisonment as part of the Decian persecution, *see* Potter (2004), p. 209 with references.

28. Drinkwater, in *CAH²* XII (2005), pp. 38–44, Potter (2004), pp. 241–257.

29. The sources for these campaigns can be found in Dodgeon & Lieu (1991), pp. 49–67.

30. For the final siege of Dura Europos, *see* James (2004), pp. 21–25, 30–39; for the asphyxiation of the Roman soldiers, *see* S. James, 'The Deposition of Military Equipment During the Final Siege at Dura-Europos, With Particular Regard to the Tower 19 Countermine', *Carnuntum Jahrbuch 2005* (2005), pp. 189–206. There will also be a summary in the same author's, *Rome and the Sword* (provisional title, forthcoming, Thames and Hudson). I am very grateful to Simon for giving me the details of his fascinating analysis.

5–Barbarians

1. Dexippus, *fragment* 28, translation from F. Millar, 'P. Herennius Dexippus: The Greek World and the Third-Century Invasions', *JRS*, 59 (1969), pp. 12–29, p. 27–28, which gives the full passage and a commentary.

2. For the Abrittus campaign, *see* Zosimus 1. 23, Zonaras 12. 20, Aurelius Victor De Caesaribus 29, Jordanes, *Getica* 101–103, the summary in D. Potter, *Prophecy and History in the Crisis of the Roman Empire* (1990), pp. 278–283, and *The Roman Empire at Bay* (2004), p. 246, P. Heather, *The Goths* (1996), p. 40, and J. Drinkwater, in *CAH²* (2005), pp. 38–39.

3. For relations between Romans and Germans, *see* T. Burns, *Rome and the Barbarians, 100 BC–AD 400* (2003), pp. 1–193, M. Todd, *The Early Germans* (2nd edn, 2004), pp. 44–61, and P. Wells, *The Barbarians Speak: How the Conquered Peoples Shaped Roman Europe* (1999), pp. 64–98; for more specific discussion of Caesar's campaigns, *see* A. Goldsworthy, *Caesar: The Life of a Colossus* (2006), pp. 224–232, 270–278, 306–310; for Augustus, *see* C. Wells, *The German Policy of Augustus* (1972).

4. On the Bastarnae, *see* Tacitus, *Germania* 46; for overviews of Germanic society and culture, *see* Todd (2004), pp. 8–43, 62–135, Wells (1999), pp. 99–170.

5. Todd (2004), pp. 64–75, *CAH*[2] (2005), pp. 447–450, and Burns (1999), pp. 244–255.

6. Tacitus, *Germania* 7, 13–14; C. Fabech, 'Booty Sacrifices in Southern Scandinavia – A History of Warfare and Ideology', in E. Björklund, *Roman Reflections in Scandinavia* (1996), pp. 135–138, Wells (1999), pp. 4–6, E. Nylam, 'Early *Gladius* Swords in Scandinavia', *Acta Archaeologia*, 34 (1963), and p. 185, J. Ilkjærm 'The Weapons' Sacrifice at Illerup Ådal, Denmark', in K. Randsbourg, *The Birth of Europe* (1989), pp. 54–61.

7. Tacitus, *Germania* 33, cf. 36; on warfare, *see* A. Goldsworthy, *The Roman Army at War, 100 BC–AD 200* (1996), pp. 42–53, and H. Elton, *Warfare in Roman Europe: AD 350–425* (1996), pp. 15–88.

8. Tacitus, *Germania* 41–42; in general, *see also* C. Whittaker, *Frontiers of the Roman Empire: A Social and Economic Study* (1994), esp. pp. 113–131, 222–240.

9. Burns (2003), pp. 167–174, 183–193, 212–247, and B. Cunliffe, *Greeks, Romans and Barbarians: Spheres of Inter-action* (1988).

10. Todd (2004), pp. 63–71, and Wells (1999), pp. 245–258.

11. Caesar, *Bellum Gallicum* 6. 23; on raiding, *see* Whittaker (1996), pp. 210–214.

12. L. Hedeager, 'The Evolution of German society 1–400 AD', in R. Jones, J. Bloemers, S. Dyson & M. Biddle (eds.), *First Millennium Papers: Western Europe in the 1st Millennium* (1988), pp. 129–401.

13. *CIL* 3. 3385.

14. For discussion, *see* S. Dyson, *The Creation of the Roman Frontier* (1985), *passim*, and A. Goldsworthy, 'War: The Late Republic and Principate', in P. Sabin, H. Van Wees & M. Whitby (eds.) *The Cambridge History of Greek and Roman Warfare*, Vol. 2 (2007), pp. 76–121.

15. On the Goths, *see* Heather (1998), pp. 11–39; on the Franks and Alamanni, *see* Burns (2003), pp. 275–290. The epitome of Dio (78. 13. 4) mentions the Alamanni in 213, but Burns argues that this is most likely a later interpolation. A stronger case for accepting the passage is made in J. Drinkwater, *The Alamanni and Rome 213–496: Caracalla to Clovis* (2007), pp. 41–44.

16. *See* Burns (2003), pp. 229–245, Todd (2004), pp. 54–56, and Wells (1999), pp. 189–191.

17. Burns (2003), pp. 244–260, Drinkwater, in *CAH*[2] (2005), pp. 28–38.

18. Goths, Zosimus 1. 24. 2, Zonaras 12. 21.

19. Zosimus 1. 27–37, SHA, *The Two Gallieni* 5. 6–6. 9; Potter (2004), pp. 252–256, Heather (1998), pp. 40–43, and Drinkwater, in *CAH*[2] (2005), pp. 40–44; *see also* chapter 4, pp. 100–101.

20. The inscription is *AE* 1993, 1231 with comments in Potter (2004), pp. 256–257, Wilkes, in *CAH*[2] (2005), pp. 222–223, and Burns (2003), pp. 281–282; *see also* Todd (2004), pp. 56–59, including discussion of abandoned plunder.

21. Orosius 7. 22. 7–8, Aurelius Victor, *De Caesaribus* 33. 3, Eutropius 9. 8. 2, with comments in J. Richardson, *The Romans in Spain* (1996), pp. 250–251, and M. Kulikowski, *Later Roman Spain and Its Cities* (2004), pp. 66–69, who argues that the impact was probably minimal.

22. Zosimus 1. 42–43, Zonaras 12. 23, Millar (1969), pp. 26–29, and J. Camp, *The Archaeology of Athens* (2001), pp. 223–231.

23. For discussions of the impact generally and in specific regions, *see* E. Wightman, *Gallia Belgica* (1985), pp. 193–199, 219–230, 243–250, G. Alfödy, *Noricum* (1974), pp. 169–171, Burns (2003), pp. 267–271, 281–300, and J. Drinkwater, 'The Germanic Threat on the Rhine Frontier: A Romano-Gallic Artefact', in R. Mathisen & H. Sivan (eds.), *Shifting Frontiers in Late Antiquity* (1996), pp. 20–30.

24. *See* J. Lander, *Roman Stone Fortification* (1984), esp. pp. 151–262, S. Johnson, *Late Roman Fortifications* (1983), *passim*, but especially pp. 9–81, H. von Petrikovits, 'Fortifications in the North-western Roman Empire From the Third to Fifth centuries AD', *JRS*, 61 (1971), pp. 178–218, M. Mackensen, 'Late Roman Fortifications and Building Programmes in the Province of Raetia', in J. Creighton & R. Wilson (eds.), *Roman Germany: Studies in Cultural Interaction* (1999), pp. 199–244, R. Wilson, *Roman Forts: An Illustrated Introduction to the Garrison Posts of Roman Britain* (1980), Wightman (1985), p. 220, Camp (2001), pp. 223–225, and R. MacMullen, *Soldier and Civilian in the Later Roman Empire* (1963), pp. 37–42.

25. For a robust defence of Gallienus, *see* L. de Blois, *The Policy of the Emperor Gallienus* (1976); on his campaigns, *see* Zosimus 1. 42–43, with Drinkwater, in *CAH*² (2005), pp. 46–47, Heather (1998), p. 41, Potter (2004), pp. 263–266 with discussion of whether the campaign was actually fought in 269; rumour of Gothic mistress, SHA, *The Two Gallieni* 21. 3.

26. See in general, J. Drinkwater, *The Gallic Empire, Historia Einzelschriften*, 52 (1987), pp. 1–270, and there is a brief summary in Potter (2004), pp. 260–262; the reference to 'assuming power over the Gallic provinces' is from Eutropius 9. 9.

27. Gallienus' supposed cavalry reserve, *see* E. Luttwak, *The Grand Strategy of the Roman Empire From the First Century AD to the Third* (1976), pp. 185–186, Y. Le Bohec, *The Imperial Roman Army* (1994), pp. 197–198, de Blois (1976), pp. 26–30, with some criticism in M. Nicasie, *Twilight of Empire* (1998), pp. 35–38.

28. Zosimus 1. 40, SHA, *The Two Gallieni* 14. 15. 3, Aurelius Victor, *De Caesaribus* 33, with Potter (2004), pp. 263–264.

29. Potter (2004), pp. 264–269, and Drinkwater, in *CAH*² (2005), pp. 48–51.

30. Drinkwater (1987), pp. 41–44, SHA, *Aurelian* 39. 1 for the employment of Tetricus in the imperial administration.

31. W. Willems, *Romans and Barbarians* (1986).

32. Burns (2003) has a good discussion of this; use of Germanic mercenaries in civil wars, examples include Herodian 8. 7. 8, 8. 8. 2, SHA, *The Two Maximini* 24. 6, *Maximus and Balbinus* 12. 3, 13. 5, 14. 6–8, *The Thirty Tyrants* 6. 2; on

bandits and deserters joining raiders, *see* R. MacMullen, *Enemies of the Roman Order* (1967), pp. 195, 211, 255–268.

33. H. Schonberger, 'The Roman Frontier in Germany: An Archaeological Survey', *JRS*, 59 (1969), pp. 144–197, esp. 175–179, and esp. L. Okamura, 'Roman Withdrawals from Three Transfluvial Frontiers', in Mathisen & Sivan (1996), pp. 11–30, esp. 13–15 on Pfünz and Niederbieder. Okamura argues that traces of undermining on one of the walls at Niederbieder provides a clear indication of siegecraft that only Roman attackers would possess. D. Baatz has recently shown that the damage to the wall was later in date and the result of natural subsidence and quarrying for stone rather than enemy action, *see* D. Baatz, 'Cuiculus – Zur Technik der Unterminierung antiker Wehrbauten' in E. Schallmayer, *Niederbieder, Postumus und der Limesfall* (1996), pp. 84–89. I am very grateful to Kurt Kleemann for bringing this to my attention.

34. A. Diaconescu, 'The towns of Roman Dacia: An Overview of Recent Archaological Research', in W. Hanson & I. Haynes, *Roman Dacia: The Making of a Provincial Society* (2004), pp. 87–142, esp. 128–137.

6–The Queen and the 'Necessary' Emperor

1. SHA, *Thirty Tyrants* 15. 8 and *Aurelian* 37. 1. Similar sentiments about Aurelian are expressed elsewhere, e.g. John of Antioch, *fragment* 155, *Fragmenta Historicorum Graecorum*, Vol. 4, p. 599.

2. Lactantius, *De mortibus persecutorum* 5, and see the other sources and references in M. Dodgeon & S. Lieu, *The Roman Eastern Frontier and the Persian Wars, AD 226–363* (1991), pp. 58–63.

3. Dodgeon & Lieu (1991), pp. 65–67, J. Drinkwater, in *CAH²* (2005), pp. 44–45, and D. Potter, *The Roman Empire at Bay, AD 180–395* (2004), p.256–259; SHA, *Thirty Tyrants* 13–14.

4. *See* F. Millar, *The Roman Near East, 31 BC–AD 337* (1993), pp. 157–158, 161–173, J. Lang, 'Two Sides of a coin', in R. Mathisen & H. Sivan (eds.), *Shifting Frontiers in Late Antiquity* (1996), pp. 59–71, esp. 61–62, Potter (2004), pp. 256, 259–261, and Drinkwater, in *CAH²* (2005), pp. 45–46.
Against Rome (1992), esp. pp. 31–49.

5. For the sources, *see* Dodgeon & Lieu (1991), pp. 68–80, and in particular SHA, *Thirty Tyrants* 15. 1–8, *Gallienus* 10. 1–8, 12. 1, Zosimus 1. 39.

6. Assassination of Odaenathus, *see* Dodgeon and Lieu (1991), pp. 80–83, and esp. SHA, *Thirty Tyrants* 15. 5–6, *Gallienus* 13. 1, Zosimus 1. 39, Zonaras 12. 24.

7. R. Stoneman, *Palmyra and its Empire: Zenobia's Revolt Against Rome* (1992), esp. pp. 31–49.

8. On the culture, *see* Millar (1993), pp. 319–336; for a well-illustrated overview of the city's architecture, *see* I. Browning, *Palmyra* (1979).

9. Stoneman (1992), pp. 61–63, 76–79; the importance of heavy cavalry, Zosimus 1 50.

10. Stoneman (1992), pp. 111–127, A. Watson, *Aurelian and the third century* (1999), pp. 59–66, Dodgeon & Lieu (1991), pp. 83–86; SHA, *Thirty Tyrants* 30.

1–3, 12–22, esp. 30. 12 claiming that she only allowed Odaenathus to lie with her in order to produce children, and would wait until she was sure she was not pregnant before letting him couple with her again; Cleoptra, *see CIS* 2. 3946, and it is also emphasised in SHA, *Thirty Tyrants* 30. 19–20, *Aurelian* 27. 3, *Probus* 9. 5.

11. Lang (1996), pp. 64–69, Dodgeon & Lieu (1991), pp. 84–85, 88–89, Potter (2004), pp. 266–267, and Millar (1993), pp. 171–172.

12. Work on temple at Bostra, *IGLS* 9107 = *AE* 1947, 165, translated in Dodgeon & Lieu (1991), p. 86; the Egyptian campaign, *see* Potter (2004), pp. 266–267, Watson (1999), pp. 61–63, Zosimus 1. 44, SHA, *Claudius* 11. 1–2.

13. Potter (2004), pp. 261, Watson (1999), pp. 65–66.

14. Lang (1996), pp. 68–69, Watson (1999), pp. 67–69.

15. Zosimus 1. 50–51, SHA, *Aurelian* 22. 1–25. 6, Dodgeon & Lieu (1991), pp. 89–95, with Watson (1999), pp. 71–75.

16. Zosimus 1. 52–53.

17. Watson, (1999), pp. 76–80, 81–84, and Dodgeon & Lieu (1991), pp. 96–101 for the key sources, including Zosimus 1. 55; on the death of Cassius Longinus, *see* Zosimus 1. 56. 2–3, SHA, *Aurelian* 30. 3.

18. Watson (1999), pp. 82–3, Dodgeon & Lieu (1991), pp. 101–105.

19. SHA, *Aurelian* 33. 1–34. 6 for a detailed – if possibly fanciful – account of the triumph; on Zenobia's fate, *see* Zosimus 1. 59, Zonaras 12. 27, SHA, *Thirty Tyrants* 30. 27, Eutropius 9. 13. 2, Jerome, *Chron.* 223, and *see also* Watson (1999), pp. 83–88, and Dodgeon & Lieu (1991), pp. 105–109.

20. SHA, *Aurelian* 18. 3–4, 21. 1–3, Zosimus 1. 48–49, Dexippus *FGH* II no. 100, *fr.* 6. 2, with Watson (1999), pp. 48–52, 54–56, Potter (2004), pp. 269–270.

21. Watson (1999), pp. 138–140 on the distributions of food to the urban population, and pp. 143–152 on the walls.

22. Eusebius, *Ecclesiastical History* 7. 11. 10, M. Edwards, in *CAH²* (2005), pp. 637–647, Potter (2004), p. 255.

23. For a full discussion of the episode, *see* F. Millar, 'Paul of Samosata, Zenobia and Aurelian, *JRS*, 61 (1971), pp. 1–17.

24. Drinkwater, in *CAH²* (2005), pp. 53–54, R. Syme, *Emperors and Biography: Studies in the Historia Augusta* (1971), pp. 245–246, Potter (2004), pp. 274–275, and Watson (1999), pp. 104–112.

25. SHA, *Tacitus* 13. 2–3, Zosimus 1. 63. 1, Zonaras 12. 28 on the raiders; Aurelius Victor, *De Caesaribus* 36, SHA, *Tacitus* 13. 5, Zosimus 1. 63.

26. Drinkwater, in *CAH²* (2005), pp. 54–57, and Potter (2004), pp. 275–279.

27. S. Mitchell, *Cremna in Pisidia: An Ancient City in Peace and War* (1995), pp. 177–218 for a full discussion of the siege and the literary and archaeological evidence for it; Zosimus' account is found in 1. 69, mentioning the shooting of Lydius.

28. Drinkwater, in *CAH²* (2005), pp. 56–58, and Potter (2004), pp. 279–280.

29. Dodgeon & Lieu (1991), pp. 112–121 for the sources.

30. Zosimus 1. 73.

31. R. Frye, in *CAH²* (2005), pp. 470–471.

32. E.g., P. Heather, *The Fall of the Roman Empire: A New History* (2005), pp. 58–67, esp. pp. 60, 64.

33. Potter (2004), p. 256, Dodgeon & Lieu (1991), pp. 67, 297, and esp. S. Lieu, 'Captives, Refugees and Exiles', in P. Freeman & D. Kennedy (eds.), *The Defence of the Roman and Byzantine East* (1986), pp. 475–505.

7—Crisis

1. Herodian 1. 1. 4–5 (Loeb translation).

2. Domitianus is mentioned in Zosimus 1. 49, SHA, *Gallienus* 2. 6, *Thirty Tyrants* 12. 14, 13. 3.

3. For discussions of the 'Third Century Crisis', *see* the useful introduction in A. Watson, *Aurelian and the Third Century* (1999), pp. 1–20, A. Jones, *The Later Roman Empire, 284–602*, Vol. 1 (1964), pp. 1–36, G. Alföldy, 'The Crisis of the Third Century As Seen By Contemporaries', in *Greek, Roman, and Byzantine Studies*, 15 (1974), pp. 89–111, W. Liebeschuetz, 'Was There a Crisis of the Third Century?', in O. Hekster, G. Kleijn & D. Slootjes (eds.), *Crises and the Roman Empire* (2007), pp. 11–20, and in general, R. MacMullen, *Roman Government's Response to Crisis, AD 235–337* (1976), and *Corruption and the Decline of Rome* (1988). A recent reassessment that still presents a fairly bleak view of the period is L. de Blois, 'The Crisis of the Third Century A.D. in the Roman Empire: A Modern Myth?', in L. de Blois & J. Rich (eds.), *The Transformation of Economic Life Under the Roman Empire* (2002), pp. 204–217. A more positive view of the period is offered in C. Witschel, 'Re-evaluating the Roman West in the 3rd c. A.D.', *Journal of Roman Archaeology*, 17 (2004), pp. 251–281. On the period as one of change rather than crisis, *see* R. Reece, 'The Third Century: Crisis or Change?', in A. King & M. Henig (eds.), *The Roman West in the Third Century: Contributions From Archaeology and History* (1981), pp. 27–38. A convenient collection of comments on this and other themes related to the end of the Roman empire is M. Chambers (ed.), *The Fall of Rome: Can it be Explained?* (1963).

4. Jones (1964), pp. 9–11, 20–23, 29–32, K. Hopkins, 'Taxes and Trade in the Roman Empire (200 BC–AD 400)', *JRS*, 70 (1980), pp. 101–125, M. Corbier, in *CAH²* (2005), pp. 360–386.

5. On devaluation and its possible consequences, *see* Corbier, in *CAH²* (2005), pp. 330–360, C. Howgego, 'Coin Circulation and the Integration of the Roman Economy,' *Journal of Roman Archaeology*, 7 (1994), pp. 6–21, esp. 12–16, de Blois (2002), pp. 215–217, R. Duncan-Jones, *Money and Government in the Roman Empire* (1994), esp. pp. 20–32, and L. de Blois, 'Monetary Politics, the Soldiers' Pay, and the Onset of Crisis in the First Half of the Third Century AD', in P. Erdkamp (ed.), *The Roman Army and the Economy* (2002), pp. 90–107.

6. C. Bruun, 'The Antonine Plague and the Third Century Crisis', in Hekster, Kleijn & Slootjes (2007), pp. 201–217, and W. Jongman, 'Gibbon was Right: The Decline and Fall of the Roman Economy', in Hekster, Kleijn & Slootjes (2007), pp. 183–199, both of which argue that there was a serious decline in

both the population and the economy of the empire during the third century.

7. R. MacMullen, 'The Epigraphic Habit in the Roman Empire,' *American Journal of Philology*, 103 (1982), pp. 233–246.

8. Hopkins (1980), pp. 105–108, and A. Parker, *Ancient Shipwrecks of the Mediterranean and the Roman provinces* (1992); on trade with India and China, *see* G. Young, *Rome's Eastern Trade* (2001), pp. 80–88, 126–128.

9. *See* Witschel (2004), esp. pp. 261–274, D. Bar, 'Was there a 3rd-C. economic crisis in Palestine?' in J. Humphrey (ed.), *The Roman and Byzantine Near East*, Vol. 3. (2002), pp. 43–54, Reece (1981), MacMullen (1988), pp. 23–35, and M. Todd, *Roman Britain* (3rd edn, 1999), pp. 156–178.

10. For the alleged German preference for older silver coins, *see* M. Todd, *The Early Germans* (2nd edn., 2004), pp. 98–101, who is sceptical.

11. A. Wilson, 'Machines, Power and the Ancient Economy', *JRS*, 92 (2002), pp. 1–32, esp. 24–31.

12. For the theory that a declining population contributed massively to the fall of Rome, *see* A. Boak, *Manpower Shortage and the Fall of the Roman Empire in the West* (1955); on the economy in general, *see* W. Jongman, 'The Roman Economy: From Cities to Empire', in de Blois & Rich (2002), pp. 28–47.

13. Aurelius Victor, *De Caesaribus* 33, 37, and *see also* L. de Blois, *The Policy of the Emperor Gallienus* (1976), pp. 37–47, and E. Lo Cascio, in *CAH²* (2005), pp. 158–165.

14. E.g., D. Potter, *The Roman Empire at Bay, AD 180–395* (2004), p. 258, Watson (1999), p. 10, F. Millar, *The Roman Empire and Its Neighbours* (1981), pp. 60–61, and Y. Le Bohec, *The Imperial Roman Army* (1994), pp. 198–199.

15. For a discussion of styles of generalship, *see* A. Goldsworthy, *In the Name of Rome* (2004), esp. pp. 336–359.

16. The unsuccessful coup of Praetorian Prefect Sejanus against Emperor Tiberius saw him gradually acquire senatorial rank and magistracies. Three inscriptions seem to suggest that Legio II Parthica was commanded by a senatorial legate at some point, *see* J. Balty & W. Van Rengen, *Apamea in Syria: The Winter Quarters of Legio II Parthica* (1993), pp. 16, 39–41.

17. For Alexander, *see* ch. 4, and for Tacitus, *see* Aurelius Victor, *De Caesaribus* 37, SHA, *Tacitus* 3. 1–9. 6.

18. *See* Watson (1999), pp. 4–6, F. Millar, 'Emperors, Frontiers and Foreign Relations', in *Britannia*, 8 (1982), pp. 1–23, esp. 11–15, J. Drinkwater, in *CAH²* (2005), pp. 58–62.

19. On the emperor's relationship with the army, *see* J. Campbell, *The Emperor and the Roman Army* (1984), esp. pp. 59–69, 120–156; J. Drinkwater, *The Alamanni and Rome 213–496: Caracalla to Clovis* (2007), pp. 28–32 argues not entirely convincingly that Marcus Aurelius was mainly motivated by a traditional desire for glory.

20. *See* F. Vervaet, 'The Reappearance of the Supra-provincial Commands in the Late Second and Early Third Centuries CE', in Hekster, Kleijn & Slootjes (2007), pp. 125–139.

21. Suetonius, *Tiberius* 25. 1.

22. Dio 79. 32. 3–4; a good discussion of the misbehaviour of soldiers during civil wars is in de Blois & Rich (eds.) (2002), pp. 209–214.

8–The Four – Diocletian and the Tetrarchy

1. SHA, *Carus, Carinus, and Numerian* 18. 3–4.

2. B. Grenfall et al, *The Oxyrhyncus Papyri* (1898–), LXIII. 4352, translation by its editor, J. Rea, *see* A. Bowman, in *CAH²* XII (2005), p. 67.

3. SHA, *Aurelian* 6. 2.

4. Aurelius Victor 39, with P. Garnsey & C. Humfress, *The Evolution of the Late Antique World* (2001), p. 26–35, and S. Corcoran, 'Before Constantine', in N. Lenski (ed.), *The Cambridge Companion to the Age of Constantine* (2006), pp. 35–58, esp. 42–46.

5. 'Restorer of eternal light' from the Arras Amedallion, *see* P. Casey, *Carausius and Allectus: The British Usurpers* (1994), p. 142; on the need for radical reform and strong centralised rule in the third century, *see* Garnsey & Humfress (2001), esp. pp. 12–13, 14–17.

6. S. Williams, *Diocletian and the Roman Recovery* (1985), pp. 24–27, 34–46, T. Barnes, *The New Empire of Diocletian* (1982), pp. 3–4, 30–35.

7. Williams (1985), pp. 45–46, Zonaras 12. 31, and also Bowman, in *CAH²* XII (2005), pp. 71–73, 78–79, and D. Potter, *The Roman Empire at Bay* (2004), pp. 282–290, 292.

8. Casey (1995), pp. 39–45, 89–105.

9. On the creation of the tetrarchy, *see* Williams (1985), pp. 58–70, Barnes (1982), pp. 35–38, and *CAH²* etc; on the end of the rebellion, *see* Casey (1995), pp. 106–114, 127–145.

10. *See* Williams (1985), pp. 80–82, and Bowman, in *CAH²* XII (2005), pp. 81–82

11. In general, *see* S. Corcoran, *The Empire of the Tetrarchs: Imperial Pronouncements and Government, AD 284–324* (1996), *passim*, but esp. pp. 254–297; on Galerius, *see* Ammianus Marcellinus 14. 11. 10, Orosius 7. 25. 9–11–these and other descriptions of the events are collected in M. Dodgeon & F. Lieu, *The Roman Eastern Frontier and the Persian Wars, AD 226–363* (1991), pp. 128–130.

12. *See* Williams (1985), pp. 148; highly recommended for all visitors to Rome is A. Claridge, *Rome: Oxford Archaeological Guides* (1998), in this case pp. 70–72.

13. Williams (1985), pp. 148–150; on the emperors' movements and residences, *see* Barnes (1982), pp. 47–64.

14. On the army, *see* H. Nicasie, *Twilight of Empire* (1998), pp. 14–22.

15. *See* Garnsey & Humfress (2001), pp. 25–51, C. Kelly, *Ruling the Later Roman Empire* (2004), *passim*, R. MacMullen, *Corruption and the Decline of Rome* (1988), pp. 144–145, A. Jones, *The Later Roman Empire, 284–602* (1964), esp. 366–410, Potter (2004), pp. 370–377; on the role of the praetorian prefect, *see* L. Howe, *The Praetorian Prefect from Commodus to Diocletian, AD 180–305* (1942), esp. 60–64; ' ... flies on sheep', *see* Libanius, *Orations* 19. 130.

16. Lactantius, *On the deaths of the persecutors* 7. 4.

17. On the role of governors, *see* Corcoran (1996), pp. 234–253; on the new administration in general, *see* Williams (1985), pp. 102–114.

18. For a detailed discussion of the creation of the dioceses and provinces, *see* Barnes (1982), pp. 195–225.

19. *See* W. Treadgold, *Byzantium and Its Army, 284–1081* (1995), pp. 9–21, 87–93.

20. *See* Kelly (2004), and Jones (1964), pp. 366–410, 563–606.

21. Jones (1964), pp. 411–469, M. Corbier, in *CAH²* XII (2005), pp. 360–386.

22. On the census and taxation, *see* Williams (1985), pp. 126–139, Barnes (1982), pp. 226–237.

23. Jones (1964), pp. 60–68,

24. Jones (1964), pp. 438–442.

25. On price edict, *see* Bowman, in *CAH²* XII (2005), pp. 83–4, 177–178 and Corcoran (1996), pp. 205–233; for a translation of a text reconstructed from several inscriptions, *see* R. Rees, *Diocletian and the Tetrarchy* (2004), pp. 139–146.

26. Prologue to price edict, *see* Corcoran (1996), pp. 207–208 incl. Quotes; on laws and courts, *see* Jones (1964), pp. 470–522, and MacMullen (1988), pp. 87–93; Justinian Code 9. 20. 7 is a law of Diocletian's ordering the summary and execution of kidnappers of slaves 'so that by the manner of the punishment the rest should be deterred'.

27. Potter (2004), 294–298.

28. Williams (1985), pp.140–150, and Garnsey & Humfress (2001), pp. 25–51.

29. On fortifications, *see* J. Lander, *Roman Stone Fortifications* (1984), esp. pp. 151–262, and S. Johnson, *Late Roman Fortifications* (1983); for a view contrasting frontier policy under Diocletian and Constantine, *see* Zosimus 2. 34. 1.

30. *See* Bowman, in *CAH²* XII (2005), pp. 81–83, Dodgeon & Lieu (1991), pp. 124–139, and Williams (1985), pp. 79–81, 84–86.

9–The Christian

1. Eusebius, *Ecclesiastical History* 9. 9. 2 (Loeb translation, J. Oulton).

2. Zosimus 2. 53 (translation R. Ridley, *Zosimus: New History* (1982)).

3. The fullest account is in Lactantius, *On the deaths of the persecutors* 18–20, but *see also* Anonymous, *De Caesaribus* 39–40, Aurelius Victor, *De Caesaribus* 39, Eusebius, *Ecclesiastical History* 8. 13. 10–11; for a fuller description, *see* C. Odahl, *Constantine and the Christian Empire* (2004), pp. 71–74.

4. For discussion of the abdication, *see* C. Grant, *The Emperor Constantine* (1993), pp. 20–23, S. Corcoran, 'Before Constantine', in N. Lenski (ed.), *The Cambridge Companion to the Age of Constantine* (2006), pp. 35–58, esp. pp. 53–54, N. Lenski, 'The Reign of Constantine', also in Lenski (2006), pp. 59–90, esp. 60–61, A. Bowman, in *CAH²* XII (2005), pp. 87–88, and D. Potter, *The Roman Empire at Bay, AD 180–395* (2004), pp. 340–342.

5. Lactantius, *On the deaths of the persecutors* 24–25, Eusebius, *Life of Constantine*

1. 20–21, Aurelius Victor, *De Caesaribus* 40, Zosimus 2. 8; with Odahl (2004), pp. 72–78, Grant (1993), pp. 22–23, and Lenski (2006), p. 61 .

6. Zosimus 2. 9, Lactantius, *On the deaths of the persecutors* 23–27, Aurelius Victor, *De Caesaribus* 41, Eutropius, *Breviarum* 10, with Potter (2004), pp. 346–348, Odahl (2004), pp. 86–88, and Lenski (2006), pp. 63–64.

7. On the question of whether or not Constantine was legitimate, *see* B. Leadbetter, 'The Illegitimacy of Constantine and the Birth of the Tetrarchy', in S. Lieu & D. Montserrat (eds.), *Constantine: History, Historiography and Legend* (1998), pp. 74–85, J. Drijvers, *Helena Augusta* (1992), pp. 14–19, T. Barnes, *The New Empire of Diocletian* (1982), p. 36, and Odahl (2004), pp. 16–17.

8. Lactantius, *On the deaths of the persecutors* 29, Zosimus 2. 10, Aurelius Victor, *De Caesaribus* 39–40, Eutropius, *Breviarum* 10. 4; A. Cameron, in *CAH²* XII (2005), pp. 91–92, Odahl (2004), pp. 80–86, 90–92, Grant (1993), pp. 25–26, T. Barnes, *Constantine and Eusebius* (1981), pp. 32–33, and Potter (2004), pp. 347–351.

9. Lactantius, *On the deaths of the persecutors* 32, 42, and S. Williams, *Diocletian and the Roman Recovery* (1985), pp. 199–200.

10. Eusebius, *Ecclesiastical History* 8. 14, 9. 9, and *Life of Constantine* 1. 38, Zosimus 2. 15–17, Lactantius, *On the deaths of the persecutors* 44, Aurelius Victor, *De Caesaribus* 40; see also Odahl (2004), pp. 98–108, Potter (2004), pp. 356–359, 363, Lenski (2006), pp. 68–70, and Grant (1993), pp. 33–40.

11. For more detailed accounts of these years, *see* Grant (1993), pp. 40–50, Odahl (2004), pp. 119–120, 162–165, 170–182, Lenski (2006), pp. 73–77, A. Jones, *The Later Roman Empire, 284–602* (1964), pp. 77–83, and Potter (2004), pp. 364–368, 377–380.

12. *See* Lenski (2006), p. 66 with references to specific orations and inscriptions.

13. For the church in Nicomedia, *see* Lactantius, *On the deaths of the persecutors* 12; for Porphyry, there is a useful survey in Potter (2004), pp. 323–332, and for more detailed analysis, *see* R. Berchman, *Porphyry Against the Christians* (2005).

14. For the persecution, *see* Eusebius, *Ecclesiastical History* 8. 1–14, Lactantius, *On the deaths of the persecutors* 10–16; *see also* Potter (2004), pp. 337–340, G. Clarke, in *CAH²* XII (2005), pp. 647–665, Jones (1964), pp. 71–76.

15. *See* Clarke, in *CAH²* XII (2005), pp. 647–648, which includes this quote; *see also* Potter (2004), pp. 302–314.

16. Quote from Lactantius, *On the deaths of the persecutors* 34 (translation J. Creed, cited in *CAH²* XII (2005), p. 656–657, and Eusebius, *Ecclesiastical History* 8. 17, who provides a Greek version of Galerius' decree, and 9. 7 for Maximinus Daia's reply.

17. For surveys of Constantius' and Constantine's religious beliefs, *see* Odahl (2004), pp. 55, 63–67, 85–86, 94–95, Lenski (2006), pp. 66–68, and Grant (1993), pp. 134–140; more detailed discussion of his conversion can be found in P. Weiss, 'The Vision of Constantine', *Journal of Roman Archaeology*, 16 (2003), pp. 237–259, and J. Bremmer, 'The Vision of Constantine', in A. Lardinois et

al. (eds.), *Land of Dreams: Greek & Latin Studies in Honour of A.H.M. Kessels* (2006), pp. 57–79.

18. *See* R. Tomlin, 'Christianity and the Roman Army', in Lieu & Montserrat (1998), pp. 21–51, esp. 25–27, and R. Lane Fox, *Pagans and Christians* (1988), pp. 613–616.

19. Lactantius, *On the deaths of the persecutors* 44, Eusebius, *Life of Constantine* 1. 28–29, with discussion in H. Drake, 'The Impact of Constantine on Christianity', in Lenski (ed.) (2006), pp. 111–136, esp. 113–115, Odahl (2004), pp. 105–108, and Potter (2004), pp. 358–360.

20. The importance of perceptions of the power of a deity in conversion are well discussed in R. MacMullen, *Christianizing the Roman Empire AD 100–400* (1984); for Maximinus Daia's policy, *see* S. Mitchell, 'Maximinus and the Christians in AD 312: A New Inscription', *JRS*, 78 (1988), pp. 105–124.

21. K. Hopkins, 'Early Christian Number and its Implications', *Journal of Early Christian Studies*, 6 (1998), pp. 184–226, and *see also* Clarke, in *CAH²* XII (2005), pp. 589–616, with M. Edwards, 'The Beginnings of Christianization', in Lenski (ed.) (2006), pp. 137–158, esp. 137–140, and S. Mitchell, 'The Cities of Asia Minor in Constantine's Time', in Lieu & Montserrat (1998), pp. 52–73, esp. 66–67.

22. *See* C. Lightfoot, in *CAH²* XII (2005), pp. 481–497 esp. 486–487, 494–495.

23. *See* Edwards (2006), esp. 138–142.

24. *See* Drake (2006), esp. pp. 111–112, 115–116, 131–132, and Edwards (2006), pp. 142–145; for the emperor reading scriptures, Eusebius, *Life of Constantine* 4. 17, *see also* Odahl (2004), pp. 137–139.

25. *See* M. Johnson, 'Architecture of Empire', in Lenski (2006), pp. 278–297, esp. 282–288, 292–295, and Grant (1993), pp. 189–207.

26. Mitchell (1998), pp. 66–68; Odahl (2004), pp. 110–112, and Johnson (2006), p. 280.

27. On the Arch, *see* Odahl (2004), pp. 141–144, Johnson (2006), p. 281, Potter (2004), pp. 360–362, S. Mitchell, *A History of the Later Roman Empire AD 284–641* (2007), pp. 158–163.

28. Johnson (2006), pp. 291–292, Grant (1993), pp. 116–122, Odahl (2004), pp. 221–223, 232–244, and Potter (2004), pp. 383–386.

29. Libanius, *Orations* 30. 6; for a good discussion of the question, *see* A. Lee, 'Traditional Religions', in Lenski (ed.) (2006), pp. 159–179, esp. pp. 174–175.

30. On sacrifice, *see* Lee (2006), pp. 173–174, esp. n. 69; on other legislation, *see* A. Cameron, in *CAH²* XII (2005), pp. 95–7, Jones (1964), p. 92, and Mitchell (2007), pp. 68–69.

31. Jones (1964), pp. 92–93, and Odahl (2004), p. 250.

32. Drake (2006), pp. 116–121, Odahl (2004), pp. 129–141, Grant (1993), pp. 164–167, and Potter (2004), pp. 402–410.

33. Drake (2006), pp. 123–125, Potter (2004), pp. 410–420, Odahl (2004), pp. 190–199, Jones (1964), pp. 86–89.

34. Jones (1964), pp. 90–92, 93–97, and Lane Fox (1988), pp. 609–662.

35. For discussion of these aspects, *see* C. Kelly, 'Bureaucracy and Government',

in Lenski (ed.) (2006), pp. 183–204, and H. Elton, 'Warfare and the Military', in Lenski (2006), pp. 325–346.

36. Grant (1993), pp. 110–115, Odahl (2004), pp. 204–208, Lenski (ed.) (2006), pp. 78–79, Potter (2004), pp. 380–382.

37. Drijvers (1992), pp. 55–72.

38. For the wars with the Goths, *see* M. Kulikowski, *Rome's Gothic Wars* (2007), pp. 80–86; for feeding Frankish kings to the wild beasts, *see Pan. Lat.* 7(6). 4. 2, 6(7). 10. 2–11.6, 4(10). 16. 5–6, Eutropius, *Breviarum* 10. 3. 2.

39. For sources for Constantine's relations with Persia, *see* M. Dodgeon & S. Lieu, *The Roman Eastern Frontier and the Persian Wars, AD 226–363* (1991), pp. 145–163. The quote is taken from the extract from Eusebius, *Life of Constantine* 4. 8–13, pp. 150–152; *see also* T. Barnes, 'Constantine and the Christians of Persia,' *JRS*, 75 (1985), pp. 126–136.

40. Odahl (2004), pp. 274–275, and Grant (1993), 211–214.

10–Rivals

1. Zosimus 2. 39 (trans. J. Buchanan & H. Davies, *Zosimus: Historia Nova: The Decline of Rome*, 1967).

2. Julian, *Letter to the Athenians* 270c–271b (trans. Wright) from N. Lenski (ed.), *The Cambridge Companion to the age of Constantine* (2006), p. 98.

3. *See* R. Burgess, 'The Summer of Blood', *Dumbarton Oaks Papers*, 61 (forthcoming, 2008).

4. The main sources for the death of Constantine II include Zosimus 2. 39–40, Aurelius Victor, *De Caesaribus* 41, who states that the army refused to accept anyone other than the sons of Constantine; for fuller accounts and discussion, *see* R. Frakes, 'The Dynasty of Constantine down to 363', in Lenski (2006) pp. 91–107, esp. 94–99, D. Potter, *The Roman Empire at Bay, AD 180–395* (2004), pp. 459–462, D. Hunt, in *CAH²* XIII (1998), pp. 1–5, and A. Jones, *The Later Roman Empire 284–603*, Vol. 1 (1964), p. 112.

5. For Constans having only one officer with him when he was captured, *see* Ammianus Marcellinus 15. 5. 16.

6. In general, *see* Frakes (2006), pp. 100–101, Potter (2004), pp. 471–474, Hunt, in *CAH²* XIII (1998), pp. 10–11, 14–22, Jones (1964), pp. 112–113; *see* Aurelius Victor, *De Caesaribus* 42, and Ammianus Marcellinus 15. 5. 33 on defection of Silvanus.

7. Quotation from Ammianus Marcellinus 15. 1. 2; for the career of Gallus, *see* Frakes (2006), pp. 101–102, Potter (2004), pp. 474–476, Hunt, in *CAH²* XIII (1998), pp. 24–25, and G. Bowersock, *Julian the Apostate* (1978), pp. 21–47; Ammianus provides the most detailed account, 14. 1, 7, 9, 11, 15. 1.

8. For differing views on Ammianus as a source *see* J. Matthews, *The Roman Empire of Ammianus* (1989), T. Barnes, *Ammianus and the Representation of Historical Reality* (1998), and the papers in J. Drijvers & D. Hunt (eds.), *The Late Roman World and its Historian* (1999); for a discussion of the military aspects of his work, *see* N. Austin, *Ammianus on Warfare: An Investigation Into*

Ammianus' Military Knowledge, Collection Latomus, 165 (1979); for a discussion of his career, *see* Barnes (1998), pp. 54–64.

9. For discussion of his coverage of Gallus, *see* Barnes (1998), pp. 129–142.

10. *See* esp. Ammianus Marcellinus 14. 1. 4–8, 5. 1–9, 15. 3. 1–11; Paul 'the chain' is first mentioned at 14. 5. 6–9, 'the count of dreams' is mentioned in 15. 3. 5.

11. For Ursicinus, *see* Ammianus Marcellinus 15. 2. 1–6; on administration in general, *see* C. Kelly, *Ruling the Later Roman Empire* (2004), and the very useful review of this by G. Greatrex in *Phoenix*, 60 (2006), pp. 178–181.

12. For Silvanus' father, *see* Ammianus Marcellinus 15. 5. 33; for specific discussion on the number of Alamanni in Roman service, *see* J. Drinkwater, *The Alamanni and Rome 213–496* (2007), pp. 145–159.

13. Ammianus Marcellinus 15. 6. 3.

14. Quote from Ammianus Marcellinus 15. 5. 23.

15. Ammianus Marcellinus 15. 5. 31–32.

16. The full account is Ammianus Marcellinus 15. 5. 1–6. 4; for the accusations against Ursicinus, *see* 15. 5. 36; for discussion, *see* D. Hunt, 'The Outsider Inside: Ammianus on the Rebellion of Silvanus', in Drijvers & Hunt (1999), pp. 51–63, and Matthews (1989), pp. 36–38, 81–83.

17. Twenty-eight-day reign from Jerome, *Chron. s.a.* 354, Aurelius Victor, *De Caesaribus* 42. 16, and Julian, *Oration* 2. 99a, who says under a month.

18. Ammianus Marcellinus 16. 10. 6–7, 9–10.

11–Enemies

1. Claudius Mamertinus, *Latin Panegyric* XI (3). 3, translation by M. Morgan in S. Lieu (ed.), *The Emperor Julian: Panegyric and Polemic* (2nd edn, 1989), p. 14.

2. M. Goodman, *The Roman World 44 BC–AD 180* (1997), pp. 81–84, argues that Augustus maintained a standing army first and foremost to defend himself against internal rivals. This was ceratinly a factor, but it does not explain why the army needed to be so large.

3. For the origin and meaning of the term, *see* B. Isaac, 'The Meaning of the Terms Limes and Limitanei', *JRS*, 78 (1988), pp. 125–147; On raiding, *see* H. Elton, *Warfare in Roman Europe AD 350–425* (1996), p. 206.

4. Zosimus 2. 33 claims that Constantine created the rank of Master of Soldiers.

5. For the army in general, *see* Elton (1996), esp. 89–117, M. Nicasie, *Twilight of Empire* (1998), K. Dixon & P. Southern, *The Late Roman Army* (1996), Y. Le Bohec, *L'armée Romaine sous le Bas-Empire* (2006), A. Lee, in *CAH²* XIII (1998), pp. 213–237, A. Jones, *The Later Roman Empire 284–603*, Vol. 1 (1964), pp. 607–686, and D. Potter, *The Roman Empire at Bay, AD 180–395* (2004), pp. 448–459.

6. For discussion of the size of the army, *see* R. MacMullen, 'How Big was the Roman Imperial Army?', *Klio*, 62 (1980), pp. 451–460, Jones (1964), pp. 679–685, and W. Treadgold, *Byzantium and its Army, 284–1081* (1995), pp. 43–59.

7. For discussion of the papyrus, *see* R. Duncan-Jones, 'Pay and Numbers in Diocletian's Army', *Chiron*, 8 (1978), pp. 541–560, and in general, T. Coello,

Unit Sizes in the Late Roman Army, BAR International Series, 645 (1996); for *XIII Gemina*, see *Notitia Dignitatum Or.* 42. 34–38, 28. 15, 8. 6 and discussion in J. Casey, 'The Legions in the Later Roman Empire', in R. Brewer (ed.), *The Second Augustan Legion and the Roman Military Machine* (2002), pp. 165–176.

8. *See* Elton (1996), pp. 89–90, Coello (1996), pp. 59–64; Ammianus Marcellinus 31. 10. 12 mentions detachments of 500 men apparently drawn from each legion, which would indicate that these units were larger than this.

9. Potter (2004), pp. 456–457 is one of very few scholars to suggest tentatively that the army may actually have been smaller in the fourth century.

10. Jones (1964), pp. 614–623, Elton (1996), pp. 128–154, Potter (2004), pp. 457–459, 687 fn. 74 for references to laws dealing with self-mutilation; Ammianus Marcellinus 15. 12. 3 claims this was especially common in Italy; for the equestrian under Augustus, *see* Suetonius, *Augustus* 24. 1; for desire to serve in the *limitanei*, *see* R. Tomlin, 'Christianity and the Roman Army', in S. Lieu & D. Montserrat (eds.), *Constantine: History, Historiography and Legend* (1998), pp. 21–51, esp. pp. 22–24.

11. Elton (1996), p. 101, Jones (1964), pp. 633–634.

12. The fullest expression of this view is in E. Luttwak, *The Grand Strategy of the Roman Empire from the First Century* AD *to the Third* (1976), pp. 127–190; for criticism, *see* amongst others D. Whittaker, *Frontiers of the Roman Empire: A Social and Economic Study* (1994), pp. 206–209, who is especially critical of the idea of 'defence in depth'; on the army in general, *see* Le Bohec (2006), esp. pp. 16–37, 97–107.

13. Zosimus 2. 34 (trans. J. Buchanan & H. Davies, *Zosimus: Historia Nova: the decline of Rome* (1967), p. 76; for the tendency of armies left idle in large camps to mutiny, *see* Tacitus, *Annals* 1. 16–17, 20–21.

14. This is fully explored in E. Wheeler, 'The Laxity of the Syrian Legions', in D. Kennedy (ed.), *The Roman Army in the East* (1996), pp. 229–276.

15. *See* Elton (1996), pp. 107–117, 250–263, M. Bishop & J. Coulston, *Roman Military Equipment from the Punic Wars to the Fall of Rome* (2nd edn, 2006), pp. 199–232, I. Stephenson, *Romano-Byzantine Infantry Equipment* (2006) and I. Stephenson & K. Dixon, *Roman Cavalry Equipment* (2003).

16. On the *comitatenses* and their deployment, *see* Elton (1996), pp. 89–99, 199–233.

17. Ammianus Marcellinus 15. 8. 1–22; the soldiers' showing their approval 15. 8. 15; on the attitude of our sources to Julian, *see* G. Bowersock, *Julian the Apostate* (1978), pp. 1–11, T. Barnes, *Ammianus Marcellinus and the Representation of Historical Reality* (1998), pp. 143–165, and the sources collected and commented upon in S. Tougher, *Julian the Apostate* (2007); on Julian's promotion to Caesar, *see* J. Matthews, *The Roman Empire of Ammianus* (1989), pp. 81–90.

18. In general, *see* Elton (1996), pp. 15–88, J. Drinkwater, *The Alamanni and Rome 213–496: Caracalla to Clovis* (2007), *passim*, T. Burns, *Rome and the Barbarians 100* BC–AD *400* (2003), pp. 309–362, H. Wolfram, *The Roman Empire*

and its Germanic Peoples (1997), pp. 51–101; forty-five captured towns, *see* Julian, *Letter to the Athenians* 278d–279b; for recovery of Roman captives, *see* Ammianus Marcellinus 17. 10. 7–8, 18. 2. 19, Zosimus 3. 3. 4–7.

19. On trade in stone and iron from east of the Rhine, *see* Drinkwater (2007), pp. 133–134; Magnentius' use of barbarians, *see* Drinkwater (2007), pp. 201–205.

20. Julian, *Letter to the Athenians* 123d–124d on reading Caesar's *Commentaries*; on his early life, *see* Bowersock (1978), pp. 12–32.

21. On the campaign in general see the analysis in Drinkwater (2007), pp. 219–224, and Barnes (1998), pp. 151–155; in the case of the *ballistarii* it remains possible that the unit had consisted of artillerymen at some earlier date, but that they were now simply ordinary infantry. In the end, we just do not know.

22. For the campaign, *see* Ammianus Marcellinus 16. 2. 1–3. 3; the delay in being admitted to Troyes is 16. 2. 7.

23. Ammianus Marcellinus 16. 4. 1–5, 7. 1–3.

24. On the campaign and battle, *see* Ammianus Marcellinus 16. 11. 1–12. 66, with Drinkwater (2007), pp. 224–242, Bowersock (1978), pp. 40–42, Barnes (1998), p. 152, and A. Goldsworthy, *In the Name of Rome* (2003), pp. 340–354 = (2004), pp. 383–399; on the misbehaviour of the Roman cavalry, *see* Zosimus 3. 3.

25. Ammianus Marcellinus 17. 1. 1–14; on frontier relations in general in this period, *see* A. Lee, (1993).

26. Ammianus Marcellinus 17. 2. 1–4.

27. For the remaining operations in Gaul, *see* the discussion in Drinkwater (2007), pp. 242–265; for taxation, *see* Ammianus Marcellinus 17. 3. 1–6.

28. Ammianus Marcellinus 17. 11. 1–5, 18. 1. 1–4, 20. 4. 1–5. 10, with Bowersock (1978), pp. 46–54.

29. For a more detailed narrative, *see* Potter (2004), pp. 505–508, Bowersock (1978), pp. 55–65, and Hunt, in *CAH²* XIII (1998), pp. 56–60; for the despatch of the *comes* to Britain and his subsequent arrest see Ammianus Marcellinus 20. 1. 1–3, 9. 9.

30. Ammianus Marcellinus 28. 5. 1–7.

31. Quotation from Ammianus Marcellinus 27. 2. 11 (Loeb translation); for raiders dyeing their hair, *see* Ammianus Marcellinus 27. 2. 1–3.

12–The Pagan

1. Julian, Letter to the Athenians 280d, 281b-c (Loeb translation, M. Wright, *The Works of the Emperor Julian*, Vol. II, 1913).

2. Ammianus Marcellinus 22. 3. 1–12; *see also* N. Lenski, *The Failure of Empire: Valens and the Roman State in the Fourth Century AD* (2002), p. 104.

3. On Julian's beliefs, *see* the discussions in G. Bowersock, *Julian the Apostate* (1978), pp. 12–20, 61–65, D. Potter, *The Roman Empire at Bay, AD 180–395* (2004), pp. 496–499, 508–509, and G. Fowden, in *CAH²* XIII (1998), pp. 543–

548; A. Murdoch, *The Last Pagan: Julian the Apostate and the Death of the Ancient World* (2003), is an accessible recent survey of Julian's life, and see pp. 9–37 on his early life and beliefs.

4. Julian, *Hymn to the Sun* 130b-c, 132c (Loeb translation, Wright, 1913).

5. Ammianus Marcellinus 22. 4. 1–10, 7. 5–8; for Maximus of Ephesus, *see* Ammianus Marcellinus 22. 7. 3–4.

6. For this period, *see* the sources in M. Dodgeon & S. Lieu, *The Roman Eastern Frontier and the Persian Wars AD 226–363* (1991), pp. 143–210.

7. Ammianus Marcellinus 16. 9. 1–4, 17. 5. 1–15, with J. Matthews, *The Roman Empire of Ammianus* (1989), pp. 39–47, and Dodgeon & Lieu (1991), pp. 211–212.

8. On the campaign and siege, *see* Ammianus Marcellinus 18. 4. 1–19. 9. 9.

9. Ammianus Marcellinus 19. 9. 9 claims that Shapur suffered 30,000 casualties during the siege of Amida; for the trail of hamstrung prisoners, *see* Ammianus Marcellinus 19. 6. 2, with A. Lee, *War in Late Antiquity: A Social History* (2007), pp. 135–138; for the capture of Singara and Bezabde, *see* Ammianus Marcellinus 20. 6. 1–7. 18.

10. Ammianus Marcellinus 20. 11. 1–25, 31–32.

11. For the war, *see* Ammianus Marcellinus 22. 12. 1–4, with Matthews (1989), pp. 134–140, Potter (2004), pp. 514–520, and D. Hunt, in *CAH²* XIII (1998), pp. 73–77.

12. The collapse of the stockpiled fodder, *see* Ammianus Marcellinus 23. 2. 8; for sacrifices, *see* Ammianus Marcellinus 22. 12. 1–3, 6–7; for Antioch, *see* Ammianus Marcellinus 22. 9. 1–10. 7; for army size, *see* Ammianus Marcellinus 23. 3. 5, 24. 7. 4, 25. 7. 2, and Zosimus 3. 13 and discussion in Matthews (1989), pp. 166–169.

13. *See* Ammianus Marcellinus 24. 2. 15–17; *see also* the discussion in J. Lendon, *Soldiers and Ghosts: A History of Battle in Classical Antiquity* (2005), pp. 290–309.

14. *See* Ammianus Marcellinus 24. 4. 1–5; for the stories about Africanus and Alexander, *see* Polybius 10. 18. 1–19. 7, Livy 26. 49. 11–50. 14, and Plutarch, *Alexander* 21.

15. For the campaign as a whole Dodgeon & Lieu (1991), pp. 231–274 surveys the sources.

16. For the Persian campaign, *see* Matthews (1989), pp. 130–179; on Julian's death, *see* Ammianus Marcellinus 25. 3. 1–23, with Potter (2004), p. 518 and Lenski (2002), p. 14 for the date.

17. *See* Ammianus Marcellinus 25. 5. 1–8; on Jovian's elevation, see Matthews (1989), pp. 180–184, Lenski (2002), pp. 14–20.

18. Ammianus Marcellinus 25. 7. 1–14, 9. 1–13 and Lenski (2002), pp. 160–161; Ammianus and the sources for the treaty are gathered in G. Greatrex & S. Lieu, *The Roman Eastern Frontier and the Persian Wars. Part 2 AD 363–630* (2002), pp. 1–9.

19. *See* Lenski (2002), pp. 214–217; for Jerusalem, *see* Ammianus Marcellinus 23. 1. 1–3.

20. Julian, *The Caesars* 336a-b (Loeb translation, Wright, 1913).

21. Ammianus Marcellinus 22. 10. 7, with Bowersock (1978), pp. 70–71, 79–93, Potter (2004), pp. 508–514, and Fowden, in *CAH²* XIII (1998), pp. 543–548.

22. *See* H. Chadwick, in *CAH²* XIII (1998), pp. 561–600 for the church in general; for the dramatic career of an especially controversial bishop of Alexandria, *see* T. Barnes, *Athanasius and Constantius: Theology and Politics in the Constantinian Empire* (1993); on monasticism, *see* P. Brown, 'The Rise and Function of the Holy Man in Late Antiquity', *JRS*, 61 (1971), pp. 801–10, and 'Asceticism: Pagan and Christian', in *CAH²* XIII (1998), pp. 601–631, and 'Christianization and Religious Conflict', in *CAH²* XIII (1998), pp. 632–664, esp. p. 639 discussing the origins of the word 'pagan'.

23. Ammianus Marcellinus 25. 11. 1–13. 1, with Lenski (2002), pp. 20–22.

24. Ammianus Marcellinus 26. 4. 1, with Lenski (2002), pp. 14–45.

25. For the sources of friction between Rome and Persia, *see* Greatrex & Lieu (2002), pp. 10–16.

26. Ammianus Marcellinus 26. 5. 13; for the rebellion as a whole, *see* the discussion in Lenski (2002), pp. 68–115, and Matthews (1989), pp. 193–203.

27. Lenski (2002), pp. 104–109.

28. *See* C. Kelly, *Ruling the Later Roman Empire* (2004), *passim*, but esp. pp. 20–34.

29. Ammianus Marcellinus 28. 5. 1–7.

30. *See* Kelly (2004), pp. 36–44, 64–104, and 107, 138–143 on the Timgad inscription; for an especially critical view of administration in this period, *see* R. MacMullen, *Corruption and the Decline of Rome* (1988), pp. 137–170.

31. Kelly (2004), p. 207, MacMullen (1988), pp. 149–150, and A. Jones, *The Later Roman Empire: 284–602*, Vol. 1 (1964), pp. 126–130, 396–401.

32. Ammianus Marcellinus 28. 6. 1–30.

33. A. Sherwin-White, *The Letters of Pliny: A Historical and Social Commentary* (1966), pp. 80–82, 525–528.

34. For instance, the discussion in P. Heather, *The Fall of the Roman Empire: A New History* (2005), pp. 103–110, who sees this as a general result of poor communications in the ancient world rather than a particular reflection of fourth-century administration.

13–Goths

1. Ammianus Marcellinus 31. 13. 10–12.

2. Ammianus Marcellinus 30. 6. 1–6.

3. On the dominance of senior officers and bureaucrats, *see* D. Potter, *The Roman Empire at Bay, AD 180–395* (2004), pp. 533–546.

4. N. Lenski, *The Failure of Empire: Valens and the Roman state in the Fourth Century AD* (2002), pp. 14–45, and esp. 56–67.

5. *See* P. Heather, *Goths and Romans 332–489* (1991), pp. 12–18, 84–121, and *The Goths* (1996), pp. 51–93, H. Wolfram, *The Roman Empire and its Germanic Peoples* (1997), pp. 69–72, M. Kulikowski, *Rome's Gothic Wars* (2007), pp. 43–

70, and T. Burns, *Barbarians Within the Gates of Rome* (1994), esp. pp. 303–304, n. 117.

6. Ammianus Marcellinus 31. 3. 8–4. 4; on the support for Procopius, *see* Ammianus Marcellinus 26. 10. 3, with Heather (1991), pp. 101–102, 109, 116, and Kulikowski (2007), pp. 112–118.

7. Ammianus Marcellinus 27. 5. 7–10, cf 30. 3. 4–6.

8. Heather (1991), pp. 118–121, Kulikowski (2007), p. 117, Burns (1994), pp. 15–19, and Wolfram (1997), pp. 64–65.

9. Ammianus Marcellinus 31. 2. 1–12, with quote from 10–11, with P. Heather, *The Fall of the Roman Empire: A New History* (2005), pp. 146–153, and (1996), pp. 97–104.

10. Ammianus Marcellinus 31. 3. 1–8, with Heather (1996), pp. 98–102, and Kulikowski (2007), pp. 124–128; note the hiring of Huns by Goths at 31. 3. 3.

11. *See* the brief comments in S. Mitchell, *A History of the Later Roman Empire AD 284–641* (2007), p. 81–84.

12. Ammianus Marcellinus 31. 4. 6, Eunapius, *fragment* 42 gives the figure 200,000; for discussion, *see* Heather (1991), p. 139, Kulikowski, p. 130–131, and H. Delbrück, *The Barbarian Invasions* (1980), pp. 275–276; as a comparison, Julius Caesar claimed that out of 368,000 migrating Helvetii, some 92,000 were adult males able to bear arms, *Bellum Gallicum* 1. 29.

13. Ammianus Marcellinus 31. 4. 1–9, 12–13, with Heather (1991), pp. 128–135, and (2005), pp. 158–163, who argues that the Romans had no choice but to admit the Tervingi because of the current dispute with Persia; *see also* Kulikowski (2007), pp. 128–130, Lenski (2002), pp. 325–328, 345–347, Wolfram (1997), pp. 81–82, and G. Halsall, *Barbarian Migrations and the Roman West 376–568* (2007), pp. 165–176.

14. *ILS* 986, *see* Campbell (1984), pp. 360–361, and for earlier cases of settling external groups, *see* S. Dyson, *The Creation of the Roman Frontier* (1985), esp. pp. 105–108, 172–173, 205–206.

15. For Caesar, *see* the discussion of this campaign in A. Goldsworthy, *Caesar: The life of a Colossus* (2006), pp. 212–223 = (2007), pp. 256–271; for the nature of surrenders, *see* Heather (1991), pp. 109–113, Burns (1994), pp. 12–13, 86, and *Rome and the Barbarians, 100 BC–AD 400* (2003), pp. 245–247, and Wolfram (1997), pp. 56–57.

16. Zosimus 4. 20. 6 claims that the Roman officers failed to disarm the Goths; *see* discussion in Burns (1994), p. 24, and Kulikowski (2007), p. 130.

17. Ammianus Marcellinus 31. 4. 11, 5. 1–2; *see* Heather (1991), pp. 140–142, and Kulikowski (2007), pp. 130–131, both of whom suggest that the Goths may deliberately have been kept short of food to keep them under control. There is no evidence for this, and it would have been an exceptionally dangerous plan; *see also* Lenski (2002), pp. 348–355; on the preparations for imperial campaigns, *see* H. Elton, *Warfare in Roman Europe: AD 350–425* (1996), pp. 236–238.

18. Ammianus Marcellinus 31. 5. 4–8, with Heather (1991), pp. 140–142, (2005), pp. 164–165, who argues that Valens most likely gave the order to secure the Gothic chieftains, and also Lenski (2002), pp. 325–328, Kulikowski (2007), pp.

132–133, and Burns (1994), p. 26; for other recent examples of Roman foul play at banquets, *see* Ammianus Marcellinus 29. 6. 5 in 374, and 30. 1. 18–21 around the same year.

19. Ammianus Marcellinus 31. 6. 4.

20. Ammianus Marcellinus 31. 6. 1–8, 8. 1–10; *see also* Lenski (2002), pp. 336–338 on divisions amongst the Goths.

21. Ammianus Marcellinus 31. 7. 1–16,, 8. 9–10, 11. 1–6; for this phase of the war, *see also* Heather (1991), pp. 142–146, Kulikowski (2007), pp. 133–138, Burns (1994), pp. 26–28, and M. Nicasie, *Twilight of Empire* (1998), pp. 233–242.

22. Ammianus Marcellinus 31. 10. 1–18.

23. Ammianus Marcellinus 31. 12. 1–11.

24. Ammianus Marcellinus 31. 12. 12–13. 19.

25. On numbers and for discussion of the battle in general, *see* Heather (1991), pp. 146–147, Burns (1994), pp. 29–33, and 'The Battle of Adrianople: A Reconsideration', *Historia*, 22 (1973), pp. 336–345, Kulikowski (2007), pp. 139–143, Nicasie (1998), pp. 241–253, Wolfram (1997), pp. 84–87, Lenski (2002), pp. 339, 354–355, W. Treadgold, *Byzantium and its Army, 284–1081* (1995), p. 57, A. Jones, *The Later Roman Empire*, Vol. 2 (1965), p. 1425, J. Matthews, *The Roman Empire of Ammianus* (1989), pp. 296–301, A. Barbero, *The Day of the Barbarians: The First Battle in the Fall of the Roman Empire* (2007), pp. 93–112, and Delbruck (1980), pp. 269–284; *see also* Y. Le Bohec, *L'armée Romaine sous le Bas-Empire* (2006), and the review by G. Greatrex in *Antiquite Tardive*, 15 (2007); in general, *see also* R. Errington, *Roman Imperial Policy from Julian to Theodosius* (2006).

26. Ammianus Marcellinus 31. 15. 1–16. 7.

27. On the massacres, *see* Ammianus Marcellinus 31. 16. 8 with Kulikowski (2007), pp. 145–147; for Theodosius, *see* S. Williams & G. Friell, *Theodosius: The Empire at Bay* (1994), pp. 20–28, Kulikowski (2007), pp. 147–150, and Burns (1994), pp. 43–45; for discussion of the aftermath of Adrianople, *see also* N. Lenski, '*Initium mali Romano imperio*: Contemporary reactions to the battle of Adrianople', *Transactions of the American Philological Association*, 127 (1997), pp. 129–168.

28. Williams & Friell (1994), pp. 28–35, Kulikowski (2007), pp. 150–153, and Burns (1994), pp. 45–72.

29. *See* Heather (1991), pp. 149–181, (2005), pp. 182–189, Wolfram (1997), pp. 87–89, and Burns (1994), pp. 73–91, with a more sceptical view in Halsall (2007), pp. 180–185.

30. The comment in Nicasie (1998), p. 254 that 'despite the Roman defeat, the campaign of Adrianople shows Roman strategy at its best' is a little surprising, although not untypical of recent views of the effectiveness of the fourth-century army and empire. He emphasises the logistical failure in supplying the Goths; *see also* Lenski (2002), pp. 355–367 on the reasons for the disaster, who puts much of the blame on Gratian for being slow and reluctant to co-operate; on the question of manpower, *see* in particular R. MacMullen, *Corruption and the Decline of Rome* (1988), pp. 173–177, 185–186, although Elton (1996), pp. 152–154 is more sceptical.

31. Ammianus Marcellinus 31. 10. 18–19, Williams & Friell (1994), pp. 36–40, Potter (2004), pp. 549–552, and J. Curran, in *CAH²* XIII (1998), pp. 104–106.

32. On living as 'father and son', *see* Ambrose, *epistulae* 24. 7.

33. Williams & Friell (1994), pp. 40–43, 61–64, Potter (2004), and Curran, in *CAH²* XIII (1998), p. 107; the story of Justina enlisting her daughter to persuade Theodosius is in Zosimus 4. 44.

34. Williams & Friell (1994), pp. 125–137, Curran, in *CAH²* XIII (1998), pp. 108–110.

35. Heather (1991), pp. 181–188, Kulikowski (2007), pp. 158–163, and Burns (1994), pp. 92–111.

14–East and West

1. Zosimus 4. 59. 3, trans. by Ridley (1982).

2. For discussion of the split, *see* S. Williams & G. Friell, *Theodosius: The Empire at Bay* (1994), pp. 137–148, S. Mitchell, *A History of the Later Roman Empire* AD *284–641* (2007), pp. 89–91, and R. Brockley, in *CAH²* XIII (1998), pp. 113–118.

3. C. Kelly, *Ruling the Later Roman Empire* (2004), pp. 26–36, 186–203.

4. For the sources, *see* G. Greatrex & N. Lieu (eds.), *The Roman Eastern Frontier and the Persian Wars: Part II* AD *363–630* (2002), pp. 20–30.

5. For a useful survey of Roman and Persian relations in this period, *see* B. Isaac, in *CAH²* XIII (1998), pp. 442–452; for the war of 421–422, *see* the collected sources in Greatrex & Lieu (2002), pp. 36–43.

6. For a summary of his career, *see* T. Burns, *Rome and the Barbarians, 100* BC–AD *400* (2003), pp. 338–339; for a discussion of the phenomenon of men moving between tribal leadership and senior posts in the Roman army, *see* J. Drinkwater, *The Alamanni and Rome 213–496: Caracalla to Clovis* (2007), pp. 145–176.

7. G. Young, *Rome's Eastern Trade* (2001), pp. 86–88, 126–130; *see also* Greatrex & Lieu (2002), pp. 33–34.

8. On saws, *see* Ausonius, *Mosella* 2. 361–363, with A. Wilson, 'Machines, Power, and the Ancient Economy', *JRS*, 92 (2002), pp. 1–32, esp. 15–17.

9. For a brief survey of the issue of rural population, *see* P. Heather, *The Fall of the Roman Empire: A New History* (2005), pp. 110–116, who justifiably points to the pioneering work of G. Tchalenko, *Villages Antiques de la Syrie du Nord* (1953–1958); also very useful on agriculture in this period is J. Banaji, *Agrarian Change in Late Antiquity: Gold, Labour, and Aristocratic Dominance* (2001), and C. Whittaker & P. Garnsey, in *CAH²* XIII (1998), pp. 277–311, who also argue against seeing the period as one of decline. While such studies make a good case for reassessing the earlier, very pessimistic view of economic life in this period, we do need to remember that our evidence is extremely limited and caution is always necessary.

10. *See* B. Ward-Perkins, in *CAH²* XIII (1998), pp. 373–382.

11. Paulinus, *Life of Ambrose* 31; for discussion, *see* Williams & Friell (1994), pp. 131–137, and in far more detail, N. McLynn, *Ambrose of Milan: Church and Court in a Christian Capital* (1994).

12. Codex Theodosianus 16. 1. 2, quoted in S. Mitchell, *A History of the Later Roman Empire AD 284–641* (2007), pp. 247–248.

13. Williams & Friell (1994), pp. 47–60.

14. *See* D. Hunt, in *CAH²* XIII (1998), pp. 240–250.

15. On synagogues, *see* Mitchell (2007), pp. 235–237.

16. On Ambrose and Theodosius, *see* Williams & Friell (1994), pp. 64–65, 68–70, and Mitchell (2007), pp. 248–250.

17. *See* C. Kelly, in *CAH²* XIII (1998), pp. 153–156, & N. Lenski, *The Failure of Empire: Valens and the Roman State in the Fourth Century AD* (2002), pp. 86–97, 142–143.

18. Gregory of Nyssa, *De Deitate Filii et Spiritus Sanctis*, in J.-P. Migne (ed.) *Patrologia Graeca* 46. 557–558.

19. For an introduction to disputes in this period, *see* H. Chadwick, in *CAH²* XIII (1998), pp. 561–600.

20. See Williams & Friell (1994), pp. 119–125, Mitchell (2007), pp. 248–251, and G. Fowden in *CAH²* XIII (1998), pp. 548–554.

21. The theme of the apparent power of Christian leaders and holy men as a major factor in conversion is explored in R. MacMullen, *Christianizing the Roman Empire AD 100–400* (1984); on the church in general, *see* H. Chadwick, *The Church in Ancient Society: From Galilee to Gregory the Great* (2001).

22. On Ulfilas, Saba and Gothic Christianity, *see* P. Heather, *The Goths* (1996), pp. 60–62, 73–74, 85, 313, H. Wolfram, *The Roman Empire and its Germanic Peoples* (1991), pp. 69–70, 72–73, 76–79, M. Kurikowski, *Rome's Gothic Wars* (2007), pp. 107–111, 118–122, G. Greatrex, 'The Gothic Arians after Theodosius (to Justinian)', *Studia Patristica*, 34 (2001), pp. 73–81, and T. Burns, *Rome and the Barbarians, 100 BC–AD 400* (2003), pp. 337–338, 368–369.

15–Barbarians and Romans: Generals and Rebels

1. Zosimus, *A New History* 5. 26. 5 (translation by Ridley (1982)).

2. Orientius, *Commonitorium* 2. 184.

3. For the *Notitia Dignitatum*, see A. Jones, *The Later Roman Empire 284–602* (1964), pp. 1417–1450, and the collection of papers in R. Goodburn & P. Bartholomew (eds.), *Aspects of the Notitia Dignitatum* (1976), and also M. Kulikowski, 'The *Notitia Dignitatum* as a Historical Source', *Historia*, 99 (2002), pp. 358–377. O. Seeck (ed.), *Notitia Dignitatum* (1876) remains one of the most readily available editions, but *see also La Notitia Dignitatum: Nueva Edición Critica y Comenatrio Histórico: Nueva Roma* 25 (2005), which has far more useful colour plates.

4. On the shields, *see* R. Grigg, 'Inconsistency and Lassitude: The shield Emblems of the *Notitia Dignitatum*', *JRS*, 73 (1983), pp. 132–142.

5. *See* J. Matthews, 'Mauretania in Ammianus and the *Notitia*', in Goodburn & Bartholomew (1976), pp. 157–186.

6. *See* R. Tomlin, '*Notitia Dignitatum omnium, tam civilium quam militarium*', in Goodburn & Bartholomew (1976), pp. 189–209; for the problem of multiple

appointments to the same command in Egypt, *see* Jones (1964), p. 393, referring to H. Bell, V. Martin, E. Turner & D. van Berchem (eds.), *The Abinnaeus Archive* (1964) 1.

7. For the suggestion that our version was prepared by the staff of the Magister Peditum in the west, *see* J. Mann, 'What was the *Notitia Dignitatum* for?' in Goodburn & Bartholomew (1976), pp. 1–9.

8. For numbers, *see* the discussion in W. Treadgold, *Byzantium and its Army 284–1081* (1995), pp. 43–64. Agathius 5. 13. 7–8 writing in the 580s claimed that the army in earlier periods numbered 645,000; on the structure of the army more generally, *see* H. Elton, 'Military Forces', in P. Sabin, H. Van Wees & M. Whitby (eds.), *The Cambridge History of Greek and Roman Warfare*, Vol. II (2007), pp. 270–309.

9. *See* in general J. O'Flynn, *Generalissimos of the Western Roman Empire* (1983), pp. 1–24, S. Williams & G. Friell, *Theodosius: The Empire at Bay* (1994), pp. 143–158, T. Burns, *Barbarians Within the Gates of Rome* (1994), pp. 148–182, and J. Matthews, *Western Aristocracies and Imperial Court: AD 364–425* (1975), pp. 253–283.

10. *See* G. Greatrex & S. Lieu, *The Roman Eastern Frontier and the Persian Wars: Part 2: AD 363–630* (2002), pp. 17–19 for the sources for this episode.

11. On the origins of Alaric and his rebellion, *see* M. Kulikowski, *Rome's Gothic Wars* (2007), pp. 154–166, Burns (1995), pp. 156–158, 176–177, 188, H. Wolfram, *The Roman Empire and its Germanic Peoples* (1997), pp. 89–94, P. Heather, *The Goths* (1996), pp. 138–146, and *Goths and Romans, 332–489* (1991), pp. 183–188, 193+; on the role of 'barbarians' in the army *see* J. Liebeschuetz, *Barbarians and Bishops* (1990), pp. 7–88.

12. Zosimus 5. 4–8.

13. Kulikowski (2007), pp. 166–168, Burns (1995), pp. 158–163, O'Flynn (1983), pp. 27–38, and J. Bury, *History of the Later Roman Empire from the Death of Theodosius I to the Death of Justinian*, Vol. 1 (1958), pp. 115–121.

14. Zosimus 5. 11, with O'Flynn (1983), pp. 36–37, Williams & Friell (1994), pp. 148–150.

15. Zosimus 5. 13–18, with Kulikowski (2007), pp. 168–169, Burns (1995), pp. 168–178, and Bury (1958), pp. 126–137.

16. Kulikowski (2007), pp. 170–171, Burns (1995), pp. 178–193, & (1996), p. 146, & O'Flynn (1983), pp. 37–42.

17. Zosimus 5. 28 for the figure of 400,000 Goths and the thirty units in Stilicho's army; for discussion of the campaign, *see* Kulikoswki (2007), p. 171, Wolfram (1997), pp. 96–97, & Burns (1995), pp. 197–198, and n. 53, p. 356 on the Roman numbers, suggesting Stilicho may have had as few as 7,500 regulars plus a few thousand auxiliaries; for the drop in price of slaves, *see* Orosius 7. 37. 13–16.

18. Zosimus 5. 27, with M. Todd, *Roman Britain* (3rd edn, 1999), pp. 208–209, Bury (1958), pp. 169–171, O'Flynn (1983), pp. 42–44, 56, Jones (1964), pp. 185–186, and Burns (1995), pp. 208–214.

19. *See* M. Kulikowski, 'Barbarians in Gaul, Usurpers in Britain', *Britannia*, 31

(2000), pp. 325–345, W. Goffart, *Barbarian Tides: The Migration Age and the Later Roman Empire* (2006), pp. 73–118, Burns (1995), pp. 203–209, and A. Birley, *The Roman Government of Britain* (2005), pp. 455–460; J. Drinkwater, *The Alamanni and Rome 213–496: Caracalla to Clovis* (2007), pp. 323–325 suggests plausibly that there may have been some warbands of Alamanni amongst the raiders.

20. Burns (1995), pp. 214–217, Kulikowski (2007), pp. 172–173, and O'Flynn (1983), pp. 55–59; the quote was made by a senator named Lampadius and is in Zosimus 5. 29.

21. Williams & Friell (1994), pp. 157–158, O'Flynn (1983), pp. 59–62, Burns (1995), pp. 215–223, Matthews (1975), pp. 270–283, and R. Blockley, in *CAH²* XIII (1998), pp. 121–125.

16–The Sister and the Eternal City

1. Jerome, *Comm. In Ezech. I praef.*

2. Orosius 7. 43. 5–7 (translation taken from S. Oost, *Galla Placidia Augusta: A Biographical Essay* (1968), p. 124).

3. Zosimus 5. 35–37, 45, with J. Matthews, *Western Aristocracies and Imperial Court: AD 364–425* (1975), pp. 284–287, T. Burns, *Barbarians within the gates of Rome* (1995), pp. 224–233.

4. Zosimus 5. 38–44, with Burns (1995), pp. 233–239, M. Kulikowski, *Rome's Gothic Wars* (2007), pp. 173–174, and Oost (1968), pp. 89–92.

5. Matthews (1975), pp. 291–298, Burns (1995), pp. 239–242, and Kulikowski (2007), pp. 174–176.

6. Zosimus 6. 8, with Matthews (1975), pp. 298–300, and Burns (1995), pp. 242–246.

7. Zosimus 6. 13, where it is stated that Sarus had only 300 men.

8. Procopius, *History of the Wars* 3. 2. 25–26 (Loeb translation, H. Dewing (1916)).

9. *See* Burns (1995), pp. 244–245, Kulikowski (2007), pp. 6–10, 176–177, P. Heather, *The Goths* (1996), pp. 148–149, H. Wolfram, *The Roman Empire and its Germanic Peoples* (1997), pp. 99–100, and P. Heather, *The Fall of the Roman Empire: A New History* (2005), pp. 227–232.

10. *See* Oost (1968), pp. 93–104.

11. Burns (1995), pp. 247–258, J. Bury, *History of the Later Roman Empire from the Death of Theodosius I to the Death of Justinian*, Vol. 1 (1958), pp. 185–194, and R. Brockley, in *CAH²* XIII (1998), pp. 129–131.

12. Oost (1968), pp. 108–135, Burns (1995), pp. 258–261, and Heather (1995), pp. 148–149.

13. Burns (1995), pp. 261–279, Brockley, in *CAH²* XIII (1998), pp. 131–133, and Bury (1958), pp. 194–209.

14. J. O'Flynn, *Generalissimos of the Western Roman Empire* (1983), pp. 63–73, Heather (2005), pp. 236–244, 251.

15. Brockley, in *CAH²* XIII (1998), pp. 133–135.

16. Army of 40,000 is Zosimus 5. 42; the handing over of 4,000 silk tunics and 3,000 red-dyed skins is used by Burns (1995), p. 234 to conjecture that Alaric may have had about 7,000 genuine warriors.

17. Zosimus 5. 41 for the 6,000 men sent to Rome; Heather (2005), pp. 246–248 has a good introductory discussion of the apparent losses and replacements in the western army suggested by the *Notitia Dignitatum* and see also A. Jones, *The Later Roman Empire, 284–602* (1964), pp. 1425–1436 for a more detailed breakdown.

18. Orosius 7. 43, with Burns (1995), pp. 258–259; a violent argument over the oaths to Rome and earlier oaths is described in Zosimus 4. 56, and Eunapius, *fragment* 59 (60), cf. Burns (1995), p. 68.

17–The Hun

1. Callinicus, *Vita S. Hypatii* (ed. G. Bartelink), *SC* 177 (1971), p. 139. 21.

2. For a discussion of the use of the word 'Hun' before and during the First World War, *see* J. Man, *Attila: The Barbarian King who Challenged Rome* (2005), pp. 302–307. Although noting that the term was more often employed by people not directly involved in the fighting, 'Hun' did become a common slang term for German aircraft and airmen in the RFC and RNAS.

3. *See* E. Thompson, *The Huns* (1996), pp. 56–59, and on Hunnic appearance, *see* O. Maenchen-Helfen, *The World of the Huns: Studies in Their History and Culture* (1973), pp. 358–375, & Man (2005), pp. 63–66.

4. Thompson (1996), pp. 79–81, and Maenchen-Helfin (1973), pp. 94–95, 125–129.

5. Maenchen-Helfin (1973), pp. 222–23 and 367–369, P. Heather, *The Fall of the Roman Empire: A New History* (2005), pp. 148–150, and Man (2005), pp. 30–54.

6. Maenchen-Helfin (1973), pp. 11–13, 18–26, Thompson (1996), pp. 19–68.

7. Attacking Huns near the end of winter, *see* Leo, *Problemata* 7. 9; on Hunnic horses, *see* Vegetius, *Mulomedicina* 3. 6. 1– 7. 1, with Maenchen-Helfin (1973), pp. 185, 204; on saddles, *see* Maenchen-Helfin (1973), pp. 208–210; Heather (2005), p. 328 repeats the claim that each warrior required ten horses, citing R. Lindner, 'Nomadism, Huns and Horses', *Past and Present* 92 (1981), pp. 1–19.

8. On bows and archery, *see* Maenchen-Helfin (1973), pp. 221–232, Heather (2005), pp. 154–158, Man (2005), p. 97–99, N. Fields, *The Hun: Scourge of God AD 375–565* (2006), pp. 30–32, 39–46, M. Bishop & J. Coulston, *Roman Military Equipment from the Punic Wars to the Fall of Rome* (2nd edn, 2006), pp. 88, 134–135, 164–168, 205–206, J. Coulston, 'Roman Archery Equipment', in M. Bishop (ed.), *The Production and Distribution of Roman Military Equipment* (1985), pp. 230–348; for effectiveness, *see* W. McLeod, 'The Range of the Ancient Bow', *Phoenix*, 19 (1965), pp. 1–14; for modern reconstructions and techniques, *see* L. Kassai, *Horseback Archery* (2002).

9. H. Elton, *Warfare in Roman Europe: AD 350–425* (1996), pp. 26–28 discusses the possibility that Hunnic lifestyle changed as they settled near the empire.

10. E.g., the generic account in Man (2005), pp. 100–103, and cf. Heather (2005), pp. 156–157.

11. *See* M. Whitby, in *CAH*² XIV (2000), pp. 704–712.

12. Maenchen-Helfin (1973), pp. 74–94, Thompson (1996), pp. 30–45, and A. Lee, in *CAH*² XIV (2000), pp. 40–41.

13. Maenchen-Helfin (1973), pp. 109–110, Thompson (1996), pp. 87–89.

14. *See* Maenchen-Helfin (1973), pp. 108–120, Thompson (1996), pp. 89–95 and Whitby, in *CAH*² XIV (2000), pp. 708–709 on sieges, with references to Priscus *fragment* 6. 2 (= Brockley 54, who suggested alternative section divisions), Jordannes, *Getica* 42. 220–221, and Procopius, *Wars* 3. 4. 30–5; on the bones at Naissus, *see* Priscus *Excerpta de legationibus Romanorum ad gentes* 123.

15. On demands for return of deserters, *see* Whitby, in *CAH*² XIV (2000), p. 705.

16. Maenchen-Helfin (1973), pp. 120–121, Thompson (1996), pp. 98–103, and J. Bury, *History of the Later Roman Empire from the Death of Theodosius I to the Death of Justinian*, Vol. 1 (1958), pp. 271–276.

17. Maenchen-Helfin (1973), pp. 123–125, Thompson (1996), pp. 104–108, and R. Blockley, *East Roman Foreign Policy* (1992), pp. 63–64.

18. On taxation of the Senate, *see* Priscus, *fragment* 9. 3. 22–33 and the comments on his attitude in Thompson (1996), pp. 203–224; on sending of frequent embassies, *see* Maenchen-Helfin (1973), pp. 185, Thompson (1996), pp. 95–97, with Priscus, *fragments* 5M. 1–10; on Attila's diplomacy, *see* also Whitby, in *CAH*² XIV (2000), pp. 706–708.

19. Bury (1958), pp. 279–288 provides a full and lively translation of this remarkable passage.

20. Thompson (1996), pp. 140–141.

21. Bury (1958), p. 287 slightly mod.

22. Maenchen-Helfin (1973), pp. 195–196, Thompson (1996), pp. 112–136, and Heather (2005), pp. 313–320, 322–324.

23. H. Wolfram, *The Roman Empire and its Germanic Peoples* (1997), pp. 123–136.

24. Bury (1958), pp. 240–244, Heather (2005), pp. 281–282, Thompson (1996), pp. 38–40, 54–56, 60, and Maenchen-Helfin (1973), pp. 33–35, 49–50; on Aetius and other Roman generals in this period, *see* P. McGeorge, *Late Roman Warlords* (2003), *passim.*

25. *See* P. Heather, in *CAH*² XIV (2000), pp. 5–8, Bury (1958), pp. 247–249, Maenchen-Helfin (1973), pp. 63–65.

26. *See* Heather (2005), pp. 266–272, Bury (1958), pp. 244–247, Wolfram (1997), pp. 165–167, and M. Todd, *The Early Germans* (2nd edn, 2004), pp. 175–178; for the figure of 80,000 for Vandal numbers, *see* Victor of Vita, *History of the Vandal Persecutions* 1. 1.

27. Procopius, *Wars* 3. 3. 22–30 claims that Boniface invited the Vandals into Africa, hoping to use them as allies in his struggle with Aetius, but subsequently repented of the decision; on St Augustine's letters, *see* Heather (2005), pp. 267 &

271; examples of letters written in these years include Augustine, *Ep.* 220, 229–231.

28. Heather (2005), pp. 272–280, and in *CAH²* XIV (2000), pp. 10–12, 288–299, Bury (1958), pp. 254–260, and A. Jones, *The Later Roman Empire, 284–602* (1964), pp. 190, 204–208.

29. Heather (2005), pp. 281–289, Maenchen-Helfin (1973), pp. 64–70, Thompson (1996), pp. 71–79; quote from Merbaudes, *Panegyric* 1.

30. Maenchen-Helfin (1973), pp. 129–132, Thompson (1996), pp. 143–148, Heather (2005), pp. 333–337, and Jones (1964), p. 194.

31. Thompson (1996), pp. 148–156, Bury (1958), pp. 288–294, and Heather (2005), pp. 336–339.

32. Maenchen-Helfin (1973), pp. 131–142, Thompson (1996), pp. 156–163, Bury (1958), pp. 294–296, and Heather (2005), pp. 339–342.

33. Maenchen-Helfin (1973), pp. 143–162, Thompson (1996), pp. 163–176, Burns (1958), pp. 296–298, and Whitby in *CAH²* XIV (2000), pp. 712–713.

34. Bury (1958), pp. 298–300, & Heather (2005), pp. 369–375.

18–Sunset on an Outpost of Empire

1. Zosimus, *Historia Nova* 6. 5 (trans. Ridley).

2. Procopius, *History of the Wars: The Vandal War* 3. 2. 38 (Loeb translation, H. Dewing).

3. Gildas, *De Excidio* 20. 1, 23–26. 1; for discussion of this and other sources, *see* A. Birley, *The Roman Government of Britain* (2005), pp. 461–465.

4. On the literary sources, *see* A. Esmonde Cleary, *The Ending of Roman Britain* (1989), pp. x, 162–165, & C. Snyder, *An Age of Tyrants: Britain and the Britons ad 400–600* (1998), *passim*, but esp. pp. 29–49, and K. Dark, *Britain and the End of the Roman Empire* (2000), pp. 27–48.

5. Dark (2000), p. 60, and Snyder (1998), p. 68.

6. For emphasis on the wider context of Britain within the empire, see esp. Dark (2000), Esmonde Cleary (1989), and N. Faulkner, *The Decline and Fall of Roman Britain* (2nd edn, 2004).

7. For Roman Britain in general, *see* S. Frere, *Britannia* (3rd edn, 1987), P. Salway, *Roman Britain* (1998), M. Todd, *Roman Britain* (3rd edn, 1999), and M. Millett, *Roman Britain* (1995).

8. On the size of the army in the second century, *see* A. Birley, 'The Economic Effects of Roman Frontier Policy', in A. King & M. Henig (eds.), *The Roman West in the Third Century*, BAR 109 (1981), p. 40; on the smaller size of third-century barrack blocks, *see* N. Hodgson & P. Bidwell, 'Auxiliary barracks in a New Light: Recent Discoveries on Hadrian's Wall', *Britannia* 35 (2004), pp. 121–157, esp. 147–154.

9. On the cathedral, *see* Dark (2000), pp. 50–51; on 'small towns', *see* the papers in T. Rodwell & T. Rowley (eds.), *Small Towns of Roman Britain*, BAR 15 (1975), and more generally J. Wacher, *The Towns of Roman Britain* (2nd edn., 1995).

10. Faulkner (2004), pp. 27–30, J. Manley, *AD 43: The Roman Invasion of Britain: A Reassessment* (2002), 64–5, 111–128; the inscription is *RIB* 91.

11. Quotes from D. Mattingly, *An Imperial Possession: Britain in the Roman Empire, 54 BC–AD 409* (2006), pp. 20 & 12; *see also* the review of this work including M. Beard, *The Times Literary Supplement*, 4 October 2006, and S. Ireland, *JRS*, 97 (2007), pp. 364–366.

12. On the organisation of the diocese and provinces, *see* S. Johnson, *Later Roman Britain* (1980), pp. 4–31, Todd (1999), pp. 179–203, Esmonde Cleary (1989), pp. 41–130, and Snyder (1998), pp. 3–16; on the army, *see* S. James, 'Britain and the Late Roman Army', in T. Blagg & A. King, *Military and Civilian in Roman Britain: Cultural Relationships in a Frontier Province* (1984), pp. 161–186. This remains an excellent article although the concept of chalet-barracks has now been discredited by Hodgson & Bidwell (2004).

13. On the Picts and other northern peoples, *see* Mattingly (2006), p. 436, Johnson (1980), pp. 51–64, and Dark (2000), pp. 211–214; for an introduction to the problems of dating St Patrick and some discussion of his life, *see* C. Thomas, 'Saint Patrick and Fifth-Century Britain: An Historical Model Explored', in P. Casey (ed.) *The End of Roman Britain* (1979), pp. 81–101, and St Patrick *Confessions* 1.

14. Ammianus Marcellinus 27. 8. 5.

15. For discussion of this question, *see* J. Coterill, 'Saxon Raiding and the Role of the Late Roman Coastal Forts of Britain', *Britannia*, 24 (1993), pp. 227–239, A. Pearson, 'Piracy in Late Roman Britain: A Perspective from the Viking Age', *Britannia* 37 (2006), pp. 337–353, J. Haywood, *Dark Age Naval Power: A Reassessment of Frankish and Anglo-Saxon Seafaring Activity* (1991), esp. pp. 15–76, and G. Grainge, *The Roman Invasions of Britain* (2005), pp. 141–160; Haywood (1991), pp. 18–22 on the question of sails and the carving from Denmark.

16. Vegetius, *Epitoma Rei Militaris* 4. 37.

17. *See* S. Johnson, *The Roman Forts of the Saxon Shore* (1976), and A. Pearson, *The Roman Shore Forts* (2002), for contrasting views of the functions of the forts.

18. On the state of the towns, *see* Esmonde Cleary (1989), pp. 131–133, Mattingly (2006), pp. 325–350, Faulkner (2004), pp. 169–185, Johnson (1980), pp. 91–97, Todd (1999), pp. 210–212.

19. Esmonde Cleary (1989), pp. 134–136, Mattingly (2006), pp. 368–370, Faulkner (2004), pp. 185–220, and Todd (1999), pp. 221–229; on Christianity, *see* Dark (2000), pp. 18–20.

20. Zosimus, *Historia Nova* 6. 5, 6, 10, with contrasting comments in Birley (2005), pp. 461–465, Snyder (1998), p. 24.

21. Esmonde Cleary (1989), pp. 136–143, Faulkner (2004), pp. 242–262, Mattingly (2006), pp. 529–539, Snyder (1998), pp. 17–25, and Johnson (1980), pp. 104–110.

22. On terminology, *see* esp. Snyder (1998), pp. 81–127.

23. For discussion of the Gallic Chronicle of 452, *see* R. Burgess, 'The Dark Ages Return to Fifth century Britain: The restored Gallic Chronicle Exploded',

Britannia, 21 (1990), pp. 185–195, with the reply by M. Jones & P. Casey, 'The Gallic Chronicle Exploded?', *Britannia*, 22 (1991), pp. 212–215. The relevant entry is for Honorius XVI.

24. K. Dark, 'A Sub-Roman Re-Defence of Hadrian's Wall?', *Britannia* 23 (1992), pp. 111–120.

25. Esmonde Cleary (1989), pp. 144–161, 172–185.

26. *See* Dark (2000), esp. pp. 150–192.

27. *See* I. Wood, 'The Fall of the Western Empire and the End of Roman Britain', *Britannia*, 18 (1987), pp. 251–262, Snyder (1998), pp. 37–40, and Johnson (1980), pp. 115–116.

28. For Pelagianism in general, *see* H. Chadwick, in *CAH²* XIII (1998), pp. 288–292; on St Germanus and the Pelagians, *see* I. Wood, 'The End of Roman Britain: Continental Evidence and Parallels', in M. Lapidge & D. Dumville (eds.), *Gildas: New Approaches* (1984), pp. 1–25, esp. 12–13.

29. For an excellent and insightful survey of the academic debate over Saxon settlement, *see* G. Halsall, *Barbarian Migrations and the Roman West, 376–568* (2007), pp. 357–370.

30. *See* the varying views in Johnson (1980), pp. 104–147, Dark (2000), pp. 58–104, and H. Wolfram, *The Roman Empire and its Germanic Peoples* (1997), pp. 240–247.

31. *See* Wolfram (1997), pp. 244–247, and Johnson (1980), pp. 119–123; The Gallic Chronicle of 452 lists under 441 (Theodosius II XVIII) that Britain fell under the control of the Saxons.

32. M. Todd, *The Early Germans* (2nd edn, 2004), pp. 202–210.

33. Sidonius Apollinaris, *Epistolae* 3. 9. 1–2 for Riothamus, with Snyder (1998), pp. 82–83; St Patrick, *Epistola* 6 for the British King Coroticus.

34. For the suggestion of Christian survival in the south-east, *see* Dark (2000), pp. 78–85.

35. On Britons and their sense of identity, *see* Snyder (1998), pp. 66–72.

36. There is a good brief introduction to the evidence and the academic attitude to Arthur in Snyder (1998), pp. 253–255. J. Morris, *The Age of Arthur: A History of the British Isles from 350 to 650* (1973) remains a good read, but has not always dated well.

19–Emperors, Kings and Warlords

1. Salvian, *De Gubernatione Dei* 4. 30, with J. Bury, *History of the Later Roman Empire from the Death of Theodosius I to the Death of Justinian* (1958), p. 308.

2. Procopius, *Wars* 3. 4. 37–38.

3. For the Vandal sack of Rome in general, *see* Bury (1958), pp. 323–326, A. Jones, *The Later Roman Empire, 284–602* (1964), p. 240, P. Barnwell, *Emperors, Prefects and Kings: The Roman West, 395–565* (1992), pp. 116–117, B. Ward-Perkins, *The Fall of Rome and the End of Civilization* (2005), p. 17, citing Victor of Vita, *Vandal Persecution* 1. 25 for the ransoming of captives, and P. Heather, *The Fall of the Roman Empire: A New History* (2005), pp. 378–379; for the sack

and the death of Petronius, *see* Priscus, *fragment* 30. 2, John of Antioch 201, Procopius, *Wars* 3. 4. 36–5. 5, and Sidonius Apollinaris, *Letters* 2. 13.

4. Barnwell (1992), pp. 61–62.

5. Bury (1958), pp. 326–328, Jones (1964), pp. 240–241, and Heather (2005), pp. 375–384, 390–391; on rumours of foul play in the death of Avitus see John of Antioch, *fragment* 86.

6. *See* M. Todd, *The Early Germans* (2nd edn, 2004), pp. 152–154, 172–175, and P. Heather, *The Goths* (1996), pp. 187–191, 194–198, and in *CAH*² XIV (2000), p. 22.

7. Bury (1958), pp. 330–332, and Heather in *CAH*² XIV (2000), p. 23.

8. For discussion, *see* Heather (2005), pp. 343–348 and in *CAH*² XIV (2000) pp. 19–23.

9. Heather (2005), pp. 392–407, and Burns (1958), pp. 332–337.

10. Ward-Perkins (2005), pp. 45–46, 54, Heather (2005), pp. 282–283, and I. Wood, in *CAH*² XIV (2000), pp. 502–505.

11. For discussion, *see* J. Drinkwater, 'The Bacaudae of Fifth Century Gaul', in J. Drinkwater & H. Elton (eds.), *Fifth Century Gaul* (1992), pp. 208–217.

12. *See* A. Lee in *CAH*² XIV (2000), pp. 45–48, and Bury (1958), pp. 316–321.

13. In general, *see* Bury (1958), pp. 348–388, and S. Mitchell, *A History of the Later Roman Empire, AD 284–641* (2007), pp. 289–293; for more detail, *see* P. Allen, in *CAH*² XIV (2000), pp. 811–820, and W. Treadgold, *A History of Byzantine State and Society* (1997), esp. pp. 1–241.

14. Mitchell (2007), pp. 275, 290, 320, and Bury (1958), pp. 215–221.

15. Sidonius Apollinaris, *Letters* 1. 2. 2–3 (Loeb translation, W. Anderson, 1936).

16. Sidonius Apollinaris, *Letters* 1. 2. 4.

17. Heather (2005), pp. 375–384, Mitchell (2007), pp. 205–208, and esp. J. Harries, *Sidonius Apollinaris and the Fall of Rome, ad 407–485* (1994).

18. Sidonius Apollinaris, *Letters* 2. 1. 1–8, and for the quoted sections 2. 9. 8–9 (Loeb translation).

19. Ward-Perkins (2005), pp. 54–56, Heather (2005), pp. 419–423, and Bury (1958), pp. 342–343; *see also* Sidonius Apollinaris, *Letters* 7. 7. 2–6 on his anger at the handover of Clermont by Nepos, & 8. 3. 2, which describes the Gothic women.

20. Eugippius, *The Life of St Severinus* 4. 1.

21. Eugippius, *The Life of St Severinus* 20. 1–2 (translation L. Bieler with L. Krestan, The Catholic University of America Press, 1965).

22. Eugippius, *The Life of St Severinus* 1. 4–2. 2.

23. *See* Heather (2005), pp. 407–415, and Ward–Perkins (2005), pp. 17–20, 134–136; for King Feva, *see* Eugippius, *The Life of St Severinus* 8. 1, 22. 2, 31. 1–6, 40. 1–3, 42. 8, 44. 4.

24. *See* Bury (1958), pp. 338–341, and Heather (2005), pp. 425–426.

25. Bury (1958), pp. 389–394, 404–406, Heather (2005), p. 426, Jones (1965), pp. 243–245, and Lee, in *CAH*² XIV (2000), pp. 49–52.

26. Heather (2005), pp. 428–430, Bury (1958), pp. 405–411, and Jones (1965), pp. 244–245.

27. On Odoacer, *see* H. Wolfram, *The Roman Empire and its Germanic Peoples* (1997), pp. 183–188; on the significance of 476, *see* B. Croke, 'AD 476–the manufacture of a turning point', *Chiron*, 73 (1983), pp. 81–119.

28. *See* M. Humphries, in *CAH*² XIV (2000), pp. 528–530, Bury (1958), pp. 422–426, and Heather (1996), pp. 216–220.

20–West and East

1. Procopius, *Wars* 5. 1. 25–27 (Loeb translation, H. Dewing).

2. Cassiodorus, *Variae* 1. 1.

3. A good introduction to such ideas is provided by the collection of extracts and articles published in T. Noble (ed.), *From Roman Provinces to Medieval Kingdoms* (2006); the work of P. Brown has also been massively influential, beginning with *The World of Late Antiquity: From Marcus Aurelius to Muhammad* (1971).

4. For an excellent discussion of warfare in this period, *see* G. Halsall, *Warfare and Society in the Barbarian West, 450–900* (2003); for a more general survey of developments throughout the empire, *see* J. Moorhead, *The Roman Empire Divided 400–700* (2001), and G. Halsall, *Barbarian Migrations and the Roman West, 376–568* (2007), pp. 284–357.

5. Suetonius, *Tiberius*, 32.

6. E.g., *see* J. Moorhead, *Theodoric in Italy* (1992), pp. 66–68, and P. Heather, *The Goths* (1996), pp. 236–242.

7. Sidonius Apollinaris, *Letters* 5. 5 on the friend fluent in the Burgundian language, and *Carmen* 5. 238–242 for using butter on hair; for Catholics dressed in Vandal fashion, *see* Victor Vitalis, *History* 2. 8.

8. The main advocate of transferral of tax revenue rather than land itself is W. Goffart, *Barbarians and Romans: The Techniques of Accommodation Revisited* (1980), who staunchly defends his position in *Barbarian Tides: The Migration Age and the Later Roman Empire* (2006), pp. 119–186. For the opposing view, *see* the insightful comments of W. Liebeschuetz, 'Cities, Taxes, and the Accommodation of the Barbarians: The Theories of Durliat and Goffart', in Noble (2006), pp. 309–323. For Theodoric's propaganda about the roles of Goths and Romans, *see* Moorhead (1992), pp. p. 71–75, and in more detail, P. Amory, *People and Identity in Ostrogothic Italy, 489–554* (1997), pp. 43–85. The quotation is from Cassiodorus, *Variae* 12. 5. 4.

9. Moorhead (1992), pp. 75–80, and T. Charles–Edwards, in *CAH*² XIV (2000), pp. 260–271.

10. *See* Moorhead (2001), pp. 54–56, 58–60, and Moorhead (1992), pp. 95–97, Amory (1997), pp. 195–276, Heather (1996), pp. 245–258, and Todd, *The Early Germans* (2nd edn, 2004), pp. 150–163, 166–171, 177–178, and H. Wolfram, *The Roman Empire and its Germanic Peoples* (1997), pp. 169–182, 199–213.

11. *See* Moorhead (1992), pp. 1–31, and Wolfram (1997), pp. 199–203; on the *legi* story, *see* anonymous Valesianus 79, with analysis in Moorhead (1992), PP. 104–105.

12. Sidonius Apollinaris, *Letters* 1. 2. 4, with P. Barnwell, *Emperors, Prefects and Kings: The Roman West, 395–565* (1992), pp. 73–74, 129–145; on legislation, *see* Charles-Edwards, in *CAH² XIV* (2000), pp. 260–287.

13. For a much fuller consideration of the impact on material culture of the fall of Rome, *see* B. Ward-Perkins, *The Fall of Rome and the End of Civilization* (2005), pp. 87–168. Although there may be some regional and local exceptions to the bleak picture he paints, the overall argument is highly convincing. For a discussion of the western provinces in the fourth and fifth centuries, *see* E. Swift, *The End of the Western Roman Empire: An Archaeological Investigation* (2000), arguing that the change from Roman to barbarian rule is not always obvious in the archaeological record.

14. *See also* B. Ward-Perkins, in *CAH² XIV* (2000), pp. 346–391 on the overall economic picture.

15. *See* A. Lee, in *CAH² XIV* (2000), pp. 49–52, M. Whitby, in *CAH² XIV* (2000), pp. 712–714, J. Bury, *History of the Later Roman Empire from the Death of Theodosius I to the Death of Justinian* (1958), pp. 389–396, 411–422 and A. Jones, *The Later Roman Empire 284–602* (1964), pp. 224–227.

16. Bury (1958), pp. 397–400, and Jones (1965), pp. 228–229.

17. Jones (1965), pp. 230–337, Lee, in *CAH² XIV* (2000), pp. 52–62, and Bury (1958), pp. 429–452; on the rebellion in Isauria against Anastasius, *see* F. Haarer, *Anastasius I: Politics and Empire in the Late Roman World* (2006), pp. 11–28.

18. W. Treadgold, *Byzantium and its Army, 284–1081* (1995), pp. 13–15, 149–157 on the army; for the administration, *see* in general C. Kelly, *Ruling the Later Roman Empire* (2004).

19. E.g., P. Heather, *The Fall of the Roman Empire: A NewHhistory* (2005), pp. 443–449.

20. *See* Ward-Perkins (2005), pp. 57–62.

21. *See* Heather (2005), pp. 110–115, discussing the pioneering work of G. Tchalenko, *Villages Antiques de la Syrie du Nord* (1953–1958); *see also* C. Roueché, in *CAH² XIV* (2000), pp. 583–585, Ward-Perkins, in *CAH² XIV* (2000), pp. 328–332, and esp. C. Foss, 'Syria in Transition, AD 550–750: An Archaeological Approach', *Dumbarton Oaks Papers*, 51 (1997), pp. 189–269.

22. *See* Moorhead (2001), pp. 186–188.

23. Moorhead (1992), pp. 144–147.

24. On Clovis, *see* R. Collins, in *CAH² XIV* (2000), p. 118.

21–Rise and Fall

1. *Nov.* 30. 11. 2 (translation from J. Evans, *The Age of Justinian: The Circumstances of Imperial Power* (1996), p. 126).

2. On Anastasius, *see* F. Haarer, *Anastasius I: Politics and Empire in the Late Roman World* (2006); on the succession, *see* J. Moorhead, *Justinian* (1994), pp. 14–18, Evans (1996), pp. 96–98, and J. Bury, *History of the Later Roman Empire from the Death of Theodosius I to the Death of Justinian* (1958), pp. 16–21; on his rise to power, *see* G. Greatrex, 'The Early Years of Justin in the Sources',

Electrum, 12 (2007), pp. 99–115; on his lack of education, *see* Procopius, *Secret History* 6. 19, 11. 5, 12. 29, and John Lydus, *On the magistracies* 3. 51.

3. Moorhead (1994), pp. 15–16, 17–18, 21–22, Evans (1996), p. 97, M. Maas, 'Roman Questions, Byzantine Answers: Contours of the Age of Justinian', in M. Maas (ed.), *The Cambridge Companion to the Age of Justinian* (2005), pp. 3–27, esp. 5–6, Bury (1958), pp. 20–21, 23–27, and A. Cameron, in *CAH*² XIV (2000), pp. 63–67; cf. Procopius, *Wars* 3. 9. 5.

4. Evans (1996), pp. 101–102, with Procopius, *Secret History* 30. 21–26.

5. J. Evans, *The Empress Theodora: Partner of Justinian* (2002), pp. 13–24, and Evans (1996), pp. 98–101, and Moorhead (1994), pp. 19–21.

6. Moorhead (1994), pp. 38–40, Evans (1996), p. 104, 138, 145–146, 152, 196–197, and Evans (2002), pp. 48–58; Procopius, *Secret History* 17. 32–36 tells of the three former actresses brought to live in the palace.

7. J. Howard-Johnston, 'The Two Great Powers in Late Antiquity: A Comparison', in A. Cameron (ed.), *The Byzantine and Early Islamic Near East III: States Resources and Armies* (1995), pp. 157–226, also reprinted in A. Howard-Johnston, *Early Rome, Sassanian Persia and the End of Antiquity* (2006); *see also* G. Greatrex, 'Byzantium and the East in the Sixth Century', in Maas (ed.) (2005), pp. 477–509, and Moorhead (1994), pp. 89–95.

8. G. Greatrex, *Rome and Persia at War, 502–532* (1998), pp. 43–59.

9. Greatrex (1998), pp. 14–17 on the question of the Caspian Gates; for the Anastasian war *see* Greatrex (1998), pp. 73–119, with sources in G. Greatrex & S. Lieu, *The Roman Eastern Frontier and the Persian Wars: Part 2 AD 363–630* (2002), pp. 62–77.

10. Procopius, *Wars* 1. 11. 1–39, with Greatrex (1998), pp. 134–138.

11. Greatrex (1998), pp. 139–221, with sources in Greatrex & Lieu (2002), pp. 82–101; on Dara and Callinicum, *see also* J. Haldon, *The Byzantine Wars* (2001), pp. 23–35, and A. Goldsworthy, *In the Name of Rome* (2003), pp. 363–371; an excellent article by C. Lillington-Martin, 'Archaeological and Ancient Literary Evidence for a Battle near Dara Gap, Turkey, AD 530', in A. Lewin & P. Pellegrini, (eds.), *The Late Roman Army in the Near East from Diocletian to the Arab Conquest* (Oxford, 2007), pp. 299–311.

12. Greatrex (2005), pp. 488–489, with Greatrex & Lieu (2002), pp. 102–111.

13. *See* P. Holden, 'Mediterranean Plague in the Age of Justinian', in Maas (ed.) (2005), pp. 134–160, B. Ward-Perkins, in *CAH*² XIV (2000), pp. 388–389, and Evans (1996), pp. 160–165; one of the most famous and detailed contemporary accounts is Procopius, *Wars* 2. 22. 1–23. 21.

14. Greatrex & Lieu (2002), pp.111–134; on allies, *see* Greatrex (1998), pp. 25–31 and (2005), pp. 490–503.

15. Evans (1996), pp. 168–169.

16. On the size of armies see Howard-Johnston (1995), pp. 165–169, and Greatrex (1998), pp. 31–34; on the Balkan frontier, *see* Moorhead (1994), pp. 145–162.

17. On the debate over risking the expedition to Africa, *see* Procopius, *Wars* 3. 10. 1–34.

18. On the Vandal War, *see* Moorhead (1994), pp. 64–70, and Evans (1996),

pp. 126–133; for Justinian's western campaigns in general, *see* W. Pohl, 'Justinian and the Barbarian Kingdoms', in Maas (ed.) (2005), pp. 448–476, and G. Halsall, *Barbarian Migrations and the Roman West, 376–568* (2007), pp. 499–518; for the triumph, *see* Procopius, *Wars* 4. 9. 1–16.

19. *See* H. Wolfram, *The Roman Empire and its Germanic Peoples* (1997), pp. 224–227, M. Humphries, in *CAH²* XIV (2000), pp. 533–535, and P. Heather, *The Goths* (1996), pp. 253–255.

20. Moorhead (1994), pp. 72–86 and Evans (1996), pp. 139–151, 153–154, 199; *see* Procopius, *Wars* 7. 1. 31–33 on the career of the notorious Alexander 'the scissors' for an example of the brutality of some of Justinian's officials, cf. A. Jones, *The Later Roman Empire, 284–602* (1964), p. 289.

21. On army discipline, *see* Haldon (2001), pp. 24–28, and Goldsworthy (2003), pp. 370–376; for examples of poor discipline, *see* Procopius, *Wars* 4. 4. 3–7, 3. 23–4. 25, 14. 7–15. 49, 5. 8. 5–10, 28. 1–29. 50.

22. Evans (1996), pp. 176–181, Moorhead (1994), pp. 107–109, Wolfram (1997), pp. 233–239, and Haldon (2001), pp. 37–40.

23. Haldon (2001), pp. 40–44.

24. *See* Moorhead (1994), pp. 109–115, Evans (1996), pp. 265–266, and Humphries, in *CAH²* XIV (2000), pp. 535–551.

25. For a discussion of administration and its failings and abuses, *see* Jones (1964), pp. 294–296; on friction caused to allies by the presence of Roman officials and troops one example is Lazica, for which *see* the summary in Greatrex (2005), pp. 497–499.

26. Moorhead (1994), pp. 40–49, Evans (1996), pp. 119–125, and (2002), pp. 40–47, and in detail, G. Greatrex, 'The *Nika* Riot: A Reappraisal', *Journal of Hellenic Studies*, 117 (1997), pp. 60–86; the quotation comes from Procopius, *Wars* 1. 24. 37.

27. For Belisarius being offered the throne, *see* Procopius, *Wars* 6. 29. 1–20, with Moorhead (1994), pp. 85–86, and Evans (1996), p. 150; on Theodora's plot against John, *see* Evans (2002), pp. 54–56.

28. Evans (1996), pp. 44–46, 194–195, and C. Kelly, *Ruling the Later Roman Empire* (2004), pp. 83–85, 95–104.

29. C. Humfress, 'Law and Legal Practice in the Age of Justinian', in Maas (ed.) (2005), pp. 161–184, Moorhead (1994), pp. 32–38, and D. Liebs, in *CAH²* XIV (2000), pp. 247–252.

30. For Justinian and the Church, *see* P. Gray, 'The Legacy of Chalcedon: Christological Problems and Their Significance', in Maas (ed.) (2005), pp. 215–238, C. Sotinel, 'Emperors and Popes in the Sixth Century: The Western View', in Maas (ed.) (2005), pp. 267–290, Moorhead (1994), pp. 116–143, Evans (1996), pp. 183–192, and P. Allen in *CAH²* XIV (2000), pp. 820–834.

31. Evans (1996), pp. 65–71, and C. Wildberg, 'Philosophy on the Age of Justinian', in Maas (ed.) (2005), pp. 316–340.

32. *See* K. Holum, 'The Classical City in the Sixth Century: Survival and Transformation', in Maas (ed.) (2005), pp. 87–112, and W. Liebeschuetz, *The Decline and Fall of the Classical City* (2001), pp. 223–248, 284–317; for eastern

Roman culture and society in general C. Mango, *Byzantium: The Empire of the New Rome* (1980) presents a wide-ranging survey.

33. Mango (1980), p. 1.

34. On the period in general, *see* M. Whitby, in *CAH²* XIV (2000), pp. 86–111; on Justin's aggression against Persia, *see* Greatrex (2005), pp. 489–490.

35. On the fall of the Roman provinces to Persia and the Roman recovery, *see* the sources in Greatrex & Lieu (2002), pp. 182–228.

36. *See* J. Moorhead, *The Roman Empire Divided 400–700* (2001), pp. 194–227, and F. Donner, 'The Background to Islam', in Maas (ed.) (2005), pp. 510–533.

Conclusion – A Simple Answer

1. This theme is most fully explored in R. MacMullen, *Corruption and Decline of Rome* (1988).

2. E.g., J. Drinkwater, 'The Principate – Lifebelt or Millstone Around the Neck of Empire?', in O. Hekster, G. Kleijn & D. Slootjes (eds.), *Crises and the Roman Empire* (2007), pp. 67–74.

Epilogue – An Even Simpler Moral

1. C. Murphy, *Are We Rome? The Fall of an Empire and the Fate of America* (2007), *passim*, but esp. pp. 189–195; an earlier attempt at drawing clear lessons for the modern USA – then still engaged in the Cold War – is E. Luttwak, *The Grand Strategy of the Roman Empire from the First Century* AD *to the Third* (1976).

2. I can remember over a decade ago working in a university and noticing a framed sign in the staff canteen. It was a mission statement, detailing the acceptable length of a queue and other vital details by which the success or failure of the management could be judged. Clearly, considerable effort had gone into the document, whose purpose was to make complicated the quite staggeringly obvious. Of course, it provided something to measure in place of an intelligent and informed impression.

Index

Abrittus 103–104, 111
Ad Salices 254–255, 260
Adrianople 178, 253, 258, 281, 294
  disaster 245, 255, 257–258, 259, 260,
  262
Aemilianus 100, 111
Aetius, Flavius 327, 328, 329, 331, 332,
  354, 355, 356, 358, 366, 384
  and Britain 335–336
  and the Huns 327–328, 330, 333
  murder of 333
Africa see North Africa
agents (agentes in rebus) 242
Agri Decumates 105, 120, 121
agriculture 107, 143, 275
Agrippina 79
Ahura-Mazda 89
Aila (Aqaba) 273
Alamanni tribe 104, 109–110, 215, 216,
  217–218, 221, 240, 255, 258, 330,
  365, 372
Alamannic state 370
Alans 248, 253, 257, 259, 295–296,
  303, 304, 318, 319, 328–329,
  332
Alaric 291–292, 293–295, 296, 298,
  299, 300, 301, 302, 307, 310, 346,
  387
  movements including sack of
  Rome 297
Alavivus 249, 253
Alba 67, 68, 71
Albinus, Decimus Clodius 65, 66, 75,
  83
Alexander, Domitius 177

Alexander, Severus see Severus
  Alexander
Alexander the Great 74, 84, 89, 192,
  229, 232, 272
Alexandria 74, 129, 161, 361, 385, 389
  population 42
  Temple of Serapis 280
Alexandria, bishop of 277, 278,
  361–362
Allectus 161, 340
amber 48, 107
Ambrose, Bishop of Milan 276,
  278–279, 362
Amida 391
  siege of (359) 227–228
Ammianus Marcellinus 198–199, 211,
  223, 235, 236, 237, 286, 341
  and Adrianople disaster 245, 255,
  258
  and Constantius II 203–204
  and Corbulo 202–203
  on Gaul 215, 216, 218, 219, 220, 221
  and the Goths 249, 251, 252, 255,
  258, 259
  and Julian 224
  and Persian war 227, 228, 229,
  234–235
  and Silvanus 201, 202
amphorae 47
Anastasius 381, 383, 384, 388, 391, 392
  nephew 400
Ancyra 237
Angles 348–349
Anglo-Saxons 349, 376
Anthemius 359, 366

Antioch 42, 76, 78–79, 100, 101, 128, 136, 139, 162–163, 179, 187, 197, 229, 237, 247, 249, 274, 381, 392, 403
Antioch, bishop of 278
Antonina 400
Antonines 50
Antoninus Pius 39, 150, 151
    daughter 53
Antony, Mark 37, 70
apartment blocks (*insulae*) 42
Aper 134
Aqaba (Aila) 273
Aquileia 196, 262, 332
    attack on (170) 51
    siege of 92–93
Aquilia Severa 79–80
Aquitania 303, 328, 355
Aquitania Secunda 304
Arab conquests 403–404
Arab groups 393
Arbogast, Master of Soldiers 262
Arcadius 261, 262, 264, 290, 292, 296
Ardashir I, King of Persia 88–89, 91–92, 93, 135, 136, 137, 181
Arelate (Arles) 303, 331, 355, 364
Argentorate (Strasbourg) 217–218, 221, 258
Ariadne 381
Arianism 238, 277, 279, 281, 376
Arians 188, 278, 281, 376
Ariminum (Rimini) 300
Aristides, Aelius 37
aristocrats 275–276
    local 34, 40
    tribal 221
Arius 188
Arles (Arelate) 303, 331, 355, 364
Armenia 36, 50, 91, 94, 100, 136, 173, 183, 234, 238, 247, 271, 272, 403
Arminius 106–107
Arria, Aurelia 88
Arsaces, King of Armenia 271

Arsacid family 88, 91
art, emperors in 157–158
Artabanus V of Parthia 88
Arthur 336, 352
Asdings 295–296
Asia Minor 128, 132, 133, 139, 361
Aspar, general 356, 361, 367
assassinations 152
Assyria 393
Astarte (god) 81
Athanaric, King of the Tervingi 247, 249
Athaulf 299, 300, 302, 303–304, 307, 312, 331
Athens 35, 41, 115
    philosophical schools 401
    sack of (267) 103, 114
Attalus, Priscus 300–301, 304
Attila the Hun 314, 315, 316, 319–320, 322, 323, 382, 406
    and Aetius 331
    appearance 326
    assassination plots 326–327
    attacks the western empire 331–332
    death of 333
    demands for gold 320, 323, 325, 326
    empire 315
    meets Roman ambassadors 324, 325–326
Augsburg (Augusta Vindelicum) 111
Augusta Emerita (Merida) 328, 378
Augusta Vindelicum (Augsburg) 111
Augustus (Octavian) 70, 83, 104, 105, 110, 129, 148, 150, 152, 158, 163, 168, 173, 203, 337, 412
    creates Principate 64
    and equestrians 39
    and appointment of new Senators 38
    'restoration of Republic' 37–38
Aurelian (Lucius Domitius Aurelianus) 118–119, 122, 123, 158, 181

brings provinces back under
control 130
and Christians 131, 132
conquests 128, 129
and god Sol Invictus 131
murder of 132
quells riot in Rome 130–131
Aurelianus, Ambrosius 335
Austria (Noricum) 364–366
Autun 196, 217
Auxerre 217
Auxerre, bishop of 348
Avars 382
Avitus 355, 356, 364

babies, abandonment of 43–44
Badon Hill 335, 336
Bagaudae rebels 159–160, 330, 331,
359
Balbinus 92, 93, 141
Balkan frontier 321, 394
Barates 32–33, 126
wife Regina 32–33, 44
barbarian hordes 119–122
barbarian invasions, initial 5th
century 308–309
barbarian kings and chieftains, sons
of 272–273
barbarians, life under 378–379
barbarians, numbers 373
barbarians and the Eastern Empire
382–383
Barbatio, Master of Soldiers 217
Barcelona 304
barrels 47, 48
Basiliscus 367, 380
Bastarnae tribe 105
Batavis 365
bath houses and complexes 43, 73, 149,
162, 185
Belgrade (Singidunum) 322
Belisarius 392, 393, 394, 396–398, 399,
400

Beloch, K. 41–42
Beowulf 106
Bezabde 228
Bithynia and Pontus province 35, 96,
127, 243
Black Sea raids 111, 114
Bleda 320, 322
widow of 324
Boniface 328, 329, 384
Borani people 111
Bosphorus 382
Bostra 127
Boudica, Queen 337
Boulogne 161
Brigonius 45
Britain 133, 139, 150, 261, 295, 360
after the end of Roman rule
345–348 *see also* Britain: in 5th
century
arrests in 199
cemeteries in 350
Channel coast, seaborne raids on
160
Christianity in 344–345, 347–348,
351–352
cities in 338, 344, 347
Constantine in 175, 176
division of 68, 340, 370
eastern 373–374
end of Roman rule in 345
in 5th century 335–336, 344–345 *see
also* Britain: after the end of
Roman rule
invaders after Roman occupation
348–352
languages in 351, 376
mining in 47, 145
nobility in 338–339
prosperity in 144
provinces 340
raids on 341–343, 346–347
rebellion of Carausius and Allectus
161

Britain—*contd*
  refuses to accept Julianus as
    emperor 59
  Roman occupation of 337–345
  'Saxon Shore' and forts 340, 341,
    342, 343–344
  Saxon war leaders in 350
  Severus in 67
  villas 344, 347
  warships patrolling Channel 343
Britons 335, 336, 345–346, 350–351, 363
Brittany 336, 347, 351, 370
buildings 33, 35
Bulgars 382
bureaucracy 244, 267, 269, 411
  central imperial 269
  growth of 164, 171, 189
bureaucrats 165, 168, 207, 223,
  240–242, 245–246, 267
Burgundian kingdom/state 356, 370
Burgundians 328, 330, 332, 356, 372,
  374

Cadiz (Gades) 39
Caecilian 187
Caesar, family name of 38
Caesar, Julius 33, 37, 74, 104–105, 108,
  337
  Commentaries on the Gallic Wars
    216, 218, 219
  and appointments to Senate 38
  and migrants 250
Caledonians 67, 70, 338, 341
Caligula 76
Callinicum, Battle of (531) 392, 397
Callinicum, synagogue 278
Callinicus 314
camels 47
Campus Mauriacus (Catalaunian
  Plains), Battle of (451) 332
Camulodunum (Colchester) 337
Cannae, Battle of (216 BC) 258
Cappadocia 101

Caracalla 66, 68, 69, 80, 110, 140, 147,
  150, 152, 153
  army pay 78, 140
  coinage introduced 141
  as emperor 70–71, 73–74, 75, 76,
    83, 84
  grant of citizenship 84, 87, 168
  murder of 74–75, 76, 88
Carausius 160, 161, 162, 176, 341
caravan routes 125, 126
Cardiff, fort 343
Carinus 134, 135, 138, 159
Carnuntum 177
Carpi tribe 105, 110
Carrhae 74, 92, 93, 100
Cartagena 398
Carthage 42, 66, 329, 396
  siege of (146 BC) 230
Carthage, bishop of 278, 355
carts and carriages 47
Carus, Marcus Aurelius Numerius 134
Caspian Gates pass 391
Cassiodorus 370
Cassius, Avidius 51, 63
Catalaunian Plains (Campus
  Mauriacus), Battle of (451) 332
Catholic Church 379
Catholicism 376
Caucasian mountain passes 391
Chalcedon, Council of 401
Cherusci tribe 106
Chief Steward (*castrensis sacri palatini*)
  171
chieftains 106–107, 108
Childeric 376–377
China 48, 49
Chnodomarius 217, 218
Christian bishops 235, 277–278,
  279–280, 385
  growing prominence of 361–363
Christian chi-rho symbol 182
Christian monastic communities 237
Christianity 95–96, 99, 194, 237

barbarians convert to 376, 379
in Britain 344–345, 347–348,
    351–352
and Constantine 174, 179, 181–183,
    184–185, 187, 188, 189, 192–193,
    194
in the empire 276–282
and the Goths 251, 281
growth of 179–180, 183, 184
and Justinian 401
organisation of 184
the Trinity 188
Christians 95, 96–97, 99, 131, 179, 187
in army 183
freedom to practise religion 181,
    182–183, 185
and Jesus' Second Coming 353
life of 237
persecution and martyrdom of 96,
    97–98, 99, 131, 180–181, 236
in North Africa 187–188
in Persia 192
Chrysopolis 178
churches, building of 179, 181, 185, 275
in barbarian times 378
churches, demolition of 180
Cilicia 101
Cirencester 338
cities
becoming a Roman town or colony
    34–35
in Britain 338, 344, 347
changes in physical shape of 402
conditions in 42–43, 50
defences of 114–115, 142, 226–227
growth of 275
hygiene in 43
population of 42, 43
civil servants see bureaucrats
civil wars 84, 119, 120, 139, 141–142,
    152, 153, 196–197, 203, 215, 216,
    307, 372, 409
Claudius 38–39, 337, 339, 350, 412

Claudius II (Marcus Aurelius
    Claudius) 118, 125, 147, 178
clerks, senior (notarii) 242
Clermont 363, 364, 367
clothing, 5th century 374
clothing of emperors and officials 240
Clovis, King of the Franks 372, 376,
    386
Cniva 103, 104, 111
coin hoards 114
coinage see also currency system
in Britain 345–346
debasing of 141, 144
Diocletian reforms 169, 170
emperors' control of 141
coins
minted in Rome 46
pagan imagery 186
Palmyrene 127
shortage of silver and bronze 145
Colchester (Camulodunum) 337
Cologne 201–202, 217
Comazon, Publius Valerius 83
comites (counts) 165, 207
Commodus 29, 51, 66, 68, 71, 150, 152,
    153
behaviour 55
court favourites 54
murder of 55, 56
skills in the Colosseum 54, 55, 73
slaves 57
succeeds Marcus Aurelius as
    emperor 53–54
unpopularity of 56
communities, reduction in size of 143
Comum 40
Constans 191, 194, 195, 196
Constans, son of usurper Constantine
    303
Constantia 178
Constantine 174, 250, 266, 322, 340,
    408
allied with Licinius 178

Constantine—*contd*
  Arch of 185–186
  and the army 206, 207, 212, 214
  attacks Licinius 178, 183
  attacks Maxentius 177, 178
  campaigns 191–192
  and Christianity 174, 179, 181–183,
    184–185, 187, 188, 189, 192–193,
    194
  and Constantinople 186
  death of 192, 194, 195, 226
  family, extended 189, 191, 194–195
  family tree 190
  harsh legal punishments 187
  in Gaul 214
  parentage 177
  as sole emperor 178–179
  style of rule 188–189
  succeeds father as emperor 175–176,
    200
Constantine (British usurper) 295,
  296, 302–303
Constantine II 189, 266
Constantine III (usurper) 340–341,
  345, 351
Constantinople 186, 223, 225–226,
  238, 255, 259, 270, 279–280, 281,
  295, 305, 312, 367, 368, 377, 379,
  380, 381
  Blues faction 323
  Burnt Column 186
  circus adjacent to palace 389
  Constantine's mausoleum 195
  earthquakes 322
  food supplies 274
  Goths in 292, 293
  Greens faction 323
  growth of 275
  and the Huns 320, 323–324, 326,
    327
  importance of 385
  plague in 392
  riots in 399–400

  Theodosian Walls 383
Constantinople, bishop of 278
Constantius 157, 164, 174, 180, 181, 358,
  366, 384
  death of 175–176, 233
Constantius (Attila's secretary) 325
Constantius (officer, later emperor)
  303, 304–305, 307, 311
Constantius, Flavius 160–161
Constantius II 191, 194, 195–196, 197,
  198, 201, 273, 277, 280
  and bureaucrats 242
  and Christianity 236
  death of 220, 223, 229
  entry into Rome 203–204
  in Gaul 216, 217, 219
  purges 198–199, 200, 202
  war with Persia 226, 227, 228–229
consuls 39, 117, 293
Corbulo 202–203
Cornwall 347, 349
Coroticus, King 351
Corsica 389
counts (*comites*) 165, 207
Cremna 133–134
Cremona, arms factory 200
'Crisis, Third Century' 112–113, 138,
  139–145
Crispus 189, 191
crucifixion, ban on 187
Ctesiphon 50, 93, 124, 134, 136,
  172–173, 232, 233, 272
  sack of (202) 67
  Trajan's sack of 36
Cumbria 347
curial class 40
currency system 46 *see also* coinage;
  coins
Cyprian, Bishop 131
Cyprus 36, 293
Cyril, bishop of Alexandria 361–362
Czech Republic, Roman army bases
  in the present 51

Dacia 105, 121–122
  mines in 145
Dacia Ripensis 323
Dacians 110
Daia, Maximinus 174, 175, 177, 178,
  181, 183
Dalmatia 358, 385
Dalmatius 191, 194, 195
Danube, River 247, 249, 251, 252,
  260–261
Danubian frontier 51, 74, 94, 100, 104,
  105, 108, 109, 110, 111, 119, 121,
  247, 271, 382
Dara 392, 393, 402
death penalty 187
Debelt (Deultum/Dibaltum) 254
Decius, Caius Messius Quintus
  94–95, 99–100, 103–104, 111, 191
denarii 141, 144, 170
Denmark, weapons as offerings in 106
Depression, Great 142
'Deserters War' 120
Deultum (Debelt) 254
Dexippus, P. Herennius 103, 114
Dibaltum (Debelt) 254
Dio Cassius
  and Caracalla 71, 73, 74, 84, 140
  and Commodus 54, 55
  consulship with Alexander 82
  and Elagabalus 79, 80
  and Marcus Aurelius 29, 52
  and Pertinax 58
  and Publius Valerius Comazon 83
  and Severus 65, 66
  and Syria 91
Diocletian (Caius Valerius Diocles)
  134, 135, 138, 139, 153, 157, 158,
  159, 176, 179, 185, 188, 189, 191,
  192, 194, 250, 266, 410
  and the army 206, 212, 214
  and ceremony 172
  and Christianity 180–181
  currency reform 169

death of 177
importance of 173
made emperor 159, 163
regulates sale price of goods
  169–170
reorganises taxation and levy
  system 169, 171, 172, 176
resignation 174, 175
statue, St Mark's Square 157–158
success of 171, 172
supports Galerius 177
and the tetrarchy 161–162, 163, 164
disease see plague
Domitian 412
Domitianus 138
Domitianus, Lucius Domitius 161
Donatists 187–188, 236, 277, 376
Dougga amphitheatre, Tunisia 43
dress, 5th century 374
dress of emperors and officials 240
duces (dukes) 165
Dura Europos 86–88, 93, 95, 101, 125,
  126, 129, 143, 158, 230, 286
  baptistry 95
  siege of 101–102
  synagogue 95

Earth, beliefs and knowledge
  regarding 32
earthquakes 322
Eastern Empire after the decline of
  Rome 381–383, 386, 387, 402
Eburacum (York) 68–69, 71, 175–176,
  200
Eclectus 55, 58
economic system 46
economy, changes in 141–142, 144–145
Edeco 326
Edessa 74, 75, 92, 93, 100, 393
education 40, 41, 45
Egypt
  challenge to tetrarchs in 161
  Christians in 237

Egypt—*contd*
  coinage in 141
  epidemic in 51, 392
  equestrian prefects in 63, 147
  exposed babies in 43–44
  grain from 141
  Jewish rebellion in 36
  knights in 40
  Palmyrene invasion 127
  Roman troops in 60
  taken by Muslim Arabs 403
  trade links with India and China
    48–49
  water-powered machinery in 48
Ejsbøl, weapons find near 106
Elagabalus (Bassianus, later Marcus
    Aurelius Antoninus) 77, 78–81,
    83, 84, 127–128, 141, 147, 151, 153
Elagabalus (god) 77, 79, 80–81, 131
elephants, war 64–65
Emesa 77
Emesa, Battle of (272) 128–129
emperor, becoming an 148
emperor, use of term 37, 38
emperors
  in art 157–158
  clothing of 240
  deaths of 147, 384
  entourage of 171–172, 410
  as figureheads 270
  and foreign wars 206
  joint rule of 149–150
  land holdings of 140, 168
  life of splendour of 203
  numbers of 138–139
  rule of 266–267
  spending by 139–140
  success in war of 149, 151
  usurpation of 203, 205 *see also*
    usurpers
  work of 54
Empire, fourth century 166–167
engineering 47, 48, 274

England, creation of 349
entertainment, human slaughter for
    50
Ephesus, Temple of Artemis 114
epidemic *see* plague
Epirus 292
Equester, Annius 45
equestrian order ('knights') 39–40, 44,
    63, 84, 147
  in the army 145–146, 148
  rise to high office of 148–149
Eudocia 330, 331, 354
Eudoxia 293, 306, 354, 355
Eugenius, Flavius 262, 263, 264, 276,
    281, 292
Euphrates, River 86, 125, 229, 230
Euric, King 356, 359, 364
Europe in early 6th century 371
Eusebius 174, 182, 185
Eutropius 292, 293

Fars (Persis) 89
Fausta 176–177, 189, 191
Faustina 38
favour 45–46, 61, 241
Felix, Master of Soldiers 328
Feva, King of the Rugi 365
fish sauce (*garum*) 143
Fishbourne palace 338
Flavius Constantinus 323
Florian (Marcus Annius Florianus) 133
fortifications in cities 114–115 *see also*
    cities, defences
Frankish kingdom 370
Frankish officer 201
Franks 104, 109–110, 114, 191, 200, 201,
    215, 217, 218–219, 328, 330, 332,
    341, 353, 356, 375, 376, 398, 406
Fravitta 293
freedmen 45, 163
French Foreign Legion 86
Frigidus River, Battle of (394) 262,
    264, 291

Frisians 160
Fritigern 249, 253, 254, 255, 257,
    258–259, 260
frontier forts 120–121
frontier garrisons 108–109, 121

Gades (Cadiz) 39
Gainas 292, 293, 294
Galerius Maximianus 157, 160–161,
    162, 172, 174, 175, 176, 177, 180,
    181, 182, 192, 226, 234, 238
    son of 121
Galla Placidia 302, 303–304, 305, 306,
    328, 333
Gallia Belgica 120
Gallic Empire 116–119
    third century 112–113
Gallienus 100, 111, 116, 117, 118, 123,
    124, 125, 131, 138, 140–141, 145,
    179
    empire of 112–113
Gallus 100, 111, 197, 198, 219
Garamantes tribe 48
Gaul 214–222, 359, 360
    arrests in 199
    barbarian kingdoms 357
    Channel coast, seaborne raids on
        160
    cities in 115
    conquest of (58–50 BC) 33
    Goths in 358, 364
    hilltop settlements in 115–116
    north-western, population in 143
    suppression of Bagaudae 159–160
Geiseric, King of the Vandals 329, 330,
    354, 357, 359, 394, 396
Genghis Khan 314, 315
Germanic mercenaries 104–105, 110
Germanic pirates 100
Germanic tribes 104, 105, 108, 109,
    114, 146, 315, 351
    life of 105–106
Germanic warriors 51, 106, 152

Germanic weapons 106
Germanus, Bishop of Auxerre 348
Germany, growing prosperity of 142
Gerontius 303
Geta 66, 68, 69, 70–71, 73, 76, 84, 150
Ghassanid Arabs 393
Ghengis Khan 314, 315
Gibbon, E. 50, 77, 412
Gildas 335–336, 346, 351
Gildo 292
Gladiator (film) 54
gladiators 54, 55, 73
Glycerius 366, 367
goods, sale price, regulation of
    169–170
goods, trade in 46–47, 48
goods, trade links for 48–49
Gordian (Marcus Antonius
    Gordianus Sempronianus
    Romanus) 86, 92, 191
    monument to 230
Gordian III 92, 93, 141
Gordians 140, 143
Gothic army 307, 310
Gothic burials 322
Gothic kingdom 356
Gothic pirates 139
Gothic War (376–382) 289, 291,
    252–260, 262–263, 276, 413
Gothic warriors 262
Goths 104, 109, 110–111, 114, 116, 146,
    191, 221, 346, 355, 356, 360, 365,
    380–381, 406 *see also* Ostrogoths;
    Visigoths
    blockade of Rome 299, 300
    and Christianity 251, 281
    cross into Spain 304
    in Gaul 358, 364
    and the Huns 248–249
    in Italy 375, 396
    migration of 246–247, 249–250,
        251–252, 260–261, 294, 316
    numbers 312

Goths—*contd*
   raid on Italy 295
   rebellion (395) 291, 292
   sack of Rome 297, 299, 301–302,
      312
   seaborne raids 132
government, growth of 162–165, 168
governors 164
governors, staffs of 163
governors of provinces 62–63
Grand Chamberlain (*praepositus sacri
   cubiculi*) 171
Gratian 245, 246, 254, 255, 259, 261,
   264, 273, 280–281
Greece 37, 139
Greek language 40
Greuthungi people 249, 250, 252, 253,
   254, 257
Gundobad 366

Hadrian 50
   affairs with boys 53
   criticises orator 38
   as dedicated hunter 40
   first emperor to wear beard 33
   petitioned by a woman 54
   predictions by 32
   Spanish origin 39, 66
   tours of provinces 150
   unpopularity 41
   withdrawal from the provinces 36
Hadrian's Wall 337, 338, 340, 347
   Arbeia Roman fort, tombstone 32,
      33, 126
   Birdoswald 347
   Housesteads 347
   Vindolanda 45
Hannibal 258
Hannibalianus 194–195, 198
Hatra 68, 91, 93, 94
Helena 189, 191, 195
Helvetii tribe 250
Hengist 349

Herculaneum 40
Herodes 124–125
Herodian 70, 79, 92, 138
Herodotus 172
Heruli tribe 114, 115, 365, 367
Hippo Regius 329
Historiae Augustae 123, 157, 159
Hitler, Adolf 290
Homer 402
homosexuality 80
honestiores ('more honourable men')
   41
Honoria 331, 333
Honorius 262, 264, 290, 291, 298, 299,
   300–303, 304, 305, 312, 345, 351
   senior notary clerk of (*primicerius
     notariorum*) 285, 288
Horace 170
Horsa 349
houses, town 40
Hsuing-Nu people 315–316
humiliores ('more humble men') 41
Huneric 330
Hunnic armies 314, 315, 319
   attacks on western empire 331–332,
     333
   horse archers 317–319
Hunnic Empire, collapse of 333
Hunnic invasion (440s) 314
Huns 247–249, 253, 259, 382, 406
   and Aetius 327–328, 330, 333
   appearance of 314–315
   attacks on cities 320, 322, 323
   bow as weapon 318, 319
   drift westwards 316
   horses and horsemanship 317–319
   image of 314
   military success 317
   origins of 315–316
   predatory bands of 291, 315, 320
   slavery under 322, 324–325
Huns, Hephthalite ('White Huns')
   382, 390, 391

Huns, Sabir 390, 391
Hypatia 362

Iceni tribe 33–34, 337
Illerup, weapons finds from 106
Illyricum 196, 246, 292, 305, 320
Immae 78–79, 128
incense 273
India 48–49, 143, 273
industrial activity 47–48
influence, political importance of 45, 61
informers 198–199
innovation 47, 48, 274
inscriptions 142
Ireland 339, 341, 351
Irish 346
Isauria 133, 380–381
Isaurians 361, 367, 380
Islamic world 403–404
Issus, battle of (194) 65
Italian campaigns, 6th century 396–398
Italy, transportation in 47
Iuthungi people 111

Japan, twentieth century prosperity of 142
Jerome, Bishop 298
Jerusalem 403
    Church of the Holy Sepulchre 191
    Temple 235, 354–355
Jesus Christ 96, 99, 174, 182, 187, 188, 191, 235–236, 277, 353, 361, 401, 403
Jews 36, 95, 187, 235, 278
John the Cappadocian 400
Jovian 234, 235, 237, 271, 272
Jovius 300
Judaea 36, 60, 191
Julia Domna 70, 76, 77, 82
Julia Maesa 76–77, 78–79, 80
Julia Mamaea 76, 80, 81, 99

Julia Soaemias 76, 77, 78–79, 80, 82
Julian 189, 194, 197, 205, 223–226, 238, 240, 242, 246, 258, 273, 280
    appearance 225
    death of 226, 233–234, 272
    and Gaul 214–215, 216, 217, 218–220, 224, 228, 229
    idolises Marcus Aurelius 225
    Persian expedition 229, 230–232, 233–234, 235
    religion 224, 225, 235–236
    The Caesars 225, 229, 235–236
Julianus, Didius 58, 59, 64, 65
Julianus, Sabinus 135
Julius Caesar *see* Caesar, Julius
Justin 388, 389–390, 391–392
Justin II 402
Justina 261–262, 278
Justinian (Petrus Sabbatius) 388–390, 392, 393, 394, 396, 398, 399, 400
    and Christianity 401
    Codex Justinianus 400–401
    empire 395, 399, 402
    legal reforms 400–401
    wars 397, 398–399
Jutes 348–349

Kavadh, King of Persia 391–392
Khusro I, King of Persia 391–392, 393, 402
kings, behaviour of 377
Kipling, Rudyard 314
'knights' *see* equestrian order
Koblenz 331–332

Lactantius 175, 177, 182
Laetus, Aemilius 55, 56, 58, 65
Lakhmid Arabs 393
Lampadius 200
landowners and bands of followers 359–360
languages 33, 40, 87, 270, 375–376, 379, 401–402

languages—*contd*
in Britain 351, 376
Latin, continued use of 270, 379, 381
Lateran, Church of St John 185
Latin, continued use of 270, 379, 381
law, barbarian 377
law, Roman 41, 85, 168
Codex Justinianus 400–401
Digest 401
Institutes 401
legates 39
Leo 355–356, 358, 359, 361, 366, 367, 384
Leo II 367
Lepcis 242, 243
Lepcis Magna 66, 67, 242, 243
letters of recommendation 45, 61
Licinius 177, 178, 182, 183, 189
Licinius (son) 189
Life of St Severinus, The 364–365
Lipari 304
literature 41
Livia 76
Lombards 398, 399
London (Londinium) 161, 337, 338, 340
Longinus 381
Longinus, Cassius 127, 129
loyalty 140, 198–199
Lucius Verus 50, 57–58, 68, 138, 150
Lugdunum (Lyons) 97, 261
Battle of (196) 65
Lupicinus, *comes* 251, 252, 253, 254, 260
Lydius 133, 134
Lyons (Lugdunum) 97, 261
Battle of (196) 65

Macedonia 292
machinery 47, 48, 274
Macrianus 123

Macrinus, Marcus Opellius 74, 75–76, 78, 79, 83, 84, 128, 140, 147
magistrates 35, 37, 44
Magnentius 196, 197, 198, 199, 214, 215–216, 218, 220
Mainz 116
Majorian 355, 356, 357–358, 359
Malarichus 200
Mamertinus, Claudius 205
Mani, prophet 180, 181
Manichaeans/Manichees 131, 180–181
Manichaeism 280
manufacturing 46, 143
Marcellus 217
Marcia 55, 65
Marcian 333, 353, 355, 380, 384
Marcianopolis 252–253, 254
Marcianus, Terentius 133
Marcomanni tribe 51, 110, 111
Marcomannic Wars 110, 120
Marcus Aurelius 29, 32, 37, 68, 150, 152, 158, 404, 412
becomes emperor 49
children 38
coinage under 141
daughter 71
death of 29, 51, 53
as dedicated hunter 40
eager to promote talent 57
idolised by Julian 225
Meditations 29, 41, 51–52
and operations against Germanic people 51
persecution of Christians 97
reign of 50
renowned for devoting time to hearing cases 54
and the Roman army 60
Spanish origin of family 39
succession 57–58
wars fought by 110
Margus, and its bishop 320

Margus, River 135
Marjorian 383
Mark Antony 37, 70
Marseilles (Massilia) 303, 353, 364
Martialis, Julius 74
Mascezel 292–293
Massilia (Marseilles) 303, 353, 364
Mauretanian troops 78
Maurice 402–403
Maxentius 176, 177–178, 181, 185
Maximian (Aurelius Maximianus)
    157, 159, 160, 161, 164, 174, 175,
    176–177, 180
Maximianus, Marcus Valerius 57
Maximinus (head of embassy) 326,
    327
Maximinus Thrax 82, 84, 92–93, 110,
    132–133, 140
Maximus, *dux* 251
Maximus, Magnus 261, 262, 264
Maximus, son of Gerontius 303
Maximus of Ephesus 224, 226
Merida (Augusta Emerita) 328, 378
Merovingian family 370, 372
Mesopotamia 67, 68, 75, 91, 92, 100,
    134, 147, 228, 229, 393, 403
Milan 117, 118, 162–163, 174, 176, 197,
    200, 201, 242, 261, 270, 278, 279,
    294, 332, 397
Milan, bishop of 276, 278–279, 362
Milan, Edict of 182–183
Minerva (god) 81
mining 47, 145
Moesia 94
Moesia, Lower 64
Moors 370, 398
Muhammad, prophet 403
Mursa 197
Muslim world 403–404

Naissus 322
Naples 396
Napoleon Bonaparte 400

Narbo (Narbonne) 303, 304
Narses (eunuch) 396–397, 398, 399,
    400
Narses, king of Persia 172, 173
Neoplatonism/Neoplatonists 224, 236
Nepos, Julius 367, 368, 385
Nepotianus 197
Nero 53, 59, 66, 79, 80, 96, 185,
    202–203, 314
Nerva 50, 53
Nibelungen 330–331
Nicaea 35, 188, 277
Nicene Creed 236, 277, 279
Nicomedia 35, 162–163, 174, 175, 186,
    195
    church in 179, 180
    palace fire 180
Niederbieber 121
Niger, Gaius Pescennius 65
Nisibis 92, 93, 173, 227, 234–235, 272,
    393
Noricum (Austria) 364–366
North Africa 92, 140–141, 292–293,
    300, 386–387, 398
    Christians in 131, 187–188, 236, 277,
    376
    in early 6th century 371
    retaken from Vandals 389, 394,
    396
    Roman attempts to recapture 357,
    359, 380, 382, 383, 386
    Vandal kingdom in 394, 396
    Vandals migration to 328–329, 330,
    356–357, 358–359
North Sea, sea levels 119
Notitia Dignitatum 285–289, 341, 343
    Roman army in 286, 288, 295, 303,
    310, 340
    command structure 287, 288
Numerian 134
Numidia 92, 329

Octavian *see* Augustus

Odaenathus, Septimius 123–124, 125,
    126, 131, 136, 151
Odoacer 367–368, 381
olive oil 143
Olybrius 366
Olympius 299, 300
Onegesius 324, 325
oratory skills 40–41
Orestes 362, 367
Orientus 285
Origen 99
Orleans 332
Orosius 298
Ostrogothic kingdom, fall of 399
Ostrogothic nobles 396
Ostrogoths 246, 366, 370, 375, 377,
    379, 382, 389, 394, 396, 397, 400
Oxfordshire 138
Oxyrhynchus festival speech 157

Padua (Patavium) 39
paganism 237
paganism and Julian 224, 225, 235–236
pagans 183–184, 188, 192
Palestine 144, 403
Palladius 242–243, 244
Palmyra (Tadmor) 32, 125–126, 129,
    143
  monarchs of 139
  siege of 129
  Temple of Bel 125
  third century 112–113
Palmyrene troops 126, 128
Palmyrenes 86, 87, 126, 129
Pannonia 111, 135, 323, 383
  raid on (167) 51
Pannonia, Upper 59
  army of 64
Pap, King of Armenia 271
Paris 225, 261
Parthia 36, 74, 78, 88, 413
Parthia, Arsacid 88
Parthian cavalry armies 36

Parthian War (197–202) 67–68
Parthians 50, 87, 89
Patavium (Padua) 39
patricians 38
patronage 45–46, 61, 211, 241
Paul of Samosata 131–132, 179
Paul the Apostle 34, 35, 96
Paul 'the chain' 199, 202, 223
Pax Romana 35
pay for professions, regulation of 170
Pelagianism/Pelagius 348
Persia, Sassanid 135, 137, 146, 172–173,
    192, 271, 272, 276, 382, 387
  Christians in 192
  fall of 403
  Julian's expedition 226–235
  re-emergence of 390–392
  6th century war against 402–403
  wars against 134, 394
Persian army 91, 123, 124, 136–137, 139,
    172, 213, 272
  and Julian's expedition 227, 228,
    230, 232, 233
Persian kings 172
Persian War 134
Persians, Sassanid 88, 89, 91, 93,
    100–101, 102, 111, 116, 135–136,
    152, 162, 192, 196, 206, 219, 226,
    281, 318, 390, 392, 397, 406
  peace with 393, 394
Persis (Fars) 89
Pertinax, Publius Helvius 56–57, 83,
    152, 159, 412
  in the army 57, 63, 64
  father 56
  father-in-law 58
  murder of 58, 65
  and the praetorian guard 57–58
  son 71
  as successor to Commodus 56, 57
Peter the Apostle 96, 185
Petronius Maximus 333–334, 354, 355
Pfünz 120–121

Philip (Marcus Julius Philippus)
93–94, 99, 100, 111, 191
older brother 93, 94
Philippopolis 94, 103
Phocas 403
Piacenza (Placentia) 130, 355
Picts 335, 341, 346, 348, 351
Placentia (Piacenza) 130, 355
Placidia 366
plague 50–51, 97, 99, 110, 118, 139, 142,
392–393, 397
Plautianus 67
Pliny the Elder 45–46, 49
Pliny the Younger 35, 96, 142
pollution 47–48, 145
Polybius 230
Pompeii 40
Pontus see Bithynia and Pontus
province
poor, conditions for 42–43, 50
pope, the 278, 299–300, 354, 361, 362,
379, 385 see also Rome, bishop of
Porphyry 179
Portchester 344
Portus 299
Postumus, Marcus Cassianus Latinius
116, 117, 138
prices, rise in 141
Principate, creation of 150
Priscus (member of delegation to
Attila) 324, 325–326, 327
Priscus (Philip's brother) 151
Probus, Marcus Aurelius 133, 134
Procopius (commander in Persian
war) 230, 234, 238, 240, 247, 266
Procopius (historian) 302, 335, 370
professions, regulation of pay for 170
provinces
civil administration of, in late 4th
century 268
creation of 34–35
division of 151, 164, 166–167
groups of (dioceses) 165, 166–167

violence and rebellions in 35–37 see
also civil wars
Pulcheria 305–306, 333, 353
Pupienus 92, 93, 141

Quadi tribe 51, 110, 111, 245
Quintillus 118

Radagaisus, King 295, 296, 300
raiding 84, 108, 109, 111, 114, 120, 172,
215, 221, 273
Raphaneae 77, 78
Ravenna 111, 270, 294, 298, 300, 301,
304, 305, 310, 313, 332, 345, 368,
385
palace 333
rebellions 36–37, 238, 240, 291
recommendation, letters of 45, 61
Rheims 217
Rhine, River 111, 114
Rhine frontier 74, 104, 105, 109, 110,
111, 119, 133, 176, 232–233, 271
Ricimer 355, 357–358, 359, 366, 384
Rimini (Ariminum) 300
Riothamus 351
roads, Roman 47
Roman army 59–64
Adrianople disaster 245, 255,
257–258, 260
African regiments 242–243
alae cavalry 59, 208
auxilia palatina 219, 221
auxilia unit 209
auxiliaries 59, 61, 62
ballistarii (artillerymen) 216
barracks 61, 212
bases 51, 60–61, 172, 211–212
billeting 212
in Britain 337–338, 339
candidati (emperor's personal
bodyguards) 210
cavalry 117, 208
centurions 63–64, 67

Roman army—*contd*
and civil war 152
cohort (*ala*) 59
Cohort, Twentieth Palmyrene 86,
87–88
comes 220, 221
Comes Britanniae 340
*Comes Litoris Saxonici per
Britannias* ('Count of the Saxon
Shore') 340
comitatenses (troops under
command of emperor) 165,
188–189, 206–207, 209, 211,
212–213, 214, 238, 242, 329, 340
comites (counts - officers) 165, 207
command structure 165
in *Notitia Dignitatum* 287, 288
decorations 62
under Diocletian 163
discharge from 61
discipline 61
donatives issued 169, 205
Dux Britanniarum 340, 347
and the emperor 62, 64, 205
employed as labour force 134
and equestrians 63, 145–146, 148
flag (*labarum*) 182, 183
food supply agents 60
frumentarii ('grain-men') 60
in Gaul 215, 217–218, 219
hazards of serving in 60
imagines (images of the emperor
and family) 62
labarum, standard with Chi-Rho
Christian symbol 182, 183
legionaries' wives and children 61
legions 59, 62, 213–214
I Parthica 67, 68
II Parthica 67, 68, 71, 78, 117, 147
III Augusta 92
III Gallica 77, 78, 80
III Parthica 67, 68
X Fretensis 273

XIII Gemina 208
limitanei (*duces'* troops) 165,
188–189, 206, 207, 208, 209, 211,
213, 286, 288, 329, 340, 345,
364–365
loyalty 140
'Master of Horse' (*Magister
Equitum*) 207
'Master of Infantry' (*Magister
Peditum*) 207
'Master of Soldiers' (*Magister
Militum*) 207
in *Notitia Dignitatum* 286, 288, 295,
303, 310, 340
palatina title 209
pay 60, 73, 78, 140
based on rations 169
deductions from 60–61
preference for established dynasties
151–152
primus pilus (commander of the
first cohort) 63
promotion 61, 67
protectores domestici (junior staff
officers) 210–211
in the provinces 60
pseudocomitatenses 213, 310
recruitment 60, 61–62, 209–210,
259, 275
self-mutilation to avoid 210, 259
restructuring of 206, 207–208, 214
and senators 62, 64
and Severus 67, 68, 78
shields, symbols on 182
soldier's diet 61
strength 59, 208–209, 289
supplies 207, 213
tortoise (testudo) formation 128
training 213
tribunes (commanders) 210
unit pride 62
vexillationes (cavalry) 208, 209
war against Persia 229–230

weapons 106, 213
Roman Empire
creation of 33–35
division of 264, 266, 270
at end of 4th century 270–276,
282
eastern frontier 90
population of 41–42, 43
at end of 4th century 274–275
in 2nd century 30–31, 32
tribesmen migrating into 250–251
of Valentinian and Valens 239
Roman navy 59
Channel Fleet (*classis Britannica*)
161
Roman Republic, creation and
expansion of 37
Roman Republic, fall of 150
Romania 402
Romanus, *comes* 242, 243–244, 259
Rome
Arch of Constantine 185–186
Arch of Severus 67–68, 186
bath complexes and houses 73, 149,
162, 185
Baths of Caracalla 73
Church of St Peter 185
Circus Maximus 43, 59, 149
coins minted in 46
Colosseum 43, 54, 149, 368
Constantius II's entry into
203–204
defences 130, 177–178
equites (cavalry) 63
equites singulares Augusti (imperial
guard cavalry) 58, 59, 74
fires 96, 162
food supplies 43, 60, 130–131, 149,
274
Forum 162
basilica 185
Goths' blockade of (408–409) 299,
300

grain ration 43, 60
imperial expenditure in 140
Milvian Bridge, Battle of 178, 182,
186
Monte Testaccio 47
900th anniversary of foundation 37
Palatine Hill, emperor's palace on
58
population 42
praetorian guard 55, 56, 57–59, 60,
63, 65, 78, 80, 147, 163, 185
retaken from Goths 397–398
riot (271) 130
sack of (410) 297, 299, 301–302, 312
Salarian Gate 301
Senate *see* Senate
Senate House (Curia) 162
Altar of Victory 280–281
siege of (535) 396
size of 176
Sol Invictus temple 131
Temple of Concord 56
Temple of Jupiter 80
Vandals plunder 354–355
vigiles (firemen and night police) 59
Rome, bishop of 187, 278, 299–300 *see
also* pope, the
Romulus 37
Romulus (Augustulus) 367
Rouen mint 160
Rua 320
Rufinus 290, 292
Rugi tribe 365, 367, 380–381
rural areas, conditions for poor in 43,
50

St Albans (Verulamium) 337, 338, 348
St Augustine 329, 348, 351
St Germanus 363
St Patrick 341, 351
St Peter 96, 185
St Saba 281
Salvian 353

Saracen cavalry 259
Saracens 226, 233
Sardinia 389, 394
Sarmatian Iazyges people 51, 111
Sarmatians 105, 121, 178, 191, 318, 319
Sarmizegethusa 122
Sarus 295, 300, 303
    brother 304
Sassanid family 135
Sassanid Persia see Persia, Sassanid
Sassanids see Persians, Sassanid
Saxon grave goods 349, 350
Saxon mercenaries 335, 336, 349
'Saxon Shore' 340, 341, 342
    forts 342, 343–344
Saxon war leaders 350
Saxons 160, 220, 332, 336, 341, 346,
    348–349, 350–351, 370, 376
Scandinavia 106, 107
schools 45 see also education
Scipio Aemilianus 230
Scipio Africanus 232
Scots 335, 341, 346, 351
Scottas 324
seaborne attacks 111, 114, 132, 160,
    341–342
Sejanus 75
Seleucia 50
Semnones people 111
Senate 37, 38–39, 56, 83, 148, 149, 368
    pagan element in 280–281, 299–300
senators 38–39, 40, 41, 79, 83, 147, 148,
    149, 153, 409
    and the army 62, 64
    clients of 45
    households 163
    political role 145, 148
    wealth of 44
Senon 217
Serapio 217, 221
Serena 290–291, 299, 302
servants, senior 171
Severinus 364–366

Severus, general 174, 176
Severus, Libius 358, 359
Severus, Lucius Septimius 64, 83, 84,
    117, 131, 135, 148, 150, 152–153,
    163, 178, 191, 338
    and the army 67, 68, 78
    career 66
    death of 68–69, 147
    dismisses praetorians 205
    as emperor 66–67, 68
    family tree 72
    and the Parthian War 67–68
    proclaimed emperor 65
    rise to power 147
    and wife 77
Severus Alexander 81–82, 83, 84, 91,
    99, 110, 127–128, 147, 148, 151, 153
    Arch of 67–68, 186
    and army pay 140, 141
    murder of 138
Seville 328
Shapur I, King of Persia 86, 93, 94,
    100, 101, 123, 124, 135, 136–137,
    181, 228, 392
Shapur II, King of Persia 192, 226,
    227, 228, 229, 230, 232, 233, 234,
    271
ships and shipping 46–47
    used by raiders on Britain 341–342
shipwrecks, Roman, finds from
    142–143
Sicily 329, 389, 394, 396, 398
Sidonius Apollinaris 363–364, 365,
    367, 374, 377
siege warfare 101–102, 133–134,
    227–228
Silchester 338
Silings 295–296, 304
Silk Road 49
silk trade 49, 143
Silvanus 197, 199–200, 201–202, 203,
    207
Singara 228, 234

Singidunum (Belgrade) 322
singulares (picked cavalrymen) 64
Sirmium 162–163, 177, 322, 325
Sirmium, bishop of 325
slave trade 107, 108
slavery 44, 49
slaves 171
   ban on tattooing faces 187
   female, death penalty for 187
Slavs 382
Sol Invictus cult 131, 181
sophistic movement, second 41
South Shields, Arbeia Roman fort,
   tombstone 32, 33, 126
Spain 302, 303, 328, 330, 356, 357, 387,
   389, 398
   agriculture in 143
   arrests in 199
   Goths cross into 304
   mining in 47, 145
spice trade 143
Sri Lanka 273
Steppes 316, 317, 318
Stilicho 290–291, 292, 293, 294, 295,
   296, 298, 302, 303, 307, 310–311,
   358, 384
   death of 298, 299
Strabo 39
Strabo, Theodoric ('Squinty') 377,
   380
Strasbourg (Argentorate) 217–218,
   221, 258
Suevi tribe 295–296, 303, 328, 330, 356,
   370
Superintendent of the Bedchamber
   (*primicerius sacri cubiculi*) 171
Syria 63, 73, 86, 100, 101, 133, 392, 403
   Aurelian in 128
   bandits in 241
   division of 68
   rebellion in (248) 94
   refuses to accept Julianus as
     emperor 59

   Roman troops in 60
   silk workshops 49
Syria Phoenice 77

Tacitus, Marcus Claudius 132, 133
Tacitus, Publius Cornelius 53, 148
   and barbarian tribes 106
   and creation of the empire 33
   and secret of empire 84
Tadmor *see* Palmyra
Tarraco (Tarragona) 114
Tarsus 34, 35
taxation 168, 169, 171, 172, 176, 267,
   346, 374–375
technology 47, 48, 274
Terentius, Julius 86, 87, 88, 93
Tertullian 96–97
Tervingi people 246–247, 249–250,
   251–253, 254, 260
tetrarchs 157, 158, 159, 171, 174
   protection for 163
   rescripts of 170–171
   statue, St Mark's Square 157–158
tetrarchy 173, 266
   changes in 174, 175
   creation of 159–162
   rule of 162–165, 168
Tetricus 118–119, 129, 130
Teutoberg Forest ambush (9) 104, 105,
   106
Themes 86
Theodora, wife of Constantius 177,
   178, 189, 195
Theodora, wife of Justinian 389–390,
   396, 400, 401
Theodoric, King of the Goths 304,
   332, 368, 369, 375, 377, 380,
   381
   grandson 396
Theodoric II 355, 356, 363
Theodosius, son of Athaulf 304
Theodosius the elder 259
   family tree 265

Theodosius the younger (II) 259, 260, 261–263, 264, 271, 272, 291, 292, 296, 305–306, 329–330, 353, 358, 401
  and Christianity 276, 277, 278–279, 280, 281, 362
  death of 333
  ministers 320
  sons 290
Thermopylae 323
Thessalonica 279
Thrace 132, 246–247, 251, 253, 255, 260, 276, 292, 293, 320, 383
Tiberius (court official) 402–403
Tiberius (emperor) 91, 151, 373
Ticinum 298
Tigris, River 173, 233
Timesitheus, Caius 93
Timgad 241
Titus 354
Togidubnus, Tiberius Claudius 338
Tolosa (Toulouse) 303, 355
tombstones 32, 33
  ages shown on 42
Totila, King 398
Toulouse (Tolosa) 303, 355
trade 125
  in barbarian times 378, 379
  with eastern frontier 107, 108
  at end of 4th century 273–274
  in goods 46–47, 48
  long-distance, decline in 142, 143
trade links 48–49
trade routes 125, 126
traders 48, 49
Trajan (Marcus Ulpius Traianus) 50, 96, 103, 104, 105, 229
  on campaign 150
  as dedicated hunter 40
  fondness for boys 53, 80
  invasion of Parthia 36
  Spanish origin 39, 66
transportation 46–47

Trier 162–163, 177, 186, 191, 245, 261, 332, 353
Tropaeum Traiani 104
Troyes 217
Tyana 128

Ulfilas, bishop 281
Ulpian 82
Ursicinus, Master of Soldiers 199, 201–202, 203, 216
usurpers 384, 408, 411

Vaballathus 124, 125, 126–127, 129, 130
Vadomarius, King of the Alamanni 216, 273
Vahran II, King of Persia 135
Valao, King of the Naristae 57
Valens 237–238, 240, 245, 246, 247, 249, 250, 251, 255, 257, 266, 271, 275, 277
  death of 258, 262, 281
  empire of 239
Valentinian I 237–238, 240, 242, 243, 246, 247, 266, 340
  death of 245
  empire of 239
  family tree 265
Valentinian II 245, 246, 261, 262, 264, 298
  death of 262
Valentinian III 304, 305, 306, 328, 329, 333, 353, 354
  murder of 334
Valerian (Publius Licinius Valerianus) 100–101, 111, 116, 123, 131, 157
Vandal kingdom in North Africa 394, 396
Vandals 328–330, 354–355, 370, 375, 376, 382, 386, 387, 394
  attack by (405/406) 295–296
  cross into Spain 303
  dress 374
  kingdom destroyed 389, 398

reach North Africa 356–357, 358–359

Vandals, Siling 295–296, 304

Vascones 370

Vegetius 343

Venice, St Mark's Square, tetrarchs' statue 157–158

Verona 94, 135, 294

Verulamium (St Albans) 337, 338, 348

Vespasian 43, 66, 203

Vestal Virgins 79–80

Vetranio 196

vicarii (prefects' subordinates) 165

victories, propaganda value of 150–151

Victorinus 116

Vienna (Vindobona) 51

Vigilas 326

Vikings 114

villas, country 40, 115, 344, 347

Vindobona (Vienna) 51

Vindolanda 45

Visigoths 246, 328, 330, 331, 366, 367, 370, 372, 375, 378

Vortigern 349

Wales 337, 347, 349
   north, mining in 47

Wallia 304

warbands 311

warfare before arrival of Romans 35

water power 47, 48

watermills 47

wealth, personal 45

weapons
   as grave goods 107, 108
   Hunnic 318, 319
   as offerings to gods 106
   Roman Army 106, 213

Western Empire after the decline of Rome 383–384, 386

wine, Falernian 170

wine makers 143

women, hairstyles of 33

women, imperial 305–306

Xiongnu people 315–316

York (Eburacum) 68–69, 71, 175–176, 200

Zabda, Septimius 127

Zabdai, Septimius 127

Zeno 367, 368, 380, 381, 384, 385

Zenobia, Queen of Palmyra 123, 124, 126, 127, 128, 129–130, 131, 132, 136, 141

Zerco 326

Zoroastrianism 89, 393

Zosimus 174, 194, 212, 264, 285, 295, 299, 335, 345